Fundamentals of Assembler Language Programming for the IBM PC and IBM XT

Fundamentals of Assembler Language Programming for the IBM PC and IBM XT

Victor E. Broquard
J. William Westley

Illinois Central College

MERRILL PUBLISHING COMPANY
A Bell & Howell Information Company
Columbus   Toronto   London   Melbourne

Published by Merrill Publishing Company
A Bell & Howell Information Company
Columbus, Ohio 43216

This book was set in Century Schoolbook

Administrative Editor: Vernon R. Anthony
Production Coordinator: Jo Ellen Gohr
Cover Designer: Brian Deep

Library of Congress Catalog Card Number: 89-61504
International Standard Book Number: 0-675-21058-5
Printed in the United States of America
1 2 3 4 5 6 7 8 9—93 92 91 90

Preface

As teachers of programming, we know that the process of learning to program can be very difficult. This is especially true of the microassembler language because of the very low level of the microassembler instruction set. The problem is compounded by the lack of instructional materials geared to the needs of the beginning student who wants to learn assembler programming for the IBM PC, IBM XT, and the clones of these models. The books we reviewed when selecting a text for our course seemed to be primarily concerned with only the instruction set coverage. In some respects they appeared to be little more than a rehash of technical reference manuals. They showed few effective coding techniques and did not explain why the code should be written in a particular way. In addition, there seemed to be little consistency in the examples that were supposed to illustrate good programming style. For these reasons we decided to undertake the task of creating a student-oriented microassembler textbook.

Our textbook uses the building-block approach. First it provides the student with an understanding of microcomputer architecture. As he or she progresses through each chapter, new instructions, language features, and techniques are introduced on a need-to-know basis. Since each chapter builds on the preceding chapters, the student receives a gradual introduction to assembler programming. This leads to an in-depth understanding of the many problem-solving techniques that are available using the microassembler language. This text is not intended to be a language reference manual, although it is comprehensive in its coverage. Rather, it is a text designed to facilitate the learning of the microassembler language. For those who want to learn about the language in greater depth, this text provides an excellent foundation for further study using reference materials.

We make one fundamental assumption regarding the student who undertakes the study of the microassembler language: We assume that he or she has had at least one course in a programming language or prior programming experience. It is hoped that this experience is with structured problem analysis and design techniques, since all example programs employ the principles of structured logic as implemented in microassembler. The student soon realizes that the ability to develop a structured solution greatly simplifies the programming task in microassembler. Without prior programming knowledge and experience, learning microassembler can be a monumental task.

All the materials are classroom-tested and have been reviewed by the most critical reviewers we could find: our students. When they didn't understand something, they were very vocal. They wanted to know why things worked the way they did, and they wanted the explanation in words they could understand. This forced us to use a clear writing style, avoiding technical jargon to the extent possible.

Some of the features that we believe make this text unique are:

- The building-block approach, which introduces new concepts, instructions, and programming techniques on a need-to-know basis.

- Examples that use simple coding sequences that solve typical problems.

- Use of simple nontechnical language.

- The presentation of all the commonly used program interrupt conditions along with a complete and clearly written explanation of how, when, and why they should be used.

- Extensive coverage of debugging techniques using SYMDEB and CODE VIEW.

- The examination of the interaction between the microcomputer and system software. The student learns why they work together as they do.

- Over 50 carefully selected programs available on disk. These programs provide examples of many common applications and techniques that are used on the job. These programs are available for unlimited duplication in microassembler classes.

- Programs that have been carefully integrated with the text so that the student is required to use them while studying the text. In each chapter the student is asked to assemble, link, and run programs that illustrate the principles and techniques presented in the chapter. The student can "plug in" many of these routines to his or her own programming applications and assignments.

- Programming tips for using Microsoft Assembler versions 4.0 and 5.0.

- A consistent reading level, which aids understanding.

- A detailed presentation of the file-handling methods for handling file I/O.

- The presentation of the latest techniques for terminating the execution of a program by using return codes. Appropriately coded examples aid in understanding each technique.

- A brief introdiction to interlanguage communication. Examples of code that interfaces assembly language with FORTRAN, PASCAL, and C are included.

We hope you receive the rich satisfaction of creating efficient, well-designed, concisely coded solutions to your programming problems by using the microassembler language.

Acknowledgments

We would like to thank those who reviewed this manuscript and offered suggestions for improvement:

Richard Borst, Mount Saint Mary's College; Arthur Geis, College of DuPage; Rusty Hollingsworth, Tarrant County Community College; Kathleen Keil, Ball State University; Maria C. Kolatis, County College of Morris; John Lane, Edinboro University of Pennsylvania; Paul LeCoq, Spokane Falls Community College; Michael Michaelson, Palomar College; William O'Toole, Mount Saint Mary's College; William A. Rodgers, Moorehead State University; Paul Ross, Millersville University; Joanna Stoskus, County College of Morris; Francis Whittle, Dutchess Community College; Dave Williamson, Indiana University–Purdue University at Indianapolis.

List of Programs

Contents

CHAPTER 2   Running the Assembler Software   36

CHAPTER 5   Subroutines and the Stack   155

CHAPTER 6   Basic DOS Screen and Keyboard Services   201

CHAPTER 7   Basic ROM-BIOS CRT Services   245

CHAPTER 8   Binary Math and Conversions   305

CHAPTER 9   Disk Basics and DOS File Handles   342

CHAPTER 10   The File Control Block Method and the Program Segment Prefix   373

CHAPTER 11   String Functions   397

CHAPTER 12   External Subroutines, Segments, and Groups   421

CHAPTER 13   Array and Table Processing   471

CHAPTER 14   Addressing Modes, Structures, and Multi-level Tables   493

CHAPTER 15   Binary Coded Decimal Math   512

CHAPTER 16   Processing Random-Access Files and Advanced File Functions   539

CHAPTER 17   The Macro Language   565

1

Introduction to Microassembler Language and Personal Computer Architecture

1.1 CHAPTER OBJECTIVES

This chapter presents a brief examination of the architecture of the personal computer and of the many technical terms that are so characteristic of the microassembler language. When you have completed this chapter, you will have an understanding of:

1. The concept of machine language and its relationship to assembler language

2. The advantages and disadvantages of programming in assembler language

3. The three major radixes needed for successful assembler programming: binary, hexadecimal, and decimal

4. The conversion process between the three number schemes used in microassembler: binary, hexadecimal, and decimal

5. Addition and subtraction in hexadecimal

6. The hardware components that make up a typical microcomputer system

7. Main storage terms: *bit, nibble, byte, word, doubleword, quadword,* and *tenbyte*

8. The way the microcomputer actually stores character data, signed binary numbers, and unsigned binary numbers

9. The way a byte in memory is addressed
10. The 14 registers in the central processing unit (CPU) and their uses in a program
11. The use of flags and the flag register
12. The typical memory map of a microcomputer

1.2 INTRODUCTION

The assembler language is perhaps the most powerful programming language available on a microcomputer. Like COBOL, PASCAL, and BASIC, it is classified as a symbolic language. A **symbolic language** is one that uses letters, characters, and numbers that are combined according to a specific set of rules to communicate what actions the computer is to perform. Unlike many other languages, assembler requires an extremely high level of detail, even when carrying out the simplest programming actions, which makes assembler difficult to learn. Yet, it is the ability to precisely control the desired processing that makes assembler so powerful.

To be able to perform effectively as a microassembler programmer, it is necessary to become familiar with several different number schemes, to have a thorough understanding of how data is stored in main storage, and to know the internal operational methods of the microcomputer. In short, to master the personal computer and microassembler, you will have to learn exactly how they work.

When learning any new subject or skill, it is best to start at the beginning. In the case of the microcomputer and the assembler language, the beginning is the actual instructions that the machine can perform. Collectively, these instructions are referred to as machine language.

1.3 MACHINE LANGUAGE

Beginning programmers commonly learn to write programs in a high-level language, such as COBOL, PL/I, C, PASCAL, or BASIC. One of the major reasons for this is that these high-level languages are generally easier to learn and faster to code than low-level languages. Unfortunately, because of the structure and syntax of these languages, many beginners falsely assume that the computer understands and executes these high-level instructions directly. This is far from the truth.

In reality, a computer can understand and execute **machine language** instructions only. Machine language instructions are the fundamental, even primitive, commands that a computer can execute. Consider the ordinary task of moving the data in a field named FIRST_NAME_IN to another field named FIRST_NAME_OUT. In high-level languages the task can be coded as

```
            LET FIRST_NAME_OUT = FIRST_NAME_IN
```

or

```
        MOVE FIRST_NAME_IN TO FIRST_NAME_OUT
```

These instructions give the impression that all the characters in the FIRST_NAME_IN field are moved at one time as a group to the receiving field. Actually, the machine language instruction that moves data is capable of moving only 1 byte of data at a time, not the whole field. In fact, the machine instruction to move data can move only 1 byte of data between storage and a high-speed work area known as a register. It never moves data directly between main storage locations!

Therefore, to move the complete field in this example, a small sequence of instructions called a subroutine must be written. In this subroutine the first instruction moves the first character of FIRST_NAME_IN into a register work area, and then another instruction moves it from the register work area into the first character of FIRST_NAME_OUT. This process is repeated until all characters have been moved.

Before any high-level language program can be executed, each of its coded statements must be converted into the computer's machine language. This is done by processing the source program through the language's compiler or interpreter, thus creating one or more machine language instructions for each source language instruction. These machine language instructions are what the computer executes.

What do machine instructions look like? Since electronic circuitry can identify only two states—on and off, plus and minus, something there or nothing there—the computer is often thought of as understanding only binary digits. To store more complex values such as letters and commands, several binary digits are combined and treated as a single unit. Thus, each machine language instruction is actually composed of long strings of binary digits (0's and 1's).

Consider the following example, in which you want to place an initial value of 1 into a counter. Assume that you are using a high-speed work area known as a register to hold the counter, register AX. (In microassembler each register is designated by a unique pair of letters.) The machine language instruction to do this is

```
    1011 1000 0000 0000 0000 0001B
```

The trailing B means the characters are in binary number format.

As you can see, the machine language format is awkward and would be difficult for most people to work with. Therefore, the computer usually shows instructions and data areas in short understandable formats, or **radixes** (a radix refers to the base of a number system). Machine instructions are often in the hexadecimal radix, or hex, format. In hex, numbers are in base 16.

The number base, or radix, that you use in daily activities is decimal, or base 10. In base 10, valid digits range from 0 to 9; there is no single digit for the number 10. Likewise, in the **binary** number system, or base 2, the only allowable digits are 0 and 1; there is no 2 digit. All number bases work the same way. Thus, in hexadecimal, or base 16, there is no digit for 16, and the largest digit has the value 15.

In **hexadecimal** the digits 0 through 9 are represented in the same way as in base 10. Since six more "digits" are required to represent the hex values 10 through 15, the letters "A" through "F" are used.

A = 10

B = 11

C = 12

D = 13

E = 14

F = 15

Reconsider the machine instruction that sets the register AX counter to 1 by using register D. If the computer is asked to display the instruction that sets the register counter to 1, it responds with

```
B8 00 01H
```

The trailing H indicates hexadecimal radix.

This is somewhat better than the binary representation—at least it is shorter! However, it is unlikely that you would want to code an entire program in this way. It is preferable to code in either a high-level language or a symbolic **assembler language.** The microassembler instruction that creates the preceding machine language instruction is

```
MOV   AX,1
```

As you can see from this example, microassembler instructions tend to be rather cryptic and terse, but they are a major improvement over machine code.

Note that two spaces follow MOV in the preceding microassembler instruction. In this line of code and in code throughout this book, space is used to enhance readability. Therefore, the same line can be written with one space or with three or more spaces. Don't be concerned if the number of spaces varies; the variation is our attempt to present the code in the format that is best for the context.

1.4 CORRELATION BETWEEN ASSEMBLER INSTRUCTIONS AND MACHINE INSTRUCTIONS

The assembler language is classified as a low-level language. In low-level languages there is a one-for-one correlation between assembler and machine instructions. For each machine instruction available, there is one and only one assembler instruction equivalent. And for every assembler instruction coded, there is one and only one machine instruction created. In contrast, high-level languages seldom have such a one-for-one ratio. In fact, it is not uncommon for one high-level language instruction to generate 50 or more machine instructions just to carry out a specific operation.

1.5 ADVANTAGES AND DISADVANTAGES OF ASSEMBLY LANGUAGE

The following is a list of some of the advantages of programming in an assembler language over programming in a high-level language:

- Assembler language programs and subroutines usually execute more efficiently and usually have the fastest execution speed.

- Programs and subroutines that are impossible or nearly impossible to write in a high-level language are easily written in an assembler language.

- The assembler language programmer is given maximum control over the system.

It is possible to create an assembler program that is slow and inefficient. Yet, overall, assembler programs and subroutines do tend to run faster than corresponding high-level language versions. It is for the second reason—that writing programs and routines in a high-level language can be difficult or impossible—that people turn to assembler as the language of choice to get the job done.

There are disadvantages to programming in an assembler language:

- Assembler coding is very tedious and repetitious.

- Assembler language is difficult to learn.

- Writing assembler programs and routines requires knowledge of the computer system and its architecture.

- The code created can be very machine dependent.

- Because of machine-dependent coding, programs may not be transportable to other computers.

- Assembler programs are often more difficult to debug than high-level programs.

Perhaps the most significant disadvantage is that assembler language is difficult to learn. As a result, there are not as many assembler programmers in the work force as there are high-level language programmers. This is especially true of microassembler programmers.

There are many different assembler languages; each manufacturer—Motorola, DEC, and Intel, for example—provides its own. Each version is different from the others. For example, the Motorola family of microprocessors uses an assembler language that closely resembles the assembler that is found on many main frame computers. Although the advantages and disadvantages described previously are true for nearly all assembler languages, this book presents the specifics for personal computers that use the Intel circuitry.

Since the study of assembler language requires a mastery of both the binary and hexadecimal number schemes and the rudiments of microcomputer architecture, this chapter first examines the number schemes. Then you will apply what you have learned to a brief look at personal computer architecture.

1.6 COMMON NUMBER SCHEMES AND CODING CONVENTIONS

The numbering schemes frequently used on the personal computer are binary, decimal, and hexadecimal. To specify the radix, or number scheme, that is being represented, the values have the letter B, H, or D at the end to indicate binary, hex, or decimal. (Usually, the letter D is omitted from decimal numbers.)

It is common practice to write binary numbers in groups of 4 bits, adding leading 0's when necessary to fill out the group, as in 0011B. (The mathematical representation for this value 0011B is: $0 \times 2^3 + 0 \times 2^2 + 1 \times 2^1 + 1 \times 2^0 = 1 \times 2 + 1 \times 1 = 3$.)

When writing hex numbers, if the number begins with a letter ("A" through "F"), a leading 0 digit is usually added. Thus, FH is written 0FH. This is done because, in microassembler, names of fields begin with letters, but numbers do not. For example, if a number is coded as FH, the assembler incorrectly interprets it as the name of a field and not a number.

Finally, hex numbers are commonly grouped into pairs, as in 45H, 01 16H, and 00 A3 4DH. The last example, 00 A3 4DH, could also be shown as 0A3 4DH.

Even if a program works perfectly, the programmer needs to understand and be able to work with these numbering schemes. This is because coding assembler instructions involves the use of all three number schemes. Thorough understanding is especially important when the program has errors, because the debugging process relies heavily upon the ability to use hexadecimal numbers.

When working with assembler and these numbering schemes, a programmer performs two major activities: the conversion of data from one number system to another and the performance of addition and subtraction in hexadecimal. There is no way to program in assembler without being able to make these conversions and math calculations. There are mathematical approaches that can be used to make conversions. In reality, nearly all programmers depend on calculators or conversion tables for this purpose. Thus, for practical reasons, mathematical conversion methods are not discussed in this text. The easiest way to do calculations, of course, is to purchase a calculator and just push the buttons. However, when a calculator is unavailable, the following manual approaches will work.

1.7 CONVERSION TO AND FROM BINARY

When converting from binary to hexadecimal, group the digits into sets of four binary digits, beginning on the right and padding with 0's to make complete sets of 4 bits. Then match each 4-bit set with the hex equivalent in Table 1–1.

(Note: All the key tables of information that a programmer needs when coding assembler programs are reproduced in the appendixes.)

Suppose that it is necessary to convert 101B into hex. First, pad the string to get 0101B, and then search the table to find the exact hex match: 5.

Practice Exercises for Binary to Hex Conversion

Use Table 1–1 to convert the following binary numbers into hex:

a) 100B   d) 0001 1001B

b) 1110B   e) 0010 1101B

c) 1001B

TABLE 1–1 Binary to hex to decimal values

Binary	Hex	Decimal
0000	0	0
0001	1	1
0010	2	2
0011	3	3
0100	4	4
0101	5	5
0110	6	6
0111	7	7
1000	8	8
1001	9	9
1010	A	10
1011	B	11
1100	C	12
1101	D	13
1110	E	14
1111	F	15

You should get these results:

a) 04H   d) 19H

b) 0EH   e) 2DH

c) 09H   □

It is possible to find the decimal equivalent of the binary number by reading across Table 1–1 to the third column. However, this can be done **only if** the binary number does not exceed four binary digits. If the binary number is larger, it is necessary to first convert the number into hex and then convert the hex number into decimal. The guidelines for doing this are shown in the next section. Alternatively, it is possible to convert from decimal into binary, using standard mathematical procedures, and then to convert binary into hex. Perhaps the easiest conversion method is to use a calculator!

Table 1–1 can also be used to convert a hex or decimal number into binary. This can be done **only if** the number is one hex digit long or a decimal value less than 16. In these cases, all that you must do is to look up the hex or decimal number and read the corresponding binary equivalent.

However, if the number is longer than one hex digit **and** the number is in hex, then it is possible to convert to binary by converting each hex digit into binary from the table and stringing the binary digits together, thus creating a rather long binary string result.

If the number is in decimal and is larger than 15, then first convert the number from decimal into hex (see the next section) and then use Table 1.1 to convert the hex digits into binary (or use a calculator or mathematical procedures). For example:

3H   becomes   0011B

0AH   becomes   1010B

13   becomes   1101B

34H   becomes   0011 0100B

Practice Exercises for Hex to Binary Conversion ————————————

Use Table 1–1 to convert the following hex digits into binary:

a) 02H   d) 9FH   g) 9

b) 0DH   e) 0FFH   h) 14

c) 23H   f) 3E 7DH   i) 3

You should get these results:

a) 0010B   c) 0010 0011B

b) 1101B   d) 1001 1111B

e) 1111 1111B   h) 1110B

f) 0011 1110 0111 1101B   i) 0011B

g) 1001B   ◻

Notice one other fact from Table 1–1. It takes a maximum of four binary digits, or 4 bits, to represent one hex digit. One hex digit is frequently referred to as a nibble.

1.8 CONVERSION BETWEEN DECIMAL AND HEXADECIMAL

The ability to make conversions from hex to decimal and vice versa is even more important than being able to make binary conversions. This will become very apparent as you work with assembler programs and routines. Conversion to and from hex is accomplished by using Table 1–2. (The table is also reproduced in Appendix B.)

The layout of the table is based on hex digit positions, or columns. Assume you want to convert the number 2D6H into decimal. The 6 is in the first column, or units position; the D is in the second column, or tens position; and the 2 is in the third column, or hundreds position. Within each

TABLE 1–2   Hex to decimal conversion

Hex digit columns

Hex ten thousands 5		Hex thousands 4		Hex hundreds 3		Hex tens 2		Hex units 1	
hex	decimal	hex	decimal	hex	decimal	hex	decimal	hex	decimal
0	0	0	0	0	0	0	0	0	0
1	65,536	1	4,096	1	256	1	16	1	1
2	131,072	2	8,192	2	512	2	32	2	2
3	196,608	3	12,288	3	768	3	48	3	3
4	262,144	4	16,384	4	1,024	4	64	4	4
5	327,680	5	20,480	5	1,280	5	80	5	5
6	393,216	6	24,576	6	1,536	6	96	6	6
7	458,752	7	28,672	7	1,792	7	112	7	7
8	524,288	8	32,768	8	2,048	8	128	8	8
9	589,824	9	36,864	9	2,304	9	144	9	9
A	655,360	A	40,960	A	2,560	A	160	A	10
B	720,896	B	45,056	B	2,816	B	176	B	11
C	786,432	C	49,152	C	3,072	C	192	C	12
D	851,968	D	53,248	D	3,328	D	208	D	13
E	917,504	E	57,344	E	3,584	E	224	E	14
F	983,040	F	61,440	F	3,840	F	240	F	15

column there are two subcolumns. The hex digit is shown in the left column; the decimal equivalent is in the right column.

1.9 CONVERTING FROM HEXADECIMAL TO DECIMAL

In many ways, converting from hex to decimal is simpler than going from decimal to hex. Consider converting 25H to decimal. The 5 is in the first hex column, or units position; the 2 is in the second, or tens position. First, find column 1 in Table 1–2 and scan down that hex subcolumn until you find a matching 5. Then read the corresponding decimal value to the right of the hex digit. In this case, it's a decimal 5. Next, take the 2; it is in the second hex position. Scan down the second hex column, looking for a match. Then read the corresponding decimal value; in this case it's 32. Finally, add the two decimal values found: 5 + 32 = 37. Thus, 37 is the decimal equivalent of the hexadecimal number 25H.

Suppose you want to convert the hexadecimal number 0DAH into its decimal equivalent. The A has a value of 10 and the D has a value of 208. After adding these two values you find that 0DAH is equivalent to decimal 218.

Practice Exercises for Hex to Decimal Conversion _____

Use Table 1–2 to convert the following hex numbers into decimal:

a)   0FFH   d)   01 00H

b)   10H   e)   01 F9H

c)   0D 4CH

You should get these results:

a)   255   d)   256

b)   16   e)   505

c)   3,404   □

1.10 CONVERTING FROM DECIMAL TO HEXADECIMAL

Converting from decimal to hex is more difficult than going from hex to decimal. The procedure is as follows.

1.   Begin by scanning down the first decimal column on the right in Table 1–2. Look for an exact match. If there is none, look for the largest decimal value less than the value to be converted. If you reach the bottom of a column, continue scanning at the top of the next column. The hex digit to be selected will be either the digit that corresponds to an exact match or the digit that corresponds to

the decimal value that is just less than the decimal value to be converted.

2. Look at the number of the colum in which you found the match or near match. The column number indicates the position of the match or near match in the new hex number.

3. If you did not find an exact match, then subtract the decimal value found from the original decimal value. This becomes the new decimal value to convert.

4. Repeat the first three steps until the entire decimal value has been used.

5. When there is an exact match, check to see if you need to append 0's to the right of the hex digit to fill out the hex number. For example, if there is an exact match in the third column, append two 0's as place holders.

Suppose, for example, that you want to convert a decimal 13 into hex. Scanning down the first column, you find an exact match at hex D. Since it is in the first, or units column, the hex equivalent of decimal 13 is 0DH.

Now try 130. Since 130 is not in column 1 of Table 1–2, scan column 2. Notice that 130 lies between hex 8 and 9. Write down the lower value, hex 8, in the second column of the new hex number. Next, take the decimal value of hex 8 from the second column of the table (that is, take 128) and subtract it from 130. The result is 2. Scan down the first column, looking for a match. Since there is a match for the 2, put the value found (hex 2) in the first hex column. Thus, 82H is the equivalent of the decimal number 130.

How about 32? There is no match in column 1 of Table 1–2, so scan the second column, to find an exact match at hex 2. Therefore, place a 2 in the second column of the new hex number. Since that hexadecimal 2 equals 32, the complete decimal value has been used. In this case, insert a trailing 0 digit to the right of the hex 2 to show that 2 is in the second hex column. Thus, 20H is equal to decimal 32.

How about a larger number? Try 900. The first hex digit that is large enough but not larger than 900 is hex 3 in the third column of Table 1–2. Hex 3 has a decimal value of 768. Subtracting 768 from 900 leaves 132. Continuing the search, find the hex digit closest to decimal 768. The closest is 8 in the second column of the table. The decimal value of hex 8 is 128. The difference between 132 and 128 is 4. Since a decimal 4 is the same as a hex 4, the last digit in the new hex number is 4. Therefore, 03 84H is equivalent to decimal 900.

Practice Exercises for Decimal to Hex Conversion _____

Use Table 1–2 to convert the following from decimal to hex:

a) 89   c) 158   e) 3,409

b) 79   d) 1,233

You should get these results:

a)   59H   d)   04 D1H

b)   4FH   e)   0D 51H

c)   9EH   □

1.11 CONVERTING TO AND FROM BINARY FROM LARGER DECIMAL VALUES

To make a conversion all the way to binary from decimal, you must first convert the decimal number into hexadecimal by using Table 1–2. Then convert each hex digit into binary using Table 1–1. For example, 127 is first converted into 7FH by using Table 1–2. Then it is converted into 0111 1111B by using Table 1–1.

Conversely, if you want to convert a binary number into decimal, first convert the binary into hexadecimal by using Table 1–1. Then convert the hex into decimal by using Table 1–2. For example, if you want to know what 0101 0011B is in decimal, convert it into 53H and then into a decimal 83.

1.12 ADDITION IN HEXADECIMAL

Frequently, in the process of debugging a program, it is necessary to compute the location of data in memory by either adding or subtracting small hex numbers. A typical problem might be

$$
\begin{array}{r}
04 \quad DEH \\
+\ 00 \quad 5AH \\
\hline
\end{array}
$$

This is handled by adding the columns from the right to the left as in a decimal addition problem. Therefore, the first addition is E + A. To do this, convert each digit into decimal. Add the decimal pairs and convert the sum back into hex. If the sum exceeds one digit, then carry the left digit into the next hex column. In this case you have 14 + 10, or 24. Convert the 24 back to 18H. Write down the 8 and carry the 1 to the next column.

$$
\begin{array}{r}
1 \quad\quad \leftarrow \textbf{Carry} \\
04 \quad DEH \\
+\ 00 \quad 5AH \\
\hline
8H
\end{array}
$$

Next, do the same for the next column: 1 + D + 5. This gives 1 + 13 + 5, or 19, which is 13H.

```
        1            ← Carry
     04  DEH
   + 00  5AH
     ─────────
         38H
```

Finally, add the carry and the 4.

```
     04  DEH
   + 00  5AH
     ─────────
     05  38H
```

Practice Exercises for Hexadecimal Addition _____

Test your understanding of hexadecimal addition with the following problems.

```
a) 03 D5H      b) 11 A3H       c)    9DH      d) 01 FCH
   +    19H       + 2 EFH          + A5H         +    2CH
   ─────────      ─────────        ─────────     ─────────
```

You should get these results:

```
a) 03 EEH      b) 14 92H      c) 01 42H      d) 02 28H      ▫
```

1.13 SUBTRACTION IN HEXADECIMAL

Subtraction in hexadecimal is similar to hexadecimal addition. Remember that when you borrow in hex subtraction, however, the value borrowed is not 10 as in decimal subtraction; rather, the value borrowed is 16.

Suppose that you have the following problem:

```
     03  D4H
   - 01  F6H
     ─────────
```

First, 1 is borrowed from the D, making it C. Then 16 is added to the 4, giving 20. When the subtraction is done, you have 14, which is E in hex.

```
         C1
     03  D4H
   - 01  F6H
     ─────────
          EH
```

Next, 1 is borrowed from the 3, leaving 2. Then 16 is added to 12 (the value of the C), giving 28. Finally, 15 (the value of the F) is subtracted from 28. The result is 13, which is D in hex.

$$
\begin{array}{cc}
 & \overset{1}{} \\
2 & \cancel{C} \\
0\cancel{3} & \cancel{0}4H \\
-01 & F6H \\
\hline
 & DEH
\end{array}
\quad \leftarrow \textbf{Borrow}
$$

Last, 1 is subtracted from 2.

$$
\begin{array}{cc}
 & \overset{1}{} \\
02 & C4H \\
0\cancel{3} & \cancel{0}4H \\
-01 & F6H \\
\hline
01 & DEH
\end{array}
\quad \leftarrow \textbf{Borrow}
$$

Practice Exercises for Hexadecimal Subtraction ———————

Test your understanding of hexadecimal subtraction with the following problems:

a)	1CH	b)	A9H	c)	63H	d)	72H	e)	01	23H
	− 06H		− 25H		− 27H		− 18H		− 00	2AH

You should get these results:

a)	16H	b)	84H	c)	3CH	d)	5AH	e)	00 F9H	□

Try to develop your ability to convert between number schemes and to perform hex addition and subtraction. It will aid not only your coding and debugging efforts, but also your understanding of how the computer works. With a basic understanding of these basic number schemes, you can begin your survey of personal computer architecture.

1.14 PERSONAL COMPUTER ARCHITECTURE

A typical microcomputer system consists of the **main processor** and a number of input/output (I/O) devices.

The main processor is composed of two parts, the **central processing unit (CPU)** and the **main storage,** or **main memory.** The CPU is where all the math, comparison, logic, data movement, and I/O instructions are executed. Main storage is where the data being processed and the machine instructions (the program) are held.

Some of the primary I/O devices are a **cathode ray tube (CRT)** with its video card; the **keyboard;** a **printer;** one or more drives for **floppy**

disks; and, possibly, a **hard disk.** The CRT is a TV-like display monitor. Some are monochrome (that is, of a single color such as black, green, or amber), some display in color, and others produce superb graphics with or without color. The keyboard is used to enter characters, numbers, and other program control information. The keyboard is a device separate from the CRT. When a key is pressed, the program must determine if a key was pressed and which one; then the value that key represents may be displayed on the CRT. (Just because a key is pressed does not automatically mean the program has received it or that it will be displayed on the monitor.) Floppy disks and the hard disk are referred to as auxiliary storage devices. This is because they are external to the main processor and are used to store large amounts of data and programs. Because access to data on these auxiliary storage devices is so fast, data and programs are transferred to and from main storage very quickly.

Each primary I/O device is controlled by its own specific set of instructions, or commands. The commands must be coded for the device to perform its input or output operations. With high-level languages, it is often sufficient to simply enter the command READ. In this case the data in a logical data record such as a customer account record is input, no matter from which device. But with assembler, the instructions for reading a record vary from device to device, adding yet another layer of complexity to the job of creating a program. Several chapters are devoted to the details of just how to code the different input and output operations.

1.15 MAIN STORAGE CONCEPTS

The smallest storage element is called a **bit.** A bit is one binary digit in size and can hold a value of 0 or 1. Functionally, a bit is often used to show an on/off status, to serve as a yes/no switch, or a set/clear flag that indicates the result of processing. The use of the bit is limited because a single bit cannot be accessed directly. When presented in video or printed form, 4 bits are commonly grouped together and shown as one hex digit. This hex digit is called a **nibble.**

The **byte** is the smallest, directly accessible unit of data. It is composed of 8 connected bits and can hold one character of data. It is the smallest unit of data that the data movement, math, and I/O instructions operate upon.

In the next two chapters, you will find that when you are debugging a program, the computer often shows the contents of a byte by displaying the data in hexadecimal. Since a byte consists of 8 bits, then 2 hex nibbles are required to display 1 byte. Thus, you have bits, nibbles, and bytes. Apparently, someone had a sense of humor when they came up with these names.

Suppose that a byte contains the number 4. Each bit can be identified by its bit number:

bit number	7	6	5	4	3	2	1	0
1 byte:	0	0	0	0	0	1	0	0

or shown in hex as

0 4

or represented as simply   04H

Thus, this example can be shown in three ways:

4   04H   0000 0100B

Notice that bit number 2 is "on" in the binary representation. This means that, actually, the third bit is a 1, not the second. With computers, all numbering schemes begin with 0 as the first number, not 1. Using this same logic, you can infer that the first byte of main storage is byte number 0, not byte number 1.

In the context of data storage in a personal computer, a **word** is composed of 2 bytes, or 16 bits. A word represents the largest field that can be entered into a register or used directly for math operations. (Larger fields can be used, but not directly.)

Small computers—like the KAYPRO II, Radio Shack Model 4, and the Commodore 64—have a word size that is only 1 byte, or 8 bits. On large microcomputers and mainframes, the word size is 4 bytes, or 32 bits. In general, the larger the word size, the faster the computer can perform math operations.

A 16-bit word containing the number 4 appears as

bit numbers within the word	15	14	13	12	11	10	9	8	7	6	5	4	3	2	1	0
1 word	0	0	0	0	0	0	0	0	0	0	0	0	0	1	0	0

or in hex as

0 0	0 4

or simply as

00 04H

On the personal computer there are three byte combinations larger than 1 word. They are the doubleword, quadword, and the tenbyte.

A **doubleword** is composed of 4 connected bytes, or 32 bits. It is frequently used when working with very large integer numbers.

A **quadword** is composed of 8 bytes, or 2 doublewords.

A **tenbyte** is 10 bytes in size.

Quadwords and tenbytes are seldom used by beginning programmers. Therefore, it is best, at this time, to concentrate on learning about bits, nibbles, bytes, words, and perhaps a few uses of doublewords.

1.16 MAIN STORAGE DATA TYPES

There are several different main storage formats for storing data on a microcomputer. Of these, two are vastly more important than the others, especially for beginning programmers: character data and integer binary number data. (Some of the others—bit data, binary coded decimal, and floating point—are discussed in later chapters.)

1.17 CHARACTER DATA

The **character data** class includes the uppercase letters "A" through "Z" and the lowercase letters "a" through "z"; the digits 0 through 9; and numerous special characters, such as

! # $ % ^ & * ( ) - _ + = ? / | \ ` ~ , . ; : ' "

and so on. All data in character format may be displayed on either a screen or a printer and may be entered directly from the keyboard. Each character is stored in 1 byte of main storage.

The representation of character data in memory is based on a mutual agreement among computer manufacturers, computer users, and various other interested groups. For most microcomputers, the unique pattern that has been agreed upon is called **ASCII,** which stands for *American Standard Code for Information Interchange.*

As previously indicated, 1 byte is composed of 8 bits. Therefore, each character is represented by one unique pattern, or combination, of bits. How many unique patterns can you have in 1 byte? The following abbreviated representation of bit patterns shows some of the various combinations in 1 byte.

```
0000   0000B
0000   0001B
0000   0010B
0000   0011B
0000   0100B
        .        .
        .        .
        .        .
1111   1110B
1111   1111B
```

There are a total of 256 unique patterns available for representing characters of data. The personal computer uses 26 combinations to store the uppercase letters of the alphabet, 26 for the lowercase letters, 10 for numbers, and perhaps two dozen for special characters (including the blank, or space). These combinations represent fewer than 100 characters. There are also several dozen control combinations that are used to implement special control functions. CTRL-C, for example, aborts a program and returns to DOS. With the addition, by IBM, of over one hundred special graphics characters, all possible combinations have now been assigned.

To see how the ASCII combinations are applied, consider the unique value 0100 0001B, or 41H. Everyone who subscribes to the ASCII code has agreed that when a byte contains 41H, and if that byte is supposed to be holding character data, it is the letter "A."

Table 1–3 shows the complete set of ASCII codes. Note that the codes above 7FH are generally used for graphic characters. (On many mainframe computers a different pattern has been agreed upon. It is called EBCDIC. The existence of the two competing coding schemes causes some problems when attempting to transfer data from a microcomputer to a mainframe computer and vice versa.)

Notice that the uppercase letter "A" is stored as 41H and the lowercase letter "a" is stored as 61H. Since this is true, the lowercase letters can be converted to uppercase very simply, by subtracting 20H from the lowercase ASCII values. This will become a useful principle later on.

The codes for digits are easily recognized because they are stored in an easily recognizable pattern: 3xH, where x represents the digit. For example, 33H is decimal 3, 34H is decimal 4, and 39H is decimal 9.

You should memorize the code for the blank, or space, character: 20H. This code is so common in main storage that it is worth remembering.

The values below 20H are commonly used as **control codes.** For example, if the code 07H is sent to the CRT, the internal bell sounds; if the code 0CH is sent to the printer, a formfeed (FF) results. When the ENTER (RETURN) key is pressed, the keyboard sends 0DH (a carriage return, CR) to the program. The code 0AH is the line feed character (LF) for the printer or CRT. The control codes for carriage return (0DH) and line feed (0AH) should also be memorized.

TABLE 1-3 ASCII Codes

Ctrl	Dec	Hex	Char	Code
^@	0	00		NUL
^A	1	01	☺	SOH
^B	2	02	☻	STX
^C	3	03	♥	ETX
^D	4	04	♦	EOT
^E	5	05	♣	ENQ
^F	6	06	♠	ACK
^G	7	07	•	BEL
^H	8	08	◘	BS
^I	9	09	○	HT
^J	10	0A	◙	LF
^K	11	0B	♂	VT
^L	12	0C	♀	FF
^M	13	0D	♪	CR
^N	14	0E	♫	SO
^O	15	0F	☼	SI
^P	16	10	►	DLE
^Q	17	11	◄	DC1
^R	18	12	↕	DC2
^S	19	13	‼	DC3
^T	20	14	¶	DC4
^U	21	15	§	NAK
^V	22	16	▬	SYN
^W	23	17	↨	ETB
^X	24	18	↑	CAN
^Y	25	19	↓	EM
^Z	26	1A	→	SUB
^[	27	1B	←	ESC
^\	28	1C	∟	FS
^]	29	1D	↔	GS
^^	30	1E	▲	RS
^_	31	1F	▼	US

Dec	Hex	Char		Dec	Hex	Char		Dec	Hex	Char
32	20	(space)		64	40	@		96	60	`
33	21	!		65	41	A		97	61	a
34	22	"		66	42	B		98	62	b
35	23	#		67	43	C		99	63	c
36	24	$		68	44	D		100	64	d
37	25	%		69	45	E		101	65	e
38	26	&		70	46	F		102	66	f
39	27	'		71	47	G		103	67	g
40	28	(		72	48	H		104	68	h
41	29	)		73	49	I		105	69	i
42	2A	*		74	4A	J		106	6A	j
43	2B	+		75	4B	K		107	6B	k
44	2C	,		76	4C	L		108	6C	l
45	2D	-		77	4D	M		109	6D	m
46	2E	.		78	4E	N		110	6E	n
47	2F	/		79	4F	O		111	6F	o
48	30	0		80	50	P		112	70	p
49	31	1		81	51	Q		113	71	q
50	32	2		82	52	R		114	72	r
51	33	3		83	53	S		115	73	s
52	34	4		84	54	T		116	74	t
53	35	5		85	55	U		117	75	u
54	36	6		86	56	V		118	76	v
55	37	7		87	57	W		119	77	w
56	38	8		88	58	X		120	78	x
57	39	9		89	59	Y		121	79	y
58	3A	:		90	5A	Z		122	7A	z
59	3B	;		91	5B	[		123	7B	{
60	3C	<		92	5C	\		124	7C	|
61	3D	=		93	5D	]		125	7D	}
62	3E	>		94	5E	^		126	7E	~
63	3F	?		95	5F	_		127	7F	⌂*

Dec	Hex	Char		Dec	Hex	Char		Dec	Hex	Char		Dec	Hex	Char
128	80	Ç		160	A0	á		192	C0	└		224	E0	α
129	81	ü		161	A1	í		193	C1	┴		225	E1	ß
130	82	é		162	A2	ó		194	C2	┬		226	E2	Γ
131	83	â		163	A3	ú		195	C3	├		227	E3	π
132	84	ä		164	A4	ñ		196	C4	─		228	E4	Σ
133	85	à		165	A5	Ñ		197	C5	┼		229	E5	σ
134	86	å		166	A6	ª		198	C6	╞		230	E6	µ
135	87	ç		167	A7	º		199	C7	╟		231	E7	τ
136	88	ê		168	A8	¿		200	C8	╚		232	E8	Φ
137	89	ë		169	A9	⌐		201	C9	╔		233	E9	Θ
138	8A	è		170	AA	¬		202	CA	╩		234	EA	Ω
139	8B	ï		171	AB	½		203	CB	╦		235	EB	δ
140	8C	î		172	AC	¼		204	CC	╠		236	EC	∞
141	8D	ì		173	AD	¡		205	CD	═		237	ED	φ
142	8E	Ä		174	AE	«		206	CE	╬		238	EE	ε
143	8F	Å		175	AF	»		207	CF	╧		239	EF	∩
144	90	É		176	B0	░		208	D0	╨		240	F0	≡
145	91	æ		177	B1	▒		209	D1	╤		241	F1	±
146	92	Æ		178	B2	▓		210	D2	╥		242	F2	≥
147	93	ô		179	B3	│		211	D3	╙		243	F3	≤
148	94	ö		180	B4	┤		212	D4	╘		244	F4	⌠
149	95	ò		181	B5	╡		213	D5	╒		245	F5	⌡
150	96	û		182	B6	╢		214	D6	╓		246	F6	÷
151	97	ù		183	B7	╖		215	D7	╫		247	F7	≈
152	98	ÿ		184	B8	╕		216	D8	╪		248	F8	°
153	99	Ö		185	B9	╣		217	D9	┘		249	F9	∙
154	9A	Ü		186	BA	║		218	DA	┌		250	FA	·
155	9B	¢		187	BB	╗		219	DB	█		251	FB	√
156	9C	£		188	BC	╝		220	DC	▄		252	FC	ⁿ
157	9D	¥		189	BD	╜		221	DD	▌		253	FD	²
158	9E	₧		190	BE	╛		222	DE	▐		254	FE	■
159	9F	ƒ		191	BF	┐		223	DF	▀		255	FF	(blank)

*ASCII code 127 has the code DEL. Under DOS, this code has the same effect as ASCII 8 (BS). The DEL code can be generated by CTRL-BACKSPACE.

As you have seen, character data is stored in main storage in ASCII, one character per byte. Now look at the storage of strings of characters, which are stored in consecutive bytes of memory.

If you enter the strings of data shown in the first column in the table that follows, they are stored as shown in the second column. Notice that the characters are enclosed in apostrophes. This is done to differentiate between the strings (which are the names of data fields,) and the data to be stored in the strings. The apostrophes do not occupy storage positions.

strings entered	actually stored as
'ABC'	41 42 43H
'JANUARY'	4A 41 4E 55 51 59H
'123'	31 32 33H
'-123'	2D 31 32 33H

1.18 BINARY NUMBER DATA

The **integer binary number** class of data represents numbers stored in true binary format. For example, the number 3 is stored in 8 bits as 0000 0011B, which is $1 \times 2^1 + 1 \times 2^0 = 2 + 1 = 3$. The number 10 is stored as 0000 1010B, or 0AH. The computer displays and accepts data in hex format instead of forcing you to create and enter the longer binary strings.

There are two forms of binary numbers: **signed** and **unsigned.** The unsigned number format uses all available bits to represent the value. The signed number format, however, uses the leftmost, or first, bit of the field to represent and hold the sign. If 0B is in the sign position, the number is positive (+); 1B in the sign position means the number is negative (−).

Thus, +3 is stored as 03H, or 0000 0011B. Since the first 0 bit of the byte is the sign, a signed 3 is exactly the same as an unsigned 3. Likewise, a +10 and an unsigned 10 are stored identically as 0AH, or 0000 1010B.

What does 7FH, or 0111 1111B, represent? Either a +127 or an unsigned 127. What if you add 1 to this binary value? It becomes 1000 0000B, or 80H. It is an unsigned 128. But wait, the sign bit now contains a 1 bit. This means that if the number is to be a signed number, it is negative.

1.19 NEGATIVE BINARY NUMBERS

Negative binary numbers in the Intel processors are always stored in the **2's complement** form, whereas other microprocessors may use the 1's complement. Suppose that you want to store a −1 in one byte. You must carry out the following procedure:

Steps to Represent Negative Binary Numbers

1. Ignore the – sign; assume the value is positive and convert it into hexadecimal.

2. Convert the hex equivalent into binary.

3. Complement all digits—that is, flip the digits by changing all 0 bits to 1 bits and all 1 bits to 0 bits.

4. Add a binary 1 to this complemented result.

5. Convert the binary string back into hex.

By following these steps for –1, you get:

Step		
		01H
1	0000	0001B
2	1111	1110B
3	1111	1110B
4	+	1B
	1111	1111B
5		0FFH

Thus, –1 is stored in binary as 1111 1111B and shown in hex as 0FFH.
Now try –7:

Step		
		07H
1	0000	0111B
2	1111	1000B
3	1111	1000B
4	+	1B
	1111	1001B
5		0F9H

And try –12:

Step		
		12H
1	0000	1100B
2	1111	0011B
3	1111	0011B
4	+	1B
	1111	0100B
5		0F4H

Practice Exercises for Converting Negative Decimal Numbers to Hex

Convert the following negative decimal numbers to hex:

a) –4   c) –9   e) –15

b) –6   d) –11   f) –16

You should get these results:

a) 0FCH   c) 0F7H   e) 0F1H

b) 0FAH   d) 0F5H   f) 0F0H   □

Notice the pattern in the preceding exercises: As the numbers become more negative, the binary value shrinks from 0FFH to 0F0H. Hence, −17 is stored as 0EFH, and 80H is stored as −128.

1.20   BYTE AND WORD FORMATS

Binary numbers are commonly stored in one of two formats, either in 1 byte or 1 word. (Later on, when handling very large numbers, you will see how to use doublewords or even larger fields.)

For a 1-byte number, the signed values can range from 0 to +127 (00H to 7FH) and from −1 to −128 (0FFH to 80H). For a 1-byte unsigned number, the values can range from 0 to 255 (00H to 0FFH).

For a word number (2 bytes), the signed values can range from 0 to 32,767 (00 00H to 7F FFH) and from −1 to −32,768 (0FF FFH to 80 00H). Unsigned word numbers can range from 0 to 65,535 (00 00H to 0FF FFH).

1.21   MAIN STORAGE RULES

When examining a byte or word in main storage, there are three fundamental concepts to remember.

Concept 1:

When examining a binary number, there is **no** way to tell if that number is to be considered a signed or an unsigned number. Only the programmer knows how he or she intends to logically handle that number.

Concept 2:

When examining a byte, there is **no** way to tell if that byte is character data or binary data. For example, assume a byte contains 41H. It could represent the letter "A," a +65, or an unsigned 65. Only the programmer knows the byte's meaning.

Concept 3:

In general, the computer can perform math operations only on numbers in binary format, **never** when they are in character format. (Some exceptions occur in translation operations and when modifying and creating character data. See chapters 13 and 14.) In addition, the computer can print, display, or enter numbers only when they are in character format, **never** when they are in binary format. Thus, there is a fundamental difference between these two forms of storage. To do math, you will need to convert character data into binary data and back again to print it.

1.22   MAIN STORAGE ADDRESSING

Think of main storage as a vast array of bytes. Because of its vastness, the computer must have a way to identify each byte. This unique identifier is called an **address.** Consider for a moment post office boxes. They are also arranged as an array, with each mailbox having a unique box number–its address. Bytes are similar to mailboxes in that each byte has an address, with the first byte having an address of 0. The next byte has an address of 1, and so on. In this way, every byte in main storage has its own unique address.

Commonly, a personal computer has 640 kilobytes (640K) of main storage. Since 1K equals 1,024 bytes, the actual number of bytes is 655,360. Therefore, valid memory addresses commonly range from 0 to 655,359, or from 0 00 00H to 9 FF FFH. All addresses are considered unsigned binary integers. (Just as a post office box number of –10 makes no sense, a memory address of –10 does not exist.)

To accommodate 640K, the format of the addresses must consist of five hex digits. This means the addresses could conceivably range from 00H to 0F FF FFH, where 0F FF FFH is 1 byte less than 1,000K. (Another way of writing 1,000K is 1 megabyte, or 1 MEG.)

This presents an immediate problem. Personal computer architecture is designed to store an address in 1 word, or 2 bytes. This means that the largest address is 0FF FFH, or 64K. Obviously, this is a long way from 1 MEG. The personal computer addressing scheme, however, has a unique way of getting around this problem.

Main storage is divided into **segments,** each 64K in size. Any given byte is located somewhere within a 64K segment. The complete address for any byte is called a **vector.** A vector is composed of two words: an **offset address** and a **segment address.**

The **offset** is the distance the byte is from the beginning of the segment containing it. Thus, to access any given byte of storage, two different addresses must be provided: the segment address that the byte is in and the offset address of where within that 64K segment the byte is located. Figure 1–1 illustrates this principle.

Offset addresses are stored in a word as an unsigned binary number from 00 00H to 0FF FFH. Segment addresses are stored in an unusual manner. All segments begin on a **paragraph boundary.** A paragraph boundary is any absolute address that is evenly divisible by 16, or 10H. Figure 1–2 shows three paragraph boundaries in one view of main storage.

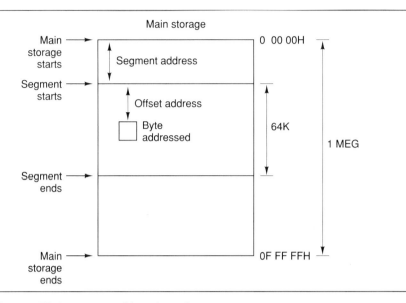

FIGURE 1-1   Main storage addressing scheme

Since a segment address always points to the start of a segment, an address may be greater than 64K in size—it can, for example, be 1 MEG. When this happens, the address does not fit in 1 word; rather, the address requires 1 word plus 1 nibble: 0F FF FFH. Because all segments are on a paragraph boundary, you know that the right nibble must be 0H (evenly divisible by 10H, or 16). Since the right nibble is always a 0 when the computer stores a segment address, it is stored by shifting it 1 nibble to the right. This "gets rid of" the extra nibble, and the resulting address can then be stored in 1 word.

For example, assume that you want to store the segment address of 128K: 131,072, or 02 00 00H. The address is stored by shifting it 1 0H nibble to the right; the address is stored as 20 00H.

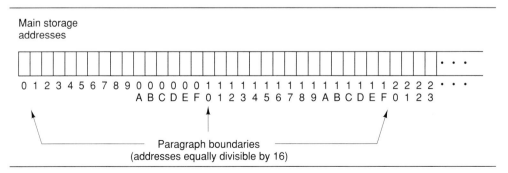

FIGURE 1-2   Paragraph boundaries

Suppose that you want to store the largest segment address possible, nearly 1 MEG, or 0F FF F0H. The segment address is shifted to the right 1 nibble and stored as 0FF FFH.

When the computer accesses main storage, it automatically computes the vector (the segment address and the offset address). In doing so, the internal circuitry first shifts the segment address to the left 1 hex digit, filling in the vacated nibble with a 0H. Now the computer has the true segment address. Finally, it adds the offset address to the true segment address to get the real main storage address of the byte. Since the computer does this automatically, beginning programmers seldom have to worry about this procedure.

1.23 STORAGE OF NUMBERS

Now comes the final confusing twist. When a word is held in a register, it appears exactly as described in this chapter. But when that word is moved into main storage, it is stored in reverse byte order.

Suppose that register AX contains hex 00 0A (this is how it would appear in the register), or 10. The hex 00 byte is the high-order (leftmost) byte of the register and the hex 0A is the low-order (rightmost) byte. When the value is placed into a word of storage, the computer stores the high-order byte of the register in the higher address of the 2 bytes of main storage and the low-order byte in the lower storage address.

```
        register AX                      storage address
                                          high      low
    high       low                      12 34H    12 35H

  +------+------+                     +------+------+
  |  00  |  0A  |                     |  0A  |  00  |
  +------+------+                     +------+------+
```

Thus, when examining a listing of the contents of main storage, the numbers appear to be stored backwards. When the values are moved back into a register, however, the computer loads the higher address's value into the high-order part of the register and the lower address's value into the register's low-order part. This tends to be very confusing to beginning programmers and is a source of interesting errors for forgetful advanced programmers.

1.24 THE CPU

The CPU is responsible for all math, comparisons, and data movement; in fact, it performs all the actual work. The CPU contains 14 high-speed word areas known as **registers,** all of which are 1 word in size (2 bytes, or 16 bits). These registers are grouped into five functional sets:

4 data registers	used as work areas for math and comparisons
4 segment registers	used for referencing data areas and code areas
3 pointer registers	used for offsets within segments
2 indexing registers	used for indexing and finding data
1 flag register	used to contain result or status information

The next sections examine each of these sets in detail.

1.25 THE DATA REGISTERS

The four *data registers* are AX, BX, CX, and DX. Each is capable of serving either as one 2-byte register or as two 1-byte registers any time the programmer desires.

The "X" suffix in the register name means the register is being used as a 2-byte, or word, register. When these 2-byte registers are used as two 1-byte registers, the suffix "H" is used for the *h*igh-order part and the suffix "L" for the *l*ow-order part. Thus, registers **AH** and **AL** make up the register AX:

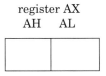

register AX
AH   AL

So, when an instruction references register AX, both bytes are used. When an instruction references register AH, only the left byte is used, and when it references AL, only the right byte is used. The other registers—BH, BL, CH, CL, DH, and DL—are named and handled in exactly the same way.

The contents of a register must always be shown as a hexadecimal. Suppose, for example, that you want to load a 10 into a register. This can be done with a MOV (move data) instruction. Carefully examine the following examples and be sure that you understand the results. (In these examples

$\leftarrow$ AX $\rightarrow$

	AH	AL
MOV AX,10	00	0A
MOV AH,10	0A	XX
MOV AL,10	XX	0A

"XX" means the previous contents are not changed; whatever value was there is still there.)

Register **AX** is known as the **primary accumulator register** and is often used in calculation operations.

Register **BX** is known as the **base register** and is also used for calculations. BX is the only register other than the index set of registers (DI and SI) and the base pointer (BP) register that can be used to reference memory locations.

Register **CX** is known as the **counter register**. It is used in calculations as well, but is also used primarily in controlling the number of times a loop is to be executed.

Register **DX** is known as the **data register.** Although it can be used in calculations (primarily with multiplication and division instructions), it is more frequently involved with I/O operations.

1.26   THE SEGMENT REGISTERS

There are four segment registers: CS, DS, SS, and ES. Each of these registers is 1 word in size and **cannot** be divided into two 1-byte registers. Their function is to hold segment addresses. Since the segment address is evenly divisible by 10H, it always has a 0 in the right hex nibble. (Remember, a segment is always aligned on a paragraph boundary—an address that is evenly divisible by 16, or 10H). All segment addresses stored in these registers are shifted 1 nibble to the right. Thus, a real segment address of 0C 10 00H is stored in a segment register as C1 00H.

Register **CS** is the **code segment register.** It points to the segment in which the current instructions of the program are being executed. (Under certain conditions, it can also point to the data segment.)

Register **DS** is the **data segment register.** It points to the program's data area or segment.

Register **SS** is the **stack segment register.** It must always point to the currently active stack segment. A **stack** is a large storage area that is used to save addresses and data in a last-value-saved, first-value-recovered, or last-in first-out (LIFO) sequence. It is heavily used to save the current contents of the registers just before calling a subroutine and for passing data to externally compiled subroutines. (The stack segment register will be covered in detail in Chapter 5.)

Register **ES** is the **extra segment register.** Like register DS, register ES points to a data area. It can be used to point to the same data area as the DS register or even to another entire 64K segment of data. Between the DS and ES registers, a program can directly reference 128K of data. ES is also used with string-handling instructions. Unless string-handling instructions are needed, register ES is seldom used by beginning programmers.

1.27 THE POINTER REGISTERS

There are three **pointer registers:** IP, SP, and BP. They are called pointer registers because they contain offset addresses that "point" to the location of items within a segment.

Register **IP**, or the **instruction pointer register,** is sometimes called the program counter (PC) register. It is *always* used with the CS register. IP contains the offset from the CS register to the current instruction to be executed. This is illustrated in Figure 1–3. The IP register is continually being updated as instructions are executed. The current instruction vector is held or retained by the CS:IP pair. Vectors are displayed by showing the segment address first, followed by the offset address, separated by a colon as in CS:IP.

Register **SP** is the **stack pointer register.** It is **always** coupled with the SS, or stack segment, register. The SP register contains the address of the next available unused byte in the stack segment. As subroutines are called, the return addresses are automatically stored in the stack and the SP is updated accordingly. The current available byte on the stack is given by the vector SS:SP. (The use of stacks will be discussed in Chapter 5.)

Register **BP,** the **base pointer register,** is also normally tied to the SS register. It permits accessing the values that are stored in the stack. Typically, these will be parameters that have been passed to external subroutines.

1.28 THE INDEXING REGISTERS

There are two **indexing registers:** the **DI,** or **destination index register,** and the **SI,** or **source index register.** These registers are used to provide a means of accessing main storage and normally contain offset addresses

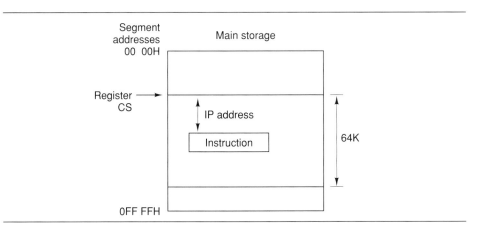

FIGURE 1–3   Using the instruction pointer register

within the data segment, indicated by DS and ES. (See also the BX register.) DI and SI are also used for indexing and for string-handling instructions.

1.29 THE FLAG REGISTER

The **flag register** contains information about the most recently executed instruction. A flag bit is said to be **set** if it contains 1, and is said to be **cleared** if it contains 0. Another way of looking at the flag register is to consider 0 as "false" and 1 as "true."

Only 9 of the 16 bits of the flag resister are actually used. The flag register's format is shown in Figure 1–4.

OF is the **overflow flag,** which indicates an overflow of a high-order bit following an arithmetic operation. OF also indicates that an error has occurred with signed numbers.

DF is the **direction flag,** which indicates the direction for moving or comparing data when using string-handling instructions.

IF is the **interrupt flag,** which indicates if an interrupt is currently disabled.

TF is the **trap flag.** If on, TF puts the CPU into the single-step mode. This mode allows a program to execute only one instruction at a time and then to examine the effects of that instruction on memory and the registers.

SF is the **sign flag,** which indicates the sign of the result of an arithmetic instruction; 0 indicates a positive result and 1 indicates a negative result.

ZF is the **zero flag,** which indicates if the result is 0. If ZF contains 0, the result is not 0; if ZF contains 1, the result is 0. Using the true/false approach, a 1 means true—the result is 0.

AF is the **auxiliary flag,** which contains any carry from bit 3 during a math operation. (This type of operation is discussed in Chapter 8.)

PF is the **parity flag,** which indicates the parity of low-order 8-bit data operations. If PF contains 1, parity is even; if PF contains 0, parity is odd.

Bit number

15	14	13	12	11	10	9	8	7	6	5	4	3	2	1	0
				OF	DF	IF	TF	SF	ZF		AF		PF		CF

FIGURE 1–4   Flag register bit assignments

        CF is the **carry flag,** which contains the carry from the high-order bit after an arithmetic operation or the value of the last bit of a shift or rotate instruction. If CF is set, it indicates that an error has occurred with unsigned numbers.

Of these flags, the most important are CF, OF, ZF, and SF.

1.30 PHYSICAL MEMORY MAP

Figure 1–5 is a typical main storage map for a personal computer. The actual values differ from one vendor to another, as does the amount of main storage that is physically available.

ROM-BIOS is the read-only memory section for the Basic Input-Output System. These low-level routines handle input and output to the various devices. They adapt the unique characteristics of a machine and its devices to the standard interface of DOS, providing a common method of programming.

Up to 640K of working RAM is usable by programs. When programs are in use this area is pointed to by the CS, SS, and DS segment registers (and sometimes by ES). Each segment register can point to 64K segments. To fully utilize all 640K, the segment registers must be reset as different segments are used.

Often a segment of 64K is not completely used, as in the case with smaller programs. The actual code, data, and stack segments usually overlap each other. If they did not, then the smallest program you could use would be 192K—three times 64K.

Suppose that the program code takes up 10K; the stack, 1K; and the data segment, 20K. In this case main storage and the segment registers appear as shown in Figure 1–6. This overlap causes no problem unless there is a program error, such as a subscript being out of bounds, a bad branch, or overflow from a stack that is too small.

Segment address	Contains
F 00 00H	ROM-BIOS
D 00 00H	Cartridge ROM
C 00 00H	Hard disk BIOS extension
B 00 00H	Conventional display memory video buffers
A 00 00H	Display expansion memory
1 00 00H	Up to 640K of working RAM for program
0 00 00H	System software work area (part of user's 640K)

FIGURE 1–5   Typical main storage map for a personal computer

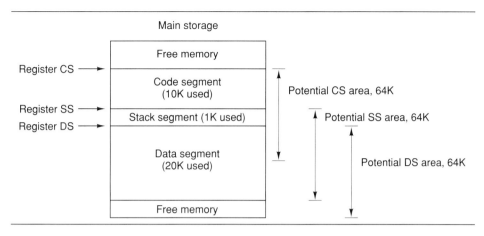

FIGURE 1–6 Main storage with segment registers

Understanding the numerous terms and concepts associated with microcomputer architecture is vital to successful assembler programming. The next chapter will outline the software needed for assembler programming, and subsequent chapters will present the instructions and how to use them.

1.31 SUMMARY

Computers execute machine language instructions. There is a one-for-one correspondence between machine language instructions and assembler instructions. Thus, coding at the assembler level provides for maximum control of the computer. If the computer is capable of a function, then an assembler program or subroutine can use that operation.

The major advantages of using assembler language include the ability to handle actions that are difficult or impossible in high-level languages, speedy program execution, and maximum control over the system. Perhaps the biggest disadvantage is that success as an assembler language programmer depends to a large degree on a thorough understanding of how the computer really functions—system internals. This understanding comes only after much study and use.

Assembler language programming utilizes numbers in the binary, hexadecimal, and decimal number systems. The ability to make conversions freely between these three systems and the ability to add and subtract in hex are crucial. The hexadecimal scheme is vital to understanding and working with the assembler language.

A microcomputer system normally consists of a main processor (including the CPU and main storage), a CRT, a keyboard, a printer, and floppy-disk or hard-disk drives.

The words *bit, nibble, byte, word, doubleword, quadword,* and *tenbyte* are used to describe and name the areas of different sizes in main storage. To access a byte in memory, a complete vector address must be specified. This address is composed of a segment address and an offset address. All segment addresses begin on a paragraph boundary in storage. A paragraph boundary is defined as any address that is evenly divisible by 16, or 10H. Segment addresses point to a 64K area of storage and are stored in a word with the value shifted to the right by 10H. The offset address contains the displacement (or distance) from the start of the 64K segment down to the desired byte.

Main storage holds two common types of data: character data and numerical data. Character data can be entered and displayed on the CRT and printer; in most cases math cannot be performed with this type of data. For beginning programmers, it is best for numeric data to be in the binary format and either signed or unsigned integers. Although numeric data are usable in math operations, they cannot be directly displayed or printed without being converted into a character format equivalent.

Character data are stored using the ASCII coding scheme, with one character per byte. Binary numbers are stored in byte, word, and—sometimes—doubleword forms. If a number is signed, the first bit of the field contains the sign: 0B indicates a positive number; 1B indicates a negative number. It is important to remember that when examining any random byte in memory, it is not possible to tell whether that byte is character data, a signed integer, an unsigned integer, or an instruction. Only the programmer knows what that byte is supposed to represent.

The CPU contains 14 word registers that are heavily used by programs. They can be grouped into several sets: the data registers (AX, BX, CX, DX), which are the only registers that can be broken down into two 1-byte registers (AH and AL and so on); the segment registers (CS, DS, ES, SS); the pointer registers (IP, SP, BP); the index registers (SI and DI); and the flag register.

There are 9-bit flags that indicate the results of certain actions. A flag is set when it contains 1B and is cleared when it contains 0B. The most important flags are the carry flag (CF), the overflow flag (OF), the zero flag (ZF), and the sign flag (SF).

1.32 REVIEW QUESTIONS

1. What are the different parts of main storage as found on a microcomputer? What are their sizes?

2. List each of the 14 registers and give its use.

3. What is the difference between the normal character set, control codes, and special keys? Where are each in the ASCII coding scheme?

4. The two main data types are character and binary numbers. Explain the differences between the two. Can two character numbers be added? Why or why not? Can a binary number be printed? Why or why not?

5. What is the difference between a signed and an unsigned number? Explain why you cannot tell if it is signed or unsigned just by looking. What ramifications do you foresee in this?

6. Suppose that you had a 3-byte binary number. What range of signed binary numbers could it hold? If it were an unsigned number, what range of numbers could it hold?

7. What is a paragraph boundary? Which of the following addresses are on paragraph boundaries: 03 40H, 9D FFH, 0D D0H, 38 F0H, 38 88H, 8A AAH

8. Explain the concept of segments and offsets. What is a vector? Why is a vector needed to fully specify any given storage location?

1.33 PRACTICE PROBLEMS

1. Convert the following from decimal to hex.
    a) 123
    b) 255
    c) 1,549
    d) 3,451
    e) 5,981

2. Convert the following from hex to decimal.
    a) 12H
    b) 34H
    c) 02 DAH
    d) 08 BFH
    e) 4D 6AH

3. Convert the following from decimal to binary.
    a) 3
    b) 12
    c) 16
    d) 4
    e) 8

4. Convert the following from binary to decimal.
    a) 0100 0011B
    b) 1010 0101B
    c) 1101 0110B
    d) 1111 1010B
    e) 0011 0111B

5. Convert the following decimal numbers into binary numbers.
   a) 12
   b) 80
   c) 100
   d) 254
   e) −12
   f) −5
   g) −100
   h) −76

6. Perform the following addition and subtraction problems.
   a) ```
         14H
       + 0DH
       ```

   b)  ```
         02 ACH
       + 03 F4H
       ```

   c) ```
         6D F3H
       + 13 3AH
       ```

   d)  ```
         05 6AH
       − 02 4BH
       ```

   e) ```
         21 32H
       − 12 45H
       ```

   f)  ```
         18H
       − 0DH
       ```

   g) ```
         02 43H
       − 01 E4H
       ```

   h)  ```
         18 18H
       + 08 18H
       ```

   i) ```
         AC EFH
       − 34 FDH
       ```

   j)  ```
         5D 41H
       + 63 ABH
       ```

7. Convert the following character fields and show what they will look like in main storage. Show two hex digits per byte.
   a) 'ABCDE'
   b) 'MAY'
   c) 'June'
   d) '123'
   e) '-123'

8. Using the conversion tables, show what the following number fields will look like in a byte of storage. Show two hex digits per byte.
   a)   123
   b)   +10
   c)   −10
   d)   155
   e)   −31
   f)   80
   g)   100

9. Using the conversion tables, show what the following number fields will look like in a word of storage. Show two hex digits per byte.
   a)   10
   b)   +13
   c)   −13
   d)   500
   e)   80
   f)   −5
   g)   1234

2

Running the
Assembler Software

2.1 CHAPTER OBJECTIVES

In this chapter you will

1. Learn what software is needed to create and execute assembler programs
2. Learn the overall assembler software system flow of control
3. Learn how to execute the MASM program
4. Learn how to execute the LINK program
5. Learn how to execute the symbolic debugging programs (SYMDEB, DEBUG, or CODE VIEW)
6. Study a simple assembler program that can be used as a model for your future programs

2.2 INTRODUCTION: THE ASSEMBLER PROGRAMMING CYCLE

A thorough knowledge of the software needed to create assembler programs plus your ability to use that software efficiently is crucial to successfully learning the assembler language.

When given a program to create, the first step is to design an optimum solution and then flowchart or pseudocode that solution. The logic of the solution should be desk-checked to make sure that it is correct. Only then should the solution be coded into the microassembler language. This coded solution is called the source program.

A source program file must then be created using a program editor or word processor and stored on a floppy disk or hard disk. Each assembler instruction must be included in the file. The word processor you use depends on your preference and what is available.

After creating the source program file, the next step is to convert the source program's assembler instructions into their machine language equivalents. This is done by running the assembler software program **MASM,** the *Macro Assembler*. Even after its conversion, the machine language program is still not ready to be run. The output of the assembler program must be further processed by the LINK program. This is a program that joins the various parts of the machine language program, making it an executable program.

After the output program is processed by LINK, it can be run to see if it executes correctly and produces the correct results. Since most programs do not work correctly the first time, the errors must be found and corrected. Generally, the best way to find assembler program errors is to run the problem program with a symbolic debugging program. A debugging program, under your guidance, executes one or more program instructions, then stops and allows you to examine the contents of the actual fields. The debugger allows you to reference the fields by their symbolic names, such as COST and TOTAL, thus eliminating the need for you to know the actual memory addresses of the fields.

When errors are found, the word processor is used to make the appropriate changes to the source program file. Then the program must be reassembled, relinked, and another debug run executed. This process is repeated until all errors have been corrected and the correct results are obtained.

You will begin your study of the assembler programming cycle by examining the software that is needed to assemble, link, and debug a program. Then you will learn how each kind of software is used. A simple program will illustrate the assembler programming cycle. This program, PGM1.ASM, is on the program disk that is available free with your text. We urge you to try the various commands with your software as you study this chapter. In addition to giving you practice, this simple program is intended to serve as a model or shell for your programs as you move into later chapters.

2.3 ASSEMBLER PROGRAMMING SOFTWARE

Assembler language programming requires a number of different development programs. They include the operating system (DOS) and several DOS utility programs, a word processor, and the assembler software. In addition, you will be using the master program disk available with this text. On this disk are the source program files for all the programming examples used in this book.

An assembler software diskette normally consists of an assembler program, a linker program, and a symbolic debugging program. There are numerous assembler packages on the market. The one we used is Microsoft Macroassembler, Version 5.1. The programs in this version are known as MASM, LINK, and CODE VIEW. However, all earlier versions of this product can be used with this text. For example, in Version 4.0 and earlier, the programs are known as MASM, LINK, and SYMDEB. We will discuss the use of both the SYMDEB and CODE VIEW debuggers when we cover the debugging process.

The programs and examples in this text are generally not version sensitive with respect to Microsoft versions and IBM versions. That is, it does not matter what version of assembler you have. There is one exception, which occurs with file handling; it is described in Chapter 9. This exception occurs because the oldest releases may support file handling only as described in Chapter 10. Where appropriate, version differences are discussed in depth.

If you are using an IBM PC, you will find that the official IBM assembler software is nearly identical to Microsoft Macroassembler. The IBM programs, however, are called MASM, LINK, and DEBUG. This package is completely compatible with this text.

If you are using another manufacturer's assembler package, you will need to follow the manufacturer's directions for running the programs. It is very likely that there will be some minor differences in the actual assembler language coding as well, so be alert for differences.

A word of caution: The DOS system provides a linker and a debugger, LINK and DEBUG. With some assembler packages (not Microsoft or IBM versions), it is possible to use the DOS system programs to link and debug programs. However, DOS LINK and DOS DEBUG do not work correctly with Microsoft and IBM versions. Be careful not to use DOS LINK and DEBUG.

2.4 SOFTWARE ORGANIZATION

All the software you will use can reside on five or six floppy disks or on a hard disk. If you are working on a floppy-disk system, then we recommend that you use the disk setup shown in Figure 2–1. In addition, create a backup copy of all the disks in case something should happen to one or all of them.

If you are running from a hard disk, then we recommend that you create separate subdirectories as shown in Figure 2–2. To use these files efficiently, you need to establish a PATH command to find these subdirectories. The path to the subdirectory for the assembler software **must** come before the subdirectory for DOS because, as indicated, DOS has programs called LINK and DEBUG. Avoid placing all files into one large

Disk	Contents
1	DOS operating system
2	Your word processor
3	Your program files
4	Text example program files
5	Assembler software (Version 4.0 and earlier)

or

Disk	Contents
5	Assembler software (Version 5.0 and later)
6	CODE VIEW (Version 5.0 and later)

FIGURE 2-1   Floppy-disk organization

Subdirectory	Contents
1	DOS operating system
2	Word processor
3	Assembler software
4	Text example program files
5	Your program files

FIGURE 2-2   Hard-disk subdirectories

subdirectory. Everything becomes difficult to find, and operation is slow because DOS must search such a large number of files.

One way to establish a subdirectory for the assembler software is by entering

```
MD C:\MASM
```

To load the assembler software into this subdirectory, use the following sequence:

```
CD C:\MASM
COPY A:*.* C:
```

The default directory is changed to \MASM, and then all programs are copied from the disk in drive A: into the subdirectory.

If the DOS utilities are already in a subdirectory called C:\UTILS and if your word processor is in a subdirectory called C:\WP, then the PATH command could be entered as

```
PATH C:\MASM;C:\WP;C:\UTILS;C:
```

Or, for example, you might build a subdirectory called C:\ASMPGMS. Then, to run the software, you change the default directory by entering

```
CD C:\ASMPGMS
```

Now the PATH command permits DOS to find the software and your program files.

2.5 THE WORD PROCESSOR

Unless you are using Microsoft Macroassembler, Version 5.1, your assembler package does not have a built-in word processor. Therefore, to enter your source code, you need to have some type of word processor. (A description of the Microsoft text editor called M is included at the end of this chapter.)

The requirements for a word processor are simple: The word processor must be able to create ASCII text files. If you use a sophisticated word processor such as WORDSTAR or WORD PERFECT, you *must* begin by entering the appropriate commands for switching the word processor to nondocument mode. When such word processors are in document mode, they insert numerous nonprintable control codes that implement special printing effects and page boundaries. If the assembler encounters any of these special codes, error messages result.

PC-WRITE is a word processor that you may want to consider for a text editor. It is easy to learn and use, it creates pure ASCII files as output, and it is inexpensive. There are other programs available on the market that are actually designed as program editors, but they are often more expensive than less specialized packages.

As a last resort, you can use the EDLIN program, which is on the DOS disk. EDLIN is the line editor program provided by IBM for entering data and programs into the computer. However, it is a relatively crude editor that allows you to enter and work with only one line of a program at a time. Word processors, on the other hand, can move quickly from line to line as the need arises.

2.6 SOURCE PROGRAM NAMES

After the program has been entered, you must give it a name and save it on your program disk. To do this, follow standard DOS file-naming conventions.

The complete name you select is made up of two parts:

filename.extension.

The filename, which must begin with a letter, may be composed of up to eight letters and/or numbers. Be sure to use program names that are meaningful and descriptive of the program. The extension *must* be the three-letter extension .ASM. If for some reason you neglect to include the .ASM extension, you can always use the command RENAME to correct the name. Again, keep your programs on a separate diskette or in a separate subdirectory, away from all other software. This will help to keep you organized.

Examples of good source program names are

PAYROLL.ASM	MATHELP.ASM	BOWLING.ASM
FUELCALC.ASM	MPG_CALC.ASM	TALLY.ASM

In naming the example program files, we elected to number the programs consecutively rather than to use descriptive names. This was necessary since many programs perform very nearly the same function, yet cannot have exactly the same name. It also simplifies cross-referencing the programs with the figure numbers in the chapters, for example: Figure 5–2, the stack example (PGM6.ASM on the program disk).

2.7   REQUIRED DOS PROGRAMS

In addition to the DOS functions that you would normally expect to have available (COPY and TYPE, for example), you may also need the MODE command to aid in printing assembler listings.

The assembler source program listing, which is created by the assembler program, is best printed on wide paper with 132 characters per line. If your printer handles only the narrower paper (80 characters per line), then it may be possible to use the MODE command to set the printer into condensed mode. This allows for printing up to 132 characters per line in condensed print. With some printers the MODE command does not send the correct printer control codes to set the printer into condensed mode. In these cases use whatever method you normally use to set the printer to condensed mode.

Note: After linking the program with the LINK program, the resultant executable program is normally a file with the extension .EXE. However, if you want to create .COM files instead of .EXE files, you need the program EXE2BIN. The differences between these two forms of the program will be discussed in a later chapter. All beginning programs introduced by this book create and use files with the .EXE extension only.

2.8   SYSTEM FLOW

Now that your software disks are organized, examine the system flowchart in Figure 2–3, which summarizes the overall operation of the software.

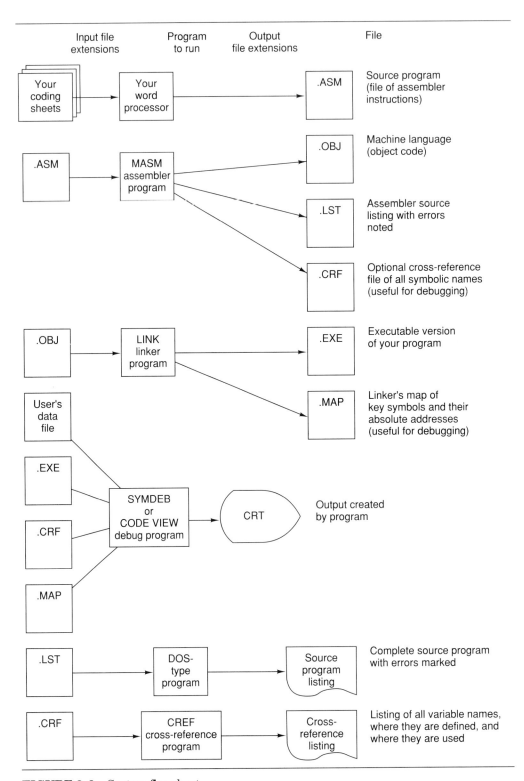

FIGURE 2–3 System flowchart

2.9   THE ASSEMBLER PROGRAMS

The MASM Program

The MASM program can create three output files. The first, an object file with the extension .OBJ, contains the machine instructions that correlate to the source code plus a few items that are needed when the program is made ready for execution. This file is always required if you want to create a program.

The second type of file that MASM produces is a list file with the extension .LST. This file contains the assembler listing of the source statements and includes all error messages, which are appropriately marked. It also shows the hex machine code that is generated. The list file is a text file that is in a format suitable for printing on the printer by using the DOS command COPY or for displaying on the screen by using the DOS command TYPE. A printout of the list file is extremely useful in debugging.

The third type of file created by MASM is a cross-reference output file with the extension .CRF. This file contains all the symbolic names used in the program. It is useful in keeping track of the many names used in large programs, and it optimizes the operation of the symbolic debugging program. For most small programs the .CRF file is not necessary except for use by the debugger. Since the .CRF file is not a text file, it requires further processing by the optional program CREF to change it to human-usable form.

The CREF Program

The optional **CREF** program uses the .CRF file as input and displays a listing that cross-references the file. This cross-reference listing shows all symbolic names and identifies the statement number where the variable is defined and all statements where that variable has been used. This information can be extremely useful when debugging and maintaining large programs.

The LINK Program

The **LINK** program builds an executable file by using the .OBJ file(s) as input. The output of the LINK program is the executable version of the program, which has the .EXE extension. In addition, LINK builds a .MAP file, which is used by the debugger program.

Running Your Program from the DOS Prompt

There are two ways to execute a completed program (the .EXE file). The first is to invoke the program from DOS. With the system prompt (A> or B> or C>) appearing on the screen, enter the name of the program. DOS then takes over and loads and executes the program. This is the normal way of executing complete, error-free programs.

The second way is used with programs that have just been written and usually have one or more errors, or bugs, in them. In such cases, the symbolic debugger program is loaded into main storage along with the .EXE program. The symbolic debugger helps find the errors.

Executing Your Program from the Symbolic Debugger

When preparing to debug your program, load the symbolic debugger into main storage. The debugger then inputs the .EXE version of your program along with the .LST, .CRF, and .MAP files, if they are present. These files are accessed by the debugger and used to provide you with the maximum information about your program during execution. The debugger enables you to step through the program one instruction at a time and to examine the results of the execution of each instruction. This lets you see the contents of the registers and the variables in main storage as each instruction is executed. It is infinitely easier to spot errors when using the debugger than when just running the program and observing the output.

2.10   A SAMPLE ASSEMBLER PROGRAM

Now that you are aware of the overall assembler flow of control, we need to discuss the specifics of how to operate the software. The adage "a picture is worth a thousand words" is appropriate at this point. To understand the operation of the software, consider a simple program. This program is on the master program disk and is named PGM1.ASM. Use the DOS command COPY to copy your program from the master program disk to your program disk or subdirectory. Then, as each command is discussed, you will be able to try it out.

This sample program provides more than a demonstration. It has been designed to serve as a model for beginning assembler programs. As such, you can use it as a shell for the programs you will be writing.

The objective of this first assembler program, PGM1.ASM, is to perform the steps required to add the contents of a field called COST to another field called TOTAL. Both are numeric fields of 1 word in size. COST currently contains the value 6 and TOTAL contains the value 4. After execution, TOTAL should contain the value 10. Remember that the computer can perform math on binary numbers only, not on ASCII (printable) numbers. Therefore, COST actually contains 00 06H and TOTAL actually contains 00 04H. After the addition, TOTAL should contain 00 0AH. This is really a very simple program. But, as you will see, it illustrates all the commands necessary to run the assembler system and provides a good program shell as well.

2.11 THE TWO VERSIONS OF THE SAMPLE PROGRAM AND YOUR DOS RELEASE

All versions of the DOS operating system are not equal. The major impact on assembler programming involves the way a program returns control to DOS after the program has finished executing.

Since Version 3.0 of DOS was released, the preferred method of ending a program is to use the DOS function END PROCESS. When a program ends, a return code is set that can be tested by batch files to determine appropriate action. Besides its ease of use, one of the primary reasons the END PROCESS function is preferred is because it is designed to facilitate coding assembler programs on the new OS/2 and PS/2 microcomputers. Prior to Version 3.0, this function was not available in DOS; another method was used to end assembler programs.

This text focuses on DOS Version 3.0 and later versions. However, this should not keep you from using one of the older releases.

To enable you to use early releases, we have included **two** versions of the sample program: one for DOS Version 3.0 and later releases and one for earlier releases. From the program disk select the program that is appropriate for your DOS release and the programs you will write. The versions are:

PGM1.ASM   For DOS Version 3.0 and later

PGM1A.ASM   For DOS version earlier than 3.0
                (Version 2.1, for example)

2.12 THE SAMPLE ASSEMBLER PROGRAM

Figure 2–4 shows PGM1.ASM, the source program after it has been created with a word processor. Figure 2–4a shows PGM1A.ASM, which is the same source program altered for early DOS releases.

You can display the source program on your screen by using the TYPE command followed by the program name.

```
A>TYPE PGM1.ASM
```

If you want a printed copy, toggle the printer to echo what appears on the screen. Do this by pressing the CTRL-P or CTRL-PRTSC and then using the DOS command TYPE. Alternatively, you can use the COPY command and copy the file to the printer.

```
A>COPY PGM1.ASM PRN
```

Or you can even type to the printer directly by entering

```
A>TYPE PGM1.ASM > PRN
```

```
        PAGE    60,132
        TITLE   PGM1    FIGURE 2-4 SAMPLE PROGRAM

;**********************************************************************
; PGM1       Title: Figure 2-4 Sample Program To Add COST to TOTAL   *
;                                                                     *
; Programmer: Vic Broquard                                           *
; Date Written:  6/11/88        Date Of Last Revision: 8/4/88        *
;                                                                     *
; Purpose: Add  two word numbers                                     *
;                                                                     *
; Special Requirements: None                                         *
;                                                                     *
;**********************************************************************


; program code segment

PGM1CD  SEGMENT

MAIN    PROC    FAR

; housekeeping section

        ASSUME  CS:PGM1CD,DS:PGM1DA,SS:PGM1SK

        MOV     AX,PGM1DA   ; ESTABLISH ADDRESSABILITY
        MOV     DS,AX       ; TO PGM1DA - THE PGM'S DATA SEGMENT

; main process section

        MOV     AX,COST     ; REG AX = COST
        ADD     AX,TOTAL    ; ADD COST TO TOTAL
        MOV     TOTAL,AX    ; STORE NEW TOTAL

; return to DOS section

        MOV     AL,0        ; SET 0 AS THE RETURN CODE FOR DOS
        MOV     AH,4CH      ; SET FOR DOS END PROCESS FUNCTION
        INT     21H         ; CALL DOS TO END PROGRAM

MAIN    ENDP

PGM1CD  ENDS


; program data segment

PGM1DA  SEGMENT
```

FIGURE 2–4   Sample assembler program

```
COST    DW    6
TOTAL   DW    4


PGM1DA  ENDS


; program stack segment

PGM1SK  SEGMENT PARA STACK 'STACK'

        DW    32 DUP (?)

PGM1SK  ENDS
        END
```

FIGURE 2–4   continued

```
        PAGE    60,132
        TITLE   PGM1A   FIGURE 2-4 ALTERNATIVE SAMPLE PROGRAM

;************************************************************************
; PGM1A       Title: Figure 2-4 Alternative Sample Program        *
;                                                                 *
; Programmer: Vic Broquard                                        *
; Date Written:  6/11/88       Date Of Last Revision: 8/4/88      *
;                                                                 *
; Purpose: Add  two word numbers                                  *
;                                                                 *
; Special Requirements: To be used for older DOS releases         *
;                                                                 *
;************************************************************************

; sample program to add cost to total

; program code segment

PGM1CD  SEGMENT

MAIN    PROC    FAR

; housekeeping section

        ASSUME  CS:PGM1CD,DS:PGM1DA,SS:PGM1SK

        PUSH    DS              ; SAVE DOS
        MOV     AX,0            ; RETURN
        PUSH    AX              ; ADDRESS
```

FIGURE 2–4a   Alternative sample assembler program   *(Continues)*

```
        MOV     AX,PGM1DA        ; ESTABLISH ADDRESSABILITY
        MOV     DS,AX            ; TO THE PGM'S DATA SEGMENT

; main process section

        MOV     AX,COST          ; REG AX = COST
        ADD     AX,TOTAL         ; ADD COST TO TOTAL
        MOV     TOTAL,AX         ; STORE NEW TOTAL

; return to DOS section

        RET                      ; RETURN TO DOS

MAIN    ENDP

PGM1CD  ENDS


; program data segment

PGM1DA  SEGMENT

COST    DW      6
TOTAL   DW      4

PGM1DA  ENDS


; program stack segment

PGM1SK  SEGMENT PARA STACK 'STACK'

        DW      32 DUP (?)

PGM1SK  ENDS
        END
```

FIGURE 2–4a   continued

Go ahead and display the source program now. Make a printed copy so you can mark it up with notes as the instructions in the program are discussed.

2.13   PGM1: THE SAMPLE PROGRAM

Now you will examine the major features of PGM1 and consider them from a general point of view. The next chapter explains each instruction in detail. The program uses two types of commands: instructions and assembler directives. **Instructions** actually create the machine language code; **directives** tell the assembler what activities it is to perform. The first command is the PAGE directive.

The **PAGE** directive causes the assembler to send a formfeed, or eject, code to the listing file (.LST). When the listing file is printed, the formfeed causes the paper to advance to a new page as needed.

In addition, the PAGE directive specifies the number of lines to be printed on a page and the number of characters on a line. The default is 66 lines, each with 80 bytes. In this case you want 60 lines, each with 132 bytes. The use of a longer print line in the source program listing is preferred because, on each line, the assembler adds to what was actually coded. As a result, many lines exceed 80 bytes. (If the shorter line length were used, the excess characters would wrap to the next line, making the listing difficult to read.)

Since most paper has a maximum of 66 lines per page, using the default of 66 lines leaves no room for page alignment errors. When errors happen, lines of code can end up being printed on the page perforations. Thus, if you specify 60 lines per page, form alignment is much easier. Having top and bottom margins also makes the listing more readable.

The next directive is the **TITLE** statement. Whatever you enter in the TITLE statement is reproduced at the top of every page. This heading serves as a form of program documentation.

Blank lines are inserted in the program by entering a carriage return—that is, by pressing the ENTER key. Blank lines separate sections of the program and so add to the program's readability.

A line that begins with a semicolon is treated as a **comment line** by the assembler. Meaningful and appropriately placed comments help a reader identify the major sections of the program and specify the overall processing that the section is to do. Use comment lines liberally.

PGM1CD SEGMENT identifies the start of the program code segment. The code segment contains all the actual instructions. Farther down the listing is a complementary statement, **PGM1CD ENDS.** This statement marks the end of the program code segment. The directives SEGMENT and ENDS are always paired.

The pair PGM1DA SEGMENT and the PGM1DA ENDS mark the beginning and the end of the data segment. This is where all the program variables are defined.

Similarly, the pair PGM1SK SEGMENT and PGM1SK ENDS mark the beginning and ending of the program stack segment. The stack is a large save area where values are temporarily stored. (Stacks will be discussed in detail in Chapter 5.)

Since this program is so small, there are no extra segments. If there were any, they would be placed after the program stack segment. (Extra segments will be discussed in a later chapter.)

The final statement, **END,** marks the physical end of the program. Nothing may follow this statement. If you unintentionally place any lines of code (including blank, or null, lines) after the END, they will be flagged as errors.

Now examine the entries in the data segment: the storage definitions for the two fields COST and TOTAL. Each is defined as a word by the **DW** (*define word*) directive. Since both fields are to have starting values, the actual values appear next: 6 and 4. (If the field were not to be initialized and had no starting value, a question mark would appear in the code. This would mean that the starting value was unknown.)

The stack segment contains an unnamed array of 32 fields, each 1 word in size. The **DUP** operator means that the value following it is to be duplicated; that is, that each of the 32 words has the same value. In Figure 2–4 a question mark appears after DUP, which means there is no starting value. Thus, all 32 words are uninitialized.

Now look at the complicated segment—the code segment. Notice that there is another pair of statements similar to SEGMENT and ENDS: MAIN PROC FAR and MAIN ENDP or **PROC FAR** and **ENDP.** The PROC FAR statement identifies the start of the procedure called MAIN.

A code segment is usually composed of one or more procedures. In this program there is only one procedure, and we arbitrarily called it MAIN. Any name could be used. The FAR option means that the procedure will be called from DOS and not from within PGM1 as a subroutine. There are many more rules about this option, but we'll save them for the next chapter.

The next directive, **ASSUME,** is required. The ASSUME statement tells the assembler and the DOS system to assume that when this program begins, the segment register CS is pointing to the program's code segment. The statement also tells the assembler that register DS is pointing to the program's data segment, PGM1DA. Further, it notifies the assembler that the SS register points to the stack segment, PGM1SK.

These statement entries are required because the assembler cannot determine this information for itself. When DOS loads and begins to execute the program, registers CS and SS point to the correct locations. Unfortunately, register DS does not. Thus, every program **must** have the next two housekeeping instructions, whose purpose is to get the DS (data segment) register pointing to the correct data segment—PGM1DA, in this example.

After the ASSUME statement, MOV moves the address of the data segment into register AX. Then, that value is moved into register DS, where it belongs. Now register DS contains the address of the data segment. (In a later chapter, you will learn exactly what the ASSUME statement and these two MOV instructions are really doing.)

It is acceptable to duplicate these two MOV instructions at the start of every program you write; the program will work if there are no errors.

Next comes the main processing section. The three instructions shown here add the contents of COST to TOTAL.

The sequence begins by using **MOV** to move the contents of COST into the accumulator, register AX. Next **ADD** adds the contents of TOTAL to register AX. The result is then in register AX. Finally, another MOV stores the new value, the sum, back into TOTAL.

Since this is all the program was intended to do, you need to end the program. The next three instructions do this by returning to DOS. DOS provides many useful capabilities. One of these is to terminate the execution of a program by setting a return code that can be tested by batch (.BAT) files. To do this, the return code for normal program end (0) must be placed in register AL where DOS can find it.

DOS is called by the **INT** (interrupt) command. In this case, INT tells DOS to execute its interrupt function number 21H (or decimal 33). This DOS interrupt is often referred to as an umbrella because it makes many totally different functions, or services, available. Since many services are available, you must tell DOS which you want. In this case you want 4CH (the number of the service to end a process). MOV AH,4CH puts 4CH into register AH. When DOS gets control, it examines register AH and invokes the proper routine to terminate the program. This routine then passes the desired return code, 0, to the command processor. (This interrupt process will be discussed in detail in a later chapter. For now, this is sufficient coverage for you to create simple programs.)

Program PGM1 can serve as a model or shell for your new programs. Just remove the three instructions that add COST to TOTAL and insert the instructions you want. Also remove the two field definitions from the data segment and add your own definitions. The stack segment can be copied as is.

2.14 PGM1A: THE ALTERNATE SAMPLE PROGRAM

If you are using a version of DOS older than Version 3.0 or if you want to write a program that will run on any version of DOS, use the alternate program (Figure 2–4a). The alternate program contains three more housekeeping instructions than PGM1 and two less return-to-DOS instructions.

The housekeeping instructions begin by saving the contents of what is currently in register DS onto the stack by using **PUSH** DS. Next an immediate value of 0 is moved into register AX. Then PUSH AX stores that value, 0, onto the stack. These instructions ensure that the program is able to return to DOS.

When the program is finished, **RET** issues the return-to-DOS command and the program returns to its caller, DOS.

2.15 RUNNING THE ASSEMBLER AND LINKER: A FIRST LOOK

To begin, examine the overall series of commands and actions needed to run the assembler and linker. Then, in the next section, you will learn the precise syntax needed for these commands.

Running MASM

After the source program has been created with a word processor, you begin by invoking the assembler. With the assembler software diskette inserted in drive A: and the program diskette in drive B:, enter

```
A>MASM B:PGM1,B:,B:,B:
```

Figure 2–5 shows the output that results on the screen. If you are running Version 4.0 from a hard disk, set the current directory to the one that holds your programs and enter

```
C>MASM PGM1,,,
```

Your PATH command is used by DOS to find the MASM program.

If you used the preceding MASM command specifying drive B:, then the following files are created by the assembly run: PGM1.OBJ, PGM1.LST, and PGM1.CRF.

Printing the .LST File by Using the MODE Command

To print the .LST file, first set the printer to print 132-byte lines. This can be done by using the MODE command:

```
A>MODE LPT1:132,6
```

If MODE does not work on your system, check your printer manual for the procedure needed to set the printer to condensed mode.

Next you must toggle the printer to echo whatever appears on the screen by pressing CTRL-P or CTRL-PRTSC. Then use TYPE to display the .LST file:

```
A>TYPE B:PGM1.LST
```

```
MASM B:PGM1,B:,B:,B:
Microsoft (R) Macro Assembler Version 5.10
Copyright (C) Microsoft Corp 1981, 1988.  All rights reserved.


   47238 + 136086 Bytes symbol space free

      0 Warning Errors
      0 Severe  Errors
```

FIGURE 2–5   Output generated by the MASM command line

Alternatively, you can copy the .LST file to the printer by entering

```
A>COPY B:PGM1.LST PRN
```

or

```
A>TYPE B:PGM1.LST >PRN
```

The result is shown in Figure 2–6.

```
Microsoft (R) Macro Assembler Version 5.10              9/1/88 09:41:38

PGM1   FIGURE 2-4 SAMPLE PROGRAM                    Page    1-1


       1                     PAGE    60,132
       2                     TITLE   PGM1   FIGURE 2-4 SAMPLE PROGRAM
       3
       4            ;**********************************************************************
       5            ; PGM1      Title: Figure 2-4 Sample Program To Add COST to TOTAL    *
       6            ;                                                                     *
       7            ; Programmer: Vic Broquard                                           *
       8            ; Date Written:  6/11/88       Date Of Last Revision: 8/4/88         *
       9            ;                                                                     *
      10            ; Purpose: Add  two word numbers                                     *
      11            ;                                                                     *
      12            ; Special Requirements: None                                         *
      13            ;                                                                     *
      14            ;**********************************************************************
      15
      16
      17            ; program code segment
      18
      19 0000           PGM1CD  SEGMENT
      20
      21 0000           MAIN    PROC    FAR
      22
      23            ; housekeeping section
      24
      25                    ASSUME  CS:PGM1CD,DS:PGM1DA,SS:PGM1SK
      26
      27 0000  B8 ---- R            MOV     AX,PGM1DA    ; ESTABLISH ADDRESSABILITY
      28 0003  8E D8               MOV     DS,AX        ; TO PGM1DA - THE PGM'S DATA SEGMENT
      29
      30            ; main process section
      31
      32 0005  A1 0000 R           MOV     AX,COST      ; REG AX = COST
      33 0008  03 06 0002 R        ADD     AX,TOTAL     ; ADD COST TO TOTAL
```

FIGURE 2–6   Sample assembler source program listing   *(Continues)*

```
34 000C  A3 0002 R              MOV     TOTAL,AX    ; STORE NEW TOTAL
35
36                ; return to DOS section
37
38 000F  B0 00                  MOV     AL,0        ; SET 0 AS THE RETURN CODE FOR DOS
39 0011  B4 4C                  MOV     AH,4CH      ; SET FOR DOS END PROCESS FUNCTION
40 0013  CD 21                  INT     21H         ; CALL DOS TO END PROGRAM
41
42 0015            MAIN    ENDP
43
44 0015            PGM1CD  ENDS
45
46
47                ; program data segment
48
49 0000            PGM1DA  SEGMENT
50
51 0000  0006      COST    DW      6
52 0002  0004      TOTAL   DW      4
53
54 0004            PGM1DA  ENDS
55
56
```

```
Microsoft (R) Macro Assembler Version 5.10               9/1/88 09:41:38
PGM1   FIGURE 2-4 SAMPLE PROGRAM                          Page    1-2


57                ; program stack segment
58
59 0000            PGM1SK  SEGMENT PARA STACK 'STACK'
60
61 0000  0020[             DW      32 DUP (?)
62     ????
63          ]
64
65
66 0040            PGM1SK  ENDS
     67                     END
```

```
Microsoft (R) Macro Assembler Version 5.10               9/1/88 09:41:38
PGM1   FIGURE 2-4 SAMPLE PROGRAM                          Symbols-1


Segments and Groups:

              N a m e          Length   Align   Combine Class

PGM1CD . . . . . . . . . . . .   0015    PARA    NONE
PGM1DA . . . . . . . . . . . .   0004    PARA    NONE
```

FIGURE 2–6   continued

```
PGM1SK . . . . . . . . . . . . .     0040    PARA    STACK    'STACK'
Symbols:
                N a m e              Type    Value   Attr

COST . . . . . . . . . . . . .       L WORD   0000   PGM1DA

MAIN . . . . . . . . . . . . .       F PROC   0000   PGM1CD    Length = 0015

TOTAL  . . . . . . . . . . . .       L WORD   0002   PGM1DA

@CPU . . . . . . . . . . . . .       TEXT   0101h
@FILENAME  . . . . . . . . . .       TEXT   B_PGM1
@VERSION . . . . . . . . . . .       TEXT   510


    64 Source  Lines
    64 Total   Lines
    12 Symbols

  47238 + 136086 Bytes symbol space free

     0 Warning Errors
     0 Severe  Errors
```

FIGURE 2–6   continued

Creating the Cross-Reference Listing: Optional

To produce the cross-reference listing, you must run the CREF program. To get printed output, be sure that the printer is toggled to echo the screen by pressing CTRL-PRTSC or CTRL-P.

Then enter

```
A>CREF B:PGM1.CRF,CON
```

It is possible to send the output of the CREF program directly to the printer by typing

```
A>CREF B:PGM1.CRF,LPT1
```

The result is shown in Figure 2–7.

Running LINK

To link the program, enter

```
A>LINK B:PGM1,B:,B:;
```

Or, if you are running from a hard disk, enter

```
C>LINK PGM1,,;
```

```
CREF B:PGM1.CRF,CON


Microsoft Cross-Reference  Version 5.10          Thu Sep 01 09:50:36 1988
PGM1   FIGURE 2-4 SAMPLE PROGRAM

   Symbol Cross-Reference       (# definition, + modification)   Cref-1

@CPU . . . . . . . . . . . . .    1#
@VERSION . . . . . . . . . . .    1#

COST . . . . . . . . . . . . .    32    51#

MAIN . . . . . . . . . . . . .    21#   42

PGM1CD . . . . . . . . . . . .    19#   25    44
PGM1DA . . . . . . . . . . . .    25    27    49#   54
PGM1SK . . . . . . . . . . . .    25    59#   66

STACK. . . . . . . . . . . . .    59

TOTAL. . . . . . . . . . . . .    33    34+   52#


 9 Symbols
```

FIGURE 2–7   Cross-reference listing

This creates the .EXE file and the .MAP file. Figure 2–8 shows the display that results from entering the LINK command from drive A:, along with a directory of drive B: that displays all the files created.

Viewing the .MAP File

The optional .MAP file can be printed by toggling the printer again (press CTRL-PRTSC or CTRL-P) and typing the .MAP file:

```
A>TYPE B:PGM1.MAP
```

Another way to view the .MAP file is by entering

```
A>TYPE B:PGM1.MAP > PRN
```

or

```
A>COPY B:PGM1.MAP PRN
```

The .MAP file is shown in Figure 2–9.

```
LINK B:PGM1,B:,B:;


Microsoft (R) Overlay Linker  Version 3.64
Copyright (C) Microsoft Corp 1983-1988.  All rights reserved.



DIR B:

 Volume in drive B has no label
 Directory of  B:\

PGM1     ASM     1809   7-19-00  10:02a
PGM1     LST     4100   9-01-88   9:41a
PGM1     OBJ      156   9-01-88   9:41a
PGM1     CRF      678   9-01-88   9:41a
PGM1     MAP      200   9-01-88   9:54a
PGM1     EXE      548   9-01-88   9:54a
         6 File(s)    340992 bytes free
```

FIGURE 2–8   LINK and the directory

```
Start  Stop   Length Name                Class
00000H 00014H 00015H PGM1CD
00020H 00023H 00004H PGM1DA
00030H 0006FH 00040H PGM1SK              STACK
```

FIGURE 2–9   .MAP file

2.16 THE COMMAND SYNTAX FOR MASM

Now that you have a feel for the software, this section will examine in detail the command syntax for each program, beginning with the assembler.

The MASM command line is highly flexible, producing only the output files desired. Further, it is acceptable to enter all the required information on the command line or to have MASM request the required entries by using prompts.

The syntax of the command line differs slightly, depending upon the assembler version you are using. The syntax for Version 4.0 or earlier follows.

> A>MASM   source filename,object filename,list filename,crf filename

The syntax for Version 5.0 or later is

> A>MASM options source filename,object filename,list filename,crf filename

The only difference between the syntax of the two versions is the location of the options; early versions place options first, recent versions place them last.

For Version 4.0, no options are needed for beginning programs. Therefore, for Version 4.0 and when working from floppies, enter

`A>MASM B:PGM1,B:,B:,B:`

In the preceding statement the first B: tells MASM to put the object file on the disk in drive B:. This is necessary because the default is the currently logged drive—presumably, drive A:. The entry PGM1 is the name of the object file. The next three entries name the .OBJ, .LST, and .CRF files. MASM assumes that the name of these files will be the same name as the source—PGM1.

If you are using Version 5.0 and want to make optimal use of the debugger program, CODE VIEW, you need to use the option /ZI. Then, when the program has been completely tested, it can be reassembled without the /ZI option to create a smaller object program. So, for Version 5.0 and CODE VIEW, enter

`A>MASM /ZI B:PGM1,B:,B:,B:`

This does exactly the same thing as the statement given for Version 4.0, except MASM writes extra debugging information such as line numbers and symbolic data into the object file. CODE VIEW uses this information.

If you do not need or want these other files to be created, just enter

`A>MASM B:PGM1,B:;`

The preceding statement establishes PGM1.OBJ as the object file. The semicolon in the statement means no further files are to be created.

If you enter

`A>MASM B:PGM1;`

the assembler assembles the program, tells of any errors, and creates an .OBJ file, but no other output files are created. (The .OBJ file is the default if you do not otherwise specify.)

If you enter

`A>MASM B:PGM1,B:,B:;`

```
A> MASM
Microsoft (R) Macro Assembler Version 5.10
Copyright (C) Microsoft Corp 1981, 1988.  All rights reserved.

Source filename  [ .ASM]: B:PGM1
Object filename  [PGM1.OBJ]: B:
Source listing     [NUL.LST]: B:
Cross-reference  [NUL.CRF]: B:

  47292 + 405103 Bytes symbol space free

     0 Warning Errors
     0 Severe  Errors
```

FIGURE 2–10   MASM interactive command

then

1.   The object file is PGM1.OBJ.

2.   The listing file is PGM1.LST.

3.   There is no .CRF file.

It is possible to have MASM issue an interactive prompt for the names by entering

A>MASM

The preceding statement displays the prompts shown in Figure 2–10.

To indicate that a given file is not wanted, just press the ENTER key.

If you choose to enter all the information on the command line and fail to enter the semicolon, then MASM jumps back into its interactive mode and begins prompting for the other files.

2.17   THE COMMAND SYNTAX FOR LINK

The syntax and method of operation for LINK are similar to the syntax and method for MASM. Again, if all the information is to be entered on the command line, the syntax differs slightly between Version 4.0 and Version 5.0. For Version 4.0, enter

A>LINK   object filename,EXE filename,MAP filename,   library filename options

For Version 5.0, enter

A>LINK   options object filename,EXE filename,MAP filename,
                                                    library filename

---

The only difference between the two syntax structures is the location of the options. For simple programs in Version 4.0, no options are needed. However, in Version 5.0 the option /CO is necessary to make full use of the debugger program CODE VIEW. This option instructs the linker to build extra symbolic debugging information for CODE VIEW. After the program is thoroughly tested, it should be reassembled and relinked without this option.

The first two file parameters are required; the last two are optional. (The use of library files will be discussed in a later chapter.) Commonly, for Version 4.0, you enter:

```
A>LINK B:PGM1,B:,B:;
```

For Version 5.0 you enter

```
A>LINK /CO B:PGM1,B:,B:;
```

This links B:PGM1.OBJ to B:PGM1.EXE, and the program is ready for execution. The .MAP file is created for use with the debugger program.

If you fail to enter the final semicolon (which says there are no more operands), then LINK prompts you for the library files just as MASM prompts you for additional files.

2.18   COMMAND SUMMARY

Assembler command line:
    Two floppy-drive system
        Version 4.0:   `MASM B:PGM1,B:,B:,B:`
        Version 5.0:   `MASM /ZI B:PGM1,B:,B:,B:`
    Hard-disk system
        Version 4.0   `MASM PGM1,,,`
        Version 5.0:   `MASM /ZI PGM1,,,`
Linker command line:
    Two floppy-drive system
        Version 4.0:   `LINK B:PGM1,B:,B:;`
        Version 5.0:   `LINK /CO B:PGM1,B:,B:`
    Hard-disk system
        Version 4.0:   `LINK PGM1,,;`
        Version 5.0:   `LINK /CO PGM1,,;`

To print a copy of the .LST file:

```
MODE  LPT1:132,6
COPY  B:PGM1.LST PRN
```

To print a copy of the cross-reference listing:

```
CREF  B:PGM1.CRF,LPT1
```

2.19 SAMPLE PROGRAM EXECUTION: RUNNING THE DEBUGGER SYMDEB

Even if you do not have SYMDEB, study this section. The concepts are important, and all the commands discussed work with CODE VIEW. Only the syntax for the display command differs slightly.

After you have created the program, execute it by entering

```
A>B:PGM1
```

What happens? The following entries are displayed on the screen:

```
A>B:PGM1
A>
```

Yes, the program has finished execution and has just added COST to TOTAL. There was no output. Therefore, you must use the debugger program to find out if the program actually worked correctly. Invoke the debugger by entering

```
A>SYMDEB B:PGM1.EXE
```

After displaying some sign-on messages and identifying the processor as an 8086 processor, the debugger's prompt, a dash, is displayed. You must now tell the debugger what to do.

There are five commonly used debugger commands:

R For *registers*

T For *trace*

G For *go*

D For *display*

Q For *quit*

Examine each of these to see what they do.

R (registers)	This command displays the contents of all registers and identifies the next instruction to be executed.

T	This command traces the execution of one or more
(trace)	instructions. As each is executed, the contents of the
	registers are displayed as is the next instruction to be
	executed.
G	This command tells DEBUG to continue program
(go)	execution uninterrupted until the breakpoint stops
	DEBUG. (A breakpoint is a specified point that stops
	program execution, displays the contents of the registers
	and the next instruction to be executed, and asks what
	you want to do next.)
D	This command displays the contents of main storage. It
(display)	shows the bytes you want to see in both hexadecimal
	format as well as ASCII, or printable, format (if the byte
	has an ASCII value).
Q	This command ends the debugging run, returning to the
	DOS (quit) command level at the A> prompt.

Now consider how these commands are used to monitor the execution of a program. Figure 2–11 shows a sample debugging run using SYMDEB. However, before you attempt to decipher what is going on, decide what it is that you want to do and see.

Begin by examining the assembly listing (Figure 2–6) once more. What you want to do is to trace the execution of the main processing section. This will enable you to follow the three steps that add COST to TOTAL to verify that it executes correctly. First, you need to allow the program to execute the housekeeping code until it gets to the main processing section, where COST is added to TOTAL. Therefore, you want the debugger to execute the program until it gets to statement 32, MOV AX,COST. Statement 32 should be the **breakpoint,** a predefined point in a program where execution is temporarily halted so that you can examine the contents of memory and registers.

To specify a breakpoint, you must know the exact storage address where you want to stop. You will recall that register CS points to the start of the code segment. If you know the offset address of the MOV instruction, you can establish the breakpoint. The offset address is given in the source listing output in the column after the line number in line 32. In this case, the address is 05H. Be sure that you can find this value in Figure 2–6.

So, your first command to the debugger must execute the program until it gets to offset 05H. The command is G 5, which means begin execution of the program and interrupt execution when control gets to the instruction at offset address 05H. This command could also be entered as G5 or G 05H.

Now examine the debug listing, Figure 2–11. What happened when G5 was entered? When the debugger gets to this command, it halts the execution of the program, displays the contents of the registers, shows the next instruction to be executed (MOV AX,[0000]), and asks what to do next by displaying the prompt (the dash) after -G 5.

```
SYMDEB B:PGM1.EXE

Microsoft (R) Symbolic Debug Utility  Version 4.00
Copyright (C) Microsoft Corp 1984, 1985.  All rights reserved.

Processor is [8086]

-G 5

AX=5947  BX=0000  CX=0024  DX=0000  SP=0040  BP=0000  SI=0000  DI=0000
DS=5947  ES=5935  SS=5948  CS=5945  IP=0005    NV UP EI PL NZ NA PO NC
5945:0005 A10000          MOV  AX,[0000]                    DS:0000=0006

-D DS:00

5947:0000  06 00 04 00 00 00 00 00-00 00 00 00 00 00 00 00   ................
5947:0010  00 00 00 00 00 00 00 00-00 00 00 00 00 00 00 00   ................
5947:0020  00 00 00 00 00 00 00 00-00 00 00 00 00 00 00 00   ................
5947:0030  00 00 00 00 00 00 00 00-00 00 00 00 00 00 00 00   ................
5947:0040  00 00 00 00 00 00 0A 00-00 00 05 00 45 59 23 50   ...........EY#P
5947:0050  00 00 00 00 00 00 00 00-00 00 00 00 00 00 00 00   ................
5947:0060  00 00 00 00 00 00 00 00-00 00 00 00 00 00 00 00   ................
5947:0070  00 00 00 00 00 00 00 00-00 00 00 00 00 00 00 00   ................


-D DS:00,03
```

        Cost   **Total**

```
5947:0000  06 00    04 00                                    ....

-T

AX=0006  BX=0000  CX=0024  DX=0000  SP=0040  BP=0000  SI=0000  DI=0000
DS=5947  ES=5935  SS=5948  CS=5945  IP=0008    NV UP EI PL NZ NA PO NC
5945:0008 03060200        ADD  AX,[0002]                    DS:0002=0004


-T

AX=000A  BX=0000  CX=0024  DX=0000  SP=0040  BP=0000  SI=0000  DI=0000
DS=5947  ES=5935  SS=5948  CS=5945  IP=000C    NV UP EI PL NZ NA PE NC
5945:000C A30200          MOV  [0002],AX                    DS:0002=0004


-T

AX=000A  BX=0000  CX=0024  DX=0000  SP=0040  BP=0000  SI=0000  DI=0000
DS=5947  ES=5935  SS=5948  CS=5945  IP=000F    NV UP EI PL NZ NA PE NC
5945:000F B000            MOV  AL,00
```

FIGURE 2–11 Sample debugging run using SYMDEB   *Continues*

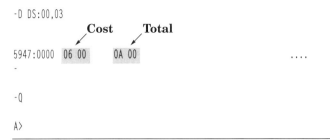

```
-D DS:00,03
                   Cost      Total
5947:0000   06 00      0A 00                        ....
-

-Q

A>
```

FIGURE 2–11   continued

The register display format is shown in hex format. For example, register AX is shown as AX 5947. This means the current value in register AX is 5947H, where 16 is the high-order byte and 47 is the low-order byte. The value is **always** presented in hex format. Since the program has not yet put COST into register AX, this value is irrelevant as far as you are concerned.

The four work registers are shown first: AX, BX, CX, and DX. Next come SP, BP, SI, and DI. These are the stack pointer, the base pointer, the source index register, and the destination index register, respectively.

The next line displays the four segment registers: DS, ES, SS, and CS. These are the data segment register, the extra segment register, the stack segment register, and the code segment register. The last register is the IP, or instruction pointer register.

The pair CS:IP points to the current instruction. IP now contains 00 05H, which is the offset from the start of the code segment to this instruction.

The IP register is followed by a series of two-letter combinations that represent the current settings of the flags. Each two-letter combination not only identifies which flag is shown, but also whether it is set or cleared (1B or 0B). The meanings of these abbreviations are shown in Table 2–1 and are also presented in Appendix A.

The next line in the sample debugging run (Figure 2–11) displays the vector address (code segment:offset address) of the next instruction to be executed, followed by the machine instruction in hex, and finally by the assembler symbolic version of the instruction (MOV AX,[0000]). Then SYMDEB gives its prompt , which looks like a dash.

At this point, you want to see the beginning contents of both COST and TOTAL, plus the starting value for register AX. AX has already been shown in the lines above and has an irrelevant value in it. That's OK, since the first instruction will be to move COST into register AX.

To display main storage, use the D (Display) command. This command is a bit complex. The syntax is:

```
        D    segment address:starting offset address,ending offset
```

TABLE 2–1 Debug flag settings

Flag*	Set (=1)		Cleared (=0)	
Overflow	OV	(yes)	NV	(no)
Direction	DN	(decrement)	UP	(increment)
Interrupt	EI	(enable)	DI	(disable)
Sign	NG	(negative)	PL	(positive)
Zero	ZR	(yes)	NZ	(no)
Auxiliary carry	AC	(yes)	NA	(no)
Parity	PE	(even)	PO	(odd)
Carry	CY	(yes)	NC	(no)

*Shown in the order that DEBUG displays the flags

To begin displaying, the data segment address must be specified. There are two ways of specifying the data segment address. You can look at the previous register display and enter the hex value that is in DS. There is less chance of error, however, if you just enter the letters DS and let the debugger find the current value in DS and automatically insert that value.

So, you can use DS as the segment address, but what do you use for the starting offset and ending offset addresses? The starting offset address is the location within the data segment where you want to begin the display of storage.

To find the starting offset address, examine the assembler listing once more (Figure 2–6). Look in the data segment where COST and TOTAL are defined. What is the offset address you need? Again, offset addresses are just to the right of the line numbers on the far left of the listing. COST is defined first and is at offset address 00 00H.

You could enter

```
-D DS:00
```

without specifying an ending address. If no ending address is given, the debugger displays the next 128 bytes in storage. These bytes may or may not be part of the data area or even the program. It simply displays bytes. How long is the sample program's data area? Look at Figure 2–6 once more. The data area is only 2 words long (COST and TOTAL), or 4 bytes. So, this display command is showing 124 bytes beyond the data area!

Examine the debug run (Figure 2–11) once more. See what SYMDEB displays in response to the display command. On the left of each of the next eight lines (each contains 16 bytes) is the vector address of the first byte on that line. The vector is composed of the segment address:offset address.

The vector is followed by the contents of the next 16 bytes. The contents are shown in hex format, with 2 hex nibbles per byte. The address of the first byte is 00H, the second is 01H, and the last on that line is 0FH. Count them and verify this. Just to test the accuracy of your counting, what is in the byte at address 5947:0002? You should see 04H. What is in the byte at address 5947:004A? You should see 05H.

On the far right is the ASCII value of each group of 16 bytes (if there is one). If there is no corresponding printable letter or number, a period is shown. In this example, the two fields in the data area are binary numbers, not ASCII characters. But remember the rule from the last chapter: The computer cannot tell if a byte contains ASCII character data, binary numbers, or even instructions. It just attempts to display any ASCII equivalent if there is one. Therefore, as you look beyond the first 4 bytes of the display, there are scattered ASCII characters like E, Y, #, and P.

If you type D again with no operands, the debugger assumes you want to continue displaying from where it just stopped. It will continue, in this case, with offset address 0080H. Go ahead and try typing D without operands.

In this program you need to see the contents of 4 bytes only. Therefore, enter

–D DS:00,03

and display 4 bytes only. (Note that the ending offset must be entered in hex format.) Examine the debug run in Figure 2–11 and see the effect of this command.

The purpose of all this displaying of main storage is to see the actual starting values of COST and TOTAL. From Figure 2–6, you learn that COST is in the first 2 bytes at offset address 00H; from Figure 2–11, you find that COST contains 06 00H.

But wait, COST is supposed to have 6 in it! It does. Remember, when words are stored in main storage, the high-order byte is stored in the higher address of the 2 bytes of storage, and the low-order byte is stored in the lower address. Thus, the word value 00 06H becomes 06 00H in storage. Remember also, that when the computer moves that word value into a register, it automatically switches the order to 00 06H.

Go ahead and find TOTAL. It is in the next 2 bytes. You should find that its starting value is 04 00H. When moved into a register, the value will appear as 00 04H.

The next step to find out if the program really works is to monitor the operation and results of each of the next three instructions. What is the instruction that is about to be executed? Look back up to where the registers were last displayed, and you should see the MOV AX,[0000] instruction that is to move COST into register AX. To execute this instruction, use the T (trace) command.

T has one operand, which specifies the decimal number of instructions to trace. If no number is coded, a default of one instruction is assumed. Since the default is precisely what you want, enter only a T. As you see in Figure 2–11, the command line looks like this.

–T

The debugger then executes the instruction and displays the contents of the registers and the next instruction to be executed. Look at the contents of register AX. COST was moved to AX and AX now contains 00 06H. The next instruction to be executed is ADD AX,[0002], which is the assembler's notation for the original instruction ADD AX,TOTAL. The 0002 is the offset address of TOTAL in the data segment.

To execute the add, enter another trace command. Again, the command line looks like this:

```
-T
```

TOTAL is now added to AX. The registers are once more displayed along with the next instruction. What is in AX? 00 0AH. But wait, you are adding 6 + 4 = 10. Since the values are added in binary and displayed in hex, you must convert 0AH into decimal to verify the addition. 0AH converts to 10. So far, so good.

The last instruction to be traced is ADD AX,[0002], which updates TOTAL in storage with the new value. To trace this instruction, enter the trace command so the command line again appears as

```
-T
```

Supposedly, storage has been updated. But has it? To find out, you need to display the data area once more. Repeat the display command:

```
-D DS:00,03
```

Now find the two fields in the data area. Notice that COST is unaltered, but TOTAL now contains 0A 00H.

At this point, you are done since you have seen that the program works correctly. To end the session, simply enter the quit command:

```
-Q
```

If you are using a different assembler, consult your debugging manual for details on your specific command syntax. If you have not yet run the debugger, go ahead and run the SYMDEB example and become familiar with it. SYMDEB is very powerful and indispensable in debugging microassembler programs.

2.20 RUNNING THE CODE VIEW DEBUGGER (VERSION 5.0 AND LATER)

Overview

The state-of-the-art CODE VIEW debugger is designed to provide a common debugging tool for many languages. Beyond just debugging programs, CODE VIEW handles and works with source programs written in microassembler, FORTRAN, BASIC, C, and PASCAL, thus providing flexibility.

Note: If you are using Version 5.0 on a two-floppy system, one disk contains the MASM and LINK programs and the other contains CODE VIEW. Drive B: always contains your program diskette. You will have to swap the assembler and CODE VIEW diskettes in drive A: as needed.

CODE VIEW is a multiwindow debugger that attempts to present as much debugging information on the screen as possible. Always present on the screen is the master menu bar (one line) that supports user-activated pull-down submenus. CODE VIEW attempts to display four windows: the dialogue window, the display window, the register window, and a watch window. The number of windows CODE VIEW can display depends on the data available.

The dialogue window is used to enter commands and to see the output.

The display window normally shows the source statements being executed and the instruction about to be executed. The current instruction is shown in reverse video. Also, any source module desired may be displayed.

The register window displays the current contents of all the registers. This display is updated after every instruction is executed.

The watch window is one of the most powerful features. In this window it is possible to display the current contents of any storage field or area desired and in the format of your choosing. The format you choose usually depends on the data type and source language (assembler, C, FORTRAN, or BASIC). Thus, you can have the data displayed in the format you are most comfortable with. You can monitor the effects of program execution with ease!

Finally, the output from the program being debugged is written to a screen area separate from the main CODE VIEW screen. Therefore, the two outputs—the CODE VIEW screens and your program—are never mixed. This is done by either screen swapping or screen flipping. (How this works will be discussed in detail in Chapter 7.) With a single keystroke, you can flip back and forth between the CODE VIEW screen and the program output screen.

CODE VIEW can be run using a mouse; function keys; pull-down menus controlled by the menu choice keys, ALT-+; and by direct dialogue commands entered in the dialogue window. The first three ways provide a quick and convenient method of controlling CODE VIEW. The dialogue commands, though more cumbersome, provide greatest control of the debugger as well as compatibility with SYMDEB commands. All the usual SYMDEB commands work in the dialogue window. The only incompatibility lies in the operands of the commands. Since CODE VIEW supports many languages, there have been some slight changes in the syntax of operand entry to align with these languages.

CODE VIEW has two different operating modes: windows and sequential. If the source has been compiled with the /ZI option and linked with the /CO option, then the source program is available to the debugger. The full capabilities of CODE VIEW are available. This is your normal choice. However, if the options were not used or if you are debugging any regular .EXE program file, then sequential mode must be used. In the sequential mode, CODE VIEW acts as if it were SYMDEB. That is, most of the window functions do not operate. Commands will have to be entered in the dialogue window. Obviously, if the source program is not present, many features that rely upon the source program are not usable.

All this power has its cost. The first difficulty is in invoking the debugger. You must choose the right set of options based upon the type of computer you have. There are three possibilities: an IBM machine, a compatible clone, and a noncompatible clone. The decision is compounded by whether or not you have a mouse and the type of display terminal you have: EGA (graphics board), CGA (color monitor), or monochrome.

The option codes and their meanings follow.

/I   Non-IBM (a compatible clone). Causes CTRL-C and CTRL-BREAK to function so that you can break out of infinite loops and the like.

/W   Use window mode.

/S   Use screen swapping (keeps debugger and program output in separate screen display areas).

/M   Your system includes a mouse, but you do not want to use it.

/B   Monochrome monitor.

/T   Use sequential mode. (It is better to use the /W option; then CODE VIEW automatically changes to sequential mode if it discovers that it cannot operate in window mode.)

/D   Use for a noncompatible system such as TANDY 1000 and AT&T 6300PLUS.

See the CODE VIEW manual for full details about the options, if necessary.

We suggest that you always use the /W, /M, and /S options. If you are comfortable with using a mouse and have one, then do not use /M. If you are using a clone, try the /I option. If any of these do not work on your computer, you will discover the fact at once; change the options and try again. Consult the CODE VIEW manual as needed.

Thus, for a color compatible, we suggest using a command line like this:

```
CV /I /W /S /M programname
```

Suppose that you want to debug a program named PGM1.EXE. The full command line is:

```
CV /I /W /S /M PGM1
```

Notice, that unlike SYMDEB, the program extension is not needed.

CODE VIEW in Sequential Mode

Now duplicate the debug run of the sample program, in which you used SYMDEB. First, use the sequential mode because it is very similar to SYMDEB. The sample program PGM1.ASM should be assembled without

the /ZI option and linked without the /CO option. Enter CODE VIEW by
typing

```
CV /I /W /S /M PGM1
```

When the debugger begins, the menu bar is shown on the top line.
Below it is the display window, while at the bottom is the dialogue window.
Examine the display window. It shows the sample program with both the
machine code and an unassembled coding. But notice that the assembler
instructions are not those that were entered in PGM1. Look at the
instruction that moved COST into register AX. The second operand is not
coded COST! What has happened is that the debugger, upon finding no
source program, has gone ahead and created an assembler version from the
machine code. In the bottom dialogue window is the confirming message: "No
symbolic information." Thus, you are in sequential mode.

The size of the two windows can be controlled by using CTRL-G and CTRL-T.
Try these control instructions and set the two windows to about equal size.

On the left side of your keyboard or at the top, there are 10 function
keys. Several of these can be used to implement some of the actions to be
taken by the debugger. The ESC key cancels any help action or returns you to
the main menu.

F1   Function key 1 brings up the help menus. Try experimenting with
     F1 now.

F2   Function key 2 opens and closes the register window. Press it once,
     and the registers are shown on the right side of the screen. Press it
     again. Now the window is removed. It is common practice to debug
     with the register window visible, so press F2 once more to get the
     window back.

F4   Function key 4 switches the screen currently being displayed. You
     are currently viewing the CODE VIEW display. Press F4 once, and
     you are viewing the original DOS screen, with any of your
     program's output. In this case there isn't any at this point. Pressing
     any key returns you to the original CODE VIEW display. At any
     time you can take a look at the real program's output just by
     pressing F4.

F5   Function key 5 generates a go command.

F6   Function key 6 changes windows from display to dialogue.

F8   Function key 8 creates a trace command.

F9   Function key 9 sets a temporary breakpoint at the point specified.

Shortly, you will try using the F5 and F8 function keys. But first, examine the
menu bar.

To activate any of the menus, you must press the ALT key and then the
first letter of the menu name. (Unlike the CTRL-C combination, it is not
necessary to hold the ALT key down while pressing the letter.) Try ALT-F for

files. A beep sounds; CODE VIEW is telling you that in sequential mode, the symbolic files are not available.

The view option, ALT-V, shows what is being displayed. Try it. The >> symbol identifies those options that are being shown. Currently, the register window is active as well as program output.

While in a pull-down menu, pressing UP ARROW or DOWN ARROW moves to the next choice; pressing RIGHT ARROW or LEFT ARROW moves the cursor to the adjacent menu. Once you have moved to the desired choice, press ENTER to activate that option. Pressing ESC cancels the menu.

Now examine the menu choice Run. The Start choice starts and runs the program. In this, Start is like a go command. The Restart choice restarts the program from the beginning, but it does not actually start program execution. This choice is often used during debugging runs to restart the program from the beginning.

Try choosing the other possible menu options, especially Help. Choosing some results in only a beep, since they are usable only in window mode when the program has been assembled with the symbolic information available from the /ZI and /CO options.

Now duplicate the SYMDEB run. Enter the command G5 to go, then stop at offset 05H. Then enter the display command

```
D DS:00
```

to examine the contents of storage. To display only 10 bytes, you must modify the SYMDEB syntax slightly. The revised command is

```
D DS:00 L 3
```

The command tells the computer to display bytes starting at offset 00H for a length of 3 bytes. Next, use the trace command. You can enter the command T or press F8. Watch the effect on register AX as you enter the three trace commands as you did in the SYMDEB example. (Remember, first move COST, which contains 6, to AX. Then add TOTAL, which contains 4, to AX. Now AX holds 0AH. Next move the result back into TOTAL.) To verify that TOTAL has been changed, enter D DS:00 L 3.

Now experiment with the menu choice Run. Try starting the program again. Notice that it executes at once to program end. Next, try the Execute option from the run menu. What you see is the program being executed in slow motion. At times this may be useful. When you are done experimenting, enter the quit command (Q).

CODE VIEW in Window Mode

Now look at an especially useful feature of CODE VIEW. Reassemble PGM1 by using the /ZI option and link with the /CO option. Then start CODE VIEW again by entering

```
CV /I /W /S /M PGM1
```

Now the register window is automatically present. But of more importance is what is in the display window at the top. It is the actual source program!

The F6 key changes windows from display to dialogue. Try pressing it a few times. Notice the effect of the arrow keys and the PGUP and PGDN keys. With this feature you can easily control the portion displayed.

Now get to the display window with the source coding and move the cursor to line 32, the MOV AX,COST instruction.

You want to cause the program to execute up to the MOV AX,COST instruction and then stop, thus permitting you to examine the registers and storage before continuing. In other words, you must set a temporary breakpoint. To do this, you need to be viewing the actual code. So, press ALT-V for View. The current setting is >> Source. Press M or A—either shows the actual code. Now use F6 to get into the display window and use the arrow keys to set the cursor on the MOV instruction.

Now press F9 to set a temporary breakpoint at this point. Notice that the instruction is highlighted in bold letters. The breakpoint is on. If you press F9 again, the breakpoint is turned off. Try it. Now make sure that it is on again. You can now execute to this point and halt. Press F6 to get back to the dialogue window; then enter G for *go*. The program executes down to this point and waits for further commands.

Now for the exciting part. Watch the TOTAL field. To do this, activate the Watch menu by pressing ALT-W. The cursor now sits on Add. This feature is selected merely by pressing the ENTER key. Do this now. Notice that the menu opens a window right in the middle of the display, asking what you want to watch. Type in the name of the field to watch—TOTAL—and press the ENTER key. Now the watch window opens up just under the menu bar line. It shows the current contents of the field, 04H. Now trace the three instructions by entering either three T commands in dialogue mode or pressing F8 three times. Watch what happens to TOTAL as the commands are executed.

Now watch the field again by using the execute mode. Press ALT-R, then move the cursor to Execute or just press E. Watch the field display of TOTAL as the program runs in slow motion once more.

This ability to monitor any field as well as the registers and the actual source code is what makes CODE VIEW so useful. You will find that debugging is much easier in window mode.

Setting fields to watch by using the dialogue watch command, W, offers an advantage because there are four useful forms of the command:

Command	Meaning
WA	Watch the following ASCII field and show the contents in character format.
WB	Watch the following bytes and show the contents in hexadecimal format.
WW	Watch the following words, and show the contents in hexadecimal format.

WD Watch the following doublewords, and show the contents in hexadecimal format.

After entering the watch code, enter the name of the field and an optional number of bytes to watch. Each of these operands is separated from the others by a space. If you define a field as

```
FILENAME DB 10 DUP(?)
```

the command to watch it is

```
WA FILENAME 10
```

Go ahead and experiment with CODE VIEW. To end, just enter Q for *quit*.

Summary of Beginning CODE VIEW Commands

Because the menu bar commands can also be entered in the dialogue window, you have two ways to execute CODE VIEW commands. Usually, the dialogue command version is more powerful, allowing additional options. The following lists summarize the major options.

keystrokes to choose menu selections	action	dialogue command
ALT - VS	Displays source listing	S+
ALT - VA	Displays machine/assembler listing	S–
ALT - RR	Restarts program but does not begin execution	L
ALT - RE	Begins execute mode	E
ALT - WA	Adds a watch field	CTRL-W
ALT - H	Provides help	H
ALT - VR	Toggles register display on/off	F2
ALT - FE	Quits	Q
F5	Goes until breakpoint or end of program is encountered	G
F7	Sets breakpoint on current line in the display window and executes the program to the breakpoint	G offset address
F8	Traces one instruction by tracing through routines	T number to trace
F10	Traces one instruction by stepping over routines	P number to do

| CTRL-G | Increases size of current window ("G" stands for *grow*.) |
| CTRL-T | Decreases size of current window ("T" stands for *tiny*.) |

dialogue-only commands for displaying data

command	action
D	Displays bytes
DB	Displays bytes
DA	Displays as ACSII character data
DW	Displays words
DD	Displays doublewords
DI	Displays as signed decimal integers
DU	Displays as unsigned decimal integers

The operand that accompanies a display-data command is either

| address1 address2 | Where address2 is in C format (which is the hex offset address preceded by 0x) |

or

| address1 L size | Where size is the decimal number to dump |

For example: if the listing is

```
0002H  FILENAME     DS   0 DUP(?)
```

then you could display, or dump, FILENAME by entering

```
DA FILENAME FILENAME+10
DA 02 0x000C
DA FILENAME L 10
```

See Chapter 7 for details and advanced commands.

2.21 M, THE MICROSOFT PROGRAM EDITOR

Beginning with Release 5.1 of Microsoft's assembler package, the M program editor provides a powerful alternative to normal text editors for program creation and modification. In addition to supporting a host of valuable text-editing features, M invokes the assembler and displays syntax error lines on the editing screen for fast repair. The editor permits the editing keys to be customized to meet your specific needs or to emulate those of several well-known text and program editors.

These fancy features are beyond the scope of this text, and many users may not have access to this latest release. Therefore, we will limit our discussion to the basics. Once familiar with these, the inquisitive can study the many help screens and the Microsoft documentation.

The editor is invoked by

```
M filename
```

For example, to build a new program called GRADESUM.ASM in drive B:, you enter

```
M B:GRADESUM.ASM
```

The editor responds by asking if you want to create a new file; if so, M begins operation.

The bottom line on the screen is the status line. It identifies the filename and the current cursor position. From time to time, a line appears just above the status line. It is known as the dialog line, and it displays messages from the editor. If this is a new file, the rest of the screen is blank, with the cursor placed in the upper-left corner, ready for you to begin entering program statements.

Begin entering the first program line. Press the ENTER key to end the current line and begin another line. The arrow keys function as expected. The HOME key moves the cursor position to the beginning of the current line you on which you are working.

There are two modes: overtype and insert. The default is overtype—that is, any character that you type replaces the current character at the cursor position. Pressing the insert key, INS, switches M to insert mode. Now the characters typed are inserted at the current cursor position. Pressing the INS key once more returns to overtype. Experiment with this feature; both options have their uses.

To save all changes and end the editing session, press the F8 key. If you want to end and **not** save any changes, first press the F9 key and then the F8 key.

To make corrections, press the delete key, DEL. DEL deletes the character at the current cursor position. CTRL-Y deletes the current line.

Many of the editor commands involve the use of the ALT key. One of the more important commands is the undo command, UNDO, which cancels the last change you made. To reverse the effects of the last command, press ALT-BACKSPACE. Pressing ALT-BACKSPACE again undoes the second to last command, and so on. M can undo up to the last 10 commands, by default. But keep in mind that not all commands can be undone.

Perhaps the most common use of the ALT key in M is in the combination ALT-A, which defines arguments. With ALT-A you can present an argument to the next command or function. For example, suppose that you had typed the following line:

```
MOV BX,COST
```

and you decide that it should be

```
MOV AX,TOTAL
```

Using the arrow keys, you can position the cursor on B and repeatedly press the DEL key. As an alternative, you can mark the block BX,COST for deletion and delete it by pressing the DEL key one time. To perform a block delete, position the cursor on B. Then press ALT-A. This marks the beginning of the block. Now use the arrow keys to position the cursor after the last character to be deleted, the T. Notice that the whole group of characters is now highlighted. Simply press the DEL key and the marked block is deleted.

Multiple lines can be deleted in a similar manner. First, position the cursor at the beginning of the first line to be deleted. Press ALT-A and move the cursor to the last line to be deleted. Press CTRL-Y and all the marked lines are deleted.

Lines can be moved around as well. To do this, position the cursor to the start of the first line to be moved. Press ALT-A and move the cursor to the end of the lines to move. Then delete them by entering CTRL-Y. Now a simple undo command puts them back where they were. To move them to another place, first move the cursor to the desired position. Then press SHIFT-INS. This will "paste" the deleted lines into the program at the new cursor position. This is a very commonly used function, so you should practice this sequence until you feel comfortable with it.

You can always get help by pressing the F1 key. Now use the arrow keys and PGUP and PGDN to move through the available information. To exit the help screens, press the F2 key.

The remaining basic command searches the text for a specific string. To invoke the command, press ALT-A and then enter the desired search string. Begin the search by pressing the F3 key. M searches from the current cursor position for the first match. If this occurrence is not the one you want, continue the search by pressing the F3 key once more. You do not have to re-enter the search string.

There are many, many more features available in M. But the features presented are enough to permit you to create and modify your programs. Once you master these features, you will want to experiment with some of the other possibilities. Do so! Just remember to experiment on a backup copy of the program, not your only master copy!

2.22 SUMMARY

To create an assembler program, you need a word processor, a DOS system disk, and the assembler software. The assembler software consists of MASM, the assembler; LINK, the link program; a debugger (SYMDEB or CODE VIEW); and the word processor M if you have version 5.1 or later.

A word processor operating in a nondocument mode is used to create the source program file. The program file must have the extension .ASM.

The MASM program assembles the source program, creating the .OBJ file of machine instructions; the .LST file (which is the source program listing); and the .CRF, or cross-reference file.

The source program listing can be displayed by using the command TYPE, or it can be printed. To print satisfactorily, you need paper wide enough to accommodate 132 characters or you must switch the printer into condensed mode. The latter can be done by using the DOS program MODE, which is available for many printers.

The object code file (.OBJ) must be linked into the executable form by using the LINK program. The program can be run from the DOS prompt by entering the program's name. However, the debugger is normally used to execute the program until all errors have been found and removed.

An assembler program consists of instructions and directives. Instructions create the actual machine instructions to carry out the job. The directives control and direct the assembler as it goes about its task of creating the machine instructions.

The instructions briefly examined in this chapter include MOV, ADD, INT, and (for the alternate program) PUSH and RET. MOV is used to move data; ADD performs addition; and INT interrupts the program and gives control to DOS so DOS can perform some service for the program, such as ending it. The PUSH instruction places data onto the stack; the RET instruction returns control to DOS only when the program is finished.

The listing control directives include PAGE and TITLE. PAGE is used to set the page dimensions and to eject the source listing to another page. TITLE is used to produce a title on every page of the source listing.

The SEGMENT directive is used to define the start of a segment of coding, such as the code segment. The ENDS directive tells the assembler where a segment physically ends. The PROC directive defines the start of a procedure or subroutine, and ENDP defines the end of that procedure.

The ASSUME directive instructs the assembler to make certain assumptions about what is in the segment registers (CS, DS, SS, and ES).

The END directive indicates the physical end of the complete program.

Fields can be defined in main storage. DW, the define word directive, can be used to allocate word variables and give them an initial value.

Chapter 3 examines the actual coding rules for assembler and re-examines directives in detail. Then, in Chapter 4, you will begin to study actual assembler instructions.

2.23 REVIEW QUESTIONS

1. In a debugging run, what pair of registers points to the current instruction?

2. In a debugging run, if you want to display the first bytes of the data area, what register is needed in the display command?

3. True/false: When DOS gives control to a program, registers CS, SS, and DS are all set to the correct starting values of the program's different segments. If not, why not?

4. True/false: Every SEGMENT directive must have a corresponding, or matching, ENDS.

5. Register AX looks like this:

Show the contents of AX after executing

```
MOV  TOTAL,AX
```

6. You use a word processor to create a new program, TRY.ASM. Then you enter the command:

```
A>MASM B:TRY;
```

The assembler finds several syntax errors. So, you attempt to view the listing to see those errors. You enter

```
A>TYPE B:TRY.LST
```

What is displayed on the screen? Why?

7. True/false: The PAGE directive sets only the number of characters per line and the number of lines per page. If not, why not?

8. Why are TITLE directives used? Doesn't the programmer know what his or her program is supposed to do?

9. The programmer makes the following error:

```
PGM1CD       END S
             END
```

What do you suppose the error messages might be?

10. Why do you not debug assembler programs by just executing them from the DOS prompt (A>PGM1)?

2.24 PRACTICE PROBLEMS

1. Outline the steps needed to convert a program known as SALECALC into an executable program. The starting point is the completed coding sheets. Where possible, show the actual commands you would give to run the necessary software.

2. Assuming that files GRADES.ASM and GRADES.OBJ exist, what files and what interactive prompts, if any, do the statements in parts a through k produce? (Assume that you are running from a hard disk; GRADES.ASM is in the current subdirectory; a PATH has been set up to find the software.)

   a) `MASM GRADES,;`
   b) `MASM GRADES,,,,`
   c) `MASM GRADES,,,,;`
   d) `MASM GRADES,,;`
   e) `MASM GRADES`
   f) `MASM GRADES,`
   g) `MASM GRADES,,`
   h) `LINK GRADES`
   i) `LINK GRADES,`
   j) `LINK GRADES,;`
   k) `LINK GRADES,,;`

3. For each of the following debugger commands (or dialogue commands, if running CODE VIEW), identify what the command is and what results the command produces.

   a) `T`
   b) `G`
   c) `D`
   d) `R`
   e) `Q`

2.25 PROGRAMMING PROBLEMS

1. Make a copy of PGM1.ASM and call it PGMTEST.ASM. Use your word processor to modify the starting values of COST and TOTAL to 8 and 20, respectively. Now assemble and link PGMTEST. Use your debugging program to see the contents of TOTAL after the last MOV instruction. Is it what you expect?

2. Make a copy of PGM1.ASM and call it SHELL.ASM. Use your word processor to remove the three main processing instructions that add COST to TOTAL. Then remove the definitions for COST and TOTAL from the data area. You should have removed five lines of coding. Finally, alter the title line to say PROGRAM SHELL. Now you have a template program that you can copy and use with your future programs. Just add main processing code and data definitions.

   Test your work. Assemble the program and link it. Now execute it to ensure that you have not made a mistake.

3

Assembler Directives

3.1 CHAPTER OBJECTIVES

In this chapter you will learn

1. The coding rules for assembler programs
2. The rules for creating names of variables and labels of instructions
3. What names are reserved by the assembler and cannot be used as names of variables
4. How to code the PAGE, TITLE, SEGMENT-ENDS, PROC-ENDP, ASSUME, and END directives
5. How to define variables or fields in main storage
6. How to code some special operators such as LABEL, EQU, SEG, OFFSET, and $

3.2 INTRODUCTION

In the last chapter the sample assembler program added the contents of the field COST to the field called TOTAL. Although the program filled a page, only eight lines contained the actual instructions, such as MOV and ADD. All the many other statements were either comments or assembler **directives.**

Comments are used to add to the readability of the program. Directives are commands to the assembler program itself and create no machine instructions. A directive, for example, may instruct the assembler to define a variable or data field, to eject the source listing to a new page, or to begin and end the code segment of the program.

Before the detailed rules for coding the many directives can be discussed, you must have a good understanding of the fundamental rules upon which the microassembler language is based. We will first present the actual coding rules for assembler and then cover the more common directives that were so briefly described in the last chapter. Then, in the next chapter, a beginning instruction set will be presented.

For easy reference, the assembler listing of the sample program given in Chapter 2 has been reproduced as Figure 3–1; it is PGM1.ASM on your program disk.

```
Microsoft (R) Macro Assembler Version 5.10          9/1/88 09:41:38


PGM1   FIGURE 3-1 SAMPLE PROGRAM                     Page    1-1



      1                        PAGE   60,132
      2                        TITLE   PGM1   FIGURE 3-1 SAMPLE PROGRAM
      3
      4              ;**************************************************************************
      5              ; PGM1       Title: Figure 3-1 Sample Program To Add COST to TOTAL   *
      6              ;                                                                     *
      7              ; Programmer: Vic Broquard                                           *
      8              ; Date Written:  6/11/88        Date Of Last Revision: 8/4/88        *
      9              ;                                                                     *
     10              ; Purpose: Add  two word numbers                                     *
     11              ;                                                                     *
     12              ; Special Requirements: None                                         *
     13              ;                                                                     *
     14              ;**************************************************************************
     15
     16
     17              ; program code segment
     18
     19 0000         PGM1CD  SEGMENT
     20
     21 0000         MAIN    PROC    FAR
     22
     23              ; housekeeping section
     24
     25                      ASSUME  CS:PGM1CD,DS:PGM1DA,SS:PGM1SK
     26
```

FIGURE 3–1   Sample assembler source program listing   *(Continues)*

```
27 0000  B8 ---- R        MOV    AX,PGM1DA   ; ESTABLISH ADDRESSABILITY
28 0003  8E D8            MOV    DS,AX       ; TO PGM1DA - THE PGM'S DATA SEGMENT
29
30                    ; main process section
31
32 0005  A1 0000 R        MOV    AX,COST     ; REG AX = COST
33 0008  03 06 0002 R     ADD    AX,TOTAL    ; ADD COST TO TOTAL
34 000C  A3 0002 R        MOV    TOTAL,AX    ; STORE NEW TOTAL
35
36                    ; return to DOS section
37
38 000F  B0 00            MOV    AL,0        ; SET 0 AS THE RETURN CODE FOR DOS
39 0011  B4 4C            MOV    AH,4CH      ; SET FOR DOS END PROCESS FUNCTION
40 0013  CD 21            INT    21H         ; CALL DOS TO END PROGRAM
41
42 0015           MAIN    ENDP
43
44 0015           PGM1CD  ENDS
45
46
47                    ; program data segment
48
49 0000           PGM1DA  SEGMENT
50
51 0000  0006     COST    DW      6
52 0002  0004     TOTAL   DW      4
53
54 0004           PGM1DA  ENDS
55
56
```

```
Microsoft (R) Macro Assembler Version 5.10          9/1/88 09:41:38
PGM1   FIGURE 3-1 SAMPLE PROGRAM                     Page    1-2


57                    ; program stack segment
58
59 0000           PGM1SK  SEGMENT PARA STACK 'STACK'
60
61 0000  0020[            DW      32 DUP (?)
62      ????
63           ]
64
65
66 0040           PGM1SK  ENDS
67                        END
```

```
Microsoft (R) Macro Assembler Version 5.10          9/1/88 09:41:38
PGM1   FIGURE 3-1 SAMPLE PROGRAM                     Symbols-1
```

FIGURE 3–1   continued

Segments and Groups:

N a m e	Length	Align	Combine	Class
PGM1CD	0015	PARA	NONE	
PGM1DA	0004	PARA	NONE	
PGM1SK	0040	PARA	STACK	'STACK'

Symbols:

N a m e	Type	Value	Attr	
COST	L WORD	0000	PGM1DA	
MAIN	F PROC	0000	PGM1CD	Length = 0015
TOTAL	L WORD	0002	PGM1DA	
@CPU	TEXT	0101h		
@FILENAME	TEXT	B_PGM1		
@VERSION	TEXT	510		

```
    64 Source  Lines
    64 Total   Lines
    12 Symbols

 47238 + 136086 Bytes symbol space free

     0 Warning Errors
     0 Severe  Errors
```

FIGURE 3–1 continued

3.3 ASSEMBLER CODING RULES

Every language has its own set of rules for coding a program. Some of these are fairly involved; however, microassembler has only a few rules. These can be summarized as follows.

1. Assembler programs consist of lines of code. A line can contain a maximum of 132 characters. However, it is realistic to limit coding to 80 characters per line. This is because the typical screen can display only this many characters on one line. No line can be continued.

2. Only one instruction can be coded on each line.

3. The command syntax is free-form and uses blanks and/or tabs as the delimiters between the various parts of an instruction.

4. Null, or blank lines, are allowed. They are inserted by pressing the ENTER key, thus creating a <CR> (carriage return). Null lines are added to the program to make the listing more readable. Use them liberally.

5. If a line begins with a semicolon, then the entire line is considered to be a comment and all text after the semicolon is ignored. It is good programming practice to use comment lines to identify the major sections of coding and to outline the major processing steps that are in each section. Examine Figure 3–1 once more and locate the comment lines.

    In addition, comments may appear on the actual instruction lines. Again, all text after the semicolon is ignored. The following lines of code illustrate comment lines.

```
; This is the Main Processing Section
      MOV  COST,AX; SAVE THE NEW VALUE OF COST(AX) IN COST
```

6. Normally it makes no difference whether the code is entered in upper- or lowercase. That is,

```
                    COST
                    Cost
                    cost
```

    refer to the same item. (There are several MASM options that can be used to make the coding partially or totally upper- or lowercase sensitive.)

7. The syntax for an assembler statement is

    name/label operation operands ;comments

    Notice that one or more blanks and/or tabs are used as the delimiters that separate these four parts of an assembler statement.

Since assembler is a relatively free-form language, there is no required column alignment for operation codes, operands, and comments. However, nearly all programmers attempt to vertically align all the operations in the same column and align the start of the operands and comments as well. Otherwise, the program is almost unreadable.

Now examine each of the four parts of an assembler statement in detail, beginning with names.

3.4   NAMES AND LABELS

The first entry on an assembler statement is the optional name field. If coded, the name must begin in the first position of the line. Names are used to identify data fields or variables and to identify the names of segments and procedures.

When names are used to identify instructions, they are called **labels.** (In BASIC, for example, each instruction is identified by a line number.) In microassembler most instructions do not have labels. Only those instructions that are referenced in conditional or unconditional branches (GO TOs) or similar instructions must have a label.

Rules for Names and Labels

Rule 1

All labels and names must be unique. There can be no duplicate names or labels in an assembler program. All subsequent duplicate names or labels generate an error message.

Rule 2

Names can be of any length, but only the first 31 characters are used.

Rule 3

Names must begin with a letter from "A" to "Z" or one of the allowed special characters, which are the question mark (?), the at sign (@), the underline (_), the period (.), and the dollar sign ($). Beginning with Version 5.0, a number of new reserved words that start with a period were added to the language. Therefore, it is probably a good idea to avoid using the period as the first character of a name.

Rule 4

The remaining characters that make up a name can also include the digits 0 through 9.

Rule 5

There are a number of **reserved words** that cannot be used as labels or names. Table 3–1 lists most of these reserved words. The list is also reproduced in Appendix B. (Note that the dollar sign and question mark are included; therefore, you cannot have a field named with just these single characters.) Also included on the list are all the register names, instruction codes, operations, and directives.

The names you create should be meaningful. A good choice of names increases program readability, lessens the chance for error, and aids in program maintenance. Use names with which you feel comfortable. Some programmers prefer long descriptive names; others opt for short names. In

TABLE 3–1   Reserved words in assembler

Register names:

AH	AL	AX	BH	BL	BP	BX	CH
CL	CS	CX	DH	DI	DL	DS	DX
ES	SI	SP	SS				

Instruction operation codes:

AAA	AAD	AAM	AAS	ADC	ADD	AND	CALL
CBW	CLC	CLD	CLI	CMC	CMP	CMPS	CWD
DAA	DAS	DEC	DIV	ESC	HLT	IDIV	IMUL
IN	INC	INT	INTO	IRET	JA	JAE	JB
JBE	JCXZ	JE	JG	JGE	JL	JLE	JMP
JNA	JNAE	JNB	JNBE	JNE	JNG	JNGE	JNL
JNLE	JNO	JNP	JNS	JNZ	JO	JP	JPE
JPO	JS	JZ	LAHF	LDS	LEA	LES	LOCK
LODS	LOOP	LOOPE	LOOPNE	LOOPNZ	LOOPZ	MOV	MOVS
MUL	NEG	NIL	NOP	NOT	OR	OUT	POP
POPF	PUSH	PUSHF	RCL	RCR	REP	REPE	REPNE
REPNZ	REPZ	RET	ROL	ROR	SAHF	SAL	SAR
SBB	SCAS	SHL	SHR	STC	STD	STI	STOS
SUB	TEST	WAIT	XCHG	XLAT	XOR		

Assembler operators and directives:

$	*	+	©	.	/	=	?	[]
ALIGN	ASSUME	BYTE	COMM	COMMENT	DB	DF	DD	
DOSSEG	DQ	DS	DT	DW	DWORD	DUP	ELSE	
END	ENDIF	ENDM	ENDMP	ENDS	EQ	EQU	EVEN	
EXITM	EXTRN	FAR	FWORD	GE	GROUP	GT	HIGH	
IF	IFB	IFDEF	IFDIF	IFE	IFIDN	IFNB	IFNDEF	
IF1	IF2	INCLUDE	INCLUDELIB		IRP	IRPC	LABEL	
LE	LENGTH	LINE	LOCAL	LOW	LT	MACRO	MASK	
MOD	NAME	NE	NEAR	NOTHING	OFFSET	ORG	PAGE	
PROC	PRT	PUBLIC	PURGE	QWORD	RECORD	REPT	REPTRD	
SEG	SEGMENT	SHORT	SIZE	STACK	STRUC	SUBTTL	TBYTE	
TITLE	THIS	TYPE	WIDTH	WORD				

.186	.286	.286P	.287	.386	.386P	.387	.8086
.8087	.ALPHA	.CODE	.CONST	.CREF	.DATA	.DATA?	.ERR
.ERR1	.ERR2	.ERRB	.ERRDEF	.ERRDIF	.ERRE	.ERRIDN	
.ERRNB	.ERRNDEF		.ERRNZ	.FARDATA	.FARDATA?		.LALL
.LFCOND	.LIST	.MODEL	%OUT	.RADIX	.SALL	.SEQ	.SFCOND
.STACK	.TFCOND	.TYPE	.XALL	.XCREF	.XLIST		

any case, the name must be meaningful. The following are examples of meaningful names.

```
COST              TALLY           INPUT            FIELD_1
WORK_AREA         TOTAL_COST      PLANT_ADDRESS    FIRST_NAME
ACTUAL_LENGTH     ACT_LENGTH      MAX_LENGTH       FNAME
```

The following examples illustrate poor choices, reserved words, or names that do not follow the rules.

```
1FIELD      *COST      F1      AL       LINE     BYTE     NAME
PAGE        C          T6      WA       TC       CLI      AND
HIGH        LOOP       LENGTH  RECORD   TYPE     A
```

Labels

As indicated, most instructions do not have a label—labels are optional.

Normally, a label ends with a colon, as shown in the examples below. If a label ends with a colon, then it is considered a NEAR label. If not, it is a FAR label. The differences between NEAR and FAR labels are covered in the next chapter.

To increase a label's visibility, it is recommended that the label be placed on a line separate from the instruction. This causes the label to stand out from the other lines of code and to enhance the program's readability by identifying the section of code in which it falls. Either of the following forms is correct:

```
BIGLOOP: MOV AX,COST
BIGLOOP:
         MOV AX,COST
```

(Note, however, that when the label is used as an operand in a conditional branching instruction, the colon is not included. Actually, there is more involved in the use of labels than this description implies. See the next chapter for more detail.)

Names That Begin with Special Characters

You will find that names and labels that begin with a special character tend to stand out from code even more than names and labels that do not begin with special characters. For example:

```
$AREA
?SCREEN
?HELP_SECTION
```

Frequently, programmers adopt a creative set of naming conventions within their programs. A common technique is to give all utility subroutine segments names that begin with a question mark—?SET_CURSOR or ?CLEAR_SCREEN, for example. This is particularly useful because the question mark provides an additional element of internal documentation.

3.5 THE OPERATION CODE

The **operation code** (**opcode,** for short) tells the assembler what action to take. Some opcodes are actual instructions, such as ADD and MOV; while others tell the assembler how to do something. For example, some opcodes tell the assembler how to print the source listing or handle some other non-executable activity such as printing titles on the source program listing. Opcodes that tell how to do something are called assembler directives. SEGMENT, PAGE, TITLE, and DW (define word) are examples.

3.6 OPERANDS

An **operand** is the address or location in main storage where data or an instruction may be found.

An instruction may have no operands, one operand, or multiple operands. If there are multiple operands, each is separated by a comma. Embedded blanks or tabs can often be used to separate operands, thereby increasing readability.

In the sample program shown in Figure 3–1, the contents of COST could be moved into register AX by entering

```
bbbbbMOVbbbAX,COST
```

or

```
tMOVtAX,COST
```

or

```
tbMOVtbbAX,COST
```

where b represents a blank and t represents a tab.

3.7 COMMENTS

Nearly all instructions should have brief comments explaining in English what is occurring. These instruction comments are preceded by a semicolon and come after the operands. They are usually aligned on a particular column for readability.

It is important to include comments on each instruction because microassembler is a terse and cryptic language. Without comments, it is often difficult to know or understand the full purpose of an instruction. Consider the following ADD instruction:

```
ADD   AX,BX
```

What does it do? It is obvious to experienced programmers that the contents of register BX are being added to the contents of register AX and the result will be placed in register AX. Knowing this, however, you still don't know what data is being added or why.

The following example contains a comment, but as you can see, it is a waste of time and effort because it gives no meaning to the instruction.

```
ADD   AX,BX      ; ADD BX TO AX
```

Get into the habit of including meaningful comments that really tell what is happening—comments such as

```
ADD   AX,BX      ; ADD COST (REG BX)  TO  TOTAL (REG AX)
```

Using informative instruction comments significantly reduces the number of errors that can find their way into a program.

Far too many programmers code the instructions first; and then, when they have the whole program working, they go back and add instruction comments. Such programmers tend to spend more time locating errors in their code than smart programmers, who include instruction comments from the start. Smart programmers have fewer errors and find their errors quickly.

3.8 THE ASSEMBLER DIRECTIVES

With the general coding rules in mind, examine the common assembler directives. They may be thought of as consisting of two categories: those that relate to overall program organization and those that define variables in main storage.

First, consider those directives that are related to program organization. Second, examine those that are used to define variables or fields in memory.

3.9 DIRECTIVES RELATING TO PROGRAM ORGANIZATION

The PAGE Directive

Primarily, the PAGE directive serves four purposes. It can be used to eject the paper in the printer to a new page, to set the number of lines per page, to set the number of bytes per line, and to increment section numbers.

The assembler listing defaults for the .LST file are 66 lines per page and 80 bytes per line. Generally, a programmer overrides these defaults to produce a readable listing. If the defaults are to be altered, change them at the beginning of the program. Enter

```
PAGE 60,132
```

In this example, the first operand specifies the number of lines per page (60) and the second operand gives the number of bytes per line (132).

The assembler can be forced to eject its source listing to a new page at any time by coding:

```
PAGE
```

Judicious use of the PAGE command enhances readability of listings. We recommend that all subroutines, all major segments and all lengthy sections of code begin on a new page. Beginning them on a new page makes them easier to find in the listing. (This was not done with the first example program because of its relatively small size.)

Examine the second line of the assembly listing (Figure 3–1), which contains the title and page number. Notice the form of the page number; it is

```
PAGE 1-1
```

The first 1 refers to the **section number** and the second 1 is the **page number.**

The use of the word PAGE with no operands automatically increments the page number portion only. On the other hand, the section number is completely user-controlled. For example, suppose that you have a very long program in which you want to identify each segment and begin each segment on a separate page. That is, let the code segment begin on page 1-1 and have subsequent pages of this segment be numbered page 1-2, 1-3, and so on. Next have the data segment begin a new section, page 2-1, with subsequent pages known as page 2-2, 2-3, and so on. Similarly, have the stack segment begin on page 3-1. To increment the section number and reset the page number back to 1, enter

```
PAGE +
```

The + option increments the section number while resetting the page number back to 1. (There is no way to decrement the section number nor is there any reason to do so.)

Another common practice is to increment the section number at the start of each major subroutine in the program. (A PROC through its ENDP delineate a complete subroutine.)

The TITLE Directive

This directive is used to print headings on each page of the assembler listing. The text following a blank after the TITLE directive in the TITLE statement is reproduced at the top of each page of the listing.

In Version 4.0 the first six characters of the title are automatically extracted by the assembler and become the module name, which is used by the linker in its error messages. Therefore, it is common practice to use these first six characters as the program name on the disk file. So, if the program name is PGM1.ASM, the title might read

```
TITLE PGM1  -  SAMPLE PROGRAM TO ADD COST TO TOTAL
```

There can be only one TITLE per module.

The SUBTTL Directive

If the program has many sections, then subtitles that identify a section are useful. Subtitles are created by using the SUBTTL directive. If TITLE has been included, a subtitle prints as a second title line after the main title line.

The syntax for SUBTTL is even simpler than that for the TITLE directive. The only operand necessary is the text of the subtitle.

```
SUBTTL  text desired
```

PAGE + and SUBTTL are frequently used in combination to identify the beginning of different sections in a large listing. The following code creates a new subtitle and then prints it on the new page with incremented section-page numbers:

```
SUBTTL  CAPITALIZATION SECTION
PAGE    +
```

What happens if these two instructions are reversed? The listing ejects to a new page with new section numbers, and the preceding subtitle and title, if any, are used. On subsequent pages, the new subtitle appears. Watch out for this minor error.

All titles and subtitles are limited to a maximum of 60 characters.

The SEGMENT-ENDS Pair

The beginning and the ending point of each segment of a program—code, data, and stack—must be given to the assembler. The beginning point of a segment is defined by the SEGMENT directive. The syntax is

```
name   SEGMENT   alignment   combine type   class name
```

The name is supplied by the programmer. The options or operands, if not coded, receive default values. Note that the operands of the SEGMENT command are separated by blanks or tabs and not by commas.

For beginning assembler programs, no options are needed except for the stack segment. The coding for the stack's SEGMENT directive is always the same. First consider the available operands and then examine this constant stack segment code.

Alignment

The **alignment parameter** can be set to several different values. PARA is used for paragraph alignment. PARA forces the segment to begin on an address that is evenly divisible by 16, or 10H. This is the default if no alignment is coded. For normal program use, paragraph alignment is fine, and—since it is the default—PARA is seldom entered in code.

The other choices are normally used when one segment is to be joined with other segments during the link operation. This is covered in Chapter 12. The other choices include BYTE, WORD, and PAGE (which align the segment on an address evenly divisible by 256, or 100H).

Combine Type

The **combine type** is used to indicate similar segments that can be combined to create one consolidated large segment. The combine type is also used to redefine variables.

In large programs with many separately assembled subroutines (see Chapter 12), it is convenient to have the data areas for all the different modules in one large segment. If no combine class is coded, the default is blank. This default means that the segment is "private" and cannot be joined to other segments.

The combine type PUBLIC is used to link external subroutines together with the main procedure. COMMON creates an external overlay area in which all common segments overlay the same physical area. See Chapter 12 for details.

The STACK option is used to define an area to be used for the stack, or save area. When used, the linker joins all stack segments into one large segment. This is the only option that you need at this time.

Class Name

The **class name** is used by the linker to place all segments of the same class name together into one large segment. The class name must be enclosed in single apostrophes.

For beginning programs, this entry is needed only with the stack segment. The objective is to join the program's stack area with the system's stack.

Normal Coding of the Code and Data Segment Directives

Until Chapter 12, when we will discuss external subroutines, normal coding of the code segment and data segment will be simply

```
name SEGMENT
```

Normal Coding of the Stack Segment Directive

The stack segment should be joined with the system's stack. The coding should be

```
            name  SEGMENT  PARA  STACK 'STACK'
```

Failure to Code a Stack Segment

What happens if a stack segment is not defined? First, the linker issues a warning message—it says there is no stack segment. Then, when the program gets control, the stack segment register (SS) points to the code segment! The SP register, which points to the next available byte, will be set to FF FFH, or the 64Kth byte of the code segment. Any values placed on the stack are stored in the 64th byte. This is usually not a problem unless the code segment is very large and the actual instructions exceed 64K. If it does exceed 64K, program instructions are overwritten by the stack, and the program terminates abnormally or generates unpredictable output!

Segment Names

Any name can be used for a segment. Yet, most programmers either pick names that are indicative of the type of segment (code, data, or stack) or choose a name that is composed partially of the program's name. Some examples are

```
CODE     SEGMENT
STACKSG  SEGMENT
DATA     SEGMENT
PGM1CD   SEGMENT
PGM1DA   SEGMENT
PGM1SK   SEGMENT
```

Matching ENDS Directive

Every segment **must** have a corresponding ENDS with a matching name. For example:

```
CODE     SEGMENT
            .
            .
            .
CODE     ENDS
```

This tells the assembler when to end a segment.

Nesting Segments

Segments are never physically nested! If for some reason another segment is started before the original segment is ended, the assembler stops the definition of the old segment, handles the new segment as if it were not nested, and then resumes working with the original segment.

Segment Order

The segments—code, data, and stack—can be in any order. Therefore, it is possible to have the segments arranged as

code, data, stack

or

data, code, stack

or

data, stack, code

and so on.

Segment order is merely a matter of programmer preference. In this text, we have used different sequences to illustrate the fact that they do not always need to be in the same order. Take your choice.

The PROC-ENDP Pair

Procedures, or subroutines, are the basic building blocks of microassembler programs. You will find that it takes an enormous number of instructions to handle even the simplest of problems. Thus, it is imperative that you organize your thinking and take the time to design an efficient solution to your problem. The use of top-down design is highly recommended. A key factor in becoming a successful assembler programmer is to develop skill in setting up procedures that avoid redundant code.

Each procedure starts with a PROC command and ends with an ENDP command. The syntax is

```
          name PROC option
                  .
                  .
                  .
          name ENDP
```

As with the ENDS directive, the ENDP notifies the assembler of the physical end of the procedure.

The name used with the PROC command should be one that is descriptive of the procedure.

PROC Options

There are two options, FAR or NEAR, that may be used with the PROC command. Their purpose is to indicate to the assembler the location of a procedure that is to be called by the assembler.

A procedure is invoked by a CALL command. The **FAR** option tells the assembler that the procedure is called from a procedure that is in another segment. This is always the case with the top, main, or first procedure in the program. Since a program is actually called by DOS and since the DOS code is certainly not a part of your code segment, the top procedure **must** use the FAR option.

The **NEAR** option is used for procedures that are called from within the same code segment. This will be the case with your beginning programs. Only when you begin to use external subroutines in Chapter 12 will the FAR option be necessary.

If an option is not specified, the assembler assumes that the NEAR option is to be used. Thus, except on the main procedure, no option is needed for all subprocedures in your beginning programs.

Ending a Procedure: the RET Instruction

All subprocedures (that is, any procedure that is not the main procedure) are ended with a RET or return command. RET means to go back to the place in the program where the procedure was called.

Different machine code is created for NEAR and FAR returns. This difference and the reasons for it will be discussed more fully in Chapter 5.

Usually, the assembler can determine from the existing code (the option on the PROC directive) which is needed—a FAR return or a NEAR return.

Standard Procedure Coding

Normally, procedures appear as

```
            name    PROC
                      .
                      .
                      .

                    RET

            name    ENDP
```

Procedure Names

Choose reasonable, meaningful procedure names. For example, a procedure to clear the screen might be coded as:

```
        CLEAR_SCREEN    PROC
                          .
                          .
                          .
```

```
                              RET

              CLEAR_SCREEN    ENDP
```

Ending the MAIN Procedure: DOS Version Differences

If you are using a DOS release prior to Version 3.0, end the MAIN procedure by returning control back to DOS with the RET instruction. (See the alternate sample program in Chapter 2, Figure 2–4a.

If you are using DOS Version 3.0 or later, do not return the main procedure to DOS; rather, terminate it and set a return code that can be checked by batch (.BAT) files. In the program in Figure 3–1, for example, the main procedure does not end with a RET as the alternate version does. Instead, it ends with the DOS interrupt INT 21H and function number 4CH. This ends the process and sets the return code to 0.

The END Directive and the First Executable Instruction

The END directive identifies the very last line of code—the physical end of the program. The END command has only one optional operand. If an operand is coded, it has the name of the first instruction in the program to be executed.

DOS has three ways of knowing where the first instruction in the program is located, or where the program is to begin executing. First, if there is no operand on the END statement, then DOS assumes the very first byte of the program contains the first instruction. This can be true only if the code segment comes first, the first item in the code segment is the main procedure, and the first thing in the main procedure is the first instruction. This is the case in the sample program in Figure 3–1.

Second, if there is a name coded in the END statement and that name is the name on a PROC statement, then DOS assumes that the first executable instruction is at the first byte in the procedure. Use this method to signal the first instruction if you code the data segment first, followed by the code segment.

Third, if there is a name coded on the END statement and that name is a label on an instruction, then DOS assumes that instruction is the first executable instruction. Such a program could be coded as shown in Example 3–1.

In Example 3–1, HERE is the option on the END directive. HERE is a label on the MOV instruction. Thus, the assembler marks this instruction as the first executable instruction rather than the first byte of the program, which is the first item in the data segment.

Remember, either the second or third method must be used if the code segment is not physically first or if the first byte of the code segment is not the first instruction. If any lines are coded after the END, they will be flagged as errors.

The ASSUME Directive

The ASSUME statement tells the assembler and the DOS system to assume that, when the program begins, the segment register CS points to the

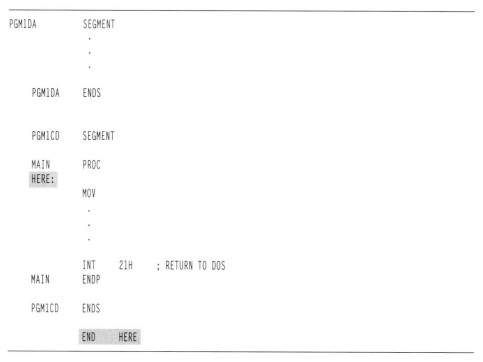

```
PGM1DA      SEGMENT
              .
              .
              .

   PGM1DA   ENDS


   PGM1CD   SEGMENT

   MAIN     PROC
   HERE:
            MOV
              .
              .
              .

            INT     21H    ; RETURN TO DOS
   MAIN     ENDP

   PGM1CD   ENDS

            END     HERE
```

EXAMPLE 3-1 Using a name in the END directive

program's code segment. Further, it tells the assembler that register DS points to the program's data segment and that the register SS points to the stack segment. These register settings are required because the assembler does not make any such assumptions itself.

As discussed in Chapter 2, when DOS loads and begins to execute a program, the CS and SS registers point to the correct locations. Unfortunately, register DS does not. Therefore, every program must perform the two housekeeping instructions to get the DS register pointing to the data segment:

```
          MOV    AX,PGM1DA ; ESTABLISH ADDRESSABILITY
          MOV    DS,AX     ; TO THE DATA SEGMENT
```

First, the address of the data segment is moved into register AX. Then, that value is moved into register DS where it belongs. In this way, register DS now contains the address of the data segment.

These two instructions **must** be included at the beginning of every program you write. A later chapter will discuss in depth exactly what these instructions along with the ending INT 21H are really doing.

There are several instructions that operate on complete strings of data rather than single characters. These are known as the string-handling

```
PGM1CD  SEGMENT

    MAIN    PROC  FAR

    ; housekeeping section

            ASSUME CS:PGM1CD,DS:PGM1DA,SS:PGM1SK,ES:PGM1DA

            MOV    AX,PGM1DA  ; ESTABLISH ADDRESSABILITY
            MOV    DS,AX      ; TO THE DATA SFGMFNT
            MOV    ES,AX      ; AND ES TO DATA SEGMENT

    ; main process section
                .
                .
                .

    ; return to DOS section

            MOV    AL,0       ; SET 0 AS THE RETURN CODE
            MOV    AH,4CH     ; SET FOR DOS END PROCESS
            INT    21H        ; CALL DOS TO END PGM

    MAIN    ENDP

PGM1CD  ENDS


PGM1DA  SEGMENT

        define all data fields

PGM1DA  ENDS
            .
            .
            .

            END
```

EXAMPLE 3–2   Establishing register ES

instructions. They are covered in detail in Chapter 11. A character **string** is
a series of ASCII characters, such as a person's name or home address or an
item description, that are treated as a single unit. If a program is going to
use some of the string-handling instructions, register ES is required to point
to the data segment. Example 3–2 shows how to set up register ES properly.

3.10 DIRECTIVES THAT DEFINE VARIABLES OR FIELDS IN MEMORY

In Chapter 1 you learned that there are different sizes of fields in storage: bytes, words, and doublewords. The table that follows shows the assembler directives that are used to define storage for these fields or variables.

Directive	Defines	A field of length
DB	a byte	1 byte
DW	a word	2 bytes
DD	a doubleword	4 bytes
DQ	a quadword	8 bytes
DT	a tenbyte	10 bytes

For each of these directives, the syntax is:

name Dn   initialvalue

where n is one of the values B, W, D, Q, or T.

The Symbolic Name

The symbolic name of a variable or field is optional. If the name is not coded, then that field cannot be accessed directly by the program. Consider how this works.

In the sample program in Figure 3–1, the variable names are COST and TOTAL. COST is defined by the directive

```
COST DW    6
```

and COST is accessed by using its name, as in

```
MOV    AX,COST
```

Suppose that no name had been coded. The directive would be

```
DW    6
```

Now, how can you directly reference that field? You cannot, since there is no name associated with the word in memory.

This technique of defining fields with no symbolic names is commonly used for setting up tables and for providing filler fields in records (as is done in many high-level languages). There are other indirect methods that use such "nameless" fields. These techniques will be presented when they are needed.

When creating variable or field names, remember that all names must be unique—no duplicate names or labels are permitted. In addition, reserved words cannot be used as field names.

Coding the Data Declaration Directive

Next Dn is coded and the symbol n is converted to the appropriate value: B for byte, W for word, D for doubleword, Q for quadword, or T for tenbyte. Be sure to use the correct field size.

Coding the Initial Value

You must keep several considerations in mind when coding initial values. First, some fields may not have or may not need an initial value. If this is the case, they are said to be uninitialized. On the other hand, some fields may have an actual starting value. Also consider that a single directive can be used to define multiple fields, some of which are initialized and some of which may not be. Examine each of these points in turn.

If the field is to be uninitialized or has no starting value, enter a question mark in place of a value. For example, the statement

```
WORK DB   ?
```

creates a 1-byte, uninitialized field known as WORK. Initially, this field contains unknown or unusable characters. Frequently, the assembler inserts 00H into such uninitialized fields, but you cannot expect that this will always be the case.

Defining Initialized Fields

Fields that are to be used as counters and totals must be initialized, usually to 0 or to some other numeric value. This is done by coding the desired value as a decimal, hexadecimal, or binary number. For example, if you need to accumulate a total of all test scores, the field TOTAL could be

```
TOTAL     DW    0
```

In this case, the initial value is written as a decimal number. If you use decimal numbers, the assembler converts them automatically into binary or hex. If you choose to code the hex value directly, add the letter H as a suffix to the hex value. This tells the assembler that the value is already in hex format and doesn't need to be converted.

```
TOTAL     DW    0000H
```

To code the binary value directly, use the suffix B after the binary value.

Note that an initial value applies only to the first time the routine is executed. TOTAL, as defined by the preceding hex value, begins with 0. Repeated executions do not reset TOTAL to 0. Only when the program is reloaded by DOS does TOTAL again begin with the initial value of 0.

However, explicit initializations that move a 0 to TOTAL permit a field to be reinitialized any time during program execution.

Defining Tables and Arrays: The DUP Operator

A **table,** or **array,** is a group of fields that have the same length and are collectively known by one name. An example is an array of month names that contains 12 entries. (Table processing will be covered fully in Chapter 13.)

Suppose that you need to store the final grades of each student in a class. Suppose also that there are a maximum of 25 students in the class. It is not practical to define 25 separate fields with 25 separate, nonduplicated names. Rather, you set up a table with 25 entries and give the table one name, such as GRADE. How is this done?

The assembler provides the DUP operand for this purpose. It says duplicate the following value as many times as specified. The DUP syntax is

```
number of fields  DUP(value desired)
```

For the table of 25 total grades, you code

```
GRADE     DW    25 DUP(0)
```

This directive defines an array of 25 words, with each word having a starting value of 00 00H.

Since the name GRADE actually refers to 25 different fields, the use of the name of the array points only to the first byte of the table. Therefore, special processing instructions are needed to access the other 24 words in the table.

If no starting values are to be inserted into GRADE, enter

```
GRADE     DW    25 DUP(?)
```

Reverse Byte Order

You recall that numeric data are stored in memory in reverse byte order, with the low-order byte of the field in the low-numbered address and the high-order byte in the high-numbered address. Then, when MOV moves data into a register, the order is reversed and data appear in the correct order.

If a line counter is to be set up with an initial value of 1, the counter is coded as

```
LINECOUNT DW    1
```

In storage, LINECOUNT contains

01 00H

Defining ASCII Character Data and Strings

Character data can be 1 byte long. However, it is more likely that character data consist of many bytes, as in a field containing a person's name. As you have learned, such multiple-byte fields are called strings.

All strings are defined with DB, the define byte directive. The initial values are either enclosed within single apostrophes or enclosed within double quotation marks. If an apostrophe is needed within the string, then the whole string is enclosed between quotation marks.

Suppose that you want to define a field that contains an error message. It could be coded as

```
ERR_MSG    DB   'THIS IS AN ERROR MESSAGE.'
WARN_MSG   DB   "FIRST NAME'S VALUE IS INCORRECT"
```

The apostrophes or quotation marks surrounding any value string tell the assembler that the data are to be stored in ASCII format. During execution, the first character is stored at the lowest string address and the last character is stored in the highest address. The name ERR_MSG points to the first byte of the string, which contains the letter T.

Be careful when coding ASCII numbers. The value 0 and the value '0' are handled very differently. A 0 means that the value is a binary number; a '0' means the value is an ASCII 0. If you had coded TOTAL in the test score example as

```
TOTAL    DB   '0'
```

then storage contains an ASCII 0 (30H, not 00H)! Confusing the radix of values is a very common source of errors.

Suppose that a field called WORK is to be 10 bytes in length with an initial value of blanks. You can code WORK in one of two ways:

```
WORK    DB   10 DUP(' ')
```

or

```
WORK    DB   '          '
```

In the first case, the assembler considers WORK to be an array of 10 elements, each of which is 1 byte long. In the second case, WORK is considered a string 10 bytes in length. Normally, both statements work equally well in beginning programs.

Defining Multiple Fields or Values

As indicated, more than one field or value can be defined with a single directive. The only requirement is that all multiple fields must be of the same directive type. That is, if you have used DW, then all multiple definitions are words.

Multiple values or fields are separated by a comma. Blanks or tabs may be added to enhance readability.

Suppose that a series of bytes containing the numbers 1 through 5 is needed and that each is to be used as a byte number. The statement

```
NUMBER     DB    1, 2, 3, 4, 5
```

defines 5 bytes in a row and appears in storage as 01 02 03 04 05H. The name NUMBER points to the byte containing 01H.

A very common use for the technique of storing multiple fields or values is to store the control characters necessary to cause a carriage return and line feed on the screen. Review the ASCII code in Table 1–3. Carriage return (CR) is 0DH and line feed (LF) is 0AH. Since this combination is so frequently used, programmers often set up a field called CRLF, which when accessed causes the desired actions. CRLF can be defined as

```
CRLF   DB   0AH,0DH      ; LF + CR CONTROL CODES
```

Character strings can be handled similarly. Suppose that four 3-byte strings are needed to contain the names of some animal types. The strings can be defined as

```
ANIMALS     DB    'DOG','CAT','PIG','RAT'
```

This allocates 12 bytes of memory containing the starting values listed. The name ANIMALS points to the D in DOG.

Initialized fields, uninitialized fields, and fields using the DUP operator can be freely mixed. Consider the following directive:

```
MIXTURE     DB    'CAT',3 DUP(?),1,'1',?
```

This defines 9 bytes of memory. The first 3 bytes contain the letters CAT; the next 3 bytes are unitialized; the next byte is a number, 01H; the next byte is ASCII 1, 31H; and the last byte is uninitialized.

Examine the definitions shown in Example 3–3. Be sure that you understand what is in main storage as a result of each definition.

One final note: With DW, DD, DQ, and DT, if character strings are used as a value, they must be either one or two characters long. They are stored in the low addresses of the field; the high addresses of the fields are filled with 00H bytes.

3.11 SOME SPECIAL OPERATORS

Storing the Address of a Variable

One special use of a word field is to store the address of another field. When the **"initialvalue"** is the name of a field or label, then the offset address for that field is stored.

The definition			Creates in storage
ID	DB	'ENTER ID:'	45 4E 54 45 52 20 49 44 3AH
TYPEL	DB	'M'	4DH
ABC	DB	'ABC'	41 42 43H
COUNT	DB	'1'	31H
TOTL	DB	1	01H
TOTAL	DW	10H	10 00H ; backwards in storage
WORK	DB	?	??H ; uninitialized but likely 00H
SET	DB	'1',"2",3	31 32 03H
AREA	DB	3 DUP(' ')	20 20 20H
AREA1	DB	3 DUP(20H)	20 20 20H
FIELDS	DW	1,2,3	01 00 02 00 03 00H
CRLF	DB	0DH,0AH	0D 0AH

EXAMPLE 3–3   Sample field definitions

Thus, the address of the field ID can be stored as:

```
ADDR_ID     DW     ID
```

Using a field to store the address of another field is a very common technique. It is particularly useful when processing strings and arrays. You will examine this further in the next chapter.

Math Operators

Simple math operators are permitted in the "initialvalue" portion of a field definition. Commonly, the operators + and – are used. For example, suppose that you need a field that contains the total length of an array. It is possible to calculate it manually and establish storage by entering

```
                    .
                    .
                    .
        TABLE_LEN DW    372
        TABLE     DW    186 DUP(?)
        TOTAL     DW    0
                    .
                    .
                    .
```

When using this manual method, you must calculate the length of TABLE in bytes—in this case, 372.

It is often easier to let the assembler do the work for you. The length of TABLE is the address of the next byte after the last byte of TABLE (TOTAL in this example) minus the address of the first byte of TABLE. Thus, the length is given by TOTAL's address minus TABLE's address. The field that contains the length of TABLE is defined as

```
TABLE_LEN    DW   TOTAL - TABLE
```

Here the value is the difference of the two addresses. The value in TOTAL − TABLE is calculated at compile time. The assembler takes the offset address of TOTAL and subtracts the offset address of the start of TABLE. The difference becomes the value contained in the word TABLE_LEN, or 372 in this case.

There is a major restriction involved in using the assembler to perform such calculations. To use the assembler in this way, it must be possible to calculate the entire expression at assembly time.

The EQU Directive

The need to change array sizes arises frequently. Suppose the number of elements in an array can vary each time the program runs. In one run, you need to have 10 entries in the array, but for another run you need 20. Between runs it is possible to go into the data area manually and alter all the array sizes and reassemble the program. However, if there are a number of arrays that need to be changed, this can become very tedious. This manual process can be eliminated by using **EQU,** the **equate directive.**

EQU does not create any machine code, but it does permit a name to be associated with a certain value. Then, whenever the assembler encounters the name associated with the EQU in the source program, it replaces that name with the equated value. The syntax is

name   EQU   value

The array size problem can be easily handled by defining ARRAY_SIZE with EQU as shown

```
                     .
                     .
                     .

ARRAY_SIZE   EQU 10
                     .
                     .
                     .

ARRAY1       DB   ARRAY_SIZE DUP(0)
ARRAY2       DB   ARRAY_SIZE DUP(0)
ARRAY3       DB   ARRAY_SIZE DUP(0)
                     .
                     .
                     .
```

As the program is assembled, the symbol ARRAY_SIZE is replaced by its current value, 10 in this case. When the program is rerun with another array size, such as 20, just change the 10 to 20 and reassemble.

Again, the value for ARRAY_SIZE must be known at assembly time. These are not program calculations, but rather assembly time calculations. Had ARRAY_SIZE been coded as

```
ARRAY_SIZE  DB   ?
```

an error message would be generated.

The EQU operator has another use. In Chapter 6 you will learn that extra coding is required to interface with the DOS operating system during any I/O operation. This interfacing is done by using the interrupt command, INT. You have already seen one example in which INT caused the return to DOS. (See the sample program, Figure 3–1 to refresh your memory.) The operand of the INT instruction is the number of the required DOS service. Since many commands need the universal DOS function 21H, there are many calls to DOS in a typical program. The code could be written

```
INT   21H   ; CALL DOS
```

However, this technique runs the risk of typographical error. Avoid this risk by using the EQU directive once early in the program, usually at the start:

```
DOS   EQU   21H
```

Then, whenever needed, just enter

```
INT   DOS   ; CALL DOS
```

With this code, there is no chance for typographical errors.

Using the $ Operator with EQU

A special value for use with the EQU is the $. The $ means the current offset, or "here," or at this byte. Both the following examples produce the same result:

```
BIGLOOP    EQU  $
           MOV  AX,COST
```

and

```
BIGLOOP:
           MOV  AX,COST
```

When used in the data area, however, $ gives a way of defining a complete record or a structure of data. Example 3–4 shows how a master record with its related fields could be defined.

```
MASTER_REC          EQU $
ITEM_NUM            DB   10 DUP(?)
DESC                DB   15 DUP(?)
QTY                 DW   ?
COST                DW   ?
MASTER_REC_LEN      DW   $ - MASTER_REC
```

EXAMPLE 3–4   Defining a master record with its related fields

Since MASTER_REC is not a storage definition, both MASTER_REC and ITEM_NUM refer to the same byte, the first byte of ITEM_NUM. Notice also that the length of the record is calculated automatically by the assembler and stored in MASTER_REC_LEN. The $ means current offset address, so $ – MASTER_REC yields the total number of bytes in the complete record.

The LABEL Operator

An alternative method of defining a structure or record is to use the **LABEL** operator in conjunction with the BYTE option. The syntax is

```
                    name  LABEL  option
```

This means that the name is another name, or label, to address the next byte in storage. The length of name is defined by the option that follows it. The option is usually either BYTE or WORD.

The MASTER_REC record shown in Example 3–4 could be defined as shown in Example 3–5. In this example LABEL says that MASTER_REC is a label that points to the next byte and that the length of MASTER_REC is 1 byte.

```
MASTER_REC          LABEL BYTE
ITEM_NUM            DB   10 DUP(?)
DESC                DB   15 DUP(?)
QTY                 DW   ?
COST                DW   ?
MASTER_REC_LEN      DW   $ - MASTER_REC
```

EXAMPLE 3–5   Alternative method for defining a master record

The techniques in examples 3–4 and 3–5 both have merit; use the technique that best suits your purpose.

The SEG and OFFSET Operators

There are many other operators that can be useful. Two of these are the **SEG** and **OFFSET** operators. The SEG operator returns the segment address of its operand. The OFFSET operator returns the offset address of its operand.

```
MOV    SEG_SAVE,SEG MASTER_REC
MOV    OFF_SAVE,OFFSET MASTER_REC
```

In these examples, the word SEG_SAVE contains the segment address of MASTER_REC, and OFF_SAVE contains the offset address of MASTER_REC.

There are numerous other directives and operators. Consult your assembler manual for details. More operators will be introduced as the need arises.

3.12   AN EXAMPLE OF DEFINING STORAGE

Figure 3–2 (PGM2.ASM on the program disk) is a listing of a simple program whose purpose is to define numerous storage fields. Consider the listing in detail.

```
Microsoft (R) Macro Assembler Version 5.10              9/1/88 13:53:41

PGM2  FIGURE 3-2  SAMPLE OF DEFINING BYTES            Page    1-1


     1                          PAGE    60,132
     2                          TITLE   PGM2  FIGURE 3-2  SAMPLE OF DEFINING BYTES
     3
     4              ;*******************************************************************
     5              ; PGM2        Title: Figure 3-2 Sample of Data Definitions        *
     6              ;                                                                  *
     7              ; Programmer: Vic Broquard                                        *
     8              ; Date Written:  6/11/88        Date Of Last Revision: 8/4/88      *
     9              ;                                                                  *
    10              ; Purpose: Shows code generated for various field definitions
    11              ;                                                                  *
    12              ; Special Requirements: None                                      *
    13              ;                                                                  *
    14              ;*******************************************************************
    15
```

FIGURE 3–2   Sample program to define fields

```
16 0000                        PGM2DA   SEGMENT
17
18                             ; BYTE FIELDS --------------------------
19
20 0000  00                    B1   DB   ?
21 0001  48 45 4C 4C 4F 20     B2   DB   'HELLO THERE'
22       54 48 45 52 45
23 000C  10                    B3   DB   16
24 000D  10                    B4   DB   10H
25 000E  10                    B5   DB   10000B
26 000F  4A 4F 48 4E           B6   DB   "JOHN"
27 0013  31 32 33 34 35 36     B7   DB   '123456'
28 0019  0005[                 B8   DB   5 DUP (1)
29       01
30              ]
31
32
33                             ; WORD FIELDS --------------------------
34
35 001E  0000                  W1   DW   ?
36 0020  0010                  W2   DW   16
37 0022  0010                  W3   DW   10H
38 0024  FFF0                  W4   DW   -16
39 0026  0010                  W5   DW   10000B
40 0028  0000 R                W6   DW   B1
41 002A  0001                  W7   DW   B2-B1
42 002C  0001 0002 0003 0004 W8   DW   1,2,3,4,5,6
43       0005 0006
44 0038  0005[                 W9   DW   5 DUP(1)
45       0001
46              ]
47
48 0042  3039                  W10  DW   12345
49
50                             ; DOUBLEWORD FIELDS --------------------
51
52 0044  00000000              D1   DD   ?
53 0048  00000010              D2   DD   16
54 004C  00000010              D3   DD   10H
55 0050  00004142              D4   DD   "AB"
56 0054  00003039              D5   DD   12345
```

Microsoft (R) Macro Assembler Version 5.10   9/1/88 13:53:41
PGM2 FIGURE 3-2 SAMPLE OF DEFINING BYTES   Page   1-2

```
57 0058  FFFFFFF0              D6   DD   -16
58 005C  0000 ---- R           D7   DD   B1
59 0060  00000001              D8   DD   B2-B1
```

FIGURE 3–2 continued   *(Continues)*

```
60 0064  0005[               D9   DD   5 DUP (1)
61        00000001
62                  ]
63


----------------------------------------------------------------------

Microsoft (R) Macro Assembler Version 5.10            9/1/88 13:53:41
PGM2  FIGURE 3-2  SAMPLE OF DEFINING BYTES            Page    1-3

64                            PAGE
65                            ; QUADWORD  FIELDS ----------------------
66
67 0078  0000000000000000  Q1   DQ   ?
68 0080  1000000000000000  Q2   DQ   16
69 0088  1000000000000000  Q3   DQ   10H
70 0090  F0FFFFFFFFFFFFFF  Q4   DQ   -16
71 0098  3930000000000000  Q5   DQ   12345
72 00A0  4241000000000000  Q6   DQ   "AB"
73
74                            ; TENBYTE FIELDS -------------------------
75
76 00A8  000000000000000000  T1   DT   ?
77       00
78 00B2  424100000000000000  T2   DT   "AB"
79       00
80 00BC  907856341200000000  T3   DT   1234567890
81       00
82 00C6  010000000000000000  T4   DT   1,2,3,4,'$';
83       00 0200000000000000
84       0000 03000000000000
85       000000 040000000000
86       00000000 2400000000
87       0000000000
88
89 00F8                      PGM2DA    ENDS
90
91 0000                      PGM2CD    SEGMENT
92 0000                      MAIN PROC FAR
93
94                           ;   housekeeping instructions
95
96                                ASSUME    CS:PGM2CD,DS:PGM2DA
97
98 0000  B8 ---- R              MOV  AX,PGM2DA ; ESTABLISH ADDRESSABILITY
99 0003  8E D8                  MOV  DS,AX    ; TO PGM2DA, THE DATA SEGMENT
100
101 0005  B0 00                 MOV  AL,0   ; SET 0 RETURN CODE
102 0007  B4 4C                 MOV  AH,4CH ; SET FOR END PROCESS FUNCTION
103 0009  CD 21                 INT  21H    ; CALL DOS
104
```

FIGURE 3-2   continued

```
    105 000B               MAIN ENDP
    106 000B               PGM2CD    ENDS
    107
    108                    END  MAIN
```

```
Microsoft (R) Macro Assembler Version 5.10          9/1/88 13:53:41
PGM2  FIGURE 3-2  SAMPLE OF DEFINING BYTES          Symbols-1
```

Segments and Groups:

N a m e	Length	Align	Combine Class
PGM2CD	000B	PARA	NONE
PGM2DA	00F8	PARA	NONE

Symbols:

N a m e	Type	Value	Attr	
B1	L BYTE	0000	PGM2DA	
B2	L BYTE	0001	PGM2DA	
B3	L BYTE	000C	PGM2DA	
B4	L BYTE	000D	PGM2DA	
B5	L BYTE	000E	PGM2DA	
B6	L BYTE	000F	PGM2DA	
B7	L BYTE	0013	PGM2DA	
B8	L BYTE	0019	PGM2DA	Length = 0005
D1	L DWORD	0044	PGM2DA	
D2	L DWORD	0048	PGM2DA	
D3	L DWORD	004C	PGM2DA	
D4	L DWORD	0050	PGM2DA	
D5	L DWORD	0054	PGM2DA	
D6	L DWORD	0058	PGM2DA	
D7	L DWORD	005C	PGM2DA	
D8	L DWORD	0060	PGM2DA	
D9	L DWORD	0064	PGM2DA	Length = 0005
MAIN	F PROC	0000	PGM2CD	Length = 000B
Q1	L QWORD	0078	PGM2DA	
Q2	L QWORD	0080	PGM2DA	
Q3	L QWORD	0088	PGM2DA	
Q4	L QWORD	0090	PGM2DA	
Q5	L QWORD	0098	PGM2DA	
Q6	L QWORD	00A0	PGM2DA	
T1	L TBYTE	00A8	PGM2DA	
T2	L TBYTE	00B2	PGM2DA	

FIGURE 3–2   continued   *(Continues)*

```
T3 . . . . . . . . . . . . . .      L  TBYTE    00BC    PGM2DA
T4 . . . . . . . . . . . . . .      L  TBYTE    00C6    PGM2DA

W1 . . . . . . . . . . . . .        L  WORD     001E    PGM2DA
W10 . . . . . . . . . . . .         L  WORD     0042    PGM2DA
W2 . . . . . . . . . . . . .        L  WORD     0020    PGM2DA
W3 . . . . . . . . . . . . .        L  WORD     0022    PGM2DA
W4 . . . . . . . . . . . . .        L  WORD     0024    PGM2DA
W5 . . . . . . . . . . . . .        L  WORD     0026    PGM2DA
W6 . . . . . . . . . . . . .        L  WORD     0028    PGM2DA
W7 . . . . . . . . . . . . .        L  WORD     002A    PGM2DA
W8 . . . . . . . . . . . . .        L  WORD     002C    PGM2DA
W9 . . . . . . . . . . . . .        L  WORD     0038    PGM2DA       Length = 0005

@CPU . . . . . . . . . . . .        TEXT  0101h
```

```
Microsoft (R) Macro Assembler Version 5.10          9/1/88 13:53:41
PGM2  FIGURE 3-2  SAMPLE OF DEFINING BYTES           Symbols-2


@FILENAME . . . . . . . . . .       TEXT  PGM2
@VERSION . . . . . . . . . . .      TEXT  510


    89 Source  Lines
    89 Total   Lines
    45 Symbols

  47236 + 398999 Bytes symbol space free

     0 Warning Errors
     0 Severe  Errors
```

FIGURE 3–2   continued

The leftmost column of the listing shows the statement number of each line. The next column shows the offset addresses within the segments. The next column shows either the machine instructions generated or, where the value is known at compile time, the actual hex contents of the storage fields.

Study this listing and be sure that you can explain what is in storage for each storage definition. Notice that when the assembler shows the contents of a numeric word on the source listing, it shows them in the proper order, not reversed as they are physically stored. Notice also that for the DD, DQ, and DT numeric fields, the values are shown as they appear in storage, not in a register like the word fields.

Finally, notice that the object code generated for field W6 contains 0000R (or at other places ----R). The R means **relocatable value.** A relocatable value is often an address that is not absolutely known at assembly time. Such values are determined by the system when the program is linked and loaded into main storage.

3.13 SUMMARY

The chapter began with a discussion of the coding rules for the assembler language. There can be only one instruction per line, and a line can contain up to 132 characters. Null, or blank, lines are permitted and aid readability. Any line that begins with a semicolon is considered a comment line by the assembler.

A line is composed of the name (optional), an op code, operands, and comments. Op codes define the operation to be performed; operands are the fields to be acted upon. Comments may be added after any operand. Comments begin with semicolons.

The name portion is used to provide names for variables in memory and to identify instructions. When used to identify instructions, names are referred to as labels. If a label ends with a colon, then it is considered to be a NEAR label. If not, it is a FAR label.

Names and labels can be of any length, but only the first 31 characters are used. The first character must be a letter and may contain the digits 0 through 9. Allowable special characters include ?, @, _, ., and $. No reserved words can be used as names or labels. The names of the registers and the operation and directive codes are the typical reserved words. No duplicate names or labels are allowed. Good programming practice demands that all names and labels be meaningful.

Directives control the source listing file. The PAGE directive controls page numbers and ejects the listing to new pages. The TITLE directive creates a heading on every page of the listing, and the SUBTTL directive creates a subheading.

Every segment—code, data, or stack—is identified by a SEGMENT-ENDS pair of directives, notifying the assembler of the starting and ending points of those segments.

In a similar manner, every subroutine or procedure must be surrounded by a PROC-ENDP pair of directives. This pair tells the assembler where that procedure begins and ends.

The END directive is used to end the program and, optionally, to tell the assembler where in the program to begin execution. That is, it can be used to identify the first executable instruction in the program. This option is used when the first byte of the program is not the first executable instruction. This occurs when a programmer prefers to have the data segment coded first in the program.

Storage fields can be defined by the DB, DW, DD, DQ, and DT directives. The name of the field is optional. Each field can be given an initial value or left uninitialized. A question mark indicates that the field has no initial value.

The DUP operator causes the assembler to insert the same value(s) through all positions of the field.

As many fields as desired can be defined with one directive. The LABEL directive associates a name with the byte or word that follows it. This is handy when creating input or output records or similar collections of fields.

3.14 REVIEW EXERCISES

1. True/false: Character data is stored in ASCII.

2. True/false: Every SEGMENT directive must have a corresponding ENDS.

3. True/false: Every PROC directive must end with an ENDS directive.

4. True/false: The following sequence prints the subtitle on the next page of a listing.

   ```
   PAGE +
   SUBTTL  THIS IS THE CALCULATION PROCEDURE
   ```

5. True/false: The following correctly sets the listing for 132 character lines and 60 lines per page:

   ```
   PAGE 132,60
   ```

6. For parts a through d, assume that the byte mentioned contains 30H.
   a) True/false: The byte could be an ASCII (printable) 0.
   b) True/false: The byte could be the unsigned number 48.
   c) True/false: The byte could be the signed number 48.
   d) True/false: The byte could be the bit string mask 0011 0000B.

7. Show what values will be defined in storage by the statements in parts a through l. Show the results in hex format, 2 nibbles per byte.
   ```
   a)  DB 'CAT'
   b)  DB 'D',' ','T'
   c)  DB 'dog'
   d)  DB 13
   e)  DB 13H
   f)  DB '35'
   g)  DW 15
   h)  ARRAY DB 7 DUP (10)
   i)  GRADES DB 10 DUP (100)
       MAXNUM DW $-ARRAY
   j)  DD 23
   k)  DW ?
   l)  MSG DB  'THIS IS AN ERROR MESSAGE', OAH, ODH, 'YOU
       GOOFED','$'
   ```

8. How do the assembler and link programs know where the first executable instruction of the program is located among the several segments in a program?

3.15 PRACTICE PROBLEMS

1. Spot all syntax errors in the following code. (Hint: There are 10 errors.)

```
        PAGE:    TITLE PGM1  INVENTORY SUMMARY
PGM1DA    SEGMENT
; INSERT DATA AREAS HERE
PGM1STK    SEGMENT PARA    STACK    'STACK'
; INSERT STACK AREA HERE
PGM1STK    ENDP
PGM1 SEG
MAIN PROC
        ASSUME CS:PGM1,DS:PGM1DA,ES;NOTHING,SS;PGM1STK
; INSERT CODING HERE
        RETURN
MAIN ENDS
PGM1 ENDS
        END
```

2. For parts a through q, indicate whether the names and labels are valid, invalid, or nondescriptive.

a) 1 COST   e) BYTE   i) sCrAmBle   m) $COST
b) I-BEAM   f) WORK.AMT j) ?WHERE   n) $cost
c) I_BEAM   g) T1   k) %COST   o) page
d) NAME   h) MOV   l) XYZ   p) segment
q) MASTER_FILE_POLICY_HOLDER_LAST_NAME_FIELD

3. Code the two directives needed to put a heading ACME INVENTORY DATA ENTRY PROGRAM on each page of a listing. Each page has 60 lines of 100 characters each.

4. Code the two directives needed to change the page number 1-1 to 2-1 and insert a second heading, INPUT ROUTINE, on that page.

5. Code the pair of directives needed to create a segment that holds the coding for WES-BRO Manufacturing Data Entry Subsystem. Use a reasonable name for the segment. Also code the pair needed to define the data area.

6. Code the pair of directives that begins and ends a subroutine called INPUT_BYTE; the routine is a NEAR routine. What would change if it were a FAR procedure?

7. Consider the following arrangement of segments.

```
        PAGE
        TITLE
WORK1DA    SEGMENT
; insert   data areas here
WORK1DA    ENDS
WORK1CD    SEGMENT
DRIVER     PROC FAR
; INSERT REST OF THE CODE AREA HERE
DRIVER     ENDP
WORK1CD    ENDS
WORK1STK   SEGMENT   PAR STACK 'STACK'
;insert stack definition here
WORK1STK   ENDS
```

Code the proper END directive.

8. Examine the coding in problem 7. Code an appropriate ASSUME directive for this program.

9. An input record consisting of 44 bytes contains six adjacent fields. The following table provides the names of the individual fields, their beginning position from the start of the record, and their length.

field name	starting position	length
SOC_SEC_NUM	3	9
RECORD_TYPE	1	2
FIRST_NAME	12	10
PREMIUM	40	5
POLICY_TYPE	37	3
LAST_NAME	22	15

Code the data definition directives to define such a record. The program refers to the record as MAST_REC. Use reasonable field names. None are binary fields; all contain character data.

10. Code the storage definition directives for parts a through g. All are binary numbers.
    a) COST is 2 bytes and is initialized with 0.
    b) WORK_AREA is 1 byte and has 33 in it.
    c) COUNT is 4 bytes with 150 as a starting value.
    d) TIME is an array of seven 1-byte entries, all set to 0.
    e) TOT_COST is an array of 25 words, each containing 0.
    f) HIGH_VAL is a byte containing the largest binary value possible.
    g) ATTRIBUTE is a byte containing 1001 0110B.

3.16 PROGRAMMING PROBLEMS

1. Using the program in Figure 3–1 as a guide, create a shell for the ACME Insurance Company Policy Data Entry Program.
   a) Code appropriate PAGE and TITLE directives.
   b) Code appropriate SEGMENT names.
   c) In the data area define the policy record as

field name	starting position	length
SOC_SEC_NUM	1	9
RECORD_TYPE	10	1
FIRST_NAME	11	10
LAST_NAME	21	15
POLICY_TYPE	36	1
PREMIUM	37	5

   All fields contain character data.
   d) In the code segment include the standard set of housekeeping instructions that begin every program.
   e) Leave the main processing section blank.
   f) Code the standard instructions to return to DOS.
   g) Finally, assembly and linking should be error-free. A test of its execution should allow the program to start and then end without error. Of course, it does not actually do real processing, yet. But the shell should work.

2. Create a complete program shell for a child's math helper program. Include all the sections, just as you did in problem 1. The data area should contain the following uninitialized fields:

   ```
   ADD_FIELD1, ADD_FIELD2, ADD_TOTAL
   SUB_FIELD1, SUB_FIELD2, SUB_TOTAL
   MUL_FIELD1, MUL_FIELD2, MUL_PRODUCT
   DIV FIELD1. DIV_FIELD2, DIV_RESULT
   ```

   The total, product, and result fields are to be words; all others are byte fields.

   Finally, several messages must be defined:

field name	contents
MSG1	CHILD'S MATH HELPER PROGRAM
MSG2	1. PERFORM ADDITION
MSG3	2. PERFORM SUBTRACTION
MSG4	3. PERFORM MULTIPLICATION
MSG5	4. PERFORM DIVISION
MSG6	5. QUIT
MSG7	ENTER THE NUMBER OF YOUR CHOICE

Test, assemble, and link the program shell. Assembly and linking should be error-free. A test execution should show that the program starts and ends successfully. (In Chapter 8 you will get a chance to add the actual code to produce a math helper program.)

3. Create a complete program shell for the Miles Per Gallon Calculator Program. Include field definitions for the following uninitialized fields:

MILES   word
GALLONS   word
MPG_NUM   word
MPG   character field of 7 bytes

Include the definitions and initial values as shown in the following table.

TEN   byte number with 10 in it
ZERO   byte number with 0 in it

MSG1   saying MILES PER GALLON CALCULATOR
MSG2   saying ENTER MILES TRAVELED
MSG3   saying ENTER GALLONS USED
MSG4   saying MILES PER GALLON WAS:

Test, assemble, and link the program shell. Assembly and linking should be error-free. A test execution should show that the program starts and ends successfully. (In Chapter 8 you will get a chance to add the coding necessary to do the calculations.)

4

A Beginning
Instruction Set

4.1 CHAPTER OBJECTIVES

In this chapter you will

1. Learn the rules for creating the operands used in the instructions
2. Examine the different forms that operands may take: registers, fields in memory, or immediate data
3. Learn the rules for coding immediate data values
4. See how the assembler determines the actual length of immediate data values
5. Learn about the indirect memory accessing of data
6. Examine the effects of indirect memory accessing upon immediate data
7. Learn the need for and use of the PTR operator in WORD PTR and BYTE PTR
8. Study a basic instruction set that includes the following instructions: MOV, LEA, INC, DEC, ADD, SUB, XCHG, JMP, CMP, LOOP, and the numerous conditional branching instructions
9. Learn the difference between a NEAR label and a FAR label
10. Examine several complete case studies to see how these instructions are applied

4.2 INTRODUCTION

Having gained an understanding of the basic assembler program presented in the last two chapters, you should now have a good foundation upon which your programs can be built. The organization and structure of the basic program can be used as a model or shell for programs you will be working with in this and subsequent chapters. By using the define storage directives introduced in the last chapter, all the necessary storage areas for program variables, constants, and messages can be established.

In this chapter a basic set of assembler instructions will be presented. These instructions consist of the common instructions that are found in nearly all assembler programs. To help you see how the instruction set can be applied, two case studies are presented and discussed in detail.

To begin your study of the basic set of assembler instructions, examine some common features of operands. The instruction set itself will follow.

4.3 OPERAND CONCEPTS

Operand Lengths

Many instructions require the use of two operands. For example, in the instruction ADD COST TO TOTAL, two operands—COST and TOTAL—are used. With all but a few exceptions, both operands **must** be the same physical size. Either both operands are 1 byte in length or they are both 1 word in size. Therefore, in an ADD instruction, it is reasonable to assume that you can add one byte to another byte or one word to another word.

If you try to add the contents of a byte to the contents of a word, however, you create an error condition. In Chapter 8 you will learn techniques that permit addition using mixed field sizes. For now, you must always make certain that the lengths of data are compatible.

Operand Forms

Normally, an operand takes one of three forms. It can be a register, a field in memory, or immediate data. If an operand is a **register,** the register can contain 1 word or 1 byte of data. It is important to remember that the four data registers—AX, BX, CX, and DX—are the only ones that can be subdivided into two 1-byte registers (such as AH and AL). This fact can have a significant impact on the way register data is handled.

An operand can also be a **field** in main storage. With the exception of character strings, a field operand is normally defined as either 1 byte or 1 word in length.

When an operand is **immediate data,** it means that the data is essentially self-defining and is physically included as a part of the instruction itself. Immediate data are commonly called **literals.** When the sample program (Figure 3–1), returned to DOS, the value 0 was needed in register AL. The instruction was coded as

```
MOV    AL,0
```

The actual value, 0, was used in this instruction. Note that the immediate data is physically a part of the instruction.

It would have been possible to define a byte number in storage and then move it into the register.

```
ZERO DB    0
           .
           .
           .

MOV    AL,ZERO
```

But this takes extra coding and uses more storage. Using the immediate data value, or literal, was much simpler.

Also in the sample program (Figure 3–1), the immediate data value of 4CH, which was used to request the DOS end process function, was moved into register AH.

```
MOV    AH,4CH
```

In both these instructions from the sample program, the second operand is immediate data—the values 0 and 4CH. Immediate data (literals) are extremely useful, and they are common in many programming languages.

Rules for Using Immediate Data

1. If the value is surrounded by apostrophes or quotation marks—either ' ' or " "—the value is assumed to be ASCII. For example, '0' becomes 30H.

2. If the value is a number with no letter after it, it is assumed to be a decimal number. For example, 10 becomes 0AH.

3. If the number ends in H, it is assumed to be a hexadecimal value; as such, there **must** be two hex digits shown per byte. For example, 15H becomes 15H, which is 21 in decimal.

4. If the number ends with B, it is assumed to be a binary string. Only the digits 0 and 1 can be used. For example, 01000001B becomes 41H.

5. Finally, when entering hex data, the first digit of the string **must not** be a letter. Therefore, if it is necessary to enter the immediate value 255, the letters FFH **cannot** be used. The value is coded as 0FFH. This idiosyncrasy arises because of the method that the assembler uses in distinguishing the difference between a number

and a name or label. The assembler always checks to see if the first byte is a letter or a number. If it is a letter, the operand is considered to be a name or label.

Length Determination of Immediate Data Operands

As you have just seen, the length of both operands must usually be the same. This poses a problem with immediate data. How does the assembler determine the length of immediate data?

If you enter

```
MOV    AX,0
```

then the value 0, as coded, is 1 byte in length, yet AX is 1 word. In this case the assembler actually uses an immediate value of 0000H, which is 1 word of 0.

The assembler determines the length of immediate data according to this rule: When immediate data is coded, the assembler determines the length of the immediate data by examining the length of the first operand.

Therefore, in the preceding example, AX is a word register, and the assembler creates the 0 value as a word: 00 00H.

On the other hand, suppose you enter the instruction as

```
MOV    AL,0
```

This time, operand1, AL, is a byte register and the 1-byte 0 value is generated: 00H.

If the assembler cannot determine the size of operand1, then an error results.

Indirect Memory Accessing

Accessing memory can be done directly by using the field name or indirectly by using a pointer, or index register, that contains the address of the field. The pointer registers commonly used for accessing main storage in the data section are registers DI, SI, and BX. (Register BP provides access to data stored on the stack. See Chapter 12.)

Suppose that field TOTAL in the sample program is defined as

```
TOTAL    DW    0
```

In the program, you stored the updated value in TOTAL by entering

```
MOV    TOTAL,AX
```

This is an example of using the name of the field directly.

Suppose, however, that somewhere in the program and prior to the MOV instruction, you load the main storage address of TOTAL into register BX. (You will see how this is done later in the chapter.) The MOV instruction can now be

```
MOV    [BX],AX
```

The brackets around the register mean that main storage is pointed to by the address in the register. This instruction says to move the contents of register AX to the field whose address is in register BX.

It is extremely important that you understand this technique because it is used frequently in microassembler programming. For example, indirect addressing is necessary when processing strings and when working with arrays and tables.

Suppose you have a table of 20 student grades, each a byte number. The table can be defined as

```
GRADES     DB     20 DUP(0)
```

Further, suppose that at the start of the routine that calculates the grades, the address of the first grade in the table is loaded into register SI. Also assume that the result of the calculation of the grade is to be placed in register AL. To store the new grade in the table, you enter

```
MOV     [SI],AL     ; STORE NEW GRADE IN THE TABLE
```

To repeat the cycle for the next student, all you need to do is to adjust register SI to point to the next entry in the table GRADES. Because each entry is only 1 byte, you can add 1 to the address in register SI:

```
ADD     SI,1     ; POINT TO THE NEXT ENTRY IN GRADES
```

Indirect addressing makes it easy to form a processing loop to do the required steps 20 times.

Indirect Memory Accessing Using Immediate Data

Combining indirect memory accessing with immediate data poses another problem. Suppose that it is necessary to move 0 into TOTAL and that register BX contains the address of TOTAL. It is tempting to enter

```
MOV     [BX],0
```

Unfortunately, this creates an error because, in this situation, the assembler cannot determine the length to move. Is the length supposed to be 1 byte or 2 bytes? The assembler cannot tell the size of operand1 because operand1 is pointing to a memory area.

In situations where an index register contains the storage address of the field and no field name is available, there are two ways of telling the assembler how many bytes are involved. The first method requires two instructions:

```
MOV     AX,0
MOV     [BX],AX
```

Here, AX is a word, so 0 becomes a word: 00 00H. The next MOV also moves a word to storage since AX is 1 word in size. Although this approach is straightforward, it has the drawback of requiring two instructions where only one is necessary.

The alternative is to use another pair of assembler operators: **WORD PTR** and **BYTE PTR.** The special operator **PTR,** or *explicit type override,* means that the memory location pointed to by the index register is to be considered the indicated size—either a byte or a word. All that the phrase WORD PTR or BYTE PTR does is to tell the assembler the number of bytes involved. Thus, the second method requires only one instruction:

```
MOV   WORD PTR [BX],0
```

Notice that a blank between PTR and [BX] increases readability.

The valid types that can occur before the word PTR when it is used to determine the size of a memory reference are BYTE, WORD, DWORD, QWORD, and TBYTE. In most assembler programs, either BYTE PTR or WORD PTR is used. If it is necessary to move only 1 byte, use BYTE PTR.

```
MOV    BYTE PTR  [BX],0
```

Keep WORD PTR and BYTE PTR in mind; they will be useful. (Later, you will see that the PTR operation can be used to modify NEAR and FAR references as well.)

Now that the essential forms of the operands have been explained, examine the basic instruction set. (Additional instructions will be discussed in Chapter 14.)

4.4   THE MOVE DATA INSTRUCTION: MOV

The MOV instruction copies the data in operand2 and places it in operand1. Unless operand1 overlaps operand2, operand2 is unchanged, and operand1 contains a new value. The syntax is

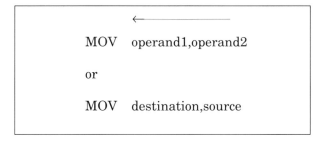

The arrow shows the direction of the move. Many assembler instructions process in this reverse direction.

The destination, operand1, can be only a register or a field name in main storage; the source, operand2, can be a register, a field name, or an immediate value. A MOV instruction does **not** alter the settings of any flags.

Not all possible combinations are allowed, however. There are three moves that are specifically **forbidden:**

- a move from memory to memory or storage to storage
- a move from immediate data to a segment register
- a move into IP, the instruction pointer register

As previously indicated, the IP register points to the next instruction to be executed. Therefore, you would not want to move anything into IP. Frequently, however, it is tempting to consider making one of the other two forbidden moves. For example, you may want to move data from one place in memory to another and it may seem appropriate to enter statements like this:

```
MOV    CURRENT_LENGTH,PRIOR_LENGTH
```

This code is invalid. To accomplish the move, you must enter

```
MOV    AX,PRIOR_LENGTH
MOV    CURRENT_LENGTH,AX
```

This may seem cumbersome, but that is how it must be done.

The other restriction, not being able to move immediate data into a segment register, impacts the housekeeping instructions. Since in every program you need to get the address of the data segment into register DS, it would be nice to be able to enter

```
MOV    DS,PGM1DA
```

But this is invalid; you must enter

```
MOV    AX,PGM1DA
MOV    DS,AX
```

Figure 4–1 will help you remember the legal moves.

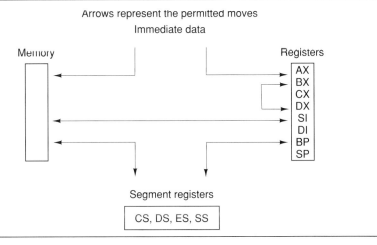

FIGURE 4–1 Allowable moves

The following are examples of valid moves. Assume that COUNT, TOTAL, and COST are defined in the data segment as shown. Further, assume that register BX contains the address of COUNT.

```
COUNT     DB    0
TOTAL     DW    10
COST      DB    0CH
     MOV  AX,BX           MOV  DH,AL
     MOV  CX,TOTAL        MOV  TOTAL,DX
     MOV  DH,COST         MOV  COUNT,BL
     MOV  DS,AX           MOV  CX,DS
     MOV  TOTAL,CS        MOV  DS,TOTAL
     MOV  COUNT,0         MOV  TOTAL,10
     MOV  BL,5            MOV  CX,5
     MOV  AL,[BX]
     MOV  [BX],DH
     MOV  BYTE PTR [BX],1
```

The last three instructions in the first column read

Move the contents of storage pointed to by register BX into register AL.

Move the contents of register DH into the byte of storage pointed to by BX.

Move a 01H byte into storage pointed to by register BX.

Notice one prominent point: It is **not** possible to move character strings directly. Suppose that you want to move FIRST_NAME to a field called OLD_NAME; both are 10 bytes long. There are only two ways that this can be done. One way is to write a small subroutine to move the fields 1 byte at a time. This requires using an intermediate register since you cannot move storage to storage. (This approach will be discussed in detail shortly.) The second approach uses the string-handling instructions that are covered in Chapter 11. String instructions do essentially the same thing and are, in effect, miniature subroutines!

4.5   THE LOAD EFFECTIVE ADDRESS INSTRUCTION: LEA

LEA, the load effective address instruction, determines the offset address of a field in storage or memory and places that address in the indicated word register. Its syntax is

```
                    ←─────────────
        LEA    word register,name of a field
```

LEA is used to get the address of character strings, such as FIRST_NAME, to get the address of tables, and even to get the address of structures of data.

Suppose the data segment contains the following declarations:

```
FIRST_NAME        DB      10 DUP (?) ; holds the client name
DEPARTMENT_CODE   DB      1,2,3,4,5,6,7,8,9,10

MSG_STRUCTURE     LABEL BYTE
ACTUAL_LEN        DB      ?   ; will contain real length
MAXIMUM_LEN       DB      20  ; maximum allowed length
MESSAGE           DB      20 DUP (?),'$' ; filled with input
```

You can enter the following:

```
LEA    DI, FIRST_NAME       ; DI = address of FIRST_NAME
LEA    BX, DEPARTMENT_CODE ; BX = address of DEPARTMENT_CODE
LEA    SI, MSG_STRUCTURE    ; SI = address of the msg structure
```

After execution, register DI contains the offset address of FIRST_NAME, register BX contains the offset address of the table of values called DEPARTMENT_CODE, and register SI contains the offset address of MSG_STRUCTURE.

There are many uses for LEA. Several examples will be shown shortly.

4.6   THE INCREMENT INSTRUCTION: INC

Frequently, it is necessary to add 1 to a counter in a program. This can be done easily by using the INC instruction, which adds 1 to either a counter that is in memory (storage) or one that is in a register. The syntax is

```
INC   operand1
```

The INC instruction adds 1 to operand1; in other words, INC increments operand1 by 1. If operand1 is a word register or a field in memory that is 1 word in size, then 00 01H is added. If operand1 is a byte register or a byte of memory, then 01H is added.

Suppose the data segment contains the following declarations:

```
COUNT        DB      0
LINE_COUNT   DW      7
```

You can code the following INC instructions:

```
INC   COUNT
INC   LINE_COUNT
```

After the instructions are executed, COUNT contains 01H and LINE_COUNT has 08 00H in storage, or—to state the value logically—00 08H.

Similarly, you can enter

```
INC   AX
INC   CX
INC   SI
INC   DI
INC   AL
INC   DH
```

The INC instruction does have an effect on the following flags: AF, OF, PF, SF, and ZF. However, with normal use of the INC instruction, you do not need to be concerned with this effect.

4.7   THE DECREMENT INSTRUCTION: DEC

The DEC instruction is similar to INC except that DEC is used to subtract 1 from a counter that is in memory (storage) or from a counter that is a register. The syntax is

```
┌─────────────────────────────────────────────┐
│                                             │
│              DEC    operand1                 │
│                                             │
└─────────────────────────────────────────────┘
```

The DEC instruction subtracts 1 from operand1; in other words, DEC decrements operand1 by 1. If operand1 is a word register or a field in memory that is 1 word in size, then 00 01H is subtracted from it. If operand1 is a byte register or a byte of storage, then 01H is subtracted from operand1.

Assume that the data segment contains the same declarations as before but with different values:

```
COUNT        DB      5
LINE_COUNT   DW      7
```

The following DEC instructions can be entered.

```
DEC    COUNT
DEC    LINE_COUNT
```

After execution, COUNT contains 04H and LINE_COUNT has 06 00H in storage, or—to state the value logically—00 06H.

Similarly, you can enter

```
DEC  AX
DEC  CX
DEC  SI
DEC  DI
DEC  AL
DEC  DH
```

In these examples, DEC affects the following flags: AF, OF, PF, SF, and ZF. DEC is sometimes used to control loops. In these cases, the zero flag is usually the flag to be tested.

4.8   THE ADD INSTRUCTION: ADD

The ADD instruction adds two binary values. The syntax is

```
                        ←───────────────
            ADD    operand1, operand2
```

The first operand, operand1, can be a register or a memory location (a field in storage). The second operand, operand2, can be a register, a memory location, or an immediate value. In all cases, operand2 is added to operand1 and the result replaces operand1. Both operands **must** be the same length—either 1 byte or 1 word (2 bytes).

Suppose a data segment contains the following fields:

```
COUNT       DB      0
PAGE_CNT    DB      1
TOTAL       DW      10
WORK        DB      3
BIGNUM      DW      8943
```

You write the following code:

```
ADD     COUNT,WORK
ADD     PAGE_CNT,1
ADD     TOTAL,5
```

After execution

COUNT   contains 03H

PAGE_CNT   contains 02H

TOTAL   contains 00 0FH (0F 00H when in memory)

An error results if you attempt to enter

```
ADD    TOTAL,WORK
```

because the two fields do not have the same length. It is permissible to enter

```
ADD    AX,CX
ADD    AL,DH
ADD    AX,5
ADD    CL,14
ADD    TOTAL,AX
ADD    AX,TOTAL
ADD    BH,COUNT
ADD    WORK,DL
```

Finally, if register BX contains the address of TOTAL, you can enter

```
ADD    [BX],AX
ADD    BIGNUM,[BX]
ADD    WORD PTR[BX],1
```

The ADD instruction affects the following flags: AF, CF, OF, PF, SF, and ZF. Because flags indicate the possibility of errors, it is necessary to be concerned about setting them. For now, however, you can ignore the issue.

There is a lot more to the ADD instruction than this description implies. At this time, however, an understanding of the complexities of the ADD instruction is not needed. Chapter 8 will return to the ADD instruction and outline all its features.

4.9   THE SUBTRACT INSTRUCTION: SUB

The SUB instruction subtracts one value from another. The syntax is

```
              ←────────────

     SUB    operand1, operand2
```

In this instruction operand1 can be a register or a memory location (a field in storage); while operand2 can be a register, a memory location, or an immediate value. SUB causes operand2 to be subtracted from operand1. The result replaces operand1. Both operands **must** be the same length—either 1 byte or 1 word (2 bytes).

Suppose that a data segment contains the following fields:

```
COUNT        DB      0
PAGE_CNT     DB      1
TOTAL        DW      10
WORK         DB      3
BIGNUM       DW      8943
```

You enter the following instructions:

```
SUB    WORK,PAGE_CNT
SUB    PAGE_CNT,1
SUB    TOTAL,5
```

After execution

    WORK   contains 02H

    PAGE_CNT   contains 00H

    TOTAL   contains 00 05H

An error results if you attempt to enter

                        SUB   TOTAL,WORK

because the two fields do not have the same length. Similarly, it is acceptable
to enter

                        SUB   AX,CX
                        SUB   AL,DH
                        SUB   AX,5
                        SUB   CL,14
                        SUB   TOTAL,AX
                        SUB   AX,TOTAL
                        SUB   BH,COUNT
                        SUB   WORK,DL

Finally, if register BX contains the address of TOTAL, the following
subtractions are permissible.

                    SUB   [BX],AX
                    SUB   BIGNUM,[BX]
                    SUB   WORD PTR[BX],1

The SUB instruction affects the following flags: AF, CF, OF, PF, SF, and
ZF. At this point it is not necessary to be concerned about the flag settings,
even though they indicate the possibility of errors. Flag settings are fully
explained in Chapter 8.

4.10 THE EXCHANGE INSTRUCTION: XCHG

XCHG, the exchange instruction, swaps the contents of two registers or the
contents of a register and a memory (storage) location. The syntax of the
XCHG instruction is

    ┌───┐
    │   │
    │   XCHG   operand1,operand2   │
    │   │
    └───┘

At least one of the operands must be a register, but neither operand can be a
segment register.

Suppose the data segment contains

```
TEMP      DW    12
SMALL     DB    2
```

and these registers contain

AX	BL	CX	SI	DH	DL
00 05	05H	00 10H	00 03H	01H	02H

Then you can enter

```
XCHG    AX,TEMP
XCHG    SMALL,BL
XCHG    CX,SI
XCHG    DH,DL
```

After execution, storage and registers contain

TEMP   = 00 05H (actually, 05 00H)

SMALL = 05H

AX	BL	CX	SI	DH	DL
00 0CH	02H	00 03H	00 10H	02H	01H

No flags are affected. XCHG is particularly useful in swapping values when doing a sort or when finding the largest or smallest value from a set of values.

4.11 BRANCHING AND LABELS

Before discussing the jump instruction, or unconditional branch, and the many different conditional branching instructions, you must have a good understanding of the concept of **NEAR** and **FAR** labels. A NEAR label is one that occurs within +127 or −128 bytes from the branching instruction itself. A FAR label occurs outside these limits. Figure 4–2 illustrates NEAR and FAR labels.

The presence or absence of a colon at the end of a label tells the assembler whether the label is a NEAR label or a FAR label. As you write programs, remember this rule: End all NEAR labels with a colon; do not end FAR labels with a colon. The following are examples of how labels look.

SMALL_LOOP: is a NEAR label

BIG_LOOP   is a FAR label

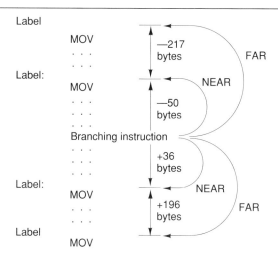

NEAR labels fall within +127 to —128
bytes of the branching instruction
FAR labels fall outside +127 to —128
bytes of the branching instruction

FIGURE 4–2   NEAR and FAR labels

The numbers +127 and –128 are the largest and smallest signed binary numbers that fit within 1 byte. Remember that 1 byte contains 8 bits and that the first bit is the sign bit, 0 for + and 1 for –. Therefore, the largest positive number that a byte holds is 0111 1111B or 7FH or +127. The smallest is 1000 0000B or 80H or –128.

Speed of execution causes this dependence on the byte. Consider a NEAR branch: The offset distance to be branched to is stored in 1 byte, and such branches execute very fast. A FAR branch, on the other hand, may need an entire word (the true offset address) and sometimes 2 words (segment and offset addresses) to find the place to branch to. This takes longer to execute.

Both NEAR and FAR adjust the IP (instruction pointer) register. The code segment register remains unchanged, unless the branch is very far. If the FAR branch leaves the current code segment, then register CS must also be changed. When this happens, the code takes longer to execute than a FAR branch that remains in the same segment. Also consider that the machine instruction for a NEAR branch, or jump, is only 2 bytes long, but the machine instruction for a jump that needs to adjust the code segment is 5 bytes long.

Unless you are certain of the distance of the branch, code all labels as NEAR labels, ending the label name with a colon. Then, if the label is too far from the branching instruction, the assembler tells you via an error message. You can then correct the label.

Do not confuse NEAR and FAR labels with NEAR and FAR procedures. NEAR and FAR procedures refer to whether the subroutine is within the current 64K segment or not. NEAR and FAR labels refer to whether the label is within +128 and −128 bytes of the conditional branching instruction.

4.12   THE UNCONDITIONAL BRANCH: JMP

The jump instruction, JMP, is an unconditional branch in which control is always transferred to the instruction at the label. JMP is sometimes called the GO TO. The syntax is

```
                    JMP    label
```

Note that no colon appears after the label operand of the JMP instruction. The colon is present only on the label itself.

Suppose you enter

```
                    MOV    AX,1
SMALL_LOOP:
                    ADD    AX,1
                    JMP    SMALL_LOOP
```

What happens? First, the value 1 is moved to AX. Next, 1 is added to AX. Then the jump instruction transfers control to SMALL_LOOP and the addition cycle is repeated. Since this creates an infinite loop, it never ends. The assembler determines which form of jump (NEAR or FAR) is needed from an examination of the label. In this case, SMALL_LOOP: is a NEAR label; thus, a NEAR jump is generated.

Some form of test and conditional branching is needed so that, under certain conditions, the loop ends. This is accomplished by a compare instruction and a conditional branching instruction.

4.13   THE COMPARE INSTRUCTION: CMP

The compare instruction, CMP, compares two values and sets a flag to indicate the result. The instruction syntax is

```
                    ←─────────
          CMP    operand1, operand2
```

In this instruction operand1 can be a register or a memory location (storage field); operand2 can be a register, a memory location, or an immediate value. Both operands must have the same length, either 1 byte or 1 word. When operand2 is compared to operand1, the flags are affected according to the relationship between the two values. In a way, this instruction operates as though operand2 were subtracted from operand1. The result is 0, positive, or negative, and the appropriate flag is set accordingly.

Assume that a data segment has been defined with the following fields:

```
CTYPE     DB     'A'
COUNT     DB     5
COST      DW     14
FNAME     DB     'SAMUEL'
```

Using these fields, the following CMP instructions have been coded:

```
      CMP   CTYPE,' '        ; IS CTYPE = A BLANK?
```
or

```
      CMP   CTYPE,20H
```

The instructions that follow compare the first character of the field FNAME to the letter "S."

```
   LEA   SI,FNAME
   CMP   [SI],'S'         ; DOES THE FIRST NAME START WITH S?
```

Other comparisons that can be made are

```
      CMP   COUNT,5        ; IS COUNT = 5?
      CMP   AX,COST        ; IS AX = COST?
      CMP   BL,COUNT       ; IS BL = COUNT?
      CMP   AL,DL          ; IS AL = DL?
      CMP   AX,CX          ; DOES AX = CX?
```

The CMP affects the following flags: AF, CF, OF, PF, SF, and ZF. The effect depends on the result of the comparison.

Obviously, the CMP is only the first half of the standard IF-THEN-ELSE programming construct.

4.14   THE CONDITIONAL BRANCHING INSTRUCTIONS

The second half of the IF-THEN-ELSE structure consists of one or more conditional branches. The syntax for the entire set of conditional branching structures is

```
            branchmnemonic   label
```

Four rules pertain to conditional branches:

1. All labels must be NEAR labels.

2. All conditional jumps are done according to the current settings of the flag registers.

3. If the jump condition is satisfied, then control is transferred to the instruction at the specified label.

4. If the jump condition is not satisfied, control passes to the next sequential instruction.

There is one bit of complexity that must be considered when using conditional branches. There are **two** sets of instructions: one to be used after comparing signed numbers and one to be used after comparing unsigned numbers. (ASCII data is considered unsigned data for comparison purposes.) The difference between signed and unsigned numbers is the effect of the first bit of the byte or word operands. If the numbers are signed, then negative numbers have a 1 as the first bit and positive numbers have a 0. Consider the effect of the following:

```
FIELD1     DB   127    ; contains 7FH
FIELD2     DB   -128   ; contains 80H

           CMP   FIELD2,FIELD1
```

If you treat this comparison as unsigned, then FIELD2 is greater than FIELD1 because the high-order bit of FIELD2 is 1 and the high-order bit of FIELD1 is 0. If you treat this comparison as signed, then FIELD2 is less than FIELD1.

Table 4–1 gives the variations of conditional jumps based on the kind of data being compared. Do not bother to memorize these lists. Just refer to them as needed. They are also reproduced in the appendix.

TABLE 4–1 Conditional JUMP instructions

Conditional Jumps Based on Unsigned Data

Operation	Meaning	Flags that are tested
JE or JZ*	jump if op1 is equal to op2 OR jump if zero flag set	ZF
JNE or JNZ*	jump if op1 is not equal to op2 OR jump if zero flag is not set	ZF
JA or JNBE	jump if op1 is above op2 OR jump if op1 is not below and is not equal to op2	CF, ZF
JAE or JNB	jump if op1 is above op2 or is equal to op2 OR jump if op1 is not below op2	CF

TABLE 4–1   continued

Operation	Meaning	Flags that are tested
JB or JNAE	jump if op1 is below op2 OR jump if op1 is not above op2 and is not equal to op2	CF
JBE or JNA	jump if op1 is below op2 or is equal to op2 OR jump if op1 is not above op2	CF, AF

Conditional Jumps Based on Signed Data

Operation	Meaning	Flags that are tested
JE or JZ*	jump if op1 is equal to op2 OR jump if the zero flag is set	ZF
JNE or JNZ*	jump if op1 is not equal to op2 OR jump if the zero flag is not set	ZF
JG or JNLE	jump if op1 is greater than op2 OR jump if op1 is not less than op2 and is not equal to op2	ZF, SF, OF
JGE or JNL	jump if op1 is greater than or equal to op2 OR jump if op1 is not less than op2	SF, OF
JL or JNGE	jump if op1 is less than op2 OR jump if op1 is not greater than op2 and is not equal to op2	SF, OF
JLE or JNG	jump if op1 is less than or equal to op2 OR jump if op1 is not greater than op2	ZF, SF, OF

*Note that the JE or JZ and JNE or JNZ are the same for unsigned and signed data, since the equal or zero condition occurs regardless of the sign.

Conditional Jumps for Special Arithmetic Conditions

Operation	Meaning	Flags that are tested
JS	jump if sign is set (negative)	SF
JNS	jump if sign is cleared (positive)	SF
JC	jump if carry flag is set (same as JB)	CF
JNC	jump if carry flag is cleared	CF
JO	jump if overflow flag is set	OF
JNO	jump if overflow flag is cleared	OF
JP or JPE	jump if parity is even (set)	PF
JNP or JPO	jump if parity is odd (cleared)	PF
JCXZ	jump if reg CX is 0	ZF and reg CX is 0

Conditional jumps can be used to implement the usual IF-THEN-ELSE and DO-WHILE structures. Consider how jumps are used in this simple version of IF-THEN-ELSE.

```
IF TOTAL IS LESS THAN ZERO THEN DO THE LOSS CALCULATION
                           ELSE DO THE PROFIT CALCULATION

        CMP    TOTAL,0       ; COMPARE TOTAL TO ZERO
        JL     LOSS_CALC     ; IF TOTAL IS NEGATIVE, IT IS A LOSS

PROFIT_CALC:
           .
           .
           .
    JMP  CONTINUE            ; JUMP AROUND THE LOSS CALCULATION

LOSS_CALC:
           .
           .
           .
CONTINUE:                    ; END OF THE IF-THEN-ELSE STRUCTURE
```

The DO-WHILE structure looks like this:

```
DO the following series WHILE COUNT is not zero

        LOOP1:
           .
           .
           .
        DEC      COUNT  ; SUBTRACT 1 FROM COUNT
        JNE      LOOP1  ; WHILE COUNT IS NOT ZERO, REPEAT LOOP1
```

With these simple skeleton structures in mind, examine some coding examples.

In this example, you want to use repetitive addition to multiply the contents of field A by 10. The code shown in Example 4–1 puts the result into the field called ANSWER.

Example 4–2 checks the field XTYPE to see if it contains A. If it contains A, then program flow goes to PROCESS_A. If XTYPE contains B, then program flow goes to PROCESS_B. If XTYPE contains neither A nor B, then program flow goes to PROCESS_C.

Example 4–3 moves the contents of the field CUST_NAME to OLD_CUST_NAME. Both fields are 20 bytes long.

In microassembler, small loops like these examples are commonplace. Therefore, be very sure that you understand the logic and coding techniques these examples employ! To simplify these loops, there is another group of instructions that can be used.

```
A      DW    5
ANSWER DW    ?



       MOV   AX,0      ; INITIALIZE REG AX TO 0
       MOV   BL,0      ; SET NUMBER OF ADDITIONS TO 0

SLOOP:
       ADD   AX,A      ; ADD A TO TOTAL (AX)
       INC   BL        ; ADD 1 TO NUMBER OF ADDITIONS
       CMP   BL,10     ; HAVE WE DONE 10 ADDS YET?
       JL    SLOOP     ; NO, DO IT AGAIN

       MOV   ANSWER,AX ; SAVE RESULT 10*A IN ANSWER
```

EXAMPLE 4–1 Calculating $10 * A$

```
XTYPE DB   ?



       CMP  XTYPE,'A'   ; IS XTYPE = A?
       JE   PROCESS_A   ; YES, GOTO PROCESS_A

       CMP  XTYPE,'B'   ; IS XTYPE = B?
       JE   PROCESS_B   ; YES, GOTO PROCESS_B

;PROCESS_C IS HERE
       .
       .
       .
       JMP  GOON        ; GOTO RESUME MAIN PROCESSING

PROCESS_A:
       .
       .
       .
       JMP  GOON        ; GOTO RESUME MAIN PROCESSING

PROCESS_B:
       .
       .
       .
GOON:                   ; CONTINUE WITH MAIN PROCESSING
```

EXAMPLE 4–2 Checking the field XTYPE

```
          LEA   DI,OLD_CUST_NAME  ; DI = ADDRESS OF OLD FIELD
          LEA   SI,CUST_NAME      ; SI = ADDRESS OF CUST_NAME
          MOV   CX,0              ; CX = NUMBER OF BYTES MOVED

NAME_LOOP:

          MOV   AH,[SI]           ; MOVE A BYTE OF CUST_NAME INTO AH
          MOV   [DI],AH           ; MOVE IT TO BYTE OF OLD_CUST_NAME

          INC   SI                ; POINT TO NEXT BYTE OF OLD_CUST_NAME
          INC   DI                ; POINT TO NEXT BYTE OF CUST_NAME
          INC   CX                ; ADD 1 TO NUMBER OF BYTES MOVED

          CMP   CX,20             ; HAVE 20 BYTES BEEN MOVED?
          JLE   NAME_LOOP         ; NO, GO MOVE ANOTHER

; HERE:  OLD_CUST_NAME = CUST_NAME
```

EXAMPLE 4-3   Moving CUST_NAME to OLD_CUST_NAME

4.15   THE LOOPING INSTRUCTIONS: LOOP, LOOPE, LOOPZ, LOOPNE, LOOPNZ

There are five looping instructions. They handle the common need for creating controlled loops that are common to high-level languages: DO LOOP, PERFORM VARYING, and FOR NEXT. In these instructions, the counter register CX is used to control the number of repetitions of the loop.

The syntax of the LOOP instruction is

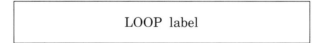

LOOP label

The label **must** be a NEAR label.

When this instruction is executed it

- Decrements register CX by 1

- Tests CX for a 0 value

- Goes to the label if CX is not equal to 0

- Falls through to the next instruction if CX = 0

Notice that the LOOP instruction automatically works its way down to 0. Thus, when the loop is entered, register CX must have been set to the total number of times the loop is to be executed.

```
      LEA  DI,OLD_CUST_NAME  ; DI = ADDRESS OF OLD FIELD
      LEA  SI,CUST_NAME      ; SI = ADDRESS OF CUST_NAME
      MOV  CX,20             ; CX = NUMBER OF BYTES MOVED

NAME_LOOP:

      MOV  AH,[SI]           ; MOVE A BYTE OF CUST_NAME INTO AX
      MOV  [DI],AH           ; MOVE IT TO BYTE OF OLD_CUST_NAME

      INC  SI               ; POINT TO NEXT BYTE OF OLD_CUST_NAME
      INC  DI               ; POINT TO NEXT BYTE OF CUST_NAME

      LOOP NAME_LOOP        ; DEC CX, IF NOT 0 THEN GOTO NAME_LOOP

; HERE:  OLD_CUST_NAME = CUST_NAME
```

EXAMPLE 4–4   Moving CUST_NAME by using a LOOP instruction

Example 4–3 can be simplified by using the LOOP instruction as illustrated in Example 4–4. There are two critical points to remember when using the LOOP instruction. First, you must make sure that register CX is given its initial value **outside** the loop itself. Can you see what would happen if MOV CX,20 was the first instruction after the label NAME_LOOP? The result would be an infinite loop! Second, notice that the LOOP ends **only** when CX contains 0. Your program will be in serious trouble if somehow register CX contains a negative number.

The four other loop instructions are variations of LOOP. These variations—LOOPE, LOOPZ, LOOPNE, and LOOPNZ—merely adjust the circumstances under which the looping process may be ended. Adding a LOOP variation is much like adding a WHILE clause to the loop.

Each variation still decrements register CX and tests it for 0 to determine whether to branch or to stop. In addition, the variations also check another condition that has been preset by the instructions within the loop itself.

Loop equal and loop zero—**LOOPE** and **LOOPZ**—transfer control to the label if CX is not 0 **and** if the zero flag is set (ZF = 1). However, if either CX = 0 or the zero flag is cleared (ZF = 0), then control passes to the next sequential instruction and the loop ends. Thus, compound loops can be given an alternate method of terminating: clearing the zero flag.

Loop not equal and loop not zero—**LOOPNE** and **LOOPNZ**—transfer control to the label if CX is not 0 **and** if the zero flag is not set (ZF = 0). If either CX = 0 or the zero flag is set (ZF = 1), then the loop ends.

For example, suppose that you want to code a loop that inputs a string of up to 10 letters. However, if the user desires fewer than 10 letters, he or she can terminate the string with an asterisk. Therefore, the loop is ended by

```
STRING   DB   10 DUP (?)


         LEA  BX,STRING      ; BX = ADDRESS OF ANSWER AREA
         MOV  CX,10          ; CX = MAX NUMBER BYTES TO ENTER

         MOV  AX,1           ; THESE TWO INSTRUCTIONS
         ADD  AX,1           ; WILL CLEAR THE ZF (ZERO FLAG)

     ENTER_LOOP:

; insert the code to get a byte and put into [BX]

         CMP  BYTE PTR [BX],'*' ; WAS BYTE AN * ?
         JNE  OK             ; NO, SO CONTINUE

         SUB  AX,AX          ; YES, SO SET ZF =1 TO END LOOP

     OK:
         INC  BX             ; POINT TO NEXT INPUT AREA BYTE
         LOOPNZ ENTER_LOOP   ; IF 10 TIMES OR ZF SET, END LOOP
```

EXAMPLE 4–5   Inputting 10 characters or fewer

either entering the 10th letter or by entering an asterisk. Since you have not yet learned how data is entered, study the pseudocode for the "get a byte" function.

> DO I = 1 TO 10 WHILE (BYTE IS NOT AN *)
>   get a byte
> END

The coding for the pseudocode is shown in Example 4–5. The highlighted instructions in the example illustrate how the zero flag is handled to control ending the loop. The MOV and ADD instructions before the beginning of the loop clear the zero flag by forcing a positive addition. Within the loop, after it has been determined that an asterisk has been entered, the zero flag is set by subtracting any register from itself. In this case the register is AX. When LOOPNZ executes, even though CX may not be 0, the zero flag is set, and the loop ends.

4.16   THE CASE STUDIES

At this point, you have seen the basic microassembler instruction set. These instructions are used in nearly every assembler program. The next step is to see how these few instructions can be combined to solve programming problems.

To assist you, two complete programming examples have been designed to demonstrate the instructions presented in this chapter. These two examples also begin to illustrate the microassembler programming "mentality," or problem-solving approaches.

Each of these programs is on the master student disk. You should copy them over to your program disk, assemble them, and link them. Execute them with the debugger, producing debugging output. There are many reasons to perform these activities. The most important is to provide you with another opportunity to become familiar with the actions of creating microassembler programs, running the assembler, running the linker, and running the debugger.

4.17   CASE STUDY: CONVERTING FROM LOWERCASE TO UPPERCASE

One common problem in a word processing program is that of converting a string of characters from lowercase to uppercase. This activity is usually needed when the program requests keyboard input from the user. For example, a user's response to yes/no questions could be Yes, YES, yes, yES, yEs, and so on. Therefore, you need to be able to convert the case of ASCII letters.

Once more examine the ASCII coding scheme shown in Table 1–3. Notice that the hex values of all the lowercase letters are exactly 20H greater than the uppercase letters. Thus, to convert from a lowercase letter to an uppercase letter, just subtract 20H, or 32, from the lowercase letters.

In this problem, only lowercase letters are converted to uppercase. That is, only the "small" letters "a" through "z" should be altered; all other values should be left as they are.

The source listing and debug run are shown in Figure 4–3 (PGM3.ASM on the program disk). Notice the order of segments. For variety, the stack segment occurs first, followed by the data segment, and the code segment is last. Since the first byte of the program is not the first executable instruction, the final END statement tells the assembler and linker that the first byte of the MAIN procedure is the first executable instruction.

The program does not produce any output on the screen. The string MSG is converted from lower- to uppercase. Thus, to find out if the program actually works, it is necessary to use the debugger to examine the string MSG before and after the conversion process. To do this, you must know where the beginning and ending of the conversion process are. These addresses are determined from the source listing. The conversion process begins in the main processing section with the MOV to CX instruction. The offset address of MOV CX,52 is 00 05H. The ending point is the return to DOS section, which begins at 00 20H.

Thus, to examine the program with the debugger, you must allow the program to execute until it gets to the start of the conversion process at 00 05H. Then you can display the contents of MSG before the conversion

```
Microsoft (R) Macro Assembler Version 5.10            9/1/88 15:06:30


PGM3  FIGURE 4-3  CONVERT FROM LOWER TO UPPER CASE           Page    1-1



     1                                 PAGE   60,132
     2                                 TITLE  PGM3  FIGURE 4-3  CONVERT FROM LOWER TO UPPER CASE
     3
     4                          ;****************************************************************
     5                          ; PGM4       Title: Figure 4-3 Convert Case To Upper        *
     6                          ;                                                            *
     7                          ; Programmer: Vic Broquard                                   *
     8                          ; Date Written: 6/11/88       Date Of Last Revision: 8/4/88  *
     9                          ;                                                            *
    10                          ; Purpose: Converts a message from lower to upper case       *
    11                          ;                                                            *
    12                          ; Special Requirements: None                                 *
    13                          ;                                                            *
    14                          ;****************************************************************
    15
    16                          ; program stack segment
    17
    18 0000                     STK   SEGMENT  PARA  STACK  'STACK'
    19
    20 0000  0020[                     DW    32 DUP (?)
    21    ????
    22         ]
    23
    24
    25 0040                     STK   ENDS
    26
    27
    28                          ; program data segment
    29
    30 0000                     DATA  SEGMENT
    31
    32 0000  54 68 69 73 20 4D  MSG   DB    'This Message is to BE changed tO uPper CaSe.'
    33        65 73 73 61 67 65
    34        20 69 73 20 74 6F
    35        20 42 45 20 63 68
    36        61 6E 67 65 64 20
    37        74 4F 20 75 50 70
    38        65 72 20 43 61 53
    39        65 2E
    40
    41 002C                     DATA  ENDS
```

FIGURE 4–3   Case study: converting to uppercase

Microsoft (R) Macro Assembler Version 5.10   9/1/88 15:06:30

PGM3 FIGURE 4-3 CONVERT FROM LOWER TO UPPER CASE   Page   1-2

```
    42                                    PAGE
    43
    44                              ; program code segment
    45
    46 0000                         CODE    SEGMENT
    47 0000                         MAIN    PROC    FAR
    48
    49                              ; housekeeping section
    50
    51                                      ASSUME CS:CODE,DS:DATA,SS:STK
    52
    53 0000  B8 ---- R                      MOV     AX,DATA  ; ESTABLISH ADDRESSABILITY
    54 0003  8E D8                          MOV     DS,AX    ; TO DATA SEGMENT
    55
    56                              ; main process section
    57
    58 0005  B9 0034                        MOV     CX,52    ; REG CX HAS LENGTH OF MSG
    59 0008  8D 1E 0000 R                   LEA     BX,MSG   ; REG BX HAS THE ADDRESS OF MSG
    60
    61 000C                         DOIT:
    62 000C  8A 27                          MOV     AH,[BX]  ; MOVE BYTE OF MSG INTO AX
    63 000E  80 FC 61                       CMP     AH,61H   ; IS BYTE LESS THAN a?
    64 0011  72 0A                          JB      NEXT     ; YES, GET NEXT CHARACTER
    65 0013  80 FC 7A                       CMP     AH,7AH   ; IS BYTE GREATER THAN z?
    66 0016  77 05                          JA      NEXT     ; YES, GET NEXT CHARACTER
    67
    68                              ; convert lower case
    69
    70 0018  80 EC 20                       SUB     AH,20H   ; SUBTRACT 20 TO CONVERT CASE
    71 001B  88 27                          MOV     [BX],AH  ; INSERT INTO MSG
    72
    73 001D                         NEXT:
    74 001D  43                             INC     BX       ; ADD 1 TO GET TO THE NEXT CHARACTER
    75 001E  E2 EC                          LOOP    DOIT     ; STOPS WHEN CX = 0
    76
    77                              ; return to DOS section
    78
    79 0020  B0 00                          MOV     AL,0     ; SET 0 AS THE RETURN CODE
    80 0022  B4 4C                          MOV     AH,4CH   ; INDICATE END PROCESS FUNCTION
    81 0024  CD 21                          INT     21H      ; CALL DOS END PROCESS
    82
    83 0026                         MAIN    ENDP
    84
    85 0026                         CODE    ENDS
    86
    87                                      END     MAIN
```

FIGURE 4–3 continued   *(Continues)*

```
Microsoft (R) Symbolic Debug Utility  Version 4.00
Copyright (C) Microsoft Corp 1984, 1985.  All rights reserved.

Processor is [8086]

-G 5

AX=7B36  BX=0000  CX=0096  DX=0000  SP=0040  BP=0000  SI=0000  DI=0000
DS=7B36  ES=7B22  SS=7B32  CS=7B39  IP=0005    NV UP EI PL NZ NA PO NC
7B39:0005 B93400        MOV CX,0034

-D DS:00,2C

7B36:0000  54 68 69 73 20 4D 65 73-73 61 67 65 20 69 73 20  This Message is
7B36:0010  74 6F 20 42 45 20 63 68-61 6E 67 65 64 20 74 4F  to BE changed tO
7B36:0020  20 75 50 70 65 72 20 43-61 53 65 2E 00           uPper CaSe..

-G 20

AX=8E36  BX=0034  CX=0000  DX=0000  SP=0040  BP=0000  SI=0000  DI=0000
DS=7B36  ES=7B22  SS=7B32  CS=7B39  IP=0020    NV UP EI PL NZ NA PO NC
7B39:0020 B000          MOV AL,00

-D DS:00,2C

7B36:0000  54 48 49 53 20 4D 45 53-53 41 47 45 20 49 53 20  THIS MESSAGE IS
7B36:0010  54 4F 20 42 45 20 43 48-41 4E 47 45 44 20 54 4F  TO BE CHANGED TO
7B36:0020  20 55 50 50 45 52 20 43-41 53 45 2E 00           UPPER CASE..

-Q
A>
```

FIGURE 4–3   continued

Next you must let the conversion routine perform its function. To do this, let the program execute until it gets to the end of the process at 00 20H. This time when you display the contents of MSG, you should see the result of the conversion process. Now you can tell if the program worked.

Examine the debugging execution portion of Figure 4–3. The first command is G5, which allows the program to execute until it gets to the main processing section. Once there, the debugger displays the contents of the registers and the next instruction to be executed. Verify that the program has indeed stopped where you want it to stop. (Compare the instruction shown to the source listing.)

Next the complete message is displayed. To determine the operands to use in the display command, examine the data segment of the source listing. You need the starting offset address of MSG within the data segment. It is 00

00H from the listing. You also need the ending address, which is 00 2CH. Thus, you enter

D DS:00,2C

to display all of MSG.

The string is full of lowercase letters. Now you enter the G20 command to execute through the conversion routine. Again, verify that the debugger halted at the correct point in the coding. To see if the conversion worked, redisplay MSG. It is indeed all uppercase letters.

This is the type of debugging procedure that you **must** be able to use proficiently. You will be doing this repeatedly when debugging microassembler programs. For additional practice, rerun the debugger and trace through the program execution instruction by instruction, following the results on a step-by-step basis. This will increase your understanding of how each instruction in the program actually works.

4.18   CASE STUDY: CONVERTING A 1-BYTE ASCII DIGIT TO A BINARY NUMBER

This case study shows a simple routine to convert a 1-byte ASCII digit (also known as a printable or keyboard-entered number) into a binary number so that math can be performed on the value. (This technique can be used only with single-digit ASCII numbers. A full discussion of ASCII-to-binary conversion can be found in Chapter 8.)

Look at Table 1–3 and examine the ASCII codes for the printable numbers. They all begin with a 30H value. The low-order nibble is the digit—that is, 4 is a 34H. To convert a 1-byte ASCII number to binary, 30H must be subtracted from the ASCII value.

The source listing and debugging run are shown in Figure 4–4 (PGM4.ASM). In this example, a string of 10 ASCII digits is converted into binary. Each digit is considered separately, not as part of one number with 10 digits. Notice that the program segments are arranged into yet a third type of order. Also, observe that there is **no** stack coded in this problem; you get a linker error message as a result. The stack becomes the highest byte of the first 64K segment, the data segment. Since the program is very small and has no subroutine calls, there is no problem. Check this for yourself. Examine the contents of the registers SS and DS just after the first program instruction has been executed. They are the same. In addition, register SP contains FFFEH, the top end of the 64K segment.

Examine the debugging run. Be sure that you understand what each debugging command does and how it is created from the offset addresses of the assembler listing. Again, it is strongly recommended that you repeat the debugging run and trace through each instruction, following exactly what occurs. This will greatly increase your understanding of the instructions.

```
Microsoft (R) Macro Assembler Version 5.10              9/1/88 15:27:07

PGM4  FIGURE 4-4 CONVERT 1 BYTE ASCII NUMBER INTO BINARY    Page    1-1


     1                                    PAGE  60,132
     2                                    TITLE PGM4  FIGURE 4-4 CONVERT 1 BYTE ASCII NUMBER INTO BINARY
     3
     4                         ;********************************************************************
     5                         ; PGM4      Title: Figure 4-4 Convert ASCII Digit Into Binary Byte Number *
     6                         ;                                                                   *
     7                         ; Programmer: Vic Broquard                                          *
     8                         ; Date Written: 6/11/88      Date Of Last Revision: 8/4/88          *
     9                         ;                                                                   *
    10                         ; Purpose: To Illustrate How An ASCII digit Could Be Converted Into *
    11                         ;          A Binary Byte Number                                     *
    12                         ; Special Requirements: Only works for single ASCII digits          *
    13                         ;                                                                   *
    14                         ;********************************************************************
    15
    16                         ; program data segment
    17
    18 0000                    DATA    SEGMENT
    19
    20 0000  30 31 32 33 34 35 FIELD  DB     '0','1','2','3','4','5','6','7','8','9'
    21       36 37 38 39
    22 000A  000A[             NUMBER DB     10 DUP (?)
    23       ??
    24         ]
    25
    26
    27 0014                    DATA    ENDS
    28
    29                         ; program code segment
    30
    31 0000                    CODE    SEGMENT
    32 0000                    MAIN  PROC   FAR
    33
    34                         ; housekeeping section
    35
    36                                 ASSUME CS:CODE,DS:DATA
    37
    38 0000  B8 ---- R                 MOV AX,DATA   ; ESTABLISH ADDRESSABILITY
    39 0003  8E D8                     MOV DS,AX     ; TO DATA SEGMENT
    40
    41                         ; main process section
    42
    43 0005  B9 000A                   MOV CX,10     ; REG CX HAS NUMBER OF BYTES TO CONVERT
    44 0008  8D 1E 0000 R              LEA BX,FIELD  ; REG BX HAS THE ADDRESS OF THE ACSII NUMS
```

FIGURE 4-4   Case study: Converting 1-byte ASCII numbers

```
45 000C  8D 3E 000A R              LEA  DI,NUMBER ; REG DI HAS THE ADDRESS OF THE ANSWERS
46
47 0010                   DOIT:
48
49 0010  8A 07                     MOV  AL,[BX]   ; MOVE ASCII NUMBER INTO AL
50 0012  2C 30                     SUB  AL,30H    ; CONVERT TO BINARY
51 0014  88 05                     MOV  [DI],AL   ; STORE BINARY INTO ANSWER
52
53 0016  47                        INC  DI        ; ADD 1 TO GET TO THE NEXT ANSWER SLOT
54 0017  43                        INC  BX        ; ADD 1 TO GET TO THE NEXT ASCII NUM
55 0018  E2 F6                     LOOP DOIT      ; STOPS WHEN CX = 0
56
```

Microsoft (R) Macro Assembler Version 5.10   9/1/88 15:27:07

PGM4 FIGURE 4-4 CONVERT 1 BYTE ASCII NUMBER INTO BINARY   Page   1-2

```
57                          ; return to DOS section
58
59 001A  B0 00                     MOV  AL,0      ; SET 0 AS THE RETURN CODE
60 001C  B4 4C                     MOV  AH,4CH    ; SET FOR END PROCESS FUNCTION
61 001E  CD 21                     INT  21H       ; CALL DOS TO END PROCESS
62
63 0020                   MAIN  ENDP
64
65 0020                   CODE  ENDS
66
67                        END   MAIN
```

Microsoft (R) Symbolic Debug Utility Version 4.00
Copyright (C) Microsoft Corp 1984, 1985. All rights reserved.

Processor is [8086]

-G 5

```
AX=18A8  BX=0000  CX=0040  DX=0000  SP=0000  BP=0000  SI=0000  DI=0000
DS=18A8  ES=1898  SS=18A8  CS=18AA  IP=0005   NV UP EI PL NZ NA PO NC
18AA:0005 B90A00        MOV   CX,000A
```

-D DS:00,14

```
18A8:0000  30 31 32 33 34 35 36 37-38 39 00 00 00 00 00 00  0123456789......
18A8:0010  00 00 00 00 00                                   .....
```

-G 1A

```
AX=1809  BX=000A  CX=0000  DX=0000  SP=0000  BP=0000  SI=0000  DI=0014
```

FIGURE 4-4   continued   *(Continues)*

```
DS=18A8  ES=1898  SS=18A8  CS=18AA  IP=001A   NV UP EI PL NZ NA PE NC
18AA:001A B000         MOV   AL,00

-D DS:00,14

18A8:0000  30 31 32 33 34 35 36 37-38 39 00 01 02 03 04 05  0123456789......
18A8:0010  06 07 08 09 00                                    .....

-Q
A>
```

FIGURE 4–4   continued

4.19 SUMMARY

Operands can take one of three forms. The forms include a register, a memory field, or immediate data (literal). This chapter discussed the various formats for immediate data and how the assembler determines the length of immediate data.

The very important concept of indirect memory accessing was presented. Either a pointer register or an index register (BX, BP, DI, and SI) can contain the offset address of a string or table. The assembler allows accessing of the data by using brackets around the register. The brackets mean that the actual storage address is pointed to by the indicated register.

Indirect memory access of operand1 when operand2 is immediate data causes a problem: The assembler does not know how many bytes to use in the instruction—a byte or a word. In such situations, use the BYTE PTR or WORD PTR operator to tell the assembler which to use.

The basic instruction set includes MOV, LEA, INC, DEC, ADD, SUB, JMP, CMP, LOOP, and the various conditional branching instructions.

At this point, you should have a good understanding of the basic instructions and the rules for using them. The next step is to learn how to create subroutines, which you will do in the next chapter.

4.20 REVIEW QUESTIONS

1. Outline the rules for coding operands in microassembler instructions.

2. What are the three forms that an operand can take?

3. If an instruction requires two operands, tell why operand1 can never be immediate data.

4. How does the assembler determine the length of immediate data?

5. What is a literal? How does it differ from immediate data?

6. What is meant by indirect memory accessing? How does it differ from direct accessing? When would you need indirect accessing?

7. What do the brackets mean in an operand? Is it possible to have brackets for both operands in an ADD instruction? In a MOV instruction? Why is there this difference between ADD and MOV?

8. What is the purpose of coding BYTE PTR [DI]? When would it be used?

9. What is wrong with the following coding?

```
BIGLOOP:
        ...
        ...
        JNE  BIGLOOP ; IF NOT ZERO, REPEAT THE LOOP
        CMP  CX,0    ; DOES THE LOOP NEED TO BE REPEATED?
```

How could you correct it?

10. A programmer defined two fields:

```
FIRST_NAME_OUT  DB   20 DUP(?)
FIRST_NAME_IN   DB   20 DUP(?)
```

After acquiring a value for FIRST_NAME_IN, the programmer wants to move it to the output area. He codes the following instruction:

```
MOV  FIRST_NAME_OUT,FIRST_NAME_IN
```

The assembler generates an error message. Why?
    In an attempt to remedy the problem, the programmer codes:

```
MOV  AX,FIRST_NAME_IN
MOV  FIRST_NAME_OUT,AX
```

Why does this fail to produce the desired effect?

11. Explain the difference between a NEAR label and a FAR label.

12. True/false: Where

```
HOLD DB ?
TEMP DB ?
```

and TEMP contains valid data, the following is valid.

```
MOV  HOLD,TEMP
```

13. True/false: The following is valid.

```
MOV ES,0
```

14. Register AX reg 00 04H in it. After executing

```
MOV   TOTAL,AX
```

a debugger storage dump display shows what in TOTAL?

15. Which registers are allowed to contain an address to a memory and be enclosed in brackets, as in MOV AX,[ ] ?

4.21 PRACTICE PROBLEMS

1. Code the instruction(s) that accomplish the following tasks.
   a) Add 1 to COUNT, where COUNT is defined to be a byte. Show how this could be done with an ADD and an INC.
   b) Subtract 1 from COUNT, where COUNT is defined to be a word. Show how this could be done with a SUB and a DEC.
   c) Test the field HOLD, which is a signed byte number, for a value of 5. If the number is equal, then jump to END_PROCESS. Otherwise, repeat the loop known as SMALL_LOOP.
   d) Load the address of MSG_WORK into register DI.
   e) Subtract 10 from COUNTER. If the result is 0, jump to END_IT.

2. Examine the problem given in Review Question 10. Code a small routine that accomplishes what the programmer desired—moving FIRST_NAME_IN to FIRST_NAME_OUT.

3. Code a routine that counts the number of blanks in WORK, where WORK is defined to be a string of length 10.

4. A programmer suspects that the values in OLD_NAME and NEW_NAME are not the same. Code a routine that compares these two fields. If they are the same, move 01H into RESULT; if they are not the same, move 00H into RESULT. Both fields are 8-byte character strings.

4.22 PROGRAMMING PROBLEMS

1. Message Decoding: Data encryption is a common application for computers. A computer can try many different schemes very rapidly in an attempt to crack a code.

   Consider a very simple coding scheme. The letter "A" is assigned the number 1, "B" is 2, "C" is 3, and so on through "Z" as 26. A blank, or space, is 0. The end of the message is the number 255. To be able to include numbers in the message, the code 35 (# in

ASCII) signals that the next series of numbers is to be treated as numbers, not converted to letters. Another 35 means that the numbers represent letters once more.

Thus, the following series

8,9,0,35,2,35,255

is decoded as

HI 2

Notice that the two 35's are omitted from the answer string.

Define the following message and answer fields in the program data area.

```
MSG  DB    14,15,23,0,9,19,0,20,8,5,0,20,9,13,5,0,6,15,18,0
     DB    1,12,12,0,7,15,15,4,0,16,5,18,19,15,14,19,0,20
     DB    15,0,3,15,13,5,0,20,15,0,20,8,5,0,1,9,4,0,15,6
     DB    0,20,8,5,9,18,0,16,1,18,20,25,0,1,14,4,0,9,6,0
     DB    25,15,21,0,2,5,12,9,5,22,5,0,20,8,9,19,0,9,0,8
   . DB    1,22,5,0,1,0,2,18,9,4,7,5,0,6,15,18,0,19,1,12
     DB    5,0,6,15,18,0,35,1,5,6,0,9,3,2,35,0,4,15,12,12
     DB    1,18,19,255

ANSR DB    142 DUP(?)
```

Your program should begin with the first byte of MSG and convert it into the corresponding decoded message, storing the valid characters in ANSR until the program encounters the 255. (Do not insert any code for the 35's in the resulting message.) Using the debugger, dump the string ANSR to display the results.

2. A CAPS Routine: Code a capitalization procedure called CAPS for use in a word processing program. When this routine is called, the following fields are already defined and filled in for use by the CAPS routine:

```
        ACTLEN   DW    ?
        WORK     DB    80 DUP(?)
```

WORK contains some word, like *cat,* while ACTLEN contains the actual length of the word. All 80 will be very seldom used.

The routine should capitalize the word by changing the first letter to a capital letter. Note: If the word is already capitalized, the program should do nothing to the remaining bytes of WORK, even if those bytes are capitalized.

Test your routine on these:

```
    CAT    cat    Cat    123    big-cat    caT
```

It should produce:

```
CAT    Cat    Cat    123    Big-cat    CaT
```

3. Full Capitalization Routine: Modify Programming Problem 2 to complete the capitalization process. The first true letter should be capitalized and all other letters should be lowercase. Therefore, the program must scan all bytes. Any that are capitalized, except the first letter, should be converted to lowercase.

    Test the routine on these:

```
CAT    cAT    123    BIG-CAT    1 CAT
```

It should produce

```
Cat    Cat    123    Big-cat    1 Cat
```

4. The Word Counter Routine: Authors and publishers often need to know how many words are in an article or book. As an aid for them, you are to write a routine that counts the number of words in a given line. Presumably, another programmer will then devise a method to complete the process for all the lines in an article.

    Your routine should define the following fields:

```
LINE  DB   'This is a sentence whose total number of words'
      DB   ' will need to be counted, including numbers - '
      DB   'such as 12345; it is ended by a period.'
TOTAL_WORDS DW      0
```

    Your routine should count the number of words in LINE and store the result in TOTAL_WORDS. Do not count the special characters: the comma, the hyphen, or the semicolon. Treat a complete number as one word. The routine should end when the period is encountered, triggering end of sentence. There are 25 words in LINE; therefore, TOTAL_WORDS should contain 25. Use the debugger to verify your results.

5

Subroutines and the Stack

5.1 CHAPTER OBJECTIVES

In this chapter you will learn

1. How to invoke and code subroutines
2. How to use the instructions CALL, RET, PUSH, and POP
3. The principles of moving strings, including truncation and padding for both ASCII character and number strings
4. What the stack is, how it is organized, and how it is used
5. What generalized subroutines are and why they are so important to microassembler programming
6. To apply the guidelines for building subroutines in case studies

5.2 INTRODUCTION

Microassembler programs usually require large numbers of relatively simple instructions, as illustrated by the case studies at the end of Chapter 4. It is not uncommon for a program listing to require 30 or more pages. With this much code, it is imperative that the program be broken down into a series of relatively small modules, which are also called routines or subroutines.

A **module, routine,** or **subroutine** is a discrete instruction or set of instructions that can be called from one or more places. The term *module* tends to be used by program designers to refer to a subroutine that performs a predefined action. Good program design suggests that each module be functional, that is, that it perform only one function.

In BASIC, a subroutine is invoked by the GOSUB instruction and, in COBOL, by the PERFORM instruction. In most other languages, it is invoked by a CALL instruction. When the subroutine has finished, it returns, or goes back, to the point from which it was originally invoked.

In this chapter the basic concepts of subroutines will be presented first. After some coding examples you will examine the stack, its operation, and its effect upon subroutines.

5.3 SUBROUTINES

In microassembler it is **mandatory** that the solution to any program be organized into many small subroutines. The extensive use of subroutines greatly aids program readability and simplifies the writing and debugging of the program. Each subroutine should be designed so that it performs only one major action, or function.

Functional subroutines don't just happen! They are planned from the very beginning of the problem-analysis stage. Either top-down design or bottom-up design can be used to design a program, since each technique identifies the required functional subroutines. The code in each subroutine should be directed toward the completion of its specific function.

All programs should be modular that is, the program designer should break complex problems into a series of functional modules. A functional module performs one specific task. By breaking your program into functional modules, you prevent yourself from creating a main section of code that is unnecessarily large.

Once the design is identified and the required modules defined, the routines can then be coded. It is bad technique to write 30 pages of code and then try to regroup that code into subroutines! It almost guarantees errors.

For example, suppose you want to write a program to build a file of names and addresses for a mailing label application. Such a program might have the top-down design shown in Example 5–1. Each of the boxes in Example 5–1 will become a module or subroutine in the final program.

The use of subroutines in microassembler involves three key concepts:

Concept 1

In microassembler, every subroutine is a procedure like the MAIN procedure in the examples shown thus far.

Concept 2

Every procedure begins with a PROC directive and ends with an ENDP directive.

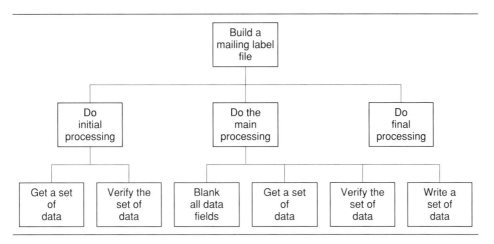

EXAMPLE 5–1   Top-down design for mailing label program

Concept 3

The name of the subroutine is the name specified in the PROC and ENDP entries.

Internal and External Subroutines

There are two forms of subroutines: internal and external. **Internal subroutines** are those whose code is physically within the same assembly as the calling routine, or driver module. **External subroutines,** on the other hand, are assembled separately in their own .OBJ files and are subsequently joined with the driver module by the LINK program, thus forming an executable program. Because the use of external subroutines is a relatively advanced topic, it will not be discussed until Chapter 12.

Invoking a Subroutine

Subroutines are invoked by a **CALL** instruction. The syntax is

CALL   name of the procedure

When CALL is executed, the normal instruction-execution sequence is suspended and control is transferred to the first instruction of the named subroutine. When the subroutine has completed its task, control returns to the instruction after the CALL instruction. When the CALL instruction is executed, the address of the next sequential instruction (the return address) is placed onto the stack, thus making the address available after the subroutine is executed. This will be fully discussed shortly.

Returning from a Subroutine

When the subroutine has finished, it must return to the instruction following the CALL instruction in the calling module. This is accomplished with **RET,** the return instruction. The syntax of the return instruction is

RET

When the RET instruction is executed, it recovers the saved return address from the stack and branches to the address.

Suppose, for example, that you want to invoke a subroutine called FILL from the MAIN procedure. The code for doing this is shown in Example 5–2. When CALL is executed, control is passed to the first instruction in the routine FILL. When FILL finally executes the RET instruction, control is passed back to the next instruction in MAIN after the CALL instruction.

Documenting Subroutines in the Source Listing

It is good practice to begin each subroutine on a separate page of the source listing. This makes the routines much easier to find. In addition, judicious use of subtitles helps show at a glance which routine is on any given page.

Notice how this is done in the example. The new subtitle is defined with the SUBTTL directive. Then the PAGE + directive ejects the listing to a new page, while incrementing the section number and resetting the page number back to 1.

NEAR and FAR Procedures

An examination of the two PROC directives in Example 5–2 shows that the option on the PROC command can be either FAR or NEAR. The functions of the FAR/NEAR operands are similar to the FAR/NEAR labels of conditional jump, or branching, instructions.

A **NEAR procedure** is one that is within the current code segment. This means that the CS register does not have to be reset to another 64K segment and that only the IP register (the instruction pointer) needs to be reset to get to the subroutine. The NEAR CALL resets the IP to the offset address of the NEAR procedure within the same code segment (CS).

On the other hand, a **FAR procedure** requires that the code segment register must also be reset to a new value. When DOS calls the main

```
PGMCD   SEGMENT

MAIN    PROC  FAR
            .
            .
            .

;  main procedure section

        CALL  FILL
            .
            .
            .

; return to DOS section
            .
            .
            .

MAIN    ENDP

        SUBTTL  FILL SUBROUTINE
        PAGE    +

; subroutine fill

FILL    PROC  NEAR
            .
            .
            .

        RET

FILL    ENDP

PGMCD   ENDS
```

EXAMPLE 5–2   Coding for a FILL subroutine

procedure of a program, it makes a FAR call. This is because DOS is not in the same code segment as the program.

Remember that both NEAR and FAR calls must reset the IP register, but only a FAR call must reset the CS register.

The default for the PROC statement is NEAR. Therefore, programmers frequently do not bother to code the operand NEAR. All FAR procedures, however, must include the option FAR as a part of the PROC statement.

5.4   A SUBROUTINE EXAMPLE: MOVING CHARACTER AND NUMERIC FIELDS

To illustrate the use of subroutines, we will use the common activity of moving fields within main storage. Very often, ASCII strings or character strings must be moved from one field to another. When dealing with character strings, there are three possible situations that must be considered.

First, both fields can be the same length. This is the usual case, and the receiving field contains an exact copy of the sending field.

Second, the receiving field can be shorter than the sending field. In this case, truncation occurs and the receiving field contains only part of the sending field. Since character fields are usually moved from the left to the right, truncation occurs on the right of the sender. Look at the following fields:

```
LONG_NAME  DB  'THOMAS'   ; 6 BYTES
SHORT_NAME DB  4 DUP(?)   ; 4 BYTES
```

If the contents of the field LONG_NAME are moved to SHORT_NAME, then the field SHORT_NAME contains only the letters THOM.

Third, if the receiving field is longer than the sending field, then padding occurs. That is, the longer field contains the characters from the shorter field in the leftmost bytes and the longer field is padded with blanks in the rightmost bytes. Suppose you have two fields:

```
BIG_NAME  DB  5 DUP(?)
SML_NAME  DB  'SAM'
```

If the contents of SML_NAME are moved to BIG_NAME, then BIG_NAME contains

```
SAMbb
```

since ASCII character strings are padded on the right. (The b means a blank, or 20H.)

Truncation and padding of numeric ASCII fields are handled quite differently. Consider the following two fields:

```
SML_NUMBER  DB  '123'
BIG_NUMBER  DB  5 DUP(?)
```

When the contents of SML_NUMBER are moved to BIG_NUMBER, they appear in BIG_NUMBER as

```
00123
```

Notice that padding occurs on the left and that the fill character is not a blank, or 20H; rather, it is 0, or 30H.

Correspondingly, if a large number field is moved to a small field, truncation occurs on the left, thus removing the more significant digits. This can certainly be a problem with some applications.

Notice that the rules for moving fields of equal and unequal lengths are straightforward. However, moves that require fill bytes are more complex. Study the following listing in Figure 5–1 (PGM5.ASM on the program disk). The main driver module calls a series of four move subprocedures; each illustrates one of the cases described above.

MOV_EQUAL moves equal-length strings—in this case, NAMEIN to NAMEOUT. Loop repetition is done manually by decrementing register CX from its initial value of 8, the length of the strings, until the value reaches 0. The other routines use the LOOP instruction.

MOV_LONG moves a longer string, CLIENT1 (5 bytes), into a shorter string, CLIENT2 (4 bytes). The resulting truncation occurs on the right. Both the MOV_EQUAL and MOV_LONG routines process the strings from left to right, because character data are padded and truncated on the right.

MOV_NUM_LONG moves a longer ASCII number field, COSTIN (4 bytes), to a shorter field, COSTOUT (3 bytes), truncating the thousands digit.

MOV_NUM_SHORT moves a shorter ASCII number field, QTY (2 bytes), to a longer field, NEWQTY (5 bytes), padding on the left with leading 0's.

Both MOV_NUM_LONG and MOV_NUM_SHORT must process the fields from right to left because padding and truncation occur on the left with numeric fields. This "reverse" direction is reflected in the LEA and incrementing instructions. In MOV_NUM_LONG, LEA puts the address of COSTIN+3 into register SI. Since COSTIN is 4 bytes long and since the name COSTIN points to the first byte of the field, then COSTIN+3 points to the last byte of the field. To get to the next byte to process, the routine must now decrement the index registers instead of incrementing them.

Further, the padding version, MOV_NUM_SHORT, requires two loops. The first loop moves all the shorter field's digits. The second loop fills the remaining bytes of the longer field with the padding character, 30H.

Notice that there is no printed or displayed output from this program. Therefore, to see if it works, you must use the debugger to examine the fields in memory before and after the move subroutines have executed.

The debugging run first allows the program to execute the housekeeping portion, establishing register DS with the address of the data segment (the G 5 instruction). At this point the contents of the entire data segment are shown. Studying the contents is a good practice when debugging programs. When errors occur, it is likely that data were moved somewhere other than to the desired receiving area. If you display the data area, you can see where the data were moved. In the data area display in Figure 5–1, you can see that all the uninitialized fields do indeed contain 00H. They are displayed as periods in the character version on the display's right side.

Rather than tracing each individual instruction within each subroutine, we will discuss the execution of the entire subroutine and then examine the

Microsoft (R) Macro Assembler Version 5.10   9/1/88 16:49:17

PGM5 FIGURE 5-1 PGM TO MOVE CHARACTER FIELDS   Page   1-1


```
    1                                 PAGE   60,132
    2                                 TITLE  PGM5  FIGURE 5-1  PGM TO MOVE CHARACTER FIELDS
    3
    4                          ;************************************************************************
    5                          ; PGM5       Title: Figure 5-1 Illustrates Effects Of Moving Character *
    6                          ;                   To Longer And Shorter Fields                        *
    7                          ; Programmer: Vic Broquard                                              *
    8                          ; Date Written:  6/11/88       Date Of Last Revision: 8/4/88            *
    9                          ;                                                                       *
   10                          ; Purpose:                                                             *
   11                          ;                                                                       *
   12                          ; MOV_EQUAL     moves equal length character fields                    *
   13                          ; MOV_LONG      moves a long character field to a shorter field         *
   14                          ; MOV_NUM_LONG  moves a long character number to a shorter field        *
   15                          ; MOV_NUM_SHORT moves a shorter character number to a longer field      *
   16                          ;                                                                       *
   17                          ; Special Requirements: None                                           *
   18                          ;                                                                       *
   19                          ;************************************************************************
   20
   21                          ; program stack segment
   22
   23 0000                     STK    SEGMENT   PARA  STACK  'STACK'
   24
   25 0000  0020[                     DW    32 DUP (?)
   26        ????
   27                    ]
   28
   29
   30 0040                     STK    ENDS
   31
   32
   33                          ; program data segment
   34
   35 0000                     DATA   SEGMENT
   36
   37 0000  42 52 4F 51 55 41  NAMEIN    DB     'BROQUARD'
   38        52 44
   39 0008  0008[             NAMEOUT   DB     8 DUP (?)
   40        ??
   41                    ]
   42
   43
   44 0010  4A 4F 4E 45 53     CLIENT1   DB     'JONES'
```

FIGURE 5–1   Moving character and numeric fields (PGM5.ASM)

```
45 0015  0004[           CLIENT2   DB   4 DUP(?)
46        ??
47              ]
48
49
50 0019  31 32 33 34     COSTIN    DB   '1234'
51 001D  0003[           COSTOUT   DB   3 DUP(?)
52        ??
53              ]
54
55
56 0020  33 32           QTY       DB   '32'
```

Microsoft (R) Macro Assembler Version 5.10   9/1/88 16:49:17

PGM5 FIGURE 5-1 PGM TO MOVE CHARACTER FIELDS   Page   1-2


```
57 0022  0005[           NEWQTY    DB   5 DUP(?)
58        ??
59              ]
60
61
62 0027                  DATA   ENDS
```

Microsoft (R) Macro Assembler Version 5.10   9/1/88 16:49:17

PGM5 FIGURE 5-1 PGM TO MOVE CHARACTER FIELDS   Page   1-3


```
63                               PAGE
64
65                       ; program code segment
66
67 0000                  CODE   SEGMENT
68
69 0000                  MAIN PROC FAR
70
71                       ; housekeeping section
72
73                               ASSUME CS:CODE,DS:DATA,SS:STK
74
75 0000  B8 ---- R               MOV   AX,DATA  ; ESTABLISH ADDRESSABILITY
76 0003  8E D8                   MOV   DS,AX    ; TO DATA SEGMENT
77
78                       ; main process section
79
80 0005  E8 0017 R               CALL MOV_EQUAL    ; MOVE EQUAL LENGTH CHARACTER FIELDS
81 0008  E8 002C R               CALL MOV_LONG     ; MOVE A LONG STRING TO A SHORT STRING
```

FIGURE 5–1   continued   *(Continues)*

```
82 000B  E8 0040 R              CALL  MOV_NUM_LONG   ; MOVE LONG NUMBER TO SHORTER NUMBER
83 000E  E8 0054 R              CALL  MOV_NUM_SHORT  ; MOVE A SHORT NUMBER TO LONGER NUMBER
84
85                        ; return to DOS section
86
87 0011  B0 00                  MOV   AL,0    ; SET A 0 RETURN CODE
88 0013  B4 4C                  MOV   AH,4CH  ; SET FOR END PROCESS
89 0015  CD 21                  INT   21H     ; CALL DOS TO END
90
91 0017             MAIN    ENDP
```

--------------------------------------   ---

Microsoft (R) Macro Assembler Version 5.10   9/1/88 16:49:17

PGM5 FIGURE 5-1 PGM TO MOVE CHARACTER FIELDS   Page   1-4


```
92                              PAGE
93
94 0017             MOV_EQUAL   PROC
95
96                        ; move character strings of equal length
97
 98 0017  8D 36 0000 R          LEA   SI,NAMEIN  ; REG SI -> NAMEIN  BYTE 1
 99 001B  8D 3E 0008 R          LEA   DI,NAMEOUT ; REG DI -> NAMEOUT BYTE 1
100 001F  B9 0008               MOV   CX,8       ; REG CX = # BYTES TO MOVE
101
102 0022             MOVE1:
103 0022  8A 04                 MOV   AL,[SI] ; MOVE A BYTE INTO AL
104 0024  88 05                 MOV   [DI],AL ; MOVE THE BYTE INTO ANSWER
105 0026  46                    INC   SI      ; ADD 1 TO GET NEXT SOURCE BYTE
106 0027  47                    INC   DI      ; ADD 1 TO GET NEXT ANSWER BYTE
107 0028  49                    DEC   CX      ; SUB 1 TO GET REMAINING NUMBER TO MOVE
108 0029  75 F7                 JNZ   MOVE1   ; CONTINUE UNTIL CX IS 0
109
110 002B  C3                    RET
111 002C             MOV_EQUAL   ENDP
112
113
114
115 002C             MOV_LONG    PROC
116
117                        ; move long character string into a shorter string
118
119 002C  8D 36 0010 R          LEA   SI,CLIENT1  ; REG SI -> CLIENT1 BYTE 1
120 0030  8D 3E 0015 R          LEA   DI,CLIENT2  ; REG DI -> CLIENT2 BYTE 1
121 0034  B9 0004               MOV   CX,4        ; REG CX = # BYTES TO MOVE
122
123 0037             MOVE2:
124 0037  8A 04                 MOV   AL,[SI]  ; MOVE A BYTE INTO AL
```

FIGURE 5–1   continued

```
125 0039  88 05                    MOV     [DI],AL      ; MOVE THE BYTE INTO ANSWER
126 003B  46                       INC     SI           ; ADD 1 TO GET NEXT SOURCE BYTE
127 003C  47                       INC     DI           ; ADD 1 TO GET NEXT ANSWER BYTE
128 003D  E2 F8                    LOOP    MOVE2        ; REPEAT UNTIL NO MORE BYTES (CX = 0)
129
130                                ; truncates on the right for character fields
131
132 003F  C3                       RET
133 0040            MOV_LONG       ENDP
```

Microsoft (R) Macro Assembler Version 5.10   9/1/88 16:49:17

PGM5 FIGURE 5-1 PGM TO MOVE CHARACTER FIELDS   Page   1-5

```
134                                PAGE
135
136 0040            MOV_NUM_LONG   PROC
137
138                                ; move long number string to shorter number string
139
140 0040  8D 36 001C R             LEA     SI,COSTIN+3  ; REG SI -> LAST BYTE OF COSTIN
141 0044  8D 3E 001F R             LEA     DI,COSTOUT+2 ; REG DI -> LAST BYTE OF COSTOUT
142 0048  B9 0003                  MOV     CX,3         ; REG CX = # BYTES TO MOVE
143
144 004B            MOVE3:
145 004B  8A 04                    MOV     AL,[SI]      ; MOVE A BYTE INTO AL
146 004D  88 05                    MOV     [DI],AL      ; MOVE THE BYTE INTO ANSWER
147 004F  4E                       DEC     SI           ; SUB 1 TO GET NEXT SOURCE BYTE
148 0050  4F                       DEC     DI           ; SUB 1 TO GET NEXT ANSWER BYTE
149 0051  E2 F8                    LOOP    MOVE3        ; REPEAT UNTIL NO MORE BYTES (CX =0)
150
151                                ; truncates on the left for numeric character strings
152
153 0053  C3                       RET
154 0054            MOV_NUM_LONG   ENDP
155
156
157 0054            MOV_NUM_SHORT  PROC
158
159                                ; moves short number string to a longer string
160
161 0054  8D 36 0021 R             LEA     SI,QTY+1     ; REG SI -> LAST BYTE OF QTY
162 0058  8D 3E 0026 R             LEA     DI,NEWQTY+4  ; REG DI -> LAST BYTE OF NEWQTY
163 005C  B9 0002                  MOV     CX,2         ; REG CX = # BYTES TO MOVE
164
165 005F            MOVE4:
166 005F  8A 04                    MOV     AL,[SI]      ; MOVE A BYTE INTO AL
167 0061  88 05                    MOV     [DI],AL      ; MOVE THE BYTE INTO ANSWER
```

FIGURE 5-1 continued   *(Continues)*

```
168 0063  4E                    DEC    SI      ; SUB 1 TO GET NEXT SOURCE BYTE
169 0064  4F                    DEC    DI      ; SUB 1 TO GET NEXT ANSWER BYTE
170 0065  E2 F8                 LOOP   MOVE4   ; REPEAT UNTIL NO MORE BYTES (CX =0)
171
172 0067  B0 30                 MOV    AL,30H  ; PUT A FILL CHAR OF 0 IN AL
173 0069  B9 0003               MOV    CX,3    ; PUT NUMBER OF BYTES TO MOVE IN CX
174
175 006C           MOVE4A:
176 006C  88 05                 MOV    [DI],AL ; MOVE IN A FILL 0 CHARACTER
177 006E  4F                    DEC    DI      ; SUB 1 TO GET TO NEXT BYTE
178 006F  E2 FB                 LOOP   MOVE4A  ; REPEAT UNTIL FIELD IS FILLED
179
180                     ; pads on the left with ASCII 0's
181
182 0071  C3                    RET
183
184 0072           MOV_NUM_SHORT   ENDP
185
186 0072           CODE   ENDS
187                        END  MAIN
```

```
Microsoft (R) Symbolic Debug Utility  Version 4.00
Copyright (C) Microsoft Corp 1984, 1985.  All rights reserved.


Processor is [8086]


-G 5


AX=5443  BX=0000  CX=00E2  DX=0000  SP=0040  BP=0000  SI=0000  DI=0000
DS=5443  ES=542F  SS=543F  CS=5446  IP=0005    NV UP EI PL NZ NA PO NC
5446:0005 E80F00        CALL   0017


-D DS:00,27


5443:0000  42 52 4F 51 55 41 52 44-00 00 00 00 00 00 00 00   BROQUARD........
5443:0010  4A 4F 4E 45 53 00 00 00-00 31 32 33 34 00 00 00   JONES....1234...
5443:0020  33 32 00 00 00 00 00 00                           32......

-G 8

AX=5444  BX=0000  CX=0000  DX=0000  SP=0040  BP=0000  SI=0008  DI=0010
DS=5443  ES=542F  SS=543F  CS=5446  IP=0008    NV UP EI PL ZR NA PE NC
5446:0008 E82100        CALL   002C

-D DS:00,27


5443:0000  42 52 4F 51 55 41 52 44-42 52 4F 51 55 41 52 44   BROQUARDBROQUARD
5443:0010  4A 4F 4E 45 53 00 00 00-00 31 32 33 34 00 00 00   JONES....1234...
```

FIGURE 5–1 continued

```
5443:0020  33 32 00 00 00 00 00 00                            32......

-G B

AX=5445  BX=0000  CX=0000  DX=0000  SP=0040  BP=0000  SI=0014  DI=0019
DS=5443  ES=542F  SS=543F  CS=5446  IP=000B   NV UP EI PL NZ NA PO NC
5446:000B E83200         CALL  0040

-D DS:00,27

5443:0000  42 52 4F 51 55 41 52 44-42 52 4F 51 55 41 52 44   BROQUARDBROQUARD
5443:0010  4A 4F 4E 45 53 4A 4F 4E-45 31 32 33 34 00 00 00   JONESJONE1234...
5443:0020  33 32 00 00 00 00 00 00                            32......

-G E

AX=5432  BX=0000  CX=0000  DX=0000  SP=0040  BP=0000  SI=0019  DI=001C
DS=5443  ES=542F  SS=543F  CS=5446  IP=000E   NV UP EI PL NZ NA PO NC
5446:000E E84300         CALL  0054

-D DS:00,27

5443:0000  42 52 4F 51 55 41 52 44-42 52 4F 51 55 41 52 44   BROQUARDBROQUARD
5443:0010  4A 4F 4E 45 53 4A 4F 4E-45 31 32 33 34 32 33 34   JONESJONE1234234
5443:0020  33 32 00 00 00 00 00 00                            32......

-G 11

AX=5430  BX=0000  CX=0000  DX=0000  SP=0040  BP=0000  SI=001F  DI=0021
DS=5443  ES=542F  SS=543F  CS=5446  IP=0011   NV UP EI PL NZ NA PE NC
5446:0011 B000          MOV   AL,00

-D DS:00,27

-------------------------------------------------------------------------

5443:0000  42 52 4F 51 55 41 52 44-42 52 4F 51 55 41 52 44   BROQUARDBROQUARD
5443:0010  4A 4F 4E 45 53 4A 4F 4E-45 31 32 33 34 32 33 34   JONESJONE1234234
5443:0020  33 32 30 30 30 33 32 00                            3200032.

-Q
A>
```

FIGURE 5-1 continued

result. If an error is spotted then, the debugging run can be restarted from the beginning and a more detailed examination made.

The offset address of the next instruction after the call to MOV_EQUAL is 00 08H. The command G 8 executes the MOV_EQUAL routine to completion. Next, study the display of that data area to see if the move was successful. To do this, find the address of the receiving field, NAMEOUT, and locate those bytes in the display.

Repeat this procedure for the other subroutines. Execute this entire debugging run on your computer to verify that the receiving fields have been handled properly. You need to be expert at this type of debugging activity to debug your own programs.

5.5 THE OPERATION OF THE STACK

As indicated earlier, the call and return instructions affect the stack. Therefore, the assembler programmer must have a thorough understanding of the stack and how it works.

The stack is a last-in, first-out (or LIFO) **program save area.** A program save area temporarily stores register or memory word values as required by the program. When DOS gives control to a program, the SS (stack segment) register contains the segment address of the program's stack segment. For beginning programs, the stack commonly contains a total of 32 words, or 64 bytes. When the size of programs increases, the size of the stack can also increase.

Study Example 5–3, which shows a stack that is about to be filled. Each box in Example 5–3 represents a word on the stack. It is a very small stack with only 5 words. The stack is filled by starting at the bottom, the highest memory address, and working toward the top, the lowest memory

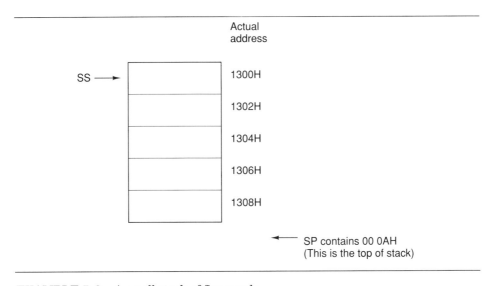

EXAMPLE 5–3   A small stack of five words

address. (Starting at the highest address is perceived by most people as working upside down). When DOS gives control to the program, the SP (stack pointer) register (which points to the current slot in the stack) is set to contain the offset address of the last word, or the highest memory address, in the stack.

Only word values can be placed onto the stack. The SP register is decremented by 2 bytes to point to the next slot. Then the word is placed onto the stack. When the SP register contains 00 00H, the stack is full and can no longer be decremented.

How are values placed onto the stack? As you learned earlier, the CALL and RET instructions do this automatically. But, in most other situations, the PUSH and POP instructions store and retrieve values.

5.6 THE PUSH INSTRUCTION

The **PUSH** instruction is used to put a word onto the stack. PUSH first subtracts 2 bytes from the SP register so that it points to the next unused slot; then it stores the word onto the stack at the word pointed to by the SP register.

The syntax is

```
PUSH    word register
```

or

```
PUSH    word of memory
```

Suppose that it is necessary to save the content of register AX and then, at a later time, retrieve the original value. Enter

```
PUSH AX
```

The stack now appears as shown in Example 5–4.

Next assume that register BX also needs to be saved. Enter

```
PUSH BX
```

Now the stack appears as shown in Example 5–5.

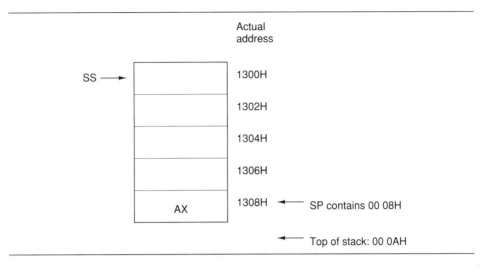

EXAMPLE 5–4   The stack after register AX has been stored

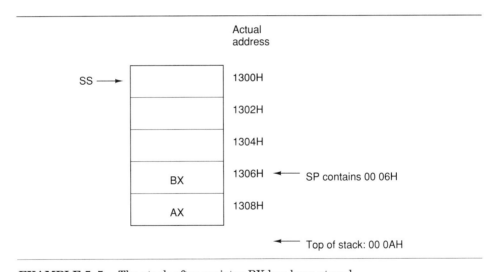

EXAMPLE 5–5   The stack after register BX has been stored

5.7 THE POP INSTRUCTION

The **POP** instruction removes words from the stack. When a POP is executed, it first extracts the word pointed to by the SP register and then adds 2 bytes to the SP register so that it points to the next word in the stack.

The syntax is

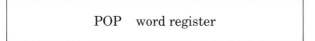

POP   word register

or

POP   word of memory

To retrieve the original value of register BX, enter

POP   BX

Register BX is assigned the value at SS:SP from the stack. The stack now appears as shown in Example 5–6.

If you want to retrieve the original value that was in register AX, also enter

POP   AX

Now SP contains 00 0AH once more.

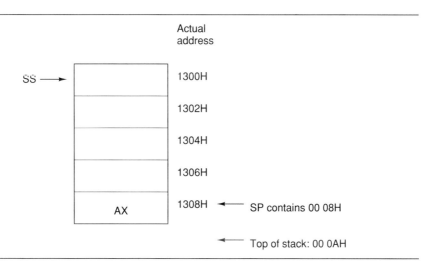

EXAMPLE 5–6   The stack after register BX has been restored

```
FILL  PROC  NEAR

      PUSH  AX     ; SAVE REG AX
      PUSH  BX     ; SAVE REG BX
      PUSH  CX     ; SAVE REG CX
      PUSH  DX     ; SAVE REG DX
        .
        .          ; SUBROUTINE CODE GOES HERE
        .
      POP   DX     ; RESTORE REG DX
      POP   CX     ; RESTORE REG CX
      POP   BX     ; RESTORE REG BX
      POP   AX     ; RESTORE REG AX

      RET          ; RETURN TO THE CALLER

FILL  ENDP
```

EXAMPLE 5–7   The FILL subroutine

5.8   SAVING AND RESTORING REGISTERS

Because there are so few registers available, it is common practice to save the contents of the work registers when a subroutine is entered and to restore them when the subroutine is finished. This practice frees the work registers for other uses within the subroutine.

In the code in Example 5–7, a series of PUSH instructions is issued when the subroutine begins. Then a reverse series of POP instructions is issued just before the RET instruction. The POPs are in the reverse order of the PUSHes because the stack is LIFO—last-in first-out.

Each routine should save and restore only those registers that it will use. It is not necessary to save all the registers.

Saving and Restoring the Flag Register

Although the flag register can also be pushed and popped, the assembler has another pair of instructions for this operation. These two instructions, **PUSHF** and **POPF,** are written with no operands. This is because the flag register does not have a register name, such as register AX. However, PUSHF and POPF operate in the same way as the PUSH and POP instructions.

5.9 NEAR AND FAR CALLS

When a call to a NEAR procedure is executed, it pushes only the IP register onto the stack, since the CS register remains unchanged. A call to a FAR procedure, however, first pushes the IP register onto the stack and then pushes the CS register as well. Then the FAR call loads the new CS register value and the new IP register values. Thus, a NEAR call places 1 word onto the stack; a FAR call places 2 words onto the stack.

To perform correctly, the RET instruction must know how many words to pop off of the stack: 1 or 2 words. Will it POP just the IP or both the IP and CS registers? The operand of PROC is used by the assembler to keep track of the number of words the RET instruction is to pop. If it is a NEAR PROC, then RET only pops the IP register. If it is a FAR PROC, then the RET pops both the IP and CS registers.

It is **vital** that the correct number of words be popped from the stack at every step in the program. If the number of PUSHes and POPs does not match, then wrong values will be popped!

5.10 STACK ERROR SITUATIONS

The need to balance the number of PUSHes and POPs leads to a number of possible error situations.

First, a jump or branch can transfer control to code within a routine without using a CALL to that routine. Study Example 5–8. What happens? The jump transfers control to a point in the subroutine called HERE. Next, the return for SUB1 is executed and a value is popped from the stack. Since no CALL (PUSH IP) is ever executed, an erroneous value is placed in the IP register. Unpredictable results can be expected.

Second, it is possible for the registers to be popped in the wrong order. Examine the code in Example 5–9. All the registers have the wrong values in them. Specifically, register AX contains the old contents of register DX. BX contains the old CX value, and so on.

Third, the called routine can fail to execute a return instruction, possibly because the programmer forgets to include it. Example 5–10 shows what happens. When the CALL is executed, the IP is pushed onto the stack. However, when SUB1 ends and no RET is executed, the next instruction is whatever is in storage after SUB1 ENDP—in this case SUB2's first instruction! So now SUB2 is executed, possibly in error. Then, when SUB2 executes its RET, the current value is popped off the stack into the IP register. That value, however, was the return address in MAIN, so control goes back to MAIN. This produces erroneous results because SUB2 was executed when it should not have been.

In addition, if the data segment or nothing comes after the SUB1 ENDP, then very strange errors occur. The IP points to the data segment or

```
MAIN  PROC
       .
       .
       .
      JMP  HERE
       .
       .              ; RETURN TO DOS CODE
       .
MAIN  ENDP

SUB1  PROC
       .
       .
       .
HERE:
       .
       .
       .
      RET
SUB1  ENDP
```

EXAMPLE 5–8   An incorrect jump into a procedure

```
SUB1 PROC

     PUSH  AX
     PUSH  BX
     PUSH  CX
     PUSH  DX

      .
      .          ; SUBROUTINE CODE GOES HERE
      .
     POP   AX
     POP   BX
     POP   CX
     POP   DX

     RET
SUB1 ENDP
```

EXAMPLE 5–9   Popping the registers in the wrong order

```
MAIN PROC
    .
    .
    .
    CALL SUB1
    .
    .          ; RETURN TO DOS CODE
    .

MAIN ENDP

SUB1 PROC
    .
    .
    .
SUB1 ENDP

SUB2 PROC
    .
    .
    .
    RET
SUB2 ENDP
```

EXAMPLE 5–10   SUB1 fails to return to the main procedure

whatever came after the last instruction, and the computer uses whatever values are in storage as its next instruction.

    Fourth, a called subroutine can issue a JMP into another procedure instead of issuing the expected RET. Example 5–11 illustrates what happens in this situation. The first thing that happens is that the return address from the CALL to SUB1 is placed onto the stack. Next, SUB1 jumps into SUB2. However, SUB2 issues a RET, which now returns—not to SUB1—but back to the next instruction after MAIN's CALL to SUB1! Flow of control is fouled up.

5.11 A STACK EXAMPLE

To reinforce your understanding of the stack, examine the short program in Figure 5–2 (PGM6.ASM on the program disk). Although it performs no useful work, it does show the effect of the CALL and RET instructions on the stack. Assemble, link, and run the debugger to produce similar output. Be sure that you understand each instruction's effect upon the stack.

```
      MAIN PROC
            .
            .
            .
      CALL SUB1
            .
            .
            .
      CALL SUB2
            .
            .      ; RETURN TO DOS CODE
            .
      MAIN ENDP


      SUB1 PROC
            .
            .
            .
      JMP SUB2
      SUB1 ENDP


      SUB2 PROC
            .
            .
            .
      RET
      SUB2 ENDP
```

EXAMPLE 5–11   SUB1 using a JMP instead of a RET instruction to terminate a subroutine

Pay particular attention to the effects on the SP register, the contents of the stack, and the IP register. What should be occurring? A quick glance shows that none of the subroutines does any real work. However, the effect of the nested CALLs is seen in the stack. When module A calls B, its return address is placed onto the stack and the stack pointer is altered. When subroutine B calls module C, the return address to B is placed onto the stack and the stack pointer is modified. When module C calls routine D, the return address for C is stored as well. When subroutine D returns to C, the return address in C is retrieved from the stack and the stack pointer is adjusted accordingly as it returns to module C. The other returns work similarly. Thus, by tracing the execution, you should be able to see the effects of CALLs and RETs on the stack and the stack pointer.

When the program starts, DOS has the SS:SP registers pointing to the top of the stack. Thus, the first command is R—to show what is in these

Microsoft (R) Macro Assembler Version 5.10   9/1/88 17:20:30

PGM6   FIGURE 5-2 PGM TO ILLUSTRATE THE USE OF A STACK   Page   1-1

```
     1                              PAGE   60,132
     2                              TITLE  PGM6  FIGURE 5-2 PGM TO ILLUSTRATE THE USE OF A STACK
     3
     4                      ;**********************************************************************
     5                      ; PGM6         Title: Figure 5-2 Illustrates The Use Of The Stack     *
     6                      ;                                                                      *
     7                      ; Programmer: Vic Broquard                                            *
     8                      ; Date Written: 6/11/88       Date Of Last Revision: 8/4/88           *
     9                      ;                                                                      *
    10                      ; Purpose: A calls B calls C Calls D to illustrate the use of the stack*
    11                      ;                                                                      *
    12                      ; Special Requirements:                                               *
    13                      ;                                                                      *
    14                      ;**********************************************************************
    15
    16                      ; stack segment defines the stack
    17
    18 0000                 STK    SEGMENT  PARA  STACK  'STACK'
    19
    20 0000  0020[                  DW     32 DUP (?)
    21        ????
    22                  ]
    23
    24
    25 0040                 STK    ENDS
    26
    27                      ; program code segment
    28
    29 0000                 CODE  SEGMENT
    30
    31 0000                 A  PROC FAR
    32
    33                             ASSUME CS:CODE,SS:STK
    34
    35 0000  E8 0009 R             CALL   B        ; CALL MODULE B
    36
    37 0003  B0 00                 MOV    AL,0     ; SET 0 AS THE RETURN CODE
    38 0005  B4 4C                 MOV    AH,4CH   ; SET FOR END PROCESS FUNCTION
    39 0007  CD 21                 INT    21H      ; CALL DOS TO END
    40
    41 0009                 A  ENDP
    42
    43
    44 0009                 B  PROC
    45
```

FIGURE 5-2   Stack example (PGM6.ASM)   *(Continues)*

```
46 0009  E8 000D R              CALL  C      ; CALL MODULE C
47
48 000C  C3                     RET
49 000D                    B    ENDP
50
51
52 000D                    C    PROC
53
54 000D  E8 0011 R              CALL  D      ; CALL MODULE D
55
56 0010  C3                     RET
```

```
57 0011                    C    ENDP
58
59
60 0011                    D    PROC
61
62 0011  C3                     RET
63 0012                    D    ENDP
64
65 0012                    CODE ENDS
66                              END   A
```

Microsoft (R) Symbolic Debug Utility Version 4.00
Copyright (C) Microsoft Corp 1984, 1985. All rights reserved.

Processor is [8086]

-R

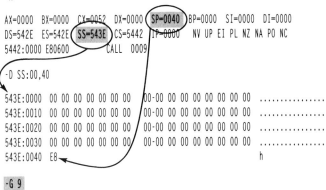

```
AX=0000  BX=0000  CX=0052  DX=0000  SP=0040  BP=0000  SI=0000  DI=0000
DS=542E  ES=542E  SS=543E  CS=5442  IP=0000   NV UP EI PL NZ NA PO NC
5442:0000 E80600            CALL  0009
```

-D SS:00,40

```
543E:0000  00 00 00 00 00 00 00 00-00 00 00 00 00 00 00 00  ................
543E:0010  00 00 00 00 00 00 00 00-00 00 00 00 00 00 00 00  ................
543E:0020  00 00 00 00 00 00 00 00-00 00 00 00 00 00 00 00  ................
543E:0030  00 00 00 00 00 00 00 00-00 00 00 00 00 00 00 00  ................
543E:0040  E8                                               h
```

-G 9

```
AX=0000  BX=0000  CX=0052  DX=0000  SP=003E  BP=0000  SI=0000  DI=0000
DS=542E  ES=542E  SS=543E  CS=5442  IP=0009   NV UP EI PL NZ NA PO NC
5442:0009 E80100            CALL  000D
```

-D SS:30,3F

```
543E:0030  00 00 00 00 00 00 00 00-09 00 42 54 1C 4B 03 00  ..........BT.K..
```

FIGURE 5–2   continued

```
-G D

AX=0000  BX=0000  CX=0052  DX=0000  SP=003C  BP=0000  SI=0000  DI=0000
DS=542E  ES=542E  SS=543E  CS=5442  IP=000D  NV UP EI PL NZ NA PO NC
5442:000D E80100         CALL  0011

-D SS:30,3F

543E:0030  00 00 00 00 00 00 0D 00-42 54 1C 4B 0C 00 03 00   ........BT.K....

-G 11

AX=0000  BX=0000  CX=0052  DX=0000  SP=003A  BP=0000  SI=0000  DI=0000
DS=542E  ES=542E  SS=543E  CS=5442  IP=0011  NV UP EI PL NZ NA PO NC
5442:0011 C3            RET

-D SS:30,3F

543E:0030  00 00 00 00 11 00 42 54-1C 4B 10 00 0C 00 03 00   ......BT.K......

-T

AX=0000  BX=0000  CX=0052  DX=0000  SP=003C  BP=0000  SI=0000  DI=0000
DS=542E  ES=542E  SS=543E  CS=5442  IP=0010  NV UP EI PL NZ NA PO NC
5442:0010 C3            RET

-D SS:30,3F

543E:0030  00 00 00 00 00 00 10 00-42 54 1C 4B 0C 00 03 00   ........BT.K....

-T

AX=0000  BX=0000  CX=0052  DX=0000  SP=003E  BP=0000  SI=0000  DI=0000
DS=542E  ES=542E  SS=543E  CS=5442  IP=000C  NV UP EI PL NZ NA PO NC

5442:000C C3            RET

-D SS:30,3F

543E:0030  00 00 00 00 00 00 00 00-0C 00 42 54 1C 4B 03 00   ..........BT.K..

-T

AX=0000  BX=0000  CX=0052  DX=0000  SP=0040  BP=0000  SI=0000  DI=0000
DS=542E  ES=542E  SS=543E  CS=5442  IP=0003  NV UP EI PL NZ NA PO NC
5442:0003 B000          MOV   AL,00

-D SS:30,3F
543E:0030  00 00 00 00 00 00 00 00-00 00 03 00 42 54 1C 4B   ............BT.K

-Q
A>
```

FIGURE 5–2   continued

registers. Next, the entire stack is displayed. As you can see, it is all 00H, uninitialized memory.

To see the effect of the CALL B instruction, enter G 9 to execute the program up to the first instruction in routine B, which is at offset address 00 09H. What happened to the SP register? It was decremented from 00 40H to 00 3EH. Displaying the stack once more shows what is in the current stack slot. It is 03 00H, which (as you learn from the source listing) is the offset address of the next instruction after the CALL B instruction.

Since module B now calls routine C, let the program run until module C gets control. From the source listing, you learn this is at offset address 00 0D. So you enter G D.

Again, notice what has happened to the SP register. It now contains 00 3CH. Examine what is on the stack at this offset. It is 0C 00H. Comparing this to the source listing, you find the address 00 0CH is at the first instruction after CALL C, as expected.

Follow the ensuing CALL to routine D with the G 11 command and display the effect on the stack.

To watch the RET action, begin tracing one instruction at a time. When D's RET is executed, register SP is incremented from 00 3AH to 00 3CH. Notice that the stack value 0010H was inserted into register IP. When C's RET is executed, register IP is loaded with the 00 0CH from the stack and SP is incremented to 00 3EH. Finally, when B's RET is executed, register IP is now loaded with 00 03H from the stack, while register SP is incremented to 00 40H.

Try experimenting with this little program shell. Add some PUSH and POP instructions and rerun the debugger to see their effects. Hint: First put some easy-to-identify values into the registers that you want to push.

5.12   GENERALIZED SUBROUTINES

Now that you more fully understand the general operation of subroutines and the stack, return once more to the design of subroutines. Re-examine Figure 5–1, which shows how four fields are moved by the various move routines. These are functional because each moves just one field and does nothing more.

However, if you approach microassembler in this way, you will create unnecessarily large programs. You may not grasp this point right now, but if you have an unexpectedly large program after doing just one of the problems in Chapter 7, we suggest that you review this section.

Suppose that it is necessary to move 10 fields. It would be highly impractical to create 10 different move subroutines; therefore, do not do it! For such functions it is best to learn how to write generalized subroutines. A generalized subroutine is one that performs a single function in such a way that it can be used in all similar situations. Instead of writing 10 move routines for 10 fields, write one move routine that moves a field and then calls it 10 times.

How can this be done? One way would be to have 20 different fields—10 sending fields and 10 receiving fields. Theoretically, there could also be 20 different lengths involved!

The key to creating generalized subroutines is to pass the fields or data items that are different from one invocation to the next to the subroutine via the registers. In the case of moving character fields, there are four items that vary from one call of the mover subroutine to the next. These are the address of the source string, the address of the receiving string, the length of the source string, and the length of the receiving string.

When the generalized subroutine gets control, it always expects that a specific register already contains the address of the receiving field. The same is true for the other three fields. The subroutine can then perform its function without knowing the symbolic names of the data. (Since the registers are being used by this subroutine, they have to be saved at the beginning of the subroutine and restored at its end.)

This is an extremely important concept; be certain that you understand it. The following two case studies show this operation. Failure to really understand what is involved in creating generalized routines will most certainly lead to failure as a microassembler programmer. If generalized subroutines are not used, a programmer can end up writing an enormous volume of very repetitious code that results in monstrous programs that cause nightmares during the debugging phase.

5.13 INVOKING GENERALIZED SUBROUTINES

Pseudocode and flowchart logic often make statements such as

IF LINE_COUNT IS GREATER THAN 55
THEN ADVANCE TO A NEW PAGE

This example reflects the common verbiage for describing the page overflow problem. When the page is full of output lines, as indicated by the field LINE_COUNT, the printer must eject the paper to a fresh page and print the report headings. Then the next output line can be written.

Assuming that LINE_COUNT is defined as a byte number, you might like to enter

```
CMP  LINE_COUNT,55
JA   CALL GET_NEW_PAGE
```

where GET_NEW_PAGE is the name of the subroutine that produces the report headings. However, conditional jumps do not issue a CALL instruction—the operand of a conditional jump must be a label.

This difficulty is often resolved by entering

```
        CMP  LINE_COUNT,55
        JNA  GO_ON
        CALL GET_NEW_PAGE
GO_ON:
```

When such situations arise in your programs, consider using this helpful technique.

5.14   CASE STUDY: A GENERALIZED ASCII CHARACTER FIELD MOVE ROUTINE

Since moving character strings is a very common function in programs, a generalized subroutine to move fields is extremely useful. Such a subroutine can be used to move any field desired. We call this subroutine ASCII_MOVE. (You can always change its name.)

ASCII_MOVE needs four pieces of information: the address of the sending field, the address of the receiving field, and the lengths of the two fields. In this example, whenever the ASCII_MOVE routine is called, it assumes that the following registers contain

SI = Address of the Source Field

DI = Address of the Destination Field

CX = Length of the Source Field

DX = Length of the Destination Field

Notice the subtle register-naming convention. The source index register (SI) contains the address of the sending or source field; the destination index register (DI) holds the address of the receiving field. This form of word and letter association helps with the readability of the program. You could have let register DI contain the address of the source field—the assembler does not really care which registers are used. But such a choice does aid the reader of the program.

One final assumption is needed to determine padding and truncation. Will the fields be character strings or will they be ASCII number strings? In this example assume that the fields are character strings.

Examine Figure 5–3 (PGM7.ASM on the program disk). The data segment contains three test cases: The first has equal-length fields, the second involves truncation, and the third involves padding on the right with blanks.

Study the MAIN procedure on pages 1-2 and 1-3 of the listing. The driver module merely loads the addresses and the lengths into the specified registers and calls ASCII_MOVE.

The next page, page 2-1, is the start of the processing routines. There is an appropriate subtitle and a series of comment lines that spell out all the register assumptions that are needed. Always document every subroutine in this way. Of course you know what the routine is receiving at the moment that you are writing the code, but 3 days later it can be very easy to forget all the details. Comments will be of great assistance and can save you from rereading all the code just to find out what values need to be where.

The subroutine saves all the registers that it is going to modify during the course of its processing. The first problem to solve is to determine which case is involved: equal lengths, padding, or truncation. The objective of this whole page of code is to determine the number of bytes of the source field that are to be moved. This value is in register CX at the end of page 2-1. Register DX contains the number of pad bytes that need to be moved into the receiving string. DX is 0 if none is needed.

Page 2-2 marks the start of the DO_IT section. Here the number of bytes contained in register CX is moved from the source field into the receiving field. The operation is controlled by register CX and a LOOP instruction.

Once this action is completed, any necessary pad bytes must be moved into the receiving field. If register DX (which contains the number of pad bytes) is 0, then the move is completed. If DX is not 0, then the second loop is executed to insert the blanks.

To fully understand this routine, draw a picture of the data fields involved and desk-check, or walk through, the program instruction by instruction. Once you fully understand the routine, you can modify and use it whenever you need to move character fields.

Also, examine the debugging run to verify that it actually works. Modify the fields and lengths to prove to yourself that the subroutine will always work. (What if the user accidentally enters a length of 0 for one of the field lengths?)

The use of generalized subroutines ultimately reduces the amount of redundant code as well as the total volume of code required to write an assembler program.

In the program design stage, similar functions must often be performed in several slightly different ways. Therefore, an attempt should be made to code one generic subroutine that determines the specific method needed as it executes. Your ability to write tight, compact assembler code depends upon careful analysis and the use of generalized subroutines. Failure to create generalized subroutines will cause your programs to be filled with enormous modules full of repetitive sequences—each of which will have to be debugged separately.

```
Microsoft (R) Macro Assembler Version 5.10              9/2/88 07:44:03

PGM7 FIGURE 5-3  GENERALIZED MOVER ROUTINE AND TEST PGM      Page    1-1


    1                                    PAGE   60,132
    2                                    TITLE  PGM7 FIGURE 5-3  GENERALIZED MOVER ROUTINE AND TEST PGM
    3
    4                             ;*************************************************************************
    5                             ; PGM7      Title: Figure 5-3 Test pgm with generalized move routine *
    6                             ;                                                                     *
    7                             ; Programmer: Vic Broquard                                            *
    8                             ; Date Written: 6/11/88      Date Of Last Revision: 8/4/88            *
    9                             ;                                                                     *
   10                             ; Purpose: Generalized ASCII String Mover Subroutine                 *
   11                             ;                                                                     *
   12                             ; Special Requirements: Routine ASCII_MOVE requires that:            *
   13                             ;    SI = address of source string   CX = length of source string    *
   14                             ;    DI = address of destination string  DX = length of destination  *
   15                             ;                                                                     *
   16                             ;*************************************************************************
   17
   18 0000                       PGM7STK  SEGMENT   PARA   STACK   'STACK'
   19
   20 0000  0020[                          DW     32 DUP(?)
   21       ????
   22                    ]
   23
   24
   25 0040                       PGM7STK  ENDS
   26
   27
   28 0000                       PGM7DATA SEGMENT
   29
   30 0000  42 52 4F 51 55 41    NAME1   DB     'BROQUARD'
   31       52 44
   32 0008  0008[               NAME1A DB     8 DUP(?)
   33       ??
   34                    ]
   35
   36
   37 0010  57 45 53 54 4C 45    NAME2   DB     'WESTLEY'
   38       59
   39 0017  0004[               NAME2A DB     4 DUP(?)
   40       ??
   41                    ]
   42
   43
   44 001B  56 49 43            NAME3   DB     'VIC'
```

FIGURE 5–3   Generalized ASCII character field move routine

```
45 001E  0009[            NAME3A DB    9 DUP(?)
46      ??
47                   ]
48
49
50 0027                   PGM7DATA ENDS
```

Microsoft (R) Macro Assembler Version 5.10   9/2/88 07:44:03

PGM7 FIGURE 5-3 GENERALIZED MOVER ROUTINE AND TEST PGM   Page   1-2

```
51                        PAGE
52
53 0000                   PGM7CODE SEGMENT
54
55 0000                   MAIN   PROC   FAR
56
57                        ; housekeeping section
58
59                                ASSUME CS:PGM7CODE,DS:PGM7DATA,SS:PGM7STK
60
61 0000  B8 ---- R                MOV    AX,PGM7DATA ; GET ADDRESSABILITY
62 0003  8E D8                    MOV    DS,AX    ; TO THE DATA SEGMENT
63
64                        ; main process section
65
66                        ; move first case 8 bytes to 8 bytes
67
68 0005  8D 36 0000 R             LEA    SI,NAME1  ; SI = ADDR OF 8 BYTE SOURCE
69 0009  8D 3E 0008 R             LEA    DI,NAME1A ; DI = ADDR OF 8 BYTE ANSWER
70
71 000D  B9 0008                  MOV    CX,8     ; CX = NUM BYTES IN SOURCE (8)
72 0010  BA 0008                  MOV    DX,8     ; DX = NUM BYTES IN ANSWER (8)
73
74 0013  E8 003E R                CALL   ASCII_MOVE  ; GO MOVE IT
```

Microsoft (R) Macro Assembler Version 5.10   9/2/88 07:44:03

PGM7 FIGURE 5-3 GENERALIZED MOVER ROUTINE AND TEST PGM   Page   1-3

```
75                        PAGE
76
77                        ; move second case 7 bytes to 4 bytes
78
79 0016  8D 36 0010 R             LEA    SI,NAME2  ; SI = ADDR OF 7 BYTE SOURCE
80 001A  8D 3E 0017 R             LEA    DI,NAME2A ; DI = ADDR OF 4 BYTE ANSWER
81
```

FIGURE 5–3   continued   (*Continues*)

```
 82 001E  B9 0007                     MOV   CX,7      ; CX = NUM BYTES IN SOURCE (7)
 83 0021  BA 0004                     MOV   DX,4      ; DX = NUM BYTES IN ANSWER (4)
 84
 85 0024  E8 003E R                   CALL  ASCII_MOVE ; GO MOVE IT
 86
 87                        ; move third case 3 bytes to 9 bytes
 88
 89 0027  8D 36 001B R                LEA   SI,NAME3  ; SI = ADDR OF 3 BYTE SOURCE
 90 002B  8D 3E 001E R                LEA   DI,NAME3A ; DI = ADDR OF 9 BYTE ANSWER
 91
 92 002F  B9 0003                     MOV   CX,3      ; CX = NUM BYTES IN SOURCE (3)
 93 0032  BA 0009                     MOV   DX,9      ; DX = NUM BYTES IN ANSWER (9)
 94
 95 0035  E8 003E R                   CALL  ASCII_MOVE ; GO MOVE IT
 96
 97                        ; return to DOS section
 98
 99 0038  B0 00                       MOV   AL,0      ; SET A 0 RETURN CODE
100 003A  B4 4C                       MOV   AH,4CH    ; SET FOR END PROCESS FUNCTION
101 003C  CD 21                       INT   21H       ; CALL DOS TO END
102
103 003E              MAIN  ENDP
104                         SUBTTL  ASCII_MOVE: GENERALIZED CHARACTER FIELD MOVER
```

Microsoft (R) Macro Assembler Version 5.10   9/2/88 07:44:03

PGM7 FIGURE 5-3 GENERALIZED MOVER ROUTINE AND TEST PGM   Page   2-1
ASCII_MOVE: GENERALIZED CHARACTER FIELD MOVER

```
105                                  PAGE   +
106
107 003E                 ASCII_MOVE    PROC
108
109                 ;    ASSUMES THAT:
110
111                 ;    SI = ADDRESS OF SOURCE STRING
112                 ;    CX = LENGTH OF SOURCE STRING
113
114                 ;    DI = ADDRESS OF DESTINATION STRING
115                 ;    DX = LENGTH OF DESTINATION STRING
116
117
118                 ; the routine will preserve the caller's registers
119
120 003E  50                          PUSH  AX        ; SAVE REG AX
121 003F  51                          PUSH  CX        ; SAVE REG CX
122 0040  52                          PUSH  DX        ; SAVE REG DX
123 0041  56                          PUSH  SI        ; SAVE REG SI
124 0042  57                          PUSH  DI        ; SAVE REG DI
125
```

FIGURE 5–3   continued

```
126 0043  3B CA                    CMP   CX,DX      ; WHICH STRING IS LONGER?
127 0045  72 10                    JB    PAD_IT     ; DESTINATION IS LONGER - GO TO PAD_IT
128 0047  74 08                    JE    SAME       ; BOTH HAVE SAME LENGTH - GO TO SAME
129
130                         ; here destination is truncated
131
132 0049  8B CA                    MOV   CX,DX      ; USE SHORTER LENGTH
133 004B  BA 0000                  MOV   DX,0       ; SET NUMBER PAD BYTES TO 0
134 004E  EB 09 90                 JMP   DO_IT      ; GO DO MOVE
135
136 0051            SAME:
137 0051  BA 0000                  MOV   DX,0       ; SET NUMBER OF PAD BYTES TO 0
138 0054  EB 03 90                 JMP   DO_IT      ; GO DO MOVE
139
140 0057            PAD_IT:
141 0057  2B D1                    SUB   DX,CX      ; CALC NUMBER OF PAD BYTES
```

Microsoft (R) Macro Assembler Version 5.10   9/2/88 07:44:03

PGM7 FIGURE 5-3 GENERALIZED MOVER ROUTINE AND TEST PGM   Page   2-2
ASCII_MOVE: GENERALIZED CHARACTER FIELD MOVER

```
142                         PAGE
143 0059            DO_IT:
144 0059  8A 24                    MOV   AH,[SI]    ; AH = NEXT BYTE OF SOURCE
145 005B  88 25                    MOV   [DI],AH    ; MOVE IT INTO DESTINATION BYTE
146
147 005D  47                       INC   DI         ; POINT TO NEXT DESTINATION BYTE
148 005E  46                       INC   SI         ; POINT TO NEXT SOURCE BYTE
149
150 005F  E2 F8                    LOOP  DO_IT      ; CONTINUE UNTIL ALL BYTES ARE MOVED
151
152                         ; now check for any needed pad bytes
153
154 0061  83 FA 00                 CMP   DX,0       ; ARE ANY NEEDED?
155 0064  74 09                    JE    DONE       ; NO, SO GO TO DONE
156
157 0066  8B CA                    MOV   CX,DX      ; SET NUMBER OF PAD BYTE TO INSERT
158 0068  B4 20                    MOV   AH,20H     ; SET THE PAD BYTE TO A BLANK
159
160 006A            FILL:
161 006A  88 25                    MOV   [DI],AH    ; MOVE IN ONE PAD BYTE
162 006C  47                       INC   DI         ; POINT TO NEXT DESTINATION BYTE
163
164 006D  E2 FB                    LOOP  FILL       ; CONTINUE WITH ALL PAD BYTES
165
166 006F            DONE:
167 006F  5F                       POP   DI         ; RESTORE DI
168 0070  5E                       POP   SI         ; RESTORE SI
```

FIGURE 5–3   continued   *(Continues)*

```
169 0071  5A                          POP    DX      ; RESTORE DX
170 0072  59                          POP    CX      ; RESTORE CX
171 0073  58                          POP    AX      ; RESTORE AX
172
173 0074  C3                          RET
174 0075               ASCII_MOVE     ENDP
175
176 0075               PGM7CODE ENDS
177
178                                   END    MAIN
```

```
Microsoft (R) Symbolic Debug Utility  Version 4.00
Copyright (C) Microsoft Corp 1984, 1985.  All rights reserved.



Processor is [8086]

-G 5

AX=543A  BX=0000  CX=00E5  DX=0000  SP=0040  BP=0000  SI=0000  DI=0000
DS=543A  ES=5426  SS=5436  CS=543D  IP=0005    NV UP EI PL NZ NA PO NC
543D:0005 8D360000     LEA   SI,[0000]                      DS:0000=5242

-D DS:00,26


543A:0000  42 52 4F 51 55 41 52 44-00 00 00 00 00 00 00 00  BROQUARD........
543A:0010  57 45 53 54 4C 45 59 00-00 00 00 56 49 43 00 00  WESTLEY....VIC..
543A:0020  00 00 00 00 00 00 00                             .......

-G 16

AX=543A  BX=0000  CX=0008  DX=0008  SP=0040  BP=0000  SI=0000  DI=0008
DS=543A  ES=5426  SS=5436  CS=543D  IP=0016    NV UP EI PL ZR NA PE NC
543D:0016 8D361000     LEA   SI,[0010]                      DS:0010=4557

-D DS:00,26

543A:0000  42 52 4F 51 55 41 52 44-42 52 4F 51 55 41 52 44  BROQUARDBROQUARD
543A:0010  57 45 53 54 4C 45 59 00-00 00 00 56 49 43 00 00  WESTLEY....VIC..
543A:0020  00 00 00 00 00 00 00                             .......

-G 27

AX=543A  BX=0000  CX=0007  DX=0004  SP=0040  BP=0000  SI=0010  DI=0017
DS=543A  ES=5426  SS=5436  CS=543D  IP=0027    NV UP EI PL ZR NA PE NC
543D:0027 8D361B00     LEA   SI,[001B]                      DS:001B=4956

-D DS:00,26
```

FIGURE 5–3   continued

```
543A:0000  42 52 4F 51 55 41 52 44-42 52 4F 51 55 41 52 44  BROQUARDBROQUARD
543A:0010  57 45 53 54 4C 45 59 57-45 53 54 56 49 43 00 00  WESTLEYWESTVIC..
543A:0020  00 00 00 00 00 00 00                              .......
```

```
-G 38
```

```
AX=543A  BX=0000  CX=0003  DX=0009  SP=0040  BP=0000  SI=001B  DI=001E
DS=543A  ES=5426  SS=5436  CS=543D  IP=0038    NV UP EI PL NZ NA PE NC
543D:0038 B000          MOV   AL,00
```

```
-D DS:00,26
```

```
543A:0000  42 52 4F 51 55 41 52 44-42 52 4F 51 55 41 52 44  BROQUARDBROQUARD
543A:0010  57 45 53 54 4C 45 59 57-45 53 54 56 49 43 56 49  WESTLEYWESTVICVI
543A:0020  43 20 20 20 20 20 20                             C
```

```
-Q
A>
```

FIGURE 5–3   continued

5.15 CASE STUDY: A CAPITALIZATION FUNCTION

Capitalization is a function commonly found in word processing programs. From the keyboard the user enters a control code that causes the word processing program to capitalize the data being entered. In Figure 5–4 (PGM8.ASM on the program disk) the subroutine CAP_RTN handles this function. When CAP_RTN is called, it expects register SI to contain the address of the character string that contains the string of ASCII characters to be capitalized. Further, CAP_RTN expects register CX to contain the length of the string to capitalize.

CAP_RTN's objective is to capitalize the first letter of the string and to ensure that all other letters are lowercase. Thus, it should accomplish the following results:

```
CAT       becomes Cat
cat       becomes Cat
caT       becomes Cat
123 cat   becomes 123 Cat
```

Notice that numbers and other special characters are ignored and the first **letter** is capitalized.

In Figure 5–4 the MAIN procedure tests the subroutine with several sets of data. CAP_RTN begins on page 2-1 of the listing. CAP_RTN assumes that register SI contains the address of the string to be capitalized. Register

```
Microsoft (R) Macro Assembler Version 5.10              9/2/88 07:58:35

PGM8  FIGURE 5-4   CAP_RTN SUBROUTINE AND TESTER PGM        Page    1-1


        1                              PAGE   60,132
        2                              TITLE  PGM8  FIGURE 5-4   CAP_RTN SUBROUTINE AND TESTER PGM
        3
        4                      ;***********************************************************************
        5                      ; PGM8       Title: Figure 5-4 Capitalization Routine With Testor Pgm *
        6                      ;                                                                      *
        7                      ; Programmer: Vic Broquard                                             *
        8                      ; Date Written: 6/11/88       Date Of Last Revision: 8/4/88           *
        9                      ;                                                                      *
       10                      ; Purpose: Capitalize an ASCII string                                 *
       11                      ;                                                                      *
       12                      ; Special Requirements:                                               *
       13                      ;    CAP_RTN requires on entry:                                       *
       14                      ;                     SI = addr of string to capitalize               *
       15                      ;                     CX = length of string                           *
       16                      ;***********************************************************************
       17
       18 0000                PGMSTK SEGMENT   PARA   STACK   'STACK'
       19
       20 0000  0020[                   DW    32 DUP(?)
       21        ????
       22                  ]
       23
       24
       25 0040                PGMSTK ENDS
       26
       27
       28 0000                PGMDA  SEGMENT
       29
       30 0000  63 61 74      FIELD1 DB      'cat'
       31 0003  43 41 54      FIELD2 DB      'CAT'
       32 0006  63 61 54      FIELD3 DB      'caT'
       33 0009  31 32 33 20 43 41   FIELD4 DB      '123 CAT'
       34        54
       35
       36 0010                PGMDA  ENDS
       37
       38
       39 0000                PGMCD  SEGMENT
       40
       41 0000                MAIN   PROC   FAR
       42
       43                     ; housekeeping section
       44
```

FIGURE 5–4   Capitalization routine

```
45                              ASSUME CS:PGMCD,DS:PGMDA,SS:PGMSTK
46
47 0000  B8 ---- R            MOV   AX,PGMDA  ; ESTABLISH ADDRESSABILITY
48 0003  8E D8               MOV   DS,AX     ; TO THE DATA SEGMENT
49
50                      ; main process section
51
52                      ; test first field
53
54 0005  8D 36 0000 R        LEA   SI,FIELD1 ; SI = ADDR OF 'cat'
55 0009  B9 0003             MOV   CX,3      ; CX = NUMBER BYTES TO DO => 3
56 000C  E8 002D R           CALL  CAP_RTN   ; GO CAPITALIZE IT
```

Microsoft (R) Macro Assembler Version 5.10   9/2/88 07:58:35

PGM8 FIGURE 5-4   CAP_RTN SUBROUTINE AND TESTER PGM   Page   1-2

```
57
58                      ; test second field
59
60 000F  8D 36 0003 R        LEA   SI,FIELD2 ; SI =ADDR OF 'CAT'
61 0013  E8 002D R           CALL  CAP_RTN   ; GO CAPITALIZE IT
62
63                      ; test third field
64
65 0016  8D 36 0006 R        LEA   SI,FIELD3 ; SI = ADDR OF 'caT'
66 001A  E8 002D R           CALL  CAP_RTN   ; GO CAPITALIZE IT
67
68                      ; test fourth field
69
70 001D  8D 36 0009 R        LEA   SI,FIELD4 ; SI = ADDR OF '123 CAT'
71 0021  B9 0007             MOV   CX,7      ; CX = 7 BYTES TO DO
72 0024  E8 002D R           CALL  CAP_RTN   ; GO CAPITALIZE IT
73
74 0027  B0 00               MOV   AL,0      ; SET A 0 RETURN CODE
75 0029  B4 4C               MOV   AH,4CH    ; SET FOR END PROCESS
76 002B  CD 21               INT   21H       ; CALL DOS TO END
77
78 002D              MAIN    ENDP
79                           SUBTTL  CAP_RTN  CAPITALIZE THE FIRST LETTER OF A STRING
```

Microsoft (R) Macro Assembler Version 5.10   9/2/88 07:58:35

PGM8 FIGURE 5-4   CAP_RTN SUBROUTINE AND TESTER PGM   Page   2-1
CAP_RTN CAPITALIZE THE FIRST LETTER OF A STRING

```
80                           PAGE  +
81
```

FIGURE 5–4   continued   (*Continues*)

```
82 002D                      CAP_RTN     PROC
83
84                           ;  assumes that  SI = address of the string
85                           ;                CX = length of the string
86
87                           ;  the routine preserves the caller's registers
88
89
90 002D  50                              PUSH    AX      ; SAVE REG AX
91 002E  51                              PUSH    CX      ; SAVE REG CX
92 002F  56                              PUSH    SI      ; SAVE REG SI
93
94 0030  B4 00                           MOV     AH,00H   ; AH = DONE 1 CAP SWITCH: 00 = NO, 01=YES
95
96 0032                      BIG_LOOP:
97
98 0032  8A 04                           MOV     AL,[SI]  ; AL = NEXT BYTE TO CHECK
99
100 0034  3C 61                          CMP     AL,61H   ; IS IT THE LETTER a?
101 0036  72 12                          JB      CHECK_CAP ; BELOW, SO GO CHECK IF IT IS A CAPITAL
102
103 0038  3C 7A                          CMP     AL,7AH   ; IS IT ABOVE A z?
104 003A  77 24                          JA      NEXT_BYTE ; YES, IGNORE IT - GO TO NEXT_BYTE
105
106                          ; here it is a small letter
107                          ; so check to see if it needs to be capitalized
108
109 003C  80 FC 00                       CMP     AH,00H   ; HAS A LETTER BEEN CAPITALIZED ALREADY?
110 003F  77 1F                          JA      NEXT_BYTE ; YES, SO IGNORE IT - GO TO NEXT_BYTE
111
112 0041  2C 20                          SUB     AL,20H   ; CONVERT IT TO UPPER CASE
113 0043  88 04                          MOV     [SI],AL  ; SAVE THE NEW BYTE IN THE STRING
114 0045  B4 01                          MOV     AH,01H   ; SET DONE 1 CAP SWITCH
115
116 0047  EB 17 90                       JMP     NEXT_BYTE ; GO TO NEXT_BYTE
```

Microsoft (R) Macro Assembler Version 5.10   9/2/88 07:58:35

PGM8 FIGURE 5-4   CAP_RTN SUBROUTINE AND TESTER PGM   Page   2-2
CAP_RTN CAPITALIZE THE FIRST LETTER OF A STRING

```
117                                      PAGE
118
119 004A                      CHECK_CAP:
120
121                          ; find out if it is a capital letter or not
122
123 004A  3C 5A                          CMP     AL,5AH   ; IS IT A Z OR LESS?
124 004C  77 12                          JA      NEXT_BYTE ; NO SO IGNORE IT - GO TO NEXT_BYTE
125
```

FIGURE 5–4   continued

```
126 004E  3C 41                      CMP   AL,41H  ; IS IT LESS THAN AN A?
127 0050  72 0E                      JB    NEXT_BYTE ; YES, SO IGNORE IT - GO TO NEXT_BYTE
128
129                       ; here it is a capital letter
130                       ; so find out if it is to be left as is or changed to lower case
131
132 0052  80 FC 00                   CMP   AH,00H  ; HAS 1 CAP BEEN DONE?
133 0055  75 05                      JNE   UNCAP   ; YES IT HAS, SO UNCAPITALIZE IT
134
135 0057  B4 01                      MOV   AH,01H  ; LEAVE IT CAPPED BUT SET 1 CAP DONE
136 0059  EB 05 90                   JMP   NEXT_BYTE ; GO ON TO NEXT_BYTE
137
138 005C              UNCAP:
139 005C  04 20                      ADD   AL,20H  ; CONVERT CAP TO LOWER CASE
140 005E  88 04                      MOV   [SI],AL ; SAVE NEW CHARACTER IN STRING
141
142 0060              NEXT_BYTE:
143
144 0060  46                         INC   SI      ; BUMP TO GET TO NEXT BYTE OF STRING
145 0061  E2 CF                      LOOP  BIG_LOOP ; CONTINUE TILL ALL BYTES DONE
146
147 0063  5E                         POP   SI      ; RESTORE SI
148 0064  59                         POP   CX      ; RESTORE CX
149 0065  58                         POP   AX      ; RESTORE AX
150
151 0066  C3                         RET           ; RETURN
152
153 0067              CAP_RTN   ENDP
154
155 0067              PGMCD  ENDS
156
157                              END   MAIN
```

```
Microsoft (R) Symbolic Debug Utility  Version 4.00
Copyright (C) Microsoft Corp 1984, 1985.  All rights reserved.

Processor is [8086]

-G 5

AX=56EB  BX=0000  CX=00B7  DX=0000  SP=0040  BP=0000  SI=0000  DI=0000
DS=56EB  ES=56D7  SS=56E7  CS=56EC  IP=0005   NV UP EI PL NZ NA PO NC
56EC:0005 8D360000     LEA   SI,[0000]                 DS:0000=6163

-D DS:00,0F

56EB:0000   63 61 74 43 41 54 63 61-54 31 32 33 20 43 41 54   catCATcaT123 CAT

-G 27
```

FIGURE 5–4 continued

(Continues)

```
AX=56EB  BX=0000  CX=0007  DX=0000  SP=0040  BP=0000  SI=0009  DI=0000
DS=56EB  ES=56D7  SS=56E7  CS=56EC  IP=0027   NV UP EI PL NZ AC PO NC
56EC:0027 B000          MOV   AL,00
```

-D DS:00,0F


```
56EB:0000  43 61 74 43 61 74 43 61-74 31 32 33 20 43 61 74   CatCatCat123 Cat
```

-Q
A>

FIGURE 5–4 continued

CX contains the length of that string. To ensure that only the first **letter** is
capitalized, register AH is going to become an indicator switch. As long as
AH contains 00H, no letter has as yet been capitalized. When the program
finds the first letter and capitalizes it, register AH will be set to 01H,
indicating that a letter has been found. Then, as subsequent capital letters
are found and if AH is equal to 01H, those letters will be converted to
lowercase.

Register SI points to the string and the next byte to check; you could
reference that byte by entering

$$[SI]$$

However, since there will be many references to that byte, faster execution
and more convenient coding will result if you put the byte to check into a
register. In this example the byte is put into register AL.

CAP_RTN begins by saving all the registers that it will use and by
setting the indicator switch, AH, to 00H. BIG_LOOP marks the start, or top,
of the master loop that will process every byte in the string. The current byte
to examine is loaded into register AL. If the byte is binarily less than an "a,"
further checking is needed to determine what must be done with it. But if it
is above a "z," skip that byte, since it is not even a letter.

If the letter is equal to or greater than "a" and less than or equal to 2,
the letter really is lowercase. Now the remaining question is whether the
letter has already been capitalized or not. If it has, then nothing further
must be done with this byte; control passes to the bottom of the loop and
repeats the process on the next byte. On the other hand, if a letter has not
yet been capitalized, then the program capitalizes it and the indicator
register AH is set to contain 01H. The new value is inserted into the string
and control passes on to get the next byte.

At the CHECK_CAP section, the program has determined that the
current value is less than an "a." But is it a capital letter or some control
code, number, or special character? If the byte is above a "Z," then it must be
a special character. If it is, then the program ignores it and gets the next byte

of the string. If it is not above "Z," then it must determine if the value is a control code—that is, below an "A." If the value is below an "A," then the program ignores it and gets the next byte.

If the byte is a capital letter, then two possibilities exist: you have already had a capital letter and this byte must be converted to lowercase, or there has not yet been a capital letter and this byte stays as is while the AH is set to 01H (indicating the presence of the first capital letter).

Study the debugging output to satisfy yourself that CAP_RTN does work correctly.

5.16 SUMMARY

You have seen that subroutines begin with a PROC directive that also provides a name to the subroutine. They end with the ENDP directive. A routine is invoked with the CALL instruction, and the module returns control back to the caller with a RET instruction.

Commonly, the first action of any subroutine is to save the contents of any register that it will modify. The final action is to restore those registers. These actions are handled by the PUSH and POP instructions, which place on and remove words from the stack.

The stack is a LIFO storage area. That is, the last word stored onto the stack is the first word removed from the stack.

Subroutine calls and returns also place words onto the stack. If the procedure to be called is within the caller's code segment, only the return offset address (for the IP register) must be placed onto the stack. Such subroutines are referred to as NEAR procedures. When the procedure is not within the caller's code segment, two words must be placed onto the stack to identify the vector address of the return point after the call. Therefore, the CS register is also pushed onto the stack in addition to the offset address or IP. Such procedures are referred to as FAR procedures.

The PROC directive allows you to specify the type of procedure that is needed. If no option is coded, then NEAR is assumed. If the procedure is to be a FAR procedure, then use the FAR option on the PROC directive.

Three cases arise when moving strings: both the sending and receiving fields can be the same length, the receiving field can be shorter (resulting in truncation of the sending field), and the receiving field can be longer (necessitating the padding of the longer string). Character fields are filled from the left to the right, with padding done with blanks on the right. ASCII number strings are filled from right to left, with padding done with 0's on the left.

These principles can be implemented in two ways: by directly using the names of the fields within the subroutine to move them or by passing the addresses and the lengths of the fields to the subroutine. You have seen that when the direct names are used within the move routine, then the subroutine cannot be used to move any fields other than those for which it was originally designed. Thus, if there are 10 fields to move, 10 similar subroutines are needed.

The best approach is to write one generalized subroutine that receives the addresses and lengths of the two fields. A generalized subroutine can be used to move any field. The generalized subroutine is the most important concept of this chapter. You must learn to design your routines in such a manner that they can be used universally.

Perhaps you have noticed that the programs presented so far do not input or output any data. In the next chapter you will discuss how I/O operations are performed.

5.17   REVIEW QUESTIONS

1. What happens if a subroutine is invoked by a JMP instruction and ends with a RET instruction? Explain by showing a drawing of the stack.

2. What is the difference between a NEAR and FAR procedure? What effects do these two types have on the stack?

3. What happens if a routine is actually a FAR procedure but is called as if it were a NEAR procedure? What happens if the routine is a NEAR procedure but is called as if it were a FAR procedure? Explain why one of these works and the other does not.

4. Explain the differences between an internal subroutine and an external subroutine.

5. What is meant by LIFO? Explain the concept of a LIFO stack. How does it differ from a last-in, last-out stack?

6. Outline the steps that occur during the execution of the instructions in parts a through g.

```
a)  PUSH   AX
b)  POP    AX
c)  CALL   CALCS    ; where CALCS is a NEAR procedure
d)  CALL   CALCS    ; where CALCS is a FAR procedure
e)  RET             ; from a NEAR procedure
f)  PUSHF
g)  POPF
```

7. What happens if a subroutine ends with a JMP instruction but was invoked by a CALL instruction? Use a drawing to show the effects of this on the stack.

8. A programmer coded the following series of instructions. What will result? How can the errors be corrected?

```
CALC PROC NEAR
     PUSH AX
     PUSH DI
     PUSH BX
     PUSH SI
     PUSH CX
     PUSH DX


     . . .

     POP DI
     POP CX
     POP BX
     POP SI
     POP AX
     POP DI
     RET
CALC ENDP
```

9. Outline the three possible situations involved with moving ASCII character strings. What differences occur if the string is actually composed of ASCII numbers?

10. What is meant by a generalized subroutine? Why is a generalized routine preferable over a routine that uses the actual field names and specific lengths?

11. What happens if the programmer enters

```
        PUSH AH
```

Why?

12. What is meant by padding and truncation of strings?

13. Why do the PAGE + and SUBTTL commands often precede a PROC directive?

5.18 PRACTICE PROBLEMS

1. Make a drawing to show the effects of executing the following series of commands:

```
        PUSH AX
        PUSH BX
        POP  CX
        CALL CALCS
        POP  DX
```

where

```
                        CALCS  PROC      NEAR
                               RET
                        CALCS  ENDP
```

2. Code the shell instructions for a subroutine to be known as OUTPUT_REC, which will output a record to a master file. At entry to the routine, register DX should contain the address of the record to output; register CX should contain the number of bytes to write.

    Code the PAGE, SUBTTL, PROC, and ENDP directives needed. Create appropriate comment lines at the start of the routine. Code the saving and restoring of the registers AX, BX, CX, and DX. Include the RET instruction as well. Do not attempt to code the actual instructions needed to do such an action (you'll learn the output instructions in a later chapter).

3. Examine the following code. Outline exactly what will occur as the program executes. Assume that the subroutines will perform the activity roughly indicated by their names. Hint: As you follow the code, sketch the effects upon the stack.

```
MAIN                          PROC   FAR
        ...

        CALL   MAIN_PROCESS_LOOP
        ...
MAIN                          ENDP


MAIN_PROCESS_LOOP   PROC

        CALL   DO_CALCS
GOON:
        CALL   OUTPUT_RESULTS
        RET

MAIN_PROCESS_LOOP   ENDP


DO_CALCS                      PROC
        ...                           ; calculations are done here
        JMP    GOON
DO_CALCS                      ENDP


OUTPUT_RESULTS                PROC
        ...                           ; results of calculations
printed
        RET
OUTPUT_RESULTS                ENDP
```

5.19   PROGRAMMING PROBLEMS

1. Write a program that sequentially calls the following subroutines:

   ADD_UP   adds COST to TOTAL
   SUB_IT   subtracts AMOUNT from TOTAL

   The fields are defined as:

   ```
   COST     DW     25
   TOTAL    DW     52
   AMOUNT   DW     18
   ```

   Be sure to include PAGE + and SUBTTL directives as appropriate. Use the debugger to show that the program works correctly.

2. One common problem is menu selection processing. A screen displays a series of possible actions, the user enters his or her choice, and the program then performs the required processing. Assume that the menu program is a child's math helper. The menu looks like this:

   ```
   1.     Addition
   2.     Subtraction
   3.     Multiplication
   4.     Division

   ENTER THE NUMBER OF YOUR CHOICE __
   ```

   The main procedure has displayed the menu and received a valid choice—an ASCII 1, 2, 3, or 4—and has stored that digit in the field CHOICE.

   Write a program that calls the appropriate subroutine based on the value of CHOICE. Of course, your program will not have any of the display and enter valid choice coding, nor will your program actually be called from one that did. Just code the needed comparisons and subroutine calls and set up the subroutines correctly.

   The names of the four routines that you will call are ADD_RTN, SUB_RTN, MUL_RTN, and DIV_RTN.

   Code each routine. However, these routines will **not** do the indicated processing; rather, move 01H to a corresponding field that can then be examined by the debugger to verify that the routine was properly invoked. The fields needed are

   ```
   CHOICE   DB     '1'
   IN_ADD   DB     0
   IN_SUB   DB     0
   IN_MUL   DB     0
   IN_DIV   DB     0
   ```

Use the debugger to verify that if CHOICE contains 1,
IN_ADD contains 01H. Then alter the contents of CHOICE with
your word processor and reassemble the code. Using the debugger,
verify that your program gets to the appropriate routine indicated
by the value in CHOICE.

Once you learn how to handle the I/O and the math, the
program can be used as a model for creating a child's math helper
program.

3. Modify the generalized ASCII character-mover subroutine to work
for ASCII number strings. You need to move the fields from right to
left, truncate on the left, and pad with 0 instead of a blank. The
routine should accept the four needed values in the same registers
as the ASCII mover routine did.

The driver, or MAIN, procedure should call this number-mover
subroutine three times, testing for the three cases: equal-length
fields, receiving string shorter than sending field, and receiving
field longer than sending field. Use the debugger to verify that the
routine works correctly.

4. For use in word processing applications, write a generalized
subroutine that converts a string completely into uppercase. Upon
subroutine entry, register SI should contain the address of the
string to be converted; register CX should contain the string's
length in bytes. The MAIN procedure should test the subroutine
with several test cases, as the case studies in this chapter did.

6
Basic DOS Screen and Keyboard Services

6.1 CHAPTER OBJECTIVES

In this chapter you will

1. Examine the three methods for handling I/O operations and understand the advantages and disadvantages of each
2. Study the fundamentals of using DOS services
3. Learn how the interrupt system functions and how the interrupt handler operates
4. Study how the INT (interrupt) command works with DOS function numbers
5. Learn to code DOS service requests for I/O operations on the keyboard, screen, and printer

6.2 INTRODUCTION

So far, you have learned about the assembler directives that define a program shell, the basic set of assembler instructions needed in nearly all programs, the fundamentals of stack operation, and—most important—how to design and code generalized and functional internal subroutines. The remaining major piece of the programming puzzle to be covered is the input/output (I/O) operation.

Until now, no input or output operations have been performed. All the required values have been defined within the data area and all results were left in the data area. The only way you could examine the results was by using the debugger program as it displayed the data area values.

This chapter presents I/O operations. It begins with a discussion of the three major methods for handling I/O operations, including their advantages and disadvantages. Then, you will learn about I/O operations in relation to the keyboard, the screen, and the printer.

6.3 THE THREE METHODS OF HANDLING I/O

Selecting the way a program will handle I/O operations can be a major decision for a programmer. Three choices are available. First, the program can request I/O services from the Disk Operating System; these services are known as **DOS services.** Second, the program may ask for an I/O operation from a set of programs held in read-only memory; these programs are called **ROM-BIOS services.** Third, it is possible to write detailed code that will directly access the device by using the assembler **direct IN and OUT I/O instructions.** These three choices are illustrated in Figure 6–1. Naturally, each technique has its advantages and disadvantages.

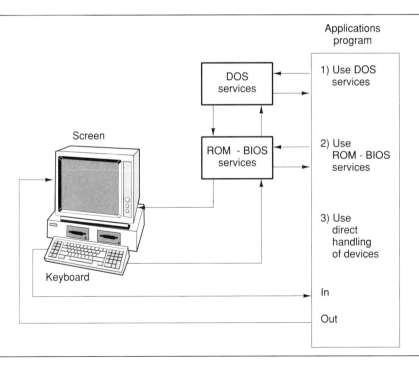

FIGURE 6–1   Three methods for handling I/O operations

6.4   THE DOS SERVICES

The DOS services are the easiest of the three to use. All you do is ask for the next entire line of input from the keyboard, or ask to print a message, or ask to read the next record from a disk file. When you make one of these requests, DOS handles all the work.

This is the preferred method when **program portability** is desired. If a program is portable, it executes correctly on many different machines. If DOS runs on a given computer and if the program uses DOS I/O services, then the program most likely will run correctly. Therefore, when MS/DOS is in control of the I/O function, the program gains maximum compatibility and portability between machines.

A further benefit occurs when new releases of DOS are made available: The program will still run. This will not necessarily be true with the other two methods.

The real drawback of DOS services is lack of flexibility. For example, with DOS services it is usually difficult to control the exact row and column where messages appear on the screen. In addition, color is difficult to control. (The ANSII.SYS driver program can be used in an attempt to remedy this deficiency.) Also, DOS services can be significantly slower than a direct write to memory, the method ROM-BIOS services uses. When it comes to processing files on disk, however, DOS file services are excellent.

6.5   ROM-BIOS SERVICES

ROM-BIOS services give the programmer a great deal of control over the various I/O devices. Particularly powerful are the services used to handle the screen display and keyboard input.

A major disadvantage is that the use of ROM-BIOS services adds a significant amount of code to the programming application. This is because the program must now furnish much of the code that DOS services normally provide. Also, if I/O requests are written at this level, some program portability is sacrificed. The program will still run on another machine but only if that machine is ROM-BIOS–compatible with IBM machines. Not all the so-called compatibles are compatible at this low level. In addition, future releases of the operating system may create a need for major program modifications or updates. This may also become a problem in maintaining the program.

Since many IBM compatibles are fully ROM-BIOS compatible and since ROM-BIOS provides substantial control over the screen, many programs use ROM-BIOS services for screen and keyboard control, thus bypassing DOS. This often results in fast programs. Yet, few programs use ROM-BIOS services for normal file handling because the code needed to program these activities is too complex. Besides, DOS—as the name Disk Operating System implies—handles file operations extremely well.

6.6 USING THE DIRECT IN AND OUT I/O INSTRUCTIONS

The third method of handling I/O operations is to write the code that will directly access any device required by the program and bypass the operating system completely. This, of course, gives the program complete control over all the steps involved. The I/O operations are handled precisely as the program directs.

Such programs are seldom, if ever, portable. It is likely that a separate version of these I/O routines must be written for each different computer on which the program is to be run. Even newer models of the same brand of computer may require a complete rewrite.

Writing at such a low level generates an enormous volume of code. Therefore, very few programmers ever attempt to write their own I/O routines; it's just not practical.

When would the use of direct I/O instructions be considered? One common situation in which it might be appropriate is when direct IN and OUT control is needed for an unsupported device that has been attached to the computer.

6.7 APPROACHES TO THE THREE DOS SERVICES

You will begin the study of basic input/output operations by using DOS services for the screen and keyboard. In the next chapter similar ROM-BIOS services will be examined for the screen only. DOS file-handling services will be covered in Chapter 9. We will not cover direct IN and OUT instructions.

6.8 THE INTERRUPT SYSTEM

The operating system handles all requests for its services (DOS or ROM-BIOS) by a unique scheme known as interrupts. The word *interrupt* means to break the continuity of an action and pursue another action. How does this apply to a program?

Normal program execution is serial. That is, the program executes each instruction sequentially, one after another. It does not alter this pattern unless it performs jumps, conditional branching, procedure calls, and so on. When an operating system service—either DOS or ROM-BIOS—is needed, normal program execution is interrupted at that point. The operating system then gives control to the part of the operating system (DOS or ROM-BIOS) that handles the type of service requested. These specialized operating system routines then perform the required task. When finished, the operating system returns control to the program and allows it to resume its normal execution from the point where the interrupt occurred.

The instruction that notifies the operating system that the program wants to use one of its services is called the INT instruction. INT is short for *interrupt*. When you see an INT instruction, interpret it as saying "Operating system, please interrupt the program at this point and perform a task for it."

6.9   THE INT INSTRUCTION

All the DOS services requests are handled by the INT instruction. The syntax is

INT   operand

The operand is a numeric identifier that indicates the system service routine required. There are literally hundreds of interrupt routines. Many of these should not be invoked by application programs because they are usable only by DOS. The operand may be written in either decimal or hexadecimal form. To avoid any confusion, this book gives all INT operands in hex format.

Theoretically, the interrupt operand numbers can range from 00H to FFH. The lower values, 00H to 19H, are used for system control and ROM-BIOS. The next group, 20H to 3FH, is reserved for DOS services. The general-use codes, which range from 40H to 67H, are reserved for applications programs in which there is a need to create separate interrupt systems. The highest numbered values, 68H to FFH, are either used by the BASIC programming language or are reserved for some special use.

When an interrupt occurs, that part of the operating system known as the **interrupt handler** finds the vector address (segment and offset addresses) of the desired routine that corresponds to the value of the operand. Control is then passed to the appropriate system subroutine.

Many of these functions require one or more parameters. For example, if you want to print a specific character on the printer, then the display routine needs to have that character passed to it. Likewise, if a string is to be displayed on the screen, then DOS needs to have the address of that string.

Parameters are passed to the interrupt routines by various registers. Therefore, skill in using the system interrupts consists of knowing the routine numbers and what belongs in which register. If incorrect values are placed in the registers, just what will occur is totally unpredictable. The vast majority of INT errors made by beginning programmers consist of having the correct information in the wrong registers or failing to supply all the required parameters.

Finally, several of the main interrupts have numerous subfunctions. DOS services has the largest number of these. Normally, most applications programs use just one DOS service interrupt—number 21H. This DOS interrupt can be called upon to perform over a hundred different subfunctions from just one invocation. To determine which subfunction is needed, the interrupt requires a subfunction number commonly known as a **DOS function number.** This number is held in register AH. Such single INTs that have many subfunctions are known as umbrella calls.

When the INT instruction is executed and an interrupt occurs, the system pushes the flag register and the CS:IP registers onto the stack, thereby preserving the path back to the program environment. When the INT is complete, it restores those registers, using the POP instruction. Therefore, each INT needs 6 bytes of stack storage. It is your responsibility, as the programmer, to make sure that the stack is large enough.

Having covered the basic concepts underlying the DOS services, now see how they are requested.

6.10   INVOKING DOS SERVICES

All DOS services are invoked by using the interrupt instruction and requesting service 21H (DOS I/O services). The code is

```
        INT  21H   ; CALL DOS
```

Since this function (21H) is used for every DOS I/O request, another parameter must be provided that identifies which subfunction is needed. The subfunction, known as the DOS function number, tells DOS I/O services whether this request is for keyboard input, displaying a line on the screen, or writing a character on the printer.

The function number of the desired DOS service **must** be in register AH. In addition, the other registers involved **must** contain any other parameters that are unique to that request, such as the character to display.
Now examine these functions in detail.

6.11   DOS KEYBOARD AND CRT FUNCTION CALLS

DOS Function 0AH: Buffered Keyboard Input

Function number 0AH is used to input a complete field. Each character is displayed, or echoed, on the screen as it is entered. When you enter a carriage return by pressing ENTER, DOS returns control to the program with the value entered being stored in the program's data area. (When the function is finished, it **does not** send a carriage return/line feed command to the CRT to move the cursor down to the next display line. The effects of this limitation are discussed later.)

From the standpoint of programming ease, using buffered keyboard input is the simplest way to input values. All DOS editing keys—such as BACKSPACE and the arrow keys—function as you normally expect. This makes correcting errors very easy.

Function 0AH requires an **input buffer area,** which tells DOS how many bytes to enter and provides a place to store those bytes. The input buffer consists of three fields defined in a precise format. Each of these fields must be the correct size and in the correct order.

The first byte of the input buffer area must contain the maximum length of the string to be entered. The value in the second byte is filled by DOS with the number of bytes that are actually input. Even though the carriage return (ASCII <CR>) is input and stored in the input string, it is not counted in the actual length. The remainder of the bytes hold the input data as they are entered, including the ending <CR>.

The carriage return has a value of 0DH and is stored at the end of the input bytes. Therefore, if a maximum of 16 bytes of data are entered, the complete input buffer area must be 19 bytes: 16 for the data, 1 for the <CR>, 1 for maximum length, and 1 for the actual length.

The maximum-length string that the command processor of DOS handles is 128 bytes plus 2 for the lengths. However, since the carriage return is also stored, the realistic maximum length for a string is 127 bytes, even though it is possible to specify 255 bytes in the maximum-length byte.

Normally, a small structure is set up in the program to define this input buffer area. Suppose that the program is to input a message that can contain up to 16 bytes. The structure that defines the input buffer area is

```
MSG_STRUC   LABEL   BYTE
MAX_LEN     DB      16
ACT_LEN     DB      ?
MSG         DB      17 DUP(?)
```

How does DOS know where the input buffer area is? Its address must be passed to function 0AH in a register. What, then, are the register requirements for function 0AH? Register AH contains 0AH. In addition, registers DS:DX must contain the vector address of the input buffer area. Since DS normally contains the data segment address in beginning programs, all that needs to be done is to load the offset address of the input buffer area into register DX. The following inputs the 16-byte field described.

```
LEA   DX,MSG_STRUC   ; DX = ADDRESS OF INPUT STRUCTURE
MOV   AH,0AH         ; SET FOR BUFFERED KEYBOARD INPUT
INT   21H            ; CALL DOS
```

This type of structure (MSG_STRUC) is a very common control block structure. Frequently, the three fields are accessed by offset from the start. If you enter

```
LEA   BX,MSG_STRUC
```

then [BX]+0 is the maximum length; [BX]+1 is the actual length; and [BX]+2 points to the first byte of the message.

Suppose, for example, you want to input several fields: first name, last name, address, and cost. Once entered, these fields are to be used to build an output record for a disk file. Since fields within a record must be in consecutive storage locations, you want to keep the four definitions together as a record structure. The fields can be defined as

```
OUT_REC LABEL BYTE
FNAME   DB    10 DUP(' ')
LNAME   DB    15 DUP(' ')
ADDRESS DB    25 DUP(' ')
COST    DB     5 DUP('0')
```

How can these be entered using function 0AH? It would be possible to define four small sets of input buffer areas, perform four INT 21Hs to input the fields, and move each value entered into its corresponding field in OUT_REC. Although this method works, it generates a lot of redundant code, it is cumbersome, and it is error-prone. In this example, defining four small areas would mean that you would have to debug four sets of DOS calls, one for each field.

As previously indicated, you should not write specific subroutines for each situation; rather, create generalized routines. Create one input subroutine that uses just one input area. The area should be large enough to hold the largest field needed, ADDRESS in this case. Then, before each function call is made, move the current maximum length to be requested into the maximum-length field. To create the required input buffer area, enter

```
IN_AREA LABEL BYTE
MAX_LEN DB    ?
ACT_LEN DB    ?
AREA    DB    26 DUP(?)
```

Thus, the maximum length for a specific entry can be inserted into MAX_LEN, and then a call to DOS can be made to input the data into AREA. After the input operation is complete and before the next input operation modifies the value in AREA, the data in AREA are moved to the corresponding field in the OUT_REC record area. This procedure can be repeated for as many fields as necessary.

The generalized input subroutine, called GET_FLD, handles the DOS input operation for all fields. It is also necessary to create a MOVER procedure to copy the data from the input buffer area (AREA) into the actual field in the OUT_REC record. Figure 6–2 (PGM9.ASM on the program disk) contains a listing of the complete program to solve this problem.

Actually, there are three more complications. First, the MOVER procedure assumes that the receiving fields already contain blanks, and it copies only the characters that are actually entered. This is the case the first time, since OUT_REC fields can be initialized to blanks. But what happens if the entire series is repeated for several sets of data? If the new values are shorter, parts of the previous values may remain at the end of the fields. Obviously, the four fields in OUT_REC must be cleared or blanked out. A solution is to use the generalized ASCII_MOVE procedure shown in the

```
        PAGE    60,132
        TITLE   PGM9 FIGURE 6-2 GET FOUR FIELDS VIA FUNCTION 0AH


;************************************************************************
; PGM9        Title: Figure 6-2 Input four fields using function 0AH  *
;                                                                     *
; Programmer: Vic Broquard                                            *
; Date Written:  6/11/88        Date Of Last Revision: 8/4/88         *
;                                                                     *
; Purpose: Inputs first and last names, address, and cost fields      *
;                                                                     *
; Special Requirements:                                               *
;                                                                     *
;   GET_FLD: inputs a field via function 0AH into a common input area *
;            AH = requested field's length on entry                   *
;            AH = actual field's length on exit                       *
;                                                                     *
;   MOVER: moves the data from the common input area to the field area*
;            AH = field's length                                      *
;            BX = address of receiving field                          *
;                                                                     *
;************************************************************************


; program code segment

PGMCD   SEGMENT

MAIN    PROC    FAR

; housekeeping section

    ASSUME  CS:PGMCD,DS:PGMDA,SS:PGMSTK

    MOV   AX,PGMDA  ; ESTABLISH ADDRESSABILITY
    MOV   DS,AX     ; TO PGMDA - THE PGM'S DATA SEGMENT

; main process section

    MOV   AH,10    ; SET AH = LENGTH NEEDED FOR FIRST NAME
    CALL GET_FLD   ; GET THE FIRST NAME FIELD
    LEA   BX,FNAME ; BX = ADDR OF FNAME FIELD TO BE FILLED
    CALL MOVER     ; MOVE DATA TO FNAME FIELD

    MOV   AH,15    ; SET AH = LENGTH NEEDED FOR LAST NAME
    CALL GET_FLD   ; GET THE LAST NAME FIELD
    LEA   BX,LNAME ; BX = ADDR OF LNAME FIELD TO BE FILLED
    CALL MOVER     ; MOVE DATA TO LNAME

    MOV   AH,25    ; SET AH = LENGTH NEEDED FOR ADDRESS
```

FIGURE 6–2 Program to input and move data by using 0AH   *(Continues)*

```
        CALL GET_FLD   ; GET THE ADDRESS FIELD
        LEA  BX,ADDRESS ; BX = ADDR OF ADDRESS FIELD TO BE FILLED
        CALL MOVER     ; MOVE DATA TO ADDRESS


        MOV  AH,5      ; SET AH = LENGTH NEEDED FOR COST

- - - - - - - - - - - - - - - - - - - - - - - - - - - - - - - - - - - - - - - - - - - - - - - - - - - - -

        CALL GET_FLD   ; GET THE COST FIELD
        LEA  BX,COST   ; BX = ADDR OF COST FIELD TO BE FILLED
        CALL MOVER     ; MOVE DATA TO COST

; return to DOS section

        MOV  AL,0      ; SET 0 AS THE RETURN CODE FOR DOS
        MOV  AH,4CH    ; SET FOR DOS END PROCESS FUNCTION
        INT  21H       ; CALL DOS TO END PROGRAM

MAIN    ENDP
        PAGE


GET_FLD  PROC


; perform DOS function 0AH buffered keyboard input


; on entry, AH = length of current request
; on exit,  AH = actual length of current entry

        PUSH DX              ; SAVE CALLER'S DX REGISTER

        MOV  MAX_LEN,AH      ; FIX MAX_LEN OF THIS REQUEST
        MOV  AH,0AH          ; SET FOR DOS BUFFERED KEYBOARD INPUT
        LEA  DX,IN_AREA      ; DX = ADDR OF BUFFER AREA

        INT  21H            ; CALL DOS TO INPUT A LINE

        MOV  AH,ACT_LEN      ; SET RETURN VALUE OF ACTUAL LENGTH

        POP  DX             ; RESTORE CALLER'S DX REGISTER

        RET                 ; RETURN TO CALLER
GET_FLD  ENDP
        PAGE

MOVER    PROC

; MOVER will move the data entered to the receiving field

; at entry, AH = number of bytes to move
; at entry, BX = address of the receiving field
```

FIGURE 6-2 continued

```
      MOV  CH,0     ; CLEAR HIGH PART OF CX
      MOV  CL,AH    ; SET NUMBER OF BYTES TO MOVE IN LOOP REG
      LEA  SI,AREA  ; SI = SENDING FIELD ADDRESS

SMALL_LOOP:

      MOV  AH,[SI]  ; GET A BYTE
      MOV  [BX],AH  ; STORE THE BYTE

      INC  SI       ; POINT TO NEXT SENDING BYTE
      INC  BX       ; POINT TO NEXT RECEIVING BYTE
----------------------------------------------------------------------------

      LOOP SMALL_LOOP ; REPEAT MOVE UNTIL CX = 0

      RET             ; RETURN WITH THE FIELD FILLED

MOVER    ENDP

PGMCD  ENDS
      PAGE

; program data segment

PGMDA   SEGMENT

OUT_REC LABEL  BYTE          ; THE CUSTOMER SET OF DATA AREA
FNAME   DB     10 DUP(' ')  ; FIRST NAME
LNAME   DB     15 DUP(' ')  ; LAST NAME
ADDRESS DB     25 DUP(' ')  ; ADDRESS OF CUSTOMER
COST    DB      5 DUP('0')  ; COST OF GOODS ORDERED


IN_AREA LABEL  BYTE         ; I/O CONTROL BLOCK USED FOR DOS BUFFERED INPUT
MAX_LEN DB     ?            ; PROVIDED BY CALLER
ACT_LEN DB     ?            ; FILLED IN BY DOS - ACTUAL NUMBER OF BYTES INPUT
AREA    DB     26 DUP(?) ; THE DATA INPUT

PGMDA  ENDS


; program stack segment

PGMSTK  SEGMENT PARA STACK 'STACK'

        DW     32 DUP (?)

PGMSTK  ENDS
        END
```

FIGURE 6–2 continued

previous chapter. It can move the new characters and then fill the remaining bytes of the receiving field with blanks.

Second, if the number field COST is to be in the proper numeric format, it needs to be filled from the right to the left and padded with 0 digits instead of blanks.

Third, when function 0AH is finished, it does not output a carriage return/line feed (a **CRLF** combination) to the CRT to skip to the beginning of the next line. What happens? Each of the input fields is displayed on top of the others on the screen. The data are entered correctly; it's just that the display is unacceptable. To see this effect first hand, copy, assemble, link, and execute program PGM9.ASM.

To remedy the display problem, you need to use the display functions that will force CRLFs after each line of data entry. How this can be done will be discussed next.

As you have seen, many steps are involved in handling even a simple action such as inputting a set of data. The only practical way to handle such a workload is to create functional subroutines. To avoid repetitive code, these subroutines should be generalized.

Now that you have created general subroutines by which data can be entered, consider how data can be displayed on the screen.

DOS Function 09H: Display String

Function 09H displays a complete message on the screen. The message can be of any length, but **must** end with a dollar sign. The dollar sign gives this function the location of the end of the string. The dollar sign itself is not displayed. If the dollar sign is erroneously omitted from the end of the string, DOS keeps on printing storage until it encounters a dollar sign. The screen appears to be displaying "garbage" until it finds a byte with a dollar sign in it. Obviously, this function cannot be used to print a string that contains a dollar sign as one of the data characters.

When the 09H function is invoked, register AH must contain 09H and registers DS:DX must hold the vector address of the message string to be displayed. Since DS normally contains the segment address of the data area, only DX must be set—typically, by a LEA instruction.

The following code causes an error message:

```
ERRMSG1  DB   'YOU HAVE ENTERED A VALUE OUT OF RANGE'
         DB   0DH, 0AH, 'PRESS ANY KEY TO CONTINUE$'


         LEA  DX,ERRMSG1    ; DX = ADDRESS OF STRING TO PRINT
         MOV  AH,09H        ; SET FOR DISPLAY STRING FUNCTION
         INT  21H           ; CALL DOS
```

Notice that there will be 2 lines printed on the screen. Why? Because you have embedded CRLF codes within the message. 0DH is the hex code for a carriage return and 0AH is hex for a line feed. Whenever possible, it is more

```
ENTER THE ADDRESS: xxxxxxxxxxxxxxxxxxxxxxxxx

THE ADDRESS ENTERED WAS:    xxxxxxxxxxxxxxxxxxxxxxxxx

IS THIS CORRECT - Y OR N? _
```

EXAMPLE 6–1   Data entry screen

efficient to use one DOS call to display several successive and related lines than to use many separate DOS calls.

Suppose the dialogue shown in Example 6–1 is being created for data entry. The storage layout for this display can be changed to make the design simpler by creating one very long message. The data areas can be defined as shown in Example 6–2.

In Example 6–2 SECOND_MSG is used for both input and output. For the input operation, function 0AH requires the first byte of ADDRESS to contain the maximum length. When the input operation is complete, DOS inserts the actual length into the second byte of ADDRESS. The data entered—including the ending carriage return, or 0DH, is placed in the remaining 26 bytes.

```
FIRST_MSG    DB 'ENTER THE ADDRESS: $'

SECOND_MSG  DB 0DH, 0AH                 ; CRLF - FORCES NEXT MSG TO NEW LINE
            DB 'THE ADDRESS ENTERED WAS:'
            DB 0DH, 0AH                 ; CRLF CODES

ADDRESS     DB 25                       ; MAX INPUT MSG LENGTH
            DB ?                        ; HOLDS THE ACTUAL LENGTH INPUT
            DB 26 DUP(?)                ; HOLDS THE MSG PLUS ENDING CR

                     ; FOR INPUT: BYTE 1 = MAX LEN    BYTE 2 = ACTUAL LEN
                     ; NEXT 26 BYTES ARE FOR THE DATA INCLUDING THE ENDING CR

                     ; FOR OUTPUT: REPLACE BYTE 1 BY 0DH AND BYTE 2 BY 0AH
                     ; TO PRODUCE A CARRIAGE RETURN AND LINE FEED COMBINATION

            DB 0DH, 0AH                 ; CRLF CODES
            DB 0DH, 0AH                 ; CRLF CODES

            DB 'IS THIS CORRECT - Y OR N? $'
```

EXAMPLE 6–2   Main storage data areas for the data entry screen

To display the SECOND_MSG, which asks for visual verification that the data have been entered correctly, the actual length must be saved in a register and the two byte lengths replaced by a carriage return and a line feed code (0DH and 0AH). Also, the carriage return that DOS stores within ADDRESS must be replaced. When the data have been verified as entered correctly, the field ADDRESS can be moved to an output record area, using the actual length that was saved in a register. Figure 6–3 (PGM10.ASM on the program disk) shows the complete program listing for this problem.

Notice that SECOND_MSG actually shows several screen lines, including the ADDRESS field (which is embedded within the display message). To accomplish this, the two byte lengths must be replaced with a CRLF. Other times, they can be replaced with blanks. In addition, the carriage return that keyboard input placed after the ADDRESS data must be replaced by a blank. If not, the remaining blanks will overprint the first characters of the address. This is because the carriage return places the cursor at the beginning of the line.

Experiment with this program. See what happens to the display if the CRLF code that replaces the two byte lengths is not included. See what the results are if the carriage return code is not removed from the end of the input buffer area. Make these changes and then run the program. Doing so will increase your understanding of the processes involved.

DOS functions 0AH (buffered keyboard input) and 09H (display string) can be used to handle many common I/O situations. However, there will be times when even more control over the I/O operation is desired. Such control is provided by these specialized functions:

DOS function 01H: keyboard input with echo and break key on
DOS function 08H: keyboard input without echo and break key on
DOS function 07H: keyboard input without echo and break key off

Functions 01H, 08H, 07H: Specialized Keyboard Input

The trio of specialized DOS functions all work in a similar way. A DOS services echo operation displays the character at the current cursor location and then advances the cursor location 1 byte. Before discussing these functions further, however, there are several keyboard concepts that must be understood.

On a personal computer the keyboard and the CRT are separate devices. When a character is input from the keyboard, it is **not** automatically printed on the screen. The character must be echoed (sent) to the CRT. There are several input services that echo the inputted character onto the screen. Function 0AH (buffered keyboard input) does this automatically. Normally, this is a highly desirable action. If the characters are not echoed, you are working in the dark because you won't know whether the correct data have been entered.

```
    PAGE    60,132
    TITLE   PGM10  FIGURE 6-3  DISPLAY STRINGS VIA FUNCTION 09H


;************************************************************************
; PGM10      Title: Display Strings Via Function 09H          *
;                                                             *
; Programmer: Vic Broquard                                    *
; Date Written:  6/11/88        Date Of Last Revision: 8/4/88 *
;                                                             *
; Purpose: To illustrate how to handle visual verification of input *
;          fields                                             *
; Special Requirements: none                                  *
;                                                             *
;************************************************************************


; program code segment

PGM10CD SEGMENT

MAIN    PROC  FAR

; housekeeping section

    ASSUME  CS:PGM10CD,DS:PGM10DA,SS:PGM10SK

    MOV  AX,PGM10DA       ; ESTABLISH ADDRESSABILITY
    MOV  DS,AX            ; TO PGM10DA - THE PGM'S DATA SEGMENT

; main process section

; display "enter data message"

    LEA  DX,FIRST_MSG     ; POINT TO BEGINNING MSG
    MOV  AH,09H           ; SET FOR DISPLAY MESSAGE
    INT  21H             ; CALL DOS TO DISPLAY THE ENTER ADDRESS MESSAGE

; input the field

    LEA  DX,ADDRESS       ; POINT TO ADDRESS INPUT BUFFER
    MOV  AH,0AH           ; SET FOR KEYBOARD BUFFERED INPUT
    INT  21H             ; CALL DOS TO INPUT ADDRESS

; remove the CR after the actual data in the field

    LEA  BX,ADDRESS+2     ; BX POINTS TO ACTUAL VALUE IN ADDRESS
    MOV  AH,00           ; 0 HIGH ORDER PART OF AX FOR NEXT ADD
    MOV  AL,ADDRESS+1     ; AL = ACTUAL LENGTH
    ADD  BX,AX           ; SET BX TO POINT TO CR IN MSG
    MOV  BYTE PTR[BX],' ' ; REPLACE CR WITH BLANK
```

FIGURE 6–3 Program to display strings by using 09H   *(Continues)*

useful when entering a series of digits into a number field. With function 0AH the program must subsequently right-justify the digits entered and left-fill with 0's. By using one of the trio, the field can be filled from the right to the left directly. Also, these functions permit the data being entered to be edited. For example, the program can force only numeric digits to be entered.

The answer to the first question depends upon the current need. Choose function 08H if the byte entered should not really be displayed on the screen. Such is the case with the response to the PRESS ANY KEY TO CONTINUE message. Similarly, it is wise to use function 08H if the program has created some special functions for some of the keys or if the program is to edit out any bad data entered. For example, if a number field is being entered, you allow only the digits 0 through 9 to be accepted. Finally, function 08H is useful for security purposes, when the display of passwords and other characters is not wanted.

Function 01H should be used when the byte is always to be displayed.

Function 07H should be used only when it is crucial that the current entry not be interrupted for any reason. Use this function very sparingly.

If a key has not yet been pressed when any one of the three input byte functions is invoked, the function waits until a key is pressed. Once entered, the character is returned in register AL.

In addition, the **type-ahead buffer** feature is in effect for these functions. This feature allows up to 16 characters to be entered rapidly, even though the program is actually inputting only the first character. The remaining characters are stored in the keyboard buffer. When the next character is requested by one of these function calls, the next sequential character is retrieved from the buffer. If more characters than the buffer can hold are entered, the keyboard refuses further entry and a beep sounds. (The keyboard buffer is also in effect for the buffered keyboard input function 0AH.)

Additional complexity arises when either a control code or a non-ASCII special key code is entered. A control code is an ASCII value that is used to control some aspect of CRT operation or a printer action. Examine Table 1–3, the ASCII coding scheme. The ASCII control codes range from 00H to 1FH plus 7FH. One of these, 03H, is the code for CTRL-C, a control break. A control code should be detected and handled or ignored as the situation dictates.

There are 97 special key actions that result in non-ASCII entry. These special codes are shown in Table 6–1. This table is also reproduced in Appendix B.

Each special key input generates a 2-byte input entry. However, register AL can hold only one of these bytes! Thus, whenever a special key is pressed, register AL contains 00H. This means that the program **must** immediately do another function call to receive the second byte of the special code, which is now in register AL. Programs using any of this trio of direct keyboard input functions must always check register AL for 00H first!

Once it has been determined that a control code or a special key has been entered, the program can handle the entry accordingly. Certain routine editing keystrokes—such as DEL, LEFT ARROW, BACKSPACE, CTRL-C, and

TABLE 6–1 The 97 Special Keys

Key pressed	Dec	Hex	Key pressed	Dec	Hex	Key pressed	Dec	Hex
F1	59	3B	ALT-1	120	78	HOME	71	47
F2	60	3C	ALT-2	121	79	UP ARROW	72	48
F3	60	3D	ALT-3	122	7A	PGUP	73	49
F4	62	3E	ALT-4	123	7B	LEFT ARROW	75	4B
F5	63	3F	ALT-5	124	7C	RIGHT ARROW	77	4D
F6	64	40	ALT-6	125	7D	END	79	4F
F7	65	41	ALT-7	126	7E	DOWN ARROW	80	50
F8	66	42	ALT-8	127	7F	PGDOWN	81	51
F9	67	43	ALT-9	128	80	INS	82	52
F10	68	44	ALT-10	129	81	DEL	83	53
SHIFT-F1	84	54	ALT-=	131	83	ALT-		
SHIFT-F2	85	55				HYPHEN	130	82
SHIFT-F3	86	56	ALT-A	30	1E			
SHIFT-F4	87	57	ALT-B	48	30	ECHO		
SHIFT-F5	88	58	ALT-C	46	2E	(CTRL-PRTSC)		
SHIFT-F6	89	59	ALT-D	32	20		114	72
SHIFT-F7	90	5A	ALT-E	18	12			
SHIFT-F8	91	5B	ALT-F	33	21	CTRL-LEFT ARROW		
SHIFT-F9	92	5C	ALT-G	34	22		115	73
SHIFT-F10	93	5D	ALT-H	35	23			
			ALT-I	23	17	CTRL-RIGHT ARROW		
CTRL-F1	94	5E	ALT-J	36	24		116	74
CTRL-F2	95	5F	ALT-K	37	25			
CTRL-F3	96	60	ALT-L	38	26	CTRL-END	117	75
CTRL-F4	97	61	ALT-M	50	32			
CTRL-F5	98	62	ALT-N	49	31	CTRL-PGDN		
CTRL-F6	99	63	ALT-O	24	18		118	76
CTRL-F7	100	64	ALT-P	25	19			
CTRL-F8	101	65	ALT-Q	16	10	CTRL-HOME		
CTRL-F9	102	66	ALT-R	19	13		119	77
CTRL-F10	103	67	ALT-S	31	1F			
			ALT-T	20	14	CTRL-PGUP		
ALT-F1	104	68	ALT-U	22	16		132	83
ALT-F2	105	69	ALT-V	47	2F			
ALT-F3	106	6A	ALT-W	17	11	NULL CHARACTER		
ALT-F4	107	6B	ALT-X	45	2D	CTRL-@	0	00
ALT-F5	108	6C	ALT-Y	21	15			
ALT-F6	109	6D	ALT-Z	44	2C	REVERSE TAB		
ALT-F7	110	6E				(SHIFT-TAB)		
ALT-F8	111	6F					15	0F
ALT-F9	112	70						
ALT-F10	113	71						

ESC—probably ought to be handled. It is at this point that a program can also handle editing of the data as they are being entered so that incorrect values are never accepted. If the entry is not a control code or special character and it is a valid entry, the program usually needs to store that character in main storage in an input area and perhaps echo it to the screen. Thus, GET_BYTE routines normally follow a checking order such as that shown in Example 6–3.

If there are only a few codes to validate, all checking and handling may be done in GET_BYTE. If there are numerous codes to check for and process, then it is best to set up several subroutines to handle the required processing of the codes.

Now consider a simple coding problem. Suppose that a menu is to be displayed on the screen to get the user's choice. That choice must be a number between 1 and 5. To input the number, DOS function 1 could be used, and no control or special codes permitted. Notice also that the entire menu can be displayed by a single display string command. Figure 6–4 (PGM11.ASM on the program disk) shows this coding.

There is one problem with this routine. If a value other than 1 through 5 is entered—9, for example—then the value 9 is rejected by the routine but is also displayed on the screen. This rejection forces the user to enter another number, such as 4. After keying the two numbers, the screen displays

94

This is because when the echo feature is on, the character is displayed at the current cursor location. Then the cursor advances one position. (Actually, only the 4 is accepted and entered into the program.) In this case, DOS function 08H is a better choice. With 08H the program will echo the value only when it is valid.

Next, consider the common PRESS ANY KEY TO CONTINUE situation. Here, function 08H is certainly the best choice. The coding is shown in Example 6–4. (The full coding is incorporated as part of PGM14.ASM on the program disk.)

Suppose you want to input a name that contains up to 10 characters. This is done by the function GET_NAME. If the name is only three characters in length, a carriage return ends the process. The carriage return can be identified by checking for 0DH in register AL. Thus, the main GET_A_BYTE loop can be terminated in two ways: 10 characters are entered or a carriage return is entered. To simplify this example, all special keys, such as the arrow keys, are ignored as are all control codes except the carriage return.

The GET_NAME procedure uses two switches to expedite control decisions. Register BL is used as the "premature done" flag: A 0 means not done and a 1 means done. Register BL is set by the CTRL_CODE procedure if a carriage return is entered. Register BH is used to represent the "good value" flag: A 0 means that the byte is not acceptable (a control code, special key, or not a letter) and a 1 means that the value is still valid. Register BH is set by various procedures when an invalid value is found.

```
GET_BYTE   PROC

    call DOS function to get next byte in AL

    if AL = 00H then call SPECIAL_KEY
    else do

        if AL < 20H or AL = 7FH then call CONTROL_CODE
        else do
            check for correct data, such as numeric
            If all is correct then do
                echo character to CRT
                move character to input work field
                INC as needed
            end do
            else either nothing needs to be done
                or perhaps the beeper could sound
        end do
    end do

GET_BYTE   ENDP

SPECIAL_KEY   PROC

    call DOS function again to get the next code in AL

    check AL for those code values that the program will
        be handling

    if one is found, call a procedure to handle that
        function or process it in-line

SPECIAL_KEY   ENDP

CONTROL_CODE   PROC

    check AL for those values that the program will be
        handling

    if one is found, call a proc to handle it or process it
        in-line

CONTROL_CODE   ENDP
```

EXAMPLE 6–3   Pseudocode for the GET_BYTE routine

```
            PAGE    60,132
            TITLE   PGM11  FIGURE 6-4  GET VALID MENU CHOICE


;**************************************************************************
; PGM11       Title: Figure 6-4 Get A Valid Menu Choice          *
;                                                                *
; Programmer: Vic Broquard                                       *
; Date Written:  6/11/88        Date Of Last Revision: 8/4/88    *
;                                                                *
; Purpose: To illustrate how to display a menu and get a valid menu  *
;          choice by using function 01H                          *
; Special Requirements: none                                     *
;                                                                *
;**************************************************************************
;

; program code segment

PGMCD   SEGMENT

MAIN    PROC    FAR

; housekeeping section

        ASSUME  CS:PGMCD,DS:PGMDA,SS:PGMSTK

        MOV  AX,PGMDA  ; ESTABLISH ADDRESSABILITY
        MOV  DS,AX     ; TO PGMDA - THE PGM'S DATA SEGMENT

; main process section

; display the menu

        MOV  AH,09H    ; SET FOR DISPLAY STRING
        LEA  DX,MENU   ; DX -> STRING TO DISPLAY
        INT  21H       ; CALL DOS TO DISPLAY MENU

; get the choice

REDO:

        MOV  AH,01H    ; SET FOR GET A BYTE FUNCTION
        INT  21H       ; CALL DOS TO GET A BYTE

        CMP  AL,00H    ; WAS A SPECIAL KEY ENTERED?
        JE   SPECIAL   ; YES, GO GET IT

        CMP  AL,31H    ; IS ENTRY LESS THAN A 1?
        JB   REDO      ; YES, GO GET IT AGAIN
```

FIGURE 6–4 Program to get valid menu choice (PGM11.ASM)

```
        CMP  AL,35H   ; IS ENTRY ABOVE A 5?
        JA   REDO     ; YES, GO GET IT AGAIN

        MOV  CHOICE,AL ; STORE GOOD VALUE IN CHOICE

---------------------------------------------------------------------

        JMP  DONE     ; GO RETURN - CHOICE IS SET

SPECIAL:

        MOV  AH,01H   ; SET FOR GET A BYTE
        INT  21H      ; CALL DOS TO GET SPECIAL CODE
        JMP  REDO     ; IGNORE IT

; return to DOS section

DONE:
        MOV  AL,0     ; SET 0 AS THE RETURN CODE FOR DOS
        MOV  AH,4CH   ; SET FOR DOS END PROCESS FUNCTION
        INT  21H      ; CALL DOS TO END PROGRAM

MAIN  ENDP

PGMCD ENDS


; program data segment

PGMDA  SEGMENT

MENU   DB  '      MASTER MENU', 0DH, 0AH, 0DH, 0AH
       DB  '1    ADD   A RECORD', 0DH, 0AH
       DB  '2    UPDATE A RECORD', 0DH, 0AH
       DB  '3    DELETE A RECORD', 0DH, 0AH
       DB  '4    PRINT  A RECORD', 0DH, 0AH
       DB  '5    QUIT',            0DH, 0AH, 0DH, 0AH
       DB  'ENTER THE NUMBER OF YOUR CHOICE ', 0DH, 0AH, '$'

CHOICE DB    ?

PGMDA  ENDS


; program stack segment

PGMSTK SEGMENT PARA STACK 'STACK'

       DW    32 DUP (?)

PGMSTK ENDS
       END
```

FIGURE 6–4   continued   *(Continues)*

```
MSG  DB    'PRESS ANY KEY TO CONTINUE$'

     MOV  AH,09H    ; SET FOR DISPLAY A STRING
     LEA  DX,MSG    ; DX -> MSG TO DISPLAY
     INT  21H       ; CALL DOS TO DISPLAY MSG

     MOV  AH,08H    ; SET FOR GET A BYTE NO ECHO
     INT  21H       ; CALL DOS TO GET A BYTE

     CMP  AL,00H    ; IS IT A SPECIAL CODE
     JNE  GOON      ; NO, SO GO PROCESS IT

     MOV  AH,08H    ; SET FOR GET A BYTE
     INT  21H       ; CALL DOS TO GET SPECIAL CODE

GOON:

      .
      .
      .
```

EXAMPLE 6–4   Partial coding to handle "PRESS ANY KEY TO CONTINUE"

The sequence for the GET_NAME routine is

> get a byte
> call SPECL_KEY to see if a special key was entered
> call CTRL_CODE to see if the byte was a control code
> call EDIT to confirm that a valid character was entered
> call MOV_BYTE to insert that value into the FNAME field

Figure 6–5 (PGM12.ASM on the program disk) shows the code to execute this sequence.

There is still one problem with the procedure. Because you used function 01H, if invalid keystrokes are entered, they are displayed on the screen even though they are neither accepted nor placed into FNAME. This can create a confusing screen display. Once more, function 08H should have been used to allow entry without displaying the character. (To effectively use function 08H, you need the ability to display a single byte. This is accomplished by using DOS function 02H, which will be covered next.)

Finally, notice that the design of the program is quite modular and can easily be adapted to more complex situations. If several special keys and control codes were allowed, additional CMP instructions in the appropriate routines would be included along with the subroutines necessary to perform those functions.

Now fix up these input routines. To do so, use functions 08H and 02H.

```
      PAGE    60,132
      TITLE   PGM12  FIGURE 6-5  INPUT FNAME BY FUNCTION 01H


;***********************************************************************
; PGM12       Title: Figure 6-5 Input first name by using function 01H *
;                                                                     *
; Programmer: Vic Broquard                                            *
; Date Written:  6/11/88        Date Of Last Revision: 8/4/88         *
;                                                                     *
; Purpose: To input first name containing up to 10 chars or a CR      *
;                                                                     *
; Special Requirements:   Calls GET_NAME to input the name            *
;                                                                     *
;   GET_NAME inputs up to 10 characters or a carriage return is entered *
;           uses BH = 0 to indicate a bad keystroke - anything other  *
;                       than a letter                                 *
;               BL = 1 to indicate that a carriage return was entered*
;                                                                     *
;   SPECL_KEY checks to see if any special key was pressed            *
;           if so, sets BH to 0                                       *
;                                                                     *
;   CTRL_CODE checks to see if any control code was entered           *
;               if so, sets BH to 0 and if CR entered, sets BL to 1   *
;                                                                     *
;   EDIT checks to see if the data is alphabetic - either case        *
;        if not, sets BH to 0                                         *
;                                                                     *
;   MOVE_BYTE moves the good character into the corresponding byte     *
;            in FNAME                                                 *
;                                                                     *
;***********************************************************************


; program code segment

PGMCD   SEGMENT

MAIN    PROC    FAR

; housekeeping section

    ASSUME  CS:PGMCD,DS:PGMDA,SS:PGMSTK

    MOV  AX,PGMDA  ; ESTABLISH ADDRESSABILITY
    MOV  DS,AX     ; TO PGMDA - THE PGM'S DATA SEGMENT

; main process section

    CALL GET_NAME  ; GET FIELD FNAME FILLED
```

FIGURE 6–5   Program to input a name by using function 01H (PGM12.ASM)   *(Continues)*

```
; test display the name

    MOV  AH,09H    ; SET FOR DISPLAY STRING
    LEA  DX,FNAME  ; DX -> STRING TO SHOW
    INT  21H       ; CALL DOS TO SHOW STRING

-----------------------------------------------------------------------

; return to DOS section

    MOV  AL,0      ; SET 0 AS THE RETURN CODE FOR DOS
    MOV  AH,4CH    ; SET FOR DOS END PROCESS FUNCTION
    INT  21H       ; CALL DOS TO END PROGRAM

MAIN    ENDP
    PAGE


GET_NAME  PROC

; GET_NAME will input until 10 chars are in FNAME or a CR is entered

    LEA  SI,FNAME  ; SI POINTS TO THE CURRENT BYTE TO FILL
    MOV  CX,10     ; CX = NUMBER OF BYTES TO INPUT
    MOV  BL,00H    ; SET DONE FLAG TO NO
    MOV  BH,00H    ; SET GOOD CHARACTER FOUND TO NO

TOP:
    CMP  CX,00H    ; HAVE CX BYTES BEEN INPUT?
    JE   DONE      ; YES, SO GOTO DONE
    CMP  BL,00H    ; HAS A CR BEEN ENTERED?
    JNE  DONE      ; YES, SO ALSO GOTO DONE

; now get the next byte

    MOV  AH,01H    ; SET FOR DOS KEYBOARD INPUT
    INT  21H       ; CALL DOS FOR 1 CHARACTER

    MOV  BH,01H    ; SET FOR A GOOD CHARACTER

    CALL SPECL_KEY ; FIND AND HANDLE ANY SPECIAL KEYS
    CMP  BH,00H    ; STILL A GOOD CHARACTER?
    JE   BOTTOM    ; NO, SO GO RETRY THE OPERATION

    CALL CTRL_CODE ; FIND AND HANDLE ANY CONTROL CODES
    CMP  BH,00H    ; STILL A GOOD CHARACTER?
    JE   BOTTOM    ; NO, SO GO RETRY THE OPERATION

    CALL EDIT      ; VERIFY BYTE IS VALID LETTER
    CMP  BH,00H    ; STILL A GOOD CHARACTER?
    JE   BOTTOM    ; NO, SO GO RETRY THE OPERATION
```

FIGURE 6–5   continued

```
        CALL MOV_BYTE  ; INSERT BYTE INTO FNAME

BOTTOM:
        JMP  TOP        ; CONTINUE PROCESS

DONE:
        RET
GET_NAME ENDP
        PAGE


;-------------------------------------------------------------------

SPECL_KEY  PROC

; this routine inputs the second byte of a special key code
; for now, they will be ignored
; sets BH = 0 if it finds a special code

        CMP  AL,00H     ; WAS A SPECIAL KEY ENTERED?
        JNE  NOT_SPCL   ; NO, SO LEAVE

        MOV  AH,01H     ; SET FOR DOS KEYBOARD INPUT
        INT  21H        ; CALL DOS FOR 1 CHARACTER

        MOV  BH,00H     ; SET FOR BAD CHARACTER

NOT_SPCL:
        RET             ; RETURN WITH BH SET

SPECL_KEY  ENDP
        PAGE


CTRL_CODE  PROC

; this proc will find and handle all control codes
; BH will be set to 0 if it finds a control code
; BL will be set to 1 if it finds a CR was entered

        CMP  AL,1FH     ; IS IT A CONTROL CODE?
        JA   CK_MORE    ; NO, BUT TRY HIGHER VALUES

        MOV  BH,00H     ; YES, SO SET BH TO FOUND A CONTROL CODE

        CMP  AL,0DH     ; WAS IT A CR?
        JNE  EXIT       ; NO, SO GO RET WITH BH SET

        MOV  BL,01H     ; YES, SO SET BL TO YES WAS A CR
        JMP  EXIT       ; SO GO RET WITH BH AND BL SET

CK_MORE:
```

FIGURE 6–5 continued   *(Continues)*

```
        CMP  AL,7FH   ; IS BYTE ABOVE ASCII CHARS?
        JB   EXIT     ; NO, SO RET WITH NOTHING TURNED ON

        MOV  BH,00H   ; YES, SO SET BH TO FOUND CONTROL CODE

EXIT:
        RET           ; RETURN WITH BH AND BL SET

CTRL_CODE ENDP
        PAGE


EDIT PROC

; verify valid character data entered
; if not, set BH to 0 for bad data

-----------------------------------------------------------------------------

        CMP  AL,41H   ; IS BYTE BELOW "A"?
        JB   NOT_VALID ; YES, SO GO SET ERROR

        CMP  AL,5AH   ; IS BYTE A "Z" OR LESS?
        JBE  GOOD     ; YES, IT'S A GOOD CHAR, GO RETURN

        CMP  AL,61H   ; IS BYTE BELOW "a"?
        JB   NOT_VALID ; YES, SO GO SET ERROR

        CMP  AL,7AH   ; IS BYTE A "z" OR LESS?
        JBE  GOOD     ; YES, IT'S A GOOD CHAR, GO RETURN

NOT_VALID:

        MOV  BH,00H   ; SET BH FOR NOT VALID

GOOD:

        RET           ; RETURN WITH BH SET

EDIT ENDP
        PAGE


MOV_BYTE  PROC

; moves the byte into FNAME

        MOV  [SI],AL  ; STORE THE BYTE
        INC  SI       ; POINT TO NEXT SLOT IN FNAME
        DEC  CX       ; DEC NUMBER OF BYTES TO GET

        RET           ; RETURN
```

FIGURE 6–5 continued

```
MOV_BYTE  ENDP

PGMCD  ENDS


; program data segment

PGMDA  SEGMENT

FNAME  DB    10 DUP(?)
       DB    '$'

PGMDA  ENDS


; program stack segment

PGMSTK SEGMENT PARA STACK 'STACK'

       DW    32 DUP (?)

PGMSTK ENDS
       END
```

FIGURE 6–5 continued

DOS Function 02H: Display Character

Frequently, there is the need to display just one character. This can be done by using DOS function 02H. As usual, register AH contains the function number—in this case, 02H. Register DL contains the character to display.

Re-examine Figure 6–5. If you replace the function 01H interrupt with function 08H, then the value entered is not displayed. This cleans up the entire program. Once the character has been determined to be valid, you then need to display the character by using function 02H. The coding to display the character is

```
MOV  DL,AL      ; PUT VALID CHARACTER INTO DL
MOV  AH,02H     ; SET FOR DISPLAY A BYTE
INT  21H        ; CALL DOS TO DISPLAY ONE BYTE
```

Figure 6–6 (PGM13.ASM on the program disk) shows the modified program.

Notice that the test display of the complete name now includes a CRLF before FNAME. This puts the display string on the next line instead of right after the original entry.

The menu choice program can also be improved by using function 08H to input the user's choice. If and when the entry is valid, function 02H can

```
      PAGE   60,132
      TITLE  PGM13  FIGURE 6-6  INPUT FNAME BY FUNCTION 08H


;************************************************************************
; PGM13      Title: Figure 6-6 Input first name by using function 08H *
;                                                                     *
; Programmer: Vic Broquard                                            *
; Date Written:  6/11/88        Date Of Last Revision: 8/4/88         *
;                                                                     *
; Purpose: To input first name containing up to 10 chars or a CR      *
;                                                                     *
; Special Requirements:   Calls GET_NAME to input the name            *
;                                                                     *
;   GET_NAME inputs up to 10 characters or a carriage return is entered *
;           uses BH = 0 to indicate a bad keystroke - anything other  *
;                       than a letter                                 *
;               BL = 1 to indicate that a carriage return was entered*
;                                                                     *
;   SPECL_KEY checks to see if any special key was pressed            *
;           if so, sets BH to 0                                       *
;                                                                     *
;   CTRL_CODE checks to see if any control code was entered           *
;           if so, sets BH to 0 and if CR entered, sets BL to 1       *
;                                                                     *
;   EDIT checks to see if the data is alphabetic - either case        *
;       if not, sets BH to 0                                          *
;                                                                     *
;   MOVE_BYTE moves the good character into the corresponding byte    *
;           in FNAME                                                  *
;                                                                     *
;************************************************************************
;

; program code segment

PGMCD  SEGMENT

MAIN   PROC    FAR

; housekeeping section

      ASSUME  CS:PGMCD,DS:PGMDA,SS:PGMSTK

      MOV  AX,PGMDA  ; ESTABLISH ADDRESSABILITY
      MOV  DS,AX     ; TO PGMDA - THE PGM'S DATA SEGMENT

; main process section

      CALL GET_NAME  ; GET FIELD FNAME FILLED
```

FIGURE 6-6   Program to input one character at a time (PGM13.ASM)

```
; test display the name

    MOV  AH,09H   ; SET FOR DISPLAY STRING
    LEA  DX,MSG   ; DX -> STRING TO SHOW
    INT  21H      ; CALL DOS TO SHOW STRING

-----------------------------------------------------------------------

; return to DOS section

    MOV  AL,0     ; SET 0 AS THE RETURN CODE FOR DOS
    MOV  AH,4CH   ; SET FOR DOS END PROCESS FUNCTION
    INT  21H      ; CALL DOS TO END PROGRAM

MAIN    ENDP
    PAGE


GET_NAME  PROC

; GET_NAME will input until 10 chars are in FNAME or a CR is entered

    LEA  SI,FNAME ; SI POINTS TO THE CURRENT BYTE TO FILL
    MOV  CX,10    ; CX = NUMBER OF BYTES TO INPUT
    MOV  BL,00H   ; SET DONE FLAG TO NO
    MOV  BH,00H   ; SET GOOD CHARACTER FOUND TO NO

TOP:
    CMP  CX,00H   ; HAVE CX BYTES BEEN INPUT
    JE   DONE     ; YES, SO GOTO DONE
    CMP  BL,00H   ; HAS A CR BEEN ENTERED?
    JNE  DONE     ; YES, SO ALSO GOTO DONE

; now get the next byte

    MOV  AH,08H   ; SET FOR DOS KEYBOARD INPUT NO ECHO
    INT  21H      ; CALL DOS FOR 1 CHARACTER

    MOV  BH,01H   ; SET FOR A GOOD CHARACTER

    CALL SPECL_KEY ; FIND AND HANDLE ANY SPECIAL KEYS
    CMP  BH,00H   ; STILL A GOOD CHARACTER?
    JE   BOTTOM   ; NO, SO GO RETRY THE OPERATION

    CALL CTRL_CODE ; FIND AND HANDLE ANY CONTROL CODES
    CMP  BH,00H   ; STILL A GOOD CHARACTER?
    JE   BOTTOM   ; NO, SO GO RETRY THE OPERATION

    CALL EDIT     ; VERIFY BYTE IS VALID LETTER
    CMP  BH,00H   ; STILL A GOOD CHARACTER?
    JE   BOTTOM   ; NO, SO GO RETRY THE OPERATION
```

FIGURE 6–6   continued   *(Continues)*

```
        CALL MOV_BYTE  ; INSERT BYTE INTO FNAME

BOTTOM:
     JMP  TOP        ; CONTINUE PROCESS

DONE:
     RET
GET_NAME ENDP
     PAGE

- - - - - - - - - - - - - - - - - - - - - - - - - - - - - - - - - - - - - - - - - - - - -

SPECL_KEY  PROC

; this routine inputs the second byte of a special key code
; for now, they will be ignored
; sets BH = 0 if it finds a special code

     CMP  AL,00H    ; WAS A SPECIAL KEY ENTERED?
     JNE  NOT_SPCL  ; NO, SO LEAVE

     MOV  AH,08H    ; SET FOR DOS KEYBOARD INPUT NO ECHO
     INT  21H       ; CALL DOS FOR 1 CHARACTER

     MOV  BH,00H    ; SET FOR BAD CHARACTER

NOT_SPCL:
     RET            ; RETURN WITH BH SET

SPECL_KEY  ENDP
     PAGE

CTRL_CODE  PROC

; this proc will find and handle all control codes
; BH will be set to 0 if it finds a control code
; BL will be set to 1 if it finds a CR was entered

     CMP  AL,1FH    ; IS IT A CONTROL CODE?
     JA   CK_MORE   ; NO, BUT TRY HIGHER VALUES

     MOV  BH,00H    ; YES, SO SET BH TO FOUND A CONTROL CODE

     CMP  AL,0DH    ; WAS IT A CR?
     JNE  EXIT      ; NO, SO GO RET WITH BH SET

     MOV  BL,01H    ; YES, SO SET BL TO YES WAS A CR
     JMP  EXIT      ; SO GO RET WITH BH AND BL SET

CK_MORE:
```

FIGURE 6–6   continued

```
        CMP  AL,7FH    ; IS BYTE ABOVE ASCII CHARS?
        JB   EXIT      ; NO, SO RET WITH NOTHING TURNED ON

        MOV  BH,00H    ; YES, SO SET BH TO FOUND CONTROL CODE

EXIT:
        RET            ; RETURN WITH BH AND BL SET

CTRL_CODE ENDP
        PAGE

EDIT PROC

; verify valid character data entered
; if not, set BH to 0 for bad data

----------------------------------------------------------------------

        CMP  AL,41H    ; IS BYTE BELOW "A"?
        JB   NOT_VALID ; YES, SO GO SET ERROR

        CMP  AL,5AH    ; IS BYTE A "Z" OR LESS?
        JBE  GOOD      ; YES, IT'S A GOOD CHAR, GO RETURN

        CMP  AL,61H    ; IS BYTE BELOW "a"?
        JB   NOT_VALID ; YES, SO GO SET ERROR

        CMP  AL,7AH    ; IS BYTE A "z" OR LESS?
        JBE  GOOD      ; YES, IT'S A GOOD CHAR, GO RETURN

NOT_VALID:

        MOV  BH,00H    ; SET BH FOR NOT VALID

GOOD:

        RET            ; RETURN WITH BH SET

EDIT ENDP
        PAGE

MOV_BYTE  PROC

; moves the byte into FNAME

        MOV  [SI],AL   ; STORE THE BYTE
        INC  SI        ; POINT TO NEXT SLOT IN FNAME
        DEC  CX        ; DEC NUMBER OF BYTES TO GET

; now display accepted character
```

FIGURE 6-6   continued

(Continues)

```
        MOV   DL,AL    ; MOVE BYTE TO DL FOR DISPLAYING
        MOV   AH,02H   ; SET FOR DISPLAY A BYTE
        INT   21H      ; CALL DOS TO DISPLAY 1 BYTE


        RET            ; RETURN

MOV_BYTE  ENDP

PGMCD  ENDS


; program data segment

PGMDA  SEGMENT

MSG    DB   0DH, 0AH  ; CRLF TO DISPLAY FNAME ON A NEW LINE

FNAME  DB   10 DUP(?)
       DB   '$'
- - - - - - - - - - - - - - - - - - - - - - - - - - - - - - - - - - - - - - - - - -

PGMDA  ENDS


; program stack segment

PGMSTK SEGMENT PARA STACK 'STACK'

       DW    32 DUP (?)

PGMSTK ENDS
       END
```

FIGURE 6–6   continued

display it on the screen. This version is shown in Figure 6–7 (PGM14.ASM on the program disk).

DOS Function 0CH: Flush Keyboard Buffer and Read Keyboard

Function 08H is not always the answer. In some situations you cannot safely use function 08H because of the type-ahead buffer. The type-ahead buffer makes it easy to unintentionally type ahead of the program and place characters in the buffer. Then, when function 08H is invoked, there is a

```
      PAGE    60,132
      TITLE PGM14  FIGURE 6-7 GET VALID MENU CHOICE USING FUN. 08H


;**************************************************************************
; PGM14      Title: Figure 6-7 Get A Valid Menu Choice          *
;                                                               *
; Programmer: Vic Broquard                                      *
; Date Written:  6/11/88      Date Of Last Revision: 8/4/88     *
;                                                               *
; Purpose: To illustrate how to display a menu and get a valid menu  *
;          choice by using function 08H                         *
; Special Requirements: none                                    *
;                                                               *
;**************************************************************************

; program code segment

PGMCD   SEGMENT

MAIN    PROC    FAR

; housekeeping section

      ASSUME  CS:PGMCD,DS:PGMDA,SS:PGMSTK

      MOV  AX,PGMDA  ; ESTABLISH ADDRESSABILITY
      MOV  DS,AX     ; TO PGMDA - THE PGM'S DATA SEGMENT

; main process section

; display the menu

      MOV  AH,09H    ; SET FOR DISPLAY STRING
      LEA  DX,MENU   ; DX -> STRING TO DISPLAY
      INT  21H       ; CALL DOS TO DISPLAY MENU

; get the choice

REDO:

      MOV  AH,08H    ; SET FOR GET A BYTE FUNCTION
      INT  21H       ; CALL DOS TO GET A BYTE

      CMP  AL,00H    ; WAS A SPECIAL KEY ENTERED?
      JE   SPECIAL   ; YES, GO GET IT

      CMP  AL,31H    ; IS ENTRY LESS THAN A 1?
      JB   REDO      ; YES, GO GET IT AGAIN
```

FIGURE 6–7 Get a valid menu choice by using function 08H (PGM14.ASM)   *(Continues)*

```
        CMP  AL,35H    ; IS ENTRY ABOVE A 5?
        JA   REDO      ; YES, GO GET IT AGAIN


        MOV  CHOICE,AL ; STORE GOOD VALUE IN CHOICE


        MOV  DL,AL     ; PUT VALUE INTO DL FOR DISPLAYING
        MOV  AH,02H    ; SET FOR DISPLAY BYTE
        INT  21H       ; CALL DOS TO DISPLAY THE BYTE


        JMP  DONE      ; GO RETURN - CHOICE IS SET

SPECIAL:

; ----------------------------------------------------------------------

        MOV  AH,08H    ; SET FOR GET A BYTE
        INT  21H       ; CALL DOS TO GET SPECIAL CODE
        JMP  REDO      ; IGNORE IT

; return to DOS section

DONE:
        MOV  AL,0      ; SET 0 AS THE RETURN CODE FOR DOS
        MOV  AH,4CH    ; SET FOR DOS END PROCESS FUNCTION
        INT  21H       ; CALL DOS TO END PROGRAM

MAIN  ENDP

PGMCD ENDS


; program data segment

PGMDA SEGMENT

MENU DB '        MASTER MENU', 0DH, 0AH, 0DH, 0AH
     DB '1    ADD   A RECORD', 0DH, 0AH
     DB '2    UPDATE A RECORD', 0DH, 0AH
     DB '3    DELETE A RECORD', 0DH, 0AH
     DB '4    PRINT A RECORD', 0DH, 0AH
     DB '5    QUIT',          0DH, 0AH, 0DH, 0AH
     DB 'ENTER THE NUMBER OF YOUR CHOICE ', 0DH, 0AH, '$'

CHOICE DB    ?

PGMDA ENDS


; program stack segment
```

FIGURE 6–7   continued

```
PGMSTK SEGMENT PARA STACK 'STACK'

        DW      32 DUP (?)

PGMSTK ENDS
        END
```

FIGURE 6–7   continued

byte(s) waiting. This allows the program to go on to the next instruction without giving the user time to read the screen display! This is what happens in the program in Figure 6–4.

Function 0CH, which flushes the keyboard buffer and reads the keyboard, is designed to correct this situation. This function clears all remaining characters from the type-ahead buffer and then, if requested, performs one of the following input services: 01H, 06H, 07H, 08H, or 0AH.

When invoked, register AH contains 0CH and register AL contains the secondary input function number 01H, 06H, 07H, 08H, or 0AH. If AL contains any other value, function 0CH does no further processing.

To properly handle the PRESS ANY KEY TO CONTINUE problem, you can use the code as shown in Example 6–5.

Next examine how a character can be sent to the printer.

```
MSG DB  'PRESS ANY KEY TO CONTINUE$'

    MOV AH,09H   ; SET FOR DISPLAY STRING
    LEA DX,MSG   ; DX -> MESSAGE
    INT 21H      ; CALL DOS TO DISPLAY THE MESSAGE

    MOV AH,0CH   ; SET FOR FLUSH KEYBOARD
    MOV AL,08H   ; SET FOR INPUT BYTE, NO ECHO
    INT 21H      ; CALL DOS TO CLEAR BUFFER AND GET BYTE

    CMP AL,00H   ; SPECIAL KEY ENTERED?
    JNE OK       ; NO, GO ON

    MOV AH,08H   ; SET TO INPUT SPECIAL KEY
    INT 21H      ; CALL DOS TO GET SPECIAL KEY CODE

OK:
```

EXAMPLE 6–5   Proper handling of "PRESS ANY KEY TO CONTINUE"

```
MSG  DB   'THIS IS A MESSAGE TO BE PRINTED'


     LEA  SI,MSG    ; SI -> STRING TO BE PRINTED
     MOV  CX,31     ; CX = NUMBER OF BYTES TO PRINT


PRT_LOOP:


     MOV  DL,[SI]   ; DL = CHARACTER TO PRINT
     MOV  AH,05H    ; SET FOR PRINT 1 BYTE
     INT  21H       ; CALL DOS TO PRINT THE BYTE


     INC  SI        ; POINT TO NEXT BYTE TO PRINT
     LOOP PRT_LOOP  ; REPEAT UNTIL WHOLE STRING IS DISPLAYED
```

EXAMPLE 6–6   Printing a message

DOS Function 05H: Print a Character on the Standard Printer Device

There is only one DOS function that permits data to be sent directly to the printer. Since this function prints only one byte at a time, it is necessary to loop through all bytes in the message, printing each in turn.

When the 05H function is invoked, register AH contains 05H and register DL contains the character to be sent to the printer.

The code shown in Example 6–6 causes the string MSG to be printed.

As with similar functions, it is best to establish a generalized subroutine that prints any string that it is given. One register should contain the number of bytes to print, using register CX whenever possible. Another register—SI, for example—should contain the address of the string to print. Don't forget to save registers AX, CX, DX, and SI.

6.12   STUB TESTING

When you create programs that utilize several subroutines, use stub testing to make debugging easier. Stub testing is the technique of building a program by adding modules sequentially to the driver, or control, module and then testing the program as each module is added. Assume the program has a MAIN procedure and three subroutines known as SUB1, SUB2, and SUB3. The incorrect approach is to write all four routines and then turn the debugger loose. Mass confusion results. The correct approach is to write the MAIN procedure with all its coding and "dummy in" the subroutines with no processing in them. For example:

```
            SUB1 PROC

                 RET

            SUB1 ENDP
```

Now debug the driver. This should be a very easy task. If necessary, you can even supply, or "plug in," values to key fields that the subroutines are to provide. You can even insert a simple message display feature in each dummy module, stating that it was invoked.

Next code SUB1 and insert it into the program. As you run the debugger, you already know that the MAIN code works, and you can concentrate solely on the SUB1 instructions. If an error does occur, then it can only be in SUB1. When SUB1 is working perfectly, code SUB2 and repeat the debugging process. Continue this sequence until the whole program is working.

Stub testing is strongly recommended; it will make your life as a programmer much more pleasant.

6.13 USING THE DEBUGGER WITH INT INSTRUCTIONS

When you use the trace command, T, and the program includes INT instructions, the debugger continues tracing instructions within the INT subroutines. At first this is interesting, since you can see what actually gets executed during the I/O operation. However, very shortly, this becomes boring and counter-productive to the job at hand.

In such cases, use the P command of the debugger when you get to the INT. The P command provides a partial trace. It traces all your program instructions, but it will **not** trace into the system code of the INTs. It merely permits the INT system code to execute to completion and returns control after the INT instruction has been carried out.

6.14 SUMMARY

You have seen that there are three methods of handling I/O operations: DOS services, ROM-BIOS services, and direct IN and OUT instructions. Of these, DOS services is the easiest to use, and DOS services offer maximum program portability to other compatible computers.

All operating system services are requested by interrupting the program by using the INT instruction. The operand of the instruction identifies the service needed. However, many of these services handle broad classes of operations known as subfunctions, or umbrella calls.

I/O requests are all processed by the DOS services interrupt function 21H. There are numerous subfunctions within this one major function. All the subfunctions are identified by a unique number called the DOS function number. These numbers are always contained in register AH during execution of the program.

Function 0AH (buffered keyboard input) inputs an entire string from the keyboard. The function requires that register DX contain the address of a structure containing the maximum number of bytes to input, the actual number entered, and the area to store the bytes as they are entered. All the DOS editing keys function as expected.

An entire message or series of lines can be displayed on the screen by use of the display string function, 09H. Register DX contains the address of the message to be shown. String messages must end with a dollar sign.

There are times when added control over the data being entered is desirable. Input byte functions 01H, 07H, and 08H provide that control. They differ in whether the byte entered is to be echoed to the screen and whether the break keys function during the request for input.

Often when using the input byte functions, the character entered must be displayed on the screen. This can be handled by the display character function, 02H. Register AL contains the character to be shown.

Function 05H sends data straight to the printer. The character to be printed is contained in register DL.

Now that you understand the basics of DOS services, you can write realistic programs that input and process data and then output the results. Use stub testing for debugging. Don't try to debug the entire program at one time.

6.15 REVIEW QUESTIONS

1. True/false: ROM-BIOS function calls should be used if widespread portability of the program is desired.

2. True/false: When calling DOS for keyboard input, register AH contains the service function code.

3. True/false: The differences between the different DOS functions for keyboard input involve whether the break keys work and whether the function waits for a key to be pressed.

4. True/false: After an INT 21H with AH = 01H, AL = 00H; this means another INT 21H with AH = 01H must be done.

5. What are the three major methods for handling I/O operations on a personal computer? If a program will be marketed to run on many different machines, which of these would be the best choice and which would be the worst choice for handling the I/O?

6. What is the difference between functions 2 and 9 of the DOS service interrupt 21H?

7. Consider DOS services 1, 7, or 8 (which get a character from the keyboard). Once a character has been received in register AL, the program must check for special codes. What is a reasonable hierarchy of special codes to check? Why is the hierarchy reasonable?

8. Explain the concept of interrupts. What is the function of the interrupt handler?

9. Why is program portability so important?

10. When DOS function 0AH is complete, it does not issue a CRLF to the screen. What impact does this have on program processing when several fields are to be entered?

11. DOS function 01H echoes the input character to the screen. When it does so, it automatically places the cursor in the next display position. What impact does this have on programming? Why?

12. When asking the user for a specific reply to an error message, why should DOS function 0CH be used?

6.16 PRACTICE PROBLEMS

1. Code the directives and instructions for a subroutine that displays a message on the screen by using function 02H. The routine should be passed the address of the message and its length.

2. Suppose you want to incorporate the ASCII_MOVE procedure shown in the last chapter in place of the crude MOVER procedure used in Figure 6–2. Outline the changes needed.

3. Code the instructions to display the following message:

```
MSG   DB   'ENTER FIVE DIGITS:$'
```

4. Code the instructions to input a client's number. It is 6 bytes long. Use buffered keyboard input.

5. Code the instructions to input the response to the following message:

```
ENTER Y OR N _
```

The code should accept Y, y, N, or n. All other responses should be rejected. The entry should be echoed to the screen. Use function 08H.

6. Write the code necessary to display MESSAGE as defined by

```
MESSAGE   DB   'This is a message to be shown'
```

7. Code a section to input a user command. The command should be limited to a maximum of 128 characters. Use DOS function 0AH to input the string.

6.17 PROGRAMMING PROBLEMS

1. CRT message handling: Write code to handle screen messages as described by the following:

    • The program should accept up to five lines entered on the keyboard. There may be 0 to 5 lines entered. Each line is a maximum of 80 characters long; it must end with a carriage return.

    • The end of input is either the fifth line entered or a CTRL-Z entered by itself on a separate line. (The presence of a CTRL-Z in any other position except the first should be ignored.)

    • The program should display the lines entered, but in reverse order. The last line entered should be the first line displayed.

    • Use DOS function 09H for the display and function 08H for the input. You should echo the character entered onto the CRT. When displaying the CTRL-Z entry, display 2 bytes: ^Z.

2. Write a routine that displays the following messages:

    ```
    DO YOU WISH TO UPDATE THE MASTER FILE NOW?

    ENTER Y FOR YES OR N FOR NO: _
    ```

    Pause for the user to read them, and then input the user's response. If the response is not valid, repeat the whole series once more. The user must enter Y or y or N or n. Any other action should cause the program to repeat the entire process.

3. Write a routine called GET_IT that inputs a field for the user. The routine receives the address of the prompt message, the address of the input area, and the maximum length of the input area. The routine should then fill up the field.

    All three fields are to be ASCII numbers. You may use any registers to pass the values desired. The values should be right-justified and left-padded with ASCII 0's. The prompts in the prompt-and-response dialogue should be

    ```
    ENTER CLIENT NUMBER
    ENTER HOURS WORKED
    ENTER TOTAL DUE
    ```

    The fields must be defined in the data segment as

```
CNUMBER   DB   8 DUP(?)
HRS_WRK   DB   6 DUP(?)
TOT_DUE   DB   7 DUP(?)
```

(The fields are going to be part of a record that will later be output to a master file.) Use buffered keyboard input to enter the fields.

4. Write a routine called VERIFY_FLD that ensures that the values entered in Programming Problem 3 are indeed ASCII numbers. The routine receives the address of a field and its maximum length. Should the field contain invalid data, sound the bell, display an error message, and display the field. Then display a message that tells the user to enter any key to continue. The program should not continue until a key is pressed.

   To sound the bell, display a byte that contains the ring bell control code, 07H.

   If you solved Programming Problem 3, you can incorporate this routine with that one to form one program.

5. Write a subroutine that prints lines on the printer. The subroutine should receive the address of the data to print and the length of that data. Both values should be in registers. The subroutine should print the line.

   Test your subroutine by creating a main procedure that calls it to print the following lines:

```
Now is the time for all good programmers to be able to
print a report on the printer. This is one such document.


Here begins another paragraph. Did it print successfully?

If it did, you win the top prize of $1,000.00. And if you
believe this, I have a bridge to sell.
```

6. Write the subroutine to display the following menu:

```
        MATH DRILL AND PRACTICE

        1. ADDITION

        2. SUBTRACTION

        3. MULTIPLICATION

        4. DIVISION

        5. QUIT

        ENTER THE NUMBER OF YOUR CHOICE:_
```

Use function 09H to display the menu.

Then write a subroutine to input the choice and store that digit in a byte field called CHOICE. Only a valid digit should be accepted. Use functions 08H and 02H for this purpose.

The main processing section of the MAIN procedure should consist of two calls: display the menu and get a valid choice. When these two are finished, the MAIN procedure should display the following message for debugging purposes:

```
THE CHOICE ENTERED WAS x
```

where x is the actual digit entered.

7

Basic ROM-BIOS CRT Services

7.1 CHAPTER OBJECTIVES

In this chapter you will

1. Learn about the architecture of CRT display terminals, including such features as the video mode, the attribute byte, and memory-mapped display

2. Learn how to use the four most common ROM-BIOS video service routines: set video mode, set cursor position, scroll up, and write character and attribute byte

3. See how these routines may be combined into a working program

4. Explore the beginnings of a full-screen data entry program

5. Examine some of the other ROM-BIOS video services

6. Learn to use some of the more powerful debugger commands to effect screen swapping, set permanent breakpoints, and modify the contents of registers and memory

7.2 INTRODUCTION

In the preceding chapters the programs and exercises have been straightforward and relatively easy. However, with this chapter the real complexity and power of the assembler language will become apparent. To gain the desired

245

level of control over the CRT, you must understand its internal operation as well as how control is implemented through ROM-BIOS. Although the ROM-BIOS functions are relatively simple in themselves, the amount of code can become very large when the functions are combined into a complete program. The features described in this chapter are often essential for creating successful and innovative programs.

Three common CRT functions—clear screen, direct cursor addressing, and set display attributes (color, reverse video, cursor size and blinking)—are not easily handled using standard DOS display services. However, each of these is handled quite easily with ROM-BIOS services.

7.3 INVOKING ROM-BIOS SERVICES

As you have seen, nearly all DOS services are implemented by invoking the umbrella function call INT 21H. In contrast, ROM-BIOS services are distributed among several different interrupt vectors. Each service also supports an umbrella of several related functions. The ROM-BIOS services INT values are

10H	video services	11H	equipment list
13H	diskette services	12H	memory size
14H	communications services	1AH	time/date services
15H	cassette tape services	05H	print screen
16H	keyboard services	18H	ROM-Basic language
17H	printer services	19H	bootstrap loader

Remember: As more of the ROM-BIOS services are used in a program, the portability of that program is greatly reduced. However, using function 10H—video services—by itself does not usually impair program compatibility. Because of this, we have limited our presentation of ROM-BIOS services to the video service functions.

These video services routines provide a program with complete control of the screen display. However, to learn how to use them, you must have a good understanding of the architecture of CRT screens and their display modes.

7.4 THE ARCHITECTURE OF VIDEO DISPLAYS

The overall screen display format is controlled by the choice of **video display mode.** When data are displayed, an **attribute byte** informs the CRT exactly how to display that data. The specific bytes to be displayed are stored in memory, allowing the program to directly modify what is currently being displayed. This is known as a **memory-mapped display.**

Now examine each of these terms in order.

Video Display Modes

The first step in using ROM-BIOS services is to determine which video display modes are available on your computer or on the machine on which the program will eventually be used. A **video display mode** represents the allowable display characteristics, including such choices as color, black-and-white, giant letters, normal-size script, and whether to show graphic characters.

The possible modes are determined by the hardware features in the form of circuit cards that are included with the computer. The more common choices include a monochrome card, a color graphics card (CGA), and/or an enhanced graphics card (EGA). Obviously, the color mode cannot be used on a machine that has only a monochrome card.

Each computer has one or more video display modes associated with the type of card it has. Figure 7–1 shows the eight common IBM modes. Monochrome cards can use only mode 7. CGA and Enhanced Color Graphics (EGA) cards can use any of the modes 0 through 6, but not 7. Text mode is used for normal character displays; graphics mode is used to produce drawings, charts, and other graphic displays. Experiment with the choices available on your computer to see which is appropriate for your needs.

Although there are several choices available, you will probably use mode 3 for most normal color work. If fancy graphics are to be displayed, then graphics mode 6 is used. As you can see from Figure 7–1, the color display in mode 3 consists of 25 lines with 80 characters per line. Throughout the text, we will assume mode 3 is being used. If mode 3 is not available on your computer, you can modify the code as required.

How is the video mode set? ROM-BIOS video services function 00H can be used to set the video mode; function 0FH can be used to find which video mode is in use. How these functions work will be examined shortly.

Mode	Type	Size	Color?
0	text	40×25	yes, gray tones
1	text	40×25	yes
2	text	80×25	yes, gray tones
3	text	80×25	yes
4	graphics	medium resolution	yes
5	graphics	medium resolution	yes, gray tones
6	graphics	high resolution	yes
7	text	80×25	no

FIGURE 7–1 IBM video display modes

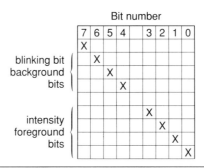

FIGURE 7–2   The attribute byte

The Attribute Byte

Each character that is displayed on the screen has an **attribute byte** that tells the device how to display that character. Each bit within the attribute byte has a specific meaning. The general format, or bit sequence, for both the monochrome and color card is shown in Figure 7–2.

The attribute byte is used in four ROM-BIOS functions of INT 10H. They are 06H (scroll up), 07H (scroll down), 08H (read character and attribute), and 09H (write character and attribute).

The Monochrome Attribute Byte

Now examine each bit as it is used to describe a monochrome attribute.

- If bit 7, the blinking bit, is on (that is, 1B) the byte blinks continuously. Similarly, if the intensity bit is on, the foreground is brighter, or more intense, than normal.

- Normal monochrome white-on-black is produced by having the foreground bits all on and the background bits all off. Thus, an attribute byte of 07H (0000 0111B) produces a display of white characters on a black background that is nonblinking and has normal intensity.

- Underlined characters can be produced by setting the foreground bits to 0000 0001B, or 01H.

- Reverse video is produced by setting the background bits on and the foreground bits off, that is, to 0111 0000B (70H).

- Invisible characters are produced by setting both the foreground and the background bits off—that is, to 0000 0000B, or 00H.

As you can see, with monochrome, the alternatives are somewhat limited.

Intensity bit off background and foreground		Intensity bit on foreground only	
Bits	Color	Bits	Color
000	black	1000	gray
001	blue	1001	light blue
010	green	1010	light green
011	cyan	1011	light cyan
100	red	1100	light red
101	magenta	1101	light magenta
110	brown	1110	light yellow
111	white	1111	high-intensity white

FIGURE 7–3   The IBM color values

The Color Attribute Byte

As with the monochrome attribute byte, if bit 7 is on, the byte blinks continuously. The background and foreground bits can be combined to produce eight different colors for the background and foreground, respectively.

In addition to brightening, or intensifying, the foreground, the intensity bit alters the color of the foreground. Thus, there are actually 16 possible foreground colors available. The color settings are identified in Figure 7–3.

For example, if you want to produce a screen with red letters on a green background, set the attribute bits to 0010 0100B, or 24H. To create light yellow letters on a blue background, use 0001 1110B, or 1EH. If you use the same color for the foreground and the background, then an invisible display results.

The Graphics Attribute Byte

When working in graphics mode, text can still be displayed with color being applied to the foreground and background. In addition, it is possible to set the border of the screen to a color different than either the foreground or background.

In graphics mode, color is handled differently. For each graphics mode, there are several available color palettes, or sets of colors. Within a specific palette, there is a limited subset of choices for foreground colors. When the palette is changed, the subset of foreground color options changes. Also, when the palette is changed, the entire screen changes. Because of this, it may be more practical to use color text mode than to change palettes if many color changes are needed on one screen display.

The palette is set by using function 0BH (set color palette). For more detail on setting the palette, consult your DOS system manuals.

7.5 MEMORY-MAPPED DISPLAY

How is the screen display actually accomplished? Personal computers use a **memory-mapped display** in which the current contents of the screen are stored in a specific section of memory. Periodically, the CRT display circuitry scans this area of memory and echoes it onto the screen. This scanning process occurs approximately 60 times per second, thereby **"refreshing the screen."** If this were not done, the images, characters, and colors would quickly fade and be lost. If it were done at a slower rate, the display would appear to flicker, much like early television sets.

Each memory location corresponds to a particular location on the screen. The first byte of storage corresponds to the first byte of the first line on the CRT, the next byte, to the second byte, and so forth up to the 81st byte. The 81st byte corresponds to the first byte of the second line in the 80-byte display mode. Thus, the name—memory-mapped.

It is possible that during normal operations of a program both the CRT controller and the program attempt to access the memory-mapped section of RAM. When this occurs, a "snowy" effect momentarily appears on the screen. (This can be avoided if the program is written so that it checks the vertical sync signal status bit. When on, this bit limits program access of the memory-mapped display to those times when the CRT is not using the display memory.)

How can a program affect the memory-mapped display? The normal DOS services discussed in the last chapter copy the data to be displayed into the appropriate bytes of the memory-mapped display area. The data is then shown on the screen during the next pass of the circuitry, approximately 1/60 of a second later.

In contrast, ROM-BIOS services provide **direct access** to any byte in the memory-mapped display area at any time. To understand how ROM-BIOS services can provide this increased control, you must grasp how the memory-mapped display corresponds to the visible image on the screen.

The CRT screen can display 25 lines, with each line having 80 characters. A coordinate system is used to identify each and every byte on the screen. The scheme is composed of rows (the lines) and columns.

The rows are numbered 0 through 24, corresponding to lines 1 through 25. The columns are numbered 0 through 79, corresponding to the positions 1 through 80. When specifying coordinates, the row number is always given first, followed by the column number. Thus, the upper-left display position is (0,0). This corresponds to the first display position on the first line. The lower-right coordinate is (24,79), corresponding to the 80th display position on the 25th line.

A given display position on the screen can be identified in one of two formats: (row,column) and (line,position). Be alert to the difference between the two numbering schemes.

The memory-mapped display area contains 2 bytes for each CRT display position. One byte contains the actual byte to be shown; the other contains the attribute byte. Thus, the memory-mapped display area consists of

4,000 bytes: 25 lines × 80 characters per line × 2. The first pair of bytes corresponds to position (0,0), the second pair to (0,1), the 81st pair to (1,0), and so on.

ROM-BIOS services permit a program to access the bytes of the video memory by specifying the row and column number of the desired byte. Therefore, it is possible to address any byte on the screen by specifying its coordinates—first the row number and then the column number. The routines permit the program to store new values or to display what is currently there.

The coordinate location system also forms the basis upon which **direct cursor addressing** is built. Direct cursor addressing permits the cursor to be directly positioned to any point on the screen and data displayed at that position. The coordinate system also facilitates scrolling up or down, clearing the screen, and creating windows.

The various color modes allow a program to create up to four different display pages and to designate which one of the four is the current page to display. The program can modify one of the pages not displayed and then switch the current page to the newly modified one. This action, called **page swapping,** gives the appearance of instantaneous changes of the screen display. The pages are numbered 0, 1, 2, and 3. ROM-BIOS always defines one of these pages as the current page. The default current page is 0. At any time, the ROM-BIOS services function (05H) can be used to change this default.

Next examine the ROM-BIOS services that perform the actions you have learned about in this section.

7.6   THE ROM-BIOS VIDEO SERVICE: INT 10H

The selection of the particular ROM-BIOS service needed is accomplished by placing the hex number of the routine into register AH, just as you did for the DOS services. The following are the more commonly used ROM-BIOS video services that are available.

function number (hex)	function name
00H	set video mode
01H	set cursor size
02H	set cursor position
03H	read cursor position
05H	set active display page
06H	scroll up
07H	scroll down
08H	read character and attribute

09H	write character and attribute
0BH	set color palette
0FH	get current video display mode

The most frequently used functions include set video mode (00H, which is usually used only once, at the start of the program), set cursor position (02H), scroll up to clear the screen (06H), and write character and attribute to display a value on the screen (09H). In addition, the functions read cursor position (03H) and read character and attribute (08H) can be useful when working with full-screen data entry applications. Whenever an INT 10H request is initiated, register AH contains one of the ROM-BIOS function numbers.

Consider the four most commonly used functions first.

Set Video Mode: Function 00H

If the program uses a nondefault video mode, such as color, the set video mode function (00H) must be invoked during the program initialization phase, that is, before any messages are displayed.

Register AL contains the number of the mode desired. The following sequence of code sets up the program for color text mode:

```
MOV AL,03H      ; SET FOR COLOR TEXT MODE
MOV AH,00H      ; SET VIDEO MODE FUNCTION
INT 10H         ; CALL BIOS TO SET THE DISPLAY MODE
```

Remember that the common video modes given in Figure 7–1 are determined by your display hardware. If you attempt to use a mode that the hardware does not support, the results will be unpredictable.

Set Cursor Position: Function 02H

The cursor can be set by the program to any point on the screen at any time. After being set, it can be followed by many forms of CRT output that will be displayed at the specific place on the screen. This CRT output can include normal DOS services as well as the CRT output.

When invoked, register AH contains the function number 02H and register BH contains the page number. Unless the multiple-page display feature in color text mode is being used, register BH should be set to 00H—the current page.

Register DX contains the coordinates of the desired position (row and column) of the cursor. Specifically, DH contains the row number and DL contains the column number. Remember that the coordinates for the upper-left corner are (00H,00H) and the coordinates for the lower-left corner are (18H,4FH)—that is, (24,79). Example 7–1 illustrates the coding that places the cursor at row 10 and column 15, that is, at line 11 and position 16.

```
MOV  AH,02H    ; SET FOR THE SET CURSOR FUNCTION
MOV  BH,00H    ; SET FOR CURRENT PAGE
MOV  DH,0AH    ; SET FOR ROW 10
MOV  DL,0FH    ; SET FOR COL 15
INT  10H       ; CALL ROM-BIOS TO SET CURSOR
```

EXAMPLE 7–1 Using BIOS to position the cursor

```
SUBTTL     SET CURSOR SUBROUTINE
PAGE       +
SET_CURSOR PROC

; set the cursor to coordinates given in reg DX

; this routine assumes that DH has the row number
;                         and DL has the column number

    PUSH AX        ; SAVE CALLER'S REGISTERS
    PUSH BX

    MOV  BH,00H    ; SET FOR CURRENT PAGE
    MOV  AH,02H    ; SET FOR THE SET CURSOR FUNCTION

    INT  10H       ; CALL ROM-BIOS TO SET THE CURSOR TO (DH,DL)

    POP  BX        ; RESTORE CALLER'S REGISTERS
    POP  AX

    RET

SET_CURSOR ENDP
```

EXAMPLE 7–2 Subroutine to set the cursor

From a program design standpoint, setting the cursor is a very frequently used subfunction and probably should be coded as a subprocedure to
which the coordinates are passed as needed. Example 7–2 presents a subroutine to set the cursor.

If it is not possible to pass coordinates in a register, then a common
word of storage can be used. In this situation, register DX must be saved and
restored, and the coordinates must be moved into register DX.

Write Character and Attribute: Function 09H

Once the cursor has been set to a particular screen position, a message must be displayed. DOS services could be used to do this. However, if color or other attributes are desired, the ROM-BIOS function 09H must be used.

Unlike DOS services, the ROM-BIOS function has no display string; it has only a display byte. Therefore, to display a complete message, a small loop must display the message byte by byte.

The message does not have to be just letters and numbers. For example, screen displays are often enhanced by drawing lines or by forming a complete box around a display area. The write character function can be used for each of these actions.

The write character function displays one or more copies of the character contained in register AL. How the character is displayed is defined by the attribute byte that is specified in register BL. The data and attribute bytes are written to the page number contained in register BH. Finally, register CX contains the number of times the character is to be displayed. Normally, register CX contains 1 when messages are shown, but it may contain other values when drawing lines and boxes.

When printing messages, remember this important rule: The cursor position does **not** change, no matter how many bytes are displayed (see register CX). Consequently, the cursor must be moved before every write function, or the characters will merely overlie each other at the current display position.

Therefore, when printing messages, set register CX to 1. Note that the routine prints only one character of a message string at a time. Thus, a loop is required to print or display an entire message. This is similar to DOS functions 02H and 05H, display a byte and print a byte. After displaying the byte, advance the cursor position before moving to the next byte of the message. Note that, since the attribute byte is written with each character, it is possible to have different colors for each byte of a message!

In the pseudocode that follows, which describes the steps to display a message, the required ROM-BIOS functions are shown in capital letters.

> (SET THE VIDEO MODE, if it has not yet been done)
> point to the first byte of the message
> get the length of the message
> get the coordinates of the first display position
>
> do while there are more bytes to display
>   SET THE CURSOR to current display position
>   DISPLAY THE BYTE at the current position
>   increment the coordinates
> enddo

Figure 7–4 (PGM15.ASM on the disk program) shows the code necessary to display the 25-byte message PRESS ANY KEY TO CONTINUE starting in row 15, column 20. First, the set mode function is invoked to allow you to set

```
   PAGE  60,132
   TITLE PGM15   FIGURE 7-4   USING BIOS TO DISPLAY 25 BYTE MESSAGE


;***************************************************************************
; PGM15       Title: Figure 7-4 Display Msg in color using BIOS     *
;                                                                   *
; Programmer: Vic Broquard                                          *
; Date Written:  6/11/88        Date Of Last Revision: 8/5/88       *
;                                                                   *
; Purpose:  display MSG in yellow on green on line 10, column 20    *
;                                                                   *
; Special Requirements:                                             *
;                                                                   *
;***************************************************************************


; program code segment

PGMCD   SEGMENT

MAIN    PROC    FAR

; housekeeping section

     ASSUME  CS:PGMCD,DS:PGMDA,SS:PGMSTK

     MOV  AX,PGMDA  ; ESTABLISH ADDRESSABILITY
     MOV  DS,AX     ; TO PGMDA - THE PGM'S DATA SEGMENT

     MOV  AH,00H    ; SET FOR SET VIDEO MODE
     MOV  AL,03H    ; SET FOR COLOR TEXT
     INT  10H       ; CALL ROM-BIOS TO SET VIDEO MODE

; main process section

     MOV  DH,0FH    ; SET FOR SCREEN ROW 15
     MOV  DL,14H    ; SET FOR SCREEN COL 20
     MOV  BH,00H    ; SET FOR CURRENT PAGE
     MOV  BL,2EH    ; SET COLOR FOR YELLOW ON GREEN

     MOV  CX,01H    ; SET REPLICATION FACTOR TO 1
     MOV  DI,25     ; DI = NUMBER OF BYTES OF MSG

     LEA  SI,MSG    ; SI -> CURRENT BYTE OF MSG

DSPLY_IT:

     MOV  AH,02H    ; SET FOR SET CURSOR FUNCTION
     INT  10H       ; CALL BIOS TO SET CURSOR POSITION
```

FIGURE 7–4   Program using ROM-BIOS to display a
25-byte message (PGM15.ASM)   *(Continues)*

```
        MOV  AL,[SI]   ; GET BYTE TO DISPLAY
        MOV  AH,09H    ; SET FOR DISPLAY BYTE FUNCTION
        INT  10H       ; CALL BIOS TO DISPLAY BYTE


        INC  DL        ; POINT TO NEXT SCREEN COLUMN
- - - - - - - - - - - - - - - - - - - - - - - - - - - - - - - - - - - - - - - - -

        INC  SI        ; POINT TO NEXT BYTE TO DISPLAY
        DEC  DI        ; DEC NUMBER OF BYTES TO DO
        JNZ  DSPLY_IT  ; REPEAT DISPLAY FOR NEXT BYTE

; return to DOS section

        MOV  AL,0      ; SET 0 AS THE RETURN CODE FOR DOS
        MOV  AH,4CH    ; SET FOR DOS END PROCESS FUNCTION
        INT  21H       ; CALL DOS TO END PROGRAM

MAIN    ENDP

PGMCD   ENDS


; program data segment

PGMDA   SEGMENT

MSG     DB 'PRESS ANY KEY TO CONTINUE'


PGMDA   ENDS


; program stack segment

PGMSTK SEGMENT PARA STACK 'STACK'

        DW      32 DUP (?)

PGMSTK ENDS
        END
```

FIGURE 7–4   continued

the display to color text. Second, notice that as much coding as possible has
been removed from the actual loop. The actions that have been removed
include establishing the starting value of the coordinate register (DX), setting BH for the current page, setting the colors desired in BL, and setting the
repeat register (CX) to 1. By doing this, the loop becomes much more efficient. The loop is controlled by the DEC DI instruction. Register DI has

been initialized as 25 bytes. As long as DEC results in a nonzero result, the JNZ (jump not zero) instruction continues the loop.

There is one major problem with this solution. Suppose that there are several messages, or lines, to be displayed. Using this approach makes it necessary to create a similar routine for each message. A disaster! A much more practical approach is to create a generalized display message routine or function. Such a generalized routine is shown in Figure 7–5 (PGM16.ASM on the program disk).

What parameters are required for a display message routine? Naturally, the routine needs the address of the message and its length. Also, the routine must have the beginning screen display coordinates and the color attribute byte(s) to be used. For simplicity, the routine in Figure 7–5 specifies that only one color attribute is used for the whole message, that only one of each character in the message is to be displayed, and that the current page for displaying the message is page 00H.

The code in Figure 7–5 is written to allow the color attribute to change from message to message. In other words, the color attribute is defined as a byte in storage. Every time a message needs to be displayed, the DSPLY_MSG procedure is invoked. Thus, only four instructions are required to print any message. The instructions set the address of the message, its length, and the coordinates at which the message is to be displayed. The fourth instruction is CALL DSPLY_MSG. Optionally, the value of the color byte could also be modified.

The driver routine in Figure 7–5 displays two messages. This is done for two reasons: to show that the DSPLY_MSG routine works and to illustrate that it is possible to place messages anywhere on the screen, almost at will. In this example, the second message is displayed on row 5 at column 3 after the first message was shown on row 15 at column 20.

Copy, assemble, link, and run program PGM16.ASM from the DOS prompt. Be sure you understand the processing performed before you continue in the text.

The effects of repeatedly displaying the same character by having register CX contain a number greater than 1 will be discussed shortly.

Scroll Window Up: Function 06H

The scroll window up function can be complicated, especially when developing pop-up screens and windows. We will ignore the topic of windowing, or creating pop-up screens, for now. In this chapter, we will use function 06H either to create a small boxed area in a full-screen data entry system or to clear the whole screen.

In its simplest form, function 06H is used first to define a rectangular window area on the screen and then to scroll the window's contents up one or more lines. The scrolling process is accomplished by inserting blank lines at the bottom of the area and moving all the other lines up one row. This makes the top row disappear. If all the lines in the window are scrolled up, then a

```
PAGE   60,132
    TITLE  PGM16 FIGURE 7-5  USING BIOS TO DISPLAY MESSAGES

;**************************************************************************
; PGM16      Title: Figure 7-5 Generalized Rtn to display a message   *
;                                                                     *
; Programmer: Vic Broquard                                            *
; Date Written:  6/11/88        Date Of Last Revision: 8/5/88         *
;                                                                     *
; Purpose:  display MSG in yellow on green on line 10, column 20      *
;                                                                     *
; Special Requirements:   DSPLY_MSG displays a string in color        *
;   at a specific screen position; it assumes the following           *
;                         AX = length of string to display            *
;                         BX = address of string to display           *
;                         DX = the coordinates to display at           *
;                         storage field COLOR contains the attribute   *
;**************************************************************************
;

; program code segment

PGMCD   SEGMENT

MAIN    PROC    FAR

; housekeeping section

      ASSUME  CS:PGMCD,DS:PGMDA,SS:PGMSTK

      MOV  AX,PGMDA  ; ESTABLISH ADDRESSABILITY
      MOV  DS,AX     ; TO PGMDA - THE PGM'S DATA SEGMENT

      MOV  AH,00H    ; SET FOR SET VIDEO MODE
      MOV  AL,03H    ; SET FOR COLOR TEXT
      INT  10H       ; CALL ROM-BIOS TO SET VIDEO MODE

; main process section

      MOV  AX,25     ; SET THE NUMBER OF BYTES TO DISPLAY
      LEA  BX,MSG    ; SET BX TO THE ADDRESS OF THE STRING
      MOV  DX,0F14H  ; SET COORDINATES OF ROW 15 COL 20
      CALL DSPLY_MSG ; CALL TO DISPLAY STRING

      MOV  AX,50     ; SET THE NUMBER OF BYTES TO DISPLAY
      LEA  BX,MSG2   ; SET BX TO THE ADDRESS OF THE STRING
      MOV  DX,0503H  ; SET COORDINATES OF ROW 5 COL 3
      CALL DSPLY_MSG ; CALL TO DISPLAY STRING
```

FIGURE 7–5 Generalized program to display messages by using ROM-BIOS (PGM16.ASM)

```
; return to DOS section

    MOV  AL,0     ; SET 0 AS THE RETURN CODE FOR DOS
    MOV  AH,4CH   ; SET FOR DOS END PROCESS FUNCTION
    INT  21H      ; CALL DOS TO END PROGRAM

----------------------------------------------------------------------

MAIN    ENDP
    PAGE

DSPLY_MSG  PROC

; display a string in color at a specific screen position

; assumes register AX = length of string to display
; assumes register BX = address of string to display
; assumes register DX = the coordinates to display at
; assumes storage field COLOR contains the attribute byte

    PUSH AX    ; SAVE ALL REGISTERS BEING USED
    PUSH BX
    PUSH CX
    PUSH DX
    PUSH SI
    PUSH DI

    MOV  SI,BX    ; SI = ADDR OF MSG TO DISPLAY
    MOV  DI,AX    ; DI = NUMBER OF BYTES TO DO

    MOV  BH,00H   ; SET FOR CURRENT PAGE
    MOV  BL,COLOR ; SET COLOR FROM USER

    MOV  CX,01H   ; SET REPLICATION FACTOR TO 1

DSPLY_IT:

    MOV  AH,02H   ; SET FOR SET CURSOR FUNCTION
    INT  10H      ; CALL BIOS TO SET CURSOR POSITION

    MOV  AL,[SI]  ; GET BYTE TO DISPLAY
    MOV  AH,09H   ; SET FOR DISPLAY BYTE FUNCTION
    INT  10H      ; CALL BIOS TO DISPLAY BYTE

    INC  DL       ; POINT TO NEXT SCREEN COLUMN
    INC  SI       ; POINT TO NEXT BYTE TO DO
    DEC  DI       ; DEC NUMBER OF BYTES TO DO
    JNZ  DSPLY_IT ; REPEAT DISPLAY FOR NEXT BYTE

    POP  DI       ; RESTORE ALL REGISTERS USED
    POP  SI
```

FIGURE 7–5   continued   *(Continues)*

```
        POP  DX
        POP  CX
        POP  BX
        POP  AX

        RET          ; RETURN TO CALLER

DSPLY_MSG  ENDP

PGMCD  ENDS
```
- -
```
; program data segment

PGMDA SEGMENT

COLOR DB 2EH    ; SET FOR YELLOW ON GREEN

MSG   DB 'PRESS ANY KEY TO CONTINUE'
MSG2  DB 'THIS IS A SECOND MESSAGE TO ENSURE DSPLY_MSG WORKS'

PGMDA ENDS


; program stack segment

PGMSTK SEGMENT PARA STACK 'STACK'

        DW      32 DUP (?)

PGMSTK ENDS
        END
```

FIGURE 7–5   continued

cleared window results. If the window has been defined to be the entire
screen and if all 25 lines are scrolled upward, then the screen is cleared.

To request function 06H, register AH must contain the value 06H and
register AL must contain the number of lines to scroll. The value in register
CX defines the upper-left corner of the window and register DX defines the
lower-right corner. In each case, the rows are specified in the high-order byte
and the columns are specified in the low-order byte of their respective registers. Thus, CH is the upper-left row number and CL is the upper-left column
number. Finally, register BH must contain the display attribute for the blank
lines that are to be inserted at the bottom and scrolled upward.

To clear the entire screen, register AL could contain 25, the total number of lines on the screen. However, the function also scrolls the entire

```
MOV  AX,0600H  ; SET FOR SCROLL UP AND FOR ENTIRE SCREEN
MOV  BH,4AH    ; SET COLOR TO RED WITH LIGHT GREEN TEXT
MOV  CX,0000H  ; SET UPPER-LEFT CORNER TO 0,0
MOV  DX,184FH  ; SET LOWER CORNER TO 24,79
INT  10H       ; CALL BIOS TO CLEAR SCREEN
```

EXAMPLE 7–3 Code to clear the screen and set the colors to light green on red

screen if AL contains 0. The coordinates required to define the entire screen
are the upper-left corner 0,0 and the lower-right corner 24,79 (18H,4FH).

Assume that you want to clear the screen and set a red background
with light green letters. The code in Example 7–3 accomplishes this task.
Normally, it is a good idea to create a subprocedure to handle such a job, perhaps moving the color attribute into BH from storage or from register AL
when the routine is invoked.

As you work with function 06H, remember this important rule: Only the
current page can be scrolled; other pages cannot. This rule is especially relevant when you create fancy page-swapping programs.

7.7 FULL-SCREEN DATA ENTRY AND BOXES

Full-screen data entry applications are commonly dressed up by drawing a
box or placing some other border design around a central working area.
Example 7–4 shows such a box.

Suppose you want a simple box outlining the central working area. You
want the upper-left corner of the box at row 5, column 70 and the lower-right

```
┌─────────────────────────────────────────────────────────────┐
│  SUPPLIER RECORD                          POSTLINE, INC.      │
│                                                               │
│  SUPPLIER CODE _ _ _  COMPANY NAME _ _ _ _ _ _ _ _ _ _ _ _ _  │
│                                                               │
│  SALES REP _ _ _ _ _ _ _ _ _ _ _ _ _ _ _ _ _                 │
│                                                               │
│  ADDRESS _ _ _ _ _ _ _ _ _ _ _ _ _ _ _ _ _                   │
│                                                               │
│  CITY _ _ _ _ _ _ _ _ _ _ _ _ _ _  STATE _ _  ZIP _ _ _ _ _  │
│                                                               │
│  AC _ _ _  PHONE _ _ _ _ _ _ _  TELEX _ _ _ _ _ _ _          │
│                                                               │
└─────────────────────────────────────────────────────────────┘
```

EXAMPLE 7–4 A data entry screen with surrounding box

corner at row 20, column 70. By knowing these two locations, you can draw the border. Of course, the box could be larger or smaller.

There are several special ASCII characters that can be used to draw a box. These include:

hex value	creates
0DAH	upper-left corner
0BFH	upper-right corner
0C0H	lower-left corner
0D9H	lower-right corner
0C4H	horizontal line
0B3H	vertical line

There are several other possibilities. Examine the ASCII graphics codes—those above 7FH—in Table B–3. The double line set is particularly effective when the colors used are different from those of the interior of the box. Also, the solid bar set could be used to create the box edge lines. Be creative.

The program in Figure 7–6 (PGM17.ASM on the program disk) defines the screen background as red, the box characters as light blue, and the foreground within the box as light green. The result looks somewhat like a Christmas tree.

The code is highly modular and functional. In the housekeeping section, SET_MODE is called to set the CRT to the color text mode 3. When the screen is cleared by CLEAR_SCREEN, the default colors of light green on red for the whole screen are set.

Next, the four corner angles are displayed using DSPLY_ANGLE. This sets the cursor to the desired location and displays the angle by using the color attribute specified in COLOR_BOX. The top and bottom lines are drawn by the DSPLY_HORIZ routine. Notice that register CX contains 59. Function 09H then displays the horizontal line character in AL 59 times.

Displaying the vertical lines is more difficult. Only one character can be shown per loop repetition. The cursor is placed at the desired location and one vertical line is drawn. Then, the row number is incremented and the cycle is repeated.

Finally, a simple message is displayed within the box to illustrate what the next steps in creating a full-screen data entry system might be. The last action places the cursor at the bottom of the screen. When the program ends, the DOS A> prompt will be at a reasonable screen location.

Figure 7–6 illustrates how a program can be designed by using subroutines. If this overall function to draw a box around the working area were to be integrated in a full-screen data entry program, then the main line coding would be set up as a subroutine, such as DRAW_BOX. Then, whenever the main procedure wanted to display a box, it would only have to call the subroutine DRAW_BOX.

```
     PAGE    60,132
     TITLE   PGM17  FIGURE 7-6  USING BIOS-SET COLORS AND DRAW A BOX


;***************************************************************************
; PGM17       Title: Figure 7-6 Set colors and draw a box          *
;                                                                  *
; Programmer: Vic Broquard                                         *
; Date Written: 6/11/88        Date Of Last Revision: 8/5/88       *
;                                                                  *
; Purpose: Set CRT colors and draw a centrally located box for full *
;          screen data entry                                       *
;                                                                  *
; Special Requirements: coordinates are hard coded; color of box is in *
;                       field COLOR_BOX while screen color is in COLOR *
;                                                                  *
;      box coordinates: (5,10) TO (5,70) AND (20,10) TO (20,70)    *
;                                                                  *
;***************************************************************************



; EQUATES FOR THE BOX COORDINATES AND CHARACTERS TO DISPLAY

UP_LEFT      EQU    050AH
UP_L_ANGLE   EQU    0DAH
UP_RIGHT     EQU    0546H
UP_R_ANGLE   EQU    0BFH

LO_LEFT      EQU    140AH
LO_L_ANGLE   EQU    0C0H
LO_RIGHT     EQU    1446H
LO_R_ANGLE   EQU    0D9H

UP_L_LINE    EQU    050BH
LO_L_LINE    EQU    140BH
NUM_COLS     EQU    59
NUM_ROWS     EQU    14
VERT_CHAR    EQU    0B3H
HOR_CHAR     EQU    0C4H




; program code segment

PGMCD     SEGMENT

MAIN PROC FAR
```

FIGURE 7–6 Program to set colors and draw a box (PGM17.ASM)   *(Continues)*

```
; housekeeping section

      ASSUME    CS:PGMCD,SS:PGMSK,DS:PGMDA

      MOV  AX,PGMDA       ; GET ADDRESSABILITY
      MOV  DS,AX          ; TO PGM DATA SEGMENT

      CALL SET_MODE       ; SET MODE TO 3 - COLOR TEXT
      CALL CLEAR_SCREEN   ; CLEAR SCREEN AND SET COLORS

; main process section


; display all four corners

; display the upper left corner angle

      MOV  DX,UP_LEFT     ; SET COORDINATES TO (5,10)
      MOV  AL,UP_L_ANGLE  ; SET AL TO THE ANGLE TO DISPLAY
      CALL DSPLY_ANGLE    ; DISPLAY THE ANGLE

; display the upper right corner angle

      MOV  DX,UP_RIGHT    ; SET COORDINATES TO (5,70)
      MOV  AL,UP_R_ANGLE  ; SET AL TO THE ANGLE TO DISPLAY
      CALL DSPLY_ANGLE    ; DISPLAY THE ANGLE

; display the lower left corner angle

      MOV  DX,LO_LEFT     ; SET COORDINATES TO (20,10)
      MOV  AL,LO_L_ANGLE  ; SET AL TO THE ANGLE TO DISPLAY
      CALL DSPLY_ANGLE    ; DISPLAY THE ANGLE

; display the lower right corner angle

      MOV  DX,LO_RIGHT    ; SET COORDINATES TO (20,70)
      MOV  AL,LO_R_ANGLE  ; SET AL TO THE ANGLE TO DISPLAY
      CALL DSPLY_ANGLE    ; DISPLAY THE ANGLE
      PAGE
; now draw in the top and bottom lines

; top line

      MOV  DX,UP_L_LINE   ; SET COORDINATES TO (5,11)
      MOV  CX,NUM_COLS    ; NUMBER OF REPETITIONS TO DISPLAY
      CALL DSPLY_HORIZ    ; DRAW THE HORIZONTAL LINE

; bottom line

      MOV  DX,LO_L_LINE   ; SET COORDINATES TO (20,11)
```

FIGURE 7–6   continued

```
        MOV   CX,NUM_COLS    ; NUMBER OF REPETITIONS TO DISPLAY
        CALL  DSPLY_HORIZ    ; DRAW THE HORIZONTAL LINE

; finally draw in the vertical lines

; left line

        MOV   DX,UP_LEFT     ; SET COORDINATES OF UPPER LEFT CORNER
        INC   DH             ; AND POINT TO NEXT ROW
        MOV   CX,NUM_ROWS    ; SET NUMBER OF ROWS TO DO
        CALL  DSPLY_VER      ; DRAW VERTICAL LINE

; right line

        MOV   DX,UP_RIGHT    ; SET COORDINATES OF UPPER RIGHT CORNER
        INC   DH             ; AND POINT TO NEXT ROW
        MOV   CX,NUM_ROWS    ; SET NUMBER OF ROWS TO DO
        CALL  DSPLY_VER      ; DRAW VERTICAL LINE

; to test out the box, display MSG in box

        LEA   BX,MSG         ; SET BX TO THE ADDRESS OF THE MSG
        MOV   AX,11          ; SET THE NUMBER OF BYTES TO DISPLAY
        MOV   DX,0A14H       ; SET THE COORDINATES OF THE DISPLAY
        CALL  DSPLY_MSG      ; DISPLAY THE MESSAGE IN THE BOX

; set cursor to line 23

        MOV   DX,1700H       ; SET COORDINATES FOR A>
        CALL  SET_CURSOR     ; SET THE CURSOR FOR PGM EXIT

; return to DOS section

        MOV   AX,4C00H       ; SET FOR RET TO DOS WITH A 0 RETURN CD
        INT   21H            ; RETURN TO DOS

MAIN ENDP



        SUBTTL    SET_MODE SUBROUTINE
        PAGE

SET_MODE  PROC

; set the vidoe display mode to type 3 - text color 25 X 80

        PUSH AX        ; SAVE CALLER'S AX
```

FIGURE 7–6   continued   *(Continues)*

```
          MOV  AX,0003H  ; SET FOR SET MODE AND MODE 3
          INT  10H       ; CALL BIOS TO SET MODE

          POP  AX        ; RESTORE AX

          RET

SET_MODE  ENDP




          SUBTTL    CLEAR_SCREEN SUBROUTINE
          PAGE

CLEAR_SCREEN  PROC

; clear screen procedure

          PUSH AX        ; SAVE CALLER'S REGISTERS
          PUSH BX
          PUSH CX
          PUSH DX

          MOV  AX,0600H  ; SET SCROLL FUNCTION AND FULL SCREEN
          MOV  BH,COLOR  ; SET COLOR FOR LIGHT GREEN ON RED
          MOV  CX,0000   ; SET COORDINATES OF UPPER LEFT CORNER
          MOV  DX,184FH  ; SET COORDINATES OF LOWER RIGHT CORNER
          INT  10H       ; CALL BIOS TO CLEAR SCREEN

          POP  DX        ; RESTORE CALLER'S RESISTERS
          POP  CX
          POP  BX
          POP  AX

          RET

CLEAR_SCREEN  ENDP




          SUBTTL    SET_CURSOR SUBROUTINE
          PAGE

SET_CURSOR  PROC    ; SET THE CURSOR POSITION

; assumes that DX has been loaded with the coordinates

          PUSH AX        ; SAVE CALLER'S REGISTERS
```

FIGURE 7–6   continued

```
        PUSH BX

        MOV  AH,02    ; SET CURSOR FUNCTION
        MOV  BH,00    ; CURRENT PAGE
        INT  10H      ; CALL BIOS

        POP  BX       ; RESTORE REGISTERS
        POP  AX

        RET

SET_CURSOR  ENDP



        SUBTTL    DSPLY_ANGLE SUBROUTINE
        PAGE

DSPLY_ANGLE    PROC

; draw a corner angle

; assumes AL holds the character to print
; assumes DX holds the coordinates

        PUSH AX            ; SAVE REGISTERS
        PUSH BX
        PUSH CX

        CALL SET_CURSOR    ; SET THE CURSOR TO THE CORNER

        MOV  AH,09H        ; SET FOR WRITE CHAR AND ATTRIBUTE
        MOV  BH,00H        ; SET FOR THE CURRENT PAGE
        MOV  BL,COLOR_BOX  ; SET FOR BOX COLOR
        MOV  CX,1          ; SET FOR DISPLAYING 1 CHAR

        INT  10H           ; CALL BIOS TO DISPLAY CORNER ANGLE

        POP  CX            ; RESTORE REGISTERTS
        POP  BX
        POP  AX

        RET

DSPLY_ANGLE    ENDP



        SUBTTL    DSPLY_HORIZ SUBROUTINE
```

FIGURE 7–6   continued   *(Continues)*

```
        PAGE

DSPLY_HORIZ    PROC

; draw a horizontal line

; assumes CX is set to number of chars to display
; assumes DX is set to the starting coordinates

        PUSH AX            ; SAVE REGISTERS
        PUSH BX

        CALL SET_CURSOR    ; SET TO STARTING COORDINATES

        MOV  AH,09H        ; SET FOR WRITE CHARACTER AND ATTRIBUTE
        MOV  AL,HOR_CHAR   ; SET THE HORIZONTAL CHAR TO DISPLAY
        MOV  BH,00H        ; SET FOR CURRENT PAGE
        MOV  BL,COLOR_BOX  ; SET THE BOX COLOR

        INT  10H           ; CALL BIOS TO DISPLAY THE LINE

        POP  BX            ; RESTORE REGISTERS
        POP  AX

        RET

DSPLY_HORIZ    ENDP


        SUBTTL    DSPLY_VER SUBROUTINE
        PAGE

DSPLY_VER   PROC ; DRAW A VERTICAL LINE

;     ASSUME DX = COORDINATES TO USE
;     ASSUME CX = NUMBER OF ROWS TO DRAW

        PUSH AX            ; SAVE REGISTERS
        PUSH BX
        PUSH CX
        PUSH DX
        PUSH DI

        MOV  DI,CX         ; SAVE THE NUMBER OF REPETITIONS TO DO

WLOOP:

        CALL SET_CURSOR    ; SET THE CURSOR
```

FIGURE 7–6   continued

```
        INC  DH            ; ADD 1 TO ROW

        MOV  DI,CX          ; SAVE REMAINING NUMBER OF REPETITIONS

        MOV  AH,09          ; SET FOR WRITE FUNCTION
        MOV  AL,VERT_CHAR   ; SET THE CHAR TO DISPLAY
        MOV  BH,00H         ; SET FOR THE CURRENT PAGE
        MOV  BL,COLOR_BOX   ; SET THE COLOR FOR THE LINE
        MOV  CX,1           ; SET FOR DRAWING 1 CHARACTER
        INT  10H            ; CALL BIOS TO DRAW IN THE CHAR

        MOV  CX,DI          ; RESTORE REMAINING NUMBER OF REPS

        LOOP WLOOP          ; DEC # OF REPETITIONS TO DRAW
                            ; REPEAT WLOOP IF NOT ZERO

        POP  DI             ; RESTORE REGISTERS
        POP  DX
        POP  CX
        POP  BX
        POP  AX

        RET

DSPLY_VER   ENDP




        SUBTTL    DSPLY_MSG SUBROUTINE
        PAGE

DSPLY_MSG   PROC

; display a string in color at a specific screen position

; assumes register AX = length of string to display
; assumes register BX = address of string to display
; assumes register DX = the coordinates to display at
; assumes storage field COLOR contains the attribute byte

        PUSH AX             ; SAVE ALL REGISTERS BEING USED
        PUSH BX
        PUSH CX
        PUSH DX
        PUSH SI
        PUSH DI

        MOV  SI,BX          ; SI = ADDR OF MSG TO DISPLAY
```

FIGURE 7–6   continued   *(Continues)*

```
        MOV  DI,AX     ; DI = NUMBER OPF BYTES TO DO

        MOV  BH,00H    ; SET FOR CURRENT PAGE
        MOV  BL,COLOR  ; SET COLOR FROM USER

        MOV  CX,01H    ; SET REPLICATION FACTOR TO 1

DSPLY_IT:

        MOV  AH,02H    ; SET FOR SET CURSOR FUNCTION
        INT  10H       ; CALL BIOS TO SET CURSOR POSITION

        MOV  AL,[SI]   ; GET BYTE TO DISPLAY
        MOV  AH,09H    ; SET FOR DISPLAY BYTE FUNCTION
        INT  10H       ; CALL BIOS TO DISPLAY BYTE

        INC  DL        ; POINT TO NEXT SCREEN COLUMN
        INC  SI        ; POINT TO NEXT BYTE TO DO
        DEC  DI        ; DEC NUMBER OF BYTES TO DO
        JNZ  DSPLY_IT  ; REPEAT DISPLAY FOR NEXT BYTE

        POP  DI        ; RESTORE ALL REGISTERS USED
        POP  SI
        POP  DX
        POP  CX
        POP  BX
        POP  AX

        RET

DSPLY_MSG  ENDP

PGMCD     ENDS



        SUBTTL    DATA AREAS
        PAGE

; program data segment

PGMDA     SEGMENT

COLOR     DB   4AH         ; COLOR LIGHT GREEN ON RED
COLOR_BOX DB   49H         ; COLOR LIGHT BLUE ON RED

MSG       DB   'ENTER NAME:' ; TEST MESSAGE

PGMDA     ENDS
```

FIGURE 7–6   continued

```
;    PROGRAM STACK SEGMENT


PGMSK     SEGMENT PARA STACK 'STACK'

    DW   32 DUP (?)

PGMSK     ENDS
    END  MAIN
```

FIGURE 7–6   continued

7.8   LESSER-USED ROM-BIOS SERVICES

Scroll Window Down: Function 07H

The scroll window down function is used to insert blank lines at the top of a window area, thereby moving all other lines down one line. For each execution of the function, one line at the bottom of the window is lost. The register usage and coding for this function are exactly the same as for function 06H, scroll window up. As with function 06H, only the current page can be scrolled.

Set Cursor Size: Function 01H

For some applications it is desirable to display a cursor that is larger than normal. Function 01H, set cursor size, can adjust the size of the cursor from one scan line in size to as large as eight scan lines (a solid block). If desired, the cursor can be made invisible by having all scan lines turned off. Scan line 0 is at the top of the display area; scan line 7 is at the bottom. The default cursor size is two lines, beginning on scan line 6 and ending on scan line 7. (On a monochrome display, the cursor uses scan lines 12 and 13 as the default settings.)

When function 01H is to be implemented, register AH must contain 01H. The contents of register CX define the size of the desired cursor, with the starting scan line number in CH and the ending scan line number in CL.

The following code sets the cursor to one line in size on scan line 7.

```
    MOV  AH,01H    ; SET FOR THE SET CURSOR SIZE FUNCTION
    MOV  CX,0707H  ; SET FOR START LINE 7, END LINE 7
    INT  10H       ; CALL BIOS TO SET THE CURSOR SIZE
```

The cursor can be made to disappear. This is done by setting bit 5 of register CH to on. If the value of the start line is greater than the end line, then a two-part cursor is created.

Read Cursor Position: Function 03H

There are times when the program may not know exactly where on the screen the cursor is currently located. This can happen when using the arrow keys and performing similar cursor movements. The read cursor function provides a quick and easy way of handling these situations.

To implement function 03H, register AH must contain the value 03H with register BH containing the page number of the display. The page number can be either the current page or any other page, so you can work with a page that is not currently being displayed.

When executed, the function returns the cursor location (row and column) and the size of the cursor (starting scan line and ending scan line). These values are contained in registers CX and DX. As a result, registers CX and DX are modified by this service.

    DH = row number
    DL = column number
    CH = starting scan line of cursor
    CL = ending scan line of cursor

Read Character and Attribute: Function 08H

Function 08H is often described as reading a character "directly from the screen." Actually, the character comes from the direct memory display area. This function works in both text and graphics modes, and the character can be from the current page or any page that is specified.

The value 08H is placed in register AH; register BH contains the number of the current page or any other page. The character and attribute are read from the current cursor position and returned in register AX. AL contains the character and AH holds the attribute.

Set Active Display Page: Function 05H

The set active display page service is used to "instantaneously" switch display pages in text mode. The 80-column mode has four pages (numbered 0, 1, 2, and 3); the 40-column mode has eight pages (numbered from 0 through 7). The default page is always 0, the current page. Register AH contains the function value 05H and AL contains the new page number.

Multiple-page displays can be used to advantage in programs that provide a help function. At any time, the user can press a specific key, often function key F1, for help messages. Typically, one or more screens of helpful information about the program commands or procedures are displayed. When the user has finished reading the messages, the program returns to the original screen and resumes processing from where it was interrupted. The following pseudocode shows how this can be accomplished.

       F1 (help) has been detected, so
             SET TO NEW ACTIVE PAGE

CLEAR SCREEN of new page
DISPLAY HELP MESSAGES on new page
GET ANY KEYSTROKE indicating user is done with help
SET TO ORIGINAL PAGE
resume processing where left off

For efficiency, programs often build the entire help screen display on a help page during the program initialization phase. Then, when help is requested, the program simply swaps the current page for the help page, thus saving execution time.

Get Current Video Mode: Function 0FH

The get current video mode function returns the current display mode. Register AH must be set to 0FH.

When the service returns to the program, BH contains the page currently in use. Register AL contains the video mode and register AH contains the screen width (40 or 80 columns).

Function 0FH is often used by "well-behaved" programs. The user may have already set the video mode as needed. A well-behaved program that needs to reset the video mode first gets the current settings and saves them in the data area. Then it changes the video mode. One of the program's last actions is to restore the user's original video mode setting, thus resetting the status to its original mode. Doing this makes it easier for the user, since he or she is returned to where they were before the function was invoked.

Set Color Palette: Function 0BH

This service is used to set the color palette in one of the graphics modes. Register AH contains the value 0BH, register BH contains a color palette number, and register BL contains a color value.

In text modes, if register BH is 0, then BL specifies the color of the border area around the working screen area. BL can be any of the 16 different colors. For further details, consult your DOS manuals.

7.9 PUTTING IT ALL TOGETHER

At first glance, none of these ROM-BIOS routines seems overly complicated. By themselves, they are not. However, to combine them into working programs requires relatively large amounts of code. If generalized routines are not used, the coding can easily become so voluminous that there may be insufficient room for coding the primary objective of the program.

This means that you must design your solution before you begin coding. It is not important which technique you use—top-down design, bottom-up design, flowcharting, pseudocoding, or the like. However, it is important that the design be created before you touch the computer. The following example illustrates how to convert from a pseudocode sketch of a module into the actual code.

Suppose that during normal processing (with the color attributes yellow on blue), an error condition occurs. It is necessary to notify the user. The error message should appear in red on green on a new screen so that it will stand out. The message is to be displayed beginning at row 10, column 20. In this example ignore whatever must be done to remedy the error situation. After the error is fixed, display the usual message PRESS ANY KEY TO CONTINUE. The "any key" value should be input by using DOS function 08H so that it is not echoed. The pseudocode is

> CLS (clear screen)
> reset the color attribute to the error scheme
> at (10,20) DISPLAY THE ERROR MESSAGE
> → the actual error handling is ignored
> reset the primary display colors
> at (20,20) DISPLAY THE CONTINUE MESSAGE
> INPUT ANYTHING

Figure 7–7 (PGM18.ASM on your program disk) shows the completed program. It makes use of several of the routines described previously. CLEAR_SCREEN, DSPLY_MSG, and SET_MODE are used to set the mode. A new module, GET_ANY, gets the user's response. To handle the color attribute swapping, two more color fields are defined. MAIN_COLOR holds the primary color attribute and ERR_COLOR holds the color scheme for error messages. The field COLOR contains the current color request for DSPLY_MSG.

Assemble and experiment with the program to reinforce your understanding of the techniques involved.

7.10 HANDLING THE SPECIAL KEYS IN FULL-SCREEN DATA ENTRY

In Chapter 6 you learned that the several "get a byte" DOS functions need to be checked when handling many of the special keys. The special keys most important in data entry include the four arrow keys (left, right, up, and down), DEL, INS, BACKSPACE, HOME-END (delete to end of line), and the ten function keys.

Suppose that the data-entry screen is as shown in Example 7–5. (Line numbers are added for discussion purposes. The actual row and column numbers would be different because the messages would be centered on the screen.) You need to design a program that meets the following specifications:

```
     PAGE    60,132
     TITLE   PGM18  FIGURE 7-7  DISPLAY ERROR MESSAGE SEQUENCE

;***********************************************************************
; PGM18         Title: Figure 7-7 Display An Error Message Sequence   *
;                                                                     *
; Programmer: Vic Broquard                                            *
; Date Written: 6/11/88         Date Of Last Revision: 8/5/88         *
;                                                                     *
; Purpose: To display an error message in a different color, then to  *
;          get any key stroke to continue                             *
;                                                                     *
; Special Requirements: uses routines DSPLY_MSG, GET_ANY, SET_MODE,   *
;                                      CLEAR_SCREEN                    *
;***********************************************************************

; program code segment

PGMCD   SEGMENT

MAIN    PROC    FAR

; housekeeping section

    ASSUME  CS:PGMCD,DS:PGMDA,SS:PGMSTK

    MOV   AX,PGMDA       ; ESTABLISH ADDRESSABILITY
    MOV   DS,AX          ; TO PGMDA - THE PGM'S DATA SEGMENT

    CALL  SET_MODE       ; SET TO MODE 3 - COLOR TEXT

; main process section

; assume that an error has occurred and pgm branches here

    CALL CLEAR_SCREEN    ; CLEAR SCREEN AND SET COLORS

; reset COLOR to the error colors

    MOV   AH,ERR_COLOR   ; GET COLOR ATTRIBUTE FOR ERROR MESSAGES
    MOV   COLOR,AH       ; SET IN COLOR FIELD FOR DISPLAYS

; display the error message

    MOV   AX,21          ; SET NUMBER OF BYTES TO DISPLAY TO 21
    LEA   BX,ERROR_MSG   ; BX = ADDR OF MESSAGE TO DISPLAY
    MOV   DX,0A14H       ; SET COORDINATES TO (10,20)
    CALL  DSPLY_MSG      ; DISPLAY ERROR MESSAGE
```

FIGURE 7–7   Program to display error message sequence
(PGM18.ASM)   *(Continues)*

```
; reset the primary colors

    MOV  AH,MAIN_COLOR  ; GET THE ORIGINAL COLOR ATTRIBUTES
    MOV  COLOR,AH       ; RESET THE COLOR BYTE

------------------------------------------------------------------------

; display continue message

    MOV  AX,25         ; SET NUMBER OF BYTES TO DISPLAY
    LEA  BX,CONT_MSG   ; BX = ADDR OF MESSAGE TO DISPLAY
    MOV  DX,1414H      ; SET COORDINATES TO (20,20)
    CALL DSPLY_MSG     ; DISPLAY THE CONTINUE MESSAGE

; get the anything entry

    CALL GET_ANY       ; PAUSE UNTIL ANY KEY IS PRESSED

; resume processing after the error is handled

; return to DOS section

    MOV  AL,0          ; SET 0 AS THE RETURN CODE FOR DOS
    MOV  AH,4CH        ; SET FOR DOS END PROCESS FUNCTION
    INT  21H           ; CALL DOS TO END PROGRAM

MAIN    ENDP



    SUBTTL    SET_MODE SUBROUTINE
    PAGE

SET_MODE  PROC

; set the video display mode to type 3 - text color 25 X 80

    PUSH AX         ; SAVE CALLER'S AX

    MOV  AX,0003H  ; SET FOR SET MODE AND MODE 3
    INT  10H       ; CALL BIOS TO SET MODE

    POP  AX         ; RESTORE AX

    RET

SET_MODE  ENDP



    SUBTTL    CLEAR_SCREEN SUBROUTINE
    PAGE
```

FIGURE 7–7 continued

```
CLEAR_SCREEN   PROC

; clear screen procedure

    PUSH AX       ; SAVE CALLER'S REGISTERS
    PUSH BX
    PUSH CX
    PUSH DX

- - - - - - - - - - - - - - - - - - - - - - - - - - - - - - - - - - - - - - - - - - - - - -

    MOV  AX,0600H ; SET SCROLL FUNCTION AND FULL SCREEN
    MOV  BH,COLOR ; SET COLOR FOR LIGHT GREEN ON RED
    MOV  CX,0000  ; SET COORDINATES OF UPPER LEFT CORNER
    MOV  DX,184FH ; SET COORDINATES OF LOWER RIGHT CORNER
    INT  10H      ; CALL BIOS TO CLEAR SCREEN

    POP  DX       ; RESTORE CALLER'S RESISTERS
    POP  CX
    POP  BX
    POP  AX

    RET

CLEAR_SCREEN   ENDP



    SUBTTL    DSPLY_MSG SUBROUTINE
    PAGE

DSPLY_MSG  PROC

; display a string in color at a specific screen position

; assumes register AX = length of string to display
; assumes register BX = address of string to display
; assumes register DX = the coordinates to display at
; assumes storage field COLOR contains the attribute byte

    PUSH AX       ; SAVE ALL REGISTERS BEING USED
    PUSH BX
    PUSH CX
    PUSH DX
    PUSH SI
    PUSH DI

    MOV  SI,BX    ; SI = ADDR OF MSG TO DISPLAY
    MOV  DI,AX    ; DI = NUMBER OF BYTES TO DO

    MOV  BH,00H   ; SET FOR CURRENT PAGE
```

FIGURE 7–7   continued   *(Continues)*

```
        MOV  BL,COLOR  ; SET COLOR FROM USER
        MOV  CX,01H    ; SET REPLICATION FACTOR TO 1

DSPLY_IT:

        MOV  AH,02H    ; SET FOR SET CURSOR FUNCTION
        INT  10H       ; CALL BIOS TO SET CURSOR POSITION

        MOV  AL,[SI]   ; GET BYTE TO DISPLAY
        MOV  AH,09H    ; SET FOR DISPLAY BYTE FUNCTION
        INT  10H       ; CALL BIOS TO DISPLAY BYTE

------------------------------------------------------------------------

        INC  DL        ; POINT TO NEXT SCREEN COLUMN
        INC  SI        ; POINT TO NEXT BYTE TO DO
        DEC  DI        ; DEC NUMBER OF BYTES TO DO
        JNZ  DSPLY_IT  ; REPEAT DISPLAY FOR NEXT BYTE

        POP  DI        ; RESTORE ALL REGISTERS USED
        POP  SI
        POP  DX
        POP  CX
        POP  BX
        POP  AX

        RET            ; RETURN TO CALLER

DSPLY_MSG  ENDP




        SUBTTL   GET_ANY - INPUT ANY KEY STROKE
        PAGE

GET_ANY   PROC

; get anything that is entered on the keyboard - no echo

        PUSH AX        ; SAVE REGISTER

        MOV  AH,08H    ; SET FOR KEYBOARD INPUT - NO ECHO
        INT  21H       ; CALL DOS TO INPUT BYTE

        CMP  AL,00H    ; SPECIAL KEY PRESSED?
        JNE  GO_ON     ; NO, CONTINUE

        MOV  AH,08H    ; SET FOR KEYBOARD INPUT - NO ECHO
```

FIGURE 7–7   continued

```
        INT  21H        ; CALL DOS TO GET ACTUAL CODE

GO_ON:
        POP  AX         ; RESTORE REGISTER
        RET
GET_ANY  ENDP

PGMCD  ENDS




; program data segment

PGMDA  SEGMENT

ERROR_MSG    DB    'YOU HAVE HAD AN ERROR'
CONT_MSG     DB    'PRESS ANY KEY TO CONTINUE'
COLOR        DB    1EH  ; YELLOW ON BLUE
MAIN_COLOR   DB    1EH  ; YELLOW ON BLUE
ERR_COLOR    DB    24H  ; RED ON GREEN

PGMDA  ENDS



; program stack segment

PGMSTK  SEGMENT PARA STACK 'STACK'

        DW    32 DUP (?)

PGMSTK  ENDS
        END
```

FIGURE 7–7   continued

```
    1    ENTER NAME     _____
    2    ENTER ADDRESS _____
    3    ENTER CITY     _____
    4    ENTER STATE    _____
    5    ENTER ZIP      _____

    6    PRESS ESC WHEN ALL DATA ARE CORRECTLY ENTERED
    7    PRESS F1  FOR HELP
```

EXAMPLE 7–5   Data entry screen with reference row numbers

- If LEFT ARROW is pressed, then the cursor should back up one column **if** the current position is not already at the first column of the field. If RIGHT ARROW is pressed, the cursor should move one column to the right **if** the current position is not already at the last column of the field.

- Whenever a carriage return is entered, indicating that the field has been completed, the cursor should move downward to the first column of the next field. If the line being entered is line 5, the next field should be line 1 to facilitate editing of a prior entry.

- If UP ARROW is entered, the cursor should be set to the first column of the field above the current one, going from line 1 to 7. If DOWN ARROW is pressed, the cursor should be positioned in the first column below the current one, going from line 7 to 1.

- If DEL is pressed, the character under the cursor should be deleted. If BACKSPACE is used, the cursor should back up (as it does with LEFT ARROW) and then blank out the character. If INS is entered, the program should accept the next characters entered and insert them at the cursor position, moving the remainder of the line to the right. When the INS key is pressed again, the keyboard should return to normal entry operation.

- When F1 is used, the screen should show some on-line help information and then return to the main screen. The help information can be shown on a page separate from the main display.

- When ESC is used, all information should be accepted as final, and the set of data should be processed.

Each of these functions can be coded as separate procedures and called when needed. As you work, remember this important rule: The screen position (which field and which byte in that field) must be coordinated to the actual data field in memory. If you back up one position on the screen, you must also back up one position in the field in memory. This amounts to double work.

Consider how a delete operation must be echoed to the screen as well as stored in the appropriate storage field. There are two common approaches to this situation. The direct method echoes the operation in the storage field as it is handled on the screen. Although this method works well, it leads to a rather large volume of code and therefore requires careful planning. The direct method offers an advantage in that when the ESC key is pressed to indicate that the screen of data is correct, all fields are immediately ready for further processing.

The second method handles the actions directly on the screen. Storage is not used. Then, when the ESC key is pressed, the program positions the cursor at the start of the first field and uses function 08H (read character and attribute), which stores the byte in the field. The process continues until all bytes of the first field have been read. Then, the process is repeated for the other fields.

To illustrate how these functions are handled, assume the user is on line 1, entering a name that which can be up to 10 characters long. To correct

```
(SET VIDEO MODE for color text, if it has not been set)

CLEAR SCREEN

DISPLAY the FNAME prompt message using the main screen colors

switch colors to the highlight style
DISPLAY FNAME (containing blanks at first)

GET THE FIELD - the user entry for FNAME

switch the colors back to the main colors
DISPLAY FNAME to reset the field display to the main colors
```

EXAMPLE 7–6   Pseudocode for handling the data entry of FNAME

mistakes, the user presses LEFT ARROW. Further, you must be able to show the user precisely how many characters can be entered in FNAME by displaying the field size. Since the program uses color mode, the columns where the user is to enter FNAME can be shown in a set of colors different from the rest of the screen. This will be done by displaying blanks in the new color scheme before permitting the user to actually enter data. Example 7–6 shows pseudocode that outlines these tasks.

The program that implements this data entry sequence must include a SET_CURSOR routine. The GET_FIELD routine can be pseudocoded as shown in Example 7–7.

Figure 7–8 (PGM19.ASM on the program disk) shows how the data entry sequence can be coded. The overall flow begins by displaying the message prompt ENTER FIRST NAME by using the DSPLY_MSG subroutine. Next, the colors are changed from the normal yellow on blue to red on green. Then, the actual FNAME field is displayed. Since the field is now blank, a window appearance is created. This significantly helps with data entry.

The major new procedure, GET_FIELD, is called to input the field. Once the data have been entered, the color is reset back to normal and the field is redisplayed. It now blends in with the rest of the screen. The entire cycle is repeated on the next field in the data entry set. Thus, the different colors keep the user constantly informed of which field is currently being entered or modified.

The GET_FIELD routine first calculates the last valid column for this field and then saves the starting and ending row and column values. The main loop, NEXT_BYTE, sets the cursor to the current column and calls GET_BYTE. This isolates the actual DOS code needed to input the byte. Register AX holds the resultant entry. Register AH indicates whether a control code, special key, or valid character was entered. The user-entered byte is in register AL. The GET_BYTE routine also validates the data to ensure that a letter, number, control code, or special key has been entered. Any other entry is ignored and a retry is requested.

```
GET THE FIELD
     do while the entry is not a <CR> and
                 while the max field length has not been reached
          SET CURSOR to next position
          GET A BYTE (indicators set: special key / control code)
          check and handle special keys
          check and handle control codes
          if ok, save character
               and echo it to CRT
     enddo
end



handle left arrow:
     can we back up?
     no, ignore request
     yes, reset coordinates
          SET CURSOR
          decrement pointer to memory area of FNAME
```

EXAMPLE 7–7   Pseudocode for the GET_FIELD routine

Thus, overall control remains in GET_FIELD. Once the byte is entered, GET_FIELD then determines what processing will be done. There is a section for control codes, special keys, and valid data. Only if a byte of data is valid does the program insert it into the FNAME field and echo it. If LEFT ARROW was entered, the special key section first checks to see if the beginning of the field has been reached. If so, the request is ignored.

With this shell as a starting point, it is possible to insert code for as many of the other special keys and control codes as desired. Yes, the routine GET_FIELD will become large, but additional subroutines can always be added as necessary. If more keys and codes are handled, then we strongly recommend creating a subprocedure for each. Otherwise, conditional branches will extend out of range and cause major difficulties. Remember that conditional branches and LOOPs can jump only +127 bytes or −128 bytes from their current locations.

Again, assemble and execute this program from the DOS prompt. Once you are comfortable with its operation, run the program from your debugger, tracing execution from procedure to procedure. If you are not using the CODE VIEW debugger (Version 5.0 or later), you will discover a major problem. The routines will set the cursor to the desired location. Then, when the debugger interrupts the program to display the registers, the display becomes completely fouled up. Try it for yourself, if you have not experienced this effect. The problem can be remedied by using the advanced debugger commands and features discussed in the next section.

```
PAGE  60,132
TITLE PGM19  FIGURE 7-8 GET A FIELD WITH OPERATIONAL LEFT ARROW

;************************************************************************
; PGM19      Title: Figure 7-8 Get a field with functional left arrow *
;                                                              key  *
; Programmer: Vic Broquard                                           *
; Date Written:  6/11/88       Date Of Last Revision: 8/5/88        *
;                                                                   *
; Purpose: To get a field and show how the arrow keys could be coded *
; input area is shown in a different color to highlight the entry size *
;                                                                   *
; Special Requirements: uses DSPLY_MSG to display msgs with the field *
;    where the field COLOR contains the current colors to use        *
;                                                                   *
;    other procedures used:                                          *
;    SET_MODE, CLEAR_SCREEN, SET_CURSOR, and GET_FIELD              *
;    GET_FIELD uses GET_BYTE, ECHO_IT, SET_CURSOR, and DSPLY_MSG    *
;************************************************************************

; program code segment

PGMCD     SEGMENT

MAIN PROC FAR

; housekeeping section

     ASSUME     CS:PGMCD,SS:PGMSK,DS:PGMDA

     MOV  AX,PGMDA      ; GET ADDRESSABILITY
     MOV  DS,AX         ; TO PGM DATA SEGMENT

     CALL SET_MODE      ; SET MODE TO 3 - COLOR TEXT
     CALL CLEAR_SCREEN  ; CLEAR SCREEN AND SET COLORS

; main process section

; display the prompt message for FNAME

     MOV  AX,MSG_LEN    ; SET THE LENGTH OF THE PROMPT
     LEA  BX,MSG_FNAME  ; SET BX = ADDR OF PROMPT
     MOV  DX,MSG_LOC    ; SET THE COORDINATES FOR PROMPT
     CALL DSPLY_MSG     ; DISPLAY THE PROMPT

; switch color default to field entry choice

     MOV  AL,COLOR_FLD  ; GET ENTRY COLOR
     MOV  COLOR,AL      ; STORE IT INTO COLOR ATTRIBUTE BYTE
```

FIGURE 7–8 Entering a field of data with left arrow operational
(PGM19.ASM)   *(Continues)*

```
; assuming FNAME is blank, display current value
; this will outline the limits of the field for clarity

        MOV  AX,FNAME_LEN  ; SET THE LENGTH OF THE ENTRY

------------------------------------------------------------------------

        LEA  BX,FNAME      ; SET BX = ADDR OF ENTRY
        MOV  DH,FNAME_ROW  ; SET ROW NUMBER
        MOV  DL,FNAME_COL  ; SET COLUMN NUMBER
        CALL DSPLY_MSG     ; DISPLAY EMPTY FIELD FOR CLARITY

; next, get the complete user entry for FNAME
; DX = coordinates of start of field
; DL + AL -1 = ending column coordinate that can be used
; BX = addr of first byte of FNAME

        CALL GET_FIELD     ; GET THE FIELD INPUT VALUE

; reset colors to main screen values

        MOV  AL,COLOR_MAIN ; GET MAIN COLOR VALUE
        MOV  COLOR,AL      ; STORE IT INTO COLOR ATTRIBUTE BYTE

; redisplay entry in main color pattern and go on to next field

        MOV  AX,FNAME_LEN  ; RESET THE LENGTH FIELD
        CALL DSPLY_MSG     ; DISPLAY FIELD AS ENTERED

; return to DOS section

        MOV  AX,4C00H      ; SET FOR RET TO DOS WITH A 0 RETURN CD
        INT  21H           ; RETURN TO DOS

MAIN ENDP




        SUBTTL   SET_MODE SUBROUTINE
        PAGE

SET_MODE  PROC

; set the video display mode to type 3 - text color 25 X 80

        PUSH AX          ; SAVE CALLER'S AX

        MOV  AX,0003H ; SET BOTH FOR SET MODE AND FOR MODE 3
        INT  10H         ; CALL BIOS TO SET MODE
```

FIGURE 7-8 continued

```
        POP  AX      ; RESTORE AX

        RET

SET_MODE  ENDP



        SUBTTL    CLEAR_SCREEN SUBROUTINE
        PAGE

---------------------------------------------------------------------

CLEAR_SCREEN  PROC

; clear screen procedure

        PUSH AX       ; SAVE CALLER'S REGISTERS
        PUSH BX
        PUSH CX
        PUSH DX

        MOV  AX,0600H ; SET SCROLL FUNCTION AND FULL SCREEN
        MOV  BH,COLOR ; SET COLOR FOR LIGHT GREEN ON RED
        MOV  CX,0000  ; SET COORDINATES OF UPPER LEFT CORNER
        MOV  DX,184FH ; SET COORDINATES OF LOWER RIGHT CORNER
        INT  10H      ; CALL BIOS TO CLEAR SCREEN

        POP  DX       ; RESTORE CALLER'S REGISTERS
        POP  CX
        POP  BX
        POP  AX

        RET

CLEAR_SCREEN  ENDP



        SUBTTL    SET_CURSOR SUBROUTINE
        PAGE

SET_CURSOR  PROC    ; SET THE CURSOR POSITION

; assumes that DX has been loaded with the coordinates

        PUSH AX       ; SAVE CALLER'S REGISTERS
        PUSH BX
```

FIGURE 7–8   continued   *(Continues)*

```
        MOV  AH,02    ; SET CURSOR FUNCTION
        MOV  BH,00    ; CURRENT PAGE
        INT  10H      ; CALL BIOS TO SET CURSOR


        POP  BX       ; RESTORE REGISTERS
        POP  AX


        RET


SET_CURSOR  ENDP




        SUBTTL    DSPLY_MSG SUBROUTINE
        PAGE


DSPLY_MSG  PROC

----------------------------------------------------------------------

; display a string in color at a specific screen position

; assumes register AX = length of string to display
; assumes register BX = address of string to display
; assumes register DX = the coordinates to display at
; assumes storage field COLOR contains the attribute byte

        PUSH AX       ; SAVE ALL REGISTERS BEING USED
        PUSH BX
        PUSH CX
        PUSH DX
        PUSH SI
        PUSH DI


        MOV  SI,BX    ; SI = ADDR OF MSG TO DISPLAY
        MOV  DI,AX    ; DI = NUMBER OF BYTES TO DO


        MOV  BH,00H   ; SET FOR CURRENT PAGE
        MOV  BL,COLOR ; SET COLOR FROM USER


        MOV  CX,01H   ; SET REPLICATION FACTOR TO 1

DSPLY_IT:

        MOV  AH,02H   ; SET AH FOR THE SET CURSOR FUNCTION
        INT  10H      ; CALL BIOS TO SET CURSOR POSITION


        MOV  AL,[SI]  ; GET BYTE TO DISPLAY
        MOV  AH,09H   ; SET FOR DISPLAY BYTE FUNCTION
        INT  10H      ; CALL BIOS TO DISPLAY BYTE
```

FIGURE 7–8 continued

```
        INC  DL        ; POINT TO NEXT SCREEN COLUMN
        INC  SI        ; POINT TO NEXT BYTE TO DO
        DEC  DI        ; DEC NUMBER OF BYTES TO DO
        JNZ  DSPLY_IT  ; REPEAT DISPLAY FOR NEXT BYTE

        POP  DI        ; RESTORE ALL REGISTERS USED
        POP  SI
        POP  DX
        POP  CX
        POP  BX
        POP  AX

        RET            ; RETURN TO CALLER

DSPLY_MSG  ENDP



        SUBTTL   GET_FIELD  WILL GET A COMPLETE FIELD ENTRY
        PAGE

GET_FIELD  PROC

----------------------------------------------------------------------

; gets a complete user entry for a field
; a CR ends the entry process or full field
; a left arrow will back up the cursor one column

; assumes the following register settings
;    AL = length of the field
;    DH = starting row number
;    DL = starting column number
;    BX = addr of the field in storage

        PUSH AX            ; SAVE REGISTERS
        PUSH BX
        PUSH CX
        PUSH DX

; calculate coordinates and store them

        MOV  START_ROW,DH  ; SAVE STARTING ROW
        MOV  START_COL,DL  ; SAVE STARTING COLUMN
        ADD  DL,AL         ; ADD LENGTH OF FIELD
        SUB  DL,1          ; DL = LAST GOOD COLUMN
        MOV  LAST_COL,DL   ; SAVE LAST GOOD COLUMN
        MOV  DL,START_COL  ; DL = STARTING COL AGAIN

; DX is now set to the current coordinate
```

FIGURE 7–8   continued   *(Continues)*

```
; main loop

NEXT_BYTE:

    CALL SET_CURSOR     ; SET CURSOR TO THE CURRENT LOCATION

; get a byte : AL = byte and AH = 0 if not a control code or
;                                    a special key
;              AL = control code if AH = 1
;              AL = special key  if AH = 2

    CAll GFT_BYTF       ; GFTS THF NFXT BYTF

    CMP  AH,2           ; WAS IT A SPECIAL CODE?
    JE   CK_SPECIAL     ; YES, GO HANDLE IT
    CMP  AH,1           ; WAS IT A CONTROL CODE?
    JE   CK_CONTROL     ; YES, GO HANDLE IT

; valid entry made, so echo it, stuff it, increment address and
;   column, check for end of field, if not reset cursor

    MOV  [BX],AL        ; STUFF CHARACTER INTO FIELD
    INC  BX             ; POINT TO NEXT FIELD BYTE

    CALL ECHO_IT        ; ECHO BYTE TO CRT

    INC  DL             ; BUMP TO NEXT COLUMN NUMBER
--------------------------------------------------------------------
    CMP  DL,LAST_COL    ; WAS THIS THE LAST COLUMN?
    JBE  NEXT_BYTE      ; NO, SO CONTINUE WITH NEXT BYTE

    JMP  DONE           ; YES, ALL FINISHED

; special keys are handled here

CK_SPECIAL:

    CMP  AL,4BH         ; WAS IT A LEFT ARROW?
    JE   BACKUP         ; YES, BACK UP ONE BYTE, IF POSSIBLE
    JMP  NEXT_BYTE      ; NO, IGNORE ALL OTHERS

BACKUP:

    DEC  DL             ; TRY TO BACK UP ONE BYTE
    CMP  DL,START_COL   ; IS NEW COL < START COL?
    JAE  CONTINUE       ; YES, IT'S IN RANGE, SO DO IT
    INC  DL             ; NO, WE'RE AT THE START
    JMP  NEXT_BYTE      ; SO IGNORE THE REQUEST

CONTINUE:
```

FIGURE 7–8 continued

```
        DEC  BX          ; BACK UP ONE BYTE IN THE STORAGE FIELD
        JMP  NEXT_BYTE   ; DONE, SO CONTINUE DATA ENTRY


; control codes are handled here


CK_CONTROL:

        CMP  AL,0DH      ; WAS IT A CARRIAGE RETURN?
        JE   DONE        ; YES, ALL FINISHED
        JMP  NEXT_BYTE   ; NO, SO IGNORE ALL OTHER POSSIBILITIES

DONE:
        POP  DX          ; RESTORE REGISTERS
        POP  CX
        POP  BX
        POP  AX


        RET
GET_FIELD ENDP


        SUBTTL  GET_BYTE  WILL GET A BYTE AND RETURN IT IN AL
        PAGE


GET_BYTE  PROC

; sets AL = byte and AH = 0 if valid byte
; sets AL = control code and AH = 1 if it is a control code
; sets AL = special key and AH = 2 if it is a special key
; accepts letters and numbers in the ASCII scheme


-------------------------------------------------------------------------
REDO:
        MOV  AH,08H    ; SET FOR KEYBOARD INPUT NO ECHO
        INT  21H       ; CALL DOS TO GET A BYTE

        MOV  AH,0      ; ASSUME IT'S VALID

        CMP  AL,0      ; SPECIAL KEY ENTERED?
        JE   SPECIAL   ; YES, GO GET IT

        CMP  AL,20H    ; IS IT A CONTROL CODE?
        JB   CONTROL   ; YES, GO SET AH
        JE   OK        ; IF IT IS A BLANK, ALL DONE
        CMP  AL,7FH    ; IS IT A DELETE?
        JE   CONTROL   ; YES, GO SET AH

        CMP  AL,30H    ; IS IT 0?
```

FIGURE 7–8 continued   *(Continues)*

```
        JB   REDO      ; NO, IT'S LESS, SO RE-ENTER IT
        CMP  AL,3AH    ; IS IT A NUMBER?
        JB   OK        ; YES, ALL DONE
        CMP  AL,41H    ; IS IT LESS THAN A?
        JB   REDO      ; YES, IT'S NOT VALID, SO REDO THE ENTRY
        CMP  AL,5BH    ; IS IT A CAP LETTER?
        JB   OK        ; YES, ALL DONE
        CMP  AL,61H    ; IS IT LESS THAN a?
        JB   REDO      ; YES, IT'S NOT VALID, SO REDO IT
        CMP  AL,7BH    ; IS IT A LOWER CASE LETTER?
        JB   OK        ; YES, ALL DONE
        JMP  REDO      ; NO, IT'S NOT VALID, SO REDO IT

SPECIAL:

        MOV  AH,08H    ; SET FOR KEYBOARD INPUT NO ECHO
        INT  21H       ; CALL DOS TO GET A BYTE

        MOV  AH,2      ; SET AH TO INDICATE AL = SPECIAL CODE
        JMP  OK        ; GO RETURN

CONTROL:

        MOV  AH,1      ; SET AH TO INDICATE CONTROL CODE

OK:
        RET

GET_BYTE  ENDP



        SUBTTL   ECHO_IT  WILL ECHO THE BYTE TO THE CRT
        PAGE

ECHO_IT   PROC
-----------------------------------------------------------------------

        PUSH AX        ; SAVE REGISTERS
        PUSH BX
        PUSH CX

        MOV  AH,09H    ; SET FOR DISPLAY BYTE
        MOV  BL,COLOR  ; SET ATTRIBUTE BYTE
        MOV  BH,00H    ; SET FOR CURRENT PAGE
        MOV  CX,1      ; SET NUMBER OF REPS TO 1
        INT  10H       ; CALL BIOS TO DISPLAY 1 CHARACTER

        POP  CX        ; RESTORE REGISTERS
        POP  BX
        POP  AX
```

FIGURE 7–8   continued

```
        RET
ECHO_IT   ENDP


PGMCD     ENDS



        SUBTTL    DATA AREAS
        PAGE

; program data segment

PGMDA     SEGMENT

COLOR       DB   1EH      ; COLOR LIGHT YELLOW ON BLUE
COLOR_MAIN DB    1EH      ; MAIN SCREEN COLOR LIGHT YELLOW ON BLUE
COLOR_FLD  DB    24H      ; FIELD ENTRY COLOR RED ON GREEN

MSG_FNAME   DB   'ENTER FIRST NAME:'
MSG_LEN     DW   17
MSG_LOC     DW   0F05H    ; DISPLAY MSG AT (15,5)

FNAME       DB   10 DUP(' ')
FNAME_LEN   DW   10
FNAME_ROW   DB   0FH      ; DISPLAY ENTRY AT ROW 15
FNAME_COL   DB   19H      ; DISPLAY ENTRY AT COL 25

; get_field's working storage area

START_ROW   DB   ?
START_COL   DB   ?
LAST_COL    DB   ?

PGMDA     ENDS

; program stack segment

PGMSK     SEGMENT PARA STACK 'STACK'

    DW   32 DUP (?)

PGMSK     ENDS
    END  MAIN
```

FIGURE 7–8 continued

7.11 ADVANCED FEATURES OF THE SYMBOLIC DEBUGGER SYMDEB (VERSION 4.0)

By this time you should have used the debugger enough to feel comfortable working with it. There are several advanced features that will greatly ease your debugging tasks. Among these are capabilities for screen swapping, utilizing breakpoints to halt execution at specific locations, and modifying the contents of registers and memory.

Screen Swapping

If you have used SYMDEB in this chapter or Chapter 6, you probably encountered a problem. The problem is the interleaving of the program's screen I/O with SYMDEB's I/O. This occurs whenever the program is using direct screen control (as in this chapter) or when there is a lot of screen I/O and SYMDEB is used to execute the program. Further, when the cursor is positioned to fixed coordinates, debugging messages get printed at that location long before the program gets to display at that same location. The screen becomes a garbled mess.

This problem can be alleviated somewhat because SYMDEB has the ability to use separate pages for screen I/O. If instructed to do so, it will put all its messages on one page and keep all the program's screen I/O on another. In this way it is possible to flip over to the program's page to examine the results at any time, then flip back and continue the debugging run. This is a very handy feature; you need to try it to appreciate it.

This screen-swapping feature is implemented by setting two switches when SYMDEB is first executed. The /I switch puts SYMDEB into the IBM mode, and the /S switch turns on page swapping. To set the switches, enter

```
A>SYMDEB /I /S B:PGM19.EXE
```

As the program executes, the debugging program swaps back and forth between the program's page and its page. At any debugging prompt you can inspect the program screen by entering a backslash. Pressing any other key brings back the debugging screen and the prompt.

Another useful option is /K, which enables the break function. This often allows you to terminate accidental infinite programming loops merely by pressing CTRL-BREAK. The message PROGRAM TERMINATED NORMALLY appears, and you can then inspect the registers and storage as desired. If interrupts are turned off, however, the break does not function. If the program is waiting for input, you can use CTRL-C to interrupt the action.

Using Breakpoints

Several debugging commands are especiallly valuable for use in longer programs. By using the Gnn command, it is possible to step around the program to any location at which you want to halt the program execution. The nnn is the address where you want to stop. This address is referred to as a **temporary breakpoint.**

In large programs it is often desirable to establish several **permanent breakpoints** at key positions. Then, whenever one of these points is reached, the debugger automatically stops and displays the contents of the registers, and awaits further instructions. Several commands are involved when setting up permanent breakpoints.

Permanent breakpoints are established by using the BP command, with each breakpoint identified by a single digit, 0 through 9. Thus, up to 10 permanent breakpoints can be established in a program. The syntax for doing this is

```
BP#    address
```

The # is the single digit identifier to be associated with this breakpoint. There can be no blanks between BP and the digit. After one or more blanks, the address of where the debugger is to halt is entered. All addresses in SYMDEB can be simple offsets within CS or they can be vectors: 14EF:005D, for example.

Generally, permanent breakpoints are established at the first SYMDEB prompt. Once all are set, they should be listed to verify that they have been entered correctly. This is done by using the BL command, which lists the current identifiers and associated addresses. BL has no operands.

Breakpoints are cleared, or removed, by the BC command. The syntax is

```
BC   *
```

The asterisk means that all breakpoints are to be eliminated. Breakpoints can be selectively removed by coding their identifiers. The instruction

```
BC 2 3 6
```

clears breakpoints 2, 3, and 6.

Breakpoints can be temporarily disabled and later reactivated by using the BD and BE commands. (See the debugger documentation.)

Where should breakpoints be established in a program? It depends on where the problems are. In Figure 7–8 assume you are sure that the program works correctly through the main call to GET_FIELD because the routines up to that point were extracted from working programs. Suggested choices for breakpoints are

7.12 ADVANCED FEATURES OF THE DEBUGGER CODE VIEW (VERSION 5.0)

CODE VIEW also permits the establishment of breakpoints and the modification of registers and memory. In addition, it has commands that allow you to search the source code for a string; search memory for a string; and compare two memory locations, looking for differences.

Handling Breakpoints in CODE VIEW

There are two simple ways to set breakpoints: by pressing function key F9 or by entering the dialogue command BP.

To use the F9 method, move to the display window, using F6 if needed. Then move the cursor to the desired instruction on which to set the breakpoint. Then press F9. The breakpoint is established. Also, the instruction is highlighted in bold. Pressing F9 again results in clearing that breakpoint.

To use the BP method, enter

> BP instructionaddress

in the dialogue window. For example:

BP BIGLOOP	sets breakpoint on the instruction with this label
BP 1A	sets breakpoint on the instruction with this offset address
BP 0x0031	sets breakpoint on the instruction with this offset address, using C notation
BP .44	sets breakpoint on the instruction with this line number (44) in the source listing

See the CODE VIEW manual for other possible operands.

The command BL lists all the breakpoints. The command BC clears breakpoints. BC has one optional operand, the breakpoint number to clear or remove. If no operands are coded, all breakpoints are removed. Otherwise, the coded breakpoint number is cleared.

BC	clears all breakpoints
BC 3	clears only breakpoint number 3

The Search and Compare Commands

Search Source for String or Label

This command attempts to find the first occurrence of a string or label in the current source module in the display window. Be sure that you are displaying the source and not the machine code–assembled version. Once found, from the search menu you can find the next or previous occurrence of that string or label. The command can be invoked by using the sequence ALT-SF in menu mode or by entering CTRL-F directly.

When the option is entered, a window is opened in the center of the screen. A message in the screen requests the string or label to be looked for. Be alert for to the case of letters and the presence of colons after label names. The following are valid entries:

```
BIGLOOP:

FIRST_NAME

ANY I/O
```

Search Memory Command: S

This command searches a memory range, looking for a specific string. It reports the address of each occurrence of the string. The syntax is

```
S    field    L    size    "string to look for"
```

Thus, coding

```
S    BUFFER L 100 "A:TEST.DAT"
```

returns a series of addresses where, between BUFFER and 100 bytes beyond the string, A:TEST.DAT is found.

Compare Memory Command: C

This command compares two areas of memory and notes any differences. The syntax is

```
C    from address    to address    with address
```

For example, entering

```
C    200    02F0    400
```

compares the data contained from 0200H to 02F0H to the data at 0400H. The command

```
C    FIELD1 L 100 FIELD2
```

compares FIELD1 for 100 bytes with FIELD2.

Examine Symbols Command: X

This instruction displays the value of the symbol or what the symbol is pointing to in storage. The value of the symbol is its vector address, that is, the segment and address and its offset address.

Entering

X?module!*

produces a handy listing of all symbols used in the program. In this instruction, module is the name of the source being displayed.

Entering

X?module!symbol

shows only the value of the indicated symbol.

Strings can be examined by entering

X?name-of-string,S

For example, entering

X? TEXT,S

displays the contents of the entire string known as TEXT.

Display Expression Command: ?

This command is very powerful because it shows the value of an expression. The expression can be many things.

The general format is

```
?    expression,format
```

If the expression is a symbol, then the value is displayed. Suppose you enter

? TEXT,S

The value of the symbol—its address—is returned. To see the contents of TEXT, enter

DA 0xnnnn,S

where nnnn is the address just returned.

If the expression is a word or byte data area, then

? RECORDSIZE

displays the current value in RECORDSIZE.

To show the contents of a register, the register name must be prefixed by an @ sign. Thus,

```
? @ES
```

displays the current contents of register ES.

If a register is supposed to point to a data area, then the data area can be displayed. If register BX contains the address of the next byte in a string, that byte is referenced by [BX] in assembler notation. However, CODE VIEW does not accept this format. Instead of brackets, you must use either BY or WO as a prefix for byte or word fields. To see the current byte pointed to by BX, enter

```
? BY BX    is equivalent to BYTE PTR [BX]
? WO BX    is equivalent to WORD PTR [BX]
```

The contents of registers and memory can be altered subtly by these commands. If an equals sign is used, then the results are calculated, stored, and then displayed, thereby altering the register or memory. If you enter

```
? @SI=81
```

then the display shows 0081 and register SI now contains the value 00 81H!

```
? BY SI=20
```

stores the value 20 at the byte pointed to by DS:SI, and then it displays the value 20.

The format option tells how to display the expression. Normally, it defaults to whatever is appropriate to the data definition. The following options alter the format of the display as indicated.

I	signed decimal integer
U	unsigned decimal integer
X	hexadecimal
A	ASCII character string
S	ASCII Z string, ended by a byte of 00H

Directly Altering Register Contents and Data Areas

The contents of a register can be altered using the R command. The syntax is

```
R    register
```

or

```
R    register = value
```

In the first case, the debugger prompts you for the new value. In the second case, the new value is provided in the command. For example:

```
R AX=0012     puts 000C into register AX
R IP          prompts you for the value
IP 00F3
:_            at the cursor you enter the new value desired
```

The command to alter memory is E for enter. The command takes several forms that are parallel to the dump (D) command:

```
E     enter a series of bytes
EB    enter a series of bytes
EA    enter an ASCII character string
EW    enter a series of words
ED    enter a series of doublewords
EI    enter a series of signed decimal integers
EU    enter a series of unsigned decimal integers
```

The operands are the address to begin filling and a list of values to be inserted there. For example:

```
EA MSG "Data is NOT correct; press enter to continue"
```

stores the long character string in a series of bytes beginning with the first byte of MSG.

```
EI 0x003E -10 53 44
```

stores 3 words at the DS:003E address.

Alternatively, the list of values can be omitted. In this case the debugger prompts you for each value. Pressing SPACEBAR moves the cursor to the next entry. Entering a backslash backs the cursor up one entry and deletes the entry. Pressing the ENTER key ends the input of values.

At this point it's a good idea to review CODE VIEW notation.

```
.line# or module:line#    references a line number in the source
@registername             references a register
&symbol                   references the address of a symbol
0x####                    provides a hex address
```

7.13   SUMMARY

The architecture of screen displays involves video modes that define how the data will be presented in terms of color, graphics, and so on. Each byte to be displayed has a corresponding attribute byte that tells the CRT what special properties, such as colors, are to be used when displaying the byte. The entire set of display bytes and attribute bytes is contained in memory and can be accessed by specifying the coordinates of the desired location on the screen. This is known as memory-mapped display.

The most commonly used ROM-BIOS services set the video mode, set the cursor position, write the character and attribute byte, and scroll up. Often these are combined in full-screen data entry programs. Due to the relatively lengthy code necessary to fully utilize these video routines, the program must be written by making judicious use of generalized subroutines.

To effectively debug programs that have screen I/O, keep the program's output on one page and the debugging information on another and switch back and forth between the two.

7.14 REVIEW QUESTIONS

1. True/false: You should not use ROM-BIOS function calls if widespread portability of the program is desired.

2. True/false: The attribute byte for a ROM-BIOS service 09H action is coded as 7EH; this means red letters on a light yellow background.

3. What is meant by *memory-mapped display?* How is it useful for programmers?

4. Why is it necessary to set the video mode before setting the colors of the background, foreground, and border?

5. With ROM-BIOS service 09H, write character and attribute, the cursor is not moved before or after the write. What is the benefit of this and why is this crucial?

6. What is an attribute byte? How is it used by the CRT? How is it used by a program?

7. Explain the concept of direct cursor addressing. How does a program make use of it?

8. Menus can be created by the DOS service display string function and by the ROM-BIOS services: clear screen, set cursor, and write character. Assuming that the time to output a byte is much longer than the time to perform any other CPU instruction, which creates the fastest routine to display a menu, DOS or ROM-BIOS? Which of the two takes the least program code?

7.15 PRACTICE PROBLEMS

1. Code the instructions that input one letter from the keyboard. The letter should be printed in light yellow on a blue background. Assume that no special characters will be entered.

2. Code instructions that place the cursor at line 12, column 35.

3. Code instructions that clear a section of the screen bordered by line 12, column 15 and line 18, column 60. The color of the area should be green with yellow letters.

4. Display MESSAGE as defined by

    ```
    MESSAGE    DB    'This is a message to be shown'
    ```

    Assume that the cursor is currently positioned in the correct position, a position defined by the value in register DX.

5. As the fields are being entered in data entry applications, the cursor position and character entered have to be echoed on the screen and in the field in main storage. We said that ROM-BIOS function 08H, read character, can be used to avoid this double duty. To do so, loop through the maximum length of the field after the field has been entered, setting the cursor position and reading the entered character from the screen. List the changes that need to be made to the program shown in Figure 7–8 to get a field with operational LEFT ARROW.

7.16 PROGRAMMING PROBLEMS

1. Full-screen data entry: Perhaps the best way to handle data entry functions is to use full-screen data entry. That is, for each set of data to be entered, the screen is cleared and a full screen is displayed. This screen shows all the fields that are to be entered, where they are to be entered, and their length.

    Code a routine called DSPLY_SCREEN that

    > clears the screen
    > draws a box around the working area
    > displays the required fields, and
    > displays the lengths of the fields to be entered

    You choose the size and characters that make up the box. The text inside the box should be as shown in Example 7–9. Use ROM-BIOS screen I/O, with direct cursor addressing. On the bottom two lines of the screen, display

    ```
    USE ENTER TO MOVE TO NEXT FIELD; USE ESC TO END ENTRY
    ENTER F1 FOR HELP; ENTER F3 TO QUIT THE PROGRAM
    ```

2. Modify the display routine of Programming Problem 1 to use reasonable colors; be creative.

3. Create a routine called BLANK_FLDS that blanks out the four fields defined in Programming Problem 1. The fields should be defined together in the data segment as

```
                    WES-BRO INVENTORY SYSTEM

      ITEM NUMBER: _____

      DESCRIPTION: _____

      QUANTITY ON HAND: ____

      ITEM COST: _____          (FORMAT 9999V99)
```

EXAMPLE 7-9 The data entry screen for Problem 1

```
            ITEM_NO   DB    5  DUP(?)
            DESC      DB   20  DUP(?)
            QTY       DB    4  DUP(?)
            COST      DB    6  DUP(?)
```

Assume that these fields will later become part of an output record.

4. Write a routine called INPUT_FLDS that uses DOS function 08H to input the fields in Programming Problem 1 and ROM-BIOS function 09H to echo the input.

   Consider a field complete when either the maximum number of characters has been entered for that field or a carriage return is entered. Then jump the cursor automatically to the start of the next field.

   When the last field has been entered, move the cursor back to the beginning of the first field again to allow the user to correct a mistake. If a carriage return is entered, move down to the next field. The routine should end when the user presses the ESC key. At this point, all the data should be properly input and stored in the four fields.

5. Modify the input routine in Programming Problem 4 to permit the use of the following special keys for data editing:

   LEFT ARROW   RIGHT ARROW BACKSPACE

   UP ARROW   DOWN ARROW

The keys should function as they normally do. UP ARROW moves the cursor to the beginning of the prior field. (If at the first field, UP ARROW moves the cursor to the beginning of the field.) Only the BACKSPACE key should destroy data.

6. Modify the input routine in Programming Problem 4 to include a help function. Call the help routine any time the user presses the F1 key. The processing steps might be

>   clear the screen
>
>   display a help screen showing all the possible entries in Programming Problems 1 through 5
>
>   wait until the user presses any key to resume
>
>   resume the original screen

Hint: Use a second page to display the help screen and return to the original page when done. Keep track of the current cursor position before you begin the help function.

7. Code a routine called GET_CHAR that inputs one letter from the keyboard and echoes it onto the screen as a red letter on a green background. No special characters, control codes, digits, or graphics are to be allowed.

8. Code a routine called CLEAR_WINDOW that clears a window with opposite corners at line 2, column 5 and line 10, column 75. The colors should be yellow on blue. The program should first clear the screen and set the colors to red on green so the window will stand out well.

9. Write a routine that

>   sets the mode to color text with 40 characters per line
>   clears the screen and sets the color to bright yellow on blue
>   displays the menu shown in Example 7–10
>   gets a valid choice from the user

WES-BRO MASTER FILE UPDATE SYSTEM

1. ADD A RECORD
2 CHANGE A RECORD
3. DELETE A RECORD
4. BROWSE A RECORD
5. QUIT

ENTER CHOICE: _

EXAMPLE 7–10   Data entry screen for Problem 9

8

Binary Math and Conversions

8.1 CHAPTER OBJECTIVES

This chapter will focus upon the problems and techniques of binary mathematics. You will

1. Review binary numbers
2. Study the effects of addition upon the flags
3. Learn to add and subtract fields that are not both bytes or words
4. Learn to use the multiplication and division instructions
5. Examine the many factors that affect the accuracy of division problems
6. Become aware of the speed of execution of binary math instructions
7. Discover possible alternative approaches to multiplication and division problems by using the shift instructions
8. Learn to convert ASCII number strings into binary
9. Learn to convert binary numbers into ASCII

8.2 INTRODUCTION

The programming problems and examples used up to this point have made very little use of math instructions. The primary emphasis has been in learning how to input and output data. You have seen that the computer inputs and displays data in ASCII format and that mathematical operations are performed only on data stored in binary. In this chapter the techniques for handling binary math will be presented first, followed by methods for converting ASCII data into binary and binary back into ASCII.

8.3 A REVIEW OF SIGNED AND UNSIGNED BINARY NUMBERS

The two types of binary numbers, signed and unsigned, were discussed in Chapter 1. You recall that the only difference between a signed and an unsigned number is the program's interpretation of the meaning of the first bit in the high-order (leftmost) byte. When the computer interprets a number as signed, the first bit is treated as the sign: 0B means the data are positive and 1B means they are negative. On the other hand, if the program interprets the 1-byte number as unsigned, then the first bit represents the value of 2^7, or 128. (Review Chapter 1, if necessary.)

The following illustrates the ranges for 1-byte binary numbers:

Signed Binary

	Range from			Range to		
	Binary	Hex	Decimal	Binary	Hex	Decimal
Positive numbers	0000 0000	00	0	0111 1111	7F	+127
Negative numbers	1111 1111	FF	−1	1000 0000	80	−128

Unsigned binary

	Binary	Hex	Decimal	Binary	Hex	Decimal
	0000 0000	00	0	1111 1111B	FF	255

8.4 EFFECTS OF THE FLAGS ON THE ADDITION PROCESS

The interpretation of signed and unsigned data can have a significant effect on the way numeric data is handled by the computer. Examine carefully the four following additions:

```
Bit #  7654 3210

 53    0011 0101B      Signed or unsigned,
+48   +0011 0000B       the results are OK
101    0110 0101B    =  101
```

```
  53   0011 0101B          Unsigned result is OK
 +96  +0110 0000B          Signed result is wrong!
 ───  ───────────
 149   1001 0101B     =  149 or −107
         ᴠ
         Carry from bit 6 into bit 7
```

Signed or unsigned

```
   53     53     0011 0101B      Signed result is OK
+(−32)  +224    +1110 0000B      Unsigned result is wrong!
 ────   ────    ───────────
   21    227     0001 0101B  =  21
                   ᴠᴠ
                Carry from bit 6 into bit 7
                External carry from bit 7 into "bit 8"
```

Signed or unsigned

```
  −96    160     1011 0000B      Signed result is wrong!
+(−64)  +192    +1100 0000B      Unsigned result is wrong!
 ────   ────    ───────────
 −160    352     0110 0101B  =  96
                   ᴠ
              No carry from bit 6 into bit 7
              External carry from bit 7 into "bit 8"
```

An **external carry** is a carry from bit 7 to the fictitious bit 8 in a byte number or bit 15 to "bit 16" in a 1-word number. It is said to be external because the value is carried beyond the boundaries of the number field.

An **overflow** is either

- an internal carry from bit 6 into bit 7 and no external carry, or
- no internal carry from bit 6 into bit 7 and an external carry.

How are the flags set in the four preceding addition problems? In the first example, neither flag is set. In the second, only the OF (overflow flag) is set. In the third, only the CF (carry flag) is set. In the fourth, both CF and OF are set.

From these examples and the definitions of *external carry* and *overflow,* you should be able to derive the following rules, which apply to math operations.

With signed numbers, an overflow condition indicates that an error has occurred.

With unsigned numbers, an external carry condition indicates that an error has occurred.

8.5   THE SIZE RANGES FOR BINARY NUMBERS

The following table lists the size ranges for byte, word, and doubleword numbers.

	signed	**unsigned**
byte	+127	0
	−128	255
word	+32,767	0
	−32,768	65,535
doubleword	+2,147,483,647	0
	−2,147,483,648	4,294,967,295

8.6   ADDITION AND SUBTRACTION

The ADD (addition) and SUB (subtraction) instructions are restricted to operations involving either byte or word operands. These instructions cannot have mixed operands, that is, data in a byte operand may not be added to or subtracted from data in a word operand. In addition, the ADD and SUB instructions may not use operands larger than a word. In situations where the operands are mixed in size or exceed a word, you must provide special coding. You will see how this is done shortly.

Further, if the numbers are considered signed and if there is the possibility of an error, you must check the overflow flag after the operation. Likewise, if the numbers are considered unsigned and if there is a chance the numbers in the result could become too large, then you should check the carry flag.

Assuming that COUNT and TOTAL are defined as

```
COUNT   DB   ?
TOTAL   DB   0
```

then the following operations are placed within a loop.

```
MOV   AL,COUNT   ; LOAD COUNT INTO AL
ADD   AL,TOTAL   ; ADD TOTAL TO COUNT
MOV   TOTAL,AL   ; UPDATE NEW TOTAL
```

If there is a chance that the values in the fields can become too large, it would be possible to check the result by inserting a jump instruction. The jump instruction can be used to test the result to see whether or not an overflow or carry condition is present. The JO tests for an overflow and the JC tests for a carry. This example can be modified as follows:

if considered signed	if considered unsigned
```MOV AL,COUNT```	```MOV AL,COUNT```
```ADD AL,TOTAL```	```ADD AL,TOTAL```
```JO NUM_ERROR```	```JC NUM_ERROR```
```MOV TOTAL,AL```	```MOV TOTAL,AL```

(See Chapter 4 for detail on conditional jumps.)

Addition of Byte to Word

When adding a byte to a word, special coding is necessary. The coding method chosen is based on whether the numbers are signed or unsigned. Assume that you have the following fields and want to add the contents of COUNT to TOTAL.

```
COUNT      DB  ?
TOTAL      DW  0
```

The first coding approach is rather crude. It is probably not the one you will normally choose. First, load the byte number into a low-order register, such as AL. Then, if the byte number is unsigned, load a 0 into the high register, AH. Or, if the number is signed, determine whether the byte number is negative or positive by adding 0 to it and checking the flags. If the number is negative, load a –1 into the high register; if not, load 0 into the high register. Finally, add the word to register AX.

A simpler approach is to use either the CBW (convert byte to word) instruction with an ADD or use the ADC (add with carry) instruction.

Convert Byte to Word : CBW

The convert byte to word instruction is used to convert a signed byte number into a signed word. CBW converts the byte number in register AL into a word in register AX. The conversion is done by propagating the sign bit through register AH. With this operation, no flags are set. To add COUNT to TOTAL, the following code can be used.

```
MOV   AL,COUNT   ; LOAD COUNT INTO AL
CBW              ; CONVERT COUNT INTO WORD
ADD   AX,TOTAL   ; ADD TOTAL TO COUNT
MOV   TOTAL,AX   ; UPDATE TOTAL
```

Note that CBW is effective only with **signed numbers.** This is because it propagates the appropriate sign into register AH.

Add with Carry: ADC

The *add* with *c*arry instruction can be used to add data stored in either byte or word operands. It usually follows a prior ADD instruction. If the carry flag was set to on by the prior instruction, ADC adds the two operands and then adds +1. If the carry flag was not set, it does not add +1. In this way, the carry can be "rolled" into the next digit. This is similar to the process followed when doing the addition by hand.

ADC affects the following flags: AF, CF, OF, PF, SF, and ZF as required.

The ADC instruction appears as

```
MOV  AX,TOTAL  ; LOAD TOTAL INTO AX FOR ADDITION
ADD  AL,COUNT  ; ADD TO LOWER BYTE - MAY SET CARRY FLAG
ADC  AH,0      ; ADD 0 AND HIGH PART OF TOTAL AND ANY CARRY
MOV  TOTAL,AX  ; UPDATE TOTAL
```

ADC works very well with either signed or unsigned numbers.

Add Word to Doubleword

Two approaches are available when it is necessary to add two fields of data where one is defined as a 1-word number and the other as a doubleword. Assume the following two fields have been defined and that COUNT is to be added to TOTAL by using the ADC instruction.

```
COUNT    DW  ?
TOTAL    DD  0
```

Remember that, when using the ADC instruction, the low-order bytes contain the low-order part of the number and must be added first. Because TOTAL is a doubleword, it cannot be moved to register AX as you would move a 1-word number. Therefore, the LEA instruction must be used to permit accessing of the first and second word of the doubleword, TOTAL. Remember also that the bytes are stored in reverse order. The first byte is the low-order byte and the last byte is the high-order byte. Study Example 8–1 to see how this is done.

```
LEA BX,TOTAL ; BX -> DOUBLEWORD
MOV AX,[BX]  ; AX = LOW-ORDER WORD
ADD AX,COUNT ; ADD COUNT TO LOW-ORDER PART OF TOTAL

MOV [BX],AX  ; UPDATE NEW LOW-ORDER PART OF TOTAL

MOV AX,[BX+2] ; AX = HIGH-ORDER PART
ADC AX,0      ; ADD ANY POSSIBLE CARRY

MOV [BX+2],AX ; UPDATE NEW HIGH-ORDER PART OF TOTAL
```

EXAMPLE 8–1   Adding a word to a doubleword

```
MOV   AX,WORD PTR [TOTAL]    ; AX = LOW ORDER WORD
ADD   AX,COUNT               ; ADD COUNT TO LOW WORD OF TOTAL

MOV   WORD PTR [TOTAL],AX    ; UPDATE NEW LOW WORD OF TOTAL

MOV   AX,WORD PTR [TOTAL+2]  ; AX = HIGH WORD OF TOTAL
ADC   AX,0                   ; ADD ANY POSSIBLE CARRY

MOV   WORD PTR [TOTAL+2],AX  ; UPDATE NEW HIGH WORD OF TOTAL
```

EXAMPLE 8–2 Simplified addition of a word to a doubleword

Note that you cannot INC or ADD 2 to BX between the ADD and the ADC instructions because the flags will be affected. Therefore, to access the high-order part, use the notation [BX+2].

An alternative to using LEA and [BX] for moving a word into a doubleword is to use the qualifier PTR [ ]. Example 8–2 illustrates the use of PTR [ ], which simplifies the code.

There is a significant advantage to the second approach because it always makes it possible to create a generalized subroutine that can be used to add a field of any size to a field of any other size. For example, if you have a large total that is 12 bytes long and need to add a doubleword to it, the addition can be performed by executing a series of ADCs.

The problem of adding a word to a doubleword can also be handled by using the convert word to doubleword instruction.

Convert Word to Doubleword: CWD

The CWD instruction converts a signed word into a signed doubleword by propagating the sign of the word. To do this, the word that is to be converted must be in register AX. The additional high-order word is placed in register DX with the sign of AX propagated through DX. Thus, the resultant doubleword is the pair DX:AX, with the high-order word in DX and the low-order word in AX. No flags are affected.

If Example 8–1 and Example 8–2 had involved signed numbers, the problem could also be coded as shown in Example 8–3. Note that CWD can be used on only **signed numbers**.

Example Addition Problem

Example 8–4 shows the calculation of the sum of the odd integers from 1 to 99.

```
MOV  AX,COUNT            ; AX = COUNT
CWD                      ; CONVERT IT TO A DOUBLEWORD IN DX:AX
MOV  CX,WORD PTR [TOTAL]  ; CX = LOW ORDER WORD

ADD  AX,CX              ; ADD LOW WORD OF TOTAL TO COUNT
MOV  WORD PTR [TOTAL],AX  ; UPDATE NEW LOW WORD OF TOTAL

MOV  CX,WORD PTR [TOTAL+2] ; CX = HIGH ORDER WORD

ADC  CX,DX              ; ADD HIGH WORD OF COUNT TO HIGH WORD OF
                       ; TOTAL AND ADD IN ANY POSSIBLE CARRY

MOV  WORD PTR [TOTAL+2],CX ; UPDATE NEW HIGH WORD OF TOTAL
```

EXAMPLE 8–3   Signed addition of a word to a doubleword

```
SUM  DW  0


    MOV  CX,50    ; SET NUMBER OF ITERATIONS TO DO
    MOV  BX,1     ; SET FIRST ODD INTEGER TO ADD
    MOV  AX,0     ; SET SUM TO 0

ADD_UP:

    ADD  AX,BX    ; ADD CURRENT ODD INTEGER
    ADD  BX,2     ; GET NEXT ODD INTEGER
    LOOP ADD_UP   ; REPEAT 50 TIMES

    MOV  SUM,AX   ; STORE SUM
```

EXAMPLE 8–4   Sum the odd integers from 1 to 99

Subtract and Subtract with Borrow: SBB

Subtraction operations are exactly parallel to addition, with the SBB (subtract with borrow) instruction corresponding to the ADC instruction. When SBB is executed, any carry value is subtracted first and then the data in operand2 are subtracted from the data in operand1.

SBB affects the following flags: AF, CF, OF, PF, SF, and ZF.

Example 8–5 shows how the data in COUNT can be subtracted from the data in TOTAL.

```
COUNT   DB   ?
TOTAL   DW   ?

        MOV    AX,TOTAL    ; LOAD TOTAL INTO AX
        SUB    AL,COUNT    ; SUBTRACT COUNT AND SET ANY CARRY (BORROW)
        SBB    AH,0        ; SUBTRACT ANY BORROW
        MOV    TOTAL,AX    ; UPDATE NEW TOTAL
```

EXAMPLE 8–5   Subtracting a byte from a word

8.7   MULTIPLICATION

There are several ways by which multiplication can be performed in micro-assembler. The choices for a multiplication instruction form a grid based upon the size of the operands and whether the operands are signed or unsigned. The IMUL instruction is used when **signed** byte or word operands are to be multiplied, and the MUL instruction is used to multiply **unsigned** byte or word operands. The size of the product is determined by the size of the operands:

$$
\begin{array}{c}
\text{byte} \\
\times\,\text{byte} \\
\hline
\text{word}
\end{array}
\qquad\qquad
\begin{array}{c}
\text{word} \\
\times\,\text{word} \\
\hline
\text{doubleword}
\end{array}
$$

An additional element increases the complexity of multiplication operations: The multiplication function makes use of hidden operands. These are operands that are assigned by the assembler by default and are not specified in the multiplication instruction itself.

Multiplication of Byte Operands

When using either MUL or IMUL, register AL (the hidden operand) must contain the multiplicand. Register AL is **not** specified in the syntax of the instruction because it is an assumed register. Therefore, only one operand is specified, the multiplier. It can be either a byte register or a byte of storage. The product, which is 1 word in size, is automatically placed in register AX.

Multiplication of Word Operands

Multiplication of word operands with either the MUL or IMUL instruction uses register AX for the multiplicand. As in the multiplication of byte operands, register AX is not specified in the instruction; AX is the hidden operand. The multiplier operand can be either a word register or a word of storage. The product is a doubleword that is stored in the pair DX:AX. The

```
UNIT_COST  DB   ?
QTY        DB   ?

TOT_COST   DW   ?


           MOV   AL,UNIT_COST   ; LOAD AL WITH UNIT_COST FOR MULTIPLY
           MUL   QTY            ; AX = AL(COST) X QTY
           MOV   TOT_COST,AX    ; STORE PRODUCT
```

EXAMPLE 8–6 Multiplying byte fields

most significant part of the result is placed in DX, and the least significant is placed in register AX.

The MUL or IMUL instruction determines whether byte-by-byte or word-by-word multiplication is to be used by examining the size of the operand specified in the multiplication instruction. For example:

```
MUL   CL   creates     AX   = AL × CL
MUL   BX   creates   DX:AX   = AX × BX
IMUL  CL   creates     AX   = AL × CL
IMUL  BX   creates   DX:AX   = AL × BX
```

Consider an example in which UNIT_COST and QTY are each defined as 1 byte in length. Assume also that both are currently unsigned binary numbers. TOT_COST, which is a word, can be calculated as shown in Example 8–6.

If the fields shown in Example 8–6 were signed, the only difference would be in the multiplication instruction, in which MUL would change to IMUL.

```
                         IMUL QTY
```

Example 8–7 demonstrates how the multiplication could be done if the fields were each defined as 1 word in size. Notice that the qualifier PTR [ ] is used as in the add instruction to avoid the syntax error that arises when attempting to move a word into a doubleword.

Sample Multiplication Problem

Example 8–8 calculates the value of N factorial, where N is an integer and the resultant value does not exceed 1 word. IMUL and MUL set the flags CF and OF. However, the contents of the following flags are unpredictable: AF, PF, SF, and ZF.

```
UNIT_COST DW  ?
QTY       DW  ?

TOTL      DD  ?

          MOV  AX,UNIT_COST      ; LOAD AX WITH UNIT_COST
          MUL  QTY               ; DX:AX = AX x QTY

          MOV  WORD PTR [TOTL],AX   ; SAVE LOW WORD IN LOW WORD OF TOT_COST
          MOV  WORD PTR [TOTL+2],DX ; SAVE HIGH WORD IN HIGH WORD OF TOT_COST
```

EXAMPLE 8–7   Word multiplication

```
N     DB  ?
NFACT DW  ?

      MOV  CX,0    ; CLEAR CX FOR HOLDING N
      MOV  CL,N    ; CX = UNSIGNED N
      MOV  AX,CX   ; AX = N
      DEC  CX      ; SET CX FOR N-1

DO_IT:
      MUL  CL      ; AX = N * N-1, ETC
      LOOP DO_IT   ; DEC CX FOR NEXT FACTORIAL, AND REPEAT

      MOV  NFACT,AX ; STORE N FACTORIAL
```

EXAMPLE 8–8   Calculating N factorial

8.8 DIVISION

The division operation closely parallels the multiplication instruction set. IDIV is used to divide signed numbers; DIV is used to divide numbers that are unsigned. It is possible to use mixed operand sizes for each form of the division instruction. They are

$$\frac{\text{word}}{\text{byte}} = \text{byte quotient} + \text{byte remainder}$$

$$\frac{\text{doubleword}}{\text{word}} = \text{word quotient} + \text{word remainder}$$

The syntax rules for division of a word by a byte with either IDIV or DIV are

```
MOV  AX,TOTAL_SALES ; LOAD TOTAL_SALES FOR DIVISION
DIV  NUM_SALES      ; CALC AVG_SALES
MOV  AVG_SALES,AL   ; SAVE AVG_SALES
```

EXAMPLE 8–9 Unsigned division: Byte into word

The dividend is placed in register AX and is not specified in the instruction.

The divisor can be in any byte register or a byte of storage.

The remainder is placed in register AH, and the quotient is placed in register AL.

The syntax rules for division of a doubleword by a word with either IDIV or DIV are

The dividend is placed in the register pair DX:AX (the most significant word is in DX; the least significant is in AX). Neither register is specified in the instruction.

The divisor can be any word register or 1 word of storage.

The remainder is placed in register DX, and the quotient is placed in register AX.

When either form of the division instruction is coded, the only operand specified is the divisor. The form of the division is determined by the size of the operand—that is, whether the division is byte into word or word into doubleword.

Suppose you want to determine the average sales for a number of salespeople or for several departments. The fields are defined as

```
TOTAL_SALES     DW     ?
NUM_SALES       DB     ?

AVG_SALES       DB     ?
```

Assuming that the numbers are unsigned, Example 8–9 shows how the division can be done.

On the other hand, suppose the fields in Example 8–9 are larger:

```
TOTAL_SALES     DD     ?
NUM_SALES       DW     ?

AVG_SALES       DW     ?
```

If the numbers are signed, the solution is as shown in Example 8–10. As with the other mathematical operations, it is necessary to use the qualifier PTR [ ] when working with a doubleword.

```
MOV   AX, WORD PTR [TOTAL_SALES]    ; LOAD LOW WORD OF TOTAL
MOV   DX, WORD PTR [TOTAL_SALES+2]  ; LOAD HIGH WORD OF TOTAL

IDIV  NUM_SALES                     ; CALC AVG_SALES
MOV   AVG_SALES,AX                  ; STORE AVG_SALES
```

EXAMPLE 8–10 Signed division: Word into doubleword

IDIV and DIV set no flags. However, the contents of the following flags are unpredictable: AF, CF, OF, PF, SF, and ZF.

Special Considerations with Division

There are some special cases to consider **before** you code a division operation. These include dividing by 0, quotient overflow, and gaining digits of accuracy.

First, if you attempt to divide by 0, an error occurs. Therefore, if there is any chance that the divisor may contain 0, the program should check the divisor before the division is attempted. This can be done by performing an ADD 0 to the divisor and testing for 0 as the result. An alternative is to use the AND instruction (discussed later in this chapter) with the divisor and 0 and test whether 0 appears as the result.

Second, the resultant quotient must be small enough to fit within the appropriate size—byte or word. Consider the following values for TOTAL_SALES and NUM_SALES:

```
TOTAL_SALES   DW   1000
NUM_SALES     DB   2

AVG_SALES     DB   ?
```

The result of dividing TOTAL_SALES by NUM_SALES is the quotient 500. Since this exceeds the space allotted for the quotient (1 byte), a division error results. Remember, the largest signed quotient can be +127; if unsigned, it can be 255. These restrictions can cause an otherwise correctly specified division operation to fail. Therefore, before deciding on the format for the division, be sure to check on the maximum size of the anticipated quotient. If the divisor contains the value 1, the quotient will be the same as the dividend.

Such a test can be automated, at least to the extent that an approximate size can be determined. A general guideline is that the divisor must be greater than the left half of the dividend. For example, if you are dividing a byte into a word, the coding is as shown in Example 8–11. Or, if you are dividing a word into a doubleword, the code can be as shown in Example 8–12. If the numbers are signed, the conditional jumps need to be modified and the absolute values need to be checked. (The AND and NEG instructions can be used to do this.)

```
MOV  AX,TOTAL_SALES ; LOAD TOTAL_SALES FOR DIVISION

CMP  AH,NUM_SALES   ; CHECK FOR AN OVERFLOW POSSIBILITY
JNB  OVERFLOW_ERROR ; YES, DIVISOR IS TOO SMALL - GO HANDLE

DIV  NUM_SALES      ; CALC AVG_SALES
MOV  AVG_SALES,AL   ; SAVE AVG_SALES
```

EXAMPLE 8–11   Division: Byte into word with overflow check

```
MOV  AX, WORD PTR [TOTAL_SALES]    ; LOAD LOW WORD OF TOTAL
MOV  DX, WORD PTR [TOTAL_SALES+2]  ; LOAD HIGH WORD OF TOTAL

CMP  DX,NUM_SALES   ; CHECK FOR AN OVERFLOW SITUATION
JNB  OVERFLOW_ERROR ; YES, DIVISOR TOO SMALL - GO HANDLE

IDIV NUM_SALES      ; CALC AVG_SALES
MOV  AVG_SALES,AX   ; STORE AVG_SALES
```

EXAMPLE 8–12   Division: Word into doubleword with overflow check

Third, it is often necessary to increase the digits of accuracy. If you use a hand calculator to divide 1 by 3, the result is .333333—six digits of accuracy. How then can a division operation that yields only a whole-number quotient and a remainder be forced to do this? If you just divide 1 by 3, the quotient is 0 and the remainder is 1.

The solution is to multiply the dividend before the division is executed by as many powers of 10 as there are digits of desired accuracy. Then manually insert the decimal point. To get a quotient of .3, first multiply by 10 and then divide by 3.

$$\frac{1 \times 10}{3} = \text{quotient of 3 and remainder of 1}$$

You must manually insert the decimal point to get the true result.

To get .333, multiply by 1,000 before dividing. The quotient is then 333 and you insert the decimal point. The result is .333.

A word of caution: It is possible for the multiplication operation to increase the number of bytes necessary to hold the dividend. It can also increase the number of bytes needed to hold the quotient! For example, an attempt to produce .333 forces the operation to be a doubleword divided by a word. Be alert to this possibility!

Suppose you want to calculate the average sales with two decimal digits of accuracy. The data definitions indicate a byte-into-word division.

```
MOV  AX,TOTAL_SALES ; LOAD TOTAL_SALES FOR MULTIPLY
MOV  CX,100         ; SET FOR MUL BY 100 TO GET .99 ACCURACY
MUL  CX             ; DX:AX = TOTAL_SALES X 100

MOV  CX,0           ; CLEAR DIVISOR REGISTER SINCE UNSIGNED
MOV  CL,NUM_SALES   ; CX = NUM_SALES IN A WORD
DIV  CX             ; CALC AVG_SALES
MOV  AVG_SALES,AX   ; SAVE AVG_SALES
```

EXAMPLE 8–13   Division with two decimals of accuracy

```
TOTAL_SALES    DW    ?
NUM_SALES      DB    ?

AVG_SALES      DW    ?
```

Example 8–13 illustrates how this can be done, assuming that the numbers are unsigned. If the numbers are signed, use CBW on NUM_SALES and IMUL and IDIV where necessary.

This technique of increasing the digits of accuracy is used when calculating percentages. In this case it is necessary to multiply by 100 to convert into percentages before the division occurs, not after. Consider the following:

$$\frac{1}{3} \quad \text{gives a quotient 0 (and a remainder 1)} \times 100 = 0\%$$

Multiplying by 100 first produces the correct result.

$$\frac{(1 \times 100)}{3} \quad \text{gives a quotient of 33\%}$$

Example Problem

An insurance company wants to display the current percentage of its policies that have lapsed. At this point in the program, the following two fields have been accumulated:

```
TOTAL_NUMBER    DB  ?       ; TOTAL NUMBER OF POLICIES IN FORCE
TOTAL_LAPSED    DB  ?       ; TOTAL NUMBER OF POLICIES THAT LAPSED

PERCENT_LAPSED  D?  ?       ; PERCENTAGE OF LAPSED POLICIES
```

The exact size of PERCENT_LAPSED has not yet been determined. The company wants to show the percentage as 99.9%, with one digit of accuracy. In this form, what is the range of values? The smallest percentage is 0.0% and the largest possible is 100.0%. However, if you assume that 100% is unrealistic (since that would mean every policy the company sold has

```
MOV  AL,TOTAL_LAPSED    ; PREPARE FOR MPY BY 1000
CBW                     ; CONVERT INTO WORD
MOV  CX,1000            ; LOAD MULTIPLIER INTO CX
MUL  CX                 ; DX:AX = TOTAL_LAPSED x 1000

MOV  CX,0               ; CLEAR CX FOR DIVISOR
MOV  CL,TOTAL_NUMBER    ; CX = DIVISOR

DIV  CX                 ; CALCULATE PERCENT LAPSED
MOV  PERCENT_LAPSED,AX  ; STORE RESULTING PERCENTAGE
```

EXAMPLE 8–14   Calculation of the percentage of lapsed policies

lapsed), you can expect a maximum of 99.9%, or three digits. This means that the quotient can exceed the capacity of a byte, thus forcing the division to be doubleword by word. The statement

```
PERCENT_LAPSED DW   ?   ; PERCENTAGE OF LAPSED POLICIES
```

determines the missing size.

The actual range of quotients is 000 to 999; therefore, you must multiply the dividend by 1,000 before the division. Multiply by 100 for percentage and 10 for the extra digit of accuracy. Because of the nature of the problem, you do not need to check for the overflow possibility. There cannot be more lapses (the dividend) than policies. This segment of the program can be coded as shown in Example 8–14.

Only one detail remains: how to convert the binary result into decimal for displaying? Before this is examined, however, there remain two other division considerations to explore: overflows and speed of execution.

Overflows

If the quotient is too large for the divisor, the division can be done by performing successive subtractions, as was done on the older Z80 and 8080 processor chips. Using this method, the divisor is repeatedly subtracted from the dividend until either the dividend is finally 0 or another subtraction cannot be done without changing the sign of the dividend. Each time a subtraction is made, 1 is added to the quotient. The remainder is the dividend when no further subtractions are possible.

Now return to Example 8–12, which calculated the average sales. When TOTAL_SALES contains 1,000 and NUM_SALES contains 2, the quotient is 500, exceeding the maximum byte size. JNB OVERFLOW_ERR checks for such an occurrence when the possibility of an overflow exists. Example 8–15 shows how OVERFLOW_ERR can be coded.

Realize that if the dividend is large and the divisor is small, there are many cycles through DIV_LOOP. This creates a relatively large quotient that

```
TOTAL_SALES DW  ?
NUM_SALES   DB  ?
AVG_SALES   DW  ?


        MOV    AX,TOTAL_SALES  ; LOAD TOTAL_SALES FOR DIVISION

        CMP    AH,NUM_SALES    ; CHECK FOR AN OVERFLOW POSSIBILITY
        JNB    OVERFLOW_ERROR  ; YES, DIVISOR IS TOO SMALL - GO HANDLE

        DIV    NUM_SALES       ; CALC AVG_SALES
        MOV    AH,0            ; SET REMAINDER PORTION TO 0
        MOV    AVG_SALES,AX    ; SAVE QUOTIENT AS AVG_SALES

        JMP    CONTINUE        ; GO ON TO NEXT ACTION


OVERFLOW_ERR:
                               ; AX = DIVIDEND
        MOV    CX,0            ; SET QUOTIENT TO 0
        MOV    BX,0            ; CLEAR DIVISOR
        MOV    BL,NUM_SALES    ; BX = DIVISOR (UNSIGNED)

DIV_LOOP:

        CMP    AX,BX           ; IS DIVIDEND < DIVISOR YET
        JB     DONE            ; YES, ALL DONE, WITH CX = QUOTIENT

        SUB    AX,BX           ; SUBTRACT DIVISOR FROM DIVIDEND
        INC    CX              ; ADD 1 TO QUOTIENT
        JMP    DIV_LOOP        ; CONTINUE PROCESS


DONE:

        MOV    AVG_SALES,CX    ; SAVE COUNT IN AVG_SALES


CONTINUE:

; HERE, AVG_SALES HAS CORRECT VALUE
```

EXAMPLE 8–15   Handling division overflow errors

does not fit within 1 byte. Therefore, even though division of a word by a byte yields a byte quotient, the answer field, AVG_SALES, has to be defined as a word. It definitely holds either result.

8.9 THE SPEED OF MULTIPLICATION AND DIVISION INSTRUCTIONS

The MUL and IMUL instructions are very slow. They require from 70 to 133 or more clock cycles as compared to the 3 to 9 required by the ADD instruction. This speed factor can be a major problem for simple multiplications.

The IDIV and DIV instructions are even slower! They can use in excess of 190 clock cycles. In addition, they are plagued by possible overflows. You have seen how to handle the overflow problem by performing the division by repetitive subtractions. Often, this method is faster than using a DIV instruction. It may also be advantageous to write multiplication routines by using a series of repetitive additions, much like division.

However, if one of the operands is a power of 2 (that is, if one operand is 2, 4, 8, 16, and so on), there are much faster techniques for performing multiplication and division. One of the ways of increasing the speed is to make use of the shift instructions.

8.10 THE SHIFT INSTRUCTIONS: SAR, SAL, SHR, SHL

There are four shift instructions that shift a register or storage field 1 or more bits either to the left or to the right in either a signed (arithmetic) or unsigned (logical) fashion.

SAR   *Shift arithmetic right*
SAL   *Shift arithmetic left*

SHR   *Shift logical right*
SHL   *Shift logical left*

In all cases the bit(s) that are shifted out of the register or storage area are moved into the CF flag. In right shifts, the new bits that are moved into the vacated bit positions are either the sign bit for arithmetic shifts or 0 bits for logical shifts. Left shifts always fill vacated bit positions with 0 bits. Thus, SAL and SHL produce identical results; SAR and SHR do not.

Any shift can work with either a byte or a word and can be either a register or a memory location. The register or memory location is the first operand. The second operand contains the number of bits to shift and is coded as either 1 or register CL.

Shifts affect the following flags: CF, OF, PF, SF, and ZF. The result in flag AF is unpredictable.

Examine the following shifts:

1. SHR   AL,1   ; SHIFT AL 1 BIT TO THE RIGHT
    Before the shift, AL contains

    > 0100 0001B,   or 41H, or 65

    After the shift, a new 0B is moved into bit 7, the 1B located at bit 0 is moved into CF, and the result in AL is divided by 2. The result is

    > 0010 0000B, or 20H, or 32 with CF = 1 (set/on)

2. COST DW   254
        SHR   COST,1

    Before the shift, COST contains

    > 0000 0000 1111 1110B,   or 00FEH, or 254

    After the shift, 0B is moved into bit 15 and the 0B from bit 0 is moved into CF. The result is

    0000 0000 0111 1111B, or 007FH, or 127 with CF = 0 (cleared/off)

3. SAR   AL,1

    Before the shift, AL contains

    > 0100 0001B, or 41H, or + 65

    After the shift, the sign (0B) is moved into bit 7, the 1B located at bit 0 is moved into CF, and the result in AL is divided by 2. The result is

    > 0010 0000B, or 20H, or + 32 with CF = 1 (set/on)

4. QTY   DB   -2
        SAR   QTY,1

    Before the shift, QTY contains

    > 1111 1110B, or FEH, or –2

    After the shift, the sign (1B) is moved into bit 7 and the 0B located at bit 0 is moved into CF. The result is

    > 1111 1111B, or FFH, or –1 with CF = 0 (cleared/off)

5. SHL   AL,1

    Before the shift, AL contains

    > 0000 0010B, or 02H, or 2

    After the shift, AL has been multiplied by 2. The result is

    > 0000 0100B, or 04H, or 4 with CF = 0

6. MOV   CL,3
    SAL   AL,CL

Before the shift, AL contains

$$0000\ 0010H,\ or\ 02H,\ or\ 2$$

After the shift, AL has been multiplied by 2^3 or 8. The result is

$$0001\ 0000H,\ or\ 10H,\ or\ 16$$

7. MOV   CL,3
    SAR   AX,CL

Before the shift, AX contains

$$0000\ 0000\ 0001\ 0000H,\ or\ 0010H,\ or\ 16$$

After the shift, AX has been divided by 8. The result is

$$0000\ 0000\ 0000\ 0010H,\ or\ 0002H,\ or\ 2$$

Shift instructions have many uses. Clearly, they can be used for multiplication and division by powers of 2, where speed is the paramount factor. The speed of shift instructions varies from 2 to just over 20 clock cycles. Shifting by 1 is fastest; however, whenever CL is used, the instruction operates more slowly.

For example, dividing a signed word in a register by 8 (in a byte register) takes about 112 clock cycles (ignoring all setup instructions); three SARs, each shifting by 1, take 6 cycles! Thus, if speed is a critical factor in the program and if the multiplication or division is by a power of 2, a series of 1-bit shifts is substantially faster, although using the series necessitates the creation of somewhat obscure code.

8.11 SOME NEW INSTRUCTIONS: NEG, AND, OR, XOR

To convert to and from binary, several new instructions are needed. The negate instruction, NEG, is used to reverse the sign of a number. AND, OR, and XOR (exclusive OR) perform logical operations on bytes and words.

The Negate Instruction: NEG

The NEG instruction is a simple instruction that negates an integer, that is, changes its sign. The operand can be either a register or a memory location and can be either a byte or a word. The syntax is

NEG   register or memory location

If register AL contains 01H, then

```
NEG    AL
```

produces FFH in register AL, changing +1 into –1. If COUNT contains FF FEH, then

```
NEG    COUNT
```

produces 00 02 in COUNT, thus changing –2 into +2.

NEG affects the following flags: AF, CF, OF, PF, SF, and ZF.

The And Instruction: AND

The AND instruction is used to perform a logical AND on either byte or word operands, which can be in a register or a memory location. Conveniently, operand2 can be immediate data. The syntax is

```
AND    operand1,operand2
```

The logical AND is a bit operation; each bit in operand2 is compared to the corresponding bit in operand1. If both bits are 1B, then 1B is placed in the result; otherwise, 0B is placed in the result. The result replaces the original value in operand1.

The AND operation is commonly used to turn a bit off, clear a bit, or set it to 0B. (Conversely, the OR instruction is used to turn a bit on or set it to 1B.)

The AND instruction affects the following flags: CF, OF, PF, SF, and ZF. Flags CF and OF contain 0B; the result in flag AF is unpredictable.

To see how AND works, suppose COUNT contains 35H (ASCII 5). The value can be converted to binary by entering

```
AND    COUNT,0FH
```

or

```
AND    COUNT,00001111B
```

Either operation results in this:

```
        COUNT    0011 0101B
    AND with     0000 1111B
                 0000 0101B
```

The following instruction shows how an entire word can be set to 00 00H.

```
AND    AX,0000H
```

The Or Instruction: OR

The OR instruction is used to perform a logical OR on either byte or word operands, which can be in a register or memory location. Conveniently, operand2 can be immediate data. The syntax is

```
OR   operand1,operand2
```

The logical OR is a bit operation; each bit in operand2 is compared to the corresponding bit in operand1. If either or both bits are 1B, then 1B is placed in the result. If not, 0B is placed in the result. The result replaces operand1.

The OR operation is commonly used to turn a bit on, set a bit, or set it to 1B.

The OR instruction affects the following flags: CF, OF, PF, SF, and ZF. Flags CF and OF contain 0B; the result in flag AF is unpredictable.

To see how OR works, suppose COUNT contains 05H. The value can be converted to 35H (ASCII 5) by entering

```
OR    COUNT,30H
```

or

```
OR    COUNT,00110000B
```

Either operation results in this

```
          COUNT   0000 0101B
        OR with    0011 0000B
                   0011 0101B
```

The following instruction shows how an entire word can be set to FF FFH.

```
OR    AX,0FFFFH
```

The Logical Exclusive OR Instruction: XOR

The XOR instruction is used to perform a logical exclusive OR on either byte or word operands, which can be in a register or memory location. As with some of the previous instructions, operand2 can be immediate data. The syntax is

```
XOR   operand1,operand2
```

The logical exclusive OR is a bit operation; each bit in operand2 is compared to the corresponding bit in operand1. If both bits are the same (that is, if both are 1B or both are 0B), then 0B is placed in the result; otherwise, 1B is placed in the result. The result replaces the contents of operand1.

The XOR operation is used to clear a byte or word. Most frequently, it is used to clear a register or set it to 00B. It is also used to mark differences in the two operands.

The XOR instruction affects the following flags: CF, OF, PF, SF, and ZF. Flags CF and OF contain 0B; the result in flag AF is unpredictable.

To see how XOR works, suppose COUNT contains 35H. The value can be cleared by entering

```
XOR   COUNT,COUNT
```

The operation results in this:

```
         COUNT   0011 0101B
     XOR with    0011 0101B
                 0000 0000B
```

Similarly, an entire register can be set to 00 00H:

```
     XOR   AX,AX
```

The preceding action, clearing a register, is probably the most common use of XOR. The register-to-register form takes 3 clock cycles compared to 4 for MOV AX,0.

8.12 CONVERSION FROM ASCII TO BINARY AND FROM BINARY TO ASCII

The final problem when working with numbers is the conversion process to and from ASCII. First consider the conversion from ASCII into binary.

Converting ASCII to Binary

Assume that you have entered the string 1234 on the keyboard and you need this value in a calculation. In memory these numbers appear as 31 32 33 34H. When converted into hex, the string appears as 04 D2H.

The method used to convert from ASCII to binary is known as **conversion by partial products**. The steps in the procedure are

1. Operate on one digit at a time, from the right to the left.
   a. Remove the 3 nibble by entering AND with 0FH, producing a 0 nibble.

    b.   Multiply that digit by the progressive power of 10 (that is, 1, 10, 100, 1,000, and so on) that represents the place value of the digit.

    c.   Sum these partial products into the final binary result.

2.   If the field is negative, then negate the final binary result with NEG.

The following shows the sequence of how 1234 is converted by this method.

```
34H → 04H ∗ 1    = 00 04H or     4
33H → 03H ∗ 10   - 00 1CH or    30
32H → 02H ∗ 100  = 00 C8H or   200
31H → 01H ∗ 1000 = 03 E8H or  1000
                   04 D2H or  1234
```

Before implementing this scheme, there are three major problems that you must examine. First, the range of values that can be entered determines the size of the binary result as well as whether the numbers are signed or unsigned. If the number is to be a signed byte, the range can be only +127 to −128.

Second, the location of the decimal point, if there is one, must be tracked manually by the programmer. The presence of a decimal point also impacts the size of the result. The value or numbers 99.99 will **not** fit in a byte number; rather, they require 1 word, since 1 word really stores 9999. Since the decimal point in one calculation creates additional problems in succeeding math operations, the programmer must constantly keep track of where the decimal is located.

Third, the conversion routine must remove all signs (− and +) in the ASCII string, and it must also handle the effects of signs on the resulting binary number. Before the conversion routine is designed, it is necessary to define exactly what forms and special characters will be allowed. Will leading blanks be permitted? Are commas to be included for readability?

For example, assume that a 6-byte ASCII string is entered. Where b means a blank, the string can contain any of the following combinations of characters.

   +9,999   +9999b   −999bb   bbb–99   9bbbbb bbbbb9 bb+9bb

   b+9.99   .99999   −bb9.9   −9.99b

Will the field be left-justified, right-justified, or centered? Will signs be allowed? Will commas be permitted? Will a decimal point be allowed, and if so, how many decimal positions will be shown? These are some of the questions that must be answered in advance.

Once the format has been fixed, then the procedure outlined at the beginning of this chapter can be implemented in one of two ways, depending upon personal preference. The two methods are known as the two-pass technique and the one-pass technique.

The two-pass technique consists of

1. Processing from right to left, finding all digits, and moving them into a work area that has been initialized to ASCII 0's. All special characters are stripped in the process.

2. Converting the work area into binary. Only digits are present.

3. Handling any negative signs.

4. Keeping track of the decimal point.

The one-pass approach handles the conversion in one pass rather than moving the characters to a work area and then converting, as in the two-pass technique. In both techniques, the negative sign and decimal point must be monitored.

The one-pass technique consists of

1. Processing from right to left to handle each byte. If the value is a digit, it is converted; if it is a special character, it is ignored.

2. Handling any negative sign.

3. Keeping track of the decimal point.

One suggestion: If a decimal point is to be included, then force all the converted numbers to have the maximum number of decimals. For example, suppose that all the following are to be allowed.

9.9   9.99   9.999   9

Convert all these entries as if they are entered as

9900   9990   9999   9000

In this way you will always know that there are three decimal places in the decimal answer. Remember, the decimal point must be added when the binary answers are converted back into ASCII.

Figure 8–1 shows a complete program with subroutines to convert from ASCII to binary and from binary to ASCII. For now, examine only the ASC2BIN procedure.

The ASC2BIN procedure converts up to 6 ASCII bytes into a binary word. Any signs must be positioned immediately in front of the first digit. Although leading blanks are ignored, there can be no trailing blanks. Commas can be included; however, no decimal points are permitted. The routine assumes upon entry that SI points to the ASCII string to convert and BX contains the actual length of the field.

The routine gets the current character by MOV AL,[SI+BX]. SI has the address of the first byte. Originally, BX holds the length. However, by subtracting 1 from BX, the address generated by adding SI and BX points to the last byte of the string. (Convince yourself of this by sketching the program's actions.) After that character has been processed, BX is decremented, thereby moving from right to left through the ASCII field.

```
        PAGE   60,132
        TITLE  PGM20  FIGURE 8-1  CONVERT ASCII TO BINARY


;*************************************************************************
;                                                                      *
; PGM20      Title: Figure 8-1  Routine to convert ASCII to Binary     *
;                                                                      *
; Programmer: Vic Broquard                                             *
; Date Written: 6/11/88         Date Of Last Revision: 8/5/88          *
;                                                                      *
; Purpose: ASC2BIN converts from ASCII to binary                       *
;          BIN2ASC converts from binary to ASCII                       *
;                                                                      *
; Special Requirements:                                                *
;                                                                      *
;          ASC2BIN expects SI = addr ASCII value, BX = length          *
;                  result will be in word field BINVAL                 *
;                                                                      *
;                                                                      *
;          BIN2ASC expects AX = bin value to convert                   *
;                  results: SI = ASCII answer slot, CX = length        *
;*************************************************************************
;

; program stack segment

STK  SEGMENT    PARA STACK      'STACK'

     DW   32 DUP (?)

STK  ENDS



; program data segment

DATA SEGMENT

MSG      LABEL  BYTE     ; I/O STRUCTURE FOR BUFFERED INOUT
MAXLEN   DB     6        ; PROVIDED BY USER - MAXIMUM LENGTH
ACTLEN   DB     ?        ; FILLED IN BY DOS - ACTUAL INPUT LENGTH
NUM      DB     7 DUP (?) ; INPUT DATA ENTERED BY USER
TENS     DW     ?        ; CURRENT POWER OF 10 FOR CONVERSION PROCESS
BINVAL   DW     0        ; THE BINARY ANSWER VALUE

MSG2HEAD DB     0DH, 0AH  ; CRLF TO NEW LINE
MSG2     DB     7 DUP (?), '$'

DATA ENDS
```

FIGURE 8–1 Program to convert from binary to ASCII
and from ASCII to binary (PGM20.ASM)

```
; program code segment

CODE SEGMENT
MAIN  PROC  FAR

; housekeeping section

    ASSUME    CS:CODE,DS:DATA,SS:STK

    MOV  AX,DATA   ; ESTABLISH ADDRESSABILITY
    MOV  DS,AX     ; TO DATA SEGMENT

----------------------------------------------------------------------

; main line

    LEA  DX,MSG    ; POINT TO MESSAGE AREA FOR INPUT
    MOV  AH,0AH    ; SET FOR EDITED INPUT
    INT  21H       ; CALL DOS TO GET A NUMBER

; set parameters for ASC2BIN call

    LEA  SI,NUM    ; SI -> 1ST BYTE OF VALUE TO CONVERT
    XOR  BX,BX     ; CLEAR BX
    MOV  BL,ACTLEN ; BX = LENGTH TO CONVERT

    CALL ASC2BIN   ; CALL CONVERT ASCII TO BINARY

; set parameters for BIN2ASC

    LEA  SI,MSG2   ; SET SI TO ADDRESS OF ANSWER SLOT
    MOV  AX,BINVAL ; LOAD BINARY VALUE TO CONVERT INTO AX
    MOV  CX,7      ; SET LENGTH OF ANSWER SLOT

    CALL BIN2ASC   ; CALL CONVERT BINARY TO ASCII

    LEA  DX,MSG2HEAD ; POINT TO MESSAGE FOR DISPLAY FUNCTION
    MOV  AH,09     ; SET FOR CRT DISPLAY FUNCTION
    INT  21H       ; CALL DOS TO PRINT MESSAGE

; return to DOS

    MOV  AX,4C00H  ; SET RETURN CODE OF 0 AND SET FOR TERMINATE
    INT  21H       ; CALL DOS TO END PROCESS

MAIN  ENDP


    SUBTTL  CONVERT ASCII TO BINARY ROUTINE
    PAGE
```

FIGURE 8–1 continued   *(Continues)*

```
ASC2BIN    PROC

; assumes SI = address of data to convert
;          BX = actual length of field to convert
; result will be in BINVAL

    PUSH AX        ; SAVE REGISTERS
    PUSH BX
    PUSH CX
    PUSH DX
    PUSH SI

    MOV    BINVAL,0    ; CLEAR BINARY NUMBER ANSWER SLOT
    MOV  TENS,1     ; INITIALIZE TENS OR POWERS FIELD
    MOV  CX,10      ; CX = MULTIPLIER TO GET NEXT POWER
    DEC  BX         ; SUB 1 SO BX = OFFSET VALUE OF LENGTH-1

LOOP1:

    MOV  AL,[SI+BX] ; AL = LAST CHAR ENTERED IN THE STRING

    CMP  AL,','     ; IS IT A COMMA?
    JE   CONTINUE   ; YES, IGNORE IT AND GO ON TO THE NEXT CHAR

    CMP  AL,20H     ; IS IT A BLANK?
    JB   ENDLOOP1   ; YES, SO THIS MUST BE ALL OF THE DIGITS

-------------------------------------------------------------------------

    AND  AX,000FH   ; REMOVE THE ASCII 3 LEFT NIBBLE
    MUL  TENS       ; MUL BY THE CORRECT POWER OF TEN FOR THIS

    ADD  BINVAL,AX  ; ADD PARTIAL PRODUCT TO THE BINARY ANSWER

    MOV  AX,TENS    ; GET NEXT DIGITS POWER OF TEN
    MUL  CX         ; MUL LAST TEN BY 10
    MOV  TENS,AX    ; SAVE NEW POWER OF DIGIT

CONTINUE:

    DEC  BX         ; POINT TO NEXT DIGIT'S OFFSET
    JNS  LOOP1      ; IS THERE ANOTHER DIGIT? YES, REPEAT
    JMP  RETURN     ; NO, SO ALL DONE AND NO SIGN ENTERED

ENDLOOP1:

    CMP  AL,'-'     ; IS DIGIT A MINUS SIGN?
    JNE  RETURN     ; NO, SO ALL DONE

    NEG  BINVAL     ; YES, SO NEGATE WHOLE BINARY NUMBER
```

FIGURE 8–1   continued

```
RETURN:

    POP  SI        ; RESTORE REGISTERS
    POP  DX
    POP  CX
    POP  BX
    POP  AX

    RET            ; RETURN WITH BINVAL HOLDING THE NUMBER

ASC2BIN  ENDP



    SUBTTL   CONVERT BINARY TO ASCII
    PAGE

BIN2ASC  PROC

; assumes SI = address of answer slot
; assumes AX = binary value to convert
; assumes CX = length of answer slot

    PUSH AX        ; SAVE REGISTERS
    PUSH BX
    PUSH CX
    PUSH DX
    PUSH SI
    PUSH DI
    PUSH BP

    PUSH SI        ; SAVE STARTING ADDRESS OF THE ANSWER AREA

    ADD  SI,CX     ; SET SI TO POINT TO LAST DIGIT'S SLOT
    DEC    SI                  ; SI = ADDR OF LAST BYTE IN ANSWER STRING
    MOV  CX,10     ; PUT DIVISOR OF 10 INTO CX

    MOV  DI,0      ; ASSUME NUMBER IS POSITIVE, SET DI = 0
    CMP  AX,0      ; IS BINARY VALUE POSITIVE?
    JNL  OK        ; YES, GOTO OK
    MOV  DI,1      ; NO, ITS NEGATIVE, SO SET DI =1
    NEG  AX        ; SET NEG BIN VALUE TO A POSITIVE VALUE

OK:
    MOV  BP,0      ; SET COUNTER FOR , INSERTION TO 0 CHARS DONE
-----------------------------------------------------------------------
    MOV  BL,','    ; SET BL TO CONTAIN THE , TO INSERT

LOOP2:
```

FIGURE 8–1   continued   *(Continues)*

```
        CMP  AX,10    ; IS REMAINDER < 10?
        JB   DO_QUOT  ; YES, NOW GO ADD IN QUOTIENT

        XOR  DX,DX    ; O HIGH ORDER FOR DIVIDE
        DIV  CX       ; DIVIDE DX,AX BY 10

        OR   DL,30H   ; INSERT ASCII 3 IN LEFT NIBBLE OF DIGIT
        MOV  [SI],DL  ; MOVE DIGIT TO ANSWER SLOT

        DEC  SI       ; POINT TO NEXT ANSWER SLOT
        INC  BP       ; ADD 1 TO NUMBER OF DIGITS

        CMP  BP,3     ; HAVE WE DONE 3 DIGITS?
        JNE  LOOP2    ; NO, SO REPEAT PROCESS

        MOV  [SI],BL  ; YES, SO INSERT A COMMA
        DEC  SI       ; POINT TO NEXT ANSWER SLOT
        MOV  BP,0     ; RESET COUNTER OF DIGITS
        JMP  LOOP2    ; GO DO ANOTHER DIGIT

DO_QUOT:

        OR   AL,30H   ; INSERT ASCII 3 LEFT NIBBLE IN QUOTIENT
        MOV  [SI],AL  ; MOVE LAST DIGIT TO ANSWER SLOT

        DEC  SI       ; POINT TO NEXT SLOT FOR POSSIBLE SIGN INSERT

        CMP  DI,0     ; IS BINVAL POSITIVE?
        JE   BLANK_FILL ; YES, SO HANDLE ANY NEEDED BLANK FILLS

        MOV  AL,'-'   ; NO, SO INSERT - SIGN
        MOV  [SI],AL  ;   INTO ANSWER
        DEC  SI       ; POINT TO NEXT SLOT

BLANK_FILL:

        MOV  BL,' '   ; PUT BLANK FILL CHAR INTO BL FOR PAD
        POP  AX       ; AX = ADDR OF FIRST BYTE OF ANSWER

LOOP3:

        CMP  AX,SI    ; ARE THERE UNFILLED SLOTS IN THE ANSWER?
        JG   FINISHED ; NO, SO NOW COMPLETELY FINISHED

        MOV  [SI],BL  ; YES, SO MOVE BLANK INTO SLOT
        DEC  SI       ; POINT TO NEXT ANSWER SLOT
        JMP  LOOP3    ; AND REPEAT PROCESS

FINISHED:
```

FIGURE 8–1   continued

```
        POP   BP        ; RESTORE REGISTERS
        POP   DI
        POP   SI
        POP   DX
        POP   CX
        POP   BX
        POP   AX


        RET             ; RETURN WITH RESULT IN ANSWER SLOT

BIN2ASC   ENDP

CODE ENDS
        END   MAIN
```

FIGURE 8–1   continued

The partial products are accumulated in BINVAL, which will hold the final answer. Finally, if the last byte in AL is a minus sign when the loop ends, then the whole field is negated.

Converting Binary to ASCII

The conversion of a binary number to ASCII is handled by a sequence of repetitive divisions by 10. Each time, the remainder becomes the next digit. For example, the table that folllows traces the conversion of AAH into ASCII.

	decimal result
$\dfrac{AA}{A} = $ 11H + remainder of 0	xx0
$\dfrac{11}{A} = $ 1H + remainder of 7	x70
final quotient of 1H	170

Therefore, AAH = decimal 170. Notice that the remainder will **always** be a decimal digit from 0 through 9. It can be converted to ASCII by adding a left 3 nibble. This can be done by using OR with the 0 left nibble of the remainder and 30H.

The procedure consists of seven steps:

1. If the binary number is negative, negate the number to make it a positive number.

2. Divide the binary number by 10.

3. OR the remainder byte with 30H to produce the ASCII digit.

4. Insert the ASCII digit into the string.

5. The quotient now becomes the binary number. Repeat steps 2 through 5 until the number (quotient) becomes less than 10.

6. Make the final remaining quotient that is less than 10 the leftmost digit of the result.

7. If the number is negative, insert a minus sign.

There are numerous other actions that can be added to enhance the resultant ASCII string. For example, leading 0's can be replaced by blanks. (Who really wants to see 000009 rather than 9?) Commas can be inserted as needed, and so on.

Re-examine Figure 8–1, noticing the second procedure, BIN2ASC. This routine converts a word binary number into ASCII. It inserts commas where needed and also inserts a minus sign if the number is negative. Finally, since the answer string may not be filled up if the number is small, any bytes that have not been used (all will be on the field's left) are blanked out.

The main processing section invokes DOS to enter a string. This ASCII string is passed to the ASC2BIN routine and converted to binary. Next, the binary value is passed to the BIN2ASC routine and converted back into ASCII. It is then displayed. Enter the program (PGM20.ASM on the program disk) into your computer and test the routine with several sets of data. This will help you to see that it works as specified.

Both procedures could be expanded to encompass larger fields and to provide fancier editing.

8.13 SUMMARY

The chapter began with an examination of the effect of addition on the flag registers. From this discussion, you have seen that a program must check the CF and OF flags after addition and subtraction instructions.

Addition and subtraction of fields that are not both bytes or words can be accomplished in several ways. Although the CBW and CWD instructions are useful in certain circumstances, procedures that utilize the add with carry (ADC) and subtract with borrow (SBB) instructions are generalized and handle operands of any size.

Multiplication is more complicated than addition and subtraction and very restrictive of operand sizes. Division is even more restrictive than multiplication. Before using division, you must consider the possibility of your program attempting to divide by 0. You must determine the size of the quotient before coding the division. Further, scaling factors or digits of accuracy must also be determined beforehand.

In certain circumstances, the shifting instructions offer both a tremendous increase in speed and a variant method of multiplication and division.

All these concepts plus the logical instructions are used in converting numbers from ASCII to binary and vice versa.

8.14 REVIEW QUESTIONS

1. True/false: The biggest signed number that fits in 1 byte is 255.

2. True/false: When adding two signed numbers, you must be alert for the overflow flag.

3. True/false: When adding two signed numbers, you must be alert for the carry flag.

4. True/false: Where

    ```
    COUNT     DW    ?
    VALUE     DB    ?
    ```

    the following code adds a 1-byte field to a 2-byte field.

    ```
    MOV   AX,COUNT
    ADD   AL,VALUE
    ADC   AH,1
    MOV   COUNT,AX
    ```

5. MUL BL multiplies BL and _____ and puts the result in _____.

6. IMUL BX multiplies BX and _____ and puts the result in _____.

7. Consider the following methods:

    ```
    MOV   AL,COUNT
    MOV   CL, 2
    MUL   CL
    ```

    and

    ```
    MOV   AL,COUNT
    SHL   AL,1
    ```

    Which is faster and why?

8. If you enter the code IDIV BX, what is divided by what and where are the quotient and remainder placed?

9. In determining your final grade, two fields have been determined: TOT_POINTS and NUM_TESTS. To calculate the grade, the two must be divided. Outline what steps are needed to determine which division instruction to use. Do not forget the possible need for redefining the number of digits of accuracy.

10. How can you determine whether the shifting instructions can be used for a multiplication or division problem?

8.15 PRACTICE PROBLEMS

1. Consider the following partial record:

    ```
    ITEMCOST        DW    ?
    NUMORDERS       DB    ?
    TOTSALES        DW    ?
    ```

    Write the code that multiplies ITEMCOST and NUMORDERS.

2. Consider the following partial record:

    ```
    TOTALSCORE      DW    ?
    NUMBERTEST      DB    ?

    AVGSCORE        DB    ?
    ```

    Write code to find the average score to the nearest whole number.
    Assume that the two fields have already been input and converted
    to binary.

3. Consider the fields

    ```
    COST         DW
    TOTAL        DB    0,0,0,0,0,0,0
    ```

    Code the instructions to add COST to TOTAL. Both are in binary
    format.

4. Consider the fields

    ```
    ORDERS          DW    ?
    CURRENT_QTY     DD    ?
    ```

    Code the instructions to subtract ORDERS from CURRENT_QTY.
    Both fields are binary.

5. Consider the fields

    ```
    SCORE           DB    ?
    TOTAL           DW    ?
    ```

    Code the instructions to add SCORE to TOTAL. Both are binary
    and both can be negative.

6. Consider the fields

    ```
    NUM_RET         DB    ?
    NUM_SOLD        DB    ?
    ```

    Write the code to calculate the ratio of the number of returned
    items to the number of items sold. The user wishes to show the
    ratio with two digits of accuracy. The fields are in binary. You may
    leave your answer in a binary field.

8.16 PROGRAMMING PROBLEMS

1. During a motoring vacation, it is necessary to fill up with gas numerous times. Create an interactive program called Trip Fuel Economy Analyzer. At each stop the user will provide the miles traveled since the last fill-up and the gallons needed to refill the tank.

   The program should use direct cursor addressing and full-screen data entry. Example 8.16 shows all the lines you will create for the display. When the program is entering data, only lines 2 through 5 should be displayed.

   If bad data are entered, then

   sound the bell

   print either line 11 or line 12

   reposition the cursor at the start of the offending field

   after the user begins to enter new data, clear out the bad field and the error message

   A carriage return entered after the first field should cause the cursor to go to the second field. A carriage return entered after the second field should cause the program to go process the data.

   The program should calculate the miles per gallon and display it in the "99.9" format on line 7. It should be accurate to one decimal. Hint: To get the miles per gallon, use doubleword by word division.

Lines

```
1    ----------------------------------------------------
2    |        TRIP FUEL ECONOMY ANALYZER                |
3    |                                                  |
4    |        ENTER MILES TRAVELED:    _____           |
5    |        ENTER GALLONS USED   :   _____            |
6    |                                                  |
7    |        MILES PER GALLON     :  _____             |
8    |                                                  |
9    |        IS THERE ANOTHER ENTRY? Y/N:  _           |
10   |                                                  |
11   |   ERROR: MILES MUST BE BETWEEN 10 AND            |
12   |   ERROR: GALLONS MUST BE BETWEEN 2 AND 25.5      |
13   ----------------------------------------------------
14
```

EXAMPLE 8–16   Data entry screen for Programming Problem 1

Finally, display line 9 and accept only a valid entry. If the user enters N or n, then put the cursor on the last screen line in the first column and end the session. If the entry is Y or y, then repeat the whole process.

2. Modify Programming Problem 1 to accumulate both the miles and gallons. At the end of all data entry, calculate the average miles per gallon for the trip and display the average with an appropriate notation.

3. Create a child's math helper program. The driver should display the master menu:

```
MATH HELPER

1. ADDITION
2. SUBTRACTION
3. MULTIPLICATION
4. DIVISION
5. QUIT

ENTER CHOICE: _
```

Accept only a valid choice and then call the appropriate subroutine, which should carry out further processing. Each routine should prompt and input two numbers. Then, each routine should carry out the required math. Finally, print the result of each routine and display a message similar to PRESS ANY KEY TO CONTINUE.

Use any reasonable method to limit the values to avoid silly errors like dividing by 0. However, you must somehow make your method clear to the user. If, for example, you want to limit the size of the numbers to add, you might display a different color around the position on the screen where the values are to be entered. Or you could display a message explaining the restrictions.

4. Code a routine that will perform the following calculations:

a) TOT_COST = UNIT_COST x QTY

where

```
UNIT_COST      DB    3 DUP(?)    ; FIELD IS IN ASCII FORMAT
QTY            DB    ?           ; FIELD IS IN ASCII FORMAT
TOT_COST       DB    4 DUP(?)    ; FIELD IS IN ASCII FORMAT
```

b) AVG_GRADE = TOTAL_GRADES / NUM_TESTS

where

```
TOTAL_GRADES    DD    ?            ; FIELD IS IN BINARY FORMAT
NUM_TESTS       DB    ?            ; FIELD IS IN BINARY FORMAT
AVG_GRADE       DB    3 DUP(?)     ; FIELD IS IN ASCII FORMAT (999)
```

    c) BIG_TOTAL = BIG_TOTAL + AMOUNT

where

```
BIG_TOTAL       DB    5 DUP(?)   ; FIELD IS IN BINARY FORMAT
AMOUNT          DW    ?          ; FIELD IS IN BINARY FORMAT
```

9

Disk Basics and
DOS File Handles

9.1 CHAPTER OBJECTIVES

In this chapter you will

1. Learn how data are stored on disk
2. Examine the organization of data on a disk, including the boot record, the file allocation table, the directory, and the data area
3. Learn how the end-of-file condition is handled
4. Study the file handle method for disk processing, including the required interrupts
5. Learn to handle common error situations

9.2 INTRODUCTION

One area in which DOS excels is in the processing of disk files. This is as it should be because, after all, it is the *Disk Operating System*. For most normal file operations, DOS services provide all that is needed to handle disk files. To understand these services, it is imperative to have an understanding of the structure and organization of data on floppy disks as they apply to the IBM PC, IBM XT, and their clones. First, the chapter will examine basic concepts of disks, and then it will discuss the DOS services that are used to handle files.

9.3 DISK BASICS

Data are recorded on a floppy disk as a series of concentric circles, known as **tracks.** The outer track is numbered 0 and the inner track is 39. When both sides are used, there are a total of 80 tracks available. A disk used on both sides is known as double sided.

When data are written on the disk surface, it is not stored uniformly around the track; rather, the tracks are divided into nine pie-shaped areas called **sectors.** A sector commonly contains 512 bytes. However, on some devices, it can contain as many as 4K. Sectors are numbered from 1 to 9, not 0 to 8. See Figure 9–1. Both reading to and writing from these sectors can be handled by DOS. To understand how this is done, you must understand the concepts of physical blocks and logical records.

DOS reads and writes only in **physical blocks** (sectors) of data. Depending on the requirements of the program, all or a portion of a block is available to the program. Suppose the program is expecting 100-byte **logical records.** (A logical record is the amount of data a program requires for processing.) With the first read, 512 bytes (a physical block) are physically input by DOS and stored in its buffer area. DOS then picks off the first 100 bytes and presents them to the program for processing. When the program executes a read and asks for the next 100-byte record, DOS extracts the second 100 bytes from its buffer—no physical input is needed since the data are already in memory. When the program asks for the sixth 100-byte record, only the first 12 bytes are in the buffer. Therefore, DOS issues another physical read operation and gets the next block, joining the first 88 bytes of this block with the other 12 bytes to present the sixth 100-byte record to the program.

Return now to considering the physical characteristics of a diskette. Side 1 of the floppy disk is referred to as side number 0. The first track is known as track 0, and the sectors are numbered beginning with sector 1. **Density** is a term that refers to the number of characters that are stored in a given area on the disk surface. It indicates how compactly the data are stored. Drives come in single density, double density, and quad density. Most personal computers use double-density drives.

In the evolution of the personal computer, floppy disks have changed from being single sided to being double sided and from having eight sectors per track to having nine sectors per track. In addition, the densities have continued to increase as the technology has improved. With such a broad spectrum of choices to discuss, space requirements in the text limit us to a discussion of only the most common choice currently in use: double-sided, double-density diskettes with nine sectors per track.

Just how many bytes can be stored on such a floppy disk? Since each disk has two sides with 40 tracks per side, each with nine sectors per track and 512 bytes per sector, then the capacity is 368,640 bytes per disk.

DOS works with collections of related records called files. Therefore, DOS services are organized primarily around file requests, such as read and

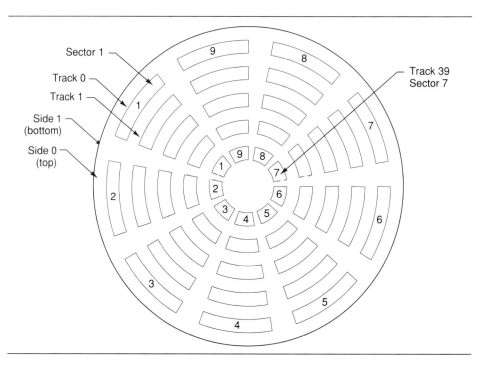

FIGURE 9–1 Floppy-disk layout

write. In performing these actions, it appears that DOS reads and writes logical records for a program and handles all the actual details. On the other
hand, ROM-BIOS reads and writes sectors, with the program determining
which sectors are to be accessed.

From a technical point of view, both DOS and BIOS physically input and output only **clusters.** A cluster consists of two adjacent sectors on a
double-sided diskette or one sector on a single-sided diskette. A cluster is
the physical block that DOS uses.

DOS and ROM-BIOS use different methods to actually find data. DOS
uses the **sector method;** ROM-BIOS uses the **side-track-sector method,**
sometimes known as the head-cylinder-sector method. In the sector method,
DOS assumes that the entire diskette consists of sectors numbered consecutively from 1 up to its maximum. (Note that, in the context of DOS, *sector*
does not have the same meaning that it has in discussions of disk configura-
tion.) To DOS, sector 1 is on side 0, track 0, sector 1. Sector 10 is on side 2,
track 0, sector 1. Sector 19 is on side 0, track 1, sector 1, and so on. The last
sector is sector 720. Therefore, with DOS, it is necessary to specify only a sector number to point to a specific block.

In contrast, the side-track-sector method used by ROM-BIOS requires
that three parameters—the absolute side, track, and sector numbers—be
specified to find data.

9.4 THE LAYOUT OF DATA ON A FLOPPY DISK

There are four functionally separate areas on any floppy disk. On the double-sided, double-density, nine-sector diskette, the areas are

	side	track	sector	total sectors
boot record	0	0	1	1
FAT	0	0	2–5	4
directory	0	0	6–9	7
	1	0	1–3	
data area	1	0	4–end of disk	708

This organization always remains the same. Because other types of disks have different sizes, the locations of these four areas vary from type to type.

9.5 THE BOOT RECORD

The boot record contains code that enables the computer to begin loading the operating system into memory when the computer is turned on. If DOS has been written onto the disk during formatting by the FORMAT A: /S command, the three required DOS system files are on the disk in the first sector of the data area. If not, user files begin at the first sector. The boot record is always included, even if the DOS system is not requested when the disk is formatted.

The contents of the boot record can be examined by using SYMDEB and its unassemble command. To do so, enter the following commands:

```
SYMDEB
L 0 0 0 1
U 0 L 2      ← This is a JMP instruction—use the address
U 2E         ← in this instruction if it is not 2E in the U's display.
```

9.6 THE FILE ALLOCATION TABLE

FAT is an acronym for the file allocation table. It contains the disk's format and a map showing the location of every file stored on the disk. There is an entry in the FAT indicating the use being made of every sector on the disk. As a precaution against the loss of the FAT, two identical copies are retained. Thus, if one FAT becomes damaged, the other can be used to recover the data. (For some unknown reason, however, most recovery utilities do not use this capability.)

9.7 THE DIRECTORY

The directory contains an entry for every file on the disk. Among the items included in the entry are filename, file size, time and date of creation or last modification, and the starting FAT entry. Each directory entry is 32 bytes in length, thus providing 16 entries per sector. Since the directory occupies seven sectors, a total of 112 files can be placed on the disk in one directory. To store more than this, subdirectories can be used. (Subdirectories are treated as though they were files.)

In the directory filenames are always stored in capital letters with no embedded blanks. When this rule is followed, DEL and COPY work as filenames, as will most other DOS commands. However, the BASIC language and a few of the DOS services will accept filenames stored as lowercase letters and with embedded blanks. When lowercase letters and blanks are used, files are created that cannot be easily erased.

The number of entries in a directory is limited. Therefore, the first byte of the filename in the directory is used to indicate the availability of the entry. Whenever a filename is erased, the first byte of the filename is changed to E5H, denoting its erased status. This indicates that the entry is available to be assigned to another filename. If an entry in the directory is empty and has never been used, the first byte contains 00H. This indicates that the entry is available. A third code, 2EH (a period) is used to indicate that the entry is a subdirectory and is not available. Any other characters in this byte mean that the entry is not available. Since the first character of the filename is used for this special purpose, DOS checks this first byte to find the first available slot.

The order of the fields in a directory entry is filename, extension, file attributes, reserved area, time, date, FAT entry, and file size.

The file attributes consist of 8 bits, which, if on, indicate the file's attributes. The attribute byte's format is

0000 0001B	01H	read-only file
0000 0010B	02H	hidden file
0000 0100B	04H	system file
0000 1000B	08H	volume label
0001 0000B	10H	subdirectory
0010 0000B	20H	archive

The high-order bits are not used. Normal files have all the attribute bits set to off, except for the **archive bit, 20H.** Whenever the file is modified, the archive bit is set, or turned on. Whenever a backup operation is done, the backup program clears the archive bit. This permits the backup of only those files that have been modified since the last backup.

9.8 THE OPERATION OF THE DIRECTORY ENTRY AND THE FAT

How do the directory entry and the FAT function? The directory entry points to the first FAT entry. That FAT entry corresponds to the first cluster of data in the file. If the file exceeds 1,024 bytes, or one cluster (normally, two sectors), the FAT entry contains the address of the next FAT entry that corresponds to the next cluster of data in the file. In this way, the FAT links all the clusters (or sectors) of the file into one long chain. The end of file (EOF) is denoted by the last FAT entry, which contains FFFH. FFFH means that the file ends somewhere within this last cluster. As previously indicated, if a FAT entry contains 00H, then the cluster is empty and available for use.

Since the last cluster's FAT entry contains FFFH to indicate EOF, one problem remains: Where within the cluster/sector does the file really end? If the file is a .COM or .EXE file, the system retrieves the entire cluster/sector, because the true EOF is not significant. However, if the file is a text, or ASCII-printable file, the last byte of the file is normally followed by a CTRL-Z marker. Therefore, when processing text files, DOS informs the program that this cluster/sector is the last one of the file and that the program should really look for the CTRL-Z byte as the true EOF.

9.9 FILE HANDLING UNDER CONTROL OF DOS

Under the control of DOS, physical I/O operations are all performed on a cluster basis. DOS stores the physical record in an internal buffer called the **DTA,** or disk transfer area. Depending on whether the operation is an input or an output, it transfers one logical record to or from the DTA and then to or from the program-specified I/O areas. Figure 9–2 illustrates this process for 100-byte records.

As the file is processed, DOS automatically updates the current offset, or location from the beginning of the file, while internally knowing the current sector number. At any time it is possible to specify a nonsequential, or direct I/O, operation by specifying an offset from the beginning of the file. This capability allows random file access.

For write operations, DOS issues a physical write to disk only when a cluster is full. Any incomplete blocks are written **only** when the file is closed. When this occurs, the FAT entry for the last cluster is updated to contain FFFH for EOF. For this reason, if the system goes down or the program ends abnormally without the file being closed, the FAT chain does not have an EOF mark and the file is damaged. In addition, the last partial physical block has not yet been actually written. To recover when this happens, special techniques must be used. Of course, when the file is damaged in this way, the partial block of data that was not yet written to the disk is lost.

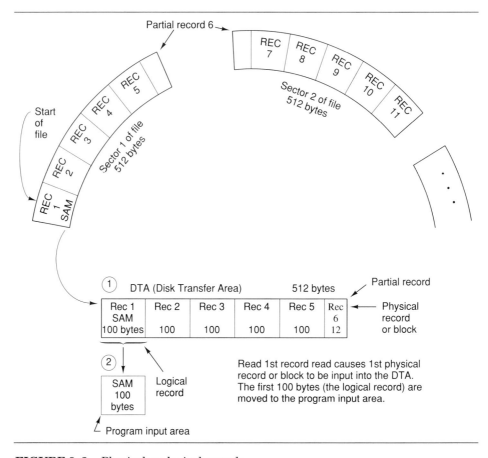

FIGURE 9–2 Physical vs. logical records

9.10 FILE-HANDLING TECHNIQUES

There are two techniques for handling files: the file control block (FCB) method and the file handle method. The FCB method is an extension of the method used by older CP/M machines with their 8-bit processors. The newer method, file handle, permits the use of paths (subdirectories) and is now the preferred approach to file-handling operations. The FCB method does not process paths. Because it is extremely easy to use and is preferred, the file handle method will be covered first. The FCB method will be discussed in the next chapter.

9.11 THE FILE HANDLE METHOD

The file handle method permits a wide range of file and path specifications that provide flexibility in accessing and working with files. A **path** is the sequence of directories that must be followed to access the desired file. Using the file handle method makes it easy to code even complex paths. The key to this flexibility is using an **ASCIIZ string** to define the file and its path.

An ASCIIZ string contains the complete path/filename followed by the byte 00H. This trailing byte marks the end of the string. The following are some examples of the ASCIIZ strings that can be used to open and/or create files.

```
FILE1    DB    'A:WORK.DAT',00H
FILE2    DB    'TEMP.TXT',00H
FILE3    DB    'C:\ACCOUNT\WORK\MASTER.WK1',00H
```

The ASCIIZ string can be simple as the first example or it can be heavily involved with subdirectories. (The FCB method will not handle FILE3 without using other DOS redirection features.)

DOS identifies all opened files with a unique binary number called a **file handle.** When a file is opened or a new file is created, the ASCIIZ string is given to DOS. DOS performs the opening cycles and returns the associated file handle for the file. A file handle is a 1-word binary number that has been assigned to the file by DOS. Every opened file has its own unique handle. All that must be done by a program to issue file operations, such as a READ, is to provide the file handle to DOS. DOS then handles all the details.

As indicated, a file handle for a specific file is obtained by either opening a file or creating a new file. DOS has five predefined standard file handles. They are numbered from 0 to 4.

handle	used for	default
0	standard input—keyboard	CON:
1	standard output—screen	CON:
2	standard error output—screen	CON:
3	standard auxiliary device	AUX:
4	standard printer	PRN:

These files are always open and these five file handles can be used by any program. Any other files are given sequentially larger handle numbers. The number of file handles allowed by Version 2.0 of DOS was limited to 20 handles for any one program. DOS Version 3.0 permits more than this number.

9.12 DOS FILE SERVICE FUNCTIONS

Since all DOS file services are invoked via the umbrella INT 21H, register AH must contain the function number. The following is a partial listing of these functions.

Service Code (in AH)	Function Performed
3CH	Create/open a file
5BH	Create a new file

3DH	Open an existing file
3EH	Close a file
3FH	Read from the file
40H	Write to the file
59H	Get extended error codes
41H	Delete a file
56H	Rename a file
42H	Move file pointer—permits random access

There are other functions, but they are used to implement advanced features that will be presented in Chapter 16.

When there is an I/O error, the carry flag, CF, is often set to on, and register AX contains an error code. Version 3.0 of DOS provides even more extensive diagnostics through function 59H. The normal codes in AX are shown in Table 9–1. After each function call, the carry flag must be checked to see if it is on. If it is, then register AX must also be examined.

Now examine the commonly used file functions.

Create/Open a file: Function 3CH

Function 3CH is used either to create and open a new file that does not yet exist or to open an existing file in the file writeover mode. Register

TABLE 9–1   File handle error codes

Code (in hex)	Meaning
1	invalid function number
2	file not found
3	path not found
4	all handles in use
5	access is denied
6	invalid file handle
7	memory control blocks are destroyed
8	insufficient memory
9	invalid memory block address
A	invalid environment (see DOS command SET)
B	invalid format
C	invalid access code (see function 3DH for details)
D	invalid data
E	not currently used
F	invalid drive specification
10	attempted to remove current directory
11	not the same device
12	no more files are to be found

AH contains 3CH, and the register pair DS:DX contains the address of the ASCIIZ string that holds the complete path/file specification. Register CL contains the file attribute(s)—normally, 20H—with the archive bit set to on. This indicates that the file has not been backed up.

This function opens any new or old file for read/write access. DOS assumes that the program will be writing to a new file and sets the file size to 0 bytes. Thus, an existing file will be overwritten.

If the carry flag (CF) is on, an error has occurred. In this case, register AX contains one of the error codes listed in Table 9–1. Otherwise, register AX contains the new file handle. The handle **must** be saved, since it will be used in all the other file operations.

Create a New File: Function 5BH

Contrast this function to 3CH. This function creates and opens a new file only. If the file already exists, the function fails. Thus, it can be used to guard against overwriting an existing file.

Register AH holds the function code 5BH, and the register pair DS:DX points to the ASCIIZ string containing the complete path/file specification. Register CL contains the file attributes, just as in function 3CH.

When finished, register AX contains the new file handle, unless the carry flag (CF) is set. If CF is set to on, then an error has occurred and register AX contains the error code.

Open File: Function 3DH

This is a general-purpose function that opens any existing file for read-only, write-only, and read/write operations. Register AH contains 3DH, and the register pair DS:DX contains the address of the ASCIIZ string with the path/filename. In addition, register AL contains the mode of operation. It includes the inheritance, sharing, and access codes. In this case the access code is used. The five high-order bits include the inheritance and sharing mode codes. All these codes are for very advanced functions that we will completely ignore for now. We also limit discussion to a program that is the only program currently executing and using the file. The lower 3 bits form the **access code:**

```
00H = read only
01H = write only
02H = read and write
```

As with all DOS functions, if there is an error, the carry flag (CF) is set and register AX contains the error code.

If the file is opened successfully, register AX contains the file handle. It should be saved because it will be needed in all other file operations.

Close File: Function 3EH

This function closes a file, empties (or flushes) all buffers, and correctly marks the end of file. Register AH contains 3EH, and register BX contains the file handle.

If there is an error, the carry flag (CF) is set and register AX contains the error code.

Read from File: Function 3FH

The read file function inputs one or more bytes from the file. Register AH contains 3FH, and register BX contains the file handle. In addition, register CX contains the number of bytes to input. The register pair DS:DX contains the address of the program's area in which to input the byte(s).

After the read is complete, register AX contains the number of bytes actually input. If register AX is less than register CX, then the program received fewer bytes than expected. Depending upon the application, this may or may not be an error. If register AX contains 0, then the program has attempted to read beyond EOF.

If there was an error, then the carry flag (CF) is set, as usual, and now AX contains the error code, not the number of bytes actually input.

Write to File: Function 40H

This function writes one or more bytes to a file. Register AH contains 40H, and BX holds the file handle. Register CX contains the number of bytes to output, and the register pair DS:DX contains the address of the data to write.

When finished, register AX contains the actual number of bytes written and should be the same as register CX.

There are two error situations that can occur with the write function. The normal error situation occurs when the carry flag (CF) is set and register AX contains the error code. The second situation occurs when the carry flag (CF) is not set, and the number of bytes actually written (given in register AX) is less than the requested number (given in CX). This means that there is not enough space on the disk to complete the file.

Now see how these functions are put to use in a program.

9.13 A SAMPLE PROGRAM

Study the program in Figure 9–3 (PGM21.ASM on the program disk). It illustrates the use of file handles in a microassembler program. It reads the program file PGM1.ASM and displays it on the screen. The main procedure first opens the file. Then, if there is no I/O error and no EOF signaled, a 128-byte record is read and displayed on the screen. At EOF, the file is closed. Each of these major functions is written as a separate procedure.

```
      PAGE   60,132
      TITLE  PGM21 FIGURE 9-3 READ & DISPLAY A FILE USING FILE HANDLE

;***********************************************************************
; PGM21       Title: Figure 9-3 Read and display a text file        *
;                                                                   *
; Programmer: Vic Broquard                                          *
; Date Written:  6/11/88        Date Of Last Revision: 8/4/88       *
;                                                                   *
; Purpose: Use file handle to read a text file and display it       *
;                                                                   *
; Special Requirements: FILENAME = ASCIIZ string, FILENUM = handle  *
;                                                                   *
;***********************************************************************


; program code segment

PGM21CD    SEGMENT
MAIN  PROC  FAR

; housekeeping section

      ASSUME    CS:PGM21CD,DS:PGM21DA,SS:PGM21SK

      MOV  AX,PGM21DA     ; ESTABLISH ADDRESSABILITY
      MOV  DS,AX          ; TO DATA SEGMENT

; main processing

      CALL OPEN           ; OPEN THE FILE
      CMP  IOERRSW,00H    ; ANY I/O ERROR?
      JNE  DONE           ; YES, HALT EXECUTION

BIGLOOP:

      CALL READREC        ; READ A RECORD

      CMP  IOERRSW,00H    ; ANY I/O ERROR?
      JNE  DONE           ; YES, HALT EXECUTION

      CMP  EOFSW,00H      ; ANY MORE DATA?
      JNE  ENDJOB         ; NO, FINISH UP

      CALL OUTPUT         ; PRINT THE RECORD

      JMP  BIGLOOP        ; CONTINUE WITH NEXT

ENDJOB:
```

FIGURE 9–3 Program to read and display a file by using a file handle
(PGM21.ASM)   *(Continues)*

```
        CALL CLOSE          ; CLOSE THE FILE

DONE:
    MOV AX,4C00H        ; SET FOR END WITH A RETURN CODE OF 0
    INT 21H             ; CALL DOS TO END PROCESS

------------------------------------------------------------------------

MAIN  ENDP



    SUBTTL  DISPLAY OUTPUT PROCEDURE
    PAGE

OUTPUT    PROC

; procedure to display a record on the CRT

    PUSH AX             ; SAVE THE REGISTERS
    PUSH BX
    PUSH CX
    PUSH DX

    MOV CX,ACTUALEN     ; SET CX = LENGTH OF RECORD
    LEA BX,INPUTAREA    ; POINT TO FIRST BYTE

PRTLOOP:

    MOV DL,[BX]         ; GET CHARACTER TO PRINT

; the next test is only needed for ASCII text files

    CMP DL,1AH          ; IS CHARACTER A ^Z?
    JE  ENDPRT          ; YES, ASCII EOF FOUND

    MOV AH,02H          ; SET FOR CRT OUTPUT
    INT 21H             ; CALL DOS TO PRINT CHARACTER

    INC BX              ; POINT TO NEXT CHARACTER TO PRINT
    LOOP PRTLOOP        ; CONTINUE WITH NEXT CHARACTER

ENDPRT:

    POP DX              ; RESTORE THE REGISTERS
    POP CX
    POP BX
    POP AX

    RET
OUTPUT  ENDP
```

FIGURE 9–3   continued

```
        SUBTTL  OPEN PROCEDURE
        PAGE


OPEN   PROC


; procedure to open file

--------------------------------------------------------------------------

        PUSH AX            ; SAVE THE REGISTERS
        PUSH BX
        PUSH CX
        PUSH DX


        MOV  AH,3DH        ; SET FOR OPEN FILE HANDLE FUNCTION
        LEA  DX,FILENAME   ; SET DX TO -> ASCIIZ FILENAME
        MOV  AL,02H        ; SET ATTRIBUTES FOR R/W
        INT  21H           ; CALL DOS TO OPEN FILE


        MOV  FILENUM,AX    ; SAVE FILE HANDLE OR ERROR CODES
        JNC  OPEN_DONE     ; ALL OK? IF SO CONTINUE

; if here, there has been an OPEN ERROR

        LEA  DX,MSG3       ; POINT TO ERROR MESSAGE TO DISPLAY
        MOV  AH,09H        ; SET FOR PRINT STRING FUNCTION
        INT  21H           ; CALL DOS TO DISPLAY A MESSAGE


        MOV  IOERRSW,01H   ; SET IOERR ON TO INDICATE ERROR


OPEN_DONE:

        POP  DX            ; RESTORE THE REGISTERS
        POP  CX
        POP  BX
        POP  AX


        RET


OPEN   ENDP




        SUBTTL    CLOSE FILE PROCEDURE
        PAGE


CLOSE     PROC

; procedure to close file
```

FIGURE 9–3 continued   *(Continues)*

```
        PUSH AX          ; SAVE THE REGISTERS
        PUSH BX
        PUSH CX
        PUSH DX


        MOV  AH,3EH      ; SET FOR CLOSE FILE FUNCTION
        MOV  BX,FILENUM  ; GIVE FILE HANDLE TO CLOSE
        INT  21H         ; CALL DOS TO CLOSE THE FILE

        JNC  CLOSEXT     ; ALL OK? IF YES, EXIT

; if here, there has been a close error

--------------------------------------------------------------------------------

        LEA  DX,MSG1     ; POINT TO ERROR MESSAGE TO DISPLAY
        MOV  AH,09H      ; SET FOR PRINT STRING FUNCTION
        INT  21H         ; CALL DOS TO DISPLAY THE MESSAGE

CLOSEXT:

        POP  DX          ; RESTORE THE REGISTERS
        POP  CX
        POP  BX
        POP  AX


        RET

CLOSE   ENDP




        SUBTTL   READ FILE PROCEDURE
        PAGE

READREC PROC

; this procedure will input 128 byte text records

        PUSH AX              ; SAVE THE REGISTERS
        PUSH BX
        PUSH CX
        PUSH DX


        MOV  AH,3FH      ; SET FOR READ NEXT RECORD
        MOV  BX,FILENUM  ; LOAD FILE HANDLE
        MOV  CX,RECORDSIZE ; SET NUMBER OF BYTES TO READ
        LEA  DX,INPUTAREA  ; SET DX -> INPUT AREA FOR READ
        INT  21H         ; CALL DOS TO INPUT A RECORD

        JC   IOERR       ; IS ALL OK? NO, SO GO TO IOERR
```

FIGURE 9–3 continued

```
        MOV   ACTUALEN,AX    ; STORE NUMBER OF BYTES ACTUALLY READ

        CMP   AX,00H         ; EOF SIGNALED ON THIS READ?
        JNE   READ_DONE      ; NO, SO LEAVE

EOF:
        MOV   EOFSW,01H      ; YES, SO SET EOFSW ON
        JMP   READ_DONE      ; AND LEAVE

IOERR:

        LEA   DX,MSG2        ; POINT TO ERROR MESSAGE
        MOV   AH,09H         ; SET FOR PRINT STRING
        INT   21H            ; CALL DOS TO PRINT THE ERROR MESSAGE

        MOV   IOERRSW,01H    ; SET IOERRSW ON

------------------------------------------------------------------------

READ_DONE:

        POP   DX             ; RESTORE THE REGISTERS
        POP   CX
        POP   BX
        POP   AX

        RET

READREC    ENDP

PGM21CD    ENDS


        SUBTTL   PROGRAM DATA AND STACK AREAS
        PAGE

; program data segment

PGM21DA    SEGMENT

FILENUM    DW   ?                   ; FILE HANDLE FOR FILE

FILENAME   DB   'B:PGM1.ASM',00H  ; ASCIIZ STRING PATH/FILE

INPUTAREA  DB   128 DUP (?)         ; INPUT RECORD AREA

ACTUALEN   DW   ?                   ; ACTUAL NUMBER OF BYTES READ
RECORDSIZE DW   128                 ; NUMBER OF BYTES TO TRY TO READ

EOFSW      DB   00H         ; ON WHEN EOF IS SIGNALED
IOERRSW    DB   00H         ; ON WHEN THERE IS AN IOERR
```

FIGURE 9–3 continued   *(Continues)*

```
MSG1      DB    '*** YOU HAVE HAD A CLOSE FILE ERROR$'
MSG2      DB    '*** YOU HAVE HAD AN I/O ERROR$'
MSG3      DB    '*** YOU HAVE HAD AN OPEN ERROR$'


PGM21DA   ENDS



; program stack segment

PGM21SK   SEGMENT PARA STACK 'STACK'


          DW    32 DUP (?)


PGM21SK   ENDS
    END   MAIN
```

FIGURE 9–3   continued

To facilitate communication of the unusual events, two switches have been established. When these switches, EOFSW and IOERRSW, have a value other than 00H, they indicate the end of file and the occurrence of an I/O error, respectively. If there is an error during opening, closing, or reading, a simple message is displayed.

RECORDSIZE contains the number of bytes to input. After the read procedure finishes, ACTUALEN contains the actual number of bytes input.

9.14 HANDLING ERROR SITUATIONS

Figure 9–3 only displayed the fact that an error occurred. Frequently, the reason for the error should also be displayed. A general error message display module can handle all error situations. Figure 9–4 (PGM22.ASM on the program disk) shows one method by which this might be accomplished.

Since register AX has the error code from DOS in it, it is simply passed to the DSPLY_ERRMSG procedure. Anytime an error occurs, the program needs only to call DSPLY_ERRMSG to have the exact corresponding error message displayed.

The error messages are contained as a series of messages in order. Each is the same size, 36 bytes. (This is actually a small table that contains the error messages; table handling is discussed in detail in Chapter 13.) The label ERR_MSG points to the first message and corresponds to error code 1. If register BX contains the address of ERR_MSG, then the pointer in register BX can be changed to the correct message by adding $(AX-1)*36$, where 36 is the length of each message.

```
     PAGE  60,132
     TITLE PGM22 FIGURE 9-4 READ/SHOW A FILE WITH ERR CODE DISPLAY

;***************************************************************************
; PGM22        Title: Figure 9-4 Read and display a text file        *
;                                                                    *
; Programmer: Vic Broquard                                           *
; Date Written:  6/11/88         Date Of Last Revision: 8/4/88       *
;                                                                    *
; Purpose: Use file handle to read a text file and display it        *
;          Use full error code for displaying error messages         *
;                                                                    *
; Special Requirements: FILENAME = ASCIIZ string, FILENUM = handle   *
;                                                                    *
;***************************************************************************


; program code segment

PGM22CD    SEGMENT
MAIN PROC FAR

; housekeeping section

     ASSUME    CS:PGM22CD,DS:PGM22DA,SS:PGM22SK

     MOV  AX,PGM22DA     ; ESTABLISH ADDRESSABILITY
     MOV  DS,AX          ; TO DATA SEGMENT

; main processing

     CALL OPEN           ; OPEN THE FILE
     CMP  IOERRSW,00H    ; ANY I/O ERROR?
     JNE  DONE           ; YES, HALT EXECUTION

BIGLOOP:

     CALL READREC        ; READ A RECORD

     CMP  IOERRSW,00H    ; ANY I/O ERROR?
     JNE  DONE           ; YES, HALT EXECUTION

     CMP  EOFSW,00H      ; ANY MORE DATA?
     JNE  ENDJOB         ; NO, FINISH UP

     CALL OUTPUT         ; PRINT THE RECORD

     JMP  BIGLOOP        ; CONTINUE WITH NEXT
```

FIGURE 9–4 Program to read/display a file with error code printed (PGM22.ASM)

(Continues)

```
ENDJOB:

    CALL CLOSE         ; CLOSE THE FILE

DONE:
    MOV  AX,4C00H      ; SET FOR END WITH A RETURN CODE OF 0
- - - - - - - - - - - - - - - - - - - - - - - - - - - - - - - - - - - - - - - - - - - - -
    INT  21H           ; CALL DOS TO END PROCESS

MAIN  ENDP



    SUBTTL  DISPLAY OUTPUT PROCEDURE
    PAGE

OUTPUT    PROC

; procedure to display a record on the CRT

    PUSH AX            ; SAVE THE REGISTERS
    PUSH BX
    PUSH CX
    PUSH DX

    MOV  CX,ACTUALEN   ; SET CX = LENGTH OF RECORD
    LEA  BX,INPUTAREA  ; POINT TO FIRST BYTE

PRTLOOP:

    MOV  DL,[BX]       ; GET CHARACTER TO PRINT

; the next test is only needed for ASCII text files

    CMP  DL,1AH        ; IS CHARACTER A ^Z?
    JE   ENDPRT        ; YES, ASCII EOF FOUND

    MOV  AH,02H        ; SET FOR CRT OUTPUT
    INT  21H           ; CALL DOS TO PRINT CHARACTER

    INC  BX            ; POINT TO NEXT CHARACTER TO PRINT
    LOOP PRTLOOP       ; CONTINUE WITH NEXT CHARACTER

ENDPRT:

    POP  DX            ; RESTORE THE REGISTERS
    POP  CX
    POP  BX
    POP  AX
```

FIGURE 9-4 continued

```
      RET
OUTPUT    ENDP




     SUBTTL  OPEN PROCEDURE
     PAGE


OPEN  PROC


; procedure to open file
----------------------------------------------------------------------


     PUSH AX            ; SAVE THE REGISTERS
     PUSH BX
     PUSH CX
     PUSH DX


     MOV  AH,3DH        ; SET FOR OPEN FILE HANDLE FUNCTION
     LEA  DX,FILENAME   ; SET DX TO -> ASCIIZ FILENAME
     MOV  AL,02H        ; SET ATTRIBUTES FOR R/W
     INT  21H           ; CALL DOS TO OPEN FILE


     MOV  FILENUM,AX    ; SAVE FILE HANDLE OR ERROR CODES
     JNC  OPEN_DONE     ; ALL OK? IF SO CONTINUE

OPEN_ERR:

     CALL DSPLY_ERRMSG  ; DISPLAY EXACT ERROR MESSAGE

     MOV  IOERRSW,01H   ; SET IOERR ON TO INDICATE ERROR

OPEN_DONE:

     POP  DX            ; RESTORE THE REGISTERS
     POP  CX
     POP  BX
     POP  AX


     RET


OPEN  ENDP




     SUBTTL   CLOSE FILE PROCEDURE
     PAGE


CLOSE    PROC
```

FIGURE 9–4 continued   *(Continues)*

```
; procedure to close file

        PUSH AX          ; SAVE THE REGISTERS
        PUSH BX
        PUSH CX
        PUSH DX

        MOV  AH,3EH      ; SET FOR CLOSE FILE FUNCTION
        MOV  BX,FILENUM  ; GIVE FILE HANDLE TO CLOSE
        INT  21H         ; CALL DOS TO CLOSE THE FILE

        JNC  CLOSEXT     ; ALL OK? IF YES, EXIT

CLOSE_ERR:

        CALL DSPLY_ERRMSG  ; DISPLAY EXACT ERROR

- - - - - - - - - - - - - - - - - - - - - - - - - - - - - - - - - - - - - - - - - - -

CLOSEXT:

        POP  DX          ; RESTORE THE REGISTERS
        POP  CX
        POP  BX
        POP  AX

        RET

CLOSE   ENDP



        SUBTTL   READ FILE PROCEDURE
        PAGE

READREC   PROC

; this procedure will input 128 byte text records

        PUSH AX          ; SAVE THE REGISTERS
        PUSH BX
        PUSH CX
        PUSH DX

        MOV  AH,3FH      ; SET FOR READ NEXT RECORD
        MOV  BX,FILENUM  ; LOAD FILE HANDLE
        MOV  CX,RECORDSIZE ; SET NUMBER OF BYTES TO READ
        LEA  DX,INPUTAREA  ; SET DX -> INPUT AREA FOR READ
        INT  21H         ; CALL DOS TO INPUT A RECORD

        JC   IOERR       ; IS ALL OK? NO, SO GO TO IOERR
```

FIGURE 9–4   continued

```
        MOV   ACTUALEN,AX    ; STORE NUMBER OF BYTES ACTUALLY READ

        CMP   AX,00H         ; EOF SIGNALED ON THIS READ?
        JNE   READ_DONE      ; NO, SO LEAVE

EOF:
        MOV   EOFSW,01H      ; YES, SO SET EOFSW ON
        JMP   READ_DONE      ; AND LEAVE

IOERR:

        CALL DSPLY_ERRMSG    ; DISPLAY THE EXACT ERROR

        MOV   IOERRSW,01H    ; SET IOERRSW ON

READ_DONE:

        POP   DX             ; RESTORE THE REGISTERS
        POP   CX
        POP   BX
```

```
        POP   AX

        RET

READREC    ENDP



        SUBTTL    ERROR MESSAGE DISPLAY MODULE
        PAGE

DSPLY_ERRMSG  PROC

; assumes that AX = DOS error number

        PUSH AX              ; SAVE REGISTERS
        PUSH BX
        PUSH DX

        SUB   AX,1           ; USE ERR CODE TO CALC OFFSET IN ERR_MSG

        CMP   AX,11H         ; IS CODE IN RANGE?
        JNA   CODE_OK        ; YES, CONTINUE

        MOV   AX,12H         ; NO, INSERT SPECIAL ERR NUMBER

CODE_OK:
```

FIGURE 9–4 continued   *(Continues)*

```
              MOV  BL,36        ; BX = SINGLE MESSAGE LENGTH
              MUL  BL           ; AX = OFFSET AMOUNT
              MOV  BX,AX        ; STORE IN OFFSET REG

              MOV  AH,09H       ; SET FOR DISPLAY STRING
              LEA  DX,ERR_HEAD  ; DX = ADDR OF FIRST ERROR MESSAGE
              INT  21H          ; CALL DOS TO DISPLAY STRING

              LEA  DX,ERR_MSG   ; GET THE CORRECT ERROR MSG TO DISPLAY
              ADD  DX,BX        ; ADD IN OFFSET TO GET TO CORRECT ONE
              MOV  AH,09H       ; SFT FOR DISPLAY FUNCTION
              INT  21H          ; DISPLAY ERROR MESSAGE

              POP  DX           ; RESTORE REGISTERS
              POP  BX
              POP  AX

              RET

DSPLY_ERRMSG  ENDP

PGM22CD  ENDS



          SUBTTL   PROGRAM DATA AND STACK AREAS

---------------------------------------------------------------------------

          PAGE

; program data segment

PGM22DA   SEGMENT

FILENUM    DW   ?                ; FILE HANDLE FOR FILE

FILENAME   DB   'B:PGM1.ASM',00H ; ASCIIZ STRING PATH/FILE

INPUTAREA DB    128 DUP (?)      ; INPUT RECORD AREA

ACTUALEN   DW  ?                 ; ACTUAL NUMBER OF BYTES READ
RECORDSIZE DW  128               ; NUMBER OF BYTES TO TRY TO READ

EOFSW      DB   00H              ; ON WHEN EOF IS SIGNALED
IOERRSW    DB   00H              ; ON WHEN THERE IS AN IOERR

ERR_HEAD   DB '*** FILE ERROR HAS OCCURRED. IT WAS:',0AH,0DH,'$'

ERR_MSG    LABEL BYTE
```

FIGURE 9–4   continued

```
        DB  'INVALID FUNCTION              $'
        DB  'FILE NOT FOUND               $'
        DB  'PATH NOT FOUND               $'
        DB  'ALL HANDLES IN USE           $'
        DB  'ACCESS IS DENIED             $'
        DB  'INVALID FILE HANDLE          $'
        DB  'MEMORY CONTROL BLOCKS ARE DESTROYED$'
        DB  'INSUFFICIENT MEMORY          $'
        DB  'INVALID MEMORY BLOCK ADDRESS   $'
        DB  'INVALID ENVIRONMENT          $'
        DB  'INVALID FORMAT               $'
        DB  'INVALID ACCESS CODE          $'
        DB  'INVALID DATA                 $'
        DB  'THIS MESSAGE SHOULD NOT APPEAR   $'
        DB  'INVALID DRIVE SPECIFICATION    $'
        DB  'ATTEMPTED TO REMOVE CURRENT DIR  $'
        DB  'NOT THE SAME DEVICE          $'
        DB  'NO MORE FILES ARE TO BE FOUND   $'
        DB  '***ERROR CODE IS BEYOND PGM TABLE  $'

PGM22DA ENDS


; program stack segment

PGM22SK  SEGMENT PARA STACK 'STACK'

     DW   32 DUP (?)

PGM22SK  ENDS
      END  MAIN
```

FIGURE 9–4   continued

The DSPLY_ERRMSG procedure first calculates the address of the correct error message to be displayed. Then it displays a general error message followed by the specific error message for the error that occurred.

It is possible that future DOS releases will make use of additional error codes. Therefore, the program in Figure 9–4 includes a simple test that displays ***ERROR CODE IS BEYOND PGM TABLE when or if an unknown error code is returned.

Get Extended Error Codes: Function 59H

This service provides detailed information on the error that occurred in the prior function call. If an error occurs and more information is desired, then this function can be used. A word of caution! This function destroys the contents of all registers except CS:IP and SS:SP. Therefore, before calling 59H,

TABLE 9–2   Extended file-handling error codes

Register AX will contain either the usual 18 codes or one of the following:

13H disk is write-protected
14H unknown unit ID
15H disk drive not ready
16H command not defined
17H disk data error
18H bad request structure length
19H disk seek error
1AH unknown disk media type
1BH disk sector not found
1CH printer out of paper
1DH write error
1EH read error
1FH general failure
20H file-sharing violation
21H file-locking violation
22H improper disk change
23H no FCB available
50H file already exists
51H reserved
52H cannot make
53H critical error interrupt failure

Register BH will contain

01H out of resource: no more of whatever you asked for
02H temporary situation; try again later
03H authorization: you aren't allowed
04H internal DOS error—not program's fault
05H hardware failure
06H system software error—other DOS problems
07H application software error—your problem
08H item requested not found
09H bad format—unrecognizable disk
0AH item locked
0BH media error—CRC error
0CH already exists
0DH error class unknown

Register BL will contain

01H try again now
02H try again later, after waiting
03H ask user to fix it—change disks
04H shut down the program gracefully
05H shut down the program at once
06H ignore the error
07H retry after user action

Register CH will contain

01H unknown
02H block device error
04H serial device error
05H memory error

TABLE 9–2 continued

save the registers you need. The function works after any 21H interrupt that sets the carry flag and after the FCB method of file I/O returns using code 255. It does not work with other DOS functions that do not set register CF to indicate that an error has occurred.

Register AH contains 59H, and BX contains the version indicator number, which is currently 0. Upon return, registers AX, BH, BL, and CH contain separate codes that give as much detail as possible about the error situation. Table 9–2 gives all the possible error codes that are returned.

Sometimes these messages can be useful in handling an error situation.

9.15 ADDITIONAL FILE HANDLE FUNCTIONS

Move File Pointer: Function 42H

The move file pointer function is used to change the logical read or write position within the file. Successive uses of the read and write functions 3FH and 40H cause the pointer to pass sequentially through the file. However, any position can be accessed by use of function 42H prior to the read or write. Thus, 42H makes random access and file merging possible.

This function sets the current location within the file by using the number of bytes from the beginning of the file, from the ending of the file, or from the current position within the file. It is possible to either advance or back up the pointer position. Register AH contains 42H, and AL contains a code that indicates the method code for direction. If register AL contains 00H, the bytes are counted from the beginning of the file. If AL contains 01H, the bytes are counted from the current position. If AL contains 02H, the number of bytes are counted from the current end of file backward.

Register BX must hold the file handle. The number of bytes to offset is contained in the register pair CX:DX. This is a 32-bit doubleword that contains in binary the number of bytes to offset.

When the function is finished, registers DX:AX contain the current file pointer, which is an offset from the beginning of the file. If the function fails, then the carry flag (CF) is set and register AX contains the appropriate error code.

It is possible to get the current file size by invoking this function with

```
CL = 02H
DX = 00H
CX = 00H
```

This moves the current position to the end of the file and backs up 0 bytes. Now DX:AX contains the file size. To move back to the start of the file, invoke this function with CL = 00H and CX:DX = 00H.

A file mod, or append, function can be done by opening the file with the read and write attribute. Then use this move file pointer function to position the pointer to the end of the file (with CX:DX = 00H). A normal write appends these records to the end of the file.

Delete File: Function 41H

A file can be deleted by passing the ASCIIZ string containing the full path/file specifications to function 41H. The registers DS:DX contain the address of the ASCIIZ string, and AH holds 41H.

Read-only files cannot be deleted and no global, or wildcard, characters (? and *) can be used.

If the carry flag (CF) is set to on, the function has failed and register AX contains the error code.

Renaming a File: Function 56H

Function 56H is used to rename a file. It can also be used to move the file's directory entry from one directory to another without moving or copying the file. The function needs two complete path/file specifications in ASCIIZ string format.

Register AH must contain 56H. Registers DS:DX point to the old name's ASCIIZ string, and ES:DI points to the new string.

Again, if the function is not successful, the carry flag (CF) is set and AX holds the error code.

9.16   SUMMARY

You have seen that disks are composed of two sides with 40 tracks per side and with nine sectors per track. Data are physically processed on a cluster basis. The first sector on a disk contains the boot record. It is followed by the FAT and the directory. The remainder of the disk is available for user files.

The directory entry for a file provides the first FAT entry for the first block, or cluster, of data in the file. Every FAT entry corresponds to another sector in the disk. The FAT entries of the file point to the next FAT entry or contain the EOF indicator, FFFH. FFFH indicates that EOF is somewhere within the cluster. For ASCII text files, a CTRL-Z code indicates the true EOF within a cluster of data.

DOS divides the entire floppy disk into sectors numbered from 1 to 720. Access is by the sector method, which requires that only the desired sector number be specified.

The file handle method is convenient. All that must be done is to provide DOS with the file handle number of the file; DOS does the rest. All opened files are given unique numbers.

To specify a file to be opened or closed, an ASCIIZ string is needed. This is the complete path/filename followed by a byte of 00H.

With most file I/O operations the file handle, the number of bytes to input or output, and the address of the appropriate program data area must be provided. If errors result, the carry flag (CF) is set and register AX contains the appropriate error code. If necessary, another DOS function can be invoked to provide additional extended error messages.

9.17 REVIEW QUESTIONS

1. True/false: A cluster consists of two adjacent tracks on a double-sided diskette.

2. True/false: The EOF marker is FFFH, and it is stored in the FAT entry for the last cluster of data.

3. True/false: The boot record is on track 0, side 0, sector 1, and it is three sectors long.

4. True/false: You can tell DOS to read in a record that is only 2 bytes long.

5. Describe the physical layout of a floppy diskette. What is the function of each section?

6. Explain how EOF is physically handled on a floppy-disk file. What programming considerations does this handling present? How does this affect detecting EOF in a text file?

7. What are the two methods that can be used to retrieve a specific block of data? Which does DOS use and which does ROM-BIOS use? Which do you suppose is easier to use? Why?

8. Explain the difference between a logical record and a physical block. What is the impact of this difference upon a program?

9. Describe the interrelated operation of the FAT and the directory. How does DOS know when a directory entry is available for use for another file? What are the key codes contained in the first byte of a directory entry?

10. What is an ASCIIZ string? What is a path? Show five examples of path/filename specifications.

11. What is a file handle? Outline the steps involved in using the file handle method for creating a new file.

12. There are several different functions for opening files. What are the differences between these? Give an example of when you would use each one.

13. What is an access code? When is it used? What is its function?

14. Explain how error situations are detected when using the file handle method. Where is the error code returned? How can you use the error code?

15. What is the DTA? Explain how DOS uses it.

9.18 PRACTICE PROBLEMS

1. Code the instructions to open an output file called A:\ASMPGMS\PGMTEST.DAT. The file should be opened whether it already exists or not.

2. Code the instructions to open an output file called A:\ASMPGMS\PGMTEST.DAT. The file should be opened only if it does not already exist.

3. Code the instructions to open an existing file called A:\ASMPGMS\PGMTEST.DAT. The file should be opened so that the program can perform both read and write operations.

4. Code the instructions to close a file whose handle is stored in the word called MASTER_FILE.

5. Code the instructions to input the next 50-byte record into ACCOUNT_REC. The file handle is stored in the word ACCT_FILE. In case of errors, jump to ACCT_ERR. If EOF is signaled, jump to EOF. Finally, if 50 bytes are not input, jump to INCORRECT_LEN.

6. Code the instructions to write the 65-byte MASTER_POLICY_REC to the file handle MASTER_FILE. If the disk is full, display an appropriate message and jump to WRAP_UP.

7. Code the instructions to delete the file B:TEST.DAT.

8. An input operation has just failed. Code the instructions to acquire detailed error codes.

9. Code the instructions to rename the file C:\WORK\TESTPGM.ASM to C:\WORK\PAYROLL.ASM.

10. After processing 10 records, which are all 89 bytes in length, the program needs to access the very last record in the file. Code the instructions to position the file to the last record and then input it into MAST_REC. The file handle is in MAST_FILE.

11. File A:MEASURE.DAT is open and has been created by the program. Its handle is in COUNT_FILE. At the end of the job and before the file is closed, code a routine that will find and display the final file size. Hint: Use function 42H.

9.19 PROGRAMMING PROBLEMS

1. Print a sequential file of inventory records. The input file can be
    created with a word processor or EDLIN. The filename should be
    INVMAST.DAT. The lines entered with the word processor are

    ```
    01011DRAIN PIPES         0050001050
    02264COUPLER JOINTS      0197000178
    39314DOWN SPOUTS W FLANGE0113003956
    56122SCREEN DOOR         0021012599
    ```

    The program should input the records into this structure:

    ```
    SALES_REC LABEL    BYTE
    ITEM_NO   DB    5  DUP(?)
    DESC      DB   20  DUP(?)
    QTY       DB    4  DUP(?)
    COST      DB    6  DUP(?)
    ```

    After displaying appropriate headings and column headings at the
    top of the screen, input and display the records.

2. Modify the full-screen data entry program from Programming
    Problem 1 in Chapter 7 to build a file containing each inventory
    record that is entered. The file should be called INVMAST.DAT. To
    show that the program works correctly, use TYPE to visually verify
    the file. (Since the record layout is the same as in problem 1 in this
    chapter, you can use the program from the preceding problem to
    display the new file.)

3. Modify the trip fuel economy analyzer, Programming Problem 1 in
    Chapter 8, to output a file called TRIP.DAT. Each record should con-
    tain an ASCII field to contain the number of miles traveled, gallons
    used, and miles per gallon. To verify that the file has been built cor-
    rectly, use the TYPE command to output the file.

4. Write a program that will sequence a set of up to 20 numbers. The
    program should have three major sections. The first will prompt
    and accept up to 20 four-digit numbers. The input is ended by
    entering the 20th number or pressing the F1 key.
        The second routine should then output a file of these numbers
    converted into binary words. The first word of the file should con-
    tain a count of the number of words to follow. The 1-word numbers
    should follow. The record size should be 2 bytes.
        The third section of the program should input the file, sort
    the numbers, convert them to ASCII, and display the sorted num-
    bers on the screen. Use appropriate headings. (Note that this prob-
    lem involves the use of tables, which is more fully covered in
    Chapter 13.)

5. Write a program that inputs a file of filenames called DELFILES.DAT, which is scheduled for deletion. Create this file of filenames with a word processor or EDLIN. Include the following names:

```
B:TEST.DAT
B:\WORK\BIG.DAT
B:\WORK\SMALL\TRY.DAT
B:\TEST\*.*
```

Create the files to be deleted by using the COPY command. For example:

```
A> COPY CON: B:TEST.DAT
```

and entering F6 (CTRL-Z) and the ENTER key.

There does not have to be any actual data in the files. The sub-directories can be created by entering

```
MD B:\WORK
MD B:\WORK\SMALL
MD B:\TEST
```

Once you create the test files and DELFILES.DAT, you can run the program. It should input a filename byte by byte until the CRLF is encountered. It should also add a byte of 00H to the end of the filename to create the ASCIIZ string. Then it should delete the file. The program should continue deleting the files until EOF is reached.

10

The File Control Block Method and the Program Segment Prefix

10.1 CHAPTER OBJECTIVES

In this chapter you will

1. Learn the layout of the file control block (FCB)

2. Study the effect of and need for the disk transfer area (DTA)

3. Use the FCB method to perform normal file I/O operations and to perform file maintenance functions

4. Learn the layout of the program segment prefix (PSP)

5. Learn what the segment registers contain when a program is given control by DOS

6. Learn the eight methods that may be used by a program to terminate and return control to DOS

7. See how to use the PSP to extract the filenames entered on the command line

8. Learn to use segment overrides when needed

10.2   INTRODUCTION

The introduction of the 16-bit microcomputer brought many changes in file-handling software. The file control block (FCB) method of handling file operations was an attempt to parallel, as nearly as possible, the file-handling techniques used with the older 8-bit CP/M-based computers.

As with any file-handling system, there are a number of parameters and values that are needed to control file-processing activities. These values are grouped together in a storage area called the file control block, or FCB. In Chapter 9 you learned that DOS maintains all these control values internally. However, with the FCB method, the program must define and maintain many of these values, thereby giving the program more direct control over file-handling operations.

Frequently, the name of the file is not known until the program is actually invoked by the user, as in a file copy or display function. In such cases, the name of the file cannot be hard-coded into the program. Therefore, the filenames must be picked up by the program from the actual command line that was entered to invoke the program. This is done through the use of the **program segment prefix** (PSP). The PSP is a control block of data created by DOS and appended to the program itself.

This chapter begins with an examination of the FCB and the fields it contains. Then, it will examine the interrupts required to process files with the FCBs. Finally, the PSP will be discussed.

10.3   THE FILE CONTROL BLOCK

The FCB consists of two parts: a 7-byte prefix and a 37-byte main data area. The primary purpose of the prefix is to tell DOS that hidden, system, or read-only files are to be processed. The main data area provides information about the control parameters necessary to correctly handle the file.

Examine Figure 10–1 carefully. It shows the layout of an FCB. The comments included for each entry identify the field and its use. The numerals in the first byte of the comments correspond to the numerals in the table of meanings. Study the table to identify when and how the entries are placed in the FCB.

The names of the fields are supplied by the programmer and can be any valid name. In Figure 10–1 descriptive names have been used. You should always use names that are appropriate and meaningful. If the program has two or more files, it would be necessary to choose a reasonable naming scheme for each file.

When working with sequential input or output files, FCB_BLKNUM, FCB_RECNUM, and FCB_RANDOM must be set to 0 in the source code. During the open function DOS sets the block number and random number to 0. However, DOS does not alter the record number. Each drive is assigned a

```
FCB_PREFX   DB  0,0,0,0,0,0,0    ;1 PREFIX SECTION
FCB         LABEL BYTE           ;  POINTER TO THE FCB
FCB_DRIVE   DB  ?                ;1 DRIVE NUMBER 0 = CURRENT, 1 = A:
FCB_FILNAM  DB  8 DUP(?)         ;1 FILE NAME 8 BYTES
FCB_EXTENS  DB  3 DUP(?)         ;1 FILE'S EXTENSION
FCB_BLKNUM  DW  0                ;2 CURRENT BLOCK NUMBER
FCB_RECSIZ  DW  ?                ;2 LOGICAL RECORD SIZE
FCB_FILSIZ  DD  ?                ;3 DOS FILE SIZE IN BYTES
FCB_DATE    DW  ?                ;3 DATE OF CREATION/MODIFICATION
FCB_TIME    DT  ?                ;3 TIME AND WORK AREA
FCB_RECNUM  DB  0                ;2 CURRENT RECORD NUMBER
FCB_RANDOM  DD  0                ;2 RANDOM RECORD NUMBER,
                                 ;  IF NOT SEQUENTIALLY USED
```

Where the codes in the comments mean

Code	Meaning
1	these bytes must be filled in before the file is opened
2	these bytes must be set by the program before each/any read or write operation
3	these bytes are filled in and updated by DOS automatically

FIGURE 10–1   The file control block

number that DOS uses to reference that drive. The current drive is known as 0, while drive A: is 1, drive B: is 2, and so on. FCB_FILNAM can also be designated as LPT1 (for line printer 1) or CON (for the console) should the program need to access these special devices.

When DOS opens a file, it automatically sets FCB_RECSIZE to 128 bytes. Thus, if the program requires a different record size, it is up to the programmer to provide an instruction that moves the required number into this field.

The 7-byte prefix should always be used in the FCB. As indicated, the prefix primarily tells DOS that hidden, system, or read-only files are to be processed. If the first byte of the prefix is 0FFH, then DOS knows that the prefix is not only present, but also that it is to be used. If the first byte does not contain 0FFH, then DOS assumes that the prefix is not there and is not to be used. DOS is given the address of the FCB itself. But since DOS **does** look at the contents of the prior seventh byte to see if it contains 0FFH, the program should always use a prefix. If not, there is a risk that some other valid program data at that spot may contain 0FFH. For this reason, it is always best to include the prefix.

10.4   THE DISK TRANSFER AREA

When an input or output operation is to be performed, an area in memory called the disk transfer area (DTA) must be available to hold the input or output data before the operation is requested. With FCBs, this area represents the program's actual input/output record area. Normally, every file has its own record area or DTA. This causes an immediate problem because DOS allows only one DTA to be active (or set) at one time. Therefore, if a program has two or more files, the DTA must be set before each file operation.

For example, if the program has a loop that inputs a record, then processes it, and outputs a new record to another file, the following sequence is necessary.

```
loop:
        set DTA to input file's record
        read input record
        process it
        set DTA to output file's record
        write the record
        jump to loop
```

If there is only one file in the program, then the DTA needs to be established only once. Preferably, this is done within the open procedure at the same time that the record size is adjusted from DOS's 128 bytes to the required size.

10.5   THE FCB FUNCTIONS

All FCB functions are invoked from the umbrella DOS function 21H (via INT 21H). As usual, register AH contains the number of the required function. Frequently, the address of the FCB needs to be in the register pair DS:DX.

The primary FCB functions for sequential processing are

service code (in hex)	function
0FH	open an existing file
16H	create a new file
10H	close file
1AH	set DTA
14H	read a sequential record
15H	write a sequential record
13H	delete a file
17H	rename a file

Open an Existing File: Function 0FH

Function 0FH is used to open an existing file. It uses drive:filename.ext as given in the FCB. The function code 0FH is in register AH, and the register pair DS:DX contains the address of the FCB. This function is normally used to open a file for input operations.

If the file is successfully opened, register AL is set to 00H and DOS automatically initializes many of the FCB fields. This includes the record size, which is 128 bytes. In addition, the file size in the FCB is set to the file's actual size in bytes. Before the FCB can be used, the program **must** reset the record size to the desired value **and** set the DTA to be used for the first read operation. If the open fails, register AL is set to 0FFH.

Create/Open a New File: Function 16H

This function is used to find an existing file or create a new file, as specified by the FCB. Register AH holds 16H, and the register pair DS:DX contains the address of the FCB. This function is primarily used to open a file for output. If the file already exists, it is reused.

If the operation is successful, register AL contains 00H. However, if the operation fails, then AL is set to 0FFH. An error at this point often means that the directory is full. The file length is set to 0 bytes.

Close a File: Function 10H

Function 10H closes a file that is open. It is important to remember that input files do not necessarily have to be closed. However, output files **must** always be closed for DOS to physically write the last partial block of data and to set the EOF flag in the FAT.

Register AH contains the function code 10H, and the register pair DS:DX contains the address of the FCB. If the close is successful, then the value 00H is placed in register AL. If it fails, register AL holds 0FFH.

Set the Disk Transfer Area: Function 1AH

Before a file can be read or written, the input or output record or area must be designated as the current DTA. Since there can be only one active DTA, this function is often coded just before a file read or write function. The value 1AH is placed in register AH, and the register pair DS:DX contains the address of the DTA desired.

Read a Sequential Record: Function 14H

Function 14H is used when a record is to be input. Before it can be invoked, the record size in the FCB must be set and the input area must be designated as the current DTA. Register AH contains the value 14H, and the register pair DS:DX contains the address of the FCB. During execution the current record and block numbers are taken from the FCB, and the record is input and moved into the DTA. The numbers are then updated in the FCB, in preparation for the next request.

After execution, register AL contains a code that indicates the result of the read operation. Notice that there are **two** EOF conditions. In the first case, there are no more data and the program can go on to the next processing. In the other, however, the last read does not input a complete physical record. This indicates that there is a partial record yet to be processed. Obviously, this complicates the EOF processing requirements.

AL	Meaning
00H	successful
01H	EOF and no data read
02H	DTA could not hold the full record
03H	EOF with a partial record read (padded with 00H bytes)

Write a Sequential Record: Function 15H

Writing records sequentially is implemented by using function 15H. Before a record can be written, the DTA must be set and the correct record size set in the FCB. Register AH contains 15H, and the register pair DS:DX contains the address of the FCB. DOS takes the current data from the DTA and moves it to its internal buffer. When the buffer is filled, a sector/cluster is written. DOS then updates the current record/block and file size numbers in the FCB so that it is ready for the next write operation.

After writing the record, register AL contains one of three codes indicating the result of the write operation. These codes are

AL	Meaning
00H	successful write
01H	error—disk is full
02H	not enough space in DOS's internal DTA to hold the program's record

Because the write operation writes to disk only after DOS's internal DTA buffer is full, a write does not necessarily mean that a physical record is written. Each write causes the record to be moved into the internal DTA buffer. Then, when the internal DTA is full, DOS writes that cluster/sector. Note: When a file is closed, all associated DOS internal DTA buffers are automatically flushed and written out.

10.6   A PROGRAMMING EXAMPLE

Recall the program presented in Figure 9–4, in which the text file named PGM1.ASM was input and displayed on the screen. This program used 128-byte records. The program in Figure 10–2 (PGM23.ASM on the program disk)

```
  PAGE  60,132
  TITLE PGM23  FIGURE 10-2 INPUT/SHOW FILE WITH FCB, BYTE BY BYTE

;*************************************************************************
; PGM23        Title: Figure 10-2 Read and display a text file       *
;                                                                     *
; Programmer: Vic Broquard                                            *
; Date Written:  6/11/88        Date Of Last Revision: 8/6/88         *
;                                                                     *
; Purpose: Use FCB method to read and display a text file            *
;                                                                     *
; Special Requirements: Structure FCB1 controls the file operations  *
;                                                                     *
;*************************************************************************


; program code segment

PGM23CD    SEGMENT

MAIN PROC FAR

; housekeeping section

     ASSUME    CS:PGM23CD,DS:PGM23DA,SS:PGM23SK

     MOV  AX,PGM23DA     ; ESTABLISH ADDRESSABILITY
     MOV  DS,AX          ; TO DATA SEGMENT

; main processing section

     CALL OPEN           ; OPEN THE FILE

     CMP  IOERRSW,00H    ; ANY I/O ERROR?
     JNE  DONE           ; YES, HALT EXECUTION

BIGLOOP:

     CALL READ_BYTE      ; READ A BYTE

     CMP  IOERRSW,00H    ; ANY I/O ERROR?
     JNE  DONE           ; YES, HALT EXECUTION

     CMP  MORE_DATA,00H  ; ANY MORE DATA?
     JNE  ENDJOB         ; NO, FINISH UP

     CMP  INPUTAREA,1AH  ; IS CHARACTER A ^Z?
     JE   ENDJOB         ; YES, ASCII EOF FOUND
```

FIGURE 10–2   Program using the FCB method and byte-by-byte input
(PGM23.ASM)   *(Continues)*

```
          CALL OUTPUT       ; PRINT THE BYTE

          CMP  EOFSW,00H    ; HAS EOF BEEN SIGNALED?
          JE   BIGLOOP      ; NO, GO GET ANOTHER BYTE

ENDJOB:

-----------------------------------------------------------------------

          CALL CLOSE        ; CLOSE THE FILE

DONE:

          MOV  AX,4C00H     ; SET FOR END WITH A 0 RETURN CODE
          INT  21H          ; CALL DOS TO END PROGRAM

MAIN  ENDP




          SUBTTL  OUTPUT: DISPLAY A BYTE ON THE SCREEN
          PAGE

OUTPUT    PROC

; procedure to display a character on the CRT

          PUSH AX           ; SAVE REGISTERS
          PUSH DX

          MOV  AH,02H       ; SET FOR CRT OUTPUT
          MOV  DL,INPUTAREA ; INSERT CHAR TO PRINT
          INT  21H          ; CALL DOS TO PRINT CHARACTER

          POP  DX           ; RESTORE REGISTERS
          POP  AX

          RET
OUTPUT    ENDP




          SUBTTL  OPEN: OPENS THE FILE USING THE FCB METHOD
          PAGE

OPEN PROC

; procedure to open file, set DTA, and set record size

          PUSH AX           ; SAVE REGISTERS
          PUSH DX
```

FIGURE 10–2   continued

```
        MOV  AH,0FH       ; SET FOR OPEN FUNCTION
        LEA  DX,FCB1      ; SET DX TO -> FCB1
        INT  21H          ; CALL DOS TO OPEN FILE

        CMP  AL,00H       ; ALL OK?
        JE   INITDTA      ; YES, CONTINUE WITH INITIALIZE DTA

; here, there is an open error, print a message

        LEA  DX,MSG3      ; POINT TO ERROR MESSAGE
----------------------------------------------------------------------
        MOV  AH,09H       ; SET FOR PRINT STRING
        INT  21H          ; CALL DOS TO DISPLAY ERR

        MOV  IOERRSW,01H  ; SET IOERR ON
        JMP  SKIPDTA      ; AND LEAVE

; here, initialize the DTA and the record size

INITDTA:

        MOV  AH,1AH       ; SET FOR DTA FUNCTION
        LEA  DX,INPUTAREA ; POINT TO DTA
        INT  21H          ; CALL DOS TO SET THE DTA

        MOV  FCBRECSZ,01H ; SET RECORD SIZE FOR 1 BYTE AT A TIME

SKIPDTA:

        POP  DX           ; RESTORE REGISTERS
        POP  AX

        RET
OPEN ENDP



        SUBTTL  CLOSE: CLOSES THE FILE USING THE FCB METHOD
        PAGE

CLOSE  PROC

; procedure to close file

        PUSH AX           ; SAVE REGISTERS
        PUSH DX

        MOV  AH,10H       ; SET FOR CLOSE FILE FUNCTION
        LEA  DX,FCB1      ; POINT TO FILE
        INT  21H          ; CALL DOS TO CLOSE THE FILE
```

FIGURE 10–2 continued   *(Continues)*

```
        CMP  AL,00H        ; ALL OK?
        JE   CLOSE_DONE    ; YES, EXIT

; here, there has been a close error, print a message

        LEA  DX,MSG1       ; POINT TO ERROR MESSAGE
        MOV  AH,09H        ; SET FOR PRINT STRING
        INT  21H           ; CALL DOS TO DISPLAY ERROR

CLOSE_DONE:

        POP  DX            ; RESTORE REGISTERS
        POP  AX

---------------------------------------------------------------------

        RET
CLOSE   ENDP



        SUBTTL   READ_BYTE: READ A BYTE USING THE FCB METHOD
        PAGE


READ_BYTE   PROC

; procedure to read a byte

        PUSH AX            ; SAVE REGISTERS
        PUSH DX

        MOV  AH,14H        ; SET FOR READ NEXT RECORD
        LEA  DX,FCB1       ; POINT TO FILE
        INT  21H           ; CALL DOS TO READ A BYTE

        CMP  AL,00H        ; ALL OK?
        JE   OK            ; YES, GO ON

        CMP  AL,01H        ; EOF?
        JE   EOF           ; YES, GOTO ENDJOB

        CMP  AL,02H        ; REC TOO BIG FOR DTA?
        JE   IOERR         ; YES, PRINT ERROR MSG

; here if EOF and some data

        MOV  EOFSW,01H     ; SET EOFSW ON
        JMP  OK            ; AND GO ON
```

FIGURE 10–2 continued

```
EOF:
    MOV  MORE_DATA,01H  ; SET MORE.DATA TO NO
    MOV  EOFSW,01H      ; SET EOFSW ON
    JMP  OK             ; AND GO ON

IOERR:

    LEA  DX,MSG2        ; POINT TO ERROR MESSAGE
    MOV  AH,09H         ; SET FOR PRINT STRING
    INT  21H            ; CALL DOS TO DISPLAY ERROR

    MOV  IOERRSW,01H    ; SET IOERRSW ON, AND GO ON

OK:
    POP  DX             ; RESTORE REGISTERS
    POP  AX

    RET
READ_BYTE  ENDP


PGM23CD  ENDS
```

```
    SUBTTL   PGM23 DATA AREA
    PAGE


; program data segment

PGM23DA   SEGMENT

FCB1PRE   DB   0,0,0,0,0,0,0  ; FCB PREFIX
FCB1    LABEL BYTE            ; FCB FOR DISK FILE
FCBDRIVE  DB   02H            ; DRIVE 0=CURRENT 1=A: 2=B:
FCBNAME   DB   'PGM1    '     ; NAME OF FILE 8 BYTES
FCBEXT    DB   'ASM'          ; EXTENSION OF FILE
FCBBLKNUM DW   0              ; CURRENT BLOCK NUMBER
FCBRECSZ  DW   ?              ; LOGICAL RECORD SIZE
FCBFILESZ DD   ?              ; FILE SIZE IN BYTES
FCBDATE   DW   ?              ; DATE FILE LAST ALTERED
FCBWORK   DT   ?              ; DOS WORK AREA
FCBRECNUM DB   0              ; CURRENT RECORD NUMBER
FCBRNDNUM DD   0              ; RANDOM RECORD NUMBER

INPUTAREA DB   ?              ; INPUT AREA WILL BE USED AS DTA

MORE_DATA DB   00H            ; ON WHEN NO MORE DATA IS AVAILABLE
EOFSW     DB   00H            ; ON WHEN EOF IS SIGNALED
IOERRSW   DB   00H            ; ON WHEN THERE IS AN IOERR
```

FIGURE 10–2 continued   *(Continues)*

```
MSG1    DB   '*** YOU HAVE HAD A CLOSE FILE ERROR$'
MSG2    DB   '*** YOU HAVE HAD AN I/O ERROR$'
MSG3    DB   '*** YOU HAVE HAD AN OPEN ERROR$'


PGM23DA  ENDS

; program stack segment

PGM23SK  SEGMENT PARA STACK 'STACK'

         DW   32 DUP (?)

PGM23SK  ENDS

    END  MAIN
```

FIGURE 10–2   continued

shows how this program can be rewritten using the FCB method and byte-by-byte input. Consequently, the record size is set to 1 byte. Since there is only one file, the DTA is established within the open routine. Notice that the extended error function (59H) can be used immediately after any commands that can return 0FFH in AL. As before, the program must check for CTRL-Z, since the file is a text file.

10.7   FILE MAINTENANCE FUNCTIONS

During normal file-processing operations, there are a number of activities that are necessary to maintain a proper file-processing environment. This section examines some of the more commonly used of these functions.

Delete a File: Function 13H

A file can be deleted by using an FCB containing the drive and filename. Register AH holds the function code 13H, and the register pair DS:DX holds the address of the FCB of the file to be deleted. If all is successful, AL contains 00H. If the operation does not succeed, AL contains 0FFH.

Rename a File: Function 17H

Frequently, it is necessary and/or desirable to change the name of a file. For the rename function the FCB is handled differently. The old file-name—consisting of the drive, name, and extension—is stored normally within the FCB. The new name and its extension are stored at offset 16 within the FCB. This is where the file size normally begins. The function code 17H is placed in register AH, and the address of the modified FCB is placed in the register pair DS:DX. If the rename operation is successful, AL holds 00H. However, if an error occurs, AL contains 0FFH.

Finally, if wildcards (* and ?) are present in the new name, they are interpreted to mean "ditto from the old name." That is, the wildcards tell the program to copy the corresponding characters from the old name into the new name, thereby shortening the amount of code required to specify the new name.

10.8   THE PROGRAM SEGMENT PREFIX

When a program is loaded into memory, DOS builds a 256-byte (100H) control block called the program segment prefix (PSP) and inserts it in front of the actual first byte of the program. This control block contains many pieces of information about the program, its execution environment, and a copy of the actual command line that invoked the program from DOS in the first place. The layout of the PSP is shown in Figure 10–3. All offsets are given in hex.

The INT 20H command (return to DOS, offset 00H) can be used by any program to return program control to DOS. The command is superseded by the 4CH return with a return code function. This feature will be covered in detail later in this chapter.

The total amount of memory, in paragraphs, is at offset 02H. The actual number of bytes needed is found by multiplying the value at 02H by 16. The command line that was entered to invoke the program is reproduced in the parameter area, beginning at offset 81H.

Suppose that the program name were XFER and the command line entered were

```
A>XFER B:TEST.DAT 06/12/88
```

Then, beginning at 81H in the PSP, the same name would be inserted as

```
B:TEST.DAT 06/12/88
```

In this way the program would acquire the parameters being passed to it from the command line—in this case, B:TEST.DAT 06/12/88.

In addition to program control, DOS performs some preliminary file-handling activities for the program. It parses the command and builds skeleton FCBs for the files given after the command XFER. Drives are converted and the names and extensions are properly set up. DOS handles the first two files only. The skeleton FCBs are called FCB #1 and FCB #2 in the PSP. At this point these FCBs are nearly ready for program use. The only problem is that the lengths of the FCBs are wrong. In fact, the first FCB, if used, would overlay most of the second FCB! Therefore, it is probably better programming style to copy these two FCB fragments into the program's true FCB areas and use the areas within the program as the FCBs. In addition, the entire parameter area, offset 80H, can be used as a DTA for 128-byte records. If there were only one file, then the first FCB could be used as is.

The Program Segment Prefix

Offset	Length	Contents
00H	2	a return to DOS instruction: INT 20H
02H	2	the number of paragraphs of all RAM—total memory
04H	1	reserved
05H	5	call to DOS function dispatcher: the second and third bytes contain the offset; the last two contain the segment address. The offset also gives the number of bytes available in the pgm code segment.
0AH	4	the terminate address IP:CS
0EH	4	the control break handler address IP:CS
12H	4	the critical error handler address IP:CS these three values can be altered by a program to modify standard DOS actions, such as attaching and calling a subprogram, which will return to the caller program (not DOS)
16H	22	DOS area
2CH	2	environment string pointer
2EH	39	DOS work area
55H	7	FCB #1 prefix
5CH	9	FCB #1
65H	7	FCB #2 prefix
6CH	20	FCB #2
80H	1	length of the parameter string
81H	127	the command string as entered

FIGURE 10–3   The program segment prefix

These two areas, the parameter area and the two skeleton FCBs, are very useful fields for a program. They speed up the process of establishing FCBs and allow the program to pick up parameters passed to it from the command line.

How does the program access the PSP? A better question might be what will the contents of the registers be when the program finally gets control at its first instruction?

When the program gets control, both registers DS and ES contain the address of the PSP. The CS:IP pair must point to the program's first instruction, and the SS:SP pair points to the program's stack segment, if one was set up.

It is now easy to see why all programs need the following two house-keeping instructions, which set register DS to point to the program's data segment.

```
MOV   AX,PGM1DA     ; ESTABLISH ADDRESSABILITY
MOV   DS,AX         ; TO PGM1'S DATA SEGMENT
```

Thus, register DS begins by pointing to the PSP, not the data area.

If for some reason the program needs to access anything in the PSP, then it must either save the original value in register DS before loading the data segment's address into it or extract the information before reloading DS. If ES is not used, then it retains the PSP address.

CODE VIEW debugger note: CODE VIEW automatically preprocesses the command line, following the rules of the C language. That is, any quotation marks are removed and only one blank is left between arguments on the command line. Normally, this is not a problem.

10.9 METHODS OF TERMINATING A PROGRAM

There are eight ways by which a program can be ended. When using DOS Version 3.0, some are now preferred over others. Take a look at each of them to identify the way they are implemented and why you would choose one over another.

Terminate the Program: INT 20H

This method ends a program and passes control back to DOS. It does not close the files that are open. The service does, however, reset the three interrupt vectors, beginning at 0AH in the PSP. The CS register **must** point to the PSP when this service is executed. This is particularly useful when terminating complex programs.

A FAR RET from the Main Procedure

Chapter 2 presented the alternative assembler shell to be used with older releases of DOS. Figure 10–4 shows that basic shell. Examine the first three instructions. When the program gets control, register DS contains the segment address of the PSP. It is pushed onto the stack. Then 1 word of zeros (00H) is pushed onto the stack. After finishing the processing, the program ends with RET. It is a FAR return because the MAIN procedure is FAR. This FAR return pops the CS:IP pair off the stack. In this case the address of the PSP is placed into register CS and an offset of 00H is loaded into the IP register. Thus, the next instruction to execute is the first byte of the PSP. What is there? The return to DOS instruction, INT 20H. In this way, the requirement that register CS point to the PSP is satisfied.

JMP to the PSP Offset 00H

It is possible for the program to issue a jump command to the PSP's INT 20H instruction. When this is done, register CS must still contain the address of the PSP.

```
MAIN     PROC    FAR

; housekeeping section

        ASSUME   CS:PGM1CD,DS:PGM1DA,SS:PGM1SK

        PUSH     DS          ; SAVE DOS
        MOV      AX,0        ; RETURN
        PUSH     AX          ; ADDRESS

        MOV      AX,PGM1DA   ; ESTABLISH ADDRESSABILITY
        MOV      DS,AX       ; TO PGM1DA - THE PGM'S DATA SEGMENT

; main process section

            .
            .
            .

; return to DOS section

        RET                  ; RETURN TO DOS

MAIN     ENDP
```

FIGURE 10–4   Alternative assembler shell

INT 21H with Function AH = 00H

The result of using this method is identical to INT 20H. CS must also point to the PSP.

The Bootstrap Loader BIOS Function: INT 19H

This BIOS service reboots the computer in a way that is similar to turning the power on. It also gives nearly the same result as keying the CTRL-ALT-DEL sequence except that the lengthy memory check is bypassed.

Use INT 19H if the logic in the program requires an immediate shutdown. For example, there are many programs that are designed to detect copy-protection violations. When detected, the program issues an INT 19H. In addition, use the service when the program requires the modification of either the memory size or the equipment list. In such situations, INT 19H reboots the program without altering these settings.

Terminate Process with a Return Code: INT 21H with AH = 4CH

This method terminates processing and was a return code. It is the method used in all examples so far in this text. With the introduction of Version 3.0 of DOS, it became the preferred method of ending programs. It is preferred because it sets a return code that any batch file can test with the ERROR-LEVEL option. The program can take alternative action based upon the value returned. In addition, DOS closes all files automatically.

To make this function work correctly, the return code desired must be placed in register AL and all files must have been opened with function 3CH and 3DH. For this reason, the use of file handles becomes even more desirable. Register CS does not have to contain the segment address of the PSP.

Terminate but Stay Resident: INT 27H

This function terminates a program, but it does not erase or remove the program from memory or close any files. DOS updates its available memory to begin with the paragraph immediately above the last byte of the program. When this happens, the program is resident but not active. Other programs will not be able to overwrite the memory area containing the program.

This is an advanced technique used by programs that are to be called later (keyboard enhancers, for example). Not only can program code be left resident, but large data blocks can be left in memory to be passed on to other programs.

Register DX contains the offset of the first byte beyond that portion of the program that is to remain resident. Thus, what stays in memory is from the beginning of the program down to the address in DX, including the PSP. Since this is an offset, up to 64K can be left resident. (If it is necessary for more code to remain resident, use INT 21H with AH = 31H as shown next.) When this function is called, register CS must contain the segment address of the PSP. This function resets the three interrupt vectors in a way that is similar to the effect of INT 20H.

Keep/Terminate but Stay Resident: INT 21H with AH = 31H

With DOS Version 3.0, this has become the preferred function for terminating and staying resident. This is an advanced version of INT 27H. In addition to all the actions that INT 27H provides, this function permits setting a return code in register AL.

Register DX must contain the number of paragraphs of memory that are to stay resident in memory. Since the PSP must remain and is included in the memory request, do not forget to include it in the request. Unlike INT 27H, this function allows more than 64K to remain resident. Further, register CS does not have to point to the PSP.

Now that you have examined the uses and effects of the PSP, consider how a program can utilize the data in the PSP.

10.10 AN EXAMPLE OF USING DATA FROM THE PSP

In this example you will see how to modify the display program in Figure 10–2 so it accepts the path/filename from the command line. Since you will

```
-d ds:00,ff
521B:0000  CD 20 00 A0 00 9A F0 FE-1D F0 8E 09 16 49 2B 0A  M ...p~.p...I+.
521B:0010  16 49 56 09 16 49 06 49-01 01 01 00 02 FF FF FF  .IV..I.I........
521B:0020  FF FF FF FF FF FF FF FF-FF FF FF FF 11 52 82 8F  .............R..
521B:0030  16 49 14 00 18 00 1B 52-FF FF FF FF 00 00 00 00  .I.....R........
521B:0040  00 00 00 00 00 00 00 00-00 00 00 00 00 00 00 00  ................
521B:0050  CD 21 CB 00 00 00 00 00-00 00 00 02 20 20 20 20  M!K.........
521B:0060  20 20 20 20 20 20 20 20-00 00 00 00 00 20 20 20       .....
521B:0070  20 20 20 20 20 20 20 20-00 00 00 00 00 00 00 00       ........
521B:0080  19 20 62 3A 5C 74 65 73-74 69 6E 67 5C 77 6F 72  . b:\testing\wor
521B:0090  6B 5C 74 65 6D 70 2E 61-73 6D 0D 00 00 0D 61 73 6D  k\temp.asm...asm
521B:00A0  0D 00 00 00 00 00 00 00-00 00 00 00 00 00 00 00  ................
521B:00B0  00 00 00 00 00 00 00 00-00 00 00 00 00 00 00 00  ................
521B:00C0  00 00 00 00 00 00 00 00-00 00 00 00 00 00 00 00  ................
521B:00D0  00 00 00 00 00 00 00 00-00 00 00 00 00 00 00 00  ................
521B:00E0  00 00 00 00 00 00 00 00-00 00 00 00 00 00 00 00  ................
521B:00F0  00 00 00 00 00 00 00 00-00 00 00 00 00 00 00 00  ................
```

FIGURE 10–5   The program segment prefix

allow any path, the FCB created by DOS is invalid. Therefore, the path/file-name must be extracted from the parameter area, beginning at 81H from the start of the PSP.

Suppose that the program is started by

```
A>PGM24 B:\TESTING\WORK\TEMP.ASM
```

Figure 10–5 shows what the PSP looks like immediately after the program has been loaded, but before the first instruction of the program executes. Notice that DOS fails to create a valid FCB beginning with 55H. You must use the parameter area beginning at 81H. This area contains the remainder of the command line, minus the program name and any redirection commands. The first byte contains a blank that separates the program name from the drive letter. Thus, the program can look for the first nonblank character beginning at offset 81H. Once found, this is the start of the string. The ending byte is 0DH, the carriage return. It is also pointed to by the length field at 80H.

The program must find the actual start of the path/filename. It is then moved byte by byte into the ASCIIZ string, until the 0DH is encountered. Then the 00H delimiter is inserted into the ASCIIZ string.

Coding Segment Overrides in Instructions

How is the PSP addressed? As you have seen, register DS holds the program's data segment address. Since we have made no changes to register ES, it still contains the PSP segment address. To get at the command part of the PSP, it might be tempting to enter

```
        MOV   SI,81H    ; GET THE OFFSET FROM THE START OF THE PSP

        MOV   AL,[SI]  ; GET THE FIRST BYTE OF THE COMMAND LINE
```

Unfortunately, the second move would fail because the assembler assumes that the segment address is in register DS, forming the pair DS:SI in the move. To fix this you could temporarily swap the contents of registers DS and ES. Now DS would have the segment address of the PSP, and the move would work correctly. But now you cannot address any program data areas to save the extracted bytes!

A better solution is to use segment overrides on those instructions that access the PSP. The following code shows how the override is coded using register ES.

```
        MOV   SI,81H     ; GET THE OFFSET FROM THE START OF THE PSP

        MOV   AL,ES: [SI] ; GET THE FIRST BYTE OF THE COMMAND LINE
```

As you can see, segment overrides can be very handy when working with the PSP.

The Example Solution

Figure 10–6 shows only the modified parts of the program (the complete version is PGM24.ASM on the program disk). Examine very carefully the various overrides that use register ES within GET_FILENAME.

Besides learning about useful features of the PSP, you now know an even more powerful assembler feature: segment overrides.

```
        PAGE 60,132
        TITLE   PGM24 - FIGURE 10-6 - ACCEPT PATH/FILE AND READ/DISPLAY IT

; program code segment

PGM24CD    SEGMENT
MAIN PROC FAR

; housekeeping section

        ASSUME    CS:PGM24CD,DS:PGM24DA,SS:PGM24SK

        MOV   AX,PGM24DA     ; ESTABLISH ADDRESSABILITY
        MOV   DS,AX          ; TO PGM1DA'S DATA SEGMENT

; ES contains the PSP address
```

FIGURE 10–6 Display a file given in the command line (PGM24.ASM) *(Continues)*

```
; main processing

    CALL GET_FILENAME   ; EXTRACT THE FILE NAME FROM PSP

    CALL OPEN           ; OPEN THE FILE
    .
    .
    .

MAIN  ENDP
      SUBTTL  EXTRACT THE FILENAME FROM THE PSP
      PAGE

GET_FILENAME  PROC

; ES -> PSP
; extract path/filename and store in FILENAME

    PUSH AX             ; SAVE REGISTERS
    PUSH BX
    PUSH SI

    LEA  BX,FILENAME    ; BX = ADDRESS OF FILENAME TO FILL UP

    MOV  SI,80H         ; ES:SI -> PSP'S LENGTH OF COMMAND

    CMP  ES: BYTE PTR [SI],00H ; WAS ANY VALUE EVEN ENTERED?
    JE   PUT_IN_00H     ; NO, SO GO FINISH UP

    INC  SI             ; SI -> FIRST BYTE OF THE COMMAND STRING

BLANK_LOOP:

    MOV  AL,ES:[SI]     ; GET THE BYTE
    CMP  AL,20H         ; IS IT A BLANK?
    JNE  GOT_START      ; NO, NOW WE'VE GOT THE START

    INC  SI             ; POINT TO NEXT BYTE
    JMP  BLANK_LOOP     ; REPEAT, UNTIL NON-BLANK IS FOUND

GOT_START:

    CMP  AL,0DH         ; IS THIS THE LAST BYTE?
    JE   PUT_IN_00H     ; YES, SO GO FINISH UP
```

```
                       ; NOTE: IF THE COMMAND STRING CONTAINED
                       ; A:TEST.ASM   B:TEST2.ASM
                       ; THIS ROUTINE WILL INSERT THE COMPLETE
                       ; STRING INTO FILENAME - OPEN WILL THEN FAIL
```

FIGURE 10–6 continued

```
                        ; AND PRODUCE THE ERROR MESSAGE
                        ; IF YOU WANT TO ACCEPT THE FIRST FILE,
                        ; INSERT CODE HERE TO COMPARE FOR A BLANK

        MOV   [BX],AL   ; STORE BYTE IN ASCIIZ STRING
        INC   SI        ; POINT TO NEXT BYTE TO CHECK
        INC   BX        ; POINT TO NEXT ANSWER BYTE

        MOV   AL,ES:[SI]    ; GET NEXT BYTE TO CHECK

        JMP   GOT_START   ; REPEAT, UNTIL CR IS FOUND

PUT_IN_00H:

        MOV   AL,00H    ; 00H IS THE DELIMITER FOR ASCIIZ STRING
        MOV   [BX],AL   ; INSERT IT INTO THE STRING

        POP   SI        ; RESTORE REGISTERS
        POP   BX
        POP   AX

        RET

GET_FILENAME   ENDP
     .
     .
     .
     SUBTTL   PROGRAM DATA AND STACK AREAS
     PAGE

; program data segment

PGM24DA   SEGMENT

FILENUM   DW   ?                    ; FILE HANDLE FOR FILE

FILENAME  DB   127 DUP(?)           ; ASCIIZ STRING
```

FIGURE 10–6 continued

10.11 SUMMARY

You have seen the layout of both the FCB and the PSP. To use the FCB method, the current program DTA must be continually set. The normal file I/O functions parallel those of the file handle method.

The PSP is an integral part of a program. At the start of every program, registers DS and ES point to it. There are eight different ways to terminate a program; many involve the PSP directly. Applications programs may also use the command line that is stored in the PSP. The most common way to do so is to extract the filenames entered on the command line.

10.12 REVIEW QUESTIONS

1. True/false: When using the FCB method, all file input and output operations require the use of a DTA.

2. Why must the record size always be moved to the FCB field after the file is opened? Why not just initialize the FCB field at compile time?

3. What byte is input when a file is opened, the FCBBLKNUM field is set to 0, the FCBRECNUM is set to 10, the FCBRECSIZE is set to 1, and an input is requested?

4. Consider a program that begins like this:

```
        . . .

        ASSUME ...
        PUSH CS
        MOV  AX,256
        PUSH AX
        MOV  AX,PGM1DA
        MOV  DS,AX
```

and ends like this:

```
        RETF
MAIN ENDP
```

What do you suppose will happen when the program attempts to end?

5. What are the following resisters set to at the time DOS gives control to your program's first executable instruction?
   a) CS
   b) SS
   c) DS
   d) ES

6. How do the standard housekeeping instructions

```
MAIN PROC FAR
     PUSH DS
     MOV  AX,0
     PUSH AX
```

relate to

```
                    RETF
            MAIN ENDP
```

Explain what is occurring.

7. What is the FCB prefix? How is it used? Why should every FCB include a prefix?

8. What are the eight ways to terminate a program? Compare and contrast these methods, paying particular attention to the effects of register DS and the closing of files.

9. What are segment overrides? Why are they used?

10.13 PRACTICE PROBLEMS

1. A program must access two files: B:ACCOUNTS.DAT and A:WORK.DAT. ACCOUNTS.DAT already exists and is to be read only. WORK.DAT is a new temporary file to be used as output. Code the FCBs needed to define these files.

2. Code the instructions to set the DTA for an input operation. The FCB is called ACCT_FCB and the input structure is called ACCT_REC.

3. Code the instructions to input the next 15 bytes from a file whose FCB is known as MASTR_FCB. Assume that the DTA has been set and points to MASTR_REC. If there is an error, call a procedure known as SHOW_ERR. If EOF is signaled, set the EOF_FLAG to 01H.

4. Code the instructions to write TEST_REC (39 bytes) to the file pointed to by TEST_FCB. Assume that the DTA has been set. If there is an error, call a procedure known as DSPLY_ERR.

5. Code the instructions to close a file whose FCB is called MOD_FCB.

6. Code the instructions to give file B:TEST.DT1 the new name of B:MSTR.DAT.

7. Code the instructions to delete file B:TEMP.TST.

8. Code a routine to extract a date from the command line stored in the PSP. The date is in the form of mm/dd/yy. It should be placed into an area called DATE_IN, which is 8 bytes long. If no date is entered, display this error message:

```
    A DATE MUST BE ENTERED OF THE FORM mm/dd/yy
```

10.14 PROGRAMMING PROBLEMS

1. Modify the inventory program in Programming Problem 1 of Chapter 9 so that it uses FCBs.

2. Modify the full-screen data entry program in Programming Problem 2 of Chapter 9 so that it uses FCBs.

3. Modify the trip fuel economy analyzer program in Programming Problem 3 in Chapter 9 so that it uses FCBs.

4. Create a file-merge, or "mod," program. The program should get two complete file specifications from the command line. Add the second file to the first file. Both files should be text files. Use the TYPE command from DOS to see if the program works. Use either FCBs or file handles. You must access the PSP to acquire the file specifications.

    The text files can be any two of your choice. If none is handy, use a word processor, EDLIN or COPY CON: to create them. The files do not have to be large; a few lines will be sufficient.

5. Create a delete file program called REMOVE that picks up the filename to delete from the command line via the PSP. The program should then display the message

    ```
    DO YOU REALLY WANT TO DELETE FILE: xxxxxxxxxxxxxxx
    ENTER y OR n: _
    ```

    and get the acceptable reply—either Y or y or N or n. If the answer is yes, then delete the file. If the answer is no, then display the message SKIPPING FILE and end the program.

    The command line syntax should be something like:

    ```
    A>REMOVE B:TEST.DAT
    ```

6. Modify the routine shown in Figure 10–6, which parses the PSP command line. The routine should now extract all the filenames entered. Assume that each filename is separated from the next by one or more blanks. Store each name in the fields called FNAME1, FNAME2, FNAME3, and FNAME4. There can be a maximum of four filenames entered.

11

String Functions

11.1   CHAPTER OBJECTIVES

In this chapter you will

1.   Learn to move strings
2.   Learn to clear strings and right- and left-justify strings
3.   Learn to code segment overrides
4.   Learn to compare and scan strings
5.   Learn to load and store strings efficiently

11.2   INTRODUCTION

String instructions enable the computer to process an entire field or group of fields as a single entity rather than a byte at a time as you have been doing. Included in this chapter are instructions to move a string, to compare two strings, and to scan a string for the presence or absence of another string. The string functions consist of five instructions plus one prefix, which is used to implement repetitive operations. These instructions are often referred to as **string primitives.**

11.3   THE EXTRA SEGMENT REGISTER: ES

The string primitives require the use of many registers in their operation. Register ES, which this text has more or less ignored until now, is vital to the operation of string instructions. When using the string primitives, register ES, the extra segment register, operates much like register DS. It must be set to point to the data segment that contains the character strings. This can be implemented within the housekeeping section as follows.

```
ASSUME     CS:PGM1CD,DS:PGM1DA,SS:PGM1SK,ES:PGM1DA

MOV   AX,PGM1DA      ; ESTABLISH ADDRESSABILITY
MOV   DS,AX          ; TO PGM1DA, THE DATA SEGMENT
MOV   ES,AX          ; ES: ALSO POINTS TO THE DATA SEG
```

Now consider the move string primitive.

11.4   THE MOVE STRING INSTRUCTION SET

In addition to the addresses of the strings to be moved, the move string instructions require other operands. Each of these operands contains parameters that will be held in certain registers. First examine each of these parameters and then consider how the move string instructions can be coded.

Move String Parameters

Consider the following situation. The data in the field NAME_IN are to be moved to NAME_OUT. Each field is 8 bytes in length. The move string instructions permit you to execute the move with a single instruction rather than by forming a small loop that moves a byte at a time as in previous examples. To use a single instruction, additional registers must be initialized.

The move string function repeatedly moves 1 byte or 1 word at a time as it proceeds through the two strings. Therefore, the first decision that must be made is how many bytes should be moved: 1 byte or 2 bytes. This is determined primarily by whether either of the strings has an odd length. If either or both have an odd length, moving a word at a time will not work. All moves of odd-length strings must use the byte form. If the length is an even number, then either the byte or the word form can be used. However, because it requires fewer iterations, the word form will be faster.

Once the number of bytes to be moved per iteration has been decided, the number of repetitions can be determined. As you might expect, this value is placed in register CX. Since the length in this example is 8 bytes (an even number), either the byte or the word form can be used. Use the word form.

This will fix the number of repetitions at $4(2 \times 4) = 8$ bytes. The operation is coded as

```
MOV   CX,4
```

Normally, when storage is referenced, brackets have been used, as in MOV AX,[BX]. With string functions, register SI, the source index, is used to hold the offset address of the source string (the sending string). Register DI, the destination index, is used to hold the offset address of the destination, or receiving, string. These can be initialized by entering:

```
LEA   DI,NAME_OUT
LEA   SI,NAME_IN
```

Unfortunately, the situation is more complex than this. To create a complete vector address, a segment register is needed. Until now, register DS was always implied. Now, however, the segment register DS is associated only with register SI, and register ES is paired with register DI. All string functions assume the following vectors: ES:DI and DS:SI.

Thus, you must use the extra segment register, ES, with string functions. You have seen that it is possible to override a segment register used within an instruction. But with the string functions, only register DS can be overridden. The segment register associated with register DI cannot be changed from register ES. Therefore, before using a string function, register ES must be given the appropriate segment address. In small beginning programs this does not present a problem because the data segment is substantially smaller than one 64K segment. Therefore, registers DS and ES contain the same value—the data segment address, as shown in the examples above.

The final variable is the direction to move: forward (from left to right) or backward (from right to left). Since you decided the direction by the way the addresses of the first bytes of the strings were moved into registers SI and DI, you must move forward. The direction flag (DF) keeps track of the direction of the string functions. The value 0B indicates forward and the value 1B indicates backward.

How can the direction flag be set or cleared?

Setting the Direction Flag: CLD and STD

Two instructions are used to change the value of the direction flag. They are CLD and STD.

CLD clears the direction flag, that is, sets it to 0B.

STD sets the direction flag, that is, sets it to 1B.

Neither instruction has any operands. As you can see, these are very simple but vital instructions that do just one thing.

11.5 THE MOVE STRING INSTRUCTIONS: MOVS, MOVSB, MOVSW

The move string instructions have three forms. **MOVSB,** move string byte, moves 1 byte per repetition. **MOVSW**, move string word, moves 1 word per repetition. The **MOVS**, move string, automatically determines which form to use from the length of the operands. It generates either MOVSB or MOVSW as required.

These move string instructions all require the following resister settings:

DS:SI	contains the address of the source string
ES:DI	contains the address of the destination string
DF	is set to indicate the direction of the move
	0B (cleared) for forward (CLD)
	1B (set) for backward (STD)
DS and ES	point to the respective segments containing the strings (in this case to the data segment)
CX	contains the number of repetitions to perform

The syntaxes of the three versions of the move string instruction are

```
MOVS    operand1,operand2

MOVSB

MOVSW
```

Only the MOVS version has coded operands. MOVS assumes that operand2 will be moved to operand1. The **only** use made of these coded operands is to determine their lengths. If the lengths are both even, then MOVS generates a MOVSW. If one or both lengths are odd, then MOVS generates a MOVSB instruction.

MOVS is seldom used because the number of repetitions must actually be determined in advance. In this example, if you intend to move 1 byte per repetition (REP), the number of REPs is eight. If you intend to move 1 word per REP, the number of REPs is 4. Therefore, it is generally considered better coding practice to explicitly code MOVSB or MOVSW to correspond with the choice of the number of REPs.

When either instruction executes, three steps are performed:

1. either a byte or a word is moved from DS:SI to ES:DI

2. depending on DF, either INC SI or DEC SI

3. depending on DF, either INC DI or DEC DI

No flags are affected by these instructions. Remember that if a MOVSW is used, the addresses are incremented by 2 bytes. Since only 1 byte or word is moved, some form of loop or repeat operation is necessary.

The Repeat Prefix: REP

The repeat prefix, **REP**, is needed to cause the instruction to be repeated the required number of times specified in register CX. The REP prefix causes the instruction that comes after it to be repeated until register CX becomes 0. This means that the REP instruction decrements CX by 1 each time. It works just like the LOOP instruction.

Note: The prefixes discussed in this chapter can only be used on the string instructions, not on other instructions. It would be convenient if they could.

The Solution to Moving NAME_IN to NAME_OUT

The problem of moving NAME_IN to NAME_OUT can be solved by any of the sequences of code shown in Example 11–1. Notice that the MOVS instruction generates a MOVSW in this case. Therefore, the number of repetitions must be set to 4.

Assume that both DS and ES have been set in the housekeeping section.

```
    LEA  DI,NAME_OUT            ; DI -> NAME_OUT
    LEA  SI,NAME_IN             ; SI ->NAME_IN
    CLD                         ; SET FOR FORWARD DIRECTION

    MOV  CX,4                   ; SET NUMBER OF REPS TO 4 WORDS
    REP MOVS NAME_OUT,NAME_IN   ; MOVE NAME_IN TO NAME_OUT


        or


    MOV  CX,8                   ; SET NUMBER OF REPS TO 8 BYTES
    REP MOVSB                   ; MOVE NAME_IN TO NAME_OUT


        or


    MOV  CX,4                   ; SET NUMBER OF REPS TO 4 WORDS
    REP MOVSW                   ; MOVE NAME_IN TO NAME_OUT
```

EXAMPLE 11–1 Moving NAME_IN to NAME_OUT

11.6 USING THE MOVE PRIMITIVES TO PROPAGATE ONE OR MORE CHARACTERS

Propagation is the process of reproducing one or more characters throughout a field until it is completely filled. This can be done with the move string instructions. The character(s) to be propagated **must** be physically contiguous and **must** immediately precede the receiving field.

The most commonly propagated character is the blank, 20H, which is used to clear a field. Suppose, for example, that a field named WORK is to be cleared and that storage is defined as

```
BLANK      DB    ' '
WORK       DB    40 DUP(?)
```

The code in Example 11–2 propagates the blank character throughout the field WORK.

On the first move, the blank is moved into the first byte of WORK. Next, both SI and DI are incremented. Now SI contains the address of the first byte of WORK, which now has a blank in it. On the next repetition, that blank is moved into WORK + 1. The process continues until WORK is filled with blanks.

This example shows why the character(s) to be propagated must be immediately in front of the receiving field. What would happen if storage had been defined as

```
BLANK      DB    ' '
MSG        DB    'ERROR'
WORK       DB    40 DUP(?)
```

WORK would contain ERROR ERROR ERROR ... , and is certainly not cleared.

It is not always possible or even desirable to define a BLANK field in storage just in front of the field to be blanked. Suppose that there are four fields to be blanked. As you can see, it would be awkward to try to place a blank in front of each of them. Example 11–3 illustrates a method of blanking

---

Assume that DS and ES are set in housekeeping.

```
    LEA  SI,BLANK    ; SI -> BLANK TO BE PROPAGATED
    LEA  DI,WORK     ; DI -> STRING TO BE BLANKED
    CLD              ; SET FOR FORWARD MOVE
    MOV  CX,40       ; SET FOR 40 REPS
    REP  MOVSB       ; BLANK OUT WORK
```

EXAMPLE 11–2 Blanking out WORK

```
MOV  AL,20H        ; PUT A BLANK
MOV  WORK,AL       ; INTO THE FIRST BYTE OF WORK
LEA  SI,WORK       ; SI -> BLANK
LEA  DI,WORK+1     ; DI -> FIRST NON-BLANK TO BE BLANKED
CLD                ; SET FOR FORWARD MOVING
MOV  CX,39         ; SET FOR 39 MORE REPS
REP  MOVSB         ; PROPAGATE BLANKS THROUGH REST OF WORK
```

EXAMPLE 11–3   Blanking out WORK—alternate method

out a field (WORK in this case) when there is no BLANK field defined in front of it. The procedure is to insert a blank in the first byte of the field and then propagate that blank throughout the rest of the field.

11.7   RIGHT AND LEFT JUSTIFICATION OF FIELDS

It is often necessary and/or desirable to position data in a field either to the right or left end of a field, contrary to the way it is normally stored. For example, when numeric data are entered through the keyboard, they are normally inserted beginning at the left side of the field, with each additional character being stored to the right. To be usable as a number, the data should be positioned on the right with the unused left positions filled with 0's. The move string instructions can be used to perform such right or left justification of fields. These functions are commonly used in spreadsheets and other numerical field data entry.

Now examine a simple problem in which a field named QTY has been defined as 10 bytes. The following are all valid examples of entries that can be made by the user.

$$1 \qquad 23 \qquad 432 \qquad 4444 \qquad 1232345 \qquad 1234567890$$

As indicated, when the data are entered, they are stored in QTY beginning on the left. Thus, when the user finishes entering a value, the value often needs to be shifted to the right with the fill character 0 inserted on the left. Therefore, if the number 123 is entered, the field contains 0000000123.

The field can be entered by the procedure GET_QTY, which uses the get buffered keyboard input function, 20H, to enter the data into a general input area.

The RIGHT_QTY procedure moves the digits entered from the general input area, WORK, into the QTY field and right-justifies them. It also left-fills the QTY field with 0's. Figure 11–1 (PGM25.ASM on the program disk) shows how this procedure can be coded.

In RIGHT_QTY the entered bytes are moved from the right to the left into the field QTY. Then the required number of fill bytes is calculated.

```
       PAGE   60,132
       TITLE  PGM25  FIGURE 11-1  RIGHT JUSTIFYING AN INPUT FIELD


;**************************************************************************
; PGM25      Title: Figure 11-1 Right justify numerical input field   *
;                                                                     *
; Programmer: Vic Broquard                                            *
; Date Written:  6/11/88        Date Of Last Revision: 8/6/88         *
;                                                                     *
; Purpose: Using string functions to right justify numerical fields   *
;                                                                     *
; Special Requirements: none                                          *
;                                                                     *
;**************************************************************************


; program code segment

PGM25CD   SEGMENT

MAIN      PROC    FAR

; housekeeping section

      ASSUME  CS:PGM25CD,DS:PGM25DA,SS:PGM25STK,ES:PGM25DA

      MOV  AX,PGM25DA ; ESTABLISH ADDRESSABILITY
      MOV  DS,AX      ; TO DATA SEGMENT
      MOV  ES,AX      ; AND SET ES FOR STRING FUNCTIONS

; main process section

      CALL GET_QTY    ; QTY IS ENTERED AND ACTLEN SET TO THE
                      ;    ACTUAL NUMBER OF BYTES ENTERED

      CALL RIGHT_QTY  ; RIGHT JUSTIFY THE NUMBER
                      ;    WITH 0 FILL CHARACTERS

; return to DOS section

      MOV  AL,0       ; SET 0 AS THE RETURN CODE FOR DOS
      MOV  AH,4CH     ; SET FOR DOS END PROCESS FUNCTION
      INT  21H        ; CALL DOS TO END PROGRAM

MAIN    ENDP


      SUBTTL   GET_QTY WILL INPUT 10 BYTE QTY FIELD
      PAGE
GET_QTY PROC
```

FIGURE 11–1   Program to right-justify and zero-fill a numeric field (PGM25.ASM)

```
    PUSH AX        ; SAVE REGISTERS
    PUSH DX

-------------------------------------------------------------------

    MOV  MAXLEN,11 ; SET MAX LENGTH FOR THIS FIELD + CR
    LEA  DX,MAXLEN ; DX -> INPUT AREA
    MOV  AH,0AH    ; SET FOR BUFFERED KEYBOARD INPUT
    INT  21H       ; CALL DOS TO INPUT FIELD

    POP  DX        ; RESTORE REGISTERS
    POP  AX

    RET
GET_QTY  ENDP


    SUBTTL    RIGHT JUSTIFY THE QTY FIELD
    PAGE

RIGHT_QTY  PROC

    PUSH AX        ; SAVE REGISTERS
    PUSH CX
    PUSH SI
    PUSH DI

    XOR  CX,CX     ; CLEAR CX
    MOV  CL,ACTLEN ; SET NUMBER OF REPS TO DO

    LEA  SI,WORK   ; SET SOURCE TO POINT TO FIRST BYTE OF QTY
    MOV  AX,CX     ; CALC OFFSET TO LAST GOOD DIGIT
    DEC  AX        ; DEC TO GET OFFSET
    ADD  SI,AX     ; SET SI TO LAST GOOD BYTE

    LEA  DI,QTY+9  ; SET DI TO LAST BYTE OF QTY

    STD            ; SET DIRECTION FOR REVERSE MOVE

    REP  MOVSB     ; MOVE GOOD DIGITS TO RIGHT OF FIELD

; DI -> first byte that needs to be 0 filled

    MOV  CX,10     ; CALC NUMBER OF BLANKS TO FILL
    SUB  CL,ACTLEN ; NUM REPS = 10 - ACTLEN

    CMP  CX,0      ; ARE ALL DIGITS ALREADY ENTERED?
    JE   DONE      ; YES, SO NOTHING NEEDS TO BE DONE, LEAVE
    MOV  AL,30H    ; AL = 0 TO INSERT
    MOV  QTY,AL    ; INSERT FIRST 0
```

FIGURE 11–1 continued   *(Continues)*

```
        DEC  CX      ; RESET NUMBER TO DO
        CMP  CX,0    ; ANY MORE TO DO?
        JE   DONE    ; NO, SO LEAVE

        LEA  SI,QTY  ; SI -> 0 TO PROPAGATE
```

```
        LEA  DI,QTY+1 ; DI -> NEXT BYTE
        CLD           ; SET DIRECTION FOR FORWARD
        REP  MOVSB    ; MOVE IN 0 FILL BYTES

DONE:
        POP  DI       ; RESTORE REGISTERS
        POP  SI
        POP  CX
        POP  AX

        RET

RIGHT_QTY  ENDP

PGM25CD  ENDS


        SUBTTL   DATA AND STACK SEGMENTS
        PAGE

; program data segment

PGM25DA  SEGMENT

; COMMON I/O STRUCTURE FOR BUFFERED INPUT

MAXLEN  DB   ?           ; MAXIMUM LENGTH PROVIDED BY USER
ACTLEN  DB   ?           ; ACTUAL LENGTH OF USER ENTRY - DOS SUPPLIES
WORK    DB   50 DUP(?)   ; THE INPUT DATA

QTY     DB   10 DUP(?)   ; RIGHT JUSTIFIED RESULT FIELD

PGM25DA  ENDS

; program stack segment

PGM25STK  SEGMENT PARA STACK 'STACK'

        DW      32 DUP (?)
PGM25STK  ENDS
        END
```

FIGURE 11–1   continued

Finally, the fill bytes are inserted. This solution has the advantage of moving the minimum number of bytes. However, the cost is that it requires a number of instructions to do it. If fewer instructions are desired, fill QTY with 0's first and then move the digits. In this way QTY is automatically left-filled with 0's. List the changes needed to do this and see how much code is eliminated.

11.8   THE LOAD STRING INSTRUCTIONS: LODS, LODSB, LODSW

In many of the examples encountered up to this point, the following instructions (or similar ones) were used.

```
MOV   AL,[BX]
INC   BX
```

Usually, these instructions were surrounded by a loop of some type that processed all the bytes in a string. The load string primitives are another set of instructions that can be used to implement this common activity. These instructions load either a byte or a word into registers AL and AX from memory.

Registers DS:SI contain the memory address from which the data are to be loaded. If a word is loaded, it is placed into register AX; if a byte is loaded, it goes into register AL.

In addition, register SI is either incremented or decremented to ready it for the next load operation, depending upon the direction flag. If DF is set, then SI is decremented; if DF is cleared, SI is incremented. If LODSW is used, SI is incremented or decremented by 2.

Just as with the move string primitives, there are three forms of the load instruction. These are similar in operation to the MOVS instruction. Their syntaxes are

```
            LODS   operand1

            LODSB

            LODSW
```

If the LODS instruction is used, then the assembler examines the length of operand1 to determine if it is an even or odd length. If it is even, a

LODSW is generated; if it is odd, a LODSB is generated. No flags are affected by these instructions.

For example, if you want to load 1 byte of NAME2 into register AL, you can enter

```
LEA  SI,NAME2  ; SI-> NAME2
CLD            ; SET FOR FORWARD DIRECTION
LODSB          ; LOAD BYTE AND INC FOR NEXT ONE
```

Thus, the LODSB replaces the commonly used series

```
MOV  AL,[SI]
INC  SI
```

An advantage of the LODSB function is that it generates only 1 byte of machine code; the MOV generates 3 bytes, not counting the INC. LODSB is more efficient.

11.9 THE STORE STRING INSTRUCTIONS: STOS, STOSB, STOSW

These three instructions store either a byte or a word into a memory location. Their function is the opposite of the LODS instructions.

Registers ES:DI contain the address of the storage location. If the byte form is used, then 1 byte from register AL is stored. If the word form is used, then register AX is stored.

Next, depending upon the direction flag, register DI is either incremented or decremented, ready for the next store operation. If DF is cleared, then DI is incremented; if DF is set, then register DI is decremented. Again, if STOSW is used, DI is incremented or decremented by 2 bytes.

The syntaxes are similar to the other string functions:

```
STOS   operand1

STOSB

STOSW
```

Again, operand1 is used only to determine whether the length is even or odd. If it is even, a STOSW is generated. If it is odd, a STOSB is generated. No flags are affected by these instructions.

The following instructions store the contents of register AL into the first byte of the field NAME1:

```
CLD                 ; SET FOR FORWARD DIRECTION
LEA  DI,NAME1  ; SI->NAME1
STOSB               ; SAVE AL BYTE IN NAME1 AND INC FOR NEXT BYTE
```

DI is also incremented, ready for the next store instruction. This is a more efficient method of storing data than the use of the MOV instructions

```
MOV  [DI],AL
INC  DI
```

11.10 THE SEG AND OFFSET OPERANDS

The SEG and OFFSET operands enable you to change or override the segment address associated with register SI (normally, register DS). Only the segment associated with register SI can be overridden.

Until now, you have been entering:

```
LEA  SI,NAME2
```

This same operation can be implemented by coding

```
MOV  SI, OFFSET NAME2 ; RETURNS THE OFFSET ADDRESS WITHIN DS
```

To get the address of the ending byte, assuming NAME2 is 8 bytes long, you can enter

```
MOV  SI, OFFSET NAME2 + 7
```

However, entering the segment operand, SEG, is more useful than the preceding code. SEG provides an alternative method of getting the segment address into register ES.

```
MOV  AX, SEG NAME2      ; GETS THE SEGMENT ADDRESS OF NAME2
MOV  ES,AX             ; STORE SEGMENT ADDR IN ES
```

You will find SEG to be a very powerful tool when developing and using external subroutines. It is also useful in simpler programs, in which the contents of register ES are not established in the housekeeping section.

11.11 THE STRING COMPARISON INSTRUCTIONS: CMPS, CMPSB, CMPSW

Often, a program needs to compare the contents of two fields. Suppose that a control break report is to be produced using the AGENT_NAME as the control field. The program must compare PRIOR_AGENT_NAME to

AGENT_NAME; if they are different, a control break has occurred. Rather than create a small subroutine to do the byte-by-byte comparison, the string comparison instruction can be used.

The register usage in these comparison operations is similar to the other string instructions. Registers DS:SI hold the address of the first string, registers ES:DI contain the address of the second string, and register CX holds the number of repetitions. The direction flag (DF) determines the direction of the comparison: if DF is set, the comparison is executed right to left; if DF is cleared, the comparison proceeds left to right through the fields.

The three forms of this instruction are

```
CMPS    operand1,operand2

CMPSB

CMPSW
```

As with the other string operations, the CMPS version uses the operands only to determine if the field lengths are both even. If so, a CMPSW instruction is implemented. If either or both of the lengths are odd, a CMPSB instruction is used.

A word of caution when using the CMPSW version: A forward comparison on DW, DD, and DQ number fields results in comparing the low-order bytes first! Such comparisons **must** be executed in the reverse direction, so that the high-order part of the field is compared first.

If the two fields are defined as

```
AGENT_NAME          DB     'TOM '
PRIOR_AGENT_NAME    DB     'DICK '
```

then the comparison can begin as

```
LEA  SI,PRIOR_AGENT_NAME   ; SI->PRIOR NAME
LEA  DI,AGENT_NAME         ; DI->THIS NAME
MOV  CX,5                  ; CX = NUMBER BYTES TO COMPARE
CLD                        ; SET FOR FORWARD DIRECTION
CMPSB                      ; COMPARE ONE BYTE OF THE NAMES
```

The preceding code compares the first bytes and sets the flags. Both registers SI and DI are incremented, ready for the next comparison.

What would happen if the CMPSB were replaced by

```
REP  CMPSB                      ; COMPARE ALL BYTES OF THE NAMES
```

The flags would be set by the first bytes' comparison. Next they would be reset by the results of the comparison of the second bytes. The final result would have the flags set as if the fields were equal, since a blank equals a blank! For this reason, you need another exit from the repetition process, an exit other than register CX becoming 0. Another prefix, REPE, provides the exit.

REPE, the repeat equal prefix, repeats the process as long as register CX is not 0 **and** as long as the bytes are equal. If either CX becomes 0 or the bytes become unequal, execution ends. An alternative to REPE is **REPZ**, the repeat zero prefix. REPZ is functionally identical to REPE.

In the preceding code the CMPSB instruction should be replaced by

```
   REPE   CMPSB      ; COMPARE ALL BYTES OF THE NAMES WHILE EQUAL
```

When control reaches the next instruction, there are two possibilities: either the strings are equal or they are not. If the repetition was ended because CX became 0, the strings are equal. Otherwise, they are unequal. Generally, the code can be written as

```
    REPE CMPSB      ; COMPARE ALL BYTES OF THE NAMES WHILE EQUAL
    JNE  NOT_EQUAL ; MUST DEC SI AND DI TO GET THE DIFFERENCES
; HERE THEY ARE EQUAL
```

To get to the bytes that are not equal, the program must undo, or reverse, the last INC or DEC instruction(s). This is because the CMPSB has already updated SI and DI, assuming there will be another repetition. If the comparison was going in the forward direction, then the program must DEC both SI and DI. The DEC occurs once if CMPSB was used and twice if CMPSW was used.

The string comparison instructions affect the following flags: AF, CF, OF, PF, SF, and ZF.

11.12 THE SCAN STRING INSTRUCTIONS: SCAS, SCASB, SCASW

These instructions enable the program to scan a string, looking for the presence of a particular byte or word. It follows the usual register conventions for the string functions, with some additions.

The register pair ES:DI contains the address of the string to be examined. The direction flag determines whether a forward or backward scan is to be executed, resulting in either an INC or DEC of register DI. Register CX contains the number of repetitions. If the byte form is used, it is the length of the string.

If the scan is looking for a byte, the byte to be found is contained in register AL. If the scan is looking for a word, the word is in AX.

There are three forms of the scan string instruction:

```
SCAS   operand1

SCASB

SCASW
```

Just as in all the other string functions, if SCAS is used, the operand is used only to determine whether SCASB or SCASW is to be generated.

The repetition operand for scanning cannot normally be either REP or REPE. If REP were used, the scan would bypass any match. If REPE were used, then the first byte that is **not** what the scan is looking for would end the scan. Therefore, one of two other prefixes, REPNE or REPNZ, is used.

REPNE, repeat not equal, repeats the scan as long as CX is not 0 and the scan string has not been found. If CX becomes 0 or the scan byte or word is found, the process is halted. **REPNZ**, repeat not zero, is functionally identical to REPNE.

After the REPNE SCASB instruction, it is necessary to determine what occurred. If register CX = 0, then the byte or word was not found; otherwise, it was found. If the byte or word was found, register DI is either incremented or decremented (depending on the direction of the scan) to get the address of the byte or word.

The scan string instructions affect the following flags: AF, CF, OF, PF, SF, and ZF.

Suppose the field NAME1 is defined as

```
NAME1 DB 'Thomas'
```

and you want to find out if the field contains the letter "a." The code can be as given in Example 11–4.

```
        LEA    DI,NAME1      ; DI->NAME1
        MOV    ES, SEG NAME1 ; ES SET TO CORRECT SEGMENT VALUE
        CLD                  ; SET FOR FORWARD DIRECTION
        MOV    AL,'a'        ; AL = BYTE TO SCAN FOR
        MOV    CX,5          ; CX = NUMBER BYTES TO SCAN
        REPNE SCASB          ; SCAN NAME1 FOR AN "A"
        JE     FOUND_IT      ; MUST DEC DI TO GET THE ACTUAL ADDRESS

; HERE IT IS NOT FOUND
```

EXAMPLE 11–4   Scanning NAME1 for an "a"

11.13 ACCEPTING THE PATH/FILENAME FROM THE COMMAND LINE

As a final example, reconsider the problem presented in Chapter 10, in which the path/filename is accepted from the command line and the file displayed. To unravel the command line in the PSP, you want to find the 0DH, the carriage return, that ended the command entry. Starting with the first nonblank byte, all the bytes preceding the carriage return are to be inserted into the ASCIIZ string.

The program can be modified to scan for the first nonblank character and then scan for the carriage return, <CR>. Once the number of valid bytes is determined, a MOVSB can move the valid data into the ASCIIZ string. This form of coding removes all the loops within the GET_FILENAME routine.

The only problem is that the scan function uses the register pair ES:DI. When the MOVSB is needed, DI must be the destination address, not the source, as it currently is. This problem can be solved by using the XCHG instruction to swap DI and SI. To swap registers DS and ES, push them onto the stack and then pop them in the wrong order, thereby reversing them.

Figure 11–2 shows the complete solution. (Note that only those portions of the program that have changed are shown; PGM26.ASM on the program disk has the full solution.) If there are two files being passed to the program, then the second scan (the one that looks for <CR>) is done twice: once when looking for <CR> and a second time when looking for the first blank after the start of the first filename. Next the results are compared. If the <CR> occurred before the blank, then no second file was entered. If the blank occurs before the <CR>, then there is a second filename.

```
        PAGE  60,132
        TITLE PGM26 FIGURE 11-2 ACCEPT PATH/FILE USING SCAN INSTRS

;*******************************************************************
; PGM26       Title: Accept path/file from command line to display    *
;                                                                     *
; Programmer: Vic Broquard                                            *
; Date Written:  6/11/88        Date Of Last Revision: 8/5/88         *
;                                                                     *
; Purpose: Use string functions to extract path/file specs from PSP   *
;          then read text file and display it on screen               *
;                                                                     *
; Special Requirements: none                                          *
;                                                                     *
;*******************************************************************
```

FIGURE 11–2 Program to accept and display path/filename from the command line by using string functions (PGM26.ASM) *(Continues)*

```
; program code segment

PGM26CD    SEGMENT
MAIN       PROC  FAR

; housekeeping section

      ASSUME    CS:PGM26CD,DS:PGM26DA,SS:PGM26SK

      MOV  AX,PGM26DA    ; ESTABLISH ADDRESSABILITY
      MOV  DS,AX         ; TO DATA SEGMENT

; ES contains the PSP address

; main processing

      CALL GET_FILENAME  ; EXTRACT THE FILE NAME FROM PSP

      CALL OPEN          ; OPEN THE FILE
      CMP  IOERRSW,00H   ; ANY I/O ERROR?
      JNE  DONE          ; YES, HALT EXECUTION

BIGLOOP:

      CALL READREC       ; READ A RECORD

      CMP  IOERRSW,00H   ; ANY I/O ERROR?
      JNE  DONE          ; YES, HALT EXECUTION

      CMP  EOFSW,00H     ; ANY MORE DATA?
      JNE  ENDJOB        ; NO, FINISH UP

      CALL OUTPUT        ; PRINT THE RECORD

      JMP  BIGLOOP       ; CONTINUE WITH NEXT

ENDJOB:
- - - - - - - - - - - - - - - - - - - - - - - - - - - - - - - - - - - - - - - - -

      CALL CLOSE         ; CLOSE THE FILE

DONE:
      MOV  AX,4C00H      ; SET FOR END WITH A RETURN CODE OF 0
      INT  21H           ; CALL DOS TO END PROCESS

MAIN  ENDP



      SUBTTL  EXTRACT THE FILENAME FROM THE PSP
      PAGE
```

FIGURE 11–2   continued

```
GET_FILENAME  PROC

; ES -> PSP
; extract path/filename and store in FILENAME

    PUSH AX             ; SAVE REGISTERS
    PUSH BX
    PUSH CX
    PUSH DX
    PUSH SI
    PUSH DI

    LEA  SI,FILENAME    ; DS:SI = ADDRESS OF FILENAME TO FILL UP

    MOV  DI,80H         ; ES:DI -> PSP'S LENGTH OF COMMAND LINE

    XOR  CX,CX          ; CLEAR CX
    MOV  CL,ES:[DI]     ; EXTRACT THE LENGTH OF COMMAND LINE

    CMP  CX,0           ; WAS ANY VALUE EVEN ENTERED?
    JE   PUT_IN_00H     ; NO, SO GO FINISH UP

    INC  DI             ; DI -> FIRST BYTE OF THE COMMAND STRING

    MOV  AL,20H         ; 20H IS THE BYTE TO LOOK FOR
    CLD                 ; CLEAR DF FOR FORWARD SCAN
    REPE SCASB          ; SCAN UNTIL CX = 0 OR NON-BLANK FOUND
    JE   PUT_IN_00H     ; NONE FOUND, SO GO FINISH UP

    INC  CX             ; ADD BACK IN THE CURRENT BYTE TO DO
    DEC  DI             ; GET TO NON-BLANK CHAR

    MOV  BX,CX          ; SAVE LENGTH OF VALID PART
    MOV  DX,DI          ; SAVE START ADDRESS OF VALID PART

    MOV  AL,0DH         ; SET TO LOOK FOR A CR

    REPNE SCASB         ; SCAN FOR CR, STOP CX=0 OR FIND CR

    SUB  BX,CX          ; CALC NUMBER OF VALID BYTES
    MOV  CX,BX          ; SET NUMBER OF REPS

;-----------------------------------------------------------------

; must reverse DI SI for MOVSB

    PUSH DS             ; SWAP SEGMENT REGISTERS
    PUSH ES
    POP  DS
    POP  ES
```

FIGURE 11–2   continued   *(Continues)*

```
        MOV  DI,DX          ; RESET TO START OF VALID PART
        XCHG SI,DI          ; SWAP OFFSET REGS

        REP  MOVSB          ; MOVE IN ALL VALID BYTES

        PUSH DS             ; SWAP SEGMENT REGS BACK
        PUSH ES
        POP  DS
        POP  ES

        XCHG DI,SI          ; SWAP BACK OFFSET REGS

PUT_IN_00H:

        MOV  AL,00H         ; 00H IS THE DELIMITER FOR ASCIIZ STRING
        MOV  [SI],AL        ; INSERT IT INTO THE STRING

        POP  DI             ; RESTORE REGISTERS
        POP  SI
        POP  DX
        POP  CX
        POP  BX
        POP  AX

        RET

GET_FILENAME  ENDP


        .
        .
        .


PGM26CD   ENDS



        SUBTTL   PROGRAM DATA AND STACK AREAS
        PAGE

; program data segment

PGM26DA   SEGMENT

FILENUM    DW   ?            ; FILE HANDLE FOR FILE

FILENAME   DB   127 DUP(?)  ; ASCIIZ STRING PATH/FILE
```

FIGURE 11–2   continued

```
INPUTAREA DB   128 DUP (?) ; INPUT RECORD AREA
ACTUALEN  DW   ?           ; ACTUAL NUMBER OF BYTES READ
RECORDSIZE DW  128         ; NUMBER OF BYTES TO TRY TO READ

EOFSW     DB   00H         ; ON WHEN EOF IS SIGNALED
IOERRSW   DB   00H         ; ON WHEN THERE IS AN IOERR


          .
          .
          .

    END  MAIN
```

FIGURE 11–2   continued

11.14 SUMMARY

The string primitives permit complex coding with few instructions. They allow a program to easily manipulate character strings. To do so, many registers are used.

Often, the pair ES:DI points to the destination string and DS:SI points to the source string. The direction flag (DF) indicates the direction of processing—forward or backward. Register CX contains the repetition factor. The primitives process either a byte or a word per repetition.

MOVSB and MOVSW move strings as well as propagate one or more characters throughout a string, thereby clearing the string. CMPSB and CMPSW compare strings, and SCASB and SCASW scan a string for the presence of another string. LODSB and LODSW load a byte or word of a string and increment or decrement the address for the next cycle. STOSB and STOSW store a byte or word and increment or decrement the address for the next repetition.

Although they use many registers, the string primitives are very useful instructions. This overshadows the fact that they require that register ES point to the data segment, that segment overrides be coded, and other additional code be written.

11.15 REVIEW QUESTIONS

1. To use string functions, outline specifically what registers are needed and what they are to contain.

2. Show how register ES can be established for use in string functions. Show two different methods.

3. When using the move string instructions to clear a field, why must the value(s) to be propagated immediately precede the receiving field? Draw a diagram of what happens if this is not the case.

4. Outline the steps involved in left-justifying a text string.

5. Discuss the steps involved in establishing a generalized routine to compare two character strings. Assume that they are the same length. How could you handle the comparison if they were not the same length?

6. The text showed a scan example involving finding the first occurrence of an "a". Normally, FIND functions must search the main string for the presence of the second string, which often is several characters long. Use pseudocode to outline the general processing steps that are needed to scan for strings longer than a byte or word.

7. Why are the load and store string instructions more efficient than the MOV and INC instructions?

11.16 PRACTICE PROBLEMS

1. Code the instructions to move the following field:

```
LAST_NAME_IN    DB    20 DUP(?)
LAST_NAME_OUT   DB    20 DUP(?)
```

2. Code the instructions to blank out LAST_NAME_OUT as defined in Practice Problem 1.

3. Code the instructions to determine if an agent's name has changed. The fields are defined as

```
AGENT_NAME          DB    25 DUP(?)
OLD_AGENT           DB    25 DUP(?)
```

If the names are different, then call a routine named AGENT_BREAK.

4. A line of text has been entered and stored in TXT_LINE, which can be a maximum of 128 bytes. Search the text to see if the value SAM is present. If it is found, call a routine named GOT_IT. Such a routine can be incorporated into a word processing program to find strings.

5. Re-examine Figure 4–3, the routine to convert from lower- to uppercase. Show how the main processing section can be redone using LODSB and STOSB instructions.

6. Re-examine Figure 4–4, the routine to convert a 1-byte ASCII digit into binary. Show how the main processing sections can be modified to use the LODSB and STOSB instructions.

11.17 PROGRAMMING PROBLEMS

1. Create a hyphenation function. When the routine is called, the following two fields have been given values:

    ```
    ACTLEN    DB    ?
    WORK      DB    80 DUP(?)
    ```

    ACTLEN provides the current length of the string contained in WORK. The string consists of 2 words separated by a blank. Use SCASB to find the blank and replace it with a hyphen.

2. Create a generalized subroutine to move a field. The fields should be pointed to by registers DS:SI and ES:DI, and register AX should contain the length. Move the SI field to the DI field.

3. Modify Programming Problem 2 to accept the length of the SI field in register AX and the length of the DI field in register BX and to move the fields accordingly. Watch out for truncation, and provide any necessary padding.

4. Write a program to sort and display a text file of your friends and their phone numbers. The file can be created by a word processor, EDLIN, or COPY CON:. The filename should be FRIENDS.DAT.

    The first field in each line should be LAST_NAME. Make it 10 characters long. The second field should be FIRST_NAME (six characters long), and the last field should be PHONE (eight characters, including the dash). An entry might look like this:

    ```
    SMITH JIM 699-9999
    ```

    Code an ascending sort on the LAST_NAME field only. Use reasonable headings. Whenever the screen is one line from full, display the message

    ```
    PRESS ANY KEY FOR MORE
    ```

    Accept any key and continue. Clear the screen and redisplay the headings before continuing the display. There can be a maximum of 50 total entries. (Note that this problem involves the use of tables, which is more fully discussed in Chapter 13.)

5. Create a word processing subroutine called WORD COUNT. The program should input a file called WORK.TXT, which consists of several paragraphs of simple text. Use a word processor to create it. The subroutine should count the number of words in the file and display a final message that reports the total. The message should look like this:

    ```
    FILE: WORK.TXT CONTAINS 99999 WORDS.
    ```

A word is one or more characters that are delimited by a blank or other punctuation. For example, the following text line contains 7 words.

Now is the time to count words.

Use the scan primitive to look for blanks or punctuation. To make the problem easier, allow only periods and commas as punctuation in the text file.

12

External Subroutines, Segments, and Groups

12.1 CHAPTER OBJECTIVES

In this chapter you will

1. Study the basic concepts of external subroutines
2. Understand the five major problems involved with such routines
3. Learn to use the EXTRN and PUBLIC directives
4. Learn to pass data either by value or by address
5. Study the three ways that data can be passed to external routines
6. Learn the new DOS commands to build programs from many external routines
7. Study the Version 5.0 enhancements for simplified segment names
8. Examine the concepts of segment groups

12.2 INTRODUCTION

Up to now you have used the structured monolithic approach to microassembler programming. That is, the programs you have created are structured, but they consist of very large source modules. The .ASM program files tend to become very large because it takes many instructions to perform relatively simple tasks. Although it is true that you have achieved "solid" program design and organization by use of many internal subroutines, it is very awkward to work with source modules that are so large.

The next step toward creating manageable programs is to convert many of the internal procedures into external, separately assembled modules. The size of these modules should be limited to an acceptable page or two of code per module. Then the linker can link these smaller modules together to form a complete program.

12.3 EXTERNAL SUBROUTINES: THE PROBLEMS INVOLVED

An **external subroutine** is a procedure that is assembled separately from the module that invokes it. Thus, the one-assembly, 30-page, source program could possibly be broken down into 15 separately assembled, 2-page routines. To build the program, all that must be done is to tell the linker the names of the 15 parts. There is even a way to expedite the creation of this bit of tedious linker code. Thus, the use of external subroutines can be of immense value to the assembly programmer.

Using external subroutines presents some new problems. Theoretically, these routines can be coded almost any way you want. However, good programming design, structured programming, and data coupling theory eliminate some methods that are really counterproductive in today's world.

There are two cardinal rules that "well-behaved" programs should follow.

1. No subroutine should modify the caller's registers, except perhaps to pass back the result in a register. That is, when module A calls module B, module B must preserve module A's environment (the current register values).

2. No module should alter the actual program code segments of another module. To do so invites errors that are extremely difficult to debug.

Within the limitations of these rules, there are many techniques available for handling external subroutines.

Begin by examining the basic problem areas. They include

1. How does the caller actually call a module that is not physically present at assembly time?

2. How does the called module preserve the register environment of the caller?

3. What happens to the stack?

4. How are data items passed between the modules?

5. What DOS commands are required to create and execute the complete program?

Each of these problem areas will be discussed in turn. Some will be easy to resolve; others are more difficult.

12.4   CALLING EXTERNAL MODULES

The Use of the CALL Instruction

The instruction used to invoke an external module is the same CALL instruction that is used for internal procedures. Assume that the driver module, or the main procedure, wants to call an external routine to do some calculations. The code for the call is

```
CALL    CALCRTN
```

Because it is not in the same code segment, the CALCRTN procedure is a FAR routine. It is going to be assembled separately.

With an internal subroutine, the called procedure is normally within the currently defined and assumed code segment. The routine can be identified by adjusting the IP (instruction pointer) register. The vector address of the internal routine is CS:IP, but register CS does not change. Thus, when the CALL is executed with internal routines, only the IP register needs to be saved on the stack (via PUSH IP).

With external subroutines, the CS register must also be altered to get to the 64K segment in which the routine is now located. (The module is placed in this location by the linker program.) Thus, register CS must also be saved. This is the difference between NEAR and FAR subroutine calls: NEAR calls to internal routines place only the IP onto the stack; FAR calls to external routines place CS and then IP onto the stack.

Even if the modules are small and all would actually fit in a 64K code segment, the assembler treats them as if they were located anywhere in memory. Therefore, the programmer does not have to be concerned with where the modules are physically located in the resultant program.

Defining External Symbols: The EXTRN Directive

The next problem involves the definition of the symbol CALCRTN. Currently, there is no such symbol within the calling program. If assembled now, the assembler will generate an error message saying that the symbol CALCRTN is undefined. Therefore, you must tell the assembler that an undefined CALCRTN is acceptable—that the undefined symbol is actually external to this assembly. This is done by the **EXTRN directive.** The syntax of the EXTRN directive is:

$$\boxed{\text{EXTRN}\quad \text{symbol:type,symbol:type, ...}}$$

One or more external symbols can be defined with one EXTRN directive. The EXTRN directives are usually coded just after the TITLE directive.

When used with subroutine names, the operand type has two possible values, NEAR and FAR. Since external subroutines are all FAR, the type must be coded as FAR.

To continue the example of calling the CALCRTN, the code with CALCRTN now reads

```
TITLE    PGMCALC    PROGRAM TO DO FINANCIAL CALCULATIONS
EXTRN    CALCRTN:FAR
  .
  .
  .
CALL     CALCRTN    ; CALCRTN FINDS THE TOTAL COST
```

Now during the assembly process, the assembler inserts an empty address for the symbol CALCRTN in the CALL instruction:

```
0000 --- E          CALL CALCRTN
```

It is the linker's task to find the symbol and replace the empty address with the actual address for CALCRTN.

Making Internal Symbols External: The PUBLIC Directive

Now examine the CALCRTN subroutine. It is likely to be

```
TITLE       CALCRTN CALCULATES TOTAL COST
  .
  .
  .
CALCRTN   PROC
    ASSUME    ...
    .
    .
    .
    RET
CALCRTN   ENDP
```

Again, trouble! The symbol CALCRTN is internal to this module, and the linker cannot find it.

For the symbol for an external subroutine to be made known to the linker, the **PUBLIC directive** must be used. This directive tells the assembler and linker that the symbols after PUBLIC are to be made external so that they are known to other modules. The syntax of the PUBLIC directive is

```
            PUBLIC   symbol,symbol, . . .
```

One or more symbols can be included in a single PUBLIC directive. However, good programming design usually restricts one module to one function and one entry point. Therefore, only one symbol, the entry point of the routine, is usually named. It is commonly coded after the ASSUME directive. Thus, the PUBLIC directive in the CALCRTN example is

```
        TITLE      CALCRTN CALCULATES TOTAL COST
               .
               .
               .
CALCRTN    PROC
        ASSUME     ...
        PUBLIC     CALCRTN
               .
               .
               .
        RET
CALCRTN    ENDP
```

Figures 12–1 and 12-1a (PGM27.ASM and PGM27A.ASM on the program disk) show these shells in detail. After examining the code, study the resulting link .MAP listing.

Notice that there are **two** code segments. Notice the two data segments as well. Now look at both "symbols" pages. Specifically, what is the combine type and class of these segments? That is, with what other type of segment and with which specific class of segments within that type will this current segment be merged? The answer is NONE. This means that the linker is not able to merge these similar segments into similar overall segments. That is, code and data segments are interspersed throughout.

Combining Code and Data Segments

A much better solution is to create one segment that contains all the program instructions and another segment for all the data. This can be accomplished by using some of the other options available in the SEGMENT definition directives. (See Chapter 3 for detail.)

```
Microsoft (R) Macro Assembler Version 5.10              9/4/88 14:30:19


PGM27    FIGURE 12-1 DRIVER MODULE TO CALL CALCRTN        Page    1-1



        1                              PAGE    60,132
        2                              TITLE   PGM27     FIGURE 12-1 DRIVER MODULE TO CALL CALCRTN
        3
        4            ;********************************************************************
        5            ; PGM27       Title: Figure 12-1 Stub driver to test CALCRTN      *
        6            ;                                                                  *
        7            ; Programmer: Vic Broquard                                         *
        8            ; Date Written:  6/11/88        Date Of Last Revision: 8/6/88      *
        9            ;                                                                  *
       10            ; Purpose: Stub driver to invoke CALCRTN, an external subroutine   *
       11            ;                                                                  *
       12            ; Special Requirements: needs external CALCRTN subroutine          *
       13            ;                                                                  *
       14            ;********************************************************************
       15
       16                              EXTRN   CALCRTN:FAR
       17
       18 0000                 PGMCD   SEGMENT
       19
       20 0000                 MAIN    PROC    FAR
       21
       22                              ASSUME  CS:PGMCD,DS:PGMDA,SS:PGMSTK
       23
       24 0000  B8 ---- R              MOV     AX,PGMDA    ; ESTABLISH ADDRESSABILITY
       25 0003  8E D8                  MOV     DS,AX       ; TO PGMDA - THE PGM'S DATA SEGMENT
       26
       27 0005  9A 0000 ---- E         CALL    CALCRTN
       28
       29 000A  B0 00                  MOV     AL,0        ; SET 0 AS THE RETURN CODE FOR DOS
       30 000C  B4 4C                  MOV     AH,4CH      ; SET FOR DOS END PROCESS FUNCTION
       31 000E  CD 21                  INT     21H         ; CALL DOS TO END PROGRAM
       32
       33 0010                 MAIN    ENDP
       34
       35 0010                 PGMCD   ENDS
       36
       37 0000                 PGMDA   SEGMENT
       38
       39 0000                 PGMDA   ENDS
       40
       41 0000                 PGMSTK  SEGMENT PARA STACK 'STACK'
       42
```

FIGURE 12–1   Driver module to call CALCRTN (PGM27.ASM)

```
43 0000  0020[                    DW    32 DUP (?)
44        ????
45                    ]
46
47
48 0040                   PGMSTK  ENDS
49                           END
```

Microsoft (R) Macro Assembler Version 5.10   9/4/88 14:30:19

PGM27   FIGURE 12-1 DRIVER MODULE TO CALL CALCRTN   Symbols-1

Segments and Groups:

                N a m e   Length Align Combine Class

PGMCD   0010   PARA NONE
PGMDA   0000   PARA NONE
PGMSTK   0040   PARA STACK   'STACK'

Symbols:

                N a m e   Type   Value Attr

CALCRTN . . . .   L FAR   0000   External

MAIN . . . .   F PROC 0000 PGMCD   Length = 0010

@CPU . . . .   TEXT 0101h
@FILENAME . . . .   TEXT pgm27
@VERSION . . . .   TEXT 510

    46 Source Lines
    46 Total   Lines
    11 Symbols

  47262 + 157501 Bytes symbol space free

     0 Warning Errors
     0 Severe Errors

FIGURE 12–1   continued

```
Microsoft (R) Macro Assembler Version 5.10              9/4/88 14:30:28

PGM27A  FIGURE 12-1a SUBROUTINE CALCRTN              Page     1-1


       1                              PAGE    60,132
       2                              TITLE   PGM27A  FIGURE 12-1a  SUBROUTINE CALCRTN
       3
       4                    ;***************************************************************************
       5                    ; PGM27A     Title: Figure 12-1a Fxternal CALCRTN subroutine      *
       6                    ;                                                                 *
       7                    ; Programmer: Vic Broquard                                        *
       8                    ; Date Written: 6/11/88      Date Of Last Revision: 8/6/88        *
       9                    ;                                                                 *
      10                    ; Purpose: Illustrates invocation of external modules            *
      11                    ;                                                                 *
      12                    ; Special Requirements: Does no actual calculations              *
      13                    ;                                                                 *
      14                    ;***************************************************************************
      15
      16 0000              PGMCD   SEGMENT
      17
      18 0000              CALCRTN PROC    FAR
      19
      20                           ASSUME  CS:PGMCD,DS:PGMDA
      21                           PUBLIC  CALCRTN
      22
      23 0000  CB                  RET
      24
      25 0001              CALCRTN ENDP
      26
      27 0001              PGMCD   ENDS
      28
      29 0000              PGMDA   SEGMENT
      30
      31 0000              PGMDA   ENDS
      32                           END
```

```
Microsoft (R) Macro Assembler Version 5.10              9/4/88 14:30:28

PGM27A  FIGURE 12-1a  SUBROUTINE CALCRTN                 Symbols-1


Segments and Groups:

            N a m e          Length   Align Combine Class
```

FIGURE 12–1a   The CALCRTN subroutine (PGM27A.ASM)

```
PGMCD  . . . . . . . . . . . .      0001   PARA   NONE
PGMDA  . . . . . . . . . . . .      0000   PARA   NONE


Symbols:


                    N a m e        Type    Value  Attr


CALCRTN  . . . . . . . . . . .     F PROC  0000   PGMCD      Global     Length = 0001


@CPU . . . . . . . . . . . . .     TEXT   0101h
@FILENAME  . . . . . . . . . .     TEXT   pgm27a
@VERSION . . . . . . . . . . .     TEXT   510



    32 Source  Lines
    32 Total   Lines
     8 Symbols


  47284 + 157479 Bytes symbol space free


     0 Warning Errors
     0 Severe  Errors


PGM27.MAP:



 Start  Stop   Length Name                   Class
 00000H 0000FH 00010H PGMCD
 00010H 00010H 00000H PGMDA
 00010H 00010H 00001H PGMCD
 00020H 00020H 00000H PGMDA
 00020H 0005FH 00040H PGMSTK                 STACK
```

FIGURE 12–1a continued

First, for each segment, set the alignment to paragraph boundaries by using PARA. Next, set the combine type to PUBLIC. This tells the linker to put all similarly named segments together into one larger segment. Finally, assign class names: CODE and DATA. The linker merges all PUBLIC segments named CODE into one large segment, and it merges all PUBLIC segments named DATA into another segment.

Figure 12–2 (PGM28.ASM on the program disk) illustrates these changes to the SEGMENT directives and the results in the .EXE module. Examine the "symbols" pages and then the .MAP listing. Notice that both code segments are merged into one, as are both data segments. Figure 12–2a (PGM28A.ASM on the program disk) is the external subroutine.

What happens if the names of the segments are not the same? In this case, suppose that one was not called PGMCD, but instead was called

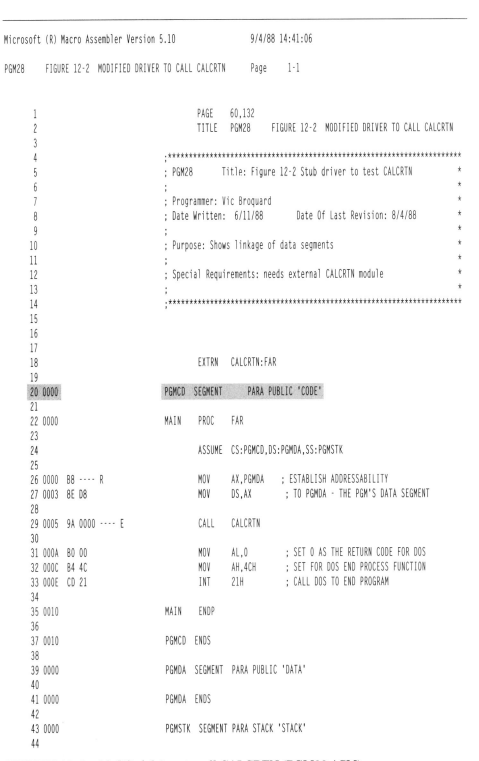

Microsoft (R) Macro Assembler Version 5.10   9/4/88 14:41:06

PGM28   FIGURE 12-2 MODIFIED DRIVER TO CALL CALCRTN   Page   1-1

```
  1                                     PAGE    60,132
  2                                     TITLE   PGM28     FIGURE 12-2  MODIFIED DRIVER TO CALL CALCRTN
  3
  4                          ;************************************************************************
  5                          ; PGM28      Title: Figure 12-2 Stub driver to test CALCRTN      *
  6                          ;                                                                *
  7                          ; Programmer: Vic Broquard                                       *
  8                          ; Date Written: 6/11/88       Date Of Last Revision: 8/4/88      *
  9                          ;                                                                *
 10                          ; Purpose: Shows linkage of data segments                       *
 11                          ;                                                                *
 12                          ; Special Requirements: needs external CALCRTN module           *
 13                          ;                                                                *
 14                          ;************************************************************************
 15
 16
 17
 18                                     EXTRN   CALCRTN:FAR
 19
 20 0000                     PGMCD   SEGMENT     PARA PUBLIC 'CODE'
 21
 22 0000                             MAIN    PROC    FAR
 23
 24                                           ASSUME  CS:PGMCD,DS:PGMDA,SS:PGMSTK
 25
 26 0000  B8 ---- R                           MOV     AX,PGMDA    ; ESTABLISH ADDRESSABILITY
 27 0003  8E D8                               MOV     DS,AX       ; TO PGMDA - THE PGM'S DATA SEGMENT
 28
 29 0005  9A 0000 ---- E                      CALL    CALCRTN
 30
 31 000A  B0 00                               MOV     AL,0        ; SET 0 AS THE RETURN CODE FOR DOS
 32 000C  B4 4C                               MOV     AH,4CH      ; SET FOR DOS END PROCESS FUNCTION
 33 000E  CD 21                               INT     21H         ; CALL DOS TO END PROGRAM
 34
 35 0010                             MAIN    ENDP
 36
 37 0010                     PGMCD   ENDS
 38
 39 0000                     PGMDA   SEGMENT  PARA PUBLIC 'DATA'
 40
 41 0000                     PGMDA   ENDS
 42
 43 0000                     PGMSTK  SEGMENT PARA STACK 'STACK'
 44
```

FIGURE 12–2   Modified driver to call CALCRTN (PGM28.ASM)

```
45 0000  0020[                      DW      32 DUP (?)
46       ????
47                     ]
48
49
50 0040                    PGMSTK  ENDS
51                                 END
```

Microsoft (R) Macro Assembler Version 5.10   9/4/88 14:41:06

PGM28   FIGURE 12-2 MODIFIED DRIVER TO CALL CALCRTN   Symbols-1

Segments and Groups:

```
              N a m e          Length  Align Combine Class

PGMCD . . . . . . . . . . . .  0010    PARA  PUBLIC  'CODE'
PGMDA . . . . . . . . . . . .  0000    PARA  PUBLIC  'DATA'
PGMSTK . . . . . . . . . . .   0040    PARA  STACK   'STACK'
```

Symbols:

```
              N a m e          Type    Value Attr

CALCRTN . . . . . . . . . . .  L FAR   0000      External

MAIN . . . . . . . . . . . . . F PROC  0000  PGMCD    Length = 0010

@CPU . . . . . . . . . . . . . TEXT    0101h
@FILENAME . . . . . . . . . .  TEXT    PGM28
@VERSION . . . . . . . . . . . TEXT    510
```

```
    48 Source  Lines
    48 Total   Lines
    13 Symbols

  47262 + 157501 Bytes symbol space free

     0 Warning Errors
     0 Severe  Errors
```

FIGURE 12–2 continued

```
Microsoft (R) Macro Assembler Version 5.10                    9/4/88 14:41:14


PGM28A FIGURE 12-2a  MODIFIED SUBROUTINE CALCRTN               Page    1-1



    1                                      PAGE   60,132
    2                                      TITLE  PGM28A FIGURE 12-2a  MODIFIED SUBROUTINE CALCRTN
    3
    4                           ;**************************************************************************
    5                           ; PGM28A      Title: Figure 12-2a CALCRTN with data segments linked   *
    6                           ;                                                                      *
    7                           ; Programmer: Vic Broquard                                             *
    8                           ; Date Written:  6/11/88        Date Of Last Revision: 8/6/88          *
    9                           ;                                                                      *
   10                           ; Purpose: To show linkage of data segments                           *
   11                           ;                                                                      *
   12                           ; Special Requirements: does no actual calculations                   *
   13                           ;                                                                      *
   14                           ;**************************************************************************
   15
   16 0000                     PGMCD  SEGMENT PARA PUBLIC  'CODE'
   17
   18 0000                     CALCRTN PROC    FAR
   19
   20                                      ASSUME  CS:PGMCD,DS:PGMDA
   21                                      PUBLIC  CALCRTN
   22
   23 0000  CB                            RET
   24
   25 0001                     CALCRTN ENDP
   26
   27 0001                     PGMCD   ENDS
   28
   29 0000                     PGMDA   SEGMENT PARA PUBLIC 'DATA'
   30
   31 0000                     PGMDA   ENDS
   32                                      END
```

```
Microsoft (R) Macro Assembler Version 5.10                    9/4/88 14:41:14


PGM28A FIGURE 12-2a  MODIFIED SUBROUTINE CALCRTN              Symbols-1



Segments and Groups:
```

FIGURE 12–2a   The CALCRTN subroutine (PGM28A.ASM)

```
                N a m e            Length  Align Combine Class
PGMCD . . . . . . . . . . . . .    0001    PARA  PUBLIC  'CODE'
PGMDA . . . . . . . . . . . . .    0000    PARA  PUBLIC  'DATA'


Symbols:

                N a m e            Type    Value Attr


CALCRTN . . . . . . . . . . .      F PROC  0000  PGMCD     Global    Length = 0001


@CPU . . . . . . . . . . . . .     TEXT    0101h
@FILENAME . . . . . . . . . .      TEXT    PGM28A
@VERSION . . . . . . . . . . .     TEXT    510



    32 Source  Lines
    32 Total   Lines
    10 Symbols

  47284 + 157479 Bytes symbol space free


    0 Warning Errors
    0 Severe  Errors



PGM28.MAP:


Start  Stop  Length Name          Class
00000H 00010H 00011H PGMCD        CODE
00020H 00020H 00000H PGMDA        DATA
00020H 0005FH 00040H PGMSTK       STACK
```

FIGURE 12–2a   continued

XXXXX? Figure 12–3 (PGM29.ASM on the program disk) shows the result. Figure 12–3a (PGM29A.ASM on the program disk) shows the external subroutine.

Notice that both code segments in Figure 12–3 are grouped into the one common code segment called CODE.XXXXX becomes a unique symbol once more, but it is still grouped with all code segments.

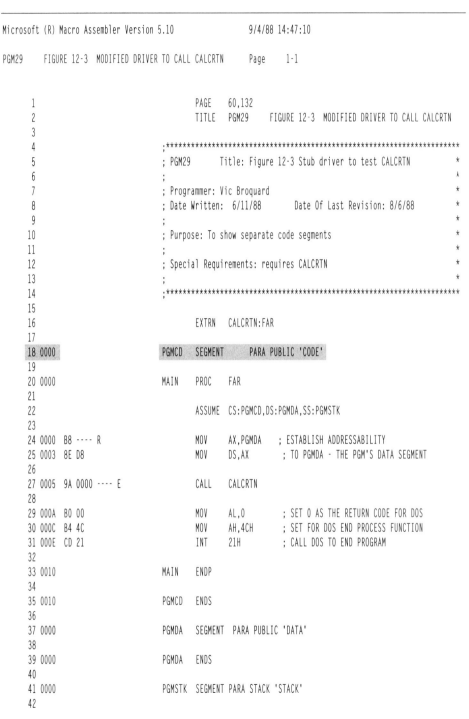

```
Microsoft (R) Macro Assembler Version 5.10            9/4/88 14:47:10

PGM29    FIGURE 12-3  MODIFIED DRIVER TO CALL CALCRTN      Page    1-1


  1                              PAGE    60,132
  2                              TITLE   PGM29    FIGURE 12-3  MODIFIED DRIVER TO CALL CALCRTN
  3
  4                      ;****************************************************************************
  5                      ; PGM29       Title: Figure 12-3 Stub driver to test CALCRTN        *
  6                      ;                                                                   *
  7                      ; Programmer: Vic Broquard                                          *
  8                      ; Date Written: 6/11/88      Date Of Last Revision: 8/6/88          *
  9                      ;                                                                   *
 10                      ; Purpose: To show separate code segments                          *
 11                      ;                                                                   *
 12                      ; Special Requirements: requires CALCRTN                            *
 13                      ;                                                                   *
 14                      ;****************************************************************************
 15
 16                              EXTRN   CALCRTN:FAR
 17
 18 0000                PGMCD   SEGMENT     PARA PUBLIC 'CODE'
 19
 20 0000                MAIN    PROC    FAR
 21
 22                              ASSUME  CS:PGMCD,DS:PGMDA,SS:PGMSTK
 23
 24 0000  B8 ---- R             MOV     AX,PGMDA    ; ESTABLISH ADDRESSABILITY
 25 0003  8E D8                 MOV     DS,AX       ; TO PGMDA - THE PGM'S DATA SEGMENT
 26
 27 0005  9A 0000 ---- E        CALL    CALCRTN
 28
 29 000A  B0 00                 MOV     AL,0        ; SET 0 AS THE RETURN CODE FOR DOS
 30 000C  B4 4C                 MOV     AH,4CH      ; SET FOR DOS END PROCESS FUNCTION
 31 000E  CD 21                 INT     21H         ; CALL DOS TO END PROGRAM
 32
 33 0010                MAIN    ENDP
 34
 35 0010                PGMCD   ENDS
 36
 37 0000                PGMDA   SEGMENT  PARA PUBLIC 'DATA'
 38
 39 0000                PGMDA   ENDS
 40
 41 0000                PGMSTK  SEGMENT PARA STACK 'STACK'
 42
```

FIGURE 12–3   Modified driver to call CALCRTN with different segments
(PGM29.ASM)

```
43 0000  0020[                   DW     32 DUP (?)
44        ????
45                  ]
46
47
48 0040                  PGMSTK ENDS
49                          END
```

Microsoft (R) Macro Assembler Version 5.10   9/4/88 14:47:10

PGM29   FIGURE 12-3 MODIFIED DRIVER TO CALL CALCRTN   Symbols-1

Segments and Groups:

N a m e	Length	Align	Combine	Class
PGMCD	0010	PARA	PUBLIC	'CODE'
PGMDA	0000	PARA	PUBLIC	'DATA'
PGMSTK	0040	PARA	STACK	'STACK'

Symbols:

N a m e	Type	Value	Attr	
CALCRTN	L FAR	0000	External	
MAIN	F PROC	0000	PGMCD	Length = 0010
@CPU	TEXT	0101h		
@FILENAME	TEXT	PGM29		
@VERSION	TEXT	510		

```
   46 Source  Lines
   46 Total   Lines
   13 Symbols

 47262 + 161085 Bytes symbol space free

    0 Warning Errors
    0 Severe  Errors
```

FIGURE 12–3 continued

```
Microsoft (R) Macro Assembler Version 5.10              9/4/88 14:47:17

PGM29A FIGURE 12-3a  MODIFIED SUBROUTINE CALCRTN              Page    1-1


      1                                    PAGE    60,132
      2                                    TITLE   PGM29A FIGURE 12-3a  MODIFIED SUBROUTINE CALCRTN
      3
      4                             ;************************************************************************
      5                             ; PGM29A     Title: Figure 12-3a CALCRTN to show code segments    *
      6                             ;                                                                  *
      7                             ; Programmer: Vic Broquard                                         *
      8                             ; Date Written: 6/11/88       Date Of Last Revision: 8/6/88        *
      9                             ;                                                                  *
     10                             ; Purpose: Illustrates separate code segments                      *
     11                             ;                                                                  *
     12                             ; Special Requirements: does no actual calculations               *
     13                             ;                                                                  *
     14                             ;************************************************************************
     15
     16 0000                       XXXXX   SEGMENT PARA PUBLIC  'CODE'
     17
     18 0000                       CALCRTN PROC    FAR
     19
     20                                    ASSUME  CS:XXXXX,DS:PGMDA
     21                                    PUBLIC  CALCRTN
     22
     23 0000  CB                           RET
     24
     25 0001                       CALCRTN ENDP
     26
     27 0001                       XXXXX   ENDS
     28
     29 0000                       PGMDA   SEGMENT PARA PUBLIC 'DATA'
     30
     31 0000                       PGMDA   ENDS
     32                                    END
-----------------------------------------------------------------------------

Microsoft (R) Macro Assembler Version 5.10              9/4/88 14:47:17

PGM29A FIGURE 12-3a  MODIFIED SUBROUTINE CALCRTN              Symbols-1


Segments and Groups:

              N a m e          Length  Align Combine Class
```

FIGURE 12–3a The CALCRTN subroutine (PGM29A.ASM)

```
PGMDA . . . . . . . . . . . . .    0000   PARA   PUBLIC   'DATA'
XXXXX . . . . . . . . . . . . .    0001   PARA   PUBLIC   'CODE'
```

Symbols:

```
                 N a m e           Type    Value  Attr

CALCRTN . . . . . . . . . . .      F PROC  0000   XXXXX    Global    Length = 0001


@CPU . . . . . . . . . . . . .     TEXT  0101h
@FILENAME . . . . . . . . . .      TEXT  PGM29A
@VERSION . . . . . . . . . . .     TEXT  510


   32 Source  Lines
   32 Total   Lines
   10 Symbols

 47284 + 161063 Bytes symbol space free

    0 Warning Errors
    0 Severe  Errors
```

PGM29.MAP:

```
Start  Stop   Length Name          Class
00000H 0000FH 00010H PGMCD          CODE
00010H 00010H 00001H XXXXX          CODE
00020H 00020H 00000H PGMDA          DATA
00020H 0005FH 00040H PGMSTK         STACK
```

FIGURE 12–3a continued

12.5 PRESERVING THE CALLER'S ENVIRONMENT

It is a wise practice not to alter the caller's registers or actual machine code segments. Therefore, the policy that we've adopted throughout this text is to save all the registers that the routine will use. A series of PUSHes becomes one of the first actions performed upon entry into an external routine. A corresponding series of POPs is the last set of instructions before the RET. Since a module should have only one entry point and only one exit point, this is easily accomplished. Besides, this is the design we have been implementing with all internal procedures.

Which registers should be saved? As a standard action, save and restore all the work registers (AX, BX, CX, and DX) plus SI and DI. In some cases, BP may also be needed. The flag register is seldom saved and restored, unless the caller module has some urgent need to have the flags preserved.

Stack Considerations

The program usually has only one stack segment that is defined in the driver, top, or main module. All subroutines merely use this LIFO area. Therefore, register SS is not normally modified by subroutines.

Notice that the CS and IP registers are saved and restored by the CALL and RET instructions.

Registers DS and ES

Registers DS and ES are usually the ones that can cause problems. The driver module loads register DS (and possibly ES) with the address of its data segment. When the subroutine gets control, neither register DS nor ES has been modified. If all data segments have been grouped into one common segment—called DATA, for example—then the linker automatically handles the situation. Nothing else must be done to either register DS or ES. This is an especially good reason to combine all data segments into one larger group by using the SEGMENT directives as shown in Figure 12–2. If it is not done, it is necessary to save register DS and/or ES in every subroutine, move the new correct value into register DS and/or ES, and restore register DS and/or ES on the way out.

12.6 PASSING DATA BETWEEN MODULES

How the driver passes data to the external subroutine and how the results are returned to the driver are the most complex part of the entire process. The first problem is to determine what should be passed. There are two choices: the actual data value itself or the address of that value. The second problem is how to actually pass the data. If good program design is to be preserved, there are three ways that data can be passed to and returned from a subroutine. There are times when each is more appropriate; therefore, you should become familiar with all three methods.

Passing Data by Value or by Address

Either the data value itself or the address to the data may be passed. In previous internal subroutine examples, registers AX and CX often contained actual values, such as the length of a field, the cost, or the total. Other times, the routines expected that registers SI, DI, and BX contained the address of the data, such as the beginning address of an ASCII character string.

Thus, your first choice is to determine if the data are to be passed by address or by value. Generally, the best criteria is to pass byte or word values as the actual value and to pass all strings, ASCII, text, or large number fields by address. However, this is not a hard-and-fast rule. Frequently, passing single byte values can be just as difficult as passing a string.

Once the choice of what to pass is determined, the next step is to decide how to actually pass it. Examine the three possibilities.

Passing Data Through the Use of Registers

With nearly all the internal routines shown so far, any data needed by a routine was passed to the routine through registers. These registers contained either the value itself (as in field lengths or binary numbers from numeric fields) or the registers contained the address of the string. Often, the work registers contained the values while the index and base register (BX) contained the addresses.

This technique is particularly useful when interfacing with DOS or BIOS interrupt routines, which expect or need certain values to be in certain registers. To do otherwise forces these modules to perform a lot of needless shuffling to get the correct values into the correct registers.

Figure 5–3 presented PGM7.ASM, a generalized string mover procedure. The internal routine was designed to move one string into another, handling padding and truncation as needed. The subroutine required four parameters: the lengths of the sending and receiving strings and the addresses of the two strings. Figure 12–4 (PGM30.ASM on the program disk) presents a revision that calls MOVSTR (an external subroutine) to perform the move. The program passes all four parameters by using registers. Figure 12–4a (PGM30A.ASM on the program disk) shows the external subroutine that calls MOVSTR.

The drawback of passing by registers is twofold. First, there is a limited number of registers. Second, many values may need to be passed. This is especially true of modules that are near the top of the program design tree.

One solution is to create a large connected block of fields in memory—that is, to define all the fields together. Then all that must be done is to pass the address of the start of this large area. Then the routine has access to the whole collection of fields. However, this approach presents two significant drawbacks. First, all the data **must** be in connected storage. That is, each field must be physically located one after another. For example, suppose that you want to pass three values: QTY, COST, and TOTAL. Storage must be defined as shown in Figure 12–5.

The address of the start of this small connected area (the address of QTY) is passed to the subroutine, which presumably is used to calculate TOTAL. The subroutine knows that QTY is the first byte of the connected area, COST is the next word, and TOTAL begins at an offset of 3 bytes from the start of the connected area. Here comes the trouble! What happens during program maintenance, when a new field needs to be added to the driver module called ITEM_DESC? It could very easily be inserted between COST and TOTAL, thus creating a different storage definition for total.

```
QTY        DB   ?
COST       DW   ?
ITEM_DESC  DB   10 DUP(?)
TOTAL      DW   0
```

Now what happens when the subroutine tries to calculate TOTAL by using the offset of 3 bytes from the start of the common area? Disaster!

```
        PAGE   60,132
        TITLE  PGM30 Figure 12-4  TEST DRIVER MODULE FOR SUBROUTINE MOVSTR


;***************************************************************************
; PGM30        Title: Figure 12-4 Stub driver to test MOVSTR, a text    *
;                     string mover subroutine                           *
;                                                                       *
; Programmer: Vic Broquard                                              *
; Date Written:  6/11/88         Date Of Last Revision: 8/6/88          *
;                                                                       *
; Purpose: this module tests the external subroutine MOVSTR, which      *
; moves one string to another                                          *
;                                                                       *
; Special Requirements: parameters are passed via the registers         *
;                                                                       *
;***************************************************************************

        EXTRN     MOVSTR:FAR

PGMSTK SEGMENT   PARA   STACK   'STACK'

        DW     32 DUP(0)

PGMSTK ENDS


PGMDA   SEGMENT

NAME1  DB      'BROQUARD'
NAME1A DB      8 DUP(?)

NAME2  DB      'WESTLEY'
NAME2A DB      4 DUP(?)

NAME3  DB      'VIC'
NAME3A DB      9 DUP(?)

PGMDA  ENDS
       PAGE
PGMCD  SEGMENT PARA PUBLIC 'CODE'

MAIN   PROC   FAR

; housekeeping section

       ASSUME CS:PGMCD,DS:PGMDA,SS:PGMSTK
```

FIGURE 12–4   Program to move string fields by using an external subroutine
(PGM30.ASM)

```
        MOV    AX,PGMDA   ; GET ADDRESSABILITY
        MOV    DS,AX      ; TO THE DATA SEGMENT

; main process section

; move first case 8 bytes to 8 bytes

--------------------------------------------------------------------

        LEA    SI,NAME1  ; SI = ADDR OF 8 BYTE SOURCE
        LEA    DI,NAME1A ; DI = ADDR OF 8 BYTE ANSWER

        MOV    CX,8       ; CX = NUM BYTES IN SOURCE (8)
        MOV    DX,8       ; DX = NUM BYTES IN ANSWER (8)

        CALL   MOVSTR     ; MOVE NAME1 TO NAME1A

; move second case 7 bytes to 4 bytes

        LEA    SI,NAME2  ; SI = ADDR OF 7 BYTE SOURCE
        LEA    DI,NAME2A ; DI = ADDR OF 4 BYTE ANSWER

        MOV    CX,7       ; CX = NUM BYTES IN SOURCE (7)
        MOV    DX,4       ; DX = NUM BYTES IN ANSWER (4)

        CALL   MOVSTR     ; MOVE NAME2 TO NAME2A

; move third case 3 bytes to 9 bytes

        LEA    SI,NAME3  ; SI = ADDR OF 3 BYTE SOURCE
        LEA    DI,NAME3A ; DI = ADDR OF 9 BYTE ANSWER

        MOV    CX,3       ; CX = NUM BYTES IN SOURCE (3)
        MOV    DX,9       ; DX = NUM BYTES IN ANSWER (9)

        CALL   MOVSTR     ; MOVE NAME3 TO NAMEA

; return to DOS section

        MOV    AL,0       ; SET A 0 RETURN CODE
        MOV    AH,4CH     ; SET FOR END PROCESS FUNCTION
        INT    21H        ; CALL DOS TO END

MAIN    ENDP

PGMCD   ENDS

        END    MAIN
```

FIGURE 12–4   continued

```
        PAGE      60,132
        TITLE    MOVSTR: SUBROUTINE TO MOVE ASCII STRINGS (PGM30A Figure 12-4a)


;***********************************************************************
; PGM30A      Title: Figure 12-4a MOVSTR routine to move ASCII strings *
;                                                                      *
; Programmer: Vic Broquard                                             *
; Date Written: 6/11/88       Date Of Last Revision: 8/6/88            *
;                                                                      *
; Purpose: Generalized ASCII string mover subroutine                   *
;                                                                      *
; Special Requirements:     upon entry:                                *
;                                                                      *
;     SI = ADDRESS OF SOURCE STRING                                    *
;     CX = LENGTH OF SOURCE STRING                                     *
;                                                                      *
;     DI = ADDRESS OF DESTINATION STRING                               *
;     DX = LENGTH OF DESTINATION STRING                                *
;                                                                      *
;***********************************************************************


PGMCD   SEGMENT PARA PUBLIC 'CODE'

MOVSTR PROC    FAR

        ASSUME CS:PGMCD

        PUBLIC MOVSTR

        PUSH    AX      ; SAVE REGISTERS
        PUSH    CX
        PUSH    DX
        PUSH    SI
        PUSH    DI


        CMP     CX,DX   ; WHICH STRING IS LONGER?
        JB      PAD_IT  ; DESTINATION IS LONGER - GO TO PAD_IT
        JE      SAME    ; BOTH HAVE SAME LENGTH - GO TO SAME

; here destination is truncated

        MOV     CX,DX   ; USE SHORTER LENGTH
        MOV     DX,0    ; SET NUMBER PAD BYTES TO 0
        JMP     DO_IT   ; GO DO MOVE
```

FIGURE 12–4a   The MOVSTR subroutine receives parameters passed via the registers (PGM30A.ASM)

```
SAME:
      MOV    DX,0        ; SET NUMBER OF PAD BYTES TO 0
      JMP    DO_IT       ; GO DO MOVE

PAD_IT:
      SUB    DX,CX       ; CALC NUMBER OF PAD BYTES

DO_IT:
      MOV    AH,[SI]     ; AH = NEXT BYTE OF SOURCE
      MOV    [DI],AH     ; MOVE IT INTO DESTINATION BYTE

      INC    DI          ; POINT TO NEXT DESTINATION BYTE
      INC    SI          ; POINT TO NEXT SOURCE BYTE

      LOOP   DO_IT       ; CONTINUE UNTIL ALL BYTES ARE MOVED

; now check for any needed pad bytes

      CMP    DX,0        ; ARE ANY NEEDED?
      JE     DONE        ; NO, SO GO TO DONE
----------------------------------------------------------------------
      MOV    CX,DX       ; SET NUMBER OF PAD BYTE TO INSERT
      MOV    AH,20H      ; SET THE PAD BYTE TO A BLANK

FILL:
      MOV    [DI],AH     ; MOVE IN ONE PAD BYTE
      INC    DI          ; POINT TO NEXT DESTINATION BYTE

      LOOP   FILL        ; CONTINUE WITH ALL PAD BYTES

DONE:
      POP    DI          ; RESTORE REGISTERS
      POP    SI
      POP    DX
      POP    CX
      POP    AX

      RET

MOVSTR ENDP

PGMCD  ENDS
       END
```

FIGURE 12–4a continued

```
QTY        DB   ?
COST       DW   ?
TOTAL      DW   0
```

FIGURE 12–5   Three fields in connected storage

The second major problem with passing data in a connected area lies in data coupling. Data coupling theory states that any module should have access to only the data it needs. Clearly, with data passed in this manner, a module can easily have access to **all** data of the program. The program could then alter data that it had no business modifying. This creates a nightmare during debugging, because the data could be modified in the most unexpected places.

On the other hand, this is a workable approach for passing input/output records, for passing tables and arrays, and for passing structures. Typically, these types of connected fields cannot easily be accidentally altered, and they contain limited data. These connected fields do not provide access to all fields in the program.

Figure 12–6 (PGM31.ASM on the program disk) shows how the general string mover subroutine can be rewritten to pass parameters by using a common area. Register BX contains the address of the four data items needed to perform the move function. Figure 12–6a (PGM31A.ASM on the program disk) shows the external subroutine.

Passing Data by Use of External Common Areas

There is another way to avoid excessive use of registers. The method is quite simple and convenient. In the module that actually defines the fields or connected areas, define the names of the fields as PUBLIC, thus making their names external in scope. Then, any external subroutine that needs the fields needs only to notify the assembler that these names are EXTERNAL. When the subroutine references external names, it accesses the original data areas. This approach is known as making the fields a **common** area—that is, common to all necessary modules.

Include the name of each variable or common area to be referenced by other external routines in the PUBLIC directive in the module that actually defines them. In the modules that need to use these fields, include the names in an EXTRN directive. However, the type operand of EXTRN is not NEAR or FAR, as before; rather, the type operand is one of the size specifiers:

```
BYTE
WORD
DWORD
QWORD
TBYTE
```

```
        PAGE   60,132
        TITLE  PGM31 Figure 12-6  TEST DRIVER MODULE FOR SUBROUTINE MOVSTR


;**************************************************************************
; PGM31        Title: Figure 12-6 Stub driver to test MOVSTR, a text   *
;                     string mover subroutine                          *
;                                                                      *
; Programmer: Vic Broquard                                             *
; Date Written:  6/11/88        Date Of Last Revision: 8/6/88          *
;                                                                      *
; Purpose: this module tests the external subroutine MOVSTR, which     *
; moves one string to another                                         *
;                                                                      *
; Special Requirements: parameters are passed via a common area that   *
;                       is pointed to by register BX                   *
;**************************************************************************

        EXTRN  MOVSTR:FAR

PGMSTK SEGMENT PARA STACK 'STACK'

        DW     32 DUP(0)

PGMSTK ENDS


PGMDA   SEGMENT

GROUP1 DW      8
NAME1  DB      'BROQUARD'
       DW      8
NAME1A DB      8 DUP(?)

GROUP2 DW      7
NAME2  DB      'WESTLEY'
       DW      4
NAME2A DB      4 DUP(?)

GROUP3 DW      3
NAME3  DB      'VIC'
       DW      9
NAME3A DB      9 DUP(?)

PGMDA   ENDS
        PAGE
PGMCD   SEGMENT PARA PUBLIC 'CODE'

MAIN   PROC    FAR
```

FIGURE 12–6   Program to pass parameters by using a common area
(PGM31.ASM)   *(Continues)*

```
; housekeeping section

        ASSUME CS:PGMCD,DS:PGMDA,SS:PGMSTK

        MOV     AX,PGMDA     ; GET ADDRESSABILITY
------------------------------------------------------------------------
        MOV     DS,AX        ; TO THE DATA SEGMENT

; main process section

; move first case 8 bytes to 8 bytes

        LEA     BX,GROUP1 ; BX = ADDR OF COMMON AREA1
        CALL    MOVSTR    ; MOVE NAME1 TO NAME1A

; move second case 7 bytes to 4 bytes

        LEA     BX,GROUP2 ; BX = ADDR OF COMMON AREA2
        CALL    MOVSTR    ; MOVE NAME2 TO NAME2A

; move third case 3 bytes to 9 bytes

        LEA     BX,GROUP3 ; BX = ADDR OF COMMON AREA3
        CALL    MOVSTR    ; MOVE NAME3 TO NAMEA

; return to DOS section

        MOV     AL,0      ; SET A 0 RETURN CODE
        MOV     AH,4CH    ; SET FOR END PROCESS FUNCTION
        INT     21H       ; CALL DOS TO END

MAIN    ENDP

PGMCD   ENDS

        END     MAIN
```

FIGURE 12–6   continued

To attempt to use external names in the move string programs shown in figures 12–4 and 12–6 would be a bad choice. External names in these programs are inappropriate because the actual values that are passed change with each invocation of MOVSTR. However, the CALCRTN example—which uses QTY, COST, and TOTAL—can effectively use common external names to pass the values. Figure 12–7 (PGM32.ASM on the program disk) shows how. Figure 12–7a (PGM32A.ASM on the program disk) shows the external subroutine.

When fields are defined as a common area, the assembler lists the symbols as GLOBAL or EXTERNAL in the module's symbol table. It is also possible to make the address of a large connected area external and reference it in a similar manner.

```
        PAGE    60,132
        TITLE   MOVSTR: PGM31A Fig.12-6a MOVE ASCII STRINGS


;************************************************************************
; PGM31A      Title: Figure 12-6a MOVSTR routine to move ASCII strings *
;                                                                      *
; Programmer: Vic Broquard                                             *
; Date Written:  6/11/88        Date Of Last Revision: 8/6/88          *
;                                                                      *
; Purpose: Generalized ASCII string mover subroutine                   *
;                                                                      *
; Special Requirements:      upon entry:                               *
;                                                                      *
;     BX = address of common area whose format is                     *
;         word length of source string                                *
;         source string bytes                                         *
;         word length of destination string                           *
;         destination string bytes                                    *
;                                                                      *
;************************************************************************

_____


PGMCD  SEGMENT PARA PUBLIC 'CODE'

MOVSTR PROC    FAR

        ASSUME CS:PGMCD
        PUBLIC MOVSTR

        PUSH    AX       ; SAVE REGISTERS
        PUSH    BX
        PUSH    CX
        PUSH    DX
        PUSH    SI
        PUSH    DI

; load parameters into work registers

        MOV     CX,[BX]  ; CX = LENGTH OF SOURCE
        ADD     BX,2     ; GET TO NEXT PARAMETER
        MOV     SI,BX    ; SI = ADDR OF SOURCE STRING
        ADD     BX,CX    ; GET TO NEXT PARAMETER
        MOV     DX,[BX]  ; DX = LENGTH OF DESTINATION STRING
        ADD     BX,2     ; GET TO NEXT PARAMETER
        MOV     DI,BX    ; DI = ADDR OF DESTINATION STRING

; begin move process
```

FIGURE 12–6a   The MOVSTR subroutine with parameters received via the common area (PGM31A.ASM)   *(Continues)*

```
        CMP     CX,DX    ; WHICH STRING IS LONGER?

        JB      PAD_IT   ; DESTINATION IS LONGER - GO TO PAD_IT
        JE      SAME     ; BOTH HAVE SAME LENGTH - GO TO SAME

; here destination is trucnated

        MOV     CX,DX    ; USE SHORTER LENGTH
        MOV     DX,0     ; SET NUMBER PAD BYTES TO 0
        JMP     DO_IT    ; GO DO MOVE

SAME:
        MOV     DX,0     ; SET NUMBER OF PAD BYTES TO 0
        JMP     DO_IT    ; GO DO MOVE

PAD_IT:
        SUB     DX,CX    ; CALC NUMBER OF PAD BYTES

DO_IT:
        MOV     AH,[SI]  ; AH = NEXT BYTE OF SOURCE
        MOV     [DI],AH  ; MOVE IT INTO DESTINATION BYTE

        INC     DI       ; POINT TO NEXT DESTINATION BYTE
        INC     SI       ; POINT TO NEXT SOURCE BYTE

        LOOP    DO_IT    ; CONTINUE UNTIL ALL BYTES ARE MOVED

; now check for any needed pad bytes

;-----------------------------------------------------------------------

        CMP     DX,0     ; ARE ANY NEEDED?
        JE      DONE     ; NO, SO GO TO DONE

        MOV     CX,DX    ; SET NUMBER OF PAD BYTE TO INSERT
        MOV     AH,20H   ; SET THE PAD BYTE TO A BLANK

FILL:
        MOV     [DI],AH  ; MOVE IN ONE PAD BYTE
        INC     DI       ; POINT TO NEXT DESTINATION BYTE

        LOOP    FILL     ; CONTINUE WITH ALL PAD BYTES

DONE:
        POP     DI       ; RESTORE REGISTERS
        POP     SI
        POP     DX
        POP     CX
        POP     BX
        POP     AX
```

FIGURE 12–6a   continued

```
        RET

MOVSTR ENDP

PGMCD   ENDS
        END
```

FIGURE 12–6a continued

```
        PAGE   60,132
        TITLE  PGM32 Figure 12-7 TEST MODULE FOR CALCRTN

;****************************************************************************
; PGM32      Title: Figure 12-7 Stub driver for CALCRTN          *
;                                                                *
; Programmer: Vic Broquard                                       *
; Date Written:  6/11/88       Date Of Last Revision: 8/6/88     *
;                                                                *
; Purpose: To test the CALCRTN                                   *
;                                                                *
; Special Requirements: Passes common fields: QTY, COST, and TOTAL  *
;                                                                *
;****************************************************************************

        EXTRN  CALCRTN:FAR
        PUBLIC QTY,COST,TOTAL

PGMSTK SEGMENT PARA STACK 'STACK'

        DW      32 DUP(0)

PGMSTK ENDS


PGMDA   SEGMENT

QTY    DB   2
COST   DW   5
TOTAL  DW   ?

PGMDA  ENDS


PGMCD  SEGMENT PARA PUBLIC 'CODE'

MAIN   PROC  FAR
```

FIGURE 12–7 Program to use common external names to pass values
(PGM32.ASM)   *(Continues)*

```
; housekeeping section

        ASSUME CS:PGMCD,DS:PGMDA,SS:PGMSTK

        MOV    AX,PGMDA    ; GET ADDRESSABILITY
        MOV    DS,AX       ; TO THE DATA SEGMENT

; main process section

        CALL   CALCRTN     ; WILL CALCULATE TOTAL
; return to DOS section

        MOV    AX,4C00H  ; SET RET CODE TO 0 AND END PROCESS FUNCTION
        INT    21H       ; CALL DOS TO END
-----------------------------------------------------------------------

MAIN    ENDP

PGMCD   ENDS
        END    MAIN
```

FIGURE 12–7 continued

.

```
        PAGE   60,132
        TITLE  CALCRTN: PGM32A Fig. 12-7a CALCULATE TOTAL

;************************************************************************
; PGM32A     Title: Figure 12-7a CALCRTN calculates total cost   *
;                                                                *
; Programmer: Vic Broquard                                       *
; Date Written: 6/11/88      Date Of Last Revision: 8/6/88       *
;                                                                *
; Purpose: to calculate TOTAL = QTY * COST                       *
;                                                                *
; Special Requirements: all three fields are external in scope   *
;                                                                *
;************************************************************************

        EXTRN  QTY:BYTE,COST:WORD,TOTAL:WORD

PGMCD   SEGMENT PARA PUBLIC 'CODE'

CALCRTN PROC  FAR

        ASSUME CS:PGMCD
        PUBLIC CALCRTN
```

FIGURE 12–7a The subroutine CALCRTN with external fields (PGM32A.ASM)

```
        PUSH    AX        ; SAVE REGISTERS
        PUSH    DX
        MOV     AL,QTY
        CBW
        MUL     COST
        MOV     TOTAL,AX

        POP     DX        ; RESTORE REGISTERS
        POP     AX

        RET CALCRTN ENDP

PGMCD   ENDS
        END
```

FIGURE 12–7a continued

A major problem with this technique surfaces when there are numerous fields to pass, as might be the case with the top modules in a large program. Coding such a large number of PUBLIC and EXTRN directives is cumbersome and error-prone. Caution: It might be tempting to solve this problem by combining all the fields into one large, contiguous block, making the first symbol of the block EXTERNAL. In this way, the subroutine can gain access to all the fields. But this creates poor data coupling and is error-prone. Don't combine fields in this way.

Passing Data Values on the Stack

The technique of passing values by using the stack solves the problems of too few registers and too much code. The technique is fairly simple. To pass values by using the stack, the required values must be pushed onto the stack when the call to the subroutine is made. Then the external procedure can access the required values directly from the stack.

There are a number of benefits of using this technique. One is that the routine can have access only to those parameters that have been pushed onto the stack. This promotes strong data coupling, which is desirable. Another benefit is that passing via the stack is exactly the way high-level languages pass data to subroutines. Therefore, if you ever need to have an assembler routine called from a high-level language such as PASCAL, all parameters to the assembler routine will be passed on the stack.

Passing via the stack does present some problems, however. Since all values must be pushed onto the stack, they must be word values. Thus, byte values become difficult to pass by value. For example, assume that a count has been stored in register AL. Since you can code only PUSH AX, not PUSH AL, byte fields passed by value often store an additional byte that is not used. (It is usually 00H.)

Given this complexity, the most common approach used when passing via the stack is to pass by address. A benefit to this approach is that you always know what is in the words in the stack: the addresses of the fields. Therefore, when passing data on the stack, we recommend that **only** addresses be pushed onto the stack, never values themselves.

Reconsider Figure 12–5. Suppose the MAIN procedure must pass the values in the fields QTY, COST, and TOTAL. Either the values or the addresses can be passed. Figure 12–8 shows both approaches.

Where does the stack pointer register (SP) point when CALCRTN gets control? The SP register points to the saved return address words for CS:IP of the MAIN procedure! How can CALCRTN get at these values? One way would be to decrement SP by the required number of words, get the addresses, and then increment SP back to where it belonged. This would be a poor way because any errors in the processing could result in wrong values being inserted into CS:IP on the return.

By value:

```
XOR  AX,AX      ; clear AX
MOV  AL,QTY     ; insert byte value
PUSH AX         ; save QTY on stack plus extra byte
PUSH COST       ; save COST on the stack
PUSH TOTAL      ; save TOTAL on the stack
CALL CALCRTN    ; calculate the new TOTAL
```

By address:

```
LEA  AX,QTY
PUSH AX         ; save QTY on stack plus extra byte
LEA  AX,COST
PUSH AX         ; save COST on the stack
LEA  AX,TOTAL
PUSH AX         ; save TOTAL on the stack
CALL CALCRTN    ; calculate the new TOTAL
```

The stack, when passing by addresses, upon entry to CALCRTN:

Register IP
Register CS
addr(TOTAL)
addr(COST)
addr(QTY)

← SP points here

FIGURE 12–8 Passing via the stack (with the callee saving BP)

The processor provides a better way to work with the stack, the BP register. This register is used to access values already on the stack. The default segment associated with BP is the stack segment register, SS. Therefore, normal use of register BP implies SS:BP for the vector.

The only problem with using register BP is getting the required value into it. There are two different methods that can be used. In one the original value of register BP is saved in the called routine; in the other it is saved in the calling routine. Let's examine each of these approaches.

Approach 1: Called Routine Saves BP

This is a common approach that moves the contents of the SP register into BP upon entry to the subroutine. This is coded as:

```
MOV  BP,SP      ; set BP to get the values passed to the sub
```

At this point the address of QTY is at BP + 8, the address of COST is at BP + 6, and the address of TOTAL is at BP + 4.

There is a problem: No registers have been saved. Normally, register BP must be saved before it is modified. Therefore, the code segment of the CALCRTN can be modified to

```
PUSH BP          ; save BP
MOV  BP,SP       ; acquire access to parameters passed
```

However, 2 more bytes have been added to the stack. At this point the address of QTY is now at BP + 10, the address of COST is at BP + 8, and the address of TOTAL is at BP + 6.

The preceding sequence is a typical way to begin an external subroutine that receives parameters from the stack. Next the program saves all the other registers that the subroutine intends to use. Note that all the normal register saves (pushes) are not done before loading BP from SP. Why? When the called routine saves BP, the last parameter passed is **always** at BP + 6. If you decide to save other registers before BP, the +6 displacement must be modified by 2 bytes for each PUSH issued. Since the number of registers saved varies from routine to routine, the displacement must be manually refigured for each module! This creates extra work, so why do it?

Figure 12–9 shows the shell coding that shows how this approach is applied to the CALCRTN example. The called routine saves register BP.

Have you spotted the major problem yet? What will the stack pointer register SP point to when CALCRTN issues RET? It will point to the parameters, not the old BP value! To get the stack back to the old BP value, the caller could issue a series of POPs after the call and then POP BP. However, the RET instruction has an option designed for this situation. The full RET syntax is

```
              RET   n
```

where n is the number of bytes by which to lower the stack pointer.

If three parameters are passed on the stack, then the called module issues

$$\text{RET} \quad 6$$

This adjusts the SP register by 6 bytes, leaving the SP pointing to the old BP value.

Approach 2: Calling Routine Saves BP

The second approach is to have the calling routine save the original value of register BP. In fact, this is exactly the method used by many high-level languages. Figure 12–10 shows the coding for the calling program and the stack upon entry to the called routine, CALCRTN. The code from Figure

```
CALCRTN  PROC
         ASSUME   CS:PGMCD
         PUBLIC   CALCRTN

    PUSH BP       ; SAVE REGISTER BP
    MOV  BP,SP    ; ACQUIRE ADDRESS OF PARAMETERS PASSED

    PUSH AX       ; SAVE REGISTERS
    PUSH BX
    ....

    PUSH SI

; get parameters into registers

    MOV  BX,[BP + 10]   ; BX = ADDR OF QTY
    MOV  SI,[BP + 8]    ; SI = ADDR OF COST
    MOV  DI,[BP + 6]    ; DI = ADDR OF TOTAL

; main body of routine

; restore all registers

    POP  SI
    ...
    POP  BX
    POP  AX
    POP  BP

    RET  6

CALCRTN  ENDP
```

FIGURE 12–9 CALCRTN shell saving register BP

The caller's coding:

```
    PUSH BP        ; SAVE ORIGINAL VALUE OF BP

    lea  ax,qty
    push ax        ; save qty on stack plus extra byte
    lea  ax,cost
    push ax        ; save cost on the stack
    lea  ax,total
    push ax        ; save total on the stack

    MOV  BP,SP     ; SET BP TO POINT TO PARAMETERS

    call calcrtn   ; calculate the new total

    POP  BP        ; RESTORE ORIGINAL VALUE OF BP
```

The stack, when passing by addresses, upon entry to CALCRTN:

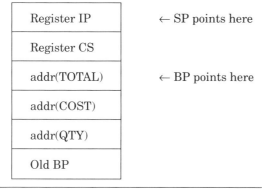

FIGURE 12–10   Passing via the stack with caller saving register BP

12–8 is in lowercase; the additional instructions are shown in capital letters. Notice that register BP points directly to the last parameter on the stack. The subroutine CALCRTN can now save its registers and begin processing using BP.

Figure 12–11 shows how the code looks if CALCRTN is called from the module shown in Figure 12–10. The calling routine saves BP.

Figure 12–12 (PGM33.ASM on the program disk) shows how the generalized string mover subroutine can be further modified to accept the four parameters from the stack. Figure 12–12a (PGM33A.ASM on the disk) shows the external subroutine.

A structure can be used to provide symbolic names to the parameters on the stack. This approach is covered near the end of Chapter 14.

```
CALCRTN  PROC
         ASSUME   CS:PGMCD
         PUBLIC   CALCRTN

     PUSH AX       ; SAVE REGISTERS
     PUSH BX
     ....

     PUSH SI

; get parameters into registers

     MOV  BX,[BP + 4]    ; BX = ADDR OF QTY
     MOV  SI,[BP + 2]    ; SI = ADDR OF COST
     MOV  DI,[BP]        ; DI = ADDR OF TOTAL

; main body of routine
     .
     .
     .

; restore all registers

     POP  SI
     ...
     POP  BX
     POP  AX

     RET  6

CALCRTN  END
```

FIGURE 12–11 CALCRTN shell without saving register BP

12.7 DOS COMMANDS FOR EXTERNAL SUBROUTINES

The driver module and each of the external subroutines are assembled normally. The typical command line to assemble the program in Figure 12–12 for MASM Version 5.0 is

```
        MASM /Z/ZI B:PGM33,B:,B:,B:
```

The typical command line to assemble the subroutine in Figure 12–12a is

```
        MASM /Z/ZI B:PGM33A,B:,B:,B:
```

```
        PAGE    61,132
        TITLE   PGM33 Figure 12-12 TEST DRIVER MODULE FOR SUBROUTINE MOVSTR


;**********************************************************************
; PGM33       Title: Figure 12-12 Stub driver to test MOVSTR, a text    *
;                    string mover subroutine                            *
;                                                                       *
; Programmer: Vic Broquard                                              *
; Date Written: 6/11/88        Date Of Last Revision: 8/6/88            *
;                                                                       *
; Purpose: this module tests the external subroutine MOVSTR, which      *
; moves one string to another                                          *
;                                                                       *
; Special Requirements: parameters are passed on the stack by address   *
;                                                                       *
;**********************************************************************


        EXTRN   MOVSTR:FAR

PGMSTK SEGMENT PARA STACK 'STACK'
        DW      32 DUP(0)
PGMSTK ENDS

PGMDA  SEGMENT

NAMEIN  DB      'VIC'
LENIN   DW      3

NAMEOUT DB      9 DUP(0)
LENOUT  DW      9

PGMDA   ENDS

PGMCD  SEGMENT PARA PUBLIC 'CODE'

MAIN   PROC    FAR

; housekeeping section

        ASSUME CS:PGMCD,DS:PGMDA,SS:PGMSTK

        MOV     AX,PGMDA   ; GET ADDRESSABILITY
        MOV     DS,AX      ; TO THE DATA SEGMENT

; main process section

; build parameters on stack
```

FIGURE 12–12   Modified test driver module for subroutine MOVSTR
(PGM33.ASM)   *(Continues)*

```
          PUSH   BP          ; SAVE ORIGINAL BP

          LEA    AX,LENIN
          PUSH   AX          ; SAVE LENGTH OF SOURCE
          LEA    AX,NAMEIN
          PUSH   AX          ; SAVE ADDR OF SOURCE

--------------------------------------------------------------------

          LEA    AX,LENOUT
          PUSH   AX          ; SAVE LENGTH OF DESTINATION
          LEA    AX,NAMEOUT
          PUSH   AX          ; SAVE ADDR OF DESTINATION STRING
          MOV    BP,SP       ; SET BP TO POINT TO PARMS

          CALL   MOVSTR      ; MOVE NAMEIN TO NAMEOUT

          POP    BP          ; RESTORE ORIGINAL BP

; return to DOS section

          MOV    AX,4C00H    ; SET FOR END PROCESS FUNCTION WITH RC = 0
          INT    21H         ; CALL DOS TO END

MAIN   ENDP
PGMCD  ENDS
       END    MAIN
```

FIGURE 12–12   continued

```
          PAGE   60,132
          TITLE  MOVSTR: PGM33A Fig. 12-12a MOVE ASCII STRINGS

;*************************************************************************
; PGM33A      Title: Figure 12-12a MOVSTR routine to move ASCII strings*
;                                                                      *
; Programmer: Vic Broquard                                             *
; Date Written:  6/11/88         Date Of Last Revision: 8/6/88         *
;                                                                      *
; Purpose: Generalized ASCII string mover subroutine                   *
;                                                                      *
; Special Requirements:      upon entry:                               *
;                                                                      *
;     STACK contains:                                                  *
;         address of word length of source string                      *
;         address of source string bytes                               *
;         address of word length of destination string                *
;         address of destination string bytes                         *
;                                                                      *
;*************************************************************************
;
```

FIGURE 12–12a   The subroutine MOVSTR with parameters passed on the stack
(PGM33A.ASM)

```
PGMCD   SEGMENT PARA PUBLIC 'CODE'

MOVSTR PROC    FAR
        ASSUME  CS:PGMCD
        PUBLIC  MOVSTR

        PUSH    AX          ; SAVE REGISTERS
        PUSH    BX
        PUSH    CX
        PUSH    DX
        PUSH    SI
        PUSH    DI

----------------------------------------------------------------------

; load parameters into work registers

        MOV     BX,[BP+6]   ; BX = ADDR OF LENIN
        MOV     CX,[BX]     ; CX = LENGTH OF SOURCE
        MOV     SI,[BP+4]   ; SI = ADDR OF SOURCE STRING
        MOV     BX,[BP+2]   ; BX = ADDR OF LENOUT
        MOV     DX,[BX]     ; DX = LENGTH OF DESTINATION STRING
        MOV     DI,[BP]     ; DI = ADDR OF DESTINATION STRING

; begin move process

        CMP     CX,DX       ; WHICH STRING IS LONGER?
        JB      PAD_IT      ; DESTINATION IS LONGER - GO TO PAD_IT
        JE      SAME        ; BOTH HAVE SAME LENGTH - GO TO SAME

; here destination is truncated

        MOV     CX,DX       ; USE SHORTER LENGTH
        MOV     DX,0        ; SET NUMBER PAD BYTES TO 0
        JMP     DO_IT       ; GO DO MOVE

SAME:
        MOV     DX,0        ; SET NUMBER OF PAD BYTES TO 0
        JMP     DO_IT       ; GO DO MOVE

PAD_IT:
        SUB     DX,CX       ; CALC NUMBER OF PAD BYTES

DO_IT:
        MOV     AH,[SI]     ; AH = NEXT BYTE OF SOURCE
        MOV     [DI],AH     ; MOVE IT INTO DESTINATION BYTE

        INC     DI          ; POINT TO NEXT DESTINATION BYTE
        INC     SI          ; POINT TO NEXT SOURCE BYTE
        LOOP    DO_IT       ; CONTINUE UNTIL ALL BYTES ARE MOVED
        PAGE
```

FIGURE 12–12a   continued   *(Continues)*

```
; now check for any needed pad bytes

        CMP    DX,0      ; ARE ANY NEEDED?
        JE     DONE      ; NO, SO GO TO DONE

        MOV    CX,DX     ; SET NUMBER OF PAD BYTE TO INSERT
        MOV    AH,20H    ; SET THE PAD BYTE TO A BLANK

FILL:
        MOV    [DI],AH   ; MOVE IN ONE PAD BYTE
        INC    DI        ; POINT TO NEXT DESTINATION BYTE

        LOOP   FILL      ; CONTINUE WITH ALL PAD BYTES

DONE:
        POP    DI        ; RESTORE REGISTERS
----------------------------------------------------------------------

        POP    SI
        POP    DX
        POP    CX
        POP    BX
        POP    AX

        RET    8

MOVSTR ENDP

PGMCD  ENDS
       END
```

FIGURE 12–12a   continued

When the linker is invoked, all the object modules must be included. A plus sign separates each object file specification on the command line. For Version 5.0, the modules in figures 12–2 and 12–2a can be linked by entering

```
        LINK /CO B:PGM33+B:PGM33A,B:,B:;
```

If there are more names of object files than fit on one line, end the line with the plus sign. The linker responds by prompting you for more entries on a new line.

  If you have several modules to include, it can be inconvenient during the debugging stage to continue to relink and resupply the same long series of object filenames. The use of a **linker response file** eliminates the need to continually re-enter such long series of entries.

Using a Linker Response File

The linker response file is a text file built prior to invoking the linker. It contains all the responses needed to normally link the prompts. To tell the linker to use a response file, enter the at sign (@) followed by the response file's name. Most programmers use an extension on the response file that is descriptive; in this case .LNK works well. Suppose the response file to link PGM33 is PGM33.LNK. To invoke the linker and the response file, enter

```
LINK /CO @PGM33.LNK
```

Suppose the response file, created with a word processor, contains

```
B:PGM33 B:PGM33A
B:PGM33
B:PGM33
<CR>
```

The first line provides the names of the object files. The plus sign connectors between the names can be omitted if desired. The second line is the name for the .EXE file; the third line is the name of the .MAP file. A carriage return is entered on the last line to indicate that no .LIB files are included.

A semicolon can be inserted as usual. Thus, if no .MAP file is desired, the response file can contain

```
B:PGM33 B:PGM33A
B:PGM33;
```

12.8   MEMORY MODELS AND DOS SEGMENT ORDER IN VERSION 5.0

The MASM supports six different memory models, or sizes of programs: tiny, small, medium, compact, large, and huge. A tiny program—code, data, and stack—all fits within one 64K segment. This is the way .COM programs are built. (This text does not include a discussion of tiny programs.) Small programs are those whose code and data segments do not exceed 64K each. Small programs can be used for all problems in this text.

The other sizes allow the code and/or data segments to exceed the 64K segment size. In all these, vector addresses (segment:offset) are needed in place of offset addresses, yielding 4-byte pointers instead of 2-byte pointers.

You must choose a memory model before defining any segments. Therefore, the .MODEL directive is one of the first directives coded. The syntax is

```
.MODEL   type
```

where type is one of the six different types: tiny, small, medium, compact, large, huge.

Consider this example:

```
PAGE 60,132
TITLE PAY20 PROGRAM TO CALCULATE THE WEEKLY PAYROLL
.MODEL SMALL
    .
    .
    .
```

If the full segment descriptions are coded—as done throughout the text to this point—then the assembler assumes the default NEAR for all PROC directives. If .MODEL is also coded, the assembler chooses the default to suit the size. It chooses NEAR for all PROCs if small or compact and FAR for all other types of models.

12.9   DOS SEGMENT NAMES

All Microsoft's high-level languages use the same standard segment names and order. Thus, interfacing Microsoft Macroassembler to high-level languages is easy. See Appendix A for interfacing requirements and techniques. Version 5.0 of MASM permits a simplified method of defining all segments. This must be done as one of the very first actions before any segments are defined. The directive is simply

```
DOSSEG
```

When this directive is used, the assembler uses predefined segment definitions and builds the program in standard segment order.

Standard directives are available to denote the beginning of these segments, and there are several predefined equates available for referencing these standard segment names in appropriate instructions. The common simplified directives are

.STACK	start of the stack segment
.CODE	start of the code segment
.DATA	start of the initialized data segment
.DATA?	start of the uninitialized data segment
.FARDATA	start of FAR data initialized segment for large models
.FARDATA?	start of FAR data uninitialized segment, large models

How these directives simplify program coding can be seen in Figure 12–13, which shows the driver module that invokes CALCRTN.

The predefined equates provide a convenient method for acquiring the segment names needed in instructions. The names are

```
        PAGE     60,132
        TITLE    PGMCALC   PROGRAM TO DO FINANCIAL CALCULATIONS


        DOSSEG
        .MODEL   SMALL


        .STACK   60H              ; DEFINE STACK OF 30 WORDS


        .DATA                     ; DEFINES DATA SEGMENT
QTY   DB      2
COST  DW      5
TOTAL DW      ?


        .CODE                     ; DEFINES CODE SEGMENT
MAIN:
        MOV      AX,DGROUP        ; NEED TO ADDRESS DATA SEGMENT HERE
        MOV      DS,AX            ; DS POINTS TO DATA SEGMENT
        ...


        EXTRN    CALCRTN:FAR


        CALL     CALCRTN          ; CALCRTN FINDS THE TOTAL COST
        ...


        END      MAIN
```

FIGURE 12–13   Program shell using simplified DOS segments

@CURSEG   name of the current segment
@CODE   code segment name defined by .CODE
@DATA   data segment name defined by .DATA and .DATA? and
             .STACK
@FARDATA   FAR data segment name defined by .FARDATA and
             .FARDATA?

If needed, these names can be used where segment names are normally used.
For example, one common use is in initializing register DS:

```
        MOV    AX,@DATA
        MOV    DS,AX
```

Figure 12–14 shows the directive, equate, and the actual names of the segments in a small memory model. Consult the MASM manuals for details of
the other model sizes.

Directive	Name	Class	Group
.CODE	_TEXT	'CODE'	
.DATA	_DATA	'DATA'	DGROUP
.DATA?	_BSS	'BSS'	DGROUP
.STACK	STACK	'STACK'	DGROUP

FIGURE 12–14   System default names for small memory model

12.10 SEGMENT GROUPS: VERSION 4.0 AND VERSION 5.0

If there are many modules in a program, register DS must usually be reinitialized upon entry to each module. That is, it must be set to point to the data segment of that module. Earlier you saw that if the data segment directives are all coded as

        PGMDA SEGMENT PARA PUBLIC 'DATA'

then the linker makes each a part of one large data segment. There is another approach that is commonly used. It is known as making a **group.**

A group is a series of segments that are associated with the same beginning address. In other words, all collected segments can be accessed by a single segment register, instead of one register for each segment. If the assembler is directed to collect all data segments into one large group, then register DS can be set to point to the beginning of the group. The assembler then calculates all offsets from the beginning of the group instead of the individual data segments.

Thus, register DS needs only to be set in the first module. All other modules calculate their data offsets from the start of the larger group and not the individual data segments. This is especially convenient in small programs. Remember that the group itself cannot exceed 64K. That is, the combined size of all the grouped data segments cannot be larger than 64K.

The standard default name for this large data group is DGROUP. DGROUP is shown in Figure 12–14 and in Figure 12–13, where it is used in the instruction MOV AX,DGROUP. The standard DOSSEG directive establishes the DGROUP. Of course, in every module, DOSSEG must be used.

If some other grouping is desired or if the program does not use the simplified DOSSEG feature, a data group can be created by using the GROUP directive. If the full segment definitions are being used, as has been the case thus far in the text, the GROUP directive must be used to create a group collection of the data segments. The syntax for the GROUP directive is

        groupname   GROUP   segment,segment, . . .

For example, suppose that in every module in the program, the data segment is coded as

```
PGMDA SEGMENT PARA PUBLIC 'DATA'
```

As shown in Figure 12–15, all the segments can be collected into the group and referenced by setting register DS once.

Grouping data segments can greatly ease the burden of external subroutine coding. The only restriction is that a group cannot exceed 65,535 bytes.

The order in which segments are linked depends upon the order in which the segments are given to the linker and the segment's class. The GROUP directive does not affect the linking order. It is possible to have nongroup segments physically within the actual 64K segment. Since this reduces the total amount of memory available to the group, be sure to use the class operand on all segment definitions. Also consider creating a separate group for the code segments.

```
        PAGE    60,132
        TITLE   MAIN PROCEDURE


DGROUP  GROUP   PGMDA


        EXTRN   SUB1:FAR


PGMDA   SEGMENT PARA  PUBLIC  'DATA'
        .
        .
        .


PGMDA   ENDS


PGMCD   SEGMENT PARA  PUBLIC  'CODE'


MAIN    PROC    FAR


        ASSUME  CS:PGMCD,DS:DGROUP,SS:PGMSTK
        MOV     AX,DGROUP
        MOV     DS,AX


        CALL    SUB1
        .
        .
        .
```

FIGURE 12–15 Creating a data group with full segment definitions   *(Continues)*

```
PGMCD    ENDS


              .
              .
              .

         PAGE    60,132
         TITLE   SUB1  EXTERNAL PROCEDURE 1

DGROUP   GROUP   PGMDA


PGMDA    SEGMENT PARA  PUBLIC  'DATA'
              .
              .
              .

PGMDA    ENDS

PGMCD    SEGMENT PARA  PUBLIC  'CODE'

SUB1     PROC    FAR

         ASSUME  CS:PGMCD,DS:DGROUP
         PUBLIC  SUB1
              .
              .
              .
```

FIGURE 12–15   Creating a data group with full segment definitions

12.11 SUMMARY

External subroutines definitely aid the assembly language programmer by reducing the program modules to a workable size, such as two pages of code per module. These modules are invoked by a CALL instruction. However, the assembler must be notified that the name on the CALL instruction is to be considered an external name; this is done by use of the EXTRN directive. Within the subroutine, the internal name of the routine must be made external by use of the PUBLIC directive.

The calling routine's environment can be preserved by pushing and popping any required registers. By use of appropriately coded segment directives or by use of groups, all the separate data segments can be combined into one large area. In this way you can avoid the constant need to alter the setting of register DS.

Data to be passed to subroutines can be passed by value or by address. More often, all data is passed by address, thus eliminating guesswork. Such values can be passed by register, by external common areas, or by use of the stack. Each technique has its own merits and drawbacks. You must become familiar with each approach because you will see all forms in use. High-level languages almost always pass by using the stack.

When using external routines, you will have numerous source modules to assemble. The command line to the linker must include the name of each separate piece, thus creating unwieldy code. The use of a linker response file removes much of this drudgery and code.

With Version 5.0 of MASM it is possible to use the simplified DOS segment names and shell formats. This reduces the number of lines that are needed in the module.

12.12 REVIEW QUESTIONS

1. What is an external subroutine? Why should an external routine never modify the caller's registers or modify the code of the caller? How do external routines benefit programmers?

2. What are the five areas of difficulty when working with external routines?

3. What is the syntax for the EXTRN and PUBLIC directives? When and why are they used?

4. Suppose the main procedure calls an external routine called WRITE_REC, which is appropriately defined with an EXTRN directive. In the subroutine the programmer forgot the PUBLIC WRITE_REC directive. What happens at assembly time? What happens at link time? What happens at execution time?

5. Do registers CS, SS, DS, and ES ever need to be saved and restored? Be specific.

6. Explain the difference between passing data by value and passing by address. When do you use each method? Show three examples of each form. Which method do you prefer? Why?

7. Describe how data can be passed by registers. What are the limitations of this method?

8. What problems or difficulties are involved when passing the address of a large section of data in connected storage? Why does this method represent poor data coupling?

9. Describe how data can be passed by external common areas. Is this a good technique? What are its benefits and weaknesses?

10. Describe the overall process of passing data via the stack. Why does it make a difference how register BP is saved?

11. Outline the steps needed to pass two parameters by address via the stack if the callee is to save register BP. Show the effects on the stack by using a drawing. Show where the involved registers are pointing.

12. Outline the steps needed to pass two parameters by address via the stack if the caller is to save register BP. Show the effects on the stack by using a drawing. Show where the involved registers are pointing.

13. What are the benefits of using a linker response file?

14. What is meant by *memory models*? What impact do you expect these to have on your programs?

15. Describe the simplified segment scheme for DOS Version 5.0. Is this something that you wish to use? Why?

16. What is a group? How are groups used? What are the benefits to making a data segment group? Are there any drawbacks?

12.13 PRACTICE PROBLEMS

1. Code an external subroutine to set the video mode. The mode should be passed in register AL.

2. Code an external subroutine to set the video mode. The mode should be defined in the main procedure as VIDEO_MODE DB 0H and contained in a PUBLIC directive. Therefore, the video mode to use should be passed as external data.

3. Code an external subroutine to set the video mode. The mode should be passed by value on the stack. Assume that the driver is saving register BP.

4. Code an external subroutine to set the video mode. The mode should be passed by value on the stack. Assume that the callee must save register BP.

5. A module needs to pass the following fields to the WRITE_REC external routine:

```
ITEM_NO         DB    5 DUP(?)
ITEM_DESC       DB    20 DUP(?)
NET_COST        DB    10 DUP(?)
RETAIL_COST     DB    5 DUP(?)
QTY_ON_HAND     DB    5 DUP(?)
```

How should the data be passed to the subroutine? Show the coding steps required.

6. A module must pass the following fields to the CALC_AREA routine:

```
ROOM_LEN  DW    ?
ROOM_WDTH DW    ?
ROOM_AREA DW    ?
```

What is a good way for the routine to pass these fields? Show the coding steps needed.

7. Convert the program shown in Figure 12–2 to use the simplified DOS segment method.

8. Show the coding necessary to convert the program shown in Figure 12–6 to use DGROUP for the data segments.

12.14 PROGRAMMING PROBLEMS

1. Figure 7–3 showed a driver module that called a function known as DSPLY_MSG. The function used BIOS to display a message in color. Rewrite DSPLY_MSG to be a generalized external routine. Four parameters should be passed on the stack:

   address of the length of the string to display

   address of the string to display

   address of the coordinates word

   address of the color attribute byte

2. The program in Figure 6–6 called a function known as GET_NAME, which used DOS function 08H to input a valid name. Rewrite GET_NAME as a generalized field input external subroutine. Pass to GET_NAME:

   address of the input string area

   address of the maximum length to be input

   These parameters should be external. Further, GET_NAME should use two external routines: EDIT and MOV_FLD. Any parameters that need to be passed to these subroutines may be passed as you think best. All program data areas should be part of a DGROUP.

3. In Figure 8–1 the main procedure called routines to convert to and from binary. Write two generalized external subroutines:

   ASC2BIN, to convert an ASCII character string into binary

   BIN2ASC, to convert a binary number into an ASCII character

Pass three parameters to each routine:

> address of the ASCII string
>
> address of the string length
>
> address of the word of binary data

All values should be passed by address on the stack.

4. Write an external subroutine that extracts the next file specification from the command line used to invoke the main procedure. You need to create a main tester module. For example, the program could be invoked by

```
B>TEST FILE1.DAT B:\WORK\FILE2.LST A:\TEST\WORK\FILE3.*
```

The first invocation of the routine should return the first file specification as in ASCIIZ string format, that is, FILE1.DAT. The next invocation should return B:\WORK\FILE2.LST. The main procedure should repeatedly call the routine until there are no more file specifications on the command line. The parameters to the routine should include the address of the resultant file specification ASCIIZ string. You may determine how the main procedure knows from the subroutine that no more specifications are present.

5. Presumably, you have solved one or more of the Programming Problems at the end of chapters 7, 8, or 9 by writing a program. Rewrite the program so it uses external subroutines. You may choose any of the three methods to pass the necessary fields and values. When you have the new version working, answer these questions:
    a) Of the original version and the new version, which is easier to manipulate and work with at the source level?
    b) Which version is easier to debug?
    c) Which version is easier to read and understand?

13

Array and Table Processing

13.1 CHAPTER OBJECTIVES

In this chapter you will

1. Study the principles of array and table processing, including basic terminology
2. Learn to define arrays and tables in storage
3. Examine the various processing steps required for each type of table
4. Learn several new assembler operators that are useful in some table-handling situations
5. Learn about the translate instruction and how it is used

13.2 INTRODUCTION

When processing data, it is often necessary to collect, or group, similar data items into a larger set known as an array and use just one data name to refer to the entire set. Familiar examples include a set of student grades, a series of test scores, a set of bowling scores, and a table of tax rates.

Beginning with Chapter 4, you have actually been using simple array-processing techniques as a way of processing fields. You loaded the address of the start of the field, worked with the byte pointed to by that address, and

471

then incremented the address to point to the next byte in the field. In effect, you considered each field to be an array of individual bytes. Now you will formally study the principles of array and table handling.

13.3 CONCEPTS OF ARRAYS AND TABLES

The term **array** refers to a group of fields in main storage that are all referenced by the same variable name. An analogy can be made between an array and a set of post office boxes. Each mailbox is identified by a unique box number on its door. Assume, for example, that you are assigned the box numbered 112. If you want to get your mail, you look for the 112th box. The number 112 serves as a pointer to your specific mailbox.

Similarly, in data processing an array refers to a set of storage locations. Each location is known by the same variable name, but each has a different number that identifies it. In an array the variable name associated with it is the first byte of the first element that makes up the array. Thus, to access a specific element within the array, it is necessary to use a pointer. The pointer is referred to as an **index** or **subscript**—the term used depends on the programming language and the way the pointer is defined.

To access a specific entry with high-level languages, it is necessary to use an index or subscript that points to the required entry. Commonly, if the index contains the value of 1, then it refers to the first entry in the array. If the index contains the value 2, it refers to the second entry in the array, and so forth.

A **table** is an array of data structures. Consider, for example, the problem of converting a code that represents a state to the state name. The data structure for the table consists of two fields: the state code and the corresponding state name. The first three entries are 01 Alabama, 02 Alaska, 03 Arkansas. There are 50 of these two-field structures. To access any state name, the index must have a value that points to the first byte of the state code field. As a result, it points indirectly to the corresponding state name, which comes after the state code.

Through the use of tables, businesses are able to use computers for jobs that would be impossible or impractical to undertake without them. Although many tables contain numeric data, it is possible to create tables to hold any data required by the application. Some examples of tables are tax tables; inventory tables; tables containing descriptions and pricing information; rate tables; and tables containing names of people, places, or things. One of the major advantages of using tables is that data can be stored compactly for easy and rapid reference and/or retrieval.

13.4 CRITERIA FOR SUITABILITY OF AN ARRAY OR TABLE

There are three tests that can be of assistance in determining whether a group of fields could or should be set up as an array or table.

1. The field(s) should have the same physical characteristics (size and data type).

2. They must be functionally related. There should be a processing reason for them to be set up as an array.

3. They must be physically contiguous. In other words, each field is stored one after the other in main storage. (Although it is possible to set up arrays with variable-length entries, the processing requirements for this situation are complex and will not be considered in this text.)

Consider an array that is set up to hold the names of the months. In such an array each entry must be nine characters in length to hold the largest month name, September. In many languages the month of May is stored as MAYbbbbbb—that is, with six trailing blanks. Now examine how this array of month names can be established.

13.5 AN EXAMPLE: MONTH TABLE AND MONTH ARRAY

A simple table-handling problem involves converting the month number code into the character month name. For example, if a month is entered as 03 it is converted into MARCH. Pictorially, such a conversion table can be defined as shown in Figure 13–1. In each case there are 12 sets of entries in the array or table. Notice that the array version has only one field per entry, whereas the table version has two fields per entry.

13.6 TABLE TERMINOLOGY

Three terms are commonly associated with tables and arrays: argument, function, and search argument. The numeric month code in the table in Figure 13–1 is the **argument**. An argument is any data item used as a

Month table	or	Month array
01 January		January
02 February		February
03 March		March
. .		.
. .		.
. .		.
12 December		December

FIGURE 13–1 Month conversions

pointer to a specific entry within a table. The argument may be either **explicit** or **implicit**. If the argument is physically a part of the table, as shown in the figure, it is explicit; such tables are known as **argument-function tables.** If the argument is not coded as part of the table, as in the array in Figure 13–1, the table is known as a **direct-reference table.** In these cases, the relative position of the data in the table serves as the argument.

The value or values that are associated with a particular argument are called the **function**. The name of the month in both examples is the function. One or more functions are nearly always present in any table or array. In arrays, functions are also called **elements**. A way of differentiating between an argument and a function is to think of the argument as the known quantity and the function as the unknown quantity.

The month number that is to be converted into the character form is known as the **search argument.** In Figure 13–1 the 03 that you want to convert is the search argument.

Now consider how arrays and tables are defined in memory and then study the processing logic necessary to access them.

13.7   DEFINING TABLES AND ARRAYS

Defining tables and arrays is similar to defining other fields, with one exception. Only one name is given to the table, and that name refers to only the first entry in the table. As with other fields, it is possible to include initial values for the fields or to define the fields as empty. When the initial value is included in a table in high-level languages, the table is called a hard-coded, or compile time, table because the values are physically coded as a part of the definition. When initial values are not included, they are called skeleton, or run time, tables because the definition provides a framework into which data may be placed during program execution.

Defining Tables and Arrays with Initial Values

For any table or array, there are several ways the definitions can be coded. Program readability and programmer preference are usually the factors in deciding which to use. The month name table can be defined as shown in Figure 13–2. Clearly, the last method, though requiring less code, is less readable, more error-prone, and less maintainable than the other two.

The direct-reference version can be defined as shown in Figure 13–3.

Defining Tables and Arrays Without Initial Values

Other times, the values in the table may be determined by calculations during execution of the program or by inputting the values from a file or other source. In these cases definitions are easier to code. If the month names are to be input from a disk file, the table can be as shown in Figure 13–4.

```
MON_NAME  DB   '01',  'JANUARY  '
          DB   '02',  'FEBRUARY '
          DB   '03',  'MARCH    '
                 .      .
                 .      .
                 .      .
          DB   '12',  'DECEMBER '
```

or as

```
MON_NAME  DB   '01'
          DB   'JANUARY  '
          DB   '02'
          DB   'FEBRUARY '
          DB   '03'
          DB   'MARCH    '
                 .      .
                 .      .
                 .      .
          DB   '12'   'DECEMBER '
```

or even as

```
MON_NAME  DB   '01','JANUARY  ',  '02','FEBRUARY ',  '03','MARCH    '
          DB   '04','APRIL    ',  . . . . .,         '12','DECEMBER '
```

FIGURE 13–2   Three ways to define a month table

```
MON_NAME  DB   'JANUARY  '
          DB   'FEBRUARY '
          DB   'MARCH    '
                 .      .
                 .      .
                 .      .
          DB   'DECEMBER '
```

or as

```
MON_NAME  DB   'JANUARY  ','FEBRUARY ','MARCH    ',...,'DECEMBER '
```

FIGURE 13–3   Defining a direct-reference table

```
MON_NAME  DB   12 DUP( 9 DUP(?))   ; TABLE OF 12 VALUES EACH 9
                                   ; BYTES LONG
```

FIGURE 13-4   Uninitialized table definition

13.8   PROCESSING LOGIC FOR ACCESSING TABLES AND ARRAYS

The following are the processing steps needed for an argument-function table:

1. Loop through each entry in the table.

2. Compare the search argument to the argument.

3. When the arguments match, then use the corresponding function.

4. If the entire table is searched and no match occurs, then there is no corresponding entry in the table. In most instances, this is an error situation.

For a direct-reference table, all function entries must be in relative order. In the case of month names, *January* must be the 1st and *December* must be the 12th. The processing steps are

1. Calculate the relative position from the start of the table.
   a. Subtract 1 from the search argument.
   b. Multiply the result by the length of an entry.

2. Access the function that is located at the calculated relative position from the start of the table.

3. Find errors by examining the range of the original search argument. In the month name example, any search argument that is not between 1 and 12 is an error.

This list points out the major difference between handling tables with a high-level language and microassembler. Typically, with the high-level languages it is necessary only to provide the search argument as a subscript or index. The subscript or index is often enclosed within parentheses: MONTH_NAME(3) or MONTH_NAME(MONTH_CODE) or MONTH_NAME(I). The language calculates the relative position from the start of the table or array and retrieves the function automatically. At the microassembler level, the program must perform all these steps.

13.9 PROCESSING GUIDELINES

When processing arrays and tables:

- All fields should be adjacent to each other or separated by a fixed number of bytes, and

- All fields should have the same length. Although it is possible to have table entries of varying lengths, the processing techniques for such entries are complex and beyond the scope of this text.

The steps in processing are

1. Establish an index register to hold the starting address of the current entry in the array or table.

2. Do the required processing by indexing the index register.

3. Increment the index register by the length of an entry.

4. Provide the proper loop controls to perform the loop the correct number of times.

13.10 ARGUMENT-FUNCTION TABLE PROCESSING

Assume that the month table is defined as an argument-function table. Further, assume that the current month to convert has been input and stored in a search argument field known as MONTH and that the result should be moved into MON_ANSR. These fields are defined as

```
MONTH    DB  2 DUP(?)      ; CURRENT ASCII MONTH TO LOOK UP
MON_ANSR DB  9 DUP(?)      ; RESULTANT ASCII CURRENT MONTH
MON_ERR  DB  '00**ERROR**' ; SET UP AS IF IT WERE A
                           ; COMPLETE TABLE ENTRY
```

Figure 13–5 (PGM34.ASM on your program disk) shows the processing needed to do a table lookup. Register DI holds the address of the answer area, MON_ANSR. Register SI points to the current entry in the table to be checked. It begins by pointing to the first entry in the table:

```
'01', 'JANUARY  '
```

Register CX contains the number of entries in the table, 12. Register BX holds the total length of the data structure containing the month code and name (11 bytes). MON_LOOP begins the start of the main search loop. The next argument to check is moved into register AX and then compared to the search argument MONTH. If they are not equal, then register SI is incremented by 11 bytes to point to the next entry. The loop is repeated.

```
        PAGE    60,132
        TITLE   PGM34 - Figure 13-5 MONTH NAME ARGUMENT-FUNCTION TABLE


;**************************************************************************
; PGM34       Title: Figure 13-5 Month name argument-function table    *
;                                          lookup program              *
; Programmer: Vic Broquard                                             *
; Date Written:  6/11/88        Date Of Last Revision: 8/6/88          *
;                                                                      *
; Purpose: program to do a table lookup of MONTH                       *
;                                                                      *
; Special Requirements: MON_ANSR holds the result, including an error  *
;                       message for bad months                         *
;                                    *                                 *
;**************************************************************************


; program code segment

PGMCD   SEGMENT

MAIN    PROC    FAR

; housekeeping section

        ASSUME  CS:PGMCD,DS:PGMDA,SS:PGMSTK

        MOV     AX,PGMDA    ; ESTABLISH ADDRESSABILITY
        MOV     DS,AX       ; TO PGMDA - THE PGM'S DATA SEGMENT

; main process section

        LEA     DI,MON_ANSR ; DI POINTS TO THE ANSWER AREA
        LEA     SI,MON_NAME ; SI POINTS TO THE CURRENT ENTRY IN THE TABLE

        MOV     CX,12       ; CX = NUMBER OF ENTRIES IN TABLE
        MOV     BX,11       ; BX = LEN OF ENTRY = 2 FOR CODE + 9 FOR MONTH NAME

MON_LOOP:

        MOV     AX,0[SI]    ; GET NEXT ARGUMENT TO COMPARE

        CMP     AX,WORD PTR MONTH ; DOES MONTH = CURRENT ENTRY?
        JE      FOUND       ; YES, SO GO MOVE IN THE FUNCTION RESULT

        ADD     SI,BX       ; INCREMENT TO NEXT TABLE ENTRY
        LOOP    MON_LOOP    ; REPEAT ON NEXT TABLE ENTRY

; here, MONTH not found in the table, so move an err msg into MON_ANSR

        LEA     SI,MON_ERR  ; RESET SI TO POINT TO ERROR MESSAGE
```

FIGURE 13–5   Month name argument-function table (PGM34.ASM)

```
FOUND:

    MOV    CX,9      ; NUMBER OF BYTES TO MOVE

---------------------------------------------------------------------

    ADD    SI,2      ; MOVE OVER ARGUMENT BYTES

MOV_LOOP:

    MOV    AL,0[SI]  ; TRANSFER ONE BYTE FROM
    MOV    [DI],AL   ; TABLE TO ANSWER AREA
    INC    SI        ; POINT TO NEXT BYTE TO MOVE
    INC    DI        ; POINT TO NEXT ANSWER BYTE
    LOOP   MOV_LOOP  ; REPEAT UNTIL ALL ARE DONE

; return to DOS section

    MOV    AL,0      ; SET 0 AS THE RETURN CODE FOR DOS
    MOV    AH,4CH    ; SET FOR DOS END PROCESS FUNCTION
    INT    21H       ; CALL DOS TO END PROGRAM

MAIN   ENDP


PGMCD  ENDS


; program data segment

PGMDA  SEGMENT

MON_NAME DB    '01','JANUARY  '
         DB    '02','FEBRUARY '
         DB    '03','MARCH    '
         DB    '04','APRIL    '
         DB    '05','MAY      '
         DB    '06','JUNE     '
         DB    '07','JULY     '
         DB    '08','AUGUST   '
         DB    '09','SEPTEMBER'
         DB    '10','OCTOBER  '
         DB    '11','NOVEMBER '
         DB    '12','DECEMBER '

MONTH    DB    '03'            ; CURRENT MONTH TO LOOK UP
MON_ANSR DB    9 DUP(?)        ; RESULTANT ASCII MONTH NAME
MON_ERR  DB    '00**ERROR**'   ; SET UP AS IF IT WERE A COMPLETE TABLE ENTRY

PGMDA  ENDS
```

FIGURE 13–5 continued   *(Continues)*

```
; program stack segment

PGMSTK SEGMENT PARA STACK 'STACK'

      DW      32 DUP (?)

PGMSTK ENDS
      END
```

FIGURE 13–5 continued

The loop can be ended in two ways. If register CX becomes 0, then no match was found. This means that the search argument MONTH has an invalid month code in it. If this happens, register SI is set to point to the error message.

If there is a match, control goes to FOUND. Here the index register SI, which currently points to the correct argument, is incremented by 2 bytes so that it now points to the function. (The length of the month code is 2 bytes.) Finally, MOV_LOOP moves either the correct function (month name) or the error message into the answer field, MON_ANSR.

13.11 DIRECT-REFERENCE TABLE PROCESSING

Now reconsider the month conversion problem by using a direct-reference table like the one in Figure 13–3. Figure 13–6 (PGM35.ASM on the program disk) shows the table and accompanying code. This time, MONTH (the search argument) is not in character form, but in binary. The argument is 03H as opposed to 30 33H. If it is not, then it can be converted from its ASCII number form into binary by following the principles outlined in Chapter 8.

The first step is to verify that the MONTH number is valid. A range check is performed, ensuring that it is between 1 and 12. Should the value be invalid, then the error value 13 is assigned. The month name array contains 13 entries, with the 13th being an error message for invalid months.

Next, at VALID, the relative offset from the start of the array is calculated. Then the beginning address of the first byte of the correct month name entry is determined. Finally, the value is moved into the answer area, MON_ANSR.

Argument-function and direct-reference table processing work well for either byte or word search arguments. However, when working with long fields, you will encounter problems.

```
        PAGE    60,132
        TITLE   PGM35 - Figure 13-6 MONTH NAME DIRECT REFERENCE TABLE


;****************************************************************************
; PGM35       Title: Figure 13-6 Month name lookup using direct reference *
;                                                                         *
; Programmer: Vic Broquard                                                *
; Date Written:  6/11/88        Date Of Last Revision: 8/6/88             *
;                                                                         *
; Purpose:  program to do a table lookup of MONTH                         *
;                                                                         *
; Special Requirements: MON_ANSR holds the result, including error msg    *
;                                                                         *
;****************************************************************************


; program code segment

PGMCD   SEGMENT

MAIN    PROC    FAR

; housekeeping section

        ASSUME  CS:PGMCD,DS:PGMDA,SS:PGMSTK

        MOV     AX,PGMDA    ; ESTABLISH ADDRESSABILITY
        MOV     DS,AX       ; TO PGMDA - THE PGM'S DATA SEGMENT

; main process section

        LEA     DI,MON_ANSR ; DI POINTS TO THE ANSWER AREA
        LEA     SI,MON_NAME ; SI POINTS TO THE CURRENT ENTRY IN THE TABLE

        MOV     AL,MONTH    ; AL = MONTH NUMBER TO CONVERT

        CMP     AL,1        ; IS MONTH < 1?
        JL      BADMONTH    ; YES, FLAG AS ERROR

        CMP     AL,12       ; IS MONTH > 12?
        JNG     VALID       ; NO, IT'S VALID

BADMONTH:

        MOV     AL,13       ; RESET TO 13TH ENTRY - ERROR MSG

VALID:

        DEC     AL          ; SUBTRACT 1 TO TURN IT INTO AN OFFSET ADDRESS
        MOV     CL,9        ; CL = LENGTH OF ARRAY ENTRY
```

FIGURE 13–6 Month name—direct reference table (PGM35.ASM)   *(Continues)*

```
        MUL    CL          ; MULTIPLY BY LENGTH OF AN ENTRY
        ADD    SI,AX       ; ADD OFFSET TO START OF TABLE TO GET FIRST BYTE

        MOV    CX,9        ; NUMBER OF BYTES TO MOVE
```

```
MOV_LOOP:

        MOV    AL,0[SI]    ; TRANSFER ONE BYTE FROM
        MOV    [DI],AL     ; TABLE TO ANSWER AREA
        INC    SI          ; POINT TO NFXT BYTE TO MOVE
        INC    DI          ; POINT TO NEXT ANSWER BYTE
        LOOP   MOV_LOOP    ; REPEAT UNTIL ALL ARE DONE

; return to DOS section

        MOV    AL,0        ; SET 0 AS THE RETURN CODE FOR DOS
        MOV    AH,4CH      ; SET FOR DOS END PROCESS FUNCTION
        INT    21H         ; CALL DOS TO END PROGRAM

MAIN  ENDP

PGMCD ENDS


; program data segment

PGMDA SEGMENT

MON_NAME DB     'JANUARY  '
         DB     'FEBRUARY '
         DB     'MARCH    '
         DB     'APRIL    '
         DB     'MAY      '
         DB     'JUNE     '
         DB     'JULY     '
         DB     'AUGUST   '
         DB     'SEPTEMBER'
         DB     'OCTOBER  '
         DB     'NOVEMBER '
         DB     'DECEMBER '
         DB     '**ERROR**' ; SET UP AS IF IT WERE A 13th TABLE ENTRY

MONTH    DB     3
MON_ANSR DB     9 DUP(?)

PGMDA ENDS


; program stack segment
```

FIGURE 13–6 continued

```
PGMSTK  SEGMENT PARA STACK 'STACK'

        DW      32 DUP (?)

PGMSTK  ENDS
        END
```

FIGURE 13–6 continued

13.12 MULTIPLE-BYTE ARGUMENTS/SEARCH ARGUMENTS

Often, the argument field consists of several ASCII bytes. For example, part numbers, policy numbers, social security numbers, and customer identifiers are all several bytes long. This creates a problem in comparing the search argument to the argument. In such cases, the string function CMPS (compare string) alleviates the problem. This function was presented in Chapter 11.

An additional complication arises when the number of entries or their sizes varies from one assembly to another. Several special operators will be very useful in these instances.

13.13 SPECIAL MICROASSEMBLER OPERATORS: LENGTH, SIZE, TYPE

The **LENGTH** operator returns the number of elements in an array that has been defined using the DUP operator. If the definition includes nested DUPs, only the outermost value is returned.

Assume the following definitions for an array of grand totals and an array of last names:

```
TOTALS    DW    10    DUP(?)
NAMES     DB    20    DUP( 15 DUP(?)) ; 20 NAMES EACH 15 CHARS
```

You can enter

```
MOV  CX,LENGTH TOTALS  ; STORES # OF ELEMENTS IN TOTAL (10)
                       ; IN CX
MOV  BX,LENGTH NAMES   ; STORES 20 IN BX - # ELEMENTS IN
                       ; NAMES
```

or

```
LENTOTALS EQU  LENGTH TOTALS
```

The **TYPE** operator returns a number that indicates the number of bytes in the definition type.

definition	return value
DB	1
DW	2
DD	4

Using the preceding storage definitions for TOTALS and NAMES, you can enter

```
MOV   AX,TYPE TOTALS   ; AX = 2 FOR WORDS
MOV   AX,TYPE NAMES    ; AX = 1 FOR BYTES
```

The **SIZE** operator returns the total number of bytes in the definition. That is, it represents the results of LENGTH times TYPE. If the definition includes nested DUPs, only the outer values are used. Thus, for arrays of strings, the SIZE result may not be accurate.

Using the preceding definitions for TOTALS and NAMES, the following results are obtained from the use of SIZE:

```
MOV   CX,SIZE TOTALS   ; CX = 20 BYTES or 10 × 2
MOV   BX,SIZE NAMES    ; CX = 20 BYTES or 20 × 1
```

The three operands LENGTH, TYPE, and SIZE are useful when handling arrays and tables whose dimensions vary from one assembly to the next. Consider a grade book program. The number of tests for each class varies. The program can be tailored as follows.

```
NUM_TESTS EQU  5    ;  RESET THIS VALUE ONLY FOR OTHER
                    ; CLASSES - ALL OTHER CODE WILL ADJUST
SCORES    DB   NUM_TESTS DUP(?)

MOV   CX,LENGTH SCORES    ; GET NUMBER OF ENTRIES IN ARRAY
```

or

```
MOV   CX,NUM_TESTS        ; ALSO PUTS NUMBER OF ENTRIES IN CX
```

Thus, only NUM_TESTS must be altered. Then the program can be reassembled. Alternatively, it is possible to define SCORES as

```
SCORES    DB   5 DUP(?)
```

and then merely alter the 5 and reassemble the program for another class.

13.14 ALTERNATIVE APPROACH FOR NON-DUP ARRAYS AND TABLES

LENGTH, TYPE, and SIZE work well for arrays and tables that are defined by the DUP operator. However, many tables are actually given starting values, and these seldom use the DUP operator. See the month tables in Figure 13–2, for example.

```
PREMTBL    DB    'A','300.00'
           DB    'B','350.00'
           DB    'C','400.00'
                  .        .
                  .        .
                  .        .

           DB    'F','500.00'
ENDTBL     EQU   $
```

FIGURE 13–7 Automobile coverage—premium table

Suppose you need to create a table of automobile insurance coverage codes and the premiums due for that coverage. The table can be defined as shown in Figure 13–7. For coverage code A, the premium due is $300.00. The problem with this approach is that the number of coverages change; more can be added at any time, and others can be deleted. Since register CX must often contain the number of entries in the table, you must also remember to modify that MOV into CX. This potential error situation can be completely removed by including the definition ENDTBL as shown in Figure 13–7.

There are two easy approaches to automate the process of moving the number of entries in the table into register CX. They are illustrated in Example 13–1. Either approach is acceptable.

Method 1:

```
LEA  AX,ENDTBL     ; AX = ADDR OF END OF THE TABLE
LEA  BX,PREMTBL    ; BX = ADDR OF START OF THE TABLE
SUB  AX,BX         ; AX = TOTAL NUMBER OF BYTES IN TABLE
MOV  BL,7          ; BL = LENGTH OF ONE ENTRY IN TABLE
DIV  BL            ; AL = NUMBER OF ENTRIES
CBW                ; CONVERT INTO WORD
MOV  CX,AX         ; CX = NUMBER OF ENTRIES IN THE TABLE
```

Method 2: Add the definition

```
TBLSIZE    DW    ENDTBL-PREMTBL ; CONTAINS THE CURRENT TBL
                               ; LENGTH
```

and code

```
MOV  AX,TBLSIZE    ; AX = SIZE OF TABLE
MOV  BL,7          ; BL = LENGTH OF ONE ENTRY IN TABLE
DIV  BL            ; AL = NUMBER OF ENTRIES
CBW                ; CONVERT INTO WORD
MOV  CX,AX         ; CX = NUMBER OF ENTRIES IN THE TABLE
```

EXAMPLE 13–1 Two methods for obtaining the number of entries in register CX

The premium table illustrates another problem. The search argument **must** be in uppercase. A lowercase "a" results in no match found. In such cases, you can use the subroutine shown in Chapter 4 to convert from lowercase to uppercase. There is a simpler approach, however: the translation instruction.

13.15 THE TRANSLATION INSTRUCTION: XLAT

When search arguments are input by a user and when they are characters (or ASCII values), the case becomes important. For example, coverage A and a are two **different** values. Since the table uses "A", entering "a" yields the message NOT IN TABLE when a match should be found. This can create needless frustration for the user.

The translation instruction, XLAT, converts a byte into a predetermined alternate value. The XLAT instruction has no coded operands. However, there are two implied operands. First, the byte to be converted must be in register AL. Then, when the translation operation is done, the converted value is in register AL. Finally, register BX must contain the address of a 256-byte conversion table. The conversion table provides a corresponding value for each value that is contained within a single byte—that is, for each value from 00H to FFH.

Translation uses the contents of register AL, the byte to be converted, as an offset within the conversion table. Assume that AL contains "a", or 61H. The XLAT returns to register AL whatever value is contained at offset 61H within the conversion table.

Converting Case with XLAT

Look again at the problem of the user entering "a" instead of "A". To convert "a" into "A", you need to code 41H ("A") at offset 61H within the conversion table. Enter the hex equivalents for the rest of the lowercase letters. You must include the equivalents of the capital letters as well so that, if the user enters "A", it will remain the same. However, in this case, assume that all other values are invalid. Replace these with a blank, or 20H. The conversion table and coding are shown in Example 13–2.

XLAT can be used in numerous situations where a value needs to be converted into another predetermined value. It is often used to convert ASCII codes into EBCDIC values to allow communication between personal computers and mainframe computers. It can be used to convert binary values into ASCII values. XLAT also plays an important role when it is necessary to display values in the standard dump format.

Using XLAT to Convert Bytes into Dump Format

If a byte contains "A" and you want to display it in dump form, it should appear as 41H. XLAT can be used to convert the 1-byte 41H into 2 display

The conversion table:

```
CNVRTBL DB   65 DUP(' ')                   ; FIRST 65 ENTRIES ARE INVALID
        DB   'ABCDEFGHIJKLMNOPQRSTUVWXYZ'  ; LEAVE CAP LETTERS AS IS
        DB   6 DUP(' ')                    ; NEXT 6 ARE INVALID
        DB   'ABCDEFGHIJKLMNOPQRSTUVWXYZ'  ; CONVERT LOWER TO UPPER CASE
        DB   133 DUP(' ')                  ; REMAINDER ARE INVALID


COV_CODE DB  'a'                           ; BYTE TO CONVERT
```

The coding could be

```
        MOV  AL,COV_CODE     ; AL = COVERAGE TO CONVERT
        LEA  BX,CNVRTBL      ; BX =TABLE OF CONVERSION VALUES
        XLAT                 ; CONVERT AL TO UPPERCASE

; now use AL to search the table of coverages
```

EXAMPLE 13–2 Conversion table and coding to translate to uppercase

bytes: 34 31H, or ASCII 41. This forms the kernel of dump programs that display the values of registers and memory in hex format.

Consider the following problem: You want to change 1 byte of 41H into 2 display bytes: 34H and 31H. The procedure is to first isolate the 4 nibble in register AL as 04H and XLAT it into 34H. Then, isolate the 1 nibble in register AL and translate it into 31H. The nibbles can be isolated by the shifting instructions. If you shift left 1 nibble (4 bits) and then shift back 1 nibble, the 1 nibble is isolated as 01H, since the fill bits are 0 bits. Conversely, if you first shift right by 4 bits, you end up with 04H in register AL. All shifting must be logical, not algebraic, since you want no fill bits.

In Figure 13–8 (PGM36.ASM on the program disk), CODE contains the original "A", or 41H. Once the XLAT process is complete, DSPLY_CODE

```
        PAGE    60,132
        TITLE   PGM36 - Figure 13-8 TRANSLATING COVERAGE INTO DUMP FORMAT
;************************************************************************
; PGM36      Title: Figure 13-8 Translate COVERAGE into dump format    *
;                                                                      *
; Programmer: Vic Broquard                                             *
; Date Written:  6/11/88        Date Of Last Revision: 8/6/88          *
;                                                                      *
; Purpose: Translate byte field into hex dump format                   *
;                                                                      *
```

FIGURE 13–8 Translating coverage into dump format (PGM36.ASM)

```
; Special Requirements:                                            *
;                                                                  *
;      the value in CODE 'A' will be converted to dump format      *
;      and appear as two bytes: 34 31H                             *
;                                                                  *
;*********************************************************************
;

; program code segment

PGMCD SEGMENT

MAIN  PROC    FAR

; housekeeping section

      ASSUME  CS:PGMCD,DS:PGMDA,SS:PGMSTK

      MOV     AX,PGMDA     ; ESTABLISH ADDRESSABILITY
      MOV     DS,AX        ; TO PGMDA - THE PGM'S DATA SEGMENT

; main process section

      LEA     DI,DSPLY_CODE ; DI -> ANSWER BYTES

; process left nibble

      MOV     AL,CODE      ; GET THE CODE
      MOV     CL,4         ; CL = NUMBER OF BITS TO SHIFT
      SHR     AL,CL        ; MOVES LEFT NIBBLE TO RIGHT NIBBLE POSITION
      LEA     BX,CNVRTBL   ; BX = ADDR OF CONVERSION TABLE
      XLAT                 ; CONVERT NIBBLE INTO ASCII VALUE
      MOV     0[DI],AL     ; SAVE CONVERTED VALUE
      INC     DI           ; POINT TO NEXT

; process right nibble

      MOV     AL,CODE      ; GET ORIGINAL CODE
      SHL     AL,CL        ; SHIFT OUT LEFT NIBBLE
      SHR     AL,CL        ; SHIFT BACK IN 0 NIBBLE
      XLAT                 ; CONVERT NIBBLE INTO ASCII VALUE
      MOV     0[DI],AL     ; SAVE CONVERTED BYTE

; here DSPLY_CODE now contains the DUMP display format of CODE

; --------------------------------------------------------------------

; return to DOS section

      MOV     AL,0         ; SET 0 AS THE RETURN CODE FOR DOS
      MOV     AH,4CH       ; SET FOR DOS END PROCESS FUNCTION
      INT     21H          ; CALL DOS TO END PROGRAM
```

FIGURE 13–8   continued

```
MAIN  ENDP

PGMCD ENDS


; program data segment

PGMDA SEGMENT

CODE       DB    'A'
DSPLY_CODE DB    2 DUP(?)

CNVRTBL    DB    '0123456789ABCDEF'
           DB    240 DUP(00H)

PGMDA ENDS


; program stack segment

PGMSTK  SEGMENT PARA STACK 'STACK'

        DW    32 DUP (?)

PGMSTK  ENDS
        END
```

FIGURE 13–8   continued

contains the display version of 34 and 31H, or '41'. Assemble this program and use your debugger to trace the program's execution. Notice in particular the effects on register AL and the DSPLY_CODE field.

13.16 SUMMARY

This chapter presented the various terms associated with array and table processing. You have seen that there are two forms that such processing can use: argument-function tables and direct-reference tables. The processing steps are very different for each type.

The operators LENGTH, SIZE, and TYPE assist in resolving the problems presented by multiple-byte search arguments. You have seen how the number of entries in a table can be calculated in cases where the number can vary.

The translation instruction, XLAT, can be used to convert a byte into a predetermined value. XLAT plays an important role when values must be displayed in the standard dump format.

13.17 REVIEW QUESTIONS

1. What is the difference between an array and a table? What is an index or subscript and how are they used?

2. Describe how arguments, functions, and search arguments are used in table processing. What is the difference between an implicit argument and an explicit argument?

3. What is the difference between an argument-function table and a direct-reference table?

4. Outline the processing steps required to access an argument-function table.

5. Outline the processing steps required to access a direct-reference table.

6. How would you process a search argument that is five characters long?

7. Explain how the LENGTH operator functions. What use do you see for the LENGTH operator in table processing?

8. What is the difference between SIZE and TYPE? How are they used in table processing?

9. Explain how the XLAT instruction works. How does the translation array operate?

10. What is the importance of the search argument in processing tables?

13.18 PRACTICE PROBLEMS

1. Outline the steps needed to compare a 6-byte CUSTOMER_ NUMBER search argument to a table's corresponding argument.

2. Show what steps are needed to modify Figure 13–5, the month name argument-function table lookup program, to determine the number of entries in the table. The table is

```
MON_NAME DB    '01','JANUARY '
         ...
         ...
         DB    '12','DECEMBER '
END_MON  EQU   $
```

3. Show the coding steps needed to use the LENGTH, SIZE, and TYPE operands with Figure 13–6, the month name direct reference table lookup program.

4. Show the coding steps needed to load the MON_NAME table shown in Figure 13–4 from a file of names.

5. Show the modifications needed to use XLAT to change the COV_CODE in Example 13–8 to lowercase.

13.19 PROGRAMMING PROBLEMS

1. Write a routine that returns the number of days in a given month. The program should prompt the user to enter a month number from 1 to 12. It should then display the number of days in that month by accessing an array that contains the corresponding number of days. Permit any two-digit number to be entered, and display BAD MONTH if the entry is out of range. (Ignore leap years.)

2. Write a routine to retrieve a student's grade point average from a table. Each entry in the table should consist of a social security number (argument) of nine ASCII digits and the corresponding grade point average (four ASCII digits in the format 9.99). The master table should be

```
GRADE_TBL DB    '111111111','4.12'
          DB    '222222222','3.56'
          DB    '333333333','4.90'
          DB    '444444444','2.54'
```

The routine should prompt the user to enter a social security number. It should respond with the appropriate grade point average. If the social security number is not in the table, display an appropriate error message. Hint: Use the CMPS string function.

3. Write a routine to convert a string to uppercase. The routine receives a string of up to 80 characters and the string's length. When the routine is called, register SI should contain the address of the string and register AX should have the string's length. Use the XLAT instruction to do the conversion. You may write an appropriate tester module to input the original string and then display the resultant string.

4. Write a routine to display in dump format the contents of any field specified by the user. Upon entry to the routine, register SI should contain the address of the string to be shown in dump format; register AX should contain the number of bytes to display. The routine should convert the bytes to dump format and display them on the screen. Use the XLAT instruction. You may create an appropriate tester module.

5. Write a routine called CRASH_VERIFY for an auto insurance company. When a client phones in a claim, the user enters the customer's

car policy number and retrieves both the number of accidents and their associated costs. The table is

```
CRASH_TABLE     LABEL       BYTE

        DB      '111','1','$ 100.50'
        DB      '222','0','$ 0.00'
        DB      '333','2','$1,234.76'
        DB      '444','1','$ 503.54'
```

The main procedure should prompt and input a three-digit policy number and then call CRASH_VERIFY. The routine should return values in two fields

```
NUM_CRASH       DB ?
CRASH_COST      DB 9 DUP(?)
```

If there is no match, return BAD NUMBR in CRASH_COST and display a 0 in the NUM_CRASH field.

14

Addressing Modes, Structures, and Multilevel Tables

14.1 CHAPTER OBJECTIVES

In this chapter you will

1. Learn about the seven addressing modes of the personal computer
2. See how the effective address of an operand is computed and how the speed of instruction execution is dependent upon the time needed to calculate the effective address
3. Learn about data structures and their importance
4. Study the way structures are defined and how memory is allocated to them
5. Learn to reference fields and arrays within a data structure
6. Apply these principles to processing multilevel arrays and tables

14.2 INTRODUCTION

In the preceding chapters you have seen that instruction operands may take on several forms, including a register value, immediate data, the name of a field, or even data pointed to by an address stored in a register (as in [SI]). In fact, these are four of the seven different **addressing schemes** available on the personal computer. It is time to formalize your understanding of these addressing schemes, examine some of their useful properties, and see how they are applied to data structures and multilevel tables.

	Addressing mode name		Coding example
1.	register addressing		MOV AX,CX
2.	immediate addressing		MOV AX,1
3.	direct addressing		MOV AX,COST
4.	register indirect addressing		MOV AX,[BX]
5.	indexed addressing		MOV AL,MONTH [SI]
		or	MOV AL,[MONTH + SI]
		or	MOV AL,[SI] + 8
6.	based addressing		MOV AX,ACCTCODE [BX]
		or	MOV AX,[ACCTCODE + BX]
		or	MOV AX,[BX] + 8
7.	based-indexed addressing		ADD AX,COSTTBL [SI] [BX]
		or	ADD AX,[SI + BX + 6]
		or	ADD AX,[SI] [BX] 6

FIGURE 14–1   Addressing modes

14.3 THE ADDRESSING MODES

Data can be addressed in seven different ways, known as addressing modes. Figure 14–1 summarizes the seven addressing modes of the personal computer. The first three modes are sufficiently familiar by now, so there is no need to discuss them further. This chapter does discuss the others.

14.4 REGISTER INDIRECT ADDRESSING MODE

Register indirect addressing consists of storing the offset address of the desired data in register BX. It is commonly used to point to a memory location within a segment. For example, the notation [BX] means the data pointed to by register BX.

    The **effective address** (EA) is calculated by the assembler as DS:BX, which means use the current data segment address plus the offset address in register BX. You know that the default segment address (DS) can be overridden by coding the segment address (45EF:BX), by coding another segment register (ES:BX), or by coding the SEG operator (SEG COST:BX). In each case the EA is found by adding the data segment address in register BX to the offset address.

The three other modes shown in Figure 14–1 are more unfamiliar than register indirect addressing. Consider the properties of these modes and some guidelines to aid in determining when each should be used. Each provides a way to calculate EA that is slightly more complex than the methods you've already studied.

Indexed Addressing

When using **indexed addressing,** registers SI and DI contain an offset value from the start of the named symbol. To see how this works, consider a simple direct-reference table that contains month names. An abbreviated data segment layout is shown in Figure 14–2.

You know from Chapter 13 that MONTH is a direct-reference table. In other words, if you want to look up the English form of the month name that corresponds to the value in MONTHCD (which has already been converted into binary and stored in MONTHCD), you must calculate the relative offset by subtracting 1 from the MONTHCD and multiplying the result by the length of a table entry (9 bytes in this case). If this offset value is then stored in register SI, the table can be accessed by entering

```
MOV    AL,MONTH [SI]
```

This moves the first byte of the corresponding month name into register AL. (That value is then stored in the answer field, register SI is incremented, and the process is repeated until all 9 bytes of the name have been moved.)

```
PGMDATA    SEGMENT

CUSTNAME   DB    8 DUP(?)          ; WILL CONTAIN THE CUSTOMER NAME

MONTH      DB    'JANUARY  '
           DB    'FEBRUARY '
           DB    'MARCH    '
            .          .
            .          .
            .          .

           DB    'DECEMBER '
            .
            .
            .

MONTHCD    DW    ?                 ; CURRENT MONTH CODE TO LOOK UP
            .
            .
            .
```

FIGURE 14–2 Month table for indexed addressing

In this case EA is calculated by adding the segment address (the contents of DS, unless overridden), the offset address of the symbol MONTH, and the contents of the index register SI. There are two index registers that can be used for such operations: SI and DI.

Using register SI, this indexing problem can be coded in one of two ways:

```
MOV    AL,[MONTH + SI]
```

or

```
MOV    AL,[SI] + 8
```

Notice that the first instruction is relatively clear and straightforward. The latter is confusing, difficult to maintain, and—consequently—error-prone. It raises the question: Where does the 8 come from? Actually, the 8 replaces the symbol MONTH. Notice in Figure 14–2 that MONTH is located 8 bytes from the start of the segment. Thus, MONTH has a location counter, or offset value, within PGMDTA of 08H bytes. This location counter value of 8 can replace the symbol MONTH. The second technique is not recommended. Suppose, for example, that a new work field, ADDRESS, is inserted somewhere before the MONTH definition. What happens to the location counter and, therefore, the absolute offset value of 8 bytes? It changes! Why make your life difficult by using the location counter when you can use the symbolic form of indexed addressing?

Indexed addressing is a technique that is commonly used to address elements within a single-dimension array or table.

Based Addressing

Based addressing is similar to indexed addressing, and they are often used interchangeably. The primary difference is the choice of registers used. Indexed addressing uses registers SI and DI; based addressing uses registers BX and BP.

When based addressing uses register BX, it functions in exactly the same manner as indexed addressing. The segment register used is DS unless it is overridden. However, when register BP is used, the segment register is SS, the stack segment. This provides a convenient method of accessing values stored in the stack, without altering the current contents of the stack pointer register, SP. The need for this became apparent in Chapter 12 on external subroutines.

Again, the EA is calculated by adding the segment address plus the offset address of the symbol (or absolute displacement) plus the contents of the base register.

$$EA = DS + BX + \text{offset address of symbol or absolute displacement}$$

or

$$EA = SS + BP + \text{offset address of symbol or absolute displacement}$$

Based-Indexed Addressing

The last addressing mode, **based-indexed addressing,** is the most complex form. It is a combination of both the based and indexed modes. One index register is used, either SI or DI, and one base register is used, either BX or BP. The presence of a symbol or a displacement is optional. If register BP is used, the default segment register is SS, the stack segment, unless a specific segment override is coded. The use of two index or two base registers generates an error.

The EA is calculated as the segment address plus the contents of the base register plus the contents of the index register plus the optional displacement provided by the symbol or the absolute numeric displacement.

The based-indexed mode is normally used for multilevel arrays and tables or for other multidimensional situations. Consider a teacher's grade book, which can be viewed as a table of at least two dimensions. One dimension represents all the students, up to a maximum of 30. For each student there is a second array of test scores, up to a maximum of five grades. Examining the SCORES array alone, you can see it is a 30 by 5 array. Commonly, it is dimensioned as SCORES(30,5). Suppose that the teacher needs to record the fourth test score for student number 17. In many languages, grade is stored by

```
SCORES(17,4) = grade
```

In microassembler, you need two indexes to point to the required location. Assume that SCORES is defined as

```
SCORES   DB   30 DUP(5 DUP(?))
```

One index or base register is needed to point to the correct first index value, 17; the second is needed to point to the correct second index value, 4.

To effectively move the new byte test score into SCORES(17,4), both indexes must be converted into relative offset format. Let register SI point to the correct student, number 17, and let register BX point to the correct score, number 4. You must put 80 in register SI: $(17 - 1) * 5$, where the length of a complete set of scores is 5 bytes. Also, register BX should contain 3: $(4 - 1) * 1$, where the length of a single score is 1 byte. (If you are in doubt about these relationships, draw a diagram of the array.) The instruction to move the new score contained in register AL is

```
MOV   SCORES [SI] [BX],AL    ; SAVE NEW SCORE IN (17,4)
```

This action can be coded in a number of different ways:

```
        MOV    SCORES [BX] [SI], AL

        MOV    [SCORES + SI + BX], AL

        MOV    SCORES [SI + BX], AL
```

```
MOV    [BX] [SI].SCORES, AL

MOV    [SI] [BX] + SCORES, AL
```

In this case the first instruction in the list is the best choice because it closely parallels the syntax of high-level languages.

14.5 EXECUTION SPEED AND THE CALCULATION OF THE EA

The calculation of the EA has a significant effect upon execution speed. Each instruction has a fixed execution speed, referred to as its clock speed. The basic unit, clocks, can be converted into nanoseconds (10^{-9} second, or 0.000 000 001 second) by the following formula:

$$1 \text{ clock cycle} = 1 \text{ microsecond/number of megahertz}$$
$$\text{at which the processor runs}$$

(where a microsecond is 10^{-6} second or 0.000 001 second). For example, on a processor that runs at 4.77 megahertz (MHz), 1 clock cycle takes 210 nanoseconds. On a faster processor, one that runs at 8 MHz, 1 clock cycle takes 125 nanoseconds.

The Microsoft MASM manuals provide the clock cycles for all instructions. They are given either as a specific number of clock cycles or as a formula. For example, a register-to-register move takes 2 clock cycles. All other moves take 2 + EA clock cycles. This means that the total time is 2 clocks plus however long it takes to calculate the EA (effective address). Herein lies the impact of the different addressing modes. Figure 14–3 summarizes these effects.

The timings in Figure 14–3 are presented for your general information only. You should not attempt to code a routine to be as speedy as possible, sacrificing maintainability or readability, unless maximum speed is part of the design criteria. Speed of execution may be of primary concern when coding certain system modules or real-time simulators.

14.6 STRUCTURES

Many high-level languages support the concept of a record, or **data structure,** which is composed of many individual fields. For example a customer order record, or data structure, might contain such fields as customer number, name, address, city, state, ZIP code, item number, quantity, description, unit cost, total cost, tax, and so on. The overall structure name, CUST_RECORD, or the individual fields within the structure can be used to access the data.

Addressing mode	Clocks to get EA	Coding example
direct addressing	6	`MOV  AX,COST`
based or indexed	5	`MOV  AX,[BX]` `MOV  AX,[SI]`
based or indexed plus displacement	9	`MOV  AX,[BX + 8]` `MOV  AX,TABLE [DI]`
based–indexed either BX + SI or BP + DI	7	`MOV  AX,[SI + BX]`
based–indexed BX + DI or BP + SI	8	`MOV  AX,[DI + BX]`
based–index + symbol BX + SI or BP + DI	11	`MOV  AX,TABLE [SI] [BX]`
based–index + displacement BX + DI or BP + SI	12	`MOV  AX,[DI + BX + 8]`
segment override	EA + 2	`MOV  AX,ES:STRING`

FIGURE 14–3 Clock timings for effective address calculations

A field within the structure can itself be an array, with as many dimensions as desired. In some cases, it is possible to have an array of records. (Note: The term *record*, in microassembler, has a totally different meaning than that used in high-level languages. In microassembler, *record* refers to a string of bits. This definition is seldom used in business applications. See your assembler documentation for more detail.)

In microassembler, these large structures are available, although in a limited scope. To utilize structures, two things must be done. First, the overall structure template, or pattern, of the structure must be defined. Next, the actual structure in storage must be defined using this template as a guide.

14.7 DEFINING A STRUCTURE TEMPLATE

First examine how the **structure template** is defined. Every structure must be defined using the STRUC and ENDS pair. This pair is much like SEGMENT-ENDS or PROC-ENDP. Between these two statements all the

individual fields that the record or structure contains are defined. The coding
for the structure template is

```
                    name  STRUC
                             .
                             .
                             .
                    name  ENDS
```

Between the field entries include field definitions with any default initial
values desired.

Structure templates can be particularly valuable when working with
files. Assume that you want to input a customer identification record. A
CUST_REC template can be defined as

```
              CUST_REC      STRUC
                               .
                               .
                               .
              CUST_REC      ENDS
```

The field definitions are handled normally, but with some special
considerations. These special considerations are more easily grasped when
examined in the second step, defining the actual structure(s) in memory.
Figure 14–4 shows some fields that might be found in a customer
identification record.

Notice that each field is given an initial value. When the structure is
defined in memory, these initial values are used, unless they are overridden
at that time. Also, the beginning values determine the length of these byte
fields.

Figure 14–5 shows an entry pattern that can be used to create the
month table for use in converting month codes into corresponding names.

Figure 14–6 shows a customer order record, which can be set up as a
structure template.

```
CREC      STRUC
CID       DB    '00000'                          ; CUSTOMER ID NUMBER
CNAME     DB    'first and last names     '      ; NAMES ARE 25 BYTES
CADDR     DB    '                    '           ; ADDR IS 20 BYTES
CCITY     DB    '          '                     ; CITY IS 10 BYTES
CSTATE    DB    '  '                             ; STATE IS 2 BYTES
CZIP      DB    '99999-9999'                     ; ZIP IN PROPER FORMAT
CREC      ENDS
```

FIGURE 14–4 A customer ID structure

```
MONTH_NAME      STRUC

         DB     'xxxxxxxxx'     ; TO BE FILLED WITH THE MONTH NAME

MONTH_NAME      ENDS
```

FIGURE 14–5 A month name structure

```
CORDER      STRUC
ITEMNO      DB   4 DUP(?)        ; ITEM NUMBER ORDERED
DESCR       DB   10 DUP(?)       ; ITEM DESCRIPTION
QTY         DB   ?               ; QUANTITY ORDERED
COST        DW   ?               ; UNIT COST OF ITEM
CORDER      ENDS
```

FIGURE 14–6   A customer's order structure

In figures 14–4, 14–5, and 14–6, only the structure template is defined. No memory locations are given for any of the structures, or fields. The next step is to actually define the structure in memory, as it is to be used.

14.8   DEFINING THE STRUCTURE IN MEMORY

The definition of a structure in memory is known as a **structure variable.** The syntax for defining a structure variable is

name   structure namc   <initialvalue1,initialval2,...>

The name is the structure variable name that will be used in the program to reference the actual structure in memory. The structure name is the name found in the STRUC-ENDS pair that defines the template.

Any initial values specified in the template are inserted into the defined fields as the structure is being defined. However, it is possible to override the original values specified in the template by inserting the new values within angle brackets (< >). The first entry in the brackets is the value for the first field in the structure, the second value is for the second, and so on. A comma is used to separate these values.

If a particular initial value of the template is not to be overridden, then its presence within the structure must still be accounted for. Therefore, commas are used to indicate the end of each field within the structure template. For example, suppose only the second and fourth fields' initial values of 45 and 46 are to be overridden and replaced by 55 and 56. In this case the initial string is

```
<,55,,56>
```

If no values are to be overridden, the angle brackets must still be present.

There are two major rules for providing override values:

- The length of the new value cannot exceed the length of the original in the template. Longer values generate error messages. Shorter strings are padded on the right with blanks.

- Fields that have multiple values in the template **cannot** be overridden. This applies specifically to fields created by the DUP operator. Thus, if the field is defined using the DUP operator in the structure template, the initial value of that field, if any, cannot be overridden.

The customer identification record of Figure 14–4, in which there are no overrides, can be established in memory by

```
CUST_REC    CREC    <>
```

The name CUST_REC can now be used to reference the customer structure in memory. It can be used conveniently as an input or output area. Since there are no overrides of the initial values in the template, the CID field contains 00000, the CNAME field contains "first and last names", and the CZIP field holds 99999-9999. Notice also that the other fields contain blanks. The CUST_REC structure is 72 bytes long.

The month conversion table needed for converting month codes of Figure 14–5 into the corresponding character names can be created as shown in Example 14–1. The name MONTH can be used to access the entire table of 12 names. This method of creating the table is superior to using a series of DBs because each DB must be exactly 9 bytes long, thus requiring padding with blanks on most values. Using a structure decreases the opportunity for errors.

The customer order structure of Figure 14–6 can be defined in memory as

```
CITEM    CORDER    <>
```

Notice that QTY and COST can be given new values. Since ITEMNO and DESCR were defined by use of the DUP operator, they cannot be overridden.

A realistic customer order entry record would likely consist of the constant customer identification information plus a series of customer order entries, as shown in Example 14–2. For this example, assume each customer order entry record is limited to a maximum of 10 item entries. This is a more

```
MONTH      MONTH_NAME    <'JANUARY'>
           MONTH_NAME    <'FEBRUARY'>
           MONTH_NAME    <'MARCH'>
           MONTH_NAME    <'APRIL'>
           MONTH_NAME    <'MAY'>
           MONTH_NAME    <'JUNE'>
           MONTH_NAME    <'JULY'>
           MONTH_NAME    <'AUGUST'>
           MONTH_NAME    <'SEPTEMBER'>
           MONTH_NAME    <'OCTOBER'>
           MONTH_NAME    <'NOVEMBER'>
           MONTH_NAME    <'DECEMBER'>
```

EXAMPLE 14–1 Defining the month conversion table

```
CUST_REC   CREC     <>
CITEMS     CORDER   <>
           CORDER   <>
           CORDER   <>
           CORDER   <>
           CORDER   <>
           CORDER   <>
           CORDER   <>
           CORDER   <>
           CORDER   <>
           CORDER   <>
```

EXAMPLE 14–2 Defining the customer order record

complex record that can be used for both input or output. See the record layout of Figure 14–7.

The complete record is now 242 bytes long. It consists of a fixed area of basic customer data and a table of up to 10 sets of order information.

14.9 REFERENCING STRUCTURES AND FIELDS

A structure in memory can be accessed by name just like any other data definition. Commonly, the address of a structure is required. For example:

```
        LEA     SI,CUST_REC
```

or

```
        LEA     DI,MONTH
```

```
CUST_REC   EQU   $
CID        DB    '00000'                       ; CUSTOMER ID NUMBER
CNAME      DB    'first and last names     '   ; NAMES ARE 25 BYTES
CADDR      DB    '                    '        ; ADDR IS 20 BYTES
CCITY      DB    '          '                  ; CITY IS 10 BYTES
CSTATE     DB    '  '                          ; STATE IS 2 BYTES
CZIP       DB    '99999-9999'                  ; ZIP IN PROPER FORMAT

CITEMS     EQU   $               ; TEN SETS OF THE FOLLOWING TABLE
ITEMNO     DB    4 DUP(?)        ; ITEM NUMBER ORDERED
DESCR      DB    10 DUP(?)       ; ITEM DESCRIPTION
QTY        DB    ?               ; QUANTITY ORDERED
COST       DW    ?               ; UNIT COST OF ITEM

ITEMNO     DB    4 DUP(?)        ; ITEM NUMBER ORDERED
DESCR      DB    10 DUP(?)       ; ITEM DESCRIPTION
QTY        DB    ?               ; QUANTITY ORDERED
COST       DW    ?               ; UNIT COST OF ITEM

.....  (7 MORE INSERTED HERE)

ITEMNO     DB    4 DUP(?)        ; ITEM NUMBER ORDERED
DESCR      DB    10 DUP(?)       ; ITEM DESCRIPTION
QTY        DB    ?               ; QUANTITY ORDERED
COST       DW    ?               ; UNIT COST OF ITEM
```

FIGURE 14–7   Complete customer order entry record

When the address of a structure is loaded into a register, the individual fields within a structure are accessible. However, each field referenced must be qualified by the structure name that contains it. The qualification syntax is

---

structure name.field name

The period separates the structure name from the field name.
      If the customer order structure is defined as

```
                    ORDER1    CORDER    <>
                    ORDER2    CORDER    <>
                    ORDER3    CORDER    <>
                    ORDER4    CORDER    <>
```

then, the following are valid

```
                    CORDER1.QTY
                    CORDER3.DESCR
                    CORDER4.ITEMNO
                    CORDER2.COST

                    MOV    AL,CORDER1.QTY

                    ADD    AX,CORDER2.COST
```

The offset address of CORDER2.COST is the sum of the offset address to the structure CORDER2 plus the offset to the field COST within CORDER2.

14.10 WORKING WITH TABLES WITHIN STRUCTURES

Consider once more the complete customer order entry record defined in Figure 14–7. Because it includes a table, the best way to handle this structure is to use the based-index addressing mode.

Register SI can be used to point to the indexed order entry table, which has a dimension of 10. That is, SI always points to the first byte of ITEMNO within the correct CITEMS structure. To reference the first table of order data, you can use

```
          LEA    SI,CITEMS
```

To move to the second set, merely add 17 bytes (the length of an order entry) to register SI.

Use register BX to move through a field within the table or to address specific fields within the table. For instance, suppose that the DESCR field is to be updated. This field is offset 4 bytes from the start of the structure CORDER. This can be coded as

```
    MOV    BX,4    ; SET BX TO POINT TO FIRST BYTE OF DESCR
```

The routine to move the new value into DESCR is

```
    MOV    [SI] [BX],AL    ; STORE NEXT BYTE INTO DESCR FIELD
```

The move routine continues to INC BX as it processes the remaining bytes of the new description.

Examine Figure 14–8 (PGM37.ASM on the program disk). It contains the preceding structure definitions for this customer order entry record. Assemble it and then experiment with some of your own based-indexed instructions. This program can be used as the basis for solving several of the Programming Problems in this chapter.

```
          PAGE    60,132
          TITLE   PGM37  Figure 14-8  Customer Order Entry Shell

;**************************************************************************
; PGM37      Title: Figure 14-8 Shell pgm for customer order entry   *
;                                                                    *
; Programmer: Vic Broquard                                           *
; Date Written:  6/11/88       Date Of Last Revision: 8/6/88         *
;                                                                    *
; Purpose: Definition of Customer Order Entry Record                 *
;                                                                    *
; Special Requirements: does no processing                          *
;                                                                    *
;**************************************************************************


;
; program data segment
;

PGMDA   SEGMENT

;
; structure templates
;

CREC    STRUC
CID     DB     '00000'                      ; CUSTOMER ID NUMBER
CNAME   DB     'first and last names    '   ; NAMES ARE 25 BYTES
CADDR   DB     '                    '       ; ADDR IS 20 BYTES
CCITY   DB     '          '                 ; CITY IS 10 BYTES
CSTATE  DB     '  '                         ; STATE IS 2 BYTES
CZIP    DB     '99999-9999'                 ; ZIP IN PROPER FORMAT
CREC    ENDS

CORDER  STRUC
ITEMNO  DB     '0000'         ; ITEM NUMBER ORDERED
DESCR   DB     '          '   ; ITEM DESCRIPTION
QTY     DB     0              ; QUANTITY ORDERED
COST    DW     0              ; UNIT COST OF ITEM
CORDER  ENDS


;
; customer order entry record
;

CUST_REC  CREC     <>
CITEMS    CORDER   <>
          CORDER   <>
```

FIGURE 14–8   Customer order entry shell (PGM37.ASM)

```
          CORDER    <>
          CORDER    <>
          CORDER    <>
          CORDER    <>
          CORDER    <>
          CORDER    <>
          CORDER    <>
          CORDER    <>

PGMDA  ENDS


;
; program code segment
;

PGMCD  SEGMENT

MAIN   PROC    FAR

; housekeeping section

          ASSUME  CS:PGMCD,DS:PGMDA,SS:PGMSTK

          MOV     AX,PGMDA    ; ESTABLISH ADDRESSABILITY
          MOV     DS,AX       ; TO PGMDA - THE PGM'S DATA SEGMENT

; main process section

; return to DOS section

          MOV     AL,0        ; SET 0 AS THE RETURN CODE FOR DOS
          MOV     AH,4CH      ; SET FOR DOS END PROCESS FUNCTION
          INT     21H         ; CALL DOS TO END PROGRAM

MAIN   ENDP

PGMCD  ENDS

;
; program stack segment
;

PGMSTK  SEGMENT PARA STACK 'STACK'

          DW      32 DUP (?)

PGMSTK  ENDS
          END     MAIN
```

FIGURE 14–8 continued

14.11 USING A STRUCTURE TO RETRIEVE PARAMETERS FROM THE STACK

A structure is often used in external subroutines to retrieve parameters that have been passed on the stack to the subroutine. In Figure 12–11 the CALCRTN was passed the addresses of QTY, COST, and TOTAL on the stack. The driver module saved register BP. Thus, the address of TOTAL is at [BP], the address of COST is at [BP + 2], and the address of QTY is at [BP + 4]. Rather than coding these relative addresses, a parameter structure can allow these parameters to be retrieved by a symbolic name. The structure can be defined as

```
PARMS          STRUCT
ADDR_TOTAL     DW?
ADDR_COST      DW?
ADDR_QTY       DW?
PARMS          ENDS
```

Such a parameter structure does not need to be actually defined in memory as other structures do. The real storage is already there. It is on the stack pointed to by register BP. Therefore, to use the structure, enter

```
MOV  SI, [BP].ADDR_TOTAL    ; SI = ADDRESS OF TOTAL
MOV  DI, [BP].ADDR_COST     ; DI = ADDRESS OF COST
MOV  BX, [BP].ADDR_QTY      ; BX = ADDRESS OF QTY
```

14.12 SUMMARY

There are seven addressing modes on the personal computer. This chapter presented the details of the more complex ones. These addressing modes combine to produce an effective address (EA). The speed of instruction execution is often dependent upon the time the computer needs to calculate the EA. The more complex forms take more time to evaluate, as you would expect. Yet, they offer real power in programming.

This power is reflected in data structures and arrays of data structures. Complete structure templates, or patterns, can be defined using the STRUC-ENDS pair of directives. The template can then be used to define actual structures or arrays of structures in memory as well as to provide initial values to the individual fields. The more complex addressing modes are required to access and process these structures.

14.13 REVIEW QUESTIONS

1. Outline the seven addressing modes of the personal computer. Give an example of each mode that has been shown in this chapter.

2. Will there be any significant difference in program execution if indexed addressing is used instead of based addressing? Justify your answer.

3. Explain the concept of the effective address. How is the EA calculated in the different addressing modes?

4. Discuss how to find the speed of your computer. What is the effect of the EA upon instruction execution speed? Should execution speed be a coding consideration?

5. What is a data structure? Give an example not shown in this chapter.

6. What is the difference between a structure template and a structure variable? Show by use of an example.

7. Outline the rules for creating a structure variable.

8. How are fields within a structure referenced directly by name? Give two examples.

9. What is a multilevel table? Give three examples of such tables that are not shown in this chapter.

10. How does based-indexed addressing relate to processing multilevel tables? Illustrate this by presenting an example not discussed in this chapter.

14.14 PRACTICE PROBLEMS

1. Review the sample programs shown in preceding chapters to find an example of each type of addressing mode except for based-index mode, which has not been used. Create an example of each type yourself. Be sure that you understand when to use each type.

2. You have been asked to create a bowling score program for four teams. The only data required are each team's final score in each of three games. First, show how this array can be defined in memory. Assume that each score is a 1-word binary number. Second, sketch the instructions to compute the total team scores. Do not use a STRUC-ENDS approach.

3. Reconsider the bowling score program you planned in Practice Problem 2. This time, code the basic array as a structure by using the STRUC-ENDS directives. Show the template and the variables as well as the instructions needed to total each team's score.

4. Using Figure 14–3, order the following instructions according to execution speed. Rank them from fastest to slowest in terms of EA determination only.

```
a)  MOV    AX,TOTAL [SI]
b)  MOV    AX,5
c)  ADD    AX,1
d)  MOV    AX,TOTAL+8
e)  MOV    AX,TOTAL [SI] [BX]
f)  MOV    AX,[SI] [BX] 8
g)  INC    AX
```

5. Code the structure template for an insurance claim program. The fields are

```
            POLICY NUMBER         5 BYTES
            FIRST NAME            8 BYTES
            LAST NAME             10 BYTES
            DATE                  6 BYTES (yymmdd)
            CLAIM COST            10 BYTES
```

   All fields have a starting value of blanks.

6. The following grocery store data structure has been defined.

```
            INVENT_REC    STRUC
            PROD_ID       DB     '00000'
            PROD_NAME     DB     '          '
            QTY_ON_HAND   DW        0
            PRICE         DW        0
            INVENT_REC    ENDS
```

   The store carries only three items:

12345	potatoes	23	1.59
14566	bananas	51	1.09
34562	lettuce	21	.89

   Code the structure variables to allocate these in memory.

7. Using the structure you created in Practice Problem 6, how might a program access the bananas entry?

14.15 PROGRAMMING PROBLEMS

1. Create a month conversion routine to convert the numeric month code into the character form, similar to the routines presented in Chapter 13. However, use a structure to define the actual table.

2. Create a customer order entry record master file. The records should consist of the fixed customer structure and one order structure. Use Figure 14–8 (PGM37.ASM on the program disk) as a

shell, since the structure definitions are provided. Note that, if desired, QTY and COST may be modified to be character fields, not binary fields.

The program should input a complete set of values for the fields and then output the record to the master file. You may use any approach desired to enter the information into the structure. However, full-screen data entry would work well for this problem. After several records have been written, end the program and examine the master file by using TYPE or a similar program. A suggestion: Use based-index addressing on the order section.

3. Modify the file you created in Programming Problem 2 to handle up to 10 sets of order information. The structures should be exactly as given in Figure 14–8.

You will need to know how many order sets are actually present in a record. This can be determined in several ways. One way is to test ITEMNO. If it contains 0000, then the entries from that point are not used. Alternatively, you may add a new byte field, NUM_ORDERS, to the main fixed structure. When the record is built, store the actual number of order entries used in it.

4. Create a grade book program that an instructor might use to record student grades. The relevant fields should be the student ID number, the student's name, and 10 test scores. Create a suitable template with appropriate fields. The scores should be stored in binary words for ease of access. There can be a maximum of 30 students in a class.

Enter the data for five students and store all data properly. Finally, calculate the average grade for each of these five students and display the results, showing only the student ID number, the name, and the average grade.

5. Now implement the file you created in Practice Problem 2. You have been asked to create a bowling score program for four teams. The only data required are each team's final score in each of three games.

Define a two-dimensional array in memory. Assume that each score is a 1-word binary number. For each of the four teams, input the three game scores (a number between 0 and 300). Calculate the total team scores and display the highest team score. Note that the relative position in the array should be the team identifier. That is, the first entry should be team 1, and so on.

15

Binary Coded Decimal Math

15.1 CHAPTER OBJECTIVES

In this chapter you will

1. Learn about another internal numeric format, binary coded decimals (BCD)

2. See how binary coded decimals are defined in storage

3. Learn to store and handle signs and decimal points

4. Understand the need for the adjustment process after any math operation performed on decimals

5. Learn about the adjustment instructions: AAA, AAS, AAM, AAD, DAA, DAS

6. Study the routines for performing the different mathematical operations on BCD forms

15.2 INTRODUCTION

Until now, all processing of mathematical applications in this text has been performed using the binary format. This is because of the greater execution speed and the relative ease of working with the binary form of math operations. However, microcomputers do have other internal numeric formats that can be used directly in math operations. This chapter will examine another form, binary coded decimal format (BCD).

You have seen that it is awkward to accept ASCII numeric fields from the user and then try to utilize ASCII digits in calculations. Not only must each ASCII field be carefully converted into a binary number field, but all answers must be converted back into ASCII character format. In addition, the numeric size of a number affects whether it is treated as a byte or word field. Many problems arise if the numbers become too large to be handled as a word.

Some of these difficulties are removed if the math is performed using the **binary coded decimal format (BCD),** which is base 10 arithmetic. The microassembler instruction set handles two forms of decimal math: **unpacked** and **packed** binary coded decimals.

You will find that in some texts and references unpacked decimals are sometimes called ASCII numbers and packed decimals are called BCD numbers or just decimals. To avoid confusion, we will use the terms *unpacked decimals* and *packed decimals* in our discussion.

15.3 UNPACKED DECIMALS

Frequently, business and financial calculations can be performed using decimal numbers, particularly when they do not require rounding. Consider the storage of the number 1,234 as it is normally entered via the keyboard. In ASCII digit format it consists of 4 bytes (in hex):

31 32 33 34H

A number in the unpacked BCD format stores only 1 decimal digit or nibble per byte, with the high-order nibble of each byte always being 0. Therefore, in unpacked format, the number 1,234 appears as

01 02 03 04H

To convert from ASCII digits into unpacked decimals, just use the **AND** instruction. This instruction changes the left 3 nibble in each ASCII byte into a 0 nibble by applying AND to each byte with a 0FH byte, leaving the decimal-digit nibbles alone.

To convert from unpacked form back into ASCII digit form, apply **OR** to each byte with a 30H byte, thus turning the 0 nibbles back into 3 nibbles. This process is much easier than converting the characters to binary and back again.

15.4 PACKED DECIMALS

The packed decimal form is the result of a further modification of the unpacked form. In the packing operation the needless 0 nibbles are removed and the decimal digits are placed together. In this case the number 1,234 now appears as (in hex):

```
12 34H
```

Notice that this form takes only half the number of bytes as the unpacked version.

15.5 VARIATIONS AND PROBLEMS

If decimal math were **only** this simple, we would have been using it instead of binary math all along. It isn't! One major problem is that the microassembler instruction set adds only 1 byte of a field at a time. Therefore, it is the programmer's responsibility to create the loops necessary to add two decimal fields together. This can be done in several ways. What's more, there is no common method for storing the sign of a number. As a result of all the possible variations, there are no real standards that deal with the storage of unpacked and packed decimal fields. What you have read so far in this chapter is perhaps the most common approach. You will find that the most significant variation lies in handling unpacked decimals. The number 1,234 can be stored forward or backward, as

```
01 02 03 04H
```

or

```
04 03 02 01H
```

according to how you intend to process the digits in your math routines. The first choice is probably the least confusing to beginning programmers, so it is the form this text will use.

Packed numbers, however, are usually stored in reverse sequence, similar to words and doublewords. Therefore, the number 1,234 is most often stored as

```
34 12H
```

To avoid confusion in the examples in this text, packed decimals will be stored in forward sequence. This will make them more readily recognized when displayed by the debugger. Stored in forward sequence, 1,234 appears in hex as

```
12 34H
```

15.6 DEFINING DECIMAL FIELDS

Defining Unpacked Decimals

How are decimal fields defined? With unpacked numbers, use the DB directive. Thus, to store 1,234 in ascending order, you enter

```
COUNT      DB    1,2,3,4
```

Remember that each of the numbers is converted into binary, giving 4 bytes:

```
01 02 03 04H
```

This is exactly what you want!

To store the digits in reverse sequence, enter

```
COUNT      DB    4,3,2,1
```

yielding

```
04 03 02 01H
```

Defining Packed Decimals

Packed decimals are created by using DT, the define ten-byte directive. This directive allocates 10 bytes of reverse-filled packed decimal numbers. If you enter

```
COUNT      DT    1234
```

the result is

```
34 12 00 00 00 00 00 00 00 00H
```

If you want to allocate storage for a packed number that does not occupy quite so many bytes, you must use the DB directive and enter the values as hex numbers:

```
COUNT      DB    34H,12H
```

This allocates 2 bytes: 34 12H.

15.7 HANDLING SIGNS AND DECIMAL POINTS

There is no standard method for handling signs when working with unpacked data. However, there is a standard for packed data. With packed decimals, after the digits are entered, another byte is added that contains the sign. If the sign is positive, the byte is 00H; if it's negative, the sign nibble is 80H. Thus, the following results.

```
COUNT1    DT    1234     ; yields: 34 12 00 00 00 00 00 00H
COUNT2    DT    -1234    ; yields: 34 12 00 00 00 00 00 80H
```

With unpacked data, the programmer must handle the effects of the sign and may use any scheme desired. However, this text will use the same sign convention for unpacked decimals as is used for packed decimals: 00H for positive and 80H for negative. Of course, this can cause some confusion. Suppose a field contains

80 12 34H

Does this represent 801,234 or does it represent –1,234? Only the programmer knows for sure how signs are handled or even if a number has a sign.

This is also true of numbers with decimal points. Of course, no decimal point character can actually be coded in either packed or unpacked format. The programmer must keep track of the decimal point manually. Here is a helpful hint: When processing fields with decimal points, **always** store the numbers as if they all had the same number of decimal places. Thus, the numbers 1.33, 1.2, and 1 are stored as

01 33H   01 20H   01 00H

This way, you always know where the decimal point is.

15.8   THE MATH PROBLEM

The problem of performing math with decimal numbers can be summed up by this statement: The computer performs only binary math. But it is possible to **adjust** the results to effectively simulate decimal math.

Suppose you want to add the contents of the COST to TOTAL fields. The current value in TOTAL is 4, and COST currently contains 6. Both fields are unpacked decimals:

TOTAL   00 04H
COST   06H

You must add the fields, beginning with the low-order digit and ending with the high-order digit. When the machine adds the first digits, the operation is

```
  04H
+06H
 ───
  0AH
```

However, you want 01 00H, or 10 in decimal, not the binary equivalent (0AH). In other words, after each byte math operation, you must adjust the result to get it back to the decimal number system.

15.9   THE ADJUST DECIMAL INSTRUCTIONS: AAA, AAS, AAM, AAD, DAA, DAS

Six instructions are available to handle this adjustment function:
For unpacked decimal fields:

	AAA	ASCII adjust after addition
	AAS	ASCII adjust after subtraction
	AAM	ASCII adjust after multiplication
	AAD	ASCII adjust before division

For packed decimal fields:

| | DAA | Decimal adjust after addition |
| | DAS | Decimal adjust after subtraction |

Examine the unpacked decimal instructions first. With the exception of AAD, these instructions adjust the value in register AL back into decimal form by putting the low-order digit in register AL and adding the carry, if any, to register AH. Thus, if the preceding addition of 04H and 06H took place in register AL, then the following results are generated:

	AH	AL
after the ADD	00H	0AH
after the AAA	01H	00H

15.10   ADDITION USING THE AAA INSTRUCTION

How does AAA work? First, the result of the addition **must** be in register AL; also, register AH should contain 00H. If the value in AL is already a decimal digit (0 through 9), then AAA clears the carry and auxiliary flags (CF and AF). If register AL does not contain a decimal digit, AAA converts the value in register AL into the appropriate low-order digit, increments register AH, and sets the carry and auxiliary flags (CF and AF). Several other flags have unpredictable values. These include SF, ZF, PF, and OF, but they have no impact on the computation.

Use the AAA instruction to convert the following binary results to their decimal format: 0BH, 0CH, 0DH, 0EH, and 0FH. You should get 01H, 02H, 03H, 04H, and 05H and a carry on each.

How can you actually add two multiple-byte fields? First, the units bytes must be added and adjusted and AL moved into the answer. When the tens bytes are added, the possible carry must also be added into the result. Thus, you must use the ADC, add with carry, instruction. Again, after adjusting, move AL into the tens position in the answer slot. This process is continued with the hundreds bytes and so on. The final action is to save register AH, since it may contain the last carry value. (This is the case if you add the single bytes 6 and 4.) This process should be placed in an addition loop.

In practice, many programmers construct one generalized routine that performs the addition for any set of fields. The code can be simplified if all fields are the same length. A 10-byte length is commonly used, but any consistent size works. The actual size is determined by the magnitude of the numbers, which varies from problem to problem.

```
; procedure to add two ten byte unpacked decimal fields
;         expects SI to contain units addr of first field
;                 DI to contain units addr of second field
;         result of addition replaces operand at DI

    MOV  CX,10     ; USE LENGTH OF FIELDS FOR NUMBER OF REPS
    CLC            ; CLEAR THE CARRY FLAG FOR USE IN ADC

ADD_LOOP:

    MOV  AH,0      ; CLEAR AH FOR ADDITION OF POSSIBLE CARRY
    MOV  AL,[SI]   ; INSERT FIRST FIELD'S DIGIT TO ADD
    ADC  AL,[DI]   ; ADD SECOND FIELD'S DIGIT
    AAA            ; ADJUST RESULT BACK INTO DECIMAL
    MOV  [DI],AL   ; STORE RESULT INTO ANSWER BYTE
    DEC  SI        ; POINT TO NEXT DIGIT
    DEC  DI        ; POINT TO NEXT DIGIT
    LOOP ADD_LOOP  ; REPEAT FOR ALL DIGITS


; ignore possible overflow into an 11th byte
```

FIGURE 15–1   The routine to add two 10-byte unpacked decimals

Figure 15–1 shows a routine that adds two 10-byte unpacked numbers. (Figure 15–1 shows part of PGM38.ASM on the program disk.) Upon entry, register SI points to the last byte of a 10-byte unpacked number. Register DI does likewise.

All registers to be used by the routine are saved and later restored. After loading register CX with the number of repetitions to perform—that is, with the length of the fields—the carry flag (CF) is cleared. This is done because all addition will be done with ADC, the add with carry instruction. Thus, there must be no inadvertent carry at the start. Remember, if this routine is inserted into a large program, the carry flag might well be set by other instructions before the ADD_DEC procedure is invoked. (Note that, under normal circumstances, the DEC SI and DEC DI instructions do not alter the carry flag setting.)

Further, since ADC uses the carry flag as an integral part of its operation, you must be extra careful not to use any other instructions within the loop that modify the carry flag. Specifically, avoid AND, OR, and XOR. All three modify the carry flag (CF). This is the reason for moving 0 into register AH instead of using XOR or AND to set AH to 00H. Moving 0 into register AH also forces any conversions to or from unpacked decimal form to be performed outside the loop itself.

If the fields are in ASCII character format—that is, if they contain left 3 nibbles—the numbers must be converted **before** entering the addition loop because the conversion using AND clears the carry flag. Likewise, if the answer is to be returned in ASCII character format, the conversion must be

```
; procedure to sub two ten byte unpacked decimal fields
;       expects SI to contain units addr of first field
;              DI to contain units addr of second field
;       result of subtraction replaces operand at DI

   MOV  CX,10     ; USE LENGTH OF FIELDS FOR NUMBER OF REPS
   CLC            ; CLEAR THE CARRY FLAG FOR USE IN SBB

SUB_LOOP:

   MOV  AH,0      ; CLEAR AH FOR POSSIBLE BORROW
   MOV  AL,[DI]   ; INSERT TOP FIELD'S DIGIT TO SUB
   SBB  AL,[SI]   ; SUB BOTTOM FIELD'S DIGIT
   AAS            ; ADJUST RESULT BACK INTO DECIMAL
   MOV  [DI],AL   ; STORE RESULT INTO ANSWER BYTE
   DEC  SI        ; POINT TO NEXT DIGIT
   DEC  DI        ; POINT TO NEXT DIGIT
   LOOP SUB_LOOP  ; REPEAT FOR ALL DIGITS


   ; ignore possible overflow into an 11th byte
```

FIGURE 15–2   Subtraction of two unpacked decimal numbers by using AAS

done on the entire result **after** the entire addition is complete because the OR clears the carry flag.

The routine ignores any possible overflow of the answer into an 11th byte. If you want to save that byte as well, then the answer area pointed to by DI must be 11 bytes long. To create this situation, insert the following instruction after the loop is complete:

```
     MOV  [DI],AH   ; SAVE THE FINAL CARRY BYTE
```

15.11 SUBTRACTION USING THE AAS INSTRUCTION

The procedure for subtraction is similar to the process for addition. Figure 15–2 shows a routine that subtracts two 10-byte unpacked decimal numbers. (It is part of PGM39.ASM on the program disk.) SBB, the subtract with borrow instruction, performs the subtraction.

15.12 HANDLING SIGNS DURING ADDITION AND SUBTRACTION OF UNPACKED DECIMALS

If the fields are signed, then problems arise. For addition, the following rules apply:

1. If both operands are positive, then use the ADD_DEC routine in Figure 15–1.

2. If they are both negative, then use the ADD_DEC routine, but do not actually add the first bytes of the fields. These bytes contain 80H to represent the sign.

3. If one operand is positive and the other negative, then use the SUB_DEC routine in Figure 15–2. In this case, subtract the smaller number from the larger number and insert the sign of the original larger number. For example:

$$
\begin{array}{ccc}
9 & 3 & -5 \\
+ -6 & + \ 6 & +3 \\
\hline
\end{array}
$$

become

$$
\begin{array}{ccc}
9 & 6 & +5 \\
- +6 & - +3 & - +3 \\
\hline
+3 & - \ 3 & - \ 2
\end{array}
$$

using the +	**using the –**	**using the –**
from the 9	**from the –6**	**from the –5**

Subtraction of signed fields is handled similarly.

A problem can arise when adding or subtracting signed numbers. When adding signed numbers, if both signs are the same, normal addition is required. If the signs are different, you need to subtract. Conversely, when subtracting signed numbers, if the signs are the same, you really need to add, and if the signs are different, then addition is also required. In all cases requiring addition, there is no real problem. However, if you try to subtract a larger signed number from a smaller number, it will generate incorrect results. For example,

$$
\begin{array}{r}
50 \\
-120 \\
\hline
-?30
\end{array}
\qquad \leftarrow \quad \textbf{an error}
$$

In order to compute correctly, the larger absolute value must be on the top.

$$
\begin{array}{r}
-120 \\
+ \ 50 \\
\hline
- \ 70
\end{array}
$$

Therefore, when you want to add or subtract signed numbers, you must first determine if you are really adding or subtracting. If you are going to subtract, you must then determine which field has the larger absolute value and subtract the smaller from the larger. (Practice Problem 4 illustrates this situation.)

15.13 MULTIPLICATION USING THE AAM INSTRUCTION

The difficulties of decimal multiplication can best be understood by examining how a simple multiplication problem is solved manually.

```
  1234        multiplicand
× 121         multiplier
  1234    ⎫   partial
  2468    ⎬   products
  1234    ⎭
149314        final product
```

Notice that each digit of the multiplier must, in turn, multiply the multiplicand to produce a partial product. However, notice that each successive partial product is, in effect, multiplied by 10, which shifts it over one decimal place. That is, the partial product 2,468 is really considered to be 24,680, and the partial product 1,234 is really 123,400. Then partial products are added to produce the product.

The multiplication process of necessity involves two loops. One creates the partial products and the other adds the partial products to get the final product.

When using multiplication, you must **always** use MUL, not IMUL, because IMUL treats each digit as if it were signed. They are not signed at this point.

The adjustment after the multiplication instruction is performed with AAM, the ASCII adjust after multiplication instruction. It converts register AL into the decimal product digit and puts any carry into register AH. This value in AH is stored in the partial answer slot as well, and the next digit's multiplication result is added to it.

Figure 15–3 (PGM40.ASM on the program disk) multiplies two ten byte unpacked fields. Because the product can contain as many as 20 digits, it is returned in a third unpacked field that is 20 bytes long.

The process involves two major loops. The outer loop (MUL_LOOP) multiplies the multiplicand field by successive digits of the multiplier field. In doing so, it invokes the inner loop (MUL_DIGIT), which multiplies the multiplicand by the units digit of the multiplier. Next, the resultant partial product is added to get the final product by using the ADD_DEC routine, which has been slightly modified to accommodate twenty byte fields. Then, the partial product field is reset to 0.

Every time the outer loop is repeated, the current offset within the partial product must be recalculated. Register DI, which points to the partial product field, is set to point to the last, or units, byte of the field. When the tens digit of the multiplier is used, DI points to the tens position in the partial product. Since the partial product is cleared, the units position contains 00H, as required.

Since this routine shown in Figure 15–3 is rather involved, you should assemble PGM40 and run it with your debugger. If you are using CODE

```
            PAGE    60,132
            TITLE   PGM40 Figure 15-3 UNPACKED DECIMAL MULTIPLICATION

;*************************************************************************
; PGM40      Title: Figure 15-3 Multiply two unpacked decimal fields  *
;                                                                      *
; Programmer: Vic Broquard                                            *
; Date Written:  6/11/88      Date Of Last Revision: 8/6/88           *
;                                                                      *
; Purpose: Routine to multiply unpacked numbers                       *
;                                                                      *
; Special Requirements: none                                          *
;                                                                      *
;*************************************************************************
; program code segment

PGMCD   SEGMENT

MAIN    PROC    FAR

; housekeeping section

        ASSUME  CS:PGMCD,DS:PGMDA,SS:PGMSTK

        MOV     AX,PGMDA     ; ESTABLISH ADDRESSABILITY
        MOV     DS,AX        ; TO PGMDA - THE PGM'S DATA SEGMENT

; main process section

; multiply PRICE by QTY, with the product in TOTCOST

        LEA     SI,PRICE+9   ; SI = ADDR OF UNITS BYTE OF PRICE
        LEA     BX,QTY+9     ; BX = ADDR OF UNITS BYTE OF QTY
        LEA     DI,TOTCOST+19 ; DI = ADDR OF UNITS BYTE OF PRODUCT RESULT

        CALL    MUL_DEC      ; ROUTINE TO MUL TWO TEN BYTE UNPACKED NUMBERS

; return to DOS section

        MOV     AL,0         ; SET 0 AS THE RETURN CODE FOR DOS
        MOV     AH,4CH       ; SET FOR DOS END PROCESS FUNCTION
        INT     21H          ; CALL DOS TO END PROGRAM

MAIN    ENDP
        SUBTTL    MULTIPLY TWO TEN BYTE UNPACKED DECIMAL NUMBERS
        PAGE
MUL_DEC PROC
```

FIGURE 15-3   Unpacked decimal multiplication (PGM40.ASM)

```
; procedure to multiply two ten byte unpacked decimal fields
;           expects SI to contain units addr of first field
;                   BX to contain units addr of second field
;                   DI to contain units addr of product field

    PUSH    AX          ; SAVE REGISTERS
    PUSH    BX
    PUSH    CX
    PUSH    DX
    PUSH    SI
    PUSH    DI

    MOV     SAVESI,SI   ; KEEP ORIGINAL BEGINNING ADDRESS OF FIELD1
    MOV     SAVEDI,DI   ; KEEP ORIGINAL BEGINNING ADDRESS OF PRODUCT FIELD

    MOV     DH,10       ; SET REPS TO THE NUMBER OF DIGITS IN THE MULTIPLIER
MUL_LOOP:

    MOV     DL,[BX]     ; DL = NEXT DIGIT OF FIELD2 TO USE IN MUL
    MOV     CX,10       ; USE LENGTH OF FIELDS FOR NUMBER OF REPS

; set offset for partial products

    MOV     AL,DH       ; GET CURRENT BYTE OFFSET OF FIELD2
    CBW
    ADD     AX,9        ; GET OFFSET ONTO PARTIAL PRODUCT FIELD
    LEA     DI,PART_PROD ; SET DI TO STARTS OF PARTIAL PRODUCT
    ADD     DI,AX       ; SET DI TO CORRECT OFFSET FOR THIS PARTIAL PRODUCT

MUL_DIGIT:

; SI -> FIELD1
; DI -> PART_PROD
; DL = MULTIPLIER DIGIT

    MOV     AL,[SI]     ; INSERT ANOTHER FIELD1 DIGIT TO MULTIPLY
    MUL     DL          ; MUL AL BY FIELD2 DIGIT - PROD IN AX
    AAM                 ; ADJUST RESULT BACK INTO DECIMAL
    ADD     AL,[DI]     ; ADD DIGIT TO PARTIAL PRODUCT
    AAA                 ; ADJUST BACK INTO DECIMAL

    MOV     [DI],AL     ; STORE RESULT INTO PARTIAL PRODUCT
    DEC     DI          ; POINT TO NEXT DIGIT IN PARTIAL PRODUCT
    MOV     [DI],AH     ; SAVE ANY CARRY FOR NEXT DIGIT IN MUL PARTIAL PROD

    DEC     SI          ; POINT TO NEXT DIGIT OF FIELD1

    LOOP    MUL_DIGIT   ; REPEAT FOR ALL DIGITS OF FIELD1

; now add in this partial product to actual product
```

FIGURE 15–3 continued   *(Continues)*

```
        LEA     SI,PART_PROD+19 ; SET SI TO UNITS OF PARTIAL PRODUCT
        MOV     DI,SAVEDI    ; SET DI TO UNITS OF FINAL PRODUCT


        CALL    ADD_DEC      ; ADD THIS PARTIAL PRODUCT TO FINAL PRODUCT

; reset for next digit of field2

------------------------------------------------------------------

        LEA     DI,PART_PROD+19 ; SET DI TO UNITS OF PARTIAL PROD

        CALL    ZERO_PP      ; RESET PARTIAL PRODUCT TO ZERO

        MOV     SI,SAVESI    ; RELOAD SI TO POINT TO UNITS OF FIELD1 FOR MUL
        DEC     BX           ; SET TO NEXT DIGIT IN FIELD2 TO MULTIPLY BY

        DEC     DH           ; ARE ALL DIGITS DONE?
        JNZ     MUL_LOOP     ; REPEAT FOR ALL DIGITS OF FIELD2
; ignore possible overflow into an 11th byte

        POP     DI           ; RESTORE REGISTERS
        POP     SI
        POP     DX
        POP     CX
        POP     BX
        POP     AX


        RET

MUL_DEC ENDP
        SUBTTL  ADD TWO TEN BYTE UNPACKED DECIMAL NUMBERS
        PAGE
ADD_DEC PROC

; procedure to add two ten byte unpacked decimal fields
;          expects SI to contain units addr of first field
;                  DI to contain units addr of second field
;          result of addition replaces operand at DI

        PUSH    AX           ; SAVE REGISTERS
        PUSH    SI
        PUSH    DI

        MOV     CX,20        ; USE LENGTH OF FIELDS FOR NUMBER OF REPS
        CLC                  ; CLEAR THE CARRY FLAG FOR USE IN ADC

ADD_LOOP:

        MOV     AH,0         ; CLEAR AH FOR ADDITION OF POSSIBLE CARRY
        MOV     AL,[SI]      ; INSERT FIRST FIELD'S DIGIT TO ADD
```

FIGURE 15–3   continued

```
        ADC     AL,[DI]   ; ADD SECOND FIELD'S DIGIT
        AAA               ; ADJUST RESULT BACK INTO DECIMAL

        MOV     [DI],AL   ; STORE RESULT INTO ANSWER BYTE
        DEC     SI        ; POINT TO NEXT DIGIT
        DEC     DI        ; POINT TO NEXT DIGIT

        LOOP    ADD_LOOP  ; REPEAT FOR ALL DIGITS

; ignore possible overflow into a 21st byte

        POP     DI        ; RESTORE REGISTERS
------------------------------------------------------------------------------
        POP     SI
        POP     AX

        RET
ADD_DEC ENDP
        SUBTTL    ZERO_PP ROUTINE TO ZERO PARTIAL PRODUCT FIELD
        PAGE
ZERO_PP PROC

; routine to reset all partial product digits to 00H
; assumes DI is set to units of partial product field

        PUSH    AX        ; SAVE REGISTERS
        PUSH    CX
        PUSH    DI

        MOV     CX,20     ; SET NUMBER OF REPS TO LENGTH OF PART_PROD
        MOV     AL,0      ; VALUE TO RESET PART_PROD = 0

ZERO_LOOP:

        MOV     [DI],AL   ; ZERO NEXT BYTE OF PARTIAL PRODUCT
        DEC     DI        ; POINT TO NEXT BYTE OF PART_PROD

        LOOP    ZERO_LOOP ; REPEAT FOR ALL OF PART_PROD

        POP     DI        ; RESTORE REGISTERS
        POP     CX
        POP     AX

        RET

ZERO_PP ENDP

PGMCD   ENDS
```

FIGURE 15–3   continued   *(Continues)*

```
; program data segment

PGMDA    SEGMENT

QTY      DB      0,0,0,0,0,0,0,1,2,1
PRICE    DB      0,0,0,0,0,0,1,2,3,4
TOTCOST  DB      20 DUP(0)

; work areas

PART_PROD DB     20 DUP(0)
SAVESI   DW      ?
SAVEDI   DW      ?

PGMDA    ENDS
; program stack segment

PGMSTK   SEGMENT PARA STACK 'STACK'

         DW      32 DUP (?)

PGMSTK   ENDS
         END
```

FIGURE 15-3   continued

VIEW, trace through the steps used to establish DS in the housekeeping section. Use a watch memory command such as

```
          WB        PART_PROD 20
          WB        TOTCUST 20
```

for both the partial product field and the final product. Use appropriate breakpoints and watch the action. Verify for yourself that the techniques work as described. Notice that the routine ignores any possible overflow conditions in the 20-byte product field and that the routine assumes that both numbers are positive.

15.14 DIVISION WITH THE AAD INSTRUCTION

The division process is even more complex than multiplication. In some cases it is easier to do the division as a repetitive subtraction process, especially if the divisor is more than one digit in size. Because of the level of complexity involved in using multidigit divisors, this text will describe only those cases in which the divisor consists of one decimal digit.

To divide, the adjustment must be done before the division instruction. AAD, the ASCII adjust before division instruction, actually converts 2 bytes of decimal data in register AX into 1 byte of binary data stored in register AL. The division, which is done in binary, yields a decimal quotient in register AL and a remainder in register AH.

Therefore, the process involves taking the first two digits of the dividend, adjusting for division, doing the actual division, and then storing the partial quotient. The next digit is loaded into register AL, keeping the prior remainder in register AH, and the entire process is repeated. Notice that this method utilizes the high-order decimal digits first, unlike the other math processes.

Figure 15–4 shows part of a division example. (This routine is part of PGM41.ASM on the program disk.) The dividend is a 5-byte field and the divisor is a 1-byte field. The quotient is stored in a 5-byte field as well. It is assumed that you will not attempt to divide by 0.

A final note: Do not use signed division when working with decimals, because the individual digits in the process are not signed numbers. The high-order nibble is always 0H.

```
SCORES    DB    0,0,3,8,0
NUM_TEST  DB    4
GRADE     DB    5 DUP(0)


; routine to divide unpacked decimal fields
;       expects SI to contain addr of five byte dividend
;               DI to contain addr of one byte divisor
;               BX to contain addr of five byte quotient

    LEA  SI,SCORES      ; SI = ADDR OF DIVIDEND
    LEA  DI,NUM_TEST    ; DI = ADDR OF DIVISOR
    LEA  BX,GRADE       ; ADDR OF ANSWER

    MOV  CX,5           ; USE LENGTH OF DIVIDEND FOR NUMBER OF REPS
    MOV  AH,0           ; CLEAR HIGH BYTE FOR FIRST DIGIT DIVISION

DIV_LOOP:

    MOV  AL,[SI]        ; INSERT FIRST FIELD'S DIGIT TO DIVIDE
    AAD
    DIV  BYTE PTR [DI]  ; DIVIDE ONE DIGIT
    MOV  [BX],AL        ; SAVE PARTIAL QUOTIENT
    INC  BX             ; POINT TO NEXT ANSWER SLOT
    INC  SI             ; POINT TO NEXT DIGIT IN DIVIDEND
    LOOP DIV_LOOP       ; REPEAT FOR NEXT DIGIT IN DIVIDEND
    .
    .
    .
```

FIGURE 15–4   Decimal division (part of PGM41.ASM)

15.15 WORKING WITH PACKED DECIMAL FIELDS

The workings of DAA, the decimal adjust after addition instruction, are parallel to those of the AAA instruction. DAA adjusts after the addition of a packed byte, which holds two decimal digits. The real problem is converting to and from packed format and ASCII characters.

Figure 15–5 (PGM42.ASM on the program disk) adds COST (a 4-byte field) to TOTAL (a 7-byte field). Both are in ASCII format. The program is organized into four functional routines: DEC_TO_PK, ZERO_PK, PK_DEC_ADD, and PK_TO_DEC.

The DEC_TO_PK routine converts any ASCII number into a packed decimal number stored in a ten-byte field. The process involves stripping the ASCII nibbles and moving the digits into adjacent bytes. For example:

31 32 33H

becomes

01 23H

in packed form. The routine first clears the ten-byte packed field. The basic conversion process converts a word of ASCII data at a time. The word is moved into register AH. Then, since the MOV word instruction has reversed the two bytes, registers AH and AL are exchanged via XCHG. Next, register AL is shifted logically to the left by 4 bits or 1 nibble, leaving the digit nibble in the high-order nibble position. Finally, register AX is shifted 4 bits logically to the left, removing the 3 nibble as well as moving the other digit into AH. The process is summarized by the following table.

in storage	MOV into AX	exchange	shift left AL	shift left AX
32 34H	34 32H	32 34H	32 40H	24 00H

The only complication arises if you must convert an odd number of digits. See the coding at the beginning of CNVRT_LOOP in Figure 15–5 to learn the special handling required in this situation.

The PK_DEC_ADD routine of Figure 15–5 is totally parallel to the unpacked addition routine in Figure 15–1. DAA, the packed decimal adjust after addition instruction, works like AAA.

The PK_TO_DEC conversion routine converts the ten-byte packed result back into an ASCII character string. The process begins by moving 1 byte of packed data into register AL. Notice that two digits are present in AL. They are separated by shifting AX 4 bits to the left. This puts the high-order digit in the correct position in AH. Next register AL must be shifted back 4 bits to put the low-order digit in its proper place. Finally, OR is applied to each register and 30H to insert the required ASCII code. This can be done more simply by entering

OR   AX,3030H

```
        PAGE    60,132
        TITLE   PGM42 Figure 15-5 PACKED DECIMAL ADDITION

;*************************************************************************
; PGM42      Title: Figure 15-5 Add two packed decimal fields       *
;                                                                    *
; Programmer: Vic Broquard                                          *
; Date Written:  6/11/88        Date Of Last Revision: 8/6/88       *
;                                                                    *
; Purpose: Add two packed fields, where original fields are ASCII digits *
;          and the result is also ASCII digits                      *
;                                                                    *
; Special Requirements: none                                        *
;                                                                    *
;*************************************************************************

; program code segment

PGMCD   SEGMENT

MAIN    PROC    FAR

; housekeeping section

    ASSUME  CS:PGMCD,DS:PGMDA,SS:PGMSTK

    MOV    AX,PGMDA        ; ESTABLISH ADDRESSABILITY
    MOV    DS,AX           ; TO PGMDA - THE PGM'S DATA SEGMENT

; main process section

;   convert cost into packed tenbyte

    LEA    DI,PCOST        ; POINT DI TO PACKED DECIMAL RESULT FIELD
    LEA    SI,COST         ; POINT SI TO ASCII DIGITS
    MOV    CX,4            ; SET LENGTH OF COST FIELD

    CALL   DEC_TO_PK       ; CONVERT FROM CHARACTER INTO PACKED TENBYTE

;   convert total into packed tenbyte

    LEA    DI,PTOTAL       ; POINT DI TO PACKED DECIMAL FIELD
    LEA    SI,TOTAL        ; POINT SI TO ASCII DIGITS
    MOV    CX,7            ; SET LENGTH OF TOTAL FIELD

    CALL   DEC_TO_PK       ; CONVERT FROM CHARACTER INTO PACKED TENBYTE

;   add two packed tenbytes
    LEA    SI,PCOST        ; DI POINTS TO ONE FIELD, SET SI TO THE OTHER
```

FIGURE 15–5 Packed decimal addition (PGM42.ASM)   *(Continues)*

```
        CALL  PK_DEC_ADD    ; ADD TWO PACKED TENBYTES

;  convert packed tenbyte back into ASCII character

------------------------------------------------------------------------

        LEA   DI,TOTAL     ; SET DI TO POINT TO THE ANSWER ASCII FIELD
        LEA   SI,PTOTAL    ; POINT SI TO THE PACKED DECIMAL FIELD
        MOV   CX,7         ; SET LENGTH OF ANSWER FIELD

        CALL  PK_TO_DEC    ; CONVERT PACKED TENBYTE ANSWER INTO CHARACTER

;  return to DOS section

        MOV   AL,0         ; SET 0 AS THE RETURN CODE FOR DOS
        MOV   AH,4CH       ; SET FOR DOS END PROCESS FUNCTION
        INT   21H          ; CALL DOS TO END PROGRAM

MAIN  ENDP
        SUBTTL    CONVERT FROM CHARACTER TO PACKED DECIMAL
        PAGE
DEC_TO_PK  PROC

;  expects SI -> ASCII character field
;          DI -> packed tenbyte field
;          CX = number of bytes in character field

        PUSH AX        ; SAVE REGISTERS
        PUSH CX
        PUSH SI
        PUSH DI

;  set to last byte of ASCII field

        MOV  BX,CX     ; SAVE LENGTH
        DEC  BX        ; CONVERT TO OFFSET
        ADD  SI,BX     ; POINT SI TO LAST BYTE OF ASCII CHARACTER FIELD
        DEC  SI        ; POINT TO LAST WORD IN CHARACTER FIELD
        ADD  DI,9      ; POINT DI TO LAST BYTE OF TENBYTE FIELD

;  clear tenbyte field

        CALL ZERO_PK   ; MOVES 00H TO TENBYTE FIELD

;  convert pairs of words into packed format

        MOV  BX,CX     ; BX = NUMBER OF BYTES TO DO

        MOV  CL,4      ; CL = # BITS TO SHIFT IN SHL = 1 NIBBLE
CNVRT_LOOP:
```

FIGURE 15–5 continued

```
        CMP  BX,1    ; IS THERE ONLY 1 BYTE LEFT OR MORE?
        JNE  DO_WORD ; NO, SO CONVERT A WORD

        INC  SI      ; OVERSHOT SO BACK UP, NOT A WORD THIS TIME
        MOV  AH,[SI] ; INSERT LAST ASCII DIGIT
        MOV  AL,0    ; INSERT 00H TO USE FOR HIGH ORDER BYTE
        JMP  CONTINUE
```

```
DO_WORD:

        MOV  AX,[SI] ; INSERT A TWO BYTES OF ASCII DATA - LOADED BACKWARDS
```

```
CONTINUE:

        XCHG AH,AL   ; REVERSE THE DIGITS
        SHL  AL,CL   ; MOVE 3 NIBBLE OUT OF AL
        SHL  AX,CL   ; MOVE 3 NIBBLE OUT OF AH AND DIGIT OF AL INTO AH

        MOV  [DI],AH ; SAVE PAIR OF PACKED DECIMAL DIGITS

        DEC  SI
        DEC  SI      ; POINT TO NEXT PAIR TO CONVERT
        DEC  DI      ; POINT TO NEXT ANSWER BYTE

        DEC  BX
        DEC  BX      ; REDUCE NUMBER TO DO BY THE 2 JUST DONE

        CMP  BX,0    ; ARE ALL DIGITS DONE?
        JG   CNVRT_LOOP ; REPEAT FOR NEXT DIGIT(S)

        POP  DI      ; RESTORE REGISTERS
        POP  SI
        POP  CX
        POP  AX

        RET

DEC_TO_PK  ENDP
        SUBTTL  ZERO_PK CLEARS A TENBYTE PACKED FIELD
        PAGE
ZERO_PK PROC

;   expects DI to point to tenbyte field

        PUSH AX      ; SAVE REGISTERS
        PUSH CX
        PUSH DI
        MOV  CX,10   ; SET NUMBER OF BYTES TO CLEAR
        MOV  AL,0    ; CLEAR BYTE IS 00H
```

FIGURE 15–5 continued   *(Continues)*

```
ZERO_IT:

    MOV [DI],AL   ; CLEAR THE BYTE
    DEC DI        ; POINT TO NEXT BYTE
    LOOP ZERO_IT  ; REPEAT FOR ALL BYTES

    POP  DI       ; RESTORE REGISTERS
    POP  CX
    POP  AX

    RET
```

```
ZERO_PK  ENDP
         SUBTTL    CONVERT PACKED TENBYTE INTO CHARACTER
         PAGE
PK_TO_DEC PROC

;   expects SI -> addr of tenbyte
;           DI -> addr of answer (character)
;           CX = number of bytes in answer field

    PUSH AX        ; SAVE REGISTERS
    PUSH BX
    PUSH CX
    PUSH SI
    PUSH DI

    ADD  SI,9      ; POINT TO UNITS BYTE IN PACKED FIELD
    ADD  DI,CX     ; POINT TO BYTE AFTER UNITS BYTE IN ANSWER
    DEC  DI        ; CORRECTED TO NOW POINT TO UNITS BYTE OF ANSWER
    MOV  BX,CX     ; BX = NUMBER OF BYTES TO DO IN ANSWER
    MOV  CL,4      ; NUMBER OF BITS TO SHIFT = 1 NIBBLE

CNVRT:

    MOV  AH,0      ; CLEAR AH FOR CONVERSION
    MOV  AL,[SI]   ; INSERT TWO DIGITS
    SHL  AX,CL     ; MOVE LEFT NIBBLE INTO AH RIGHT NIBBLE
    SHR  AL,CL     ; SHIFT AL NIBBLE INTO RIGHT NIBBLE POSITION

    OR   AL,30H    ; CONVERT INTO ASCII CHARACTER
    OR   AH,30H    ; CONVERT INTO ASCII CHARACTER

    MOV  [DI],AL   ; SAVE DIGIT INTO ANSWER
    DEC  DI        ; POINT TO NEXT DIGIT
    DEC  BX        ; DEC NUMBER TO DO
    CMP  BX,0      ; ANY MORE IN ANSWER?
    JE   DONE      ; NO, SO IGNORE LAST DIGIT
```

FIGURE 15–5 continued

```
    MOV  [DI],AH   ; SAVE SECOND DIGIT
    DEC  DI        ; POINT TO NEXT ANSWER SLOT
    DEC  BX        ; DEC NUMBER TO DO
    DEC  SI        ; POINT TO NEXT PAIR TO CONVERT

    CMP  BX,0      ; ANY MORE DIGITS TO DO?
    JG   CNVRT     ; YES, GO CONVERT THESE

DONE:

    POP  DI        ; RESTORE REGISTERS
    POP  SI
    POP  CX
    POP  BX
    POP  AX

--------------------------------------------------------------------------

    RET

PK_TO_DEC  ENDP
           SUBTTL  ADD TWO TENBYTE PACKED DECIMAL NUMBERS
           PAGE
PK_DEC_ADD PROC

; procedure to add two tenbyte packed decimal fields
;        expects SI to contain addr of first field
;                DI to contain addr of second field
;        result of addition replaces operand at DI

    PUSH AX        ; SAVE REGISTERS
    PUSH CX
    PUSH SI
    PUSH DI

    ADD  SI,9      ; SET TO UNITS BYTE
    ADD  DI,9      ; SET TO UNITS BYTE

    MOV  CX,10     ; USE LENGTH OF FIELDS FOR NUMBER OF REPS
    MOV  AH,0      ; CLEAR CARRY BYTE
    CLC            ; CLEAR THE CARRY FLAG FOR USE IN ADC

PK_ADD_LOOP:

    MOV  AL,[SI]   ; INSERT FIRST FIELD'S DIGITS TO ADD
    ADC  AL,[DI]   ; ADD SECOND FIELD'S DIGITS
    DAA            ; ADJUST RESULT BACK INTO DECIMAL
    MOV  [DI],AL   ; STORE RESULT INTO ANSWER BYTE
    DEC  SI        ; POINT TO NEXT SET OF DIGITS
    DEC  DI        ; POINT TO NEXT SET OF DIGITS
```

FIGURE 15–5 continued   *(Continues)*

```
        LOOP PK_ADD_LOOP ; REPEAT FOR ALL DIGITS

; ignore possible overflow into an 11th byte

        POP  DI      ; RESTORE REGISTERS
        POP  SI
        POP  CX
        POP  AX

        RET

PK_DEC_ADD ENDP

PGMCD  ENDS


; program data segment

PGMDA  SEGMENT

--------------------------------------------------------------------------

COST   DB   '1','2','3','4'
TOTAL  DB   '0','0','0','1','1','1','1'

PCOST  DT   ?
PTOTAL DT   ?

PGMDA  ENDS


; program stack segment

PGMSTK SEGMENT PARA STACK 'STACK'

       DW    32 DUP (?)

PGMSTK ENDS
       END
```

FIGURE 15–5 continued

PGM42 is well worth running with the debugger. You should watch the fields: COST, TOTAL, PCOST, and PTOTAL. Initially, main procedure break-points can be established on each instruction just after every CALL. In this way you can monitor the effects. Also, to solidify your understanding of the process, trace through the instructions that actually convert and pack the ASCII numbers.

The workings of DAS, the decimal adjust after subtraction instruction, are parallel to those of AAS. If you are subtracting packed decimals, use DAS.

There are no instructions for adjusting packed decimal multiplication or division. You will have to create your own algorithms for these if you want to multiply or divide packed fields.

15.16 COMMON TECHNIQUES FOR DECIMAL MATH

Programmers who must often deal with decimal math write several generalized routines. Depending upon accuracy and the number of digits required, thye write a routine that converts from ASCII characters to unpacked decimals and stores the results in either a ten-byte field or a twenty-byte field. Then the four math routines all operate similarly, utilizing either ten-byte or twenty-byte fields. These programmers also write a routine to convert the fields back into ASCII character form. Some programmers add some editing routines to insert or strip appropriate editing characters such as commas, decimal points, pluses or minuses, and dollar signs.

15.17 SUMMARY

There are two forms of binary coded decimals (BCDs): unpacked decimals and packed decimals. You have seen how both appear in memory and how such fields are actually defined, often using the define 10-byte directive, DT. Special consideration must be given to storing and processing the sign as well as any decimal points.

After every math operation, the byte result must be adjusted to convert the binary result back into decimal. This is accomplished using the "adjust" set of instructions: AAA, AAS, AAM, AAD, DAA, and DAS.

Although coding BCD math operations is more complex than coding similar operations, generalized routines can easily be created to do BCD addition, subtraction, and so on. With careful design you can have just one routine to add any size of BCD number.

15.18 REVIEW QUESTIONS

1. Explain the differences between unpacked and packed decimal formats. Show how the number 23,467 is stored in both formats.

2. How are signs handled? Illustrate how the packed and unpacked forms of the following numbers are defined in the data area and appear in memory.
    a) +12,345
    b) −12,345
    c) −56
    d) 889
    e) −945,845

3.   How are decimal points handled in the decimal format? Assume
     that the values in parts a through e are allowable user entries for
     the field COST. How do you store each of these in memory?
     a) 12   b) 34.5   c) 55.67   d) 12,678.9   e) 1,568.09

4.   Assume you are to add two signed unpacked numbers. Discuss the
     rules you need to follow. Would the rules change if the data were
     packed decimals?

5.   Why does every math operation upon any decimal field need to be
     adjusted after the operation is complete? Provide illustrations that
     explain your answer.

6.   Outline the adjustment procedure you need to use when adding
     two 7-byte unpacked decimals.

7.   Outline the adjustment procedure you need to use when subtract-
     ing two 6-byte packed decimals.

8.   Outline the adjustment procedure you need to use when multiply-
     ing two 8-byte unpacked decimals.

9.   Why is the adjustment for division done before instead of after the
     operation? Show what steps need to be done to divide unpacked
     decimals.

10. Outline what steps are needed to divide a 10-byte field by a divisor
     that is 4 bytes long. Show how your procedure works by using a
     sample division problem. Use only unpacked decimals.

15.19 PRACTICE PROBLEMS

1.   Code the instructions needed to add the following unsigned
     unpacked decimal fields:

```
SALES_AMT    DB    3,4,6,8,9,0
TOTAL_AMT    DB    0,0,6,7,8,3,0,5
```

2.   Code the instructions needed to add the following signed unpacked
     decimal fields:

```
QTY_ON_HAND    DB    0,0,3,5,6
ORDERS_IN      DB    80H,3,5
```

3.   Code the instructions needed to subtract the following unsigned
     unpacked decimals:

```
TOTAL_SALES    DB    6 DUP(?)
REFUNDS        DB    5 DUP(?)
```

4. Code the instructions needed to subtract the following signed unpacked decimals:

    ```
    TOTAL_PROFITS   DB    8 DUP(?)
    TOTAL_LOSSES    DB    8 DUP(?)
    ```

    The sign will be in the first byte and is 80H if negative.

5. Code the instructions needed to multiply the following unsigned unpacked decimal fields:

    ```
    UNIT_PRICE      DB    6 DUP(?)
    NUM_SOLD        DB    3 DUP(?)
    ```

    The result should be placed in TOTAL, which is defined as

    ```
    TOTAL           DB    9 DUP(?)
    ```

6. Code the instructions needed to divide the following unsigned unpacked decimals:

    ```
    TOTAL_GRADE     DB    4 DUP(?)
    NUM_TESTS       DB    ?
    ```

7. Code the instructions needed to add the following unsigned packed decimal fields:

    ```
    SALES_AMT     DT    ?
    TOTAL_AMT     DT    ?
    ```

8. Code the instructions needed to subtract the following unsigned packed decimals:

    ```
    TOTAL_SALES   DB    6 DUP(?)
    REFUNDS       DB    5 DUP(?)
    ```

15.20 PROGRAMMING PROBLEMS

1. Write a routine that converts ASCII character number fields into unpacked decimals of 10 bytes. Upon entry into the routine, the contents of the registers are as follows.

    SI   address of the first byte of the ASCII string

    DI   address of the first byte of the ten-byte string

    CX   length of the ASCII string

    Be sure to clear the ten-byte field before moving unpacked data into it.

2. Write a routine to add signed unpacked 10-byte decimals. The sign should always be the first byte of the 10-byte field. A 00H byte is a plus sign and a 80H byte is a minus sign. Thus, the maximum number of digits is nine. Assume that registers SI and DI contain the addresses of the two signed 10-byte unpacked decimal fields. Place the answer into the field pointed to by register DI. Hint: Use PGM31.ASM or PGM32.ASM on your program disk as a shell. Use the signs of the two operands to determine which program is appropriate. Test your routine on the following values:

    ```
    1245        1133       1233       123444
    +345       + -99     + 745     +   -123
    ─────      ─────     ─────     ────────
    1590        1034       -488      -123567
    ```

3. Write a routine to subtract two unsigned 10-byte packed decimal fields pointed to by registers SI and DI. The result should replace the field pointed to by DI. This time, store the digits in reverse sequence. For example, 1,234 should be stored in hex as

    ```
    34 12 00 00 00 00 00 00 00 00
    ```

    Use the DAS instruction to adjust the answer bytes.

4. Write a routine to multiply two signed unpacked 10-byte fields. Registers SI and DI should point to the two fields. Register BX points to the 20-byte answer field. The signs should be defined exactly as in Programming Problem 2. Therefore, you must really multiply only 9 bytes × 9 bytes in the worst case.

5. In Programming Problem 3 in Chapter 8, you created a child's math helper program. Rework this program so it uses only decimal math. Limit the size of any divisor to one digit.

6. In Programming Problem 1 in Chapter 8, you created a trip fuel economy analyzer. Rework the program so it uses only decimal math. Be careful of the multiple-byte division.

16

Processing Random-Access Files and Advanced File Functions

16.1 CHAPTER OBJECTIVES

In this chapter you will

1. Learn the basics of random file processing
2. Study how a file index is created and maintained
3. Learn to perform inquiry, addition, update, and file deletion processes
4. Examine several advanced DOS file functions for the file handle method, the FCB method, and for manipulating subdirectories.

16.2 INTRODUCTION

Although sequential file processing is frequently needed, there are many applications that require the ability to directly access one specific record in a file. Among these applications are inquiry processing, file maintenance and update programs, and order entry systems. With each of these, records must be read, added, updated, or written randomly.

From a conceptual point of view, the processing of sequential and random-access files is completely different. However, at the DOS level, there is almost no difference between processing a file sequentially or randomly. This is particularly true when using the file handle approach to file processing rather than the older FCB (file control block) method.

16.3   CHARACTERISTICS OF A RANDOM FILE

The first general characteristic of a **random-access file,** or one that is to be accessed randomly, is that all the records are **fixed** in length. The second is that there must be a way of identifying each specific record, a **key.** Consider the significance of these two characteristics.

A record in a random file is retrieved by its **relative record number.** The first record in a file is number 0, the second is 1, and so on. All records must be fixed in length for each successive record to be located by using a relative record number. Suppose that all records in a particular file are 40 bytes long. To find relative record number 2, the file is positioned to byte 80 (2 × 40); the next 40 bytes are relative record 2.

If the file contained variable-length records, it would be impossible to know precisely where relative record 2 began; the length used to calculate the starting location would be different for each record. (With variable-length records the length of the record is usually stored as the first byte or two of the record.)

The usual approach to finding the starting point of direct-access files with variable-length records is to write physical records that are always the maximum length any record could ever be. In other words, the unused bytes are padded with 00H to fill out the physical record. In this way, relative records can be located because they are really fixed as far as the file is concerned, yet the actual length is present in the first byte or word.

An alternative approach to handling variable-length records is to create an index table that provides the relative record number and corresponding offset from the beginning of the file to the desired record.

16.4   RANDOM-FILE KEYS

Records are identified by some form of unique key. These keys are generally one of two types: a **relative record number** or a **characteristic field.** A social security number, client number, and part number are examples of characteristic fields. Through appropriate processing, however, the distinctive character field key ultimately becomes associated with a relative record number.

16.5   INQUIRY PROCESSING WITH RELATIVE RECORD NUMBERS

Inquiry processing with relative record number keys is extremely simple. First, position the file to the specific record needed. This is done by finding the record's offset from the beginning of the file, the relative record number multiplied by the fixed record length. Second, read the record. This method works as long as the relative record number is known in advance.

Using a relative record number as the key presents a significant problem: Relative record numbers seldom have any meaning to the application. For example, suppose a customer wants to know the status of his or her account and provides the account number. But what is the relative record number of the record in the file? From the information provided, you just don't know.

16.6 INQUIRY PROCESSING WITH UNIQUE FIELD KEYS

The use of keys that represent unique fields is a more common way around the problem of meaningless data in a record. Assume a client number is to be used as the associated key field. How can a random-access file be accessed when only a client number is given? Create an **index,** or conversion table, that contains all the client numbers and their associated relative record numbers. The index makes the relative record number readily available for random processing of the file.

Depending on the size or number of entries in the file, the indexes and their associated fields may be stored as a separate file. In some cases involving small master files, the first few relative records in the file itself may be reserved to store the index for that file.

To find a record for a specific client, the client number key that matches that key in the index is input and the corresponding relative record number is obtained. Then, that number is multiplied by the fixed length of the records, the file is positioned to the calculated offset, and the record is read.

Speed of execution is usually a major problem when using an index. If the keys in the index are in random order, then the matching process must compare against each entry until a match is found. To improve on this comparison process, the index is often sorted into numeric or alphabetic order. This sorting makes the matching process go faster because not all entries must be compared. There are a number of quick lookup techniques available—binary searches for numeric keys and alphabetic searches by individual letters in the key, for example.

16.7 ADDING NEW RECORDS TO A RANDOM-ACCESS FILE

Adding records to an existing random-access file is quite easy. All you do is move to the very end of the file and write the new record. Determining the new key is more of a problem, however.

A new relative record number can be determined in a number of ways. One way is to divide the total length of the file by the fixed record length, thus yielding the relative record number.

If an index is used, adding records can present some problems. Suppose that a new client record with a key of client number 3214 is added. The new relative record number must be combined with the client number to form a new entry in the index. If the index is stored randomly, there is no problem: Just create the new index and place it at the end of the index file. However, if the index has been sorted for speed, the new index entry must be created and then inserted in its proper position. (This is a somewhat tedious task at best.) Then the modified index must be saved.

16.8 UPDATING RECORDS IN A RANDOM-ACCESS FILE

To update a record, input the key and position the file to that record. Read the required record into memory and update it. Then write the record back out to the same position. The new information overwrites the older data. No changes are made to the index if an index is used.

16.9 DELETING RECORDS FROM A RANDOM-ACCESS FILE

The ability to delete records from a random-access file is perhaps the most difficult random-access function to implement. More is involved than just removing a record from a file.

Suppose you have a file that contains three records, each 100 bytes in length and with relative record numbers of 0, 1, and 2. Now assume that relative record 1 is to be deleted. How can this record be physically removed? First, all records up to the relative record number to be deleted are copied to a new, reorganized file. Second, all records after the relative record number to be deleted are copied to the new file. Third, the original file is deleted and the new file is given the name of the original file. The record is now deleted.

But wait! What has happened to the relative record numbers? In this example record number 2 has now become record number 1. Since the records are accessed by their keys—their relative record numbers—and since all the relative record numbers beyond 0 are now different, accessing random records becomes a major problem.

If the records are accessed by an index that correlates an ASCII key to the relative record numbers, the relative record numbers in the index can be reorganized. This makes the fact that a record has been deleted irrelevant to the numbering.

An alternative solution to the problem of how to delete a record from a random-access file lies in marking records as being deleted, but not physically removing them. With this approach, a unique value, often 00H or FFH, is inserted into one or more fields in the record to indicate that the record has been deleted. Now all subsequent accessing functions must check for the presence of the unique value during all forms of access: inquiry, addition, updating, and deletion. If a deleted record is accessed during an inquiry, updating, or deletion action, the program produces an error message similar to ERROR—RECORD HAS BEEN DELETED.

Since flagging deleted records rather than physically removing them is much easier to implement than the other method, it is often the choice for random files. Periodically, a reorganization program removes all flagged records and updates the index.

16.10 THE INTERRUPTS FOR RANDOM-ACCESS FILE PROCESSING

All the DOS interrupts required for random-access file processing were discussed in Chapter 9. These include open file handle (3DH), create file handle (3CH), close file handle (3EH), and read from file handle (3FH). Refer to Chapter 9 or Appendix C to review these interrupts.

16.11 RANDOM-ACCESS FILE PROCESSING CASE STUDY

The client's account file is an excellent example to illustrate the principles of random-access file processing. Assume that an account record contains three fields: client number (4 digits), client name (20 digits), and balance due (8 digits). The fixed record length is 32 bytes.

The main menu display is

```
1. INQUIRY TO A CLIENT'S BALANCE
2. ADD A NEW CLIENT
3. QUIT
ENTER CHOICE:
```

The inquiry function reads records directly; the add function adds new records to the file randomly.

The index is always stored in relative record 0, or the first record in the file. Each 6-byte entry in the index contains the client number (4 bytes) plus the relative record number stored as a word. Since each fixed-length record is 32 bytes, the index can hold only five records ($5 \times 6 = 30$ bytes).

Any attempt to add more clients than five results in an error message. (This restriction can be avoided in many ways, but we are keeping the index intentionally small for illustrative purposes.)

Figure 16–1 shows the top-down design of the program. Each module is an external subroutine. The number of modules benefits the program in that

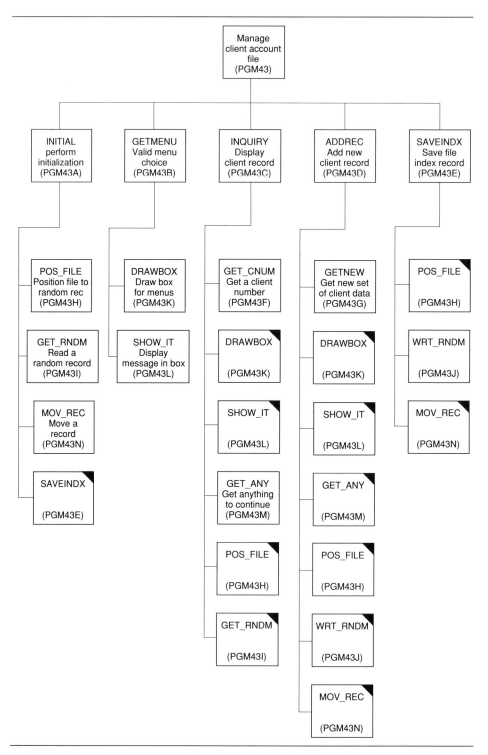

FIGURE 16–1   Top-down design for random processing of client files

each consists of only a page or two of code and each has only one major function to perform.

For simplicity, all parameters that are needed by the external routines have been made external in scope and are defined in the driver module.

The initial module and its subordinate modules open the random client account file and retrieve the index record, if the file exists. If the file does not exist, the module creates the file and prepares the index record.

The POS_FILE module is used frequently. It accepts a random relative record number and positions the file to the correct record.

The inquiry module inputs the client number desired, verifies that there is such a client in the file, positions the file to that client number, inputs the record, and displays the data.

The ADDREC module inputs a set of new client data, positions the file to the end of the file, writes the new data, and updates the index.

When QUIT is chosen, the main module sees that the new index is written to the file before the file is closed.

Figure 16–2 shows a partial listing of this program. Shown are the key portions that handle the random file-processing steps. The complete program is on the program disk as PGM43.ASM and PGM43A.ASM through PGM43N.ASM. In addition, there is a linker file, PGM43.LNK, to help you with the linking process. We strongly recommend that you assemble the program and experiment with it.

There is one potential problem with the logic in the INITIAL module. Can you spot it? Exactly how does the program determine if the master file exists or not? If the create file function is used and the file exists, DOS assumes that you wish to write over the existing file. DOS sets the file size to 0 bytes and positions itself to the beginning of the file. If this happens, all data in the file are lost. If the file does not exist and an attempt is made to open the nonexistent file, an error results. DOS provides the easiest solution to this problem by providing a find file function.

```
DRIVER PROGRAM: partial listing - FOR CLIENTS MASTER FILE - PGM43


    ......   ......

; this module controls the Client's Account Program operation
; See Figure 16-1 for the Top Down Design of this program

DGROUP GROUP   PGMDA
       EXTRN   INITIAL:FAR,GETMENU:FAR,INQUIRY:FAR,ADDREC:FAR,SAVEINDX:FAR
       PUBLIC  INDEX,FILE_HANDLE,CHOICE,REC_SIZE,CLIENT,KEY,COLOR,BOX_COLOR


    ......   .....
```

FIGURE 16–2   Partial listing of random client account file program
(PGM43.ASM and subroutines PGM43A through PGM43N)   *(Continues)*

```
INDEX       DB  32 DUP(0)    ; RANDOM FILE INDEX CONSISTING OF 5 ENTRIES:
                             ; 4 BYTE CLIENT NUM + WORD OF REL REC NUM

FILE_HANDLE DW  0
REC_SIZE    DW  32

CHOICE      DB  0

KEY         DW  0
CLIENT      LABEL BYTE
CLIENT_NO   DB  4  DUP('0')
CLIENT NM   DB  20 DUP(' ')
CLIENT_AMT  DB  8  DUP(' ')

COLOR       DB  4AH          ; GREEN ON RED
BOX_COLOR   DB  49H          ; BLUE ON RED

    ....  ....




MAIN   PROC  FAR

       ASSUME CS:PGMCD,DS:DGROUP,SS:PGMSTK

       MOV    AX,DGROUP   ; GET ADDRESSABILITY
       MOV    DS,AX       ; TO THE DATA GROUP

       CALL   INITIAL     ; PERFORM INITIAL STEPS: OPEN/CREATE FILE, GET INDEX

       CMP    AX,0        ; ANY ERRORS?
       JNE    DONE        ; YES, ABORT

       CALL   GETMENU     ; GET A VALID MENU CHOICE

MAIN_LOOP:

       CMP    CHOICE,3    ; CHOICE TO QUIT?
-------------------------------------------------------------------------------
       JE     FINISH_UP   ; YES, PERFORM FINAL STEPS

       CMP    CHOICE,1    ; IS IT INQUIRE?
       JE     DOINQ       ; YES, CALL INQUIRY ROUTINE

       CMP    CHOICE,2    ; IS IT ADD?
       JE     DOADD       ; YES, CALL ADD ROUTINE

CONTINUE:
```

FIGURE 16–2   continued

```
        CALL    GETMENU    ; GET A VALID MENU CHOICE

        JMP     MAIN_LOOP  ; REPEAT UNTIL CHOICE QUIT


DOINQ:
        CALL    INQUIRY    ; PERFORM THE INQUIRY PROCESS
        JMP     CONTINUE
DOADD:
        CALL    ADDREC     ; PERFORM ADD A RECORD PROCESS
        JMP     CONTINUE

FINISH_UP:
        CALL    SAVEINDX   ; SAVE UPDATED INDEX

; close the random file

        MOV     BX,FILE_HANDLE
        MOV     AH,3EH     ; SET FOR DOS CLOSE
        INT     21H        ; CALL DOS TO CLOSE FILE

; ignore any errors

DONE:
        MOV     AX,4C00H   ; SET FOR END PROCESS FUNCTION WITH RC = 0
        INT     21H        ; CALL DOS TO END

MAIN    ENDP
        ....    ....



INITIAL: partial listing - PGM43A Fig 16-2 OPEN/CREATE FILE, SET INDEX

        .....   ....

        EXTRN   POS_FILE:FAR,GET_RNDM:FAR,SAVEINDX:FAR,MOV_REC:FAR
        EXTRN   INDEX:BYTE,FILE_HANDLE:WORD,CLIENT:BYTE,KEY:WORD
        PUBLIC  INITIAL

        ...     ....
--------------------------------------------------------------------------

FILENM  DB      'A:CLIENTS.DAT',00H
ERRMSG  DB      'FILE CANNOT BE OPENED - PROGRAM ABORTED$'
DUMMY   DB      32 DUP(0)

        ...     ...
```

FIGURE 16–2   continued   *(Continues)*

```
INITIAL PROC    FAR

; this routine handles the beginning steps and returns a success or
; failure code in AX

        ....   .....
        CALL   EXIST    ; DOES RANDOM FILE EXIST YET?

        CMP    AX,0     ; WAS FILE FOUND?
        JE     GOTFILE  ; YES, FILE EXISTS, SO OPEN IT

        CALL   CREATE   ; NO FILE, SO CREATE A FILE

        JMP    AFTER_OPEN

GOTFILE:

        CALL   OPEN     ; OPENS AN EXISTING FILE

AFTER_OPEN:

        CMP    AX,0     ; OPENED OK?
        JNE    DONE     ; NO, SO RETURN

        CALL   FINDBYTES ; FIND OUT IF THE FILE HAS 0 BYTES = NO INDEX
        CMP    AX,0     ; ANY BYTES IN FILE?
        JA     GET_INDEX ; YES, SO GO LOAD INDEX RECORD
        CMP    DX,0     ; ANY BYTES IN FILE, CHECK HIGH ORDER PART
        JA     GET_INDEX ; YES, SO GO LOAD INDEX RECORD

        CALL   BUILD    ; BUILD FIRST INDEX FOR NEW FILE
        MOV    AX,0     ; SET ALL OK ERROR CODE

        JMP    DONE

GET_INDEX:

        CALL READ_INDEX ; INPUT INDEX TABLE
        MOV    AX,0     ; SET ALL OK ERROR CODE

DONE:
        ...   ....

        RET

------------------------------------------------------------------------

        ...   ....
```

FIGURE 16–2 continued

```
EXIST   PROC

; this routine determines if the random file already exists or not

        LEA    DX,FILENM ; DX POINTS TO THE FILE NAME
        XOR    CX,CX     ; SET FILE ATTRIBUTES
        MOV    AH,4EH    ; SET FOR FIND FILE
        INT    21H       ; CALL DOS TO FIND THE FILE
        RET
EXIST   ENDP




CREATE  PROC

; this routine creates a new random file

        LEA    DX,FILENM ; ADDR OF ASCIIZ STRING FILE NAME
        XOR    CX,CX     ; SET FILE ATTRIBUTES
        CLC              ; CLEAR THE CARRY FLAG - SET IF ERROR OCCURS
        MOV    AH,3CH    ; DOS CREATE FILE HANDLE
        INT    21H       ; CALL DOS TO OPEN/CREATE THE FILE
        JC     CREATE_ER ; IF ERRORS, GO SHOW ERROR MSG

        MOV    FILE_HANDLE,AX ; SAVE THE FILE HANDLE

        MOV    AX,00H    ; SET ERROR CODE AS OK
        JMP    CR_RET    ; AND RETURN

CREATE_ER:
        CALL   SHOWERR   ; DISPLAY ERROR MESSAGE AND IGNORE IT -
        MOV    AX,01H    ; SET ERROR CODE FOR DRIVER TO ABORT

CR_RET:
        RET
CREATE  ENDP




OPEN    PROC

; this routine opens an existing random file

        LEA    DX,FILENM ; DX = ADDR OF FILE NAME
        XOR    CX,CX     ; SET ATTRIBUTES
        CLC              ; CLEAR CARRY FLAG FOR ERROR INDICATION
```

FIGURE 16–2   continued   *(Continues)*

```
        MOV    AX,3D02H  ; SET FOR OPEN FUNCTION AS READ/WRITE
        INT    21H       ; CALL DOS TO OPEN FILE
        JC     OPEN_ER   ; OPEN FAILED, SHOW ERROR MSG

        MOV    FILE_HANDLE,AX ; SAVE THE FILE HANDLE

        MOV    AX,00H    ; SET ERROR CODE AS OK
        JMP    OPEN_RET  ; AND RETURN

OPEN_ER:
        CALL   SHOWERR   ; DISPLAY ERROR MESSAGE AND IGNORE IT -
        MOV    AX,01H    ; SET ERROR CODE FOR DRIVER TO ABORT

OPEN_RET:
        RET
OPEN    ENDP



FINDBYTES PROC

; this routine returns the file size in bytes in regs DX:AX

        MOV    AX,4202H  ; SET FOR MOVE FILE PTR TO EOF
        MOV    BX,FILE_HANDLE
        MOV    CX,0      ; SET FOR NO OFFSET BEYOND EOF
        MOV    DX,0
        INT    21H       ; CALL DOS TO SUPPLY FILE LENGTH

        RET
FINDBYTES ENDP



BUILD   PROC

; this routine builds an index table for a new file

        LEA    DI,INDEX  ; DI = ADDR OF INDEX
        MOV    CX,32     ; CX = NUMBER OF BYTES TO MOVE
        LEA    SI,DUMMY  ; SI = ADDR OF DUMMY INDEX TABLE
        CALL   MOV_REC   ; MOVE NEW INDEX INTO REAL INDEX TABLE

        CALL   SAVEINDX  ; WRITE INITIAL INDEX TO FILE

        RET
BUILD   ENDP
```

FIGURE 16-2   continued

```
READ_INDEX PROC

; this routine inputs the index table of an existing random file

        MOV     KEY,0       ; KEY = CURRENT RECORD NUMBER TO POSITION TO
        CALL    POS_FILE    ; POSITION FILE TO REL RECORD NUM IN KEY
        CALL    GET_RNDM    ; READ RANDOM RECORD INTO CLIENT

        LEA     DI,INDEX    ; DI -> INDEX TABLE
        LEA     SI,CLIENT   ; SI -> INPUT RECORD
        MOV     CX,32       ; CX = NUMBER OF BYTES TO MOVE
        CALL    MOV_REC     ; MOVE INDEX RECORD INTO THE INDEX TABLE

        RET

READ_INDEX ENDP




INQUIRY: partial listing - PGM43C Figure 16-2 PERFORM AN INQUIRY

        .....  .....

        EXTRN   CLIENT:BYTE,KEY:WORD
        EXTRN   DRAWBOX:FAR,GET_CNUM:FAR,POS_FILE:FAR
        EXTRN   GET_ANY:FAR,SHOW_IT:FAR,GET_RNDM:FAR
        PUBLIC  INQUIRY

        ...... ......

; this routine performs an inquiry on the random file

        ...... ......

; get the client number to view

        CALL    GET_CNUM    ; GET A VALID CLIENT NUMBER
                            ; KEY IS FILLED WITH RELATIVE RECORD NUM
        CMP     KEY,0       ; KEY IS 0 IF INVALID KEY FOUND
        JE      DONE        ; YES, SO ABORT PROCESS

; retrieve client data

        CALL    POS_FILE    ; POSITION RANDOM FILE TO KEY
        CALL    GET_RNDM    ; READ THE DESIRED RECORD

; display client data
```

FIGURE 16–2   continued   *(Continues)*

```
        CALL   DRAWBOX   ; REDRAW BOX FOR DISPLAY
        CALL   DISPLAY   ; SHOW CLIENT RECORD IN BOX

        ...... ......


        RET
```

```
        ...... ......




ADDREC: partial listing - PGM43D Fig 16-2 ADD A NEW CLIENT RECORD

        ...... ......

; this routine adds a new client record to the random file

        CALL   GETSLOT   ; GET NEXT SLOT IN THE INDEX
        CMP    KEY,0     ; ANY SLOT FOUND? DI = ADDR OF SLOT
        JE     ERR_RET   ; NO, FULL, PRINT ERROR AND LEAVE

        CALL   GETNEW    ; GET NEW CLIENT IN CLIENT RECORD AREA

; insert client number into index slot - DI = ADDR SLOT

        LEA    SI,CLIENT ; SI = ADDR OF CLIENT NUMBER
        MOV    CX,4      ; SET NUMBER OF BYTES TO MOVE
        CALL   MOV_REC   ; MOVE CLIENT NUMBER INTO INDEX TABLE

        CALL   POS_FILE  ; POSITION FILE TO NEW KEY POSITION
        CALL   WRT_RDM   ; WRITE RANDOM RECORD TO FILE
        JMP    DONE      ; AND LEAVE

ERR_RET:
        CALL   DRAWBOX   ; CLEAR SCREEN AND MAKE BOX

        MOV    DX,0A0CH  ; SET COORDINATES 10,12
        LEA    BX,MSG1   ; ADDR OF ERR MSG1
        MOV    AX,56     ; LENGTH OG MSG
        CALL   SHOW_IT   ; DISPLAY LINE IN BOX

        MOV    DX,0C1AH  ; SET COORDINATES 12,26
        LEA    BX,MSG2   ; ADDR OF ERR MSG2
        MOV    AX,26     ; LENGTH OF MSG
        CALL   SHOW_IT   ; DISPLAY LINE IN BOX
        CALL   GET_ANY   ; GET ANYTHING TO CONTINUE
```

FIGURE 16–2   continued

```
        RET
        ...... ......




POS_FILE: partial listing - PGM43H Fig 16-2 POSITION FILE TO RANDOM RECORD


        ...... ......

        EXTRN  FILE_HANDLE:WORD,REC_SIZE:WORD,KEY:WORD
        PUBLIC POS_FILE

--------------------------------------------------------------------------

        ...... ......

; this routine positions the random file to the desired relative record
; it assumes that KEY = relative record number desired

        MOV    AX,KEY     ; AX = KEY
        MUL    REC_SIZE   ; CALC THE OFFSET TO THIS RECORD
        MOV    CX,DX      ; SAVE HIGH ORDER PART
        MOV    DX,AX      ; SAVE LOW ORDER PART
        MOV    AX,4200H   ; SET FOR MOVE FILE POINTER FROM BEGINNING OF FILE
        MOV    BX,FILE_HANDLE
        INT    21H        ; CALL DOS TO POSITION FILE

; ignore any possible errors for now, since program should only ask for
; valid relative records, unless index gets corrupted

        RET
        ...... ......




GET_RNDM: partial listing - PGM43I Fig 16-2 READ A RANDOM RECORD


        ...... ......

        EXTRN  CLIENT:BYTE,FILE_HANDLE:WORD,REC_SIZE:WORD
        PUBLIC GET_RNDM


        ...... ......

; this routine reads a random record from the client file
; it assumes that the file is positioned to the correct record

        MOV    BX,FILE_HANDLE
```

FIGURE 16–2   continued   *(Continues)*

```
        MOV    AH,3FH      ; SET FOR READ FILE
        MOV    CX,REC_SIZE ; CX = NUMBER OF BYTES TO READ
        LEA    DX,CLIENT   ; DX = ADDR INPUT RECORD AREA
        INT    21H         ; CALL DOS TO INPUT THE RECORD

; ignore possible errors for now

        RET
        ......  ......




WRT_RDM: partial listing - PGM43J Fig 16-2 WRITE A RANDOM RECORD


        ......  ......

        EXTRN  CLIENT:BYTE,FILE_HANDLE:WORD,REC_SIZE:WORD
        PUBLIC WRT_RDM

--------------------------------------------------------------------------

        ......  ......

; this routine writes a random record to the client file
; it assumes that the file is positioned at the desired record

        MOV    BX,FILE_HANDLE
        MOV    AH,40H              ; SET FOR WRITE FILE
        LEA    DX,CLIENT
        MOV    CX,REC_SIZE
        INT    21H         ; CALL DOS TO WRITE THE RECORD

; ignore any errors for now

        RET
        ......  ......
```

FIGURE 16-2   continued

16.12 ADVANCED DOS FILE FUNCTIONS

There are several advanced DOS file features that can be very useful. Each is invoked by the standard INT 21H. These advanced functions include

File Handle Functions

Function	Name
4EH	Find first, start file search
4FH	Continue search

2FH	Get DTA address
5BH	Create new file
46H	Force handle duplication

Subdirectory Functions

Function	Name
47H	Get current directory
3BH	Change current directory (CHDIR)
39H	Make subdirectory (MKDIR)
3AH	Remove subdirectory (RMDIR)

Disk Functions

Function	Name
0EH	Select current drive
19H	Report current drive
1BH	Get FAT information, current drive
1CH	Get FAT information, any drive
36H	Get disk free space
0DH	Reset disk

FCB Functions

Function	Name
24H	Set random record field, FCB
21H	Read random file record, FCB
27H	Read random file records, FCB
22H	Write random file record, FCB
28H	Write random file records, FCB
11H	Search for first matching file, FCB
12H	Search for next matching file, FCB
23H	Get file size, FCB

16.13 ADDITIONAL FILE HANDLE FUNCTIONS

In all the additional file handle functions, register AH contains the function code. All are invoked by INT 21H.

Find First, Start File Search: Function 4EH

This function searches the disk for the first file(s) that match the given file specification(s). The file specifications may include the usual wildcards: ? and *.

Register DS:DX points to the ASCIIZ string that gives the file path and specifications. Sample ASCIIZ strings are

```
A:TEST.DAT

C:\UTILS\TEST?.EXE

B:WORK

C:\WP\MASTER\*.TXT
```

Remember that such strings must end with a byte of 00H.

Register CL contains the file attribute specification used in the search. Unless you are searching for a special hidden file, a system file, or other special type of file, the byte is coded as 00H.

Register CF is not used to indicate an error; register AX is used for this purpose. If a file is found, AX is set to 00H; if there is no file, AX is set to 02H.

If a file is found, then the current disk transfer area (DTA) is filled with 43 bytes of information:

offset	length	contents
0	21	used by DOS for find next function (4FH)
21	1	attribute byte for found file
22	2	time stamp of file
24	2	date stamp of file
26	4	file size in bytes
30	13	ASCIIZ string file specifier of file

Continue File Search: Function 4FH

This function continues the search for the next file that matches the file specification in the search begun with function 4EH.

Register DS:DX points to the formatted DTA given by the results of function 4EH. (The address of the DTA can be retrieved using function 2FH.) If a file is found, register AX contains 00H and the DTA has the 43 bytes that identify this file. If no more files are found, AX contains 18.

Get DTA Address: Function 2FH

The address of the current DTA used by DOS is returned in register ES:BX. Since register ES is used, the program's normal data segment register, DS, is not affected. (The DTA can be set by use of function 1AH; see Chapter 10 for details about file control blocks.)

Create New File: Function 5BH

This function differs from the normal file create function, 3CH, in one major aspect. If there is an existing file, function 5BH returns an error code and does not open the file. Therefore, this function is purely a new file creation process. Its biggest use is in applications in which existing files should not be disturbed but new files should be opened.

Register DS:DX points to the ASCIIZ string file specification, and CL contains the file attribute byte. The carry flag, CF, is set if there has been an error and register AX then holds the error code.

Force File Handle Duplication: Function 46H

This function forces a duplication of an existing file handle. If the original file is open, the function closes it. All actions to the original handle are rerouted to the new handle. This is useful for redirection of I/O. For example, suppose you want to "capture" the display output and store it in a data file on disk. The new file is opened and then function 46H is used, forcing closure of the display file and redirecting all I/O to the disk file.

Register BX contains the old file handle and CX contains the new file handle. When the function is completed, the file handle in register CX refers to the same file as BX; it should be used for I/O operations. The error code 06, invalid file handle, is returned in register AX.

16.14 SUBDIRECTORY FUNCTIONS

Get Current Directory: Function 47H

This function returns the name of the directory in use in an ASCIIZ string form. Register DL contains the drive number (0 = default drive, 1 = drive A:, 3 = drive C:, and so on). Register DS:SI points to a 64-byte area in which DOS will return the ASCIIZ string directory name. It does not contain the drive letter, the colon, or the initial backslash from the root in path names. The only error code, 15 (invalid drive), is returned in register AX.

Change Current Directory: Function 3BH

This function, like the DOS command CHDIR, changes the current directory. The address of the ASCIIZ string containing the path name to the new directory is contained in register DS:DX. If the path is not found, register AX contains error code 3.

Make Subdirectory: Function 39H

This function, like the DOS command MKDIR, creates a new subdirectory. Register DS:DX points to the ASCIIZ string containing the complete path name of the new subdirectory. If the path is not found, register AX contains error code 3.

Remove Subdirectory: Function 3AH

This function, like the DOS command RMDIR, removes a subdirectory. Register DS:DX contains the address of the ASCIIZ string that contains the full path name of the subdirectory to delete. If the path is not found, register AX contains error code 3. If the directory cannot be deleted—if there are files within it, for example, or it is the current directory—AX contains 5.

16.15 ADDITIONAL DISK FUNCTIONS

Select Current Drive: Function 0EH

Function 0EH selects the current default drive and also reports the total number of drives installed. Register DL contains the drive number to select (0 = A:, 1 = B:, and so on). On return, register AL contains the number of drives installed. The current drive can be a number from 0 to one less than the maximum number of drives installed. The drive number can be converted into the drive letter by adding 41H, the value of the letter "A," to the drive number.

Report Current Drive: Function 19H

The current drive number is returned in register AL. Drive number 0 is drive A:, and so on.

Get FAT Information on Current Drive: Function 1BH

This function provides useful information about the current drive. The following table shows what the registers contain on return.

AL	the number of sectors per cluster (1 for SS, 2 for DS)
CX	the number of bytes on a sector (512)
DX	the total number of clusters on the disk
DS:BX	points to a byte in a DOS work area containing the FAT ID

Note that DS is modified; therefore, you must PUSH DS before using this function. After using the FAT ID, you must POP DS.

Get FAT Information on Any Drive: Function 1CH

This function works like function 1BH except that register DL contains the drive number to be reported. The current drive is 0, drive A: is 1, and so on. The results are identical to function 1BH.

Get Free Disk Space: Function 36H

Much useful information on the disk is returned by this function. Register DL contains the drive number, where the current drive is 0, drive A: is 1, and so on. An invalid drive error results in register AX containing FFFFH. If the drive is valid, the registers contain the values shown in the following table.

AX   the number of sectors per cluster

CX   the number of bytes per sector (512)

BX   the number of available clusters

DX   the total number of clusters

Reset Disk: Function 0DH

Using this function resets the disk and flushes all file buffers without closing the files. Therefore, all output files should be closed before using this function.

16.16 ADDITIONAL FCB FUNCTIONS

Set Random Record Field: Function 24H

This function enables a program to switch from sequential file operation into random file processing mode. Register DS:DX contains the address of the FCB. The function sets the random FCB record field to the equivalent point given in the current block and record fields.

Read Random File Record: Function 21H

One record is read from a random file. Register DS:DX points to the FCB. The random record in the FCB field must be set to the desired record before the function is invoked. The record is read into the current DTA. Register AL contains the same codes as a sequential FCB read:

0   successful read

1   EOF and no more data

2   insufficient DTA space

3   EOF and some data

Read Random File Records: Function 27H

This function reads one or more direct records into the DTA. Register CX contains the number of records to be read and must not be 0. DS:DX points to the FCB. When complete, CX is set to contain the total number of records, full and partial, that were actually input. All other results are as in function 21H.

Write Random File Record: Function 22H

This function writes one record to a random file from the DAT. Register DS:DX must point to the FCB, and the random record number in the FCB field must point to the desired file position. Register AL contains the return codes found in a sequential write:

0   successful write

1   disk is full

2   DTA contains insufficient space

Write Random File Records: Function 28H

This function writes one or more successive records to the file, beginning at the random position contained in the FCB. Register CX contains the number of records to write. If CX contains 0, then DOS assumes that this write is now the new EOF marker and that some records have been deleted from the very end of the file. DS:DX points to the FCB. All other features are the same as in function 22H.

Search for First Matching File: Function 11H

This function searches the system for the first file matching the given file specification contained in the FCB. Register DS:DX points to the FCB. The filename can contain wildcards: ? and *. Register AL contains 00H if successful and FFH if no files are found. If files are found, the FCB contains information that is needed if the search is to continue with function 12H.

Search for Next Matching File: Function 12H

This function continues the file search started with function 11H. All parameters and results are as given in function 11H.

Get File Size: Function 23H

This function returns the size of the file in terms of the total number of records it contains. The FCB should be opened and contain the correct record size. (If that size is 1 byte, then the returned value is the file size in bytes.) Register DS:DX points to the FCB. If the function is successful, the file size is inserted into the FCB and AL contains 0. If the operation fails, AL contains FFH.

16.17   SUMMARY

Random files generally have fixed-length records or data structures. Specific records are identified by either a relative record number or by a key field. All key fields have a corresponding relative record number. Usually, an index table holds the key values and their record numbers.

Random access to files is gained by positioning the file to the relative record desired. This is done by multiplying the relative record number desired by the length of the record or data structure. Once the file has been positioned, the specific record can be read or rewritten.

New records can be added to the end of the file by positioning the file to the end and writing the new record. If an index is used to access the file, then a new entry must be placed into the index. Eventually, the new index data must be written as well.

There are numerous other advanced DOS file-handling functions. For the file handle method, several new functions permit searching for specific files. There are several subdirectory functions to change, create, and remove subdirectories. The older FCB method offers parallel advanced functions similar to those of the file handle method.

16.18 REVIEW QUESTIONS

1. How does the file organization of a random file differ from that of a sequential file?

2. What is meant by a relative record number? How can it be used to find a specific record?

3. What is the difference between a relative record number and a characteristic field key? How can a characteristic key be used to locate a specific record?

4. Describe the method for adding new records to a random file whose keys are social security numbers.

5. Describe the method for modifying records in a random file whose keys are social security numbers.

6. Describe the method for reading a specific record in a random file whose keys are social security numbers.

7. Describe the method for deleting records from a random file whose keys are social security numbers.

8. What is a subdirectory? What DOS services are available for processing subdirectories? When would each be used?

9. Consider the file search function. Describe three applications that can use these services.

10. What applications can you think of for the force handle duplication function?

11. In what type of applications can the FAT functions (1BH and 1CH) be used?

16.19 PRACTICE PROBLEMS

Practice Problems 1 through 5 use the following random-access file:

```
filename;    B:MASTER.DAT
filehandle;  MASTER    DW ?

records;     MAST_REC   LABEL BYTE
             STOCK_NUM  DW    ?
             PART_DESC  DB    15 DUP(?)
             QTY        DB    ?
             UNIT_COST  DB    4 DUP(?)
             LOCATION   DB    6 DUP(?)
```

Assume that the file has been properly opened for read/write operations.

1. Code the instructions to add a new MAST_REC to the random file. Assume that the STOCK_NUM key contains the relative record number.

2. Code the instructions needed to update the random file. Assume that the user has entered the key into a field called NEW_KEY, which is 1 word long. Position the file to the record, retrieve the record, call UPDATE_IT, and then update the file. Do not code the UPDATE_IT procedure; assume that this routine updates any needed fields in MAST_REC. Again, the STOCK_NUM key contains the relative record number.

3. The user has requested that the relative record number contained in DEL_KEY, 1 word long, should be deleted. A deleted record should be indicated when all fields except STOCK_NUM contain ASCII 0 digits. Code the instructions to delete the requested record. STOCK_NUM contains the relative record number.

4. An inquiry program calls a routine named FIND_REC. The routine is passed the word FIND_KEY. Code the instructions to find the record and fill up MAST_REC. The key is the relative record number.

5. Management has decided that the stock numbers can no longer be the relative record number; they should be the company product ID. Design an index structure and a scheme to store the index table on the disk. The company expects to have 1,000 separate parts.

6. Code the instructions to change the default drive to drive B:.

7. Code the instructions to change the current directory to C:\WORK.

8. Code the instructions to create a new subdirectory, C:\TEMP\WORK.

9. Code the instructions to remove the subdirectory A:\TEMP\MODS.

10. Code the instructions to find if the file B:TEST.DAT exists.

16.20 PROGRAMMING PROBLEMS

1. Modify the case study in section 16.11 to include another menu option, UPDATE A CLIENT. You will need to make slight modifications to the menu modules and add a new subprocess to the program to handle the file update.

2. Modify the case study in section 16.11 to use a sorted index. The index should be sorted into client number order. (Optional: Use a binary search procedure for the table lookup function, if you are familiar with that technique.)

3. Modify the case study in section 16.11 to store the index in a separate file, CLIENTS.IDX. Caution: Either or both the .DAT and .IDX files may or may not be present on the disk.

4. Using your word processor, create three files:

file name	contains
TEST1.DAT	HI FROM TEST1.DAT
TEST2.DAT	HI FROM TEST2.DAT
TEST3.DAT	HI FROM TEST3.DAT

   Now write a program that searches for the first file that matches the specification TEST?.DAT. Display that file and repeat the process until there are no more files that match the specification.

5. Write two programs to carry out the following series of DOS commands.

   Program 1:

   ```
   B:
   MD \WORK
   MD \WORK\TEST1
   CD \WORK\TEST1
   ```

   Program 2:

   ```
   B:
   CD \
   RD \WORK\TEST1
   RD \WORK
   ```

6. Write a program that reports the drive statistics associated with the driver you are using as the default drive. Use function 1BH and display the results returned with appropriate column headings. You may ignore the FAT ID.

7. Many word processing programs have a file maintenance function. The routine you will write in this exercise is the beginning of such a program. Write a routine that finds all the files on the current default drive (and path). The filenames and their sizes should be displayed at the top of the screen. Display a menu permitting the user to rename, delete, or view any of the displayed files. Hint: Use the find file function (4EH and 4FH), using the filename *.*.

17

The Macro Language

17.1 CHAPTER OBJECTIVES

In this chapter you will

1. Study the two forms for preprocessing assembler programs: the macro language and the conditional assembly directives

2. Learn how to define a macro, how to call or invoke a macro, and how to determine what the macro expansion will be

3. Examine the components of a macro definition, including the MACRO, ENDM, LOCAL, and EXITM directives; parameters and arguments; and the three source listing controls that affect macro listings

4. Learn how to use the INCLUDE feature to include macro libraries and other assembler coding

5. Learn the rules for parameter and argument substitution along with the substitute operator (&)

6. See how macros can be redefined, nested, and recursive

7. Learn about the conditional assembly directives for repeating blocks of coding and for creating various IF-THEN-ELSE constructs

8. Learn how to create a DO-WHILE structured programming macro

17.2 INTRODUCTION

One of the powerful features of any language is the ability to preprocess the source program file, creating or modifying the source code before it is actually assembled or compiled. Such preprocessing might involve including source code that is extracted from other files, adding some new instructions that are not originally in the source program, or creating alternative coding that depends upon the current values of some variable. In the microassembler language this preprocessing takes two forms: the **macro language** and the **conditional assembly** feature. These facilities are the most complex features of the assembler language. You will examine some of the key macro facilities first and then some that make up the conditional assembly.

A macro invocation is an assembler instruction that copies, brings in, or creates assembler source instructions. The simplest macros merely drop predetermined assembler instructions at the place in the program where the macro is invoked. Fancier macros first substitute values into the assembler instructions to be created; others drop different assembler instructions, depending on the values that are supplied to the macro.

The macro language is basically a preprocessor—that is, it operates on the source program statements before actual assembly into machine instructions occurs. First, the assembler examines the source program and locates all macros and expands them into the assembler instructions that they generate. Then, on a second pass through the source program, the assembler proceeds with the normal assembly process and translates what is currently in the newly generated source program into machine instructions.

When writing microassembler programs, the use of macros provides a number of benefits. First, macros tend to simplify or reduce the amount of code in the source program (although they increase the amount of actual machine instructions in the program). When used properly, they tend to produce more readable programs. Macros can also reduce the chance of error caused by including the same set of code in many places within the source program. In addressing this problem, macros provide an alternative to the use of external subroutines.

17.3 MACRO TERMS

A **macro** is a block of coding that will be referenced, used, or invoked later on in the actual source program. It is initialized by the **MACRO directive** and ended by the **ENDM** (end macro) **directive.** The coding within the macro is referred to as the **macro definition.** A macro generates no actual instructions until it is called, or invoked. When the macro is invoked, the contents of the macro are placed at the indicated position in the source program. These dropped-in, or generated, instructions are known as the **macro generation** or **macro expansion.**

17.4 THE MACRO DEFINITION AND CALLING THE MACRO

A macro definition is created by using the MACRO-ENDM directives. The syntax of the MACRO directive is

name   MACRO   parameter1,parameter2, . . .

The name must be unique, and it must be a valid symbolic name. It is used to invoke the macro proper. The parameters are optional and permit variables to be passed to the macro. We will discuss the passing of variables later in the chapter.

The syntax of the end macro directive is

ENDM

It has no operands or field names.

To invoke or call a macro, enter the name used on the MACRO directive as the instruction operations code. If parameters are expected, they are coded as the operands. The syntax is

name   argument1,argument2, . . .

One common macro saves the most frequently used registers: AX, BX, CX, DX, SI, and DI. We'll call this macro SAVEREGS. Example 17–1 represents how the directives can be stated.

In this example the coding within the macro definition, SAVEREGS, is inserted in two places: at the start of MOVESUB and at the start of CALCSUB. Notice the difference between the use of a macro and the use of a subroutine. The subroutine replaces repetitive coding by a single set of code and links to it whenever required. Macros insert the same set of code wherever called, multiple times if required. The use of macros increases the actual size of the program; the use of subroutines decreases the actual program size. However, the benefits and convenience of macros are often worth the additional program size. In the case of the SAVEREGS macro, it is not necessary to code the six PUSH instructions every time a new procedure is entered.

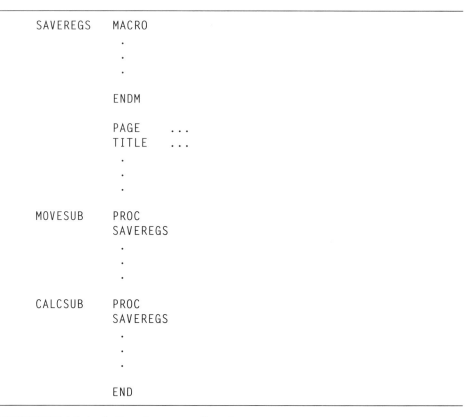

```
SAVEREGS    MACRO
              .
              .
              .
            ENDM
            PAGE    ...
            TITLE   ...
              .
              .
              .
MOVESUB     PROC
            SAVEREGS
              .
              .
              .
CALCSUB     PROC
            SAVEREGS
              .
              .
              .
            END
```

EXAMPLE 17–1 Coding the macro directives

Of course, to be fully useful, there must be a macro to restore the contents of the registers. This macro, RESTOREGS, reverses the process and pops the six registers.

Four principles apply to macro definition:

- All macro definitions must physically occur before they are invoked by the source program. The standard practice followed by many assembler programmers is to include all macro definitions at the very beginning of the program.

- Macros can be nested as deeply as required. That is, one macro can call another macro. The only restriction is that sufficient main storage be available for the assembler.

- Macros can be recursive. That is, one macro can invoke itself from within itself. You will learn how this works later in the chapter.

- Macros can redefine themselves. After the first invocation of a macro, part of the code within the macro definition can alter the code that generated on future invocations of the macro. This feature will be presented later in the chapter.

17.5 THE INSTRUCTIONS WITHIN A MACRO DEFINITION

The instructions that are coded within a macro definition are copied into the source program at the point that the macro is called. These instructions can be expanded without any modification, or they can be altered by the parameters passed to the macro. Begin by examining a simple SAVEREGS macro.

In this version of SAVEREGS, the macro saves the four data registers and the two index registers. The RESTOREGS macro restores these registers. The body of the macro is as shown in Figure 17–1 (PGM44.ASM on the program disk). Page 1-1 of the listing shows the two macro definitions. They are called from SUB1 and SUB2 on page 1-3 of the listing.

```
Microsoft (R) Macro Assembler Version 5.10              8/7/88 16:04:59


PGM44 - FIGURE 17-1 - SIMPLE SAVEREGS MACRO              Page    1-1



                     PAGE    60,132
                     TITLE   PGM44 - FIGURE 17-1 - SIMPLE SAVEREGS MACRO


          ;********************************************************************
          ; PGM44      Title: Figure 17-1 Illustrates SAVEREGS macro       *
          ;                                                                *
          ; Programmer: Vic Broquard                                      *
          ; Date Written:  6/11/88       Date Of Last Revision: 8/6/88     *
          ;                                                                *
          ; Purpose: To show the usage of a SAVEREGS macro                *
          ;                                                                *
          ; Special Requirements: none                                   *
          ;                                                                *
          ;********************************************************************
          SAVEREGS  MACRO

          ;; THIS MACRO WILL SAVE REGS AX, BX, CX, DX, SI, DI

                   PUSH   AX     ; SAVE REGISTERS
                   PUSH   BX
                   PUSH   CX
                   PUSH   DX
                   PUSH   SI
                   PUSH   DI
```

FIGURE 17–1 Simple SAVEREGS and RESTOREGS macro (PGM44.ASM) *(Continues)*

```
                          ENDM


             RESTOREGS MACRO

             ;; THIS MACRO WILL RESTORE REGS AX, BX, CX, DX, SI, DI

                     POP   DI      ; RESTORE REGISTERS
                     POP   SI
                     POP   DX
                     POP   CX
                     POP   BX
                     POP   AX

                     ENDM
```
- -

```
Microsoft (R) Macro Assembler Version 5.10              8/7/88 16:04:59

PGM44 - FIGURE 17-1 - SIMPLE SAVEREGS MACRO             Page    1-2


                          PAGE
  0000                    PGMSK   SEGMENT  PARA STACK 'STACK'
  0000  0020[                     DW    32 DUP(?)
        ????
                      ]

  0040                    PGMSK   ENDS


  0000                    PGMDA   SEGMENT
  0000                    PGMDA   ENDS




  0000                    PGMCD   SEGMENT
  0000                    MAIN    PROC   FAR

                          ; housekeeping section

                             ASSUME  CS:PGMCD,DS:PGMDA,SS:PGMSK

  0000  B8 ---- R             MOV    AX,PGMDA   ; ESTABLISH ADDRESSABILITY
  0003  8E D8                 MOV    DS,AX      ; TO PGMDA - THE PGM'S DATA SEGMENT

                          ; main process section
```

FIGURE 17-1   continued

```
0005  E8 0010 R               CALL    SUB1        ; CALL DUMMY SUBROUTINE 1
0008  E8 001D R               CALL    SUB2        ; CALL DUMMY SUBROUTINE 2


                        ; return to DOS section


000B  B8 4C00                 MOV     AX,4C00H    ; SET FOR DOS END PROCESS FUNCTION, RC=0
000E  CD 21                   INT     21H         ; CALL DOS TO END PROGRAM


0010                  MAIN    ENDP
```

Microsoft (R) Macro Assembler Version 5.10   8/7/88 16:04:59

PGM44 - FIGURE 17-1 - SIMPLE SAVEREGS MACRO   Page   1-3


```
                              PAGE
0010                  SUB1    PROC

                              SAVEREGS
0010  50              1       PUSH  AX    ; SAVE REGISTERS
0011  53              1       PUSH  BX
0012  51              1       PUSH  CX
0013  52              1       PUSH  DX
0014  56              1       PUSH  SI
0015  57              1       PUSH  DI


                              RESTOREGS
0016  5F              1       POP   DI    ; RESTORE REGISTERS
0017  5E              1       POP   SI
0018  5A              1       POP   DX
0019  59              1       POP   CX
001A  5B              1       POP   BX
001B  58              1       POP   AX


001C  C3                      RET

001D                  SUB1    ENDP



001D                  SUB2    PROC

                              SAVEREGS
001D  50              1       PUSH  AX    ; SAVE REGISTERS
001E  53              1       PUSH  BX
001F  51              1       PUSH  CX
0020  52              1       PUSH  DX
0021  56              1       PUSH  SI
```

FIGURE 17-1   continued   *(Continues)*

```
0022  57                  1       PUSH  DI

                                  RESTOREGS
0023  5F                  1       POP   DI    ; RESTORE REGISTERS
0024  5E                  1       POP   SI
0025  5A                  1       POP   DX
0026  59                  1       POP   CX
0027  5B                  1       POP   BX
0028  58                  1       POP   AX

0029  C3                          RET

002A                      SUB2    ENDP

002A                      PGMCD   ENDS

                                  END   MAIN
```

Microsoft (R) Macro Assembler Version 5.10   8/7/88 16:04:59

PGM44 - FIGURE 17-1 - SIMPLE SAVEREGS MACRO   Symbols-1

Macros:

                N a m e   Lines

RESTOREGS   7
SAVEREGS   7

Segments and Groups:

                N a m e   Length Align Combine Class

PGMCD . . . .   002A   PARA NONE
PGMDA   0000   PARA NONE
PGMSK   0040   PARA STACK   'STACK'

Symbols:

                N a m e   Type   Value Attr

MAIN . . . .   F PROC 0000 PGMCD   Length = 0010

SUB1 . . . .   N PROC 0010 PGMCD   Length = 000D
SUB2 . . . .   N PROC 001D PGMCD   Length = 000D

@CPU . . . .   TEXT   0101h
@FILENAME . . . .   TEXT   PGM44

FIGURE 17–1   continued

```
@VERSION . . . . . . . . . . .        TEXT  510


    103 Source  Lines
    131 Total   Lines
     14 Symbols

  47760 + 251404 Bytes symbol space free

      0 Warning Errors
      0 Severe  Errors
```

FIGURE 17-1 continued

Macro comments are comments that appear only in the macro definitions, not in the actual macro expansion code. Macro comments begin with two semicolons. All other comments appear in the actual macro expansion. Examine Figure 17–1 once more. Each macro has one macro comment that identifies what that macro is supposed to do. They do not appear in the expansions on page 1-3 of the listing. Notice that the other comments appear in both the macro definitions and the actual expansions on page 1-3.

17.6 CONTROLLING THE MACRO EXPANSIONS

The code from the macro that is printed on the source listing is controllable by the programmer. Initially, for debugging purposes, it is advantageous to have all statements printed. Later, when all is working, you might want to reduce the amount of code that is printed on the source listing. Three assembler directives affect the printing of statements. They are

    .LALL   lists all the source statements

    .XALL   lists only those that create code or data

    .SALL   suppresses all statements that are generated

.LALL prints everything that is generated. This is the option to use when debugging a macro. .XALL suppresses printing of comments, directives, and equates. It is the normal default when MASM begins. Only the actual instructions and storage definitions are printed. .SALL suppresses all statements, leaving only the macro call on the listing. However, all the instructions are in the .OBJ file; they are just not printed on the listing, thus creating much shorter listings. This option is often used once a macro has been fully debugged, because it results in much shorter source listings.

Figure 17–2 (PGM45.ASM on the program disk) shows DUMMY, a macro that contains a little of everything to illustrate the effect of these three options. The first invocation of DUMMY uses the default value, .XALL.

DUMMY is reinvoked using .XALL, .LALL, and .SALL. Assemble and run this program to observe the results.

```
Microsoft (R) Macro Assembler Version 5.10                8/7/88 16:05:08


PGM45 - FIGURE 17-2 - ILLUSTRATES LISTING CONTROLS          Page    1-1



                              PAGE    60,132
                              TITLE   PGM45 - FIGURE 17-2 - ILLUSTRATES LISTING CONTROLS


                      ;**************************************************************************
                      ; PGM45    Title: Figure 17-2 Illustrates listing control directives    *
                      ;                                                                        *
                      ; Programmer: Vic Broquard                                               *
                      ; Date Written:  6/11/88       Date Of Last Revision: 8/6/88             *
                      ;                                                                        *
                      ; Purpose: Shows the effects of listing controls on macro generation     *
                      ;                                                                        *
                      ; Special Requirements: none                                             *
                      ;                                                                        *
                      ;**************************************************************************


                      DUMMY MACRO

                      ;; DUMMY MACRO THAT GENERATES CODE, EQUATES, DIRECTIVES, AND COMMENTS

                      ; housekeeping section

                              ASSUME  CS:PGMCD,DS:PGMDA

                              MOV     AX,PGMDA     ; ESTABLISH ADDRESSABILITY
                              MOV     DS,AX        ; TO PGMDA - THE PGM'S DATA SEGMENT

                      ONE EQU     1

                              ENDM

                      ;----------------------------------------------------------------

0000                          PGMCD SEGMENT

0000                          MAIN  PROC    FAR

                              DUMMY
0000  B8 ---- R        1      MOV     AX,PGMDA     ; ESTABLISH ADDRESSABILITY
0003  8E D8            1      MOV     DS,AX        ; TO PGMDA - THE PGM'S DATA SEGMENT
```

FIGURE 17–2 Listing controls (PGM45.ASM)

```
                         .XALL
                         DUMMY
0005  B8 ---- R       1    MOV    AX,PGMDA   ; ESTABLISH ADDRESSABILITY
0008  8E D8           1    MOV    DS,AX      ; TO PGMDA - THE PGM'S DATA SEGMENT

                         .LALL
                         DUMMY
                     1  ;
                     1  ; housekeeping section
                     1     ASSUME  CS:PGMCD,DS:PGMDA
000A  B8 ---- R       1    MOV    AX,PGMDA   ; ESTABLISH ADDRESSABILITY
000D  8E D8           1    MOV    DS,AX      ; TO PGMDA - THE PGM'S DATA SEGMENT
= 0001               1 ONE EQU    1

                         .SALL
                         DUMMY
```

```
Microsoft (R) Macro Assembler Version 5.10          8/7/88 16:05:08

PGM45 - FIGURE 17-2 - ILLUSTRATES LISTING CONTROLS    Page    1-2



0014                     MAIN   ENDP

0014                     PGMCD  ENDS

0000                     PGMDA  ENDS
0000                     PGMDA  SEGMENT

                                END    MAIN
```

FIGURE 17-2   continued

We recommend that you use the .LALL option first. Then, when the program is fully debugged, you can switch to the .SALL option for a cleaner, shorter source listing.

17.7 USING THE INCLUDE FEATURE

Quite often, programmers want to use the same macros in several programs. This is conveniently done by placing the macros in a separate file, which can be included or appended to an actual source program. This helps reduce the physical size of a source program.

Macro definitions (or other code, for that matter) can be inserted into a program by using the **INCLUDE** option. The syntax is

```
                    ┌─────────────────────────────────────────┐
                    │                                         │
                    │    INCLUDE   file specification         │
                    │                                         │
                    └─────────────────────────────────────────┘
```

The file specification can be either simple or complex, depending on the use of paths. The following are examples of valid INCLUDE options:

```
            INCLUDE   B:MACROS.ASM
            INCLUDE   MACROS.MAC
            INCLUDE   C:\ASM\MACROS\TEST1.MAC
            INCLUDE   C:\ASM\DEFINES\MACROS.INC
```

The extensions that are commonly given to macro files include .ASM, .MAC, and .INC.

Again, these INCLUDEs must appear before the first macro call that references the macro definition that is contained in the included file. Thus, the INCLUDEs are commonly placed very near the beginning of the program. Figure 17–3 (PGM46.ASM on the program disk) illustrates the use of the INCLUDE feature.

Notice in Figure 17–3 that all statements that are copied into the source program from an INCLUDE file are preceded by a letter "C". This means that the statement was Copied in. All the macro-generated instructions are preceded by a number representing the macro nesting level.

17.8 USING PARAMETERS AND ARGUMENTS

Often, the tedious task of coding DOS and ROM-BIOS interrupts is circumvented by using macros. Suppose it is necessary to display one character on the screen by using DOS function 02H. Every time that function is needed in the program, it is necessary to remember what belongs in which register. Mistakes do occur rather easily, particularly due to lapses of memory. However, if you write a macro called DSPLY_BYTE, for example, then you are freed from having to remember what is to be in the registers. The macro handles it for you.

Such a DSPLY_BYTE macro will have the character to be displayed passed to it, and the macro will code the appropriate move instruction to copy that character into register DL for the interrupt.

The macro definition then asks for one parameter. When the macro is called, one corresponding argument is passed. This is shown in Example 17–2. The macro expects one parameter, SHOW_BYTE, which is used in the move to DL instruction. When the macro is called, whatever is coded as the argument to DSPLY_BYTE is inserted for SHOW_BYTE. If no argument is used, then a null string replaces SHOW_BYTE. If this happens, an assembly-time error message is generated.

```
Microsoft (R) Macro Assembler Version 5.10               8/7/88 16:05:16

PGM46 - FIGURE 17-3 - ILLUSTRATES THE USE OF INCLUDE        Page    1-1


                        PAGE    60,132
                        TITLE   PGM46 - FIGURE 17-3 - ILLUSTRATES THE USE OF INCLUDE


               ;************************************************************************
               ; PGM46      Title: Figure 17-3 Illustrates the use of the INCLUDE   *
               ;                                                        directive    *
               ; Programmer: Vic Broquard                                           *
               ; Date Written:  6/11/88        Date Of Last Revision: 8/6/88         *
               ;                                                                    *
               ; Purpose: To show the usage of the INCLUDE feature                  *
               ;                                                                    *
               ; Special Requirements: none                                        *
               ;                                                                    *
               ;************************************************************************
               ;

                       INCLUDE  PGM46.MAC
           C  SAVEREGS  MACRO
           C
           C  ;; THIS MACRO WILL SAVE REGS AX, BX, CX, DX, SI, DI
           C
           C       PUSH  AX    ; SAVE REGISTERS
           C       PUSH  BX
           C       PUSH  CX
           C       PUSH  DX
           C       PUSH  SI
           C       PUSH  DI
           C
           C           ENDM
           C
           C
           C
           C  RESTOREGS MACRO
           C
           C  ;; THIS MACRO WILL RESTORE REGS AX, BX, CX, DX, SI, DI
           C
           C       POP   DI    ; RESTORE REGISTERS
           C       POP   SI
           C       POP   DX
           C       POP   CX
           C       POP   BX
           C       POP   AX
           C
           C           ENDM
```

FIGURE 17–3 Using INCLUDE files (PGM46.ASM)   *(Continues)*

```
Microsoft (R) Macro Assembler Version 5.10            8/7/88 16:05:16


PGM46 - FIGURE 17-3 - ILLUSTRATES THE USE OF INCLUDE        Page    1-2



                              PAGE
0000                          PGMSK    SEGMENT  PARA STACK 'STACK'
0000  0020[                            DW    32 DUP(?)
       ????
                    ]


0040                          PGMSK    ENDS



0000                          PGMDA    SEGMENT
0000                          PGMDA    ENDS





0000                          PGMCD    SEGMENT


0000                          MAIN     PROC    FAR


                              ; housekeeping section


                                  ASSUME  CS:PGMCD,DS:PGMDA,SS:PGMSK


0000  B8 ---- R                   MOV     AX,PGMDA    ; ESTABLISH ADDRESSABILITY
0003  8E D8                       MOV     DS,AX       ; TO PGMDA - THE PGM'S DATA SEGMENT


                              ; main process section


0005  E8 0010 R                   CALL    SUB1        ; CALL DUMMY SUBROUTINE 1
0008  E8 001D R                   CALL    SUB2        ; CALL DUMMY SUBROUTINE 2


                              ; return to DOS section


000B  B8 4C00                     MOV     AX,4C00H    ; SET FOR DOS END PROCESS FUNCTION, RC=0
000E  CD 21                       INT     21H         ; CALL DOS TO END PROGRAM


0010                          MAIN     ENDP

-----------------------------------------------------------------------------------
```

FIGURE 17–3   continued

```
                               PAGE
0010                     SUB1     PROC

                         SAVEREGS
0010  50            1        PUSH  AX      ; SAVE REGISTERS
0011  53            1        PUSH  BX
0012  51            1        PUSH  CX
0013  52            1        PUSH  DX
0014  56            1        PUSH  SI
0015  57            1        PUSH  DI


                         RESTOREGS
0016  5F            1        POP   DI      ; RESTORE REGISTERS
0017  5E            1        POP   SI
0018  5A            1        POP   DX
0019  59            1        POP   CX
001A  5B            1        POP   BX
001B  58            1        POP   AX

001C  C3                     RET

001D                     SUB1     ENDP



001D                     SUB2     PROC

                         SAVEREGS
001D  50            1        PUSH  AX      ; SAVE REGISTERS
001E  53            1        PUSH  BX

001F  51            1        PUSH  CX
0020  52            1        PUSH  DX
0021  56            1        PUSH  SI
0022  57            1        PUSH  DI

                         RESTOREGS
0023  5F            1        POP   DI      ; RESTORE REGISTERS
0024  5E            1        POP   SI
0025  5A            1        POP   DX
0026  59            1        POP   CX
0027  5B            1        POP   BX
0028  58            1        POP   AX
```

FIGURE 17–3   continued   *(Continues)*

```
0029  C3                    RET

002A              SUB2    ENDP

002A              PGMCD   ENDS

                  END     MAIN
```

FIGURE 17-3 continued

Notice one safety feature: The registers to be used are saved and restored. Since using interrupts is register intensive, it is wise to save and restore the registers within the macro. That way, the main line program does not have to concern itself with what the invoked macro and interrupt do with the register contents.

Figure 17-4 (PGM47.ASM on the program disk) shows the complete coding for this example. First examine the macro definition. Next, look at the main process section. The DSPLY_BYTE macro is called four times, using various arguments. When the macro is invoked to pass LETTERA, notice that the generated move instruction becomes

```
                  MOV     DL,LETTERA
```

In the second call, the argument is register AL; the letter "B" is currently in the register. In this macro expansion, the move instruction becomes

```
                  MOV     DL,AL
```

In the third case, a more complex value is used as the argument, and the move generated is

```
                  MOV     DL,[BX]
```

```
DSPLY_BYTE        MACRO     SHOW_BYTE

;; DSPLY_BYTE WILL DISPLAY ONE CHARACTER ON CRT VIA 02H

                  PUSH      AX              ; SAVE REGISTERS
                  PUSH      DX

                  MOV       DL,SHOW_BYTE    ; MOVE BYTE TO DL
                  MOV       AH,02H          ; SET FOR DSPLY BYTE
                  INT       21H             ; CALL DOS TO DSPLY BYTE

                  POP       DX              ; RESTORE REGISTERS
                  POP       AX

                  ENDM
```

EXAMPLE 17-2 DSPLY_BYTE macro

```
Microsoft (R) Macro Assembler Version 5.10              8/10/88 18:31:34
PGM47 - FIGURE 17-4 - DSPLY_BYTE MACRO                  Page     1-1


                        PAGE    60,132
                        TITLE   PGM47 - FIGURE 17-4 - DSPLY_BYTE MACRO


                ;*************************************************************************
                ; PGM47       Title: Figure 17-4 Illustrates DSPLY_BYTE macro        *
                ;                                                                     *
                ; Programmer: Vic Broquard                                           *
                ; Date Written:  6/11/88        Date Of Last Revision: 8/7/88        *
                ;                                                                     *
                ; Purpose: To show the usage of a DSPLY_BYTE macro                   *
                ;                                                                     *
                ; Special Requirements: none                                         *
                ;                                                                     *
                ;*************************************************************************
                ;

                DSPLY_BYTE  MACRO  SHOW_BYTE

                        ;; DSPLY_BYTE WILL DISPLAY ONE CHARACTER ON CRT VIA 02H

                        PUSH   AX              ; SAVE REGISTERS
                        PUSH   DX

                        MOV    DL,SHOW_BYTE    ; MOVE BYTE TO DL
                        MOV    AH,02H          ; SET FOR DSPLY BYTE
                        INT    21H             ; CALL DOS TO DSPLY BYTE

                        POP    DX              ; RESTORE REGISTERS
                        POP    AX

                        ENDM
```

```
Microsoft (R) Macro Assembler Version 5.10              8/10/88 18:31:34
PGM47 - FIGURE 17-4 - DSPLY_BYTE MACRO                  Page     1-2


                                PAGE
0000                   PGMCD    SEGMENT

0000                   MAIN     PROC    FAR

                       ; housekeeping section

                                ASSUME CS:PGMCD,DS:PGMDA,SS:PGMSK
```

FIGURE 17–4 Using the DSPLY_BYTE macro (PGM47.ASM)   *(Continues)*

```
0000  B8 ---- R                    MOV    AX,PGMDA      ; ESTABLISH ADDRESSABILITY
0003  8E D8                        MOV    DS,AX         ; TO PGMDA - THE PGM'S DATA SEGMENT


                    ; main process section


                                   DSPLY_BYTE  LETTERA  ; DISPLAY AN "A"
0005  50                      1    PUSH   AX            ; SAVE REGISTERS
0006  52                      1    PUSH   DX
0007  8A 16 0000 R            1    MOV    DL,LETTERA    ; MOVE BYTE TO DL
000B  B4 02                   1    MOV    AH,02H        ; SET FOR DSPLY BYTE
000D  CD 21                   1    INT    21H           ; CALL DOS TO DSPLY BYTE
000F  5A                      1    POP    DX            ; RESTORE REGISTERS
0010  58                      1    POP    AX


0011  A0 0001 R                    MOV    AL,LETTERB    ; GET LETTER "B" INTO REG AL
                                   DSPLY_BYTE  AL       ; DISPLAY A "B"
0014  50                      1    PUSH   AX            ; SAVE REGISTERS
0015  52                      1    PUSH   DX
0016  8A D0                   1    MOV    DL,AL   ; MOVE BYTE TO DL
0018  B4 02                   1    MOV    AH,02H        ; SET FOR DSPLY BYTE
001A  CD 21                   1    INT    21H           ; CALL DOS TO DSPLY BYTE
001C  5A                      1    POP    DX            ; RESTORE REGISTERS
001D  58                      1    POP    AX


001E  8D 1E 0002 R                 LEA    BX,LETTERC    ; SET BX = ADDRESS OF LETTERC
                                   DSPLY_BYTE  [BX]     ; DISPLAY LETTER "C"
0022  50                      1    PUSH   AX            ; SAVE REGISTERS
0023  52                      1    PUSH   DX
0024  8A 17                   1    MOV    DL,[BX] ; MOVE BYTE TO DL
0026  B4 02                   1    MOV    AH,02H        ; SET FOR DSPLY BYTE
0028  CD 21                   1    INT    21H           ; CALL DOS TO DSPLY BYTE
002A  5A                      1    POP    DX            ; RESTORE REGISTERS
002B  58                      1    POP    AX


                                   DSPLY_BYTE  'D'      ; DISPLAY LETTER "D"
002C  50                      1    PUSH   AX            ; SAVE REGISTERS
002D  52                      1    PUSH   DX
002E  B2 44                   1    MOV    DL,'D'  ; MOVE BYTE TO DL
0030  B4 02                   1    MOV    AH,02H        ; SET FOR DSPLY BYTE
0032  CD 21                   1    INT    21H           ; CALL DOS TO DSPLY BYTE
0034  5A                      1    POP    DX            ; RESTORE REGISTERS
0035  58                      1    POP    AX


                    ; return to DOS section


0036  B8 4C00                      MOV    AX,4C00H      ; SET FOR DOS END PROCESS FUNCTION, RC=0
0039  CD 21                        INT    21H           ; CALL DOS TO END PROGRAM
```

FIGURE 17–4   continued

```
Microsoft (R) Macro Assembler Version 5.10          8/10/88 18:31:34
PGM47 - FIGURE 17-4 - DSPLY_BYTE MACRO               Page    1-3


003B                        MAIN     ENDP

003B                        PGMCD    ENDS


0000                        PGMDA    SEGMENT

0000  41                    LETTERA  DB      'A'
0001  42                    LETTERB  DB      'B'
0002  43                    LETTERC  DB      'C'

0003                        PGMDA    ENDS


0000                        PGMSK    SEGMENT  PARA STACK 'STACK'
0000  0020[                          DW      32 DUP(?)
      ????
                      ]

0040                        PGMSK    ENDS

                            END      MAIN
```

FIGURE 17–4   continued

Finally, a literal is used. It is enclosed in apostrophes. The move now uses immediate data

$$\text{MOV} \quad \text{DL,'D'}$$

Five principles apply to the use of parameters and arguments:

- The assembler replaces all occurrences of a parameter within the macro with the corresponding argument value.

- The first parameter is replaced with the value of the first argument, the second by the second, and so on.

- If there are too few arguments, then the remaining parameters are given a null string value—that is, a string of no length. This often results in assembly errors.

- If there are too many arguments, the excess are ignored.

- If an argument consists of either a series of values or a value that contains a comma, then the whole argument must be enclosed in angle brackets (<>). Remember that all arguments are separated by commas.

Consider the following macro, which defines several byte numbers:

```
DEFN_BYTES     MACRO     VAL1,VAL2,VAL3

NUMBERS        DB        VAL1
               DB        VAL2
               DB        VAL3

               ENDM
```

Suppose that DEFN_BYTES is invoked by

```
DEFN_BYTES   1,<2,3,4>,<'A','B'>
```

A total of 6 bytes are created. It is as if the code had been

```
NUMBERS     DB     1
            DB     2,3,4
            DB     'A','B'
```

17.9 SPECIAL OPERATORS AND DIRECTIVES WITHIN MACRO DEFINITIONS

The Substitute Operator: &

There are times when the parameter within the macro definition follows immediately after other characters or appears within apostrophes in macro statements. To identify these to the assembler, the substitute operator (&) is used. The substitute operator notifies the assembler to replace the substitute parameter with the argument value as usual. Consider the following macro, which creates error message storage definitions:

```
ERRDEF      MACRO     NUM,VAL

ERROR&NUM   DB        '*** ERROR #&NUM - &VAL'

            ENDM
```

In the first parameter usage (in the label of the DB directive), the ERROR&NUM is replaced by ERRORxxxx, where xxxx is the argument value of NUM. The second use of NUM and VAL occurs within a string defined by apostrophes. Without the embedded &, the assembler would think that the string was to be generated as is. With the &s, the corresponding argument values are inserted. The substitute operator is sometimes referred to as the concatenation or join operator.

If the macro ERRDEF was called by

```
         ERRDEF    1,<FILE NOT FOUND ON THE DISK>
```

the macro expands to create

```
   ERROR1    DB    '*** ERROR #1 - FILE NOT FOUND ON THE DISK'
```

This is a common way of creating standard error messages. All are guaranteed to have the same standard, uniform format. Figure 17–5 (PGM48.ASM on the program disk) is a program that uses macros to display error messages.

The LOCAL Directive

A word of caution: You must remember that all names and labels must be unique. If the message

```
         ERRDEF    1,<FILE CANNOT BE OPENED, DISK ERROR>
```

were added to those in Figure 17–5, an error would occur because there would be a duplicate name, ERROR1. In this case the duplication of names is obvious. Less obvious duplication occurs in Example 17–3, in which CALC_AVG computes the average of five scores. The macro works as

```
Microsoft (R) Macro Assembler Version 5.10            8/10/88 18:31:57
PGM48 - FIGURE 17-5 - ERROR MESSAGE DEFINITION MACRO   Page     1-1


                        PAGE    60,132
                        TITLE   PGM48 - FIGURE 17-5 - ERROR MESSAGE DEFINITION MACRO


            ;*********************************************************************
            ; PGM48       Title: Figure 17-5 Illustrates Error Message Definition  *
            ;                                                                   *
            ; Programmer: Vic Broquard                                          *
            ; Date Written:  6/11/88        Date Of Last Revision: 8/8/88       *
            ;                                                                   *
            ; Purpose: To show how error messages can be created by macros      *
            ;                                                                   *
            ; Special Requirements: none                                        *
            ;                                                                   *
            ;*********************************************************************


            ERRDEF    MACRO  NUM,VAL

                    ;; MACRO TO DEFINE ERROR MESSAGES
```

FIGURE 17–5   Macro for error message definition (PGM48.ASM)   *(Continues)*

```
                          ERROR&NUM DB    '*** ERROR #&NUM - &VAL'

                                     ENDM



0000                      PGMDA     SEGMENT

                                     ERRDEF  1,<FILE NOT FOUND ON DISK>
0000  2A 2A 2A 20 45 52   1 ERROR1 DB    '*** ERROR #1 - FILE NOT FOUND ON DISK'
                                     ERRDEF  2,<NOT ABLE TO OPEN FILE>
0025  2A 2A 2A 20 45 52   1 ERROR2 DB    '*** ERROR #2 - NOT ABLE TO OPEN FILE'
                                     ERRDEF  3,<BAD PATH TO FILE>
0049  2A 2A 2A 20 45 52   1 ERROR3 DB    '*** ERROR #3 - BAD PATH TO FILE'

0068                      PGMDA     ENDS

                                     END
```

FIGURE 17–5   continued

```
          CALC_AVG  MACRO       SCORES,AVERAGE

                ;; MACRO TO COMPUTE THE AVERAGE SCORE
                ;; SCORES IS A TABLE OF 5 UNSIGNED BINARY BYTE NUMS
                ;; AVERAGE IS A BYTE NUMBER RESULT

                LEA  BX,SCORES       ; BX = ADDRESS OF SCORES TABLE
                MOV  CX,5            ; CX = NUMBER OF ENTRIES
                MOV  AX,0            ; AX = TOTAL SCORES

          LOOP1:
                ADD  AL,[BX]         ; ADD IN CURRENT SCORE
                ADC  AH,0            ; ADD IN ANY CARRY
                INC  BX              ; POINT TO NEXT SCORE
                LOOP LOOP1           ; REPEAT FOR FIVE SCORES

                MOV  CX,5            ; DIVISOR = 5 SCORES
                DIV  CL             ; DIVIDE AX (TOTAL) BY 5
                MOV  AVERAGE,AL      ; SAVE QUOTIENT

                ENDM
```

EXAMPLE 17–3 Macro to calculate the average score

expected on the first invocation. But what happens when it is called a second or third time? Duplicate labels called LOOP1 are generated, thus creating assembly-time errors.

The solution is to designate the label LOOP1 as local in scope. There are two scopes for names and labels: global and local. If a name or label is defined as global, then the name or label is used as is and can be used or referenced from anywhere within the macro and the program. The default scope for all names and labels used within a macro is global.

If the name or label is specifically defined as local, then that name or label is replaced by a unique name known only within the macro. (If you know the method by which these substitute names are created, then it is possible to use them directly from other points within the program.)

The syntax for the LOCAL directive is

```
LOCAL   name1,name2,...
```

The LOCAL directive **must** precede all other statements in the definition, including comment lines. Then, every time the macro is expanded, the local name or label is replaced by a different value.

The LOCAL directive should be added to the CALC_AVG macro. The complete macro and its generation are shown in Figure 17–6 (PGM49.ASM on the program disk). Every time the macro is expanded, all occurrences of LOOP1 are replaced by a unique value. The first local value becomes ??0000. If the macro were invoked a second time, the second occurrence would be replaced by ??0001, and so on. Of course, you should avoid using such nondescriptive names and labels. If you are using descriptive names and labels in your programs, the problem of duplicating nondescriptive names is unlikely to occur.

Macro Redefinition

Occasionally, a macro must be fully expanded the first time that it is used, but only partially expanded on all subsequent expansions. This situation occurs mainly when the macro is used to define one or more temporary work areas and these need to be defined only once in the program. To see how this works, consider a modification of the CALC_AVG macro that restricts register usage. Assume that only registers AX and BX are available for use. (One solution is to use a series of PUSH and POP instructions.) Example 17–4 represents a first approach to such a macro.

With this macro every expansion results in local values for both LOOP1 and for GOAHEAD. However, the field COUNT presents a problem. COUNT could also be made local. However, if it is, it would be redefined continuously

```
Microsoft (R) Macro Assembler Version 5.10              8/10/88 18:32:04
PGM49 - FIGURE 17-6 - CALCULATE AVERAGE SCORE           Page    1-1


                        PAGE    60,132
                        TITLE   PGM49 - FIGURE 17-6 - CALCULATE AVERAGE SCORE


             ;**************************************************************************
             ; PGM49       Title: Figure 17-6 Calculate average score macro        *
             ;                                                                      *
             ; Programmer: Vic Broquard                                            *
             ; Date Written:  6/11/88         Date Of Last Revision: 8/9/88        *
             ;                                                                      *
             ; Purpose: To calculate the average score from a table of 5 scores    *
             ;                                                                      *
             ; Special Requirements: none                                          *
             ;                                                                      *
             ;**************************************************************************


             CALC_AVG MACRO   SCORES,AVERAGE
                      LOCAL   LOOP1


                      ;; MACRO TO COMPUTE THE AVERAGE SCORE
                      ;; SCORES IS A TABLE OF 5 UNSIGNED BINARY BYTE NUMS
                      ;; AVERAGE IS A BYTE NUMBER RESULT


                      LEA     BX,SCORES     ; BX = ADDRESS OF SCORES TABLE
                      MOV     CX,5          ; CX = NUMBER OF ENTRIES
                      MOV     AX,0          ; AX = TOTAL SCORES


             LOOP1:
                      ADD     AL,[BX]       ; ADD IN CURRENT SCORE
                      ADC     AH,0          ; ADD IN ANY CARRY
                      INC     BX            ; POINT TO NEXT SCORE
                      LOOP    LOOP1         ; REPEAT FOR FIVE SCORES


                      MOV     CX,5          ; DIVISOR = 5 SCORES
                      DIV     CL            ; DIVIDE AX (TOTAL) BY 5
                      MOV     AVERAGE,AL    ; SAVE QUOTIENT


                      ENDM
```

FIGURE 17–6 The CALC_AVE macro for calculating the average score
(PGM49.ASM)

Microsoft (R) Macro Assembler Version 5.10   8/10/88 18:32:04
PGM49 - FIGURE 17-6 - CALCULATE AVERAGE SCORE   Page   1-2

```
                                  PAGE

0000                   PGMCD    SEGMENT

0000                   MAIN     PROC    FAR

                       ; housekeeping section

                            ASSUME CS:PGMCD,DS:PGMDA,SS:PGMSK

0000  B8 ---- R                 MOV     AX,PGMDA      ; ESTABLISH ADDRESSABILITY
0003  8E D8                     MOV     DS,AX         ; TO PGMDA - THE PGM'S DATA SEGMENT

                       ; main process section

                            CALC_AVG  GRADES,AVG_GRD ; CALCULATE AVERAGE GRADE
0005  8D 1E 0000 R      1       LEA     BX,GRADES     ; BX = ADDRESS OF SCORES TABLE
0009  B9 0005          1       MOV     CX,5          ; CX = NUMBER OF ENTRIES
000C  B8 0000          1       MOV     AX,0          ; AX = TOTAL SCORES
000F                   1 ??0000:
000F  02 07            1       ADD     AL,[BX]       ; ADD IN CURRENT SCORE
0011  80 D4 00         1       ADC     AH,0          ; ADD IN ANY CARRY
0014  43               1       INC     BX            ; POINT TO NEXT SCORE
0015  E2 F8            1       LOOP    ??0000        ; REPEAT FOR FIVE SCORES
0017  B9 0005          1       MOV     CX,5          ; DIVISOR = 5 SCORES
001A  F6 F1            1       DIV     CL            ; DIVIDE AX (TOTAL) BY 5
001C  A2 0005 R        1       MOV     AVG_GRD,AL    ; SAVE QUOTIENT

                       ; return to DOS section

001F  B8 4C00                  MOV     AX,4C00H      ; SET FOR DOS END PROCESS FUNCTION, RC=0
0022  CD 21                    INT     21H           ; CALL DOS TO END PROGRAM

0024                   MAIN     ENDP

0024                   PGMCD    ENDS


0000                   PGMDA    SEGMENT

0000  5A 50 46 50 50    GRADES  DB      90,80,70,80,80
0005  00                AVG_GRD DB      ?

0006                   PGMDA    ENDS
```

FIGURE 17–6   continued   *(Continues)*

```
0000                           PGMSK   SEGMENT  PARA STACK 'STACK'
0000   0020[                           DW    32 DUP(?)
        ????
                      ]

0040                           PGMSK   ENDS

                                       END     MAIN
```

FIGURE 17–6   continued

```
CALC_AVG   MACRO        SCORES,AVERAGE
           LOCAL        LOOP1,GOAHEAD

           ;; MACRO TO COMPUTE THE AVERAGE SCORE
           ;; ONLY REGISTERS AX AND BX ARE AVAILABLE FOR USE
           ;; SCORES IS A TABLE OF 5 UNSIGNED BINARY BYTE NUMS
           ;; AVERAGE IS A BYTE NUMBER RESULT

           JMP   GOAHEAD            ; CONTINUE AROUND THE DATA FIELD

COUNT      DB    ?

GOAHEAD:

           LEA   BX,SCORES          ; BX = ADDRESS OF SCORES TABLE
           MOV   COUNT,5            ; COUNT HOLDS THE NUMBER OF ENTRIES
           MOV   AX,0               ; AX = TOTAL SCORES

LOOP1:
           ADD   AL,[BX]            ; ADD IN CURRENT SCORE
           ADC   AH,0               ; ADD IN ANY CARRY
           INC   BX                 ; POINT TO NEXT SCORE
           DEC   COUNT              ; DECREMENT AND
           JNZ   LOOP1              ; REPEAT FOR FIVE SCORES

           MOV   COUNT,5            ; DIVISOR = 5 SCORES
           DIV   COUNT              ; DIVIDE AX (TOTAL) BY 5
           MOV   AVERAGE,AL         ; SAVE QUOTIENT

           ENDM
```

EXAMPLE 17–4   Register-limited average score calculation

in every macro expansion. A better solution is to allow the macro to be expanded as coded the first time, thereby defining COUNT. Then **redefine** the macro for the second and subsequent invocations so that it does not define COUNT but reuses the original field whenever needed.

To redefine a macro, you must fully code the new version, complete with MACRO and ENDM directives, and place the new definition immediately in front of the ENDM directive of the first version. The macro to calculate the average score can be redefined as shown in Figure 17–7 (PGM50.ASM on the program disk).

On the second and all subsequent macro invocations, the redefined CALC_AVG macro is used. In the redefinition, the local label, GOAHEAD, and the COUNT field have been omitted. Also no LOCAL directive can be coded, since it **must** be the very first statement in the outermost macro. Examine the two expansions beginning at offsets 0005 and 0031. Notice the absence of COUNT in the second expansion.

Macro Nesting

Macros can be nested, that is, other macros can be called from within a macro. Of course, the nested macro calls are not invoked unless the outer macro is called first.

Recursive Macros

Macros can be recursive, that is, a macro can call or invoke itself. Recursion is one method of performing repeated operations, and it is often used with mathematical computations. The number of times a macro recursively invokes itself is frequently controlled by other conditional directives. An example of recursion will be presented in the section on conditional assembly features.

Phase Errors

When working with macros, a common error is the **phase error.** A phase error occurs when the assembler has made an assumption about a name or label type only to discover that the assumption is not true. To more fully grasp this situation, you must understand more about how the assembler translates a source program.

The assembler is actually a two-pass translator. On the first pass, no code is generated. Rather, the assembler constructs a table of all names and labels. Suppose the assembler encounters a symbol before it encounters the symbol's definition. This is known as a forward reference. Forward references happen frequently when the data segment comes after the code segment. In this case the assembler makes certain assumptions about the symbol and generates an error message regarding it. Often, the assumptions involve whether the label is long or short or whether it is a byte or a word. When the assembler encounters a statement that defines a name or label, it

```
Microsoft (R) Macro Assembler Version 5.10              8/10/88 18:32:15
PGM50 - FIGURE 17-7 - CALCULATE AVERAGE SCORE MULTIPLE TIMES Page    1-1


                        PAGE    60,132
                        TITLE   PGM50 - FIGURE 17-7 - CALCULATE AVERAGE SCORE MULTIPLE
TIMES


            ;***************************************************************************
            ; PGM50      Title: Figure 17-7 Calculate average score macro       *
            ;                              with limited registers               *
            ; Programmer: Vic Broquard                                          *
            ; Date Written: 6/11/88        Date Of Last Revision: 8/9/88        *
            ;                                                                   *
            ; Purpose: To calculate the average score from a table of 5 scores  *
            ;                                                                   *
            ; Special Requirements: Use only registers AX and BX               *
            ;                                                                   *
            ;***************************************************************************

            CALC_AVG MACRO    SCORES,AVERAGE
                     LOCAL    LOOP1,GOAHEAD,LOOP2

                     ;; MACRO TO COMPUTE THE AVERAGE SCORE
                     ;; ONLY REGISTERS AX AND BX ARE AVAILABLE FOR USE
                     ;; SCORES IS A TABLE OF 5 UNSIGNED BINARY BYTE NUMS
                     ;; AVERAGE IS A BYTE NUMBER RESULT

                     JMP     GOAHEAD       ; BRANCH AROUND TEMPORARY DATA

            COUNT    DB      ?

            GOAHEAD:
                     LEA     BX,SCORES   ; BX = ADDRESS OF SCORES TABLE
                     MOV     COUNT,5     ; COUNT HOLDS THE NUMBER OF ENTRIES
                     MOV     AX,0        ; AX = TOTAL SCORES

            LOOP1:
                     ADD     AL,[BX]     ; ADD IN CURRENT SCORE
                     ADC     AH,0        ; ADD IN ANY CARRY
                     INC     BX          ; POINT TO NEXT SCORE
                     DEC     COUNT       ; DECREMENT AND
                     JNZ     LOOP1       ; REPEAT FOR FIVE SCORES

                     MOV     COUNT,5     ; DIVISOR = 5 SCORES
                     DIV     COUNT       ; DIVIDE AX (TOTAL) BY 5
                     MOV     AVERAGE,AL  ; SAVE QUOTIENT

            CALC_AVG MACRO    SCORES,AVERAGE
```

FIGURE 17-7 Calculating the average score with limited registers (PGM50.ASM)

```
                                ;; MACRO TO COMPUTE THE AVERAGE SCORE
                                ;; ONLY REGISTERS AX AND BX ARE AVAILABLE FOR USE
                                ;; SCORES IS A TABLE OF 5 UNSIGNED BINARY BYTENUMS
                                ;; AVERAGE IS A BYTE NUMBER RESULT

                                LEA     BX,SCORES   ; BX = ADDRESS OF SCORES TABLE
                                MOV     COUNT,5     ; COUNT = NUMBER OF ENTRIES
                                MOV     AX,0        ; AX = TOTAL SCORES

                         LOOP2:
                                ADD     AL,[BX]     ; ADD IN CURRENT SCORE
```

Microsoft (R) Macro Assembler Version 5.10   8/10/88 18:32:15
PGM50 - FIGURE 17-7 - CALCULATE AVERAGE SCORE MULTIPLE TIMES Page   1-2

```
                                ADC     AH,0        ; ADD IN ANY CARRY
                                INC     BX          ; POINT TO NEXT SCORE
                                DEC     COUNT       ; DECREMENT AND
                                JNZ     LOOP2       ; REPEAT FOR FIVE SCORES

                                MOV     COUNT,5     ; DIVISOR = 5 SCORES
                                DIV     COUNT       ; DIVIDE AX (TOTAL) BY 5
                                MOV     AVERAGE,AL  ; SAVE QUOTIENT
                                ENDM

                         ENDM
```

Microsoft (R) Macro Assembler Version 5.10   8/10/88 18:32:15
PGM50 - FIGURE 17-7 - CALCULATE AVERAGE SCORE MULTIPLE TIMES Page   1-3

```
                                      PAGE
0000                          PGMCD   SEGMENT

0000                          MAIN    PROC    FAR

                              ; housekeeping section

                              ASSUME CS:PGMCD,DS:PGMDA,SS:PGMSK

0000 B8 ---- R                        MOV     AX,PGMDA    ; ESTABLISH ADDRESSABILITY
0003 8E D8                            MOV     DS,AX       ; TO PGMDA - THE PGM'S DATA SEGMENT

                              ; main process section

                                      CALC_AVG GRADES,AVG_GRD ; CALCULATE AVERAGE GRADE
0005 EB 02 90            1             JMP     ??0001      ; BRANCH AROUND TEMPORARY DATA
```

FIGURE 17-7 continued   *(Continues)*

```
0008  00                    1 COUNT    DB    ?
0009                        1 ??0001:
0009  8D 1E 0000 R          1          LEA    BX,GRADES    ; BX = ADDRESS OF SCORES TABLE
000D  2E: C6 06 0008 R 05   1          MOV    COUNT,5      ; COUNT HOLDS THE NUMBER OF ENTRIES
0013  B8 0000              1          MOV    AX,0         ; AX = TOTAL SCORES
0016                        1 ??0000:
0016  02 07               1          ADD    AL,[BX]      ; ADD IN CURRENT SCORE
0018  80 D4 00            1          ADC    AH,0         ; ADD IN ANY CARRY
001B  43                  1          INC    BX           ; POINT TO NEXT SCORE
001C  2E: FE 0E 0008 R    1          DEC    COUNT        ; DECREMENT AND
0021  75 F3               1          JNZ    ??0000        ; REPEAT FOR FIVE SCORES
0023  2E: C6 06 0008 R 05 1          MOV    COUNT,5      ; DIVISOR = 5 SCORES
0029  2E: F6 36 0008 R    1          DIV    COUNT        ; DIVIDE AX (TOTAL) BY 5
002E  A2 0005 R           1          MOV    AVG_GRD,AL   ; SAVE QUOTIENT

                                     CALC_AVG  TABLE,AVG_TBL  ; CALCULATE AVERAGE TABLE
0031  8D 1E 0006 R        1          LEA    BX,TABLE     ; BX = ADDRESS OF SCORES TABLE
0035  2E: C6 06 0008 R 05 1          MOV    COUNT,5      ; COUNT = NUMBER OF ENTRIES
003B  B8 0000            1          MOV    AX,0         ; AX = TOTAL SCORES
003E                       1 ??0002:
003E  02 07              1          ADD    AL,[BX]      ; ADD IN CURRENT SCORE
0040  80 D4 00           1          ADC    AH,0         ; ADD IN ANY CARRY
0043  43                 1          INC    BX           ; POINT TO NEXT SCORE
0044  2E: FE 0E 0008 R   1          DEC    COUNT        ; DECREMENT AND
0049  75 F3              1          JNZ    ??0002        ; REPEAT FOR FIVE SCORES
004B  2E: C6 06 0008 R 05 1          MOV    COUNT,5      ; DIVISOR = 5 SCORES
0051  2E: F6 36 0008 R   1          DIV    COUNT        ; DIVIDE AX (TOTAL) BY 5
0056  A2 000B R          1          MOV    AVG_TBL,AL   ; SAVE QUOTIENT

                                   ; return to DOS section

0059  B8 4C00                      MOV    AX,4C00H     ; SET FOR DOS END PROCESS FUNCTION, RC=0
005C  CD 21                        INT    21H          ; CALL DOS TO END PROGRAM

005E                      MAIN     ENDP

005E                      PGMCD    ENDS


0000                      PGMDA    SEGMENT
```

Microsoft (R) Macro Assembler Version 5.10   8/10/88 18:32:15
PGM50 - FIGURE 17-7 - CALCULATE AVERAGE SCORE MULTIPLE TIMES Page   1-4


```
0000  5A 50 46 50 50      GRADES   DB    90,80,70,80,80
0005  00                  AVG_GRD  DB    ?
```

FIGURE 17–7   continued

```
0006  64 5A 50 5A 5A      TABLE   DB    100,90,80,90,90
000B  00                  AVG_TBL DB    ?

000C                      PGMDA   ENDS


0000                      PGMSK   SEGMENT  PARA STACK 'STACK'
0000  0020[                       DW    32 DUP(?)
       ????
                 ]

0040                      PGMSK   ENDS

                          END     MAIN
```

FIGURE 17-7 continued

adds that name to its symbol table. By the end of pass 1, the assembler has encountered all symbol definitions in the program as well as all uses of those symbols.

On the second pass, the assembler actually creates the corresponding machine instructions. As it encounters a symbol, it can refer to the symbol dictionary for the specifics of that name or label, such as offset address or size. During the second pass two situations can occur. First, if the symbol table provides a definition for a forward reference, the assembler removes the previously generated error message, which was SYMBOL NOT FOUND.

The second situation involves incorrect assumptions. Suppose that on pass 1 the assembler assumes that the length associated with a forward reference is 1 byte and on pass 2 discovers that the true length is 1 word. All the offset addresses it creates from this point forward through the program are off by 1 byte. This is a terminal error known as a **phase error**.

Some remedies for phase error involve placing the actual definition in front of the first use of the symbol by using the LABEL, BYTE, or WORD directives and the SHORT or LONG operators. In other words, restructuring the program or explicitly identifying lengths, sizes, and distances can usually eliminate most phase errors.

17.10 ELEMENTS OF THE CONDITIONAL ASSEMBLY LANGUAGE

Conditional assembly language is a feature of the assembly language that allows repetition directives, IF-THEN-ELSE directives, and conditional error directives. All can be found either within macros or outside macros.

This chapter will present the major features of the repetition directives first and then some of the IF-THEN-ELSE directives. For more complete details of the IF directives and for the conditional error directives, consult your assembler reference manuals.

17.11 REPEATING ONE OR MORE STATEMENTS

The REPT-ENDM Pair

Often, it is desirable to generate a series of statements whose execution is similar to that of a DO loop. For example, suppose that you want to define a series of bytes that contain the collating sequence—256 bytes with the numeric values from 0 to 255. (These data are frequently useful when performing translation operations.) The task of generating such a repeated series of statements can be implemented by using **REPT-ENDM**, the repeat block directives.

The REPT directive has one 16-bit unsigned operand, which is used to control the number of times to repeat the block of statements that follow. The ENDM directive is used to mark the end of the block scheduled for repetition. The syntax is

```
        REPT    number of repeats

        statements to be repeated

        ENDM
```

Consider XLAT_TABLE, the macro shown in Figure 17–8 (PGM51.ASM on the program disk). First, the symbol COUNT is given an initial value of 0. Then the REPT directive causes the block of statements that follow it to repeat 256 times. The block first defines a byte containing 0 and COUNT is incremented by 1. The next repetition defines a byte containing 1, and so on. Notice also that there are two ENDM directives. The first ENDM ends the repeat block, and the second ends the macro.

Examine the code that is generated. A quick glance shows that all the expanded DB directives have the same operand, COUNT! However, look at the object code–generated column, the second column from the far left. It clearly shows the expected hex sequence, beginning with 00H and continuing through FFH. (We truncated the listing for convenience.)

Also note that the table could have been coded directly in the data area without the use of a macro. It could have been coded as shown in Example 17–5.

```
Microsoft (R) Macro Assembler Version 5.10            8/10/88 18:32:26
PGM51 - FIGURE 17-8 - TRANSLATE TABLE                 Page    1-1


                        PAGE    60,132
                        TITLE   PGM51 - FIGURE 17-8 - TRANSLATE TABLE


                ;************************************************************************
                ; PGM51      Title: Figure 17-8 Illustrates defining translate table  *
                ;                                                                      *
                ; Programmer: Vic Broquard                                            *
                ; Date Written:  6/11/88        Date Of Last Revision: 8/9/88         *
                ;                                                                      *
                ; Purpose: To show how to use a macro to define a translate table     *
                ;                                                                      *
                ; Special Requirements: none                                          *
                ;                                                                      *
                ;************************************************************************


                XLAT_TABLE MACRO

                    ;; DEFINE A TRANSLATION TABLE OF ALL HEX VALUES FROM
                    ;;       00H TO 255H

                XLAT_TBL LABEL BYTE

                    COUNT = 0

                    REPT    256
                    DB      COUNT
                    COUNT = COUNT + 1

                    ENDM

                    ENDM



0000                    PGMDA    SEGMENT

                                 XLAT_TABLE
0000                    1 XLAT_TBL LABEL BYTE
0000  00                2    DB      COUNT
0001  01                2    DB      COUNT
0002  02                2    DB      COUNT
0003  03                2    DB      COUNT
0004  04                2    DB      COUNT
0005  05                2    DB      COUNT
0006  06                2    DB      COUNT
```

FIGURE 17–8 Defining a translation table (PGM51.ASM)   *(Continues)*

```
0007  07                  2      DB      COUNT
0008  08                  2      DB      COUNT
0009  09                  2      DB      COUNT
000A  0A                  2      DB      COUNT
```

```
**** WE HAVE REMOVED SEVERAL PAGES OF THE LISTING AT THIS POINT ****
```

```
00F8  F8                  2      DB      COUNT
00F9  F9                  2      DB      COUNT
00FA  FA                  2      DB      COUNT
00FB  FB                  2      DB      COUNT
00FC  FC                  2      DB      COUNT
00FD  FD                  2      DB      COUNT
00FE  FE                  2      DB      COUNT
00FF  FF                  2      DB      COUNT
```

```
0100                           PGMDA    ENDS
                                        END
```

FIGURE 17–8   continued

The IRP-ENDM Pair

Not all situations can be handled by internally calculating the next value. Sometimes the specific values are known only when the macro is to be called. Consider a macro called DEFN_BYTES. Suppose that on the first invocation, DEFN_BYTES should hold a series of even bytes containing 2, 4, 6, and 8. On the second invocation, the bytes defined should contain the odd numbers 1, 3, 5, and 7. In this case, the **IRP-ENDM** pair can be used to repeatedly generate the indicated block of statements according to the number of times specified.

The syntax is

```
PGMDA      SEGMENT

XLAT_TBL   LABEL       BYTE
COUNT      =           0
           REPT        256
           DB          COUNT
COUNT      =           COUNT + 1
           ENDM

PGMDA      ENDS
```

EXAMPLE 17–5   Alternate coding of the translation table of Figure 17–8

```
IRP    name,<value1,value2,value3, . . . >

statements to generate

ENDM
```

The values can be hard-coded as values on the IRP directive or they can be parameters that are substituted during macro expansion.

Figure 17–9 (PGM52.ASM on the program disk) shows how the IRP-ENDM pair can be used to define the macro DEFN_BYTES.

Consider the results of the two macro calls

```
DEFN_BYTES    <2,4,6,8>

DEFN_BYTES    <1,3,5,7>
```

For the even bytes, the IRP statement becomes

```
IRP    VAL,<2,4,6,8>
```

This generates a series of 4 bytes whose initial values are 2, 4, 6, and 8. For the odd bytes, the IRP becomes

```
IRP    VAL,<1,3,5,7>
```

creating 4 bytes containing 1, 3, 5, and 7.

The IRP makes one copy of the repeated statements for each parameter in the enclosed list. While copying the statements, it makes all substitutions indicated by any parameters.

17.12 CONDITIONAL ASSEMBLY DIRECTIVES

In a manner similar to the repeat directives, which implement iterative processes, the conditional directives implement the IF-THEN-ELSE structures. There are 10 different IF directives. This chapter will present only the more frequently used versions. Consult your assembler manuals for more details.

Each of the conditional IF directives is ended with the **ENDIF** directive and all have the following general sequence:

```
IFxxx  expression
    ...
... block of statements
    ...
```

```
Microsoft (R) Macro Assembler Version 5.10              8/10/88 18:32:41
PGM52 - FIGURE 17-9 - DEFINING BYTES MACRO WITH IRP      Page    1-1


                              PAGE    60,132
                              TITLE   PGM52 - FIGURE 17-9 - DEFINING BYTES MACRO WITH IRP


                    ;*************************************************************************
                    ; PGM52      Title: Figure 17-9 Illustrates IRP Directive          *
                    ;                                                                  *
                    ; Programmer: Vic Broquard                                         *
                    ; Date Written: 6/11/88        Date Of Last Revision: 8/9/88       *
                    ;                                                                  *
                    ; Purpose: To show the usage of the IRP macro directive            *
                    ;                                                                  *
                    ; Special Requirements: none                                       *
                    ;                                                                  *
                    ;*************************************************************************


                    DEFN_BYTES  MACRO  BYTE_VAL

                            ;; MACRO TO DEFINE A SERIES OF BYTES

                            IRP    VAL,<BYTE_VAL>
                            DB     VAL
                            ENDM

                        ENDM


  0000                    PGMDA    SEGMENT

  0000                    EVEN_BYTES LABEL BYTE

                            DEFN_BYTES    <2,4,6,8>
  0000  02          2      DB     2
  0001  04          2      DB     4
  0002  06          2      DB     6
  0003  08          2      DB     8


  0004                    ODD_BYTES   LABEL BYTE

                            DEFN_BYTES    <1,3,5,7>
  0004  01          2      DB     1
  0005  03          2      DB     3
  0006  05          2      DB     5
  0007  07          2      DB     7


  0008                    PGMDA    ENDS
                                   END
```

FIGURE 17–9   Using the IRP directive (PGM52.ASM)

```
                              ELSE
                                ...
                              ... block of statements
                                ...
                              ENDIF
```

The ELSE clause is optional, and the ending ENDIF directive is required. The xxx represents one of the 10 different variations available. Begin by examining the simplest form.

The IF-ENDIF and IFE-ENDIF Directives

Both the IF and IFE directives test the value of an expression. The **IF** directive generates the statements that follow it only if the value of the expression is true, 1B, or nonzero. The **IFE** directive generates its statements only if the value of the expression is false, 0B, or 0. Therefore, it follows that the expression **must** ultimately produce an absolute value at compile time. It cannot evaluate the contents of a register or field in memory when the program runs. In all IF conditional directives, the expression to be evaluated is resolved at assembly time.

One very common coding mistake is

```
            IF      AX=0
                     .
                     .
                     .

            ENDIF
```

This, in effect, asks the assembler to examine the contents of register AX while the program is executing. It cannot do this. As a matter of fact, the assembler is not even "present" when the program is actually executing.

One common use of the IF directive is to insert coding that is to be used for debugging purposes only. For example, when debugging a program that involves many calculations, it may be useful to call a DSPLY_TEMP_VALUES subroutine that prints the contents of key intermediate fields or registers. After the program is debugged and ready to go into production, this extra code must be removed. It is possible to manually insert such code and then manually remove it. However, what happens when an error is discovered after the program is already in production? It would certainly be useful to have the debugging code reinserted. By using an IF directive, any debugging code can automatically be inserted and removed.

The key to this feature is to define a control field called DEBUG, for example. Then, when the program needs the debugging features, the control field can be equated to 1. When the debugging code is to be removed, the equate can be changed to 0 and the program reassembled. Example 17–6 shows some partial coding to implement this feature.

```
     DEBUG       EQU  1     ; 1 = INSERT DEBUGGING CODE
                           ; 0 = REMOVE DEBUGGING CODE
                  .
                  .
                  .

                 IF DEBUG
                    EXTRN  DSPLY_TEMP_VALUES
                    CALL   DSPLY_TEMP_VALUES
                 ENDIF
                  .
                  .
                  .
```

EXAMPLE 17–6 Using the IF directive to control debugging

Code Generation

The IF directives can also be used to control recursion. An earlier section stated that IFs can be used with recursive macros. Examine one such macro that can be used to accumulate the even numbers in a sequence from 1 to MAX. For example, if MAX is set to 6, then the macro is expected to calculate the sum of 2 + 4 + 6. The only requirement for the macro SUM_SEQUENCE is that the MAX number of the sequence be in register AX, the accumulator register. When completed, the total is in register AX.

Examine the code for the SUM_SEQUENCE macro, which is shown in Figure 17–10 (PGM53.ASM on the program disk). When the macro is invoked the first time, the macro parameter MAX holds the equated value, 6. Since MAX-2 (MAX minus 2) is not 0, the statements within the IF block are generated, creating ADD AX,MAX-2 which adds 4 to the contents of register AX, (ADD AX,4). Then, when SUM_SEQUENCE is reinvoked using MAX-2 as the argument, MAX has the value 4. Again, MAX-2 is not 0; therefore, the IF block is generated. The IF block results in another ADD instruction: ADD AX,MAX-2-2 or simply ADD AX,2. Finally, SUM_SEQUENCE is reinvoked using MAX-2-2, or 2. This time, MAX-2 is 0 and IF MAX-2 is 0. Therefore, nothing is generated and the macro ends, returning to the previous invocation, which also ends. Thus, the additional code that is generated consists of the two ADD instructions.

The IFDEF and IFNDEF Directives

The **IFDEF** and **IFNDEF** directives test whether or not an indicated name has been defined. IFDEF generates the code that follows it only if the indicated name has already been defined, either as a name, label, or symbol. IFNDEF will generate the code only if the name has not yet been defined within the program.

```
Microsoft (R) Macro Assembler Version 5.10            8/10/88 18:32:48
PGM53 - FIGURE 17-10 - CALCULATE THE SUM OF A SEQUENCE     Page    1-1


                            PAGE    60,132
                            TITLE    PGM53 - FIGURE 17-10 - CALCULATE THE SUM OF A SEQUENCE


                    ;****************************************************************************
                    ; PGM53        Title: Figure 17-10 Calculate the sum of a sequence of   *
                    ;                        even numbers                                   *
                    ; Programmer: Vic Broquard                                              *
                    ; Date Written:  6/11/88        Date Of Last Revision: 8/9/88           *
                    ;                                                                       *
                    ; Purpose: To calculate the sum of a sequence of even numbers, using IF*
                    ;          and recursion                                                *
                    ; Special Requirements: Register AX contains the MAX number in the      *
                    ;                        series and the result will be in AX            *
                    ;****************************************************************************


                    SUM_SEQUENCE MACRO MAX

                    ;; MACRO TO CALCULATE THE SUM OF A SEQUENCE OF EVEN INTEGERS
                    ;; THE MAXIMUM VALUE IS CONTAINED IN REGISTER AX
                    ;; THE SUM IS LEFT IN REGISTER AX

                            IF MAX-2             ; IF MAX - 2 IS NOT 0 THEN
                                ADD  AX,MAX-2    ; ADD IN NEXT VALUE IN THE SEQUENCE
                                SUM_SEQUENCE MAX-2  ; REPEAT FOR REST OF THE SEQUENCE
                            ENDIF

                            ENDM
```

```
Microsoft (R) Macro Assembler Version 5.10            8/10/88 18:32:48
PGM53 - FIGURE 17-10 - CALCULATE THE SUM OF A SEQUENCE     Page    1-2


                                    PAGE
0000                        PGMCD   SEGMENT

0000                        MAIN    PROC    FAR

                            ; housekeeping section

                                ASSUME CS:PGMCD,DS:PGMDA,SS:PGMSK

0000  B8 ---- R                 MOV    AX,PGMDA     ; ESTABLISH ADDRESSABILITY
0003  8E D8                     MOV    DS,AX        ; TO PGMDA - THE PGM'S DATA SEGMENT
```

FIGURE 17–10   Macro to calculate the sum of a sequence of even numbers
(PGM53.ASM)   *(Continues)*

```
                                        ; main process section

= 0006                                  MAXIMUM  =     6            ; SET UPPER LIMIT OF SERIES
0005  B8 0006                           MOV   AX,MAXIMUM    ; SET AX FOR MACRO USE
                                        SUM_SEQUENCE MAXIMUM ; CALCULATE SUM
0008  05 0004          1                  ADD  AX,MAXIMUM-2      ; ADD IN NEXT VALUE IN THE SEQUENCE
000B  05 0002          2                  ADD  AX,MAXIMUM-2-2     ; ADD IN NEXT VALUE IN THE SEQUENCE


                                        ; return to DOS section

000E  B8 4C00                           MOV   AX,4C00H       ; SFT FOR DOS END PROCESS FUNCTION, RC=0
0011  CD 21                             INT   21H           ; CALL DOS TO END PROGRAM


0013                         MAIN    ENDP


0013                         PGMCD   ENDS


0000                         PGMDA   SEGMENT


0000                         PGMDA   ENDS


0000                         PGMSK   SEGMENT   PARA STACK 'STACK'
0000  0020[                          DW     32 DUP(?)
        ????

                    ]


0040                         PGMSK   ENDS


                                     END     MAIN
```

FIGURE 17–10   continued

The IFB and IFNB Directives

The **IFB** and **IFNB** directives are meant to be used in macros. They test for a blank argument value on the original macro directive. Each has one operand. The IFB generates the block of statements if the indicated argument was not passed to the macro. If the argument was passed (that is, has a value), the IFBN generates the statements.

The IFNB can be used to create a "smart" register-save macro. In Figure 17–1, the SAVE_REGS macro, all the registers were saved. A better approach is to save only those registers indicated during the macro call. (Usually, the maximum number of registers to be saved is six—the four data registers and SI and DI.) The coding for this improved macro is shown in Figure 17–11 (PGM54.ASM on the program disk). By using IFNB and recursively invoking itself, the SAVE_REGS macro generates only the required PUSH instructions.

The macro tests the first register argument to see if the value is blank (not present) or if it has a value. If it is not blank, the block is generated,

```
Microsoft (R) Macro Assembler Version 5.10          8/10/88 18:32:57
PGM54 - FIGURE 17-11 - IMPROVED SAVE_REGS MACRO     Page    1-1


                         PAGE    60,132
                         TITLE   PGM54 - FIGURE 17-11 - IMPROVED SAVE_REGS MACRO


                 ;*************************************************************************
                 ;
                 ; PGM54      Title: Figure 17-11 A SAVE_REGS macro that only PUSHes   *
                 ;                     the needed registers                            *
                 ; Programmer: Vic Broquard                                           *
                 ; Date Written:  6/11/88       Date Of Last Revision: 8/9/88          *
                 ;                                                                     *
                 ; Purpose: To save only those registers it is invoked with - uses IFNB *
                 ;           and recursion                                             *
                 ; Special Requirements: none                                         *
                 ;                                                                     *
                 ;*************************************************************************
                 ;

                 SAVE_REGS MACRO REG1,REG2,REG3,REG4,REG5,REG6

                 ;; MACRO TO PUSH ONLY THOSE REGISTERS PASSED TO THE MACRO

                         IFNB  <REG1>      ;; IF THE REGISTER IS NOT BLANK THEN

                           PUSH  REG1 ;; SAVE THE REGISTER
                           SAVE_REGS REG2,REG3,REG4,REG5,REG6 ;; REPEAT FOR THE OTHER
REGISTERS

                         ENDIF

                         ENDM
----------------------------------------------------------------------------

Microsoft (R) Macro Assembler Version 5.10          8/10/88 18:32:57
PGM54 - FIGURE 17-11 - IMPROVED SAVE_REGS MACRO     Page    1-2


                                PAGE
0000                     PGMCD   SEGMENT

0000                     MAIN    PROC    FAR

                         ; housekeeping section

                         ASSUME CS:PGMCD,DS:PGMDA,SS:PGMSK

0000 B8 ---- R                   MOV  AX,PGMDA    ; ESTABLISH ADDRESSABILITY
```

FIGURE 17–11 SAVE_REGS macro that pushes only the needed registers
(PGM54.ASM)   *(Continues)*

```
0003  8E D8                              MOV   DS,AX         ; TO PGMDA - THE PGM'S DATA SEGMENT

                        ; main process section

                                 SAVE_REGS AX,BX,CX
0005  50                    1          PUSH  AX ;
0006  53                    2          PUSH  BX ;
0007  51                    3          PUSH  CX ;

                             SAVE_REGS AX,BX,CX,DX,SI,DI
0008  50                    1          PUSH  AX ;
0009  53                    2          PUSH  BX ;
000A  51                    3          PUSH  CX ;
000B  52                    4          PUSH  DX ;
000C  56                    5          PUSH  SI ;
000D  57                    6          PUSH  DI ;

                               SAVE_REGS AX
000E  50                    1          PUSH  AX ;

                        ; return to DOS section

000F  B8 4C00                           MOV   AX,4C00H      ; SET FOR DOS END PROCESS FUNCTION, RC=0
0012  CD 21                             INT   21H           ; CALL DOS TO END PROGRAM

0014                        MAIN    ENDP

0014                        PGMCD   ENDS

0000                        PGMDA   SEGMENT

0000                        PGMDA   ENDS

0000                        PGMSK   SEGMENT  PARA STACK 'STACK'
0000  0020[                         DW    32 DUP(?)
      ????
                      ]

0040                        PGMSK   ENDS

                            END   MAIN
```

FIGURE 17–11   continued

creating a PUSH instruction and reinvoking the SAVE_REGS macro. However, this time, it only passes the arguments beyond this first register. Thus, on the second recursion, the original second register value becomes the first register value. As long as the new first register value is not blank the process repeats, passing the original third register value as the new first register value. When the "first" register finally has no value, all the PUSHes have been generated, the IFNB fails, and the macro recursions end one by one.

The IFIDN and IFDIF Directives

The **IFIDN** (if identical) and **IFDIF** (if different) directives are used to compare the values of two arguments that are also normally found within the macro. The IFIDN directive generates the block of statements if the two arguments are identical. The IFDIF does so only if the two arguments are different.

17.13 TERMINATING A MACRO

There may be situations in which the macro should end prematurely because of abnormal occurrences. The **EXITM** directive (exit macro) notifies the assembler either to end the repeat block that is currently active or to end the macro if no repeat block is active. No remaining statements are generated.

17.14 GENERATING MESSAGES TO THE SCREEN

The **%OUT** directive, which is normally used to communicate error information, displays on the screen any text following the directive. This directive is normally used to communicate error information to the programmer.

17.15 CREATING A DO-WHILE MACRO

There is one frequently needed programming logic structure that is noticeably absent from the assembler language. It is the DO-WHILE iterative structure. To determine whether a macro can be created to handle the DO-WHILE logic, you must be able to state the problem in the following form:

DO WHILE (op1 condition op2)

CALL subroutine

ENDDO

This means that the called subroutine is executed repeatedly as long as the condition is true. There must be two operands to compare and the condition used **must** correspond to the normal conditional jump mnemonics without the "J". For example, JE is E, JNE is NE, JA is A, JAE is AE, JB is B, JBE is BE, and so on.

The macro needs to be passed the following: op1, op2, the condition to be used in a conditional jump command, and the name of the procedure to call.

In the following code, the procedure PERFORM_AVERAGE is called repetitively as long as COUNT is not equal to 0.

```
DO WHILE (COUNT NE 0)
      CALL PERFORM_AVERAGE
ENDDO
```

Figure 17–12 (PGM55.ASM on the program disk) shows how this simple macro can be implemented. This version of DO-WHILE can be used as frequently as required. All labels are local. To test the macro, the sum of five test scores is computed. OP1 becomes register CX, and OP2 becomes the literal 5. The condition used is NE. Thus, the code says, in effect

```
DO WHILE (CX IS NOT EQUAL TO 5)
      CALL CALC_SUM
ENDDO
```

Notice that provision must be made within CALC_SUM to increment the counter register CX. Failure to do so results in an infinite loop.

17.16 SUMMARY

The macro language is a powerful feature within the microassembler language. Macros begin and are defined by the MACRO directive, which specifies a name for the macro and defines the parameters that potentially are passed to it. All macros end with an ENDM directive. Macros can be nested, redefined, and recursive.

All macro definitions must be physically located in the source program before the statements that invoke or call them. Normally, macros are inserted at the beginning of the source program. Frequently, they are stored as files that have the .MAC extension and are inserted into the source program by an INCLUDE statement.

A macro is invoked by coding its name as the operations code. The statements that the macro creates are collectively referred to as the macro expansion or macro generation. One or more values, known as arguments, may be passed to the macro when it is called. They correspond, one for one, with the designated parameters coded on the MACRO definition directive. The argument values replace all occurrences of the corresponding parameters within the body of the macro.

Conditional assembler directives can be coded anywhere within the source program, but most frequently they are found within the macros. The repeat directives repeatedly generate a block of statements the indicated

```
Microsoft (R) Macro Assembler Version 5.10          8/10/88 18:33:04
PGM55 - FIGURE 17-12 - A DO WHILE MACRO              Page    1-1


                         PAGE    60,132
                         TITLE   PGM55 - FIGURE 17-12 - A DO WHILE MACRO

           ;***************************************************************************
           ; PGM55       Title: Figure 17-12 A general DO WHILE macro        *
           ;                                                                 *
           ; Programmer: Vic Broquard                                        *
           ; Date Written:  6/11/88        Date Of Last Revision: 8/9/88     *
           ;                                                                 *
           ; Purpose: To illustrate the implementation of a simple DO WHILE macro *
           ;                                                                 *
           ; Special Requirements: none                                      *
           ;                                                                 *
           ;***************************************************************************

           DOWHILE  MACRO   OP1,COND,OP2,CALLEE
                    LOCAL   TOP_OF_LOOP,DO_IT,ALL_DONE

           ;; MACRO TO IMPLEMENT A SIMPLE DO WHILE STRUCTURE
           ;;
           ;; EXPECTS COND TO BE PART OF THE CONDITIONAL JUMPS, LESS THE J
           ;; INCLUDING E, NE, A, AE, B, BE, AND SO ON - IF NOT VALID, ERROR RESULTS

           TOP_OF_LOOP:

                    CMP     OP1,OP2      ; IS LOOP DONE?
                    J&COND  DO_IT        ; NO, GO PERFORM PROCESS ONCE MORE
                    JMP     ALL_DONE     ; YES, DO WHILE IS COMPLETE

           DO_IT:

                    CALL    &CALLEE      ; PERFORM THE PROCESS
                    JMP     TOP_OF_LOOP  ; REPEAT THE DO WHILE

           ALL_DONE:

                    ENDM
           ------------------------------------------------------------------------

Microsoft (R) Macro Assembler Version 5.10          8/10/88 18:33:04
PGM55 - FIGURE 17-12 - A DO WHILE MACRO              Page    1-2


                         PAGE
           0000                 PGMCD   SEGMENT
```

FIGURE 17–12 A general DO-WHILE macro (PGM55.ASM)   *(Continues)*

```
0000                              MAIN    PROC    FAR

                                  ; housekeeping section

                                          ASSUME CS:PGMCD,DS:PGMDA,SS:PGMSK

0000  B8 ---- R                           MOV    AX,PGMDA       ; ESTABLISH ADDRESSABILITY
0003  8E D8                               MOV    DS,AX          ; TO PGMDA - THE PGM'S DATA SEGMENT

                                  ; main process section

0005  8D 1E 0000 R                        LEA    BX,SCORES      ; POINT TO THE FIRST SCORE
0009  B9 0000                             MOV    CX,0           ; SET NUMBER OF ADDED SCORES TO 0
000C  B8 0000                             MOV    AX,0           ; SET TOTAL SCORE TO 0

                                          DOWHILE CX,NE,5,CALC_SUM ; ADD THE SCORES - TOTAL IS IN AX
000F                              1 ??0000:
000F  83 F9 05                    1        CMP    CX,5        ; IS LOOP DONE?
0012  75 03                       1        JNE ??0001         ; NO, GO PERFORM PROCESS ONCE MORE
0014  EB 06 90                    1        JMP    ??0002      ; YES, DO WHILE IS COMPLETE
0017                              1 ??0001:
0017  E8 0024 R                   1        CALL   CALC_SUM       ; PERFORM THE PROCESS
001A  EB F3                       1        JMP    ??0000  ; REPEAT THE DO WHILE
001C                              1 ??0002:

001C  A3 000A R                           MOV    TOTAL,AX       ; SAVE THE SUM IN TOTAL

                                  ; return to DOS section

001F  B8 4C00                             MOV    AX,4C00H       ; SET FOR DOS END PROCESS FUNCTION, RC=0
0022  CD 21                               INT    21H            ; CALL DOS TO END PROGRAM

0024                              MAIN    ENDP


0024                              CALC_SUM PROC

                                  ; PROCEDURE TO SUM THE SCORES

0024  03 07                               ADD    AX,[BX]  ; ADD IN CURRENT SCORE
0026  43                                  INC    BX       ; POINT TO
0027  43                                  INC    BX       ; THE NEXT SCORE IN TABLE
0028  41                                  INC    CX       ; +1 TO THE COUNTER

0029  C3                                  RET

002A                              CALC_SUM ENDP


002A                              PGMCD   ENDS
```

FIGURE 17–12   continued

```
Microsoft (R) Macro Assembler Version 5.10          8/10/88 18:33:04
PGM55 - FIGURE 17-12 - A DO WHILE MACRO             Page    1-3


 0000                         PGMDA    SEGMENT

 0000  0001 0002 0003 0004    SCORES   DW    1,2,3,4,5  ; THE TABLE OF SCORES TO SUM
       0005
 000A  0000                   TOTAL    DW    ?          ; WILL HOLD THE SUM OF THE SCORES

 000C                         PGMDA    ENDS


 0000                         PGMSK    SEGMENT  PARA STACK 'STACK'
 0000  0020[                           DW    32 DUP(?)
       ????
                       ]

 0040                         PGMSK    ENDS

                              END      MAIN
```

FIGURE 17–12   continued

number of times, eliminating much tedious coding. The IF-THEN-ELSE series of directives use this conditional structure to generate one of two possible blocks of coding.

By now, you should have a good understanding of the basics of the macro and conditional assembly language. From this point, we encourage you to explore the additional, more complex, features of the microassembler language.

17.17 REVIEW QUESTIONS

1. A programmer coded a SAVE_REGS macro and included it at the end of a program. The program called the macro upon entry to four internal subroutines. What will occur when the programmer attempts to assemble the program? Why? What must be done to remedy the problem?

2. Outline the rules for defining macros.

3. Explain the difference between a parameter and an argument. What happens if there are not enough arguments on the macro call to match the parameters on the macro definition? What happens if there are more arguments than parameters?

4. Under what circumstances is the & operator needed? Why?

5. What is meant by recursion? How can recursion be useful?

6. What is meant by macro redefinition? Under what circumstances does a macro definition employ redefinition?

7. What is meant by *phase error?* What measures can a programmer take to resolve a phase error?

8. A programmer coded the following IF directive:

```
IF  AX          ; IF AX IS NOT EQUAL TO 0 THEN
    ADD  BX,AX   ; ADD COST TO TOTAL
ENDIF
```

What will happen when this code is compiled? Why? Is there any way that the coding can be made to work?

17.18 PRACTICE PROBLEMS

1. Code a simple macro that displays a byte to the printer. Use Figure 17–4 as a model.

2. Using Figure 17–5 as a guide, code a macro that defines a month-name table entry. Show how it would be called 12 times to create the table.

3. Using Figure 17–7 as a model, sketch a macro that can be used to compute the average temperature for a city. There will be 12 temperature entries (one signed byte each) for a city.

4. Code the statement to call the DEFN_BYTES macro shown in Figure 17–9 to define a series of 5 bytes that contain 'H', 'E', 'L', 'L', 'O' respectively.

17.19 PROGRAMMING PROBLEMS

1. Write a macro that sums a sequence of numbers: 1 + 2 + 3 + 4, and so on. Test the macro with 5, 10, and 25 as the largest numbers in the sequence.

2. Write a macro called RESTORE, which restores only those registers that are coded as arguments on the macro call. It should parallel the SAVE_REGS macro shown in Figure 17–11. The maximum number of registers is six.

3. Prepare a macro called INITIAL_CODE, which generates all the common initial coding that is done, including definition of the code segment, the register assigns, and the establishment of register DS. Then code FINAL_CODE, a macro that returns to DOS and ends the code segment.

4. Code a data segment macro to define a small translation table consisting of the uppercase letters only. The table should consist of 26 bytes with appropriate initial values.

5. Following the guidelines used for the DO-WHILE macro, shown in Figure 17–12, code a DO-UNTIL macro.

6. Code a macro that can be used to clear the screen and set the colors. Accept the color attribute byte as an argument. Also, accept a control field that indicates whether or not the macro is to save and restore all registers that it will use. Be sure to test both options.

7. Code a macro that can be used to set the cursor. Accept the coordinates as arguments.

Appendix A
Interlanguage Calls

Interfacing assembler external subroutines to high-level languages is a relatively easy task. Perhaps the most common interface occurs when a high-level language calls an assembler routine, although it is possible to have an assembler program call a high-level language.

In this appendix discussion focuses on three of the more popular high-level languages that commonly call assembler language routines. They are C, PASCAL, and FORTRAN. This discussion refers to the Microsoft versions of these languages. If you need to interface to other languages or other vendor's products, this discussion is still relevant because the problems and guidelines, while specific to Microsoft, apply equally to other languages and products.

Calling an Assembler External Subroutine from a High-Level Language Program

There are three major considerations when invoking an external assembler routine from another language. They are the memory model used, the procedure naming conventions, and the methods used to pass data.

Memory Models

The DOSSEG directive is used for creating simple segment directives and coding a .MODEL directive that is appropriate for the language. PASCAL uses only large models, and FORTRAN supports medium, large, and huge models. C supports all types, but small models are often used.

The assembler routine uses the directives .CODE and .DATA as well. The stack provides the high-level language.

The Procedure Naming Conventions

With most Microsoft languages, procedure names are translated to uppercase. To avoid any confusion, use uppercase on the external procedure name. C is the only language that is case sensitive. C requires that the external name be in all capital letters and prefixed by an underscore. Thus, in a C routine, if an assembler module known as CALCS is called, the actual name coded on the external assembler procedure is _CALCS.

The maximum length of the external procedure name varies according to the language.

FORTRAN uses the first 6 bytes of the external procedure name. PASCAL and C use the first 8 bytes.

Methods Used to Pass Data

How data are passed is the single most important and divergent topic among languages. First, consider what is passed and then how it is passed.

Data can be passed either by value or by address. Remember that when data are passed by value, the callee has no access to the variable, only its value.

C passes arrays either by NEAR addresses or by FAR addresses, but all other data types are passed by value. FORTRAN passes data either by FAR addresses or by value, depending upon your FORTRAN coding. PASCAL passes items that are VAR or CONST by NEAR addresses and items that are VARS or CONSTS by FAR addresses. All others are passed by value. Remember that a NEAR address reference is given only by a word offset address, but a far address involves the offset address and the segment address or 2 words.

How the data are passed is known as the calling convention. The FORTRAN and PASCAL calling conventions are the same, but the convention for C is different. Both FORTRAN and PASCAL push the parameters onto the stack in the order in which the parameters appear in the source code. These parameters are accessed using register BP. Thus, after the return address, the next entry on the stack is the last parameter pushed. Access to the parameters is in reverse order. This is similar to the methods used in Chapter 12. In addition, when the assembler routine returns, the parameters must be removed from the stack with a RET n instruction.

On the other hand, C pushes the parameters onto the stack in the reverse order from the source code. This means that the first parameter on the stack after the return is the first parameter referenced in the C source code. The C routine is responsible for removing the parameters from the stack after the assembler routine has finished. Thus, RET n is not used.

Functions that Return a Value

Sometimes the subroutine is intended to be used as a function that returns a value. This function is similar to that provided by the sine function available in many languages. You can code such a statement as

$$X = SIN(ANGLE)$$

The sine routine is passed the field ANGLE but returns a value that is then stored in field X. How are values returned? If the value is a byte, it is returned in register AL. If the value is a word, it is returned in register AX. If the value is a doubleword, it is returned in DX:AX.

Assembler Coding Details

The assembler procedure should begin with the following type of coding

```
        DOSSEG
        .MODEL LARGE
        PUBLIC CALCS

        .CODE

        CALCS PROC FAR

        .DATA
```

The first two instructions in CALCS must save register BP and establish addressability to the stack:

```
PUSH BP    ; SAVE BP REG
MOV  BP,SP ; SET BP TO POINT TO
             PARAMETERS
```

Next, some of the registers must be saved. If the routine intends to use registers SI, DI, and DS, they need to be saved. Also, if the stack segment is going to be altered, SS:SP needs to be saved. Work registers do not need to be saved, particularly if DX:AX is expected to hold a return value as in the case of a function.

Parameters are then accessed using register BP (see Chapter 12 for details.) To find the parameters, use

parm c =   2
+ size of the return address (2 or 4)
+ # bytes between first parm and parm c

The size of the return depends upon whether the procedure was NEAR (2 bytes) or FAR (4 bytes). In the FAR case, the offset address is stored on the stack below the old BP register and the segment address is stored below the offset word.

For example, to acquire the first parm on the stack from a FAR call, enter

```
MOV BX, [BP + 6]
```

that is, 2 + 4 + 0. The third parm is

```
MOV BX, [BP + 10]
```

that is, 2 + 4 + 4. Note that if the parm is passed by FAR address, then you must extract first the offset address and then the segment address. Suppose that the first parameter is a word value and the second parameter is a FAR address. Below the return address on the stack is the vector address of the second parameter, followed by the word value of the first parameter. The coding to extract these is

```
MOV BX, [BP + 6] ; GET OFFSET
                       OF SECOND
                       PARM
MOV AX, [BP + 8] ; GET SEGMENT
                       OF SECOND
                       PARM
MOV ES,AX      ; AND PLACE IN
                       REGISTER ES
MOV AX, [BP + 10] ; GET FIRST
                       PARAMETER'S
                       VALUE
```

Finally, remember that, in terms of FORTAN and PASCAL, C parameters are passed in reverse order. So, in this example, [BP + 6] points to first parameter's word value and [BP + 8] points to the offset of the second parameter and the segment address, [BP + 10].

If a value is to be returned to the high-level language after performing the main process of the subroutine, leave the value in registers AL, AX, or DX:AX, depending upon its size. Next,

pop all saved registers and code the return instruction. PASCAL and FORTRAN require that the assembler routine remove the parameters from the stack by using the RET n instruction; C does not.

Assembler MAIN Procedures that Call a High-Level Language Subroutine

Occasionally, it is the assembler program that calls a high-level language subroutine. For example, math calculations are more conveniently done in a high-level language than in assembler. However, there is one major problem with this approach: the establishment of the run-time environment for the high-level language. All high-level languages have a special run-time environment that supports program execution. When a high-level language program begins execution, the very first thing that occurs is the establishment of its run-time environment. Once the run-time environment is created, then the first program instruction can be executed. A frequent function of this environment is to monitor math errors.

The run-time environment is established only once for high-level languages. This is done as the MAIN program procedure begins. If the MAIN procedure is assembler, however, this special environment does not need to be established. To make sure that the run-time environment has been established and is available for use in calling a high-level language routine, simply create a dummy high-level language driver module. The only instruction in this module is one that calls the assembler driver routine. In this way, the dummy module establishes the required run-time environment.

Coding Examples

To briefly illustrate interlanguage call principles, we have coded three versions of a simple program that adds the numbers 2 and 3, yielding 5.

The C Version

The C driver module is

```
extern int Calcs(int, int);
main()
```

```
{
  printf("2 plus 3 is %d\n", Calcs(2,3));
}
```

The assembler subroutine is

```
        DOSSEG
        .MODEL SMALL
        PUBLIC _Calcs

.CODE

_Calcs PROC

        PUSH BP
        MOV BP,SP

        MOV AX,[BP+4]
        MOV CX,[BP+6]
        ADD AX,CX     ; LEAVE SUM IN
                        AX FOR C

        POP BP
        RET

_Calcs ENDP
        END
```

The FORTRAN Version

The FORTRAN driver module is

```
        INTERFACE TO INTEGER*2
         CALCS(A,B)
        INTEGER*2 A,B
        END
  C
        INTEGER*2 A,B
        A=2
        B=3
        WRITE (*,*) ' 2 PLUS 3 IS',
         CALCS(A,B)
        END
```

The assembler subroutine is

```
        DOSSEG
        .MODEL LARGE
        PUBLIC CALCS

    .CODE
```

```
    CALCS:

        PUSH BP
        MOV   BP,SP

        LES   BX,[BP+10]
        MOV   AX,ES:[BX]
        LES   BX,[BP+6]
        MOV   CX,ES:[BX]
        ADD   AX,CX   ; LEAVE RESULT IN AX
                            FOR FORTRAN

        POP BP
        RET 8

        END
```

The PASCAL Version

The PASCAL driver module is

```
        program testasm(input, output);
        function Calcs (a,b : integer) : integer; extern;
        begin
            writeln('2 plus 3 is ',Calcs(3,5));
        end.
```

The assembler subroutine is

```
        DOSSEG
        .MODEL LARGE
        PUBLIC CALCS

    .CODE

    CALCS:
        PUSH BP
        MOV BP,SP

        MOV AX,[BP+8]
        MOV CX,[BP+6]
        ADD AX,CX     ; LEAVE RESULT IN
                        AX FOR PASCAL

        POP BP
        RET 4

        END
```

Appendix B
Useful Tables and Personal Computer Characteristics

TABLE B–1 Binary to hex to decimal values

Binary	Hex	Decimal
0000	0	0
0001	1	1
0010	2	2
0011	3	3
0100	4	4
0101	5	5
0110	6	6
0111	7	7
1000	8	8
1001	9	9
1010	A	10
1011	B	11
1100	C	12
1101	D	13
1110	E	14
1111	F	15

TABLE B–2   Hex to decimal conversion

Hex digit columns

Hex ten thousands 5		Hex thousands 4		Hex hundreds 3		Hex tens 2		Hex units 1	
hex	decimal	hex	decimal	hex	decimal	hex	decimal	hex	decimal
0	0	0	0	0	0	0	0	0	0
1	65,536	1	4,096	1	256	1	16	1	1
2	131,072	2	8,192	2	512	2	32	2	2
3	196,608	3	12,288	3	768	3	48	3	3
4	262,144	4	16,384	4	1,024	4	64	4	4
5	327,680	5	20,480	5	1,280	5	80	5	5
6	393,216	6	24,576	6	1,536	6	96	6	6
7	458,752	7	28,672	7	1,792	7	112	7	7
8	524,288	8	32,768	8	2,048	8	128	8	8
9	589,824	9	36,864	9	2,304	9	144	9	9
A	655,360	A	40,960	A	2,560	A	160	A	10
B	720,896	B	45,056	B	2,816	B	176	B	11
C	786,432	C	49,152	C	3,072	C	192	C	12
D	851,968	D	53,248	D	3,328	D	208	D	13
E	917,504	E	57,344	E	3,584	E	224	E	14
F	983,040	F	61,440	F	3,840	F	240	F	15

TABLE B-3 ASCII codes

Ctrl	Dec	Hex	Char	Code
^@	0	00		NUL
^A	1	01		SOH
^B	2	02		STX
^C	3	03		ETX
^D	4	04		EOT
^E	5	05		ENQ
^F	6	06		ACK
^G	7	07		BEL
^H	8	08		BS
^I	9	09		HT
^J	10	0A		LF
^K	11	0B		VT
^L	12	0C		FF
^M	13	0D		CR
^N	14	0E		SO
^O	15	0F		SI
^P	16	10		DLE
^Q	17	11		DC1
^R	18	12		DC2
^S	19	13		DC3
^T	20	14		DC4
^U	21	15		NAK
^V	22	16		SYN
^W	23	17		ETB
^X	24	18		CAN
^Y	25	19		EM
^Z	26	1A		SUB
^[	27	1B		ESC
^\	28	1C		FS
^]	29	1D		GS
^^	30	1E		RS
^_	31	1F		US

Dec	Hex	Char
32	20	(space)
33	21	!
34	22	"
35	23	#
36	24	$
37	25	%
38	26	&
39	27	'
40	28	(
41	29	)
42	2A	*
43	2B	+
44	2C	,
45	2D	-
46	2E	.
47	2F	/
48	30	0
49	31	1
50	32	2
51	33	3
52	34	4
53	35	5
54	36	6
55	37	7
56	38	8
57	39	9
58	3A	:
59	3B	;
60	3C	<
61	3D	=
62	3E	>
63	3F	?

Dec	Hex	Char
64	40	@
65	41	A
66	42	B
67	43	C
68	44	D
69	45	E
70	46	F
71	47	G
72	48	H
73	49	I
74	4A	J
75	4B	K
76	4C	L
77	4D	M
78	4E	N
79	4F	O
80	50	P
81	51	Q
82	52	R
83	53	S
84	54	T
85	55	U
86	56	V
87	57	W
88	58	X
89	59	Y
90	5A	Z
91	5B	[
92	5C	\
93	5D	]
94	5E	^
95	5F	_

Dec	Hex	Char
96	60	`
97	61	a
98	62	b
99	63	c
100	64	d
101	65	e
102	66	f
103	67	g
104	68	h
105	69	i
106	6A	j
107	6B	k
108	6C	l
109	6D	m
110	6E	n
111	6F	o
112	70	p
113	71	q
114	72	r
115	73	s
116	74	t
117	75	u
118	76	v
119	77	w
120	78	x
121	79	y
122	7A	z
123	7B	{
124	7C		
125	7D	}
126	7E	~
127	7F	⌂ *

Dec	Hex	Char
128	80	Ç
129	81	ü
130	82	é
131	83	â
132	84	ä
133	85	à
134	86	å
135	87	ç
136	88	ê
137	89	ë
138	8A	è
139	8B	ï
140	8C	î
141	8D	ì
142	8E	Ä
143	8F	Å
144	90	É
145	91	æ
146	92	Æ
147	93	ô
148	94	ö
149	95	ò
150	96	û
151	97	ù
152	98	ÿ
153	99	Ö
154	9A	Ü
155	9B	¢
156	9C	£
157	9D	¥
158	9E	₧
159	9F	ƒ

Dec	Hex	Char
160	A0	á
161	A1	í
162	A2	ó
163	A3	ú
164	A4	ñ
165	A5	Ñ
166	A6	ª
167	A7	º
168	A8	¿
169	A9	⌐
170	AA	¬
171	AB	½
172	AC	¼
173	AD	¡
174	AE	«
175	AF	»
176	B0	░
177	B1	▒
178	B2	▓
179	B3	│
180	B4	┤
181	B5	╡
182	B6	╢
183	B7	╖
184	B8	╕
185	B9	╣
186	BA	║
187	BB	╗
188	BC	╝
189	BD	╜
190	BE	╛
191	BF	┐

Dec	Hex	Char
192	C0	└
193	C1	┴
194	C2	┬
195	C3	├
196	C4	─
197	C5	┼
198	C6	╞
199	C7	╟
200	C8	╚
201	C9	╔
202	CA	╩
203	CB	╦
204	CC	╠
205	CD	═
206	CE	╬
207	CF	╧
208	D0	╨
209	D1	╤
210	D2	╥
211	D3	╙
212	D4	╘
213	D5	╒
214	D6	╓
215	D7	╫
216	D8	╪
217	D9	┘
218	DA	┌
219	DB	█
220	DC	▄
221	DD	▌
222	DE	▐
223	DF	▀

Dec	Hex	Char
224	E0	α
225	E1	ß
226	E2	Γ
227	E3	π
228	E4	Σ
229	E5	σ
230	E6	µ
231	E7	τ
232	E8	Φ
232	E9	Θ
233	EA	Ω
234	EB	δ
235	EC	∞
236	ED	φ
237	EE	ε
238	EF	∩
239	F0	≡
240	F1	±
241	F2	≥
242	F3	≤
243	F4	⌠
244	F5	⌡
245	F6	÷
246	F7	≈
247	F8	°
248	F9	∙
249	FA	·
250	FB	√
251	FC	ⁿ
252	FD	²
253	FE	■
254	FF	

*ASCII code 127 has the code DEL. Under DOS, this code has the same effect as ASCII 8 (BS). The DEL code can be generated by CTRL-BACKSPACE.

Portions © copyright 1987 Microsoft Corporation. Reprinted with permission from Microsoft Corporation.

TABLE B–4   Debug flag settings

Flag*	Set (=1)		Cleared (=0)	
Overflow	OV	(yes)	NV	(no)
Direction	DN	(decrement)	UP	(increment)
Interrupt	EI	(enable)	DI	(disable)
Sign	NG	(negative)	PL	(positive)
Zero	ZR	(yes)	NZ	(no)
Auxiliary carry	AC	(yes)	NA	(no)
Parity	PE	(even)	PO	(odd)
Carry	CY	(yes)	NC	(no)

*Shown in the order that DEBUG displays the flags

TABLE B–5   Reserved words in assembler

Register names:

AH	AL	AX	BH	BL	BP	BX	CH
CL	CS	CX	DH	DI	DL	DS	DX
ES	SI	SP	SS				

Instruction operation codes:

AAA	AAD	AAM	AAS	ADC	ADD	AND	CALL
CBW	CLC	CLD	CLI	CMC	CMP	CMPS	CWD
DAA	DAS	DEC	DIV	ESC	HLT	IDIV	IMUL
IN	INC	INT	INTO	IRET	JA	JAE	JB
JBE	JCXZ	JE	JG	JGE	JL	JLE	JMP
JNA	JNAE	JNB	JNBE	JNE	JNG	JNGE	JNL
JNLE	JNO	JNP	JNS	JNZ	JO	JP	JPE
JPO	JS	JZ	LAHF	LDS	LEA	LES	LOCK
LODS	LOOP	LOOPE	LOOPNE	LOOPNZ	LOOPZ	MOV	MOVS
MUL	NEG	NIL	NOP	NOT	OR	OUT	POP
POPF	PUSH	PUSHF	RCL	RCR	REP	REPE	REPNE
REPNZ	REPZ	RET	ROL	ROR	SAHF	SAL	SAR
SBB	SCAS	SHL	SHR	STC	STD	STI	STOS
SUB	TEST	WAIT	XCHG	XLAT	XOR		

Assembler operators and directives:

$	*	+	©	.	/	=	?	[]	
ALIGN	ASSUME	BYTE	COMM	COMMENT	DB	DF	DD		
DOSSEG	DQ	DS	DT	DW	DWORD	DUP	ELSE		
END	ENDIF	ENDM	ENDMP	ENDS	EQ	EQU	EVEN		
EXITM	EXTRN	FAR	FWORD	GE	GROUP	GT	HIGH		

(Continues)

Assembler operators and directives (continued):

```
IF       IFB       IFDEF     IFDIF     IFE       IFIDN     IFNB     IFNDEF
IF1      IF2       INCLUDE   INCLUDELIB          IRP       IRPC     LABEL
LE       LENGTH    LINE      LOCAL     LOW       LT        MACRO    MASK
MOD      NAME      NE        NEAR      NOTHING   OFFSET    ORG      PAGE
PROC     PRT       PUBLIC    PURGE     QWORD     RECORD    REPT     REPTRD
SEG      SEGMENT   SHORT     SIZE      STACK     STRUC     SUBTTL   TBYTE
TITLE    THIS      TYPE      WIDTH     WORD
```

```
.186     .286      .286P     .287      .386      .386P     .387     .8086
.8087    .ALPHA    .CODE     .CONST    .CREF     .DATA     .DATA?   .ERR
.ERR1    .ERR2     .ERRB     .ERRDEF   .ERRDIF   .ERRE     .ERRIDN
.ERRNB   .ERRNDEF            .ERRNZ    .FARDATA  .FARDATA?          .LALL
.LFCOND  .LIST     .MODEL    %OUT      .RADIX    .SALL     .SEQ     .SFCOND
.STACK   .TFCOND   .TYPE     .XALL     .XCREF    .XLIST
```

TABLE B–5   continued

TABLE B–6   Conditional JUMP instructions

Conditional Jumps Based on Unsigned Data

Operation	Meaning	Flags that are tested
JE or JZ*	jump if op1 is equal to op2 OR jump if zero flag set	ZF
JNE or JNZ*	jump if op1 is not equal to op2 OR jump if zero flag is not set	ZF
JA or JNBE	jump if op1 is above op2 OR jump if op1 is not below and is not equal to op2	CF, ZF
JAE or JNB	jump if op1 is above op2 or is equal to op2 OR jump if op1 is not below op2	CF
JB or JNAE	jump if op1 is below op2 OR jump if op1 is not above op2 and is not equal to op2	CF
JBE or JNA	jump if op1 is below op2 or is equal to op2 OR jump if op1 is not above op2	CF, AF

(Continues)

Conditional Jumps Based on Signed Data

Operation	Meaning	Flags that are tested
JE or JZ*	jump if op1 is equal to op2 OR jump if the zero flag is set	ZF
JNE or JNZ*	jump if op1 is not equal to op2 OR jump if the zero flag is not set	ZF
JG or JNLE	jump if op1 is greater than op2 OR jump if op1 is not less than op2 and is not equal to op2	ZF, SF, OF
JGE or JNL	jump if op1 is greater than or equal to op2 OR jump if op1 is not less than op2	SF, OF
JL or JNGE	jump if op1 is less than op2 OR jump if op1 is not greater than op2 and is not equal to op2	SF, OF
JLE or JNG	jump if op1 is less than or equal to op2 OR jump if op1 is not greater than op2	ZF, SF, OF

*Note that the JE or JZ and JNE or JNZ are the same for unsigned and signed data, since the equal or zero condition occurs regardless of the sign.

Conditional Jumps for Special Arithmetic Conditions

Operation	Meaning	Flags that are tested
JS	jump if sign is set (negative)	SF
JNS	jump if sign is cleared (positive)	SF
JC	jump if carry flag is set (same as JB)	CF
JNC	jump if carry flag is cleared	CF
JO	jump if overflow flag is set	OF
JNO	jump if overflow flag is cleared	OF
JP or JPE	jump if parity is even (set)	PF
JNP or JPO	jump if parity is odd (cleared)	PF
JCXZ	jump if reg CX is 0	ZF and reg CX is 0

TABLE B–6   continued

TABLE B–7   The 97 special keys

Key pressed	Dec	Hex	Key pressed	Dec	Hex	Key pressed	Dec	Hex
F1	59	3B	ALT-1	120	78	HOME	71	47
F2	60	3C	ALT-2	121	79	UP ARROW	72	48
F3	60	3D	ALT-3	122	7A	PGUP	73	49
F4	62	3E	ALT-4	123	7B	LEFT ARROW	75	4B
F5	63	3F	ALT-5	124	7C	RIGHT ARROW	77	4D
F6	64	40	ALT-6	125	7D	END	79	4F
F7	65	41	ALT-7	126	7E	DOWN ARROW	80	50
F8	66	42	ALT-8	127	7F	PGDOWN	81	51
F9	67	43	ALT-9	128	80	INS	82	52
F10	68	44	ALT-10	129	81	DEL	83	53
SHIFT-F1	84	54	ALT-=	131	83	ALT-		
SHIFT-F2	85	55				HYPHEN	130	82
SHIFT-F3	86	56	ALT-A	30	1E			
SHIFT-F4	87	57	ALT-B	48	30	ECHO		
SHIFT-F5	88	58	ALT-C	46	2E	(CTRL-PRTSC)		
SHIFT-F6	89	59	ALT-D	32	20		114	72
SHIFT-F7	90	5A	ALT-E	18	12			
SHIFT-F8	91	5B	ALT-F	33	21	CTRL-LEFT ARROW		
SHIFT-F9	92	5C	ALT-G	34	22		115	73
SHIFT-F10	93	5D	ALT-H	35	23			
			ALT-I	23	17	CTRL-RIGHT ARROW		
CTRL-F1	94	5E	ALT-J	36	24		116	74
CTRL-F2	95	5F	ALT-K	37	25			
CTRL-F3	96	60	ALT-L	38	26	CTRL-END	117	75
CTRL-F4	97	61	ALT-M	50	32			
CTRL-F5	98	62	ALT-N	49	31	CTRL-PGDN		
CTRL-F6	99	63	ALT-O	24	18		118	76
CTRL-F7	100	64	ALT-P	25	19			
CTRL-F8	101	65	ALT-Q	16	10	CTRL-HOME		
CTRL-F9	102	66	ALT-R	19	13		119	77
CTRL-F10	103	67	ALT-S	31	1F			
			ALT-T	20	14	CTRL-PGUP		
ALT-F1	104	68	ALT-U	22	16		132	83
ALT-F2	105	69	ALT-V	47	2F			
ALT-F3	106	6A	ALT-W	17	11	NULL CHARACTER		
ALT-F4	107	6B	ALT-X	45	2D	CTRL-@	0	00
ALT-F5	108	6C	ALT-Y	21	15			
ALT-F6	109	6D	ALT-Z	44	2C	REVERSE TAB		
ALT-F7	110	6E				(SHIFT-TAB)		
ALT-F8	111	6F					15	0F
ALT-F9	112	70						
ALT-F10	113	71						

TABLE B–8   File handle error codes

Code
(in hex) Meaning

1	invalid function number
2	file not found
3	path not found
4	all handles in use
5	access is denied
6	invalid file handle
7	memory control blocks are destroyed
8	insufficient memory
9	invalid memory block address
A	invalid environment (see DOS command SET)
B	invalid format
C	invalid access code (see function 3DH for details)
D	invalid data
E	not currently used
F	invalid drive specification
10	attempted to remove current directory
11	not the same device
12	no more files are to be found

TABLE B–9   Extended file-handling error codes

Register AX will contain either the usual 18 codes or one of the following:

13H disk is write-protected
14H unknown unit ID
15H disk drive not ready
16H command not defined
17H disk data error
18H bad request structure length
19H disk seek error
1AH unknown disk media type
1BH disk sector not found
1CH printer out of paper
1DH write error
1EH read error
1FH general failure
20H file-sharing violation
21H file-locking violation
22H improper disk change   *(Continues)*

23H no FCB available
50H file already exists
51H reserved
52H cannot make
53H critical error interrupt failure

Register BH will contain

01H out of resource: no more of whatever you asked for
02H temporary situation; try again later
03H authorization: you aren't allowed
04H internal DOS error—not program's fault
05H hardware failure
06H system software error—other DOS problems
07H application software error—your problem
08H item requested not found
09H bad format—unrecognizable disk
0AH item locked
0BH media error—CRC error
0CH already exists
0DH error class unknown

Register BL will contain

01H try again now
02H try again later, after waiting
03H ask user to fix it—change disks
04H shut down the program gracefully
05H shut down the program at once
06H ignore the error
07H retry after user action

Register CH will contain

01H unknown
02H block device error
04H serial device error
05H memory error

TABLE B–9   continued

The Attribute Byte

Every character that is displayed on the screen has an attribute byte that tells the device how to display the character. Each bit has a specific meaning. Figure B–1 shows the general layout for either monochrome or color adapters.

The Monochrome Attribute Byte

If the blinking bit is on—that is, if it equals 1—the byte blinks. If the intensity bit is on, the foreground is brighter or more intense.

Normal white on black is produced by having all the foreground bits on and all the background

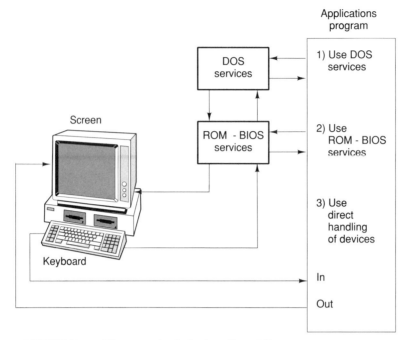

FIGURE B–1   Three methods for handling I/O operations

bits off. Thus, an attribute byte of 07H (0000 0111B) produces a white-on-black display that is nonblinking and normal intensity.

Underlined characters can be produced by setting the foreground bits to 001B.

Reverse video is produced by setting the background bits on and the foreground bits off, that is, to 0111 0000B, or 70H.

Invisible characters can be produced by setting both the foreground and the background bits off, that is, to 00H.

The attribute is used in four functions of INT 10H: 06H (scroll up), 07H (scroll down), 08H (read character and attribute), and 09H (write character and attribute).

The Color Attribute Byte

The color blinking bit functions like the monochrome blinking bit.

The background bits produce eight different colors for the background.

The foreground bits generate eight possible colors for the character.

The intensity bit, besides brightening the foreground, alters the color of the foreground. Thus, there are actually 16 possible foreground colors available.

Table B–10 show the IBM color settings.

TABLE B–10   The IBM color values

Intensity bit off backgrnd & foregrnd		Intensity bit on foreground only	
Bits	Color	Bits	Color
000	black	1000	gray
001	blue	1001	light blue
010	green	1010	light green
011	cyan	1011	light cyan
100	red	1100	light red
101	magenta	1101	light magenta
110	brown	1110	light yellow
111	white	1111	high-intensity white

TABLE B-11   The file attribute bits

0000 0001B	01H	read-only file
0000 0010B	02H	hidden file
0000 0100B	04H	system file
0000 1000B	08H	volume label
0001 0000B	10H	subdirectory
0010 0000B	20H	archive (on if changed since last backup operation)

TABLE B-12   Standard DOS I/O handles

handle	used for	default
0	standard input, keyboard	CON:
1	standard output, screen	CON:
2	standard error output, screen	CON:
3	standard auxiliary device	AUX:
4	standard printer	PRN:

For example, to produce red letters on a green background, use 0010 0100, or 24H. To create light yellow letters on a blue background, use 0001 1110B, or 1EH.

If you use the same color for the foreground and the background, an invisible display results.

The color attribute byte is used in four functions of INT 10H: 06H (scroll up), 07H (scroll down), 08H (read character and attribute), and 09H (write character and attribute).

The Graphics Attribute Byte

In graphics mode, text can be displayed, and color can be applied to the foreground and background. You can also set the border of the screen to a different color than either the foreground or background.

In graphics mode, color is handled differently than in the text mode. For each graphics mode, there are several color palettes available. Within a specific palette, there may be limited choices for foreground colors. When the palette is changed, the entire screen is changed. Thus, using color text mode may be more practical than using color graphics mode if many color changes are needed on one screen display.

The palette is set by using function 0BH (set color palette). The attribute is used in four functions of INT 10H: 06H (scroll up), 07H (scroll down), 08H (read character and attribute), and 09H (write character and attribute).

DOS File Handle Error Codes

Tables B-8 and B-9 summarize the codes in AX. The file attributes consist of eight bits, which, if on, indicate the file's attributes. Table B-11 shows the attribute byte's format.

The high-order bits are not used. Normal files have all attributes set to off, except the archive bit: 20H.

Table B-12 shows the standard DOS I/O handles.

Table B-13 shows the file control block. The numeral 1 in the comment line indicates a field for which you must provide a starting value. The numeral 2 indicates a field you must modify after the file is opened. The numeral 3 indicates a field that is maintained by DOS.

Table B-14 shows the elements of the program segment prefix.

The calculation of the effective address (EA) has a significant effect upon execution speed. Every instruction has a fixed execution speed, referred to as clock speed. The basic unit, clocks, can be converted into nanoseconds (10^{-9} second, or 0.000 000 001 second) by the following formula:

$$1 \text{ clock cycle} = 1 \text{ microsecond/number of megahertz at which the processor runs}$$

where a microsecond is 10^{-6} second, or 0.000 001 second.

For example, on a processor that runs at 4.77 megahertz (MHz), 1 clock cycle will be 210 nanoseconds, but on a faster processor that runs at 8 MHz, 1 clock cycle takes 125 nanoseconds.

The Microsoft MASM manuals provide the clock cycles for every instruction. A register-to-

TABLE B-13   The file control block

```
FCB_PREFX       DB      0,0,0,0,0,0,0       ;1 PREFIX SECTION
FCB             LABEL BYTE                  ;  POINTER TO THE FCB
FCB_DRIVE       DB      ?                   ;1 DRIVE NUMBER 0 = CURRENT, 1 = A:
FCB_FILNAM      DB      8 DUP(?)            ;1 FILE NAME 8 BYTES
FCB_EXTENS      DB      3 DUP(?)            ;1 FILE'S EXTENSION
FCB_BLKNUM      DW      0                   ;2 CURRENT BLOCK NUMBER
FCB_RECSIZ      DW      ?                   ;2 LOGICAL RECORD SIZE
FCB_FILSIZ      DD      ?                   ;3 DOS FILE SIZE IN BYTES
FCB_DATE        DW      ?                   ;3 DATE OF CREATION/MODIFICATION
FCB_TIME        DT      ?                   ;3 TIME AND WORK AREA
FCB_RECNUM      DB      0                   ;2 CURRENT RECORD NUMBER
FCB_RANDOM      DD      0                   ;2 RANDOM RECORD NUMBER,
                                            ;   IF NOT SEQUENTIALLY USED
```

TABLE B-14   The program segment prefix

offset	length	contents
00H	2	A return to DOS instruction: INT 20H
02H	2	The number of paragraphs of all RAM—total memory
04H	1	Reserved
05H	5	Call to DOS function dispatcher: the second and third bytes contain the offset; the last two contain the segment address. The offset also gives the number of bytes available in the program code segment.
0AH	4	The terminate address, IP:CS
0EH	4	The control break handler address, IP:CS
12H	4	The critical error handler address, IP:CS. These three values can be altered by a program to modify standard DOS actions, such as attaching and calling a subprogram, which will return to the caller program, not DOS.
16H	22	DOS area
2CH	2	Environment string pointer
2EH	39	DOS work area
55H	7	FCB #1 prefix
5CH	9	FCB #1
65H	7	FCB #2 prefix
6CH	20	FCB #2
80H	1	Length of the parameter string
81H	127	The command string as entered

TABLE B–15 Timings for effective address calculations

addressing mode	clocks to get EA	use example	
direct addressing	6	MOV	AX,COST
based or indexed	5	MOV	AX,[BX]
		MOV	AX,[SI]
based or indexed plus displacement	9	MOV	AX,[BX + 8]
		MOV	AX,TABLE [DI]
based-indexed either BX+SI or BP+DI	7	MOV	AX,[SI + BX]
based-indexed BX+DI or BP+SI	8	MOV	AX,[DI + BX]
based-index + displacement BX+SI or BP+DI	11	MOV	AX,TABLE [SI] [BX]
based-index + displacement BX+DI or BP+SI	12	MOV	AX,[DI + BX + 8]
segment override	EA + 2	MOV	AX,ES:STRING

register move takes 2 clock cycles, for example. However, many instructions simply state 2 + EA. This means that the total time is 2 clocks plus however long it takes to calculate the EA.

Herein lies the impact of the different addressing modes. Table B–15 summarizes these effects.

Appendix C
Instruction Summary

In this appendix operands are represented as follows.

Abbreviation for Operand	Meaning
reg8/mem8	Either a byte register or a byte of storage
imm8	A byte of immediate data
reg16/mem16	Either a word register or a word of meaning
imm16	A word of immediate data

AAA   ASCII adjust after addition

AAA

Adjusts the results of a decimal addition after adding.

AL contains the resultant decimal digit.

If sum is greater than 9, AH is incremented and CF and AF are set.

Flags: AF and CF (unpredictable are OF, SF, ZF, and PF).

AAD   ASCII adjust before division

AAD

Converts unpacked decimal digits in AX into binary. Result is in AX, ready for division.

Flags: PF, SF, ZF (unpredictable are AF, CF, and OF).

AAM   ASCII adjust after multiplication

AAM

Converts binary number in AL into unpacked decimal in AL. Any digits greater than 9 are stored in AH.

Flags: PF, SF, ZF (unpredictable are AF, CF, and OF).

AAS   ASCII adjust after subtraction

AAS

Converts binary result of subtraction in AL to unpacked decimal in AL.

If result is greater than 9, AH is decremented and CF and AF are set.

Flags: AF and CF (unpredictable are OF, SF, ZF, and PF).

ADC   Add with carry two binary numbers of the same length

ADC op1,op2

In this instruction op2 is added to op1, then the carry flag is added to op1. The result replaces op1.

op1: reg8/mem8   reg16/mem16

op2: reg8/mem8/imm8   reg16/mem16/
                                              imm16

Flags: AF, CF, OF, PF, SF, ZF.

ADD   Add two binary numbers of the same length

ADD op1,op2

In this instruction op2 is added to op1. The result replaces op1.

op1: reg8/mem8   reg16/mem16

op2: reg8/mem8/imm8   reg16/mem16/
                                              imm16

Flags: AF, CF, OF, PF, SF, ZF.

AND   Logical AND

AND op1,op2

A logical AND is done between op2 and op1; the result replaces op1. If both correspond-ing bits are 1B, then the result is 1B, other-wise the result is OB). AND is commonly used to turn a bit off.

op1: reg8/mem8   reg16/mem16

op2: reg8/mem8/imm8   reg16/mem16/
                                             imm16

Flags: AF, CF, OF, PF, SF, ZF. Flags CF and OF contain OB, and flag AF is unpredictable.

CALL   Call a subroutine or procedure

CALL name of procedure

For a NEAR procedure, decrement SP by 2, push IP onto the stack, and load IP with the destination offset address.

For a FAR procedure, decrement SP by a total of 4, push CS:IP onto the stack, and load CS:IP with the destination vector.

Control is passed to the first instruction in the routine.

Flags: none.

CBW   Converts a signed byte binary number into a word

CBW

Register AL is converted to a word in AX, by propagating the sign in AL throughout all bits of AH.

Flags: none.

CLD   Clear the direction flag

CLD

The direction flag is reset to 0B.

Flags: DF is cleared.

CMP   Compare two operands

CMP op1,op2

In this instruction op2 is compared to op1 and the flags set as if op2 were subtracted from op1.

op1: reg8/mem8   reg16/mem16

op2: reg8/mem8/imm8   reg16/mem16/
                                              imm16

Flags: AF, CF, OF, PF, SF, ZF.

CMPS, CMPSB, CMPSW   Compare string,
                                                    byte or word

CMPS   op1,op2
CMPSB
CMPSW

Compares two strings either a byte or a word at a time and sets the flags with the results.

DS:SI = address of the first string.

ES:DI = address of the second string.

DF controls the direction of the comparison.

> If DF is set, then SI and DI are decre-mented.

> If DF is cleared, then SI and DI are incremented (by 1 if byte, or by 2 if word).

CX = number of repetitions for REPE prefix.

In this instruction op1 and op2 are used only to determine the length of the operands. If both are even, then CMPSW is generated; otherwise, a CMPSB is created.

The comparison ends if CX = 0 or if the ZF flag is set, indicating an unequal condition.

The prefix REPE or REPZ repeats the function while CX is not 0 and the ZF is cleared. See REPE and REPZ.

Flags: AF, CF, OF, PF, SF, ZF.

CWD   Convert a word signed binary number into a doubleword

The word in register AX is converted into a doubleword and stored in DX:AX.

The sign of AX is propagated throughout DX.

Flags: none.

DAA   Decimal adjust after addition

DAA

Adjusts the result of a packed decimal addition in AL into packed decimal form in AL.

If the results are greater than 99, then the AF and CF flags are set.

Flags: AF, CF, PF, SF, ZF   (OF is unpredictable).

DAS   Decimal adjust after subtraction

DAS

Adjusts the result of a packed decimal subtraction in AL into packed decimal form in AL.

If the results are greater than 99, then the AF and CF flags are set.

Flags: AF, CF, PF, SF, ZF   (OF is unpredictable).

DEC   Decrement by 1

DEC op1

In this instruction op1 is decremented by 1. The result replaces op1.

op1: reg8/mem8   reg16/mem16

Flags: AF, OF, PF, SF, ZF.

DIV   Division of unsigned numbers

DIV op2

Word by byte division: Register AX is divid-

ed by op2 (1 byte). The quotient is in AL; the remainder is in AH.

Doubleword by word division: Register DX:AX is divided by op2 (1 word). The quotient is in AX; the remainder is in DX.

op2: reg8/mem8   assumes op1 is AX

op2: reg16/mem16   assumes op1 is DX:AX

Flags: none, except that AF, CF, PF, OF, SF, ZF are all undefined after the division.

IDIV   Division of signed numbers

IDIV op2

Word by byte division: Register AX is divided by op2 (1 byte). The quotient is in AL; the remainder is in AH.

Doubleword by word division: Register DX:AX is divided by op2 (1 word). The quotient is in AX; the remainder is in DX.

op2: reg8/mem8   assumes op1 is AX

op2: reg16/mem16   assumes op1 is DX:AX

Flags: none, except that AF, CF, PF, OF, SF, ZF are all undefined after the division.

IMUL   Multiplication of signed numbers

IMUL op2

Byte multiplication: AL is multiplied by op2 (1 byte). The result is in AX.

Word multiplication: AX is multiplied by op2 (1 word). The result is in DX:AX, with the low-order part in AX and the high-order part in DX.

op2: reg8/mem8   assumes op1 is AL

op2: reg16/mem16   assumes op1 is AX

Flags: CF, OF. AF, PF, SF, and ZF are undefined afterwards.

INC   Increment by 1

INC op1

In this instruction op1 is incremented by 1. The result replaces op1.

op1: reg8/mem8   reg16/mem16

Flags: AF, OF, PF, SF, ZF.

JMP   Jump, unconditional branch, branch

JMP label

Goes to label. The label can be NEAR or FAR.

Flags: none.

Jnnn   Conditional jumps

Jnnn label

Labels must be NEAR labels.

Table C.1 presents the conditional jump instructions.

LEA   Load effective address

LEA op1,op2

Loads the offset address of op2 into op1.

op1   reg16/mem16

op2   name/label/value

Flags: none.

LODS, LODSB, LODSW   Load string, byte or word

LODS   op1

LODSB

LODSW

DS:SI = address of the string to load

Byte: Loads a byte into AL.

Word: Loads a word into AX.

DF controls the direction. If DF is set, SI is decremented; if DF is cleared, SI is incremented (by 1 if byte or by 2 if word).

In this instruction op1 is used only to determine the type of load. If the length of op1 is even, then LODSW is generated; if the length is odd, then LODSB is used.

Flags: none.

TABLE C–1   Conditional JUMP instructions

Conditional Jumps Based on Unsigned Data

Operation	Meaning	Flags that are tested
JE or JZ*	jump if op1 is equal to op2 OR jump if zero flag set	ZF
JNE or JNZ*	jump if op1 is not equal to op2 OR jump if zero flag is not set	ZF
JA or JNBE	jump if op1 is above op2 OR jump if op1 is not below and is not equal to op2	CF, ZF
JAE or JNB	jump if op1 is above op2 or is equal to op2 OR jump if op1 is not below op2	CF
JB or JNAE	jump if op1 is below op2 OR jump if op1 is not above op2 and is not equal to op2	CF
JBE or JNA	jump if op1 is below op2 or is equal to op2 OR jump if op1 is not above op2	CF, AF

(Continues)

Conditional Jumps Based on Signed Data

Operation	Meaning	Flags that are tested
JE or JZ*	jump if op1 is equal to op2 OR jump if the zero flag is set	ZF
JNE or JNZ*	jump if op1 is not equal to op2 OR jump if the zero flag is not set	ZF
JG or JNLE	jump if op1 is greater than op2 OR jump if op1 is not less than op2 and is not equal to op2	ZF, SF, OF
JGE or JNL	jump if op1 is greater than or equal to op2 OR jump if op1 is not less than op2	SF, OF
JL or JNGE	jump if op1 is less than op2 OR jump if op1 is not greater than op2 and is not equal to op2	SF, OF
JLE or JNG	jump if op1 is less than or equal to op2 OR jump if op1 is not greater than op2	ZF, SF, OF

*Note that the JE or JZ and JNE or JNZ are the same for unsigned and signed data, since the equal or zero condition occurs regardless of the sign.

Conditional Jumps for Special Arithmetic Conditions

Operation	Meaning	Flags that are tested
JS	jump if sign is set (negative)	SF
JNS	jump if sign is cleared (positive)	SF
JC	jump if carry flag is set (same as JB)	CF
JNC	jump if carry flag is cleared	CF
JO	jump if overflow flag is set	OF
JNO	jump if overflow flag is cleared	OF
JP or JPE	jump if parity is even (set)	PF
JNP or JPO	jump if parity is odd (cleared)	PF
JCXZ	jump if reg CX is 0	ZF and reg CX is 0

TABLE C–1   continued

LOOPnn   Loop control, repeat a process

LOOP	label	
LOOPE	label	
LOOPZ	label	
LOOPNE	label	
LOOPNZ	label	

LOOP goes to label while CX is not 0.

LOOPE and LOOPZ go to label while CX is not 0 and the zero flag is set (ZF = 1).

LOOPNE and LOOPNZ go to label while CX is not 0 and the zero flag is cleared (ZF = 0).

All decrement CX first, then test for 0. The label must be a NEAR label.

Flags: none.

MOV   Move data

MOV op1,op2

The contents of op2 are moved into op1.

op1: reg8/mem8   reg16/mem16

op2: reg8/mem8/imm8   reg16/mem16/
                         imm16

No memory-to-memory moves.

No moves of immediate data to segment register.

No moves into the IP register.

Flags: none.

MOVS, MOVSB, MOVSW   Move string, byte or word

MOVS op1,op2   REP MOVS op1,op2

MOVSB   REP MOVSB

MOVSW   REP MOVSW

DS:SI = address of the source string.

ES:DI = address of the destination string.

DF controls the direction of the move operation.

  If DF is cleared, SI and DI are incremented;

  if DF is set, SI and DI are decremented (by 1 if byte or by 2 if word).

CX = number of repetitions to do; used by REP prefix.

REP prefix controls the number of times to execute the move string instruction. The instruction repeats while CX is not 0. *See* REP.

Flags: DF controls direction.

MUL   Multiplication of unsigned numbers

MUL op2

Byte multiplication: AL is multiplied by op2 (one byte). The result is in AX.

Word multiplication: AX is multiplied by op2 (one word). The result is in DX:AX, with the low-order part in AX and the high-order part in DX.

op2: reg8/mem8   assumes op1 is AL

op2: reg16/mem16   assumes op1 is AX

Flags: CF, OF. Afterwards, AF, PF, SF, and ZF are undefined.

NEG   Negate an integer (binary number)

NEG op1

The contents of op1 are negated, that is, 00H – op1.

op1: reg8/mem8   reg16/mem16

Flags: AF, CF, OF, PF, SF, ZF.

OR   Logical OR

OR op1,op2

A logical OR is done between op2 and op1. The result replaces op1. If either or both corresponding bits are 1B, then the result is 1B; otherwise, the result is a 0B. This instruction is commonly used to turn a bit on.

op1: reg8/mem8   reg16/mem16

op2: reg8/mem8/imm8   reg16/mem16/
                         imm16

Flags: AF, CF, OF, PF, SF, ZF. Flags CF and OF contain 0B, and flag AF is unpredictable.

POP   Pop a word off the stack

POP op1

The contents of the current word on the stack are placed in op1, and the SP is incremented by 2.

Segment registers are allowed.

Flags: none.

POPF   Pop the flag register off the stack

POPF

The contents of the current word on the stack are placed into the flags register, and the SP is incremented by 2.

Flags: none

PUSH   Push a word onto the stack

PUSH op1

The contents of op1 are pushed onto the stack.

op1: reg16/mem16

The SP is decremented by 2 and the word stored on the stack.

Segment registers are allowed.

Flags: none.

PUSHF   Push the flag register onto the stack

PUSHF

The contents of the flag register are stored on the stack.

The SP is decremented by 2 and the word is stored on the stack.

Flags: none.

REP, REPE, REPNE, REPNZ, REPZ
Repeat string function prefix

REP MOVSB   REPE CMPSB   REPNE
SCASB

Repeats the string function that follows it (MOVS, CMPS, SCAS).

Requires that CX be set to the number of repetitions.

REP repeats while CX is not 0. REP is used with MOV strings.

REPE and REPZ repeat while CX is not 0 and ZF is set (byte or word is equal). REP and REPZ are used with comparison and scan strings.

REPNE and REPNZ repeat while CX is not 0 and the ZF is cleared (byte or word is not equal). REPNE and REPNZ are used with scan strings.

Flags: Set per string function being repeated.

RET   Return from procedure

RET

From a NEAR call, pops IP and increments SP by 2.

From a FAR call, pops CS:IP and increments SP by 4.

Control returns to the next instruction after the call.

Flags: none.

RET n   Return from procedure, popping n bytes off the stack

RET 4

This instruction pops 4 bytes off the stack.

RET n functions like RET except for removal of passed parameters that were stored on the stack.

Flags: none.

SAL   Shift algebraic left (signed number)

SAL   op1,1

SAL   op1,CL

In this instruction op1 is shifted either 1 bit to the left or by the number of bits contained in CL. Vacated bits are filled with 0B. A common use is to multiply op1 by powers of 2.

op1: reg8/mem8   reg16/mem16

The results are identical to SHL.

Flags: CF, OF, PF, SF, ZF. Flag AF is unpredictable.

SAR   Shift algebraic right (signed number).

SAR   op1,1

SAR   op1,CL

In this instruction op1 is shifted either 1 bit to the right or by the number of bits contained in CL. Vacated bits are replaced by the sign bit. A common use is to divide a signed op1 by powers of 2.

op1: reg8/mem8   reg16/mem16

Flags: CF, OF, PF, SF, ZF. Flag AF is unpredictable.

SBB   Subtract with borrow two binary numbers of the same length

SBB op1,op2

In this instruction op2 is subtracted from op1, then the carry flag is subtracted from op1. The result replaces op1.

op1: reg8/mem8   reg16/mem16

op2: reg8/mem8/imm8   reg16/mem16/
                          imm16

Flags: AF, CF, OF, PF, SF, ZF.

SCAS, SCASB, SCASW   Scan strings, byte or
word

SCAS op1	REPNE SCAS op1	REPNZ SCAS op1
SCASB	REPNE SCASB	REPNZ SCASB
SCASW	REPNE SCASW	REPNZ SCASW
	REPE SCAS op1	REPZ SCAS op1
	REPE SCASB	REPZ SCASB
	REPE SCASW	REPZ SCASW

A string is scanned for the presence or
absence of a byte or word.

ES:DI = address of the string to be scanned.

AL = byte or AX = word to be scanned for.

DF controls the direction.

If DF is set, DI is decremented;

if DF is cleared, DI is incremented

(by 1 if byte or by 2 if word).

CX = number of repetitions, used by REPE
or REPNE.

In this instruction op1 is used only to determine which type to do.

If the length of op1 is even, SCASW is
generated; if it's odd, a SCASB is
generated.

If REPE is used, the scan stops when either
CX is 0 or when the byte or word is not found.

If REPNZ is used, the scan ends when
either CX is 0 or when the byte or word is
found.

Flags: AF, CF, OF, PF, SF, ZF.

SHL   Shift logical left (unsigned number)

SHL op1,1

SHL op1,CL

In this instruction op1 is shifted either 1
bit to the left or by the number of bits in
CL. Vacated bits are filled with 0B. SHL
and SAL produce identical results. A common use is to multiply unsigned op1 by
powers of 2.

op1: reg8/mem8   reg16/mem16

Flags: CF, PF, OF, SF, ZF. Flag AF is unpredictable.

SHR   Shift logical right (unsigned number)

SHR op1,1

SHR op1,CL

In this instruction op1 is shifted either 1
bit to the right or by the number of bits in
CL. Vacated bits are filled with 0B. A common use is to divide unsigned op1 by powers of 2.

op1: reg8/mem8   reg16/mem16

Flags: CF, PF, OF, SF, ZF. Flag AF is unpredictable.

STD   Set the direction flag

STD

The direction flag is set to 1B.

Flags: DF is set.

STOS, STOSB, STOSW   Store string, byte or
word

STOS op1

STOSB

STOSW

ES:DI = address of the receiving string.

Byte: AL = byte to store.

Word: AX = byte to store.

DF controls the direction.

If DF is set, then DI is decremented;

if DF is cleared, then DI is incremented

(by 1 if byte or by 2 if word).

In this instruction op1 is used only to determine whether a byte or a word is to be
moved. If op1's length is even, STOSW is
generated; if the length is odd, STOSB is
generated.

Flags: none.

SUB   Subtract two binary numbers of the same
length

SUB op1,op2

In this instruction op2 is subtracted from
op1. The result replaces op1.

op1: reg8/mem8   reg16/mem16

op2: reg8/mem8/imm8   reg16/mem16/
                                     imm16

Flags: AF, CF, OF, PF, SF, ZF.

XCHG   Exchange memory or register with
                register

XCHG op1,op2

The contents of op2 are swapped with op1.

op1 reg8/mem8   reg16/mem16

op2 reg8/mem8   reg16/mem16

At least one operand must be a register.

No segment registers are allowed.

Flags: none.

XLAT   Translate

XLAT

Converts a byte into a predetermined alternate value.

AL contains the byte to be converted.

BX contains the address of a 256-byte conversion table.

When done, AL contains the converted byte.

XLAT uses the contents of register AL as an offset within the conversion table.

Flags: none.

XOR   Logical exclusive OR

XOR op1,op2

A logical exclusive OR is done between op2 and op1. The result replaces op1. If both corresponding bits are the same, 0B is the result; otherwise, the result is 1B. XOR is commonly used to clear a register or field by applying XOR to the register or field.

op1: reg8/mem8   reg16/mem16

op2: reg8/mem8/imm8   reg16/mem16/
                                     imm16

Flags: CF, OF, PF, SF, ZF.

Flags CF and OF contain 0B. Flag AF is unpredictable.

Appendix D
Interrupt Summary

DOS Interrupt Summary

INT 20H   Terminate program

CS must point to PSP.

Returns control back to DOS.

Files are not closed.
Interrupt vectors are reset.

Used prior to DOS Version 3.0.

INT 27H   Terminate program but keep part
resident in memory

CS = address of PSP.

DX = offset address of first byte beyond that
portion that is to remain resident in
memory. Keeps PSP through this
offset; a maximum of 64K remains.

Files are not closed.
Interrupt vector are reset.

Used prior to DOS Version 3.0.

INT 21H   The major DOS functions are handled
through the umbrella interrupt
number 21H. The function number
desired is contained in register AH.

AH = 00H   Terminate program

CS must point to PSP.

Returns control back to DOS.

Files are not closed.
Interrupt vectors are reset.

Used prior to DOS Version 3.0.
Identical to INT 20H.

AH = 01H   Keyboard input byte

AL = character input.

Echo is on, and the break key works.

If a special key is entered, AL contains 00H.
The program must then issue a second INT
21H with AH = 01H to get the special key
code byte.

The cursor is positioned just after the
character is echoed on the screen.

The type-ahead buffer functions, but DOS
editing keys functions, such as LEFT ARROW,
do not.

AH = 02H   Display a character

DL = character to display.

This function displays the byte in DL at the current cursor location, then advances the cursor one position.

AH = 05H   Print a character on the standard printer

DL = character to print

The character in DL is printed at the current position on the print line.

AH = 07H   Keyboard input byte

AL = character inputed.

Echo is off, and the break key does not function.

All other functions are the same as in function AH = 01H.

AH = 08H   Keyboard input byte

AL = character input

Echo is off, but the break key functions.

All other functions are the same as in function AH = 01H.

AH = 09H   display string

DS:DX = address of string to display

Successive characters are displayed on the screen until a dollar sign is encountered.

The cursor is positioned just after the last character is displayed.

AH = 0AH   Buffered keyboard input

DS:DX = address of the input structure

Byte 1 =   maximum length of input string

Byte 2 =   actual length of input string, supplied by DOS

Byte 3 on = input area, filled with input characters, must be 1 byte longer than maximum length, because DOS stores the carriage return (0DH) at the end of the string

Echo is on, the break key works.

Normal DOS editing keys, such as LEFT ARROW, function.

The cursor is positioned just after the last character entered.

AH = 0CH   Flush keyboard buffer and read keyboard

AL = function number to use to input byte: 01H, 07H, 08H

AL = character input

First all remaining keystrokes stored in the type-ahead buffer are flushed, then the appropriate input byte function is invoked.

AL contains the byte entered, just as it does with the input byte functions. The program should check for 00H in AL, since special keys may have been pressed, just as in the 01H function.

AH = 0DH   Reset disk

Resets the disk and flushes all file buffers but does not close files. Hence, all output files should be closed before using this function.

AH = 0EH   Select current drive

DL = the drive number to select (0 = A:, 1 = B:)

Returns:
AL = the number of drives installed

Selects the current default drive and also reports on the total number of drives installed.

AH = 0FH   Open an existing file (FCB)

DS:DX = address of FCB

Returns:
AL = FFH = an error has occurred
or
AL = 00H = open was successful

Normally used for input operations.

Before FCB can be used, set desired record size and set the DTA to be used.

AH = 10H   Close file (FCB)

DS:DX = address of the FCB

Returns:
AL = FFH = an error has occurred
or
AL = 00H = open was successful

Flushes all buffers and sets the EOF marker in the FAT

AH = 11H   Search for first matching file

DS:DX = address of the FCB, which contains the filename, which can contain wildcards: (? and *)

Returns:

AL = FFH if no files are found

AL = 00H if a file is found to match and the FCB now contains information that is needed if the search is to continue with function 12H

Searches the system for the first file matching the given file specification contained in the FCB.

AH = 12H   search for next matching file

Continues the file search begun with function 11H. All parameters and results are as given in AH = 11H.

AH = 13H   Delete a file (FCB)

DS:DX = address of the FCB

Returns:
AL = FFH = an error has occurred
or
AL = 00H = open was successful

Note the name of the file to delete is contained in the FCB.

AH = 14H   Read a sequential record (FCB)

DS:DX = address of the FCB

Returns:
AL = 00H successful
     01H EOF and no data read
     02H DTA could not hold the record
     03H EOF and no data read

Requires that FCB record size, current DTA to be used, FCB record number, and block number are set. These last two are automatically adjusted by DOS for sequential processing.

AH = 15H   Write a sequential record (FCB)

DS:DX = address of the FCB

Returns:

AL = 00H successful write
     01H disk-is-full error
     02H not enough space in DOS's internal DTA to hold the current record

Note: Data are not necessarily physically written at this point; they are written only when a cluster or sector is full. Use CLOSE to flush all DOS internal buffers.

AH = 16H   Create/open a new file (FCB)

DS:DX = address of FCB

Returns:
AL = FFH = an error has occurred, possibly no more directory space available
or
AL = 00H = open was successful.

Normally used for output operations.

Before FCB can be used, set desired record size and set the DTA to be used.

Creates new files and opens existing files, resetting file size to 0 bytes.

AH = 17H   Rename a file (FCB)

DS:DX = address of the modified FCB

Returns:
AL = FFH = an error has occurred
or
AL = 00H = open was successful.

The old name is at the normal position in the FCB; the new name is located at offset 16H, where the file size is normally kept.

Wildcards (? and *) in the new name mean "ditto from the old name."

AH = 19H   Report current drive

Returns:
AL = the current drive number, where 0 is drive A

AH = 1AH   Set the DTA, disk transfer area (FCB)

DS:DX = address of the DTA to be used

There can be only one current DTA. If two or more files are being used, set DTA before each file operation.

AH = 1BH   Get FAT information on current
              drive

Returns:

AL   = the number of sectors per cluster
        (1 for SS, 2 for DS)

CX   = the number of bytes on a sector
        (512)

DX   = the total number of clusters on the
        disk

DS:BX = points to a byte in a DOS work
        area containing the FAT ID

Note that DS is modified; hence, before
using this function, push DS and pop DS
after using the FAT ID.

AH = 1CH   Get FAT information on any drive

DL = drive number to report (current drive
     is 0, A: is 1)

Returns:

AL   = the number of sectors per cluster
        (1 for SS, 2 for DS)

CX   = the number of bytes on a sector (512)

DX   = the total number of clusters on the
        disk

DS:BX = points to a byte in a DOS work
        area containing the FAT ID

Note that DS is modified; hence, before
using this function, push DS and pop DS
after using the FAT ID.

AH = 21H   read random file record

DS:DX = address of the FCB

Returns:

AL = 0 successful read
     1 EOF and no more data
     2 insufficient DTA space
     3 EOF and some data

One record is read from a random file. The
FCB field random record must be set to the
desired record before the function is invoked.
The record is read into the current DTA.

AH = 22H   Write random file record

DS:DX = address of the FCB

Returns:

AL = 0 successful write
     1 disk is full
     2 DTA contains insufficient space

This function writes one record to a random
file from the DAT. The FCB field random
record number must point to the desired file
position.

AH = 23H   Get file size

DS:DX points to the FCB.

Returns:

AL = 0 and FCB contains the file size

AL = FF operation failed

This function returns the size of the file in
terms of the total number of records it
contains. The FCB should be opened and
contain the correct record size. (If that size
is 1 byte, then the returned value is the file
size in bytes.)

AH = 24H   Set random record field

DS:DX = address of the FCB.

The function sets the random record FCB
field to the equivalent point given in the
current block and record fields. This
function enables a program to switch from
sequential file operation into random file
processing mode.

AH = 27H   Read random file records

DS:DX = address of the FCB

CX   = number of records to input

Returns:

AL = 0 successful read
     1 EOF and no more data
     2 insufficient DTA space
     3 EOF and some data

CX = the total number of records, full and
     partial

This function reads one or more direct
records into the DTA. The FCB field random
record must be set to the desired record
before the function is invoked.

AH = 28H   Write random file records

DS:DX = address of the FCB

CX   = the number of records to write

Returns:

AL = 0 successful write
     1 disk is full
     2 DTA contains insufficient space

This function writes one or more successive records to the file, beginning at the random position contained in the FCB. If CX contains 0, then DOS assumes that this is not the new EOF marker and some records have been deleted from the very end of the file.

AH = 2FH   Get DTA address

Returns:
ES:BX = the address of the current DTA
used by DOS

AH = 31H   Keep, terminate program, but stay resident in memory

AL = return code

DX = number of paragraphs to keep resident, including the PSP

CS does not have to point to the PSP.

This is the preferred method, after DOS Version 3.0.

AH = 36H   Get free disk space

DL = the drive number (current drive is 0, drive A: is 1)

Returns:
AX = FFFFH invalid drive error
or
AX = the number of sectors per cluster
CX = the number of bytes per sector (512)
BX = the number of available clusters
DX = the total number of clusters

AH = 39H   Make subdirectory

DS:DX = address of the ASCIIZ string containing the complete path name of the new subdirectory

Returns:
AX = 3   the path is not found
AX = 0   no errors

Like the DOS command MKDIR, this function creates a new subdirectory.

AH = 3AH   Remove subdirectory

DS:DX = address of the ASCIIZ string containing the complete path name of the subdirectory to delete

Returns:
AX = 3   the path is not found
AX = 5   directory cannot be deleted
AX = 0   no errors

Like the DOS command RMDIR, this function removes a subdirectory.

AH = 3BH   Change current directory

DS:DX = address of the ASCIIZ string containing the complete path name of the new subdirectory

Returns:
AX = 3   the path is not found
AX = 0   no errors

Like the DOS command CHDIR, this function changes the current directory.

AH = 3CH   Create/open a file (file handle) normally for writes

DS:DX = address of an ASCIIZ string that contains the complete drive\path\file-name.extension

CL = file attributes, normally 20H, indicating that it has not yet been backed up

Returns:
CF set = an error has occurred
    AX = error code
or
CF cleared = file is opened
AX   = file handle

This function is used to create and open a file that does not yet exist or to open and reuse an existing file.

AH = 3DH   Open a file (file handle) normally for a read

DS:DX = address of an ASCIIZ string that contains the complete drive\path\file-name.extension

AL = mode of operation: 00H read only, 01H write only, 02H read and write

Returns:
CF set = an error has occurred
    AX = error code
or
CF cleared = file is opened
AX   = file handle

This function opens an existing file for reading, appending, or updating.

AH = 3EH   Close file (file handle)

BX = file handle

Returns:
CF set = an error has occurred
    AX = error code
or
CF cleared = close was successful

AH = 3FH   Read from file (file handle)

BX   = file handle
CX   = number of bytes to read
DS:DX = address of input area to fill

Returns:
CF set = an error has occurred
    AX = error code
or
CF cleared = read was successful
        AX = actual number of bytes read
        AX = 0, EOF has occurred

AH = 40H   Write to a file (file handle)

BX   = file handle
CX   = number of bytes to write
DS:DX = address of bytes to output

Returns:
CF set = an error has occurred
    AX = error code
or
CF cleared = write may have been
           successful
        AX= actual number of bytes written

If AX is less than CX, then there is not enough space on the disk to store all of the record; only part was written.

AH = 41H   Delete a file (file handle)

DS:DX = address of ASCIIZ string that provides the complete drive\path\file-name.extension needed

Returns:
CF set = an error has occurred
    AX = error code
or
CF cleared = delete was successful

AH = 42H   Move file pointer (file handle)

AL   = direction code: 00H from the beginning, 01H from the current position, 02H from the end of the file
BX   = file handle
CX:DX = number of bytes to offset (high-order part in CX, low-order in DX)

Returns:
CF set = an error has occurred
    AX = error code
or
CF cleared = move was successful
        DX:AX = current file position from the beginning of the file (DX has the high-order part; AX has the low-order part.)

AH = 46H   Force file handle duplication

BX = old file handle
CX = new file handle

Returns:
AX = 0 done, the file handle in register CX now refers to the same file as BX
AX = 6 invalid file handle

This function forces a duplication of an existing file handle. If the original file is open, the function closes it. Now all actions to the original handle are rerouted to the new handle. This is useful for redirection of I/O.

AH = 47H   Get current directory

DL = drive number (0 = default drive, 1 = drive A:)
DS:SI = address of a 64-byte area in which DOS returns the ASCIIZ string directory name

Returns:
AX = 15 invalid drive
AX = 0 no error

This function returns the name of the current directory in use in an ASCIIZ string form. It does not contain the drive letter, the colon, or the initial back slash to start from the root in path names.

AH = 4CH   Terminate program or process

AL = return code to DOS

Closes all opened files, if opened by 3CH and 3DH.
CS does not have to point to the PSP.
Interrupt vectors are reset.

After DOS Version 3.0, this is the preferred method to end a program.

AH = 4EH   Start file search

DS:DX = address ASCIIZ string file specification

CL   = the file attribute specification used in the search

Returns:
AX   = 2 if there is no file
AX   = 0 and the current DTA has 43 bytes of information:

offset	length	contents
0	21	used by DOS for find next function (4FH)
21	1	attribute byte for found file
22	2	time stamp of file
24	2	date stamp of file
26	4	file size in bytes
30	13	ASCIIZ string file specifier of file

This function searches the disk for the first file(s) that match the given file specification(s). The file specifications may include the usual wildcards, ? and *.

AH = 4FH   Continue file search

DS:DX = address of the formatted DTA given by the results of function 4EH

Returns:
AX = 0 and DTA has 43 bytes of next file found
AX = 18 no more files found

This function continues the search for the next file that matches the file specification in the search begun with function 4EH.

AH = 56H   Rename a file (file handle)

DS:DX = address of the ASCIIZ string that

defines the old file to rename
ES:DI = address of the ASCIIZ string that defines the new filename

Returns:
CF set = an error has occurred
    AX = error code
or
CF cleared = action was successful

AH = 59H   Get extended error codes

Can be used after all types that either set CF or set AL = FFH when an error occurs.
BX = current version number, which is 00H.

Returns:
All registers destroyed, except CS:IP and SS:SP.

AX = error code
BH = more specific error information
BL = retry information
CH = other error types

AH = 5BH   Create a new file (file handle)

DS:DX = address of the ASCIIZ string that defines the complete drive\path\ filename.extension needed
    CL = file attributes, normally 20H, indicating that it has not yet been backed up

Returns:
CF set = an error has occurred
    AX = error code
or
CF cleared = file is opened

AX   – file handle

This function creates a file that does not yet exist; if the file exists, an error results.

ROM-BIOS Interrupt Summary

All ROM-BIOS video services are handled through the umbrella INT 10H. Register AH contains the function number desired.

AH = 00H   Set video mode

AL = video mode desired

TABLE D–1   IBM video display modes

Mode	Type	Size	Color?
0	text	40 × 25	yes, gray tones
1	text	40 × 25	yes
2	text	80 × 25	yes, gray tones
3	text	80 × 25	yes
4	graphics	medium resolution	yes
5	graphics	medium resolution	yes, gray tones
6	graphics	high resolution	yes
7	text	80 × 25	no

AH = 01H   Set cursor size

CH = starting line for cursor

CL = ending line for cursor

Scan line 0 is at the top, while scan line 7 is the bottom.

Default is 06H, 07H.

If bit 5 of CH is on, cursor disappears.

If starting line is greater than ending line, then a two-part cursor is created.

AH = 02H   Set cursor position

BH = page number, 0 = current page
DH = row number for cursor
DL = column number

The coordinates of the upper left are row 0, column 0.

The coordinates of the lower right are row 24, column 79 (18H,4FH).

AH = 03H   Read cursor position

BH = display page to use

Returns:
DX = coordinates of the cursor's position, DH = row, DL = column
CX = cursor's size, CH = starting scan line, CL = ending scan line

AH = 05H   Set active display page

AL = new page number to display

The new page is instantaneously displayed, and it becomes the current page.

AH = 06H   Scroll up

AL = number of lines to scroll, 0 = whole screen
CX = coordinates of the upper-left corner of the window or screen, CH = row, CL = column
DX = coordinates of the lower-right corner of the window or screen, DH = row, DL = column
BH = display attributes for the window or screen lines that are added

Note that it scrolls only the current display page.

AH = 07H   Scroll down

AL = number of lines to scroll, 0 = whole screen
CX = coordinates of the upper-left corner of the window or screen, CH = row, CL = column
DX = coordinates of the lower-right corner of the window or screen, DH = row, DL = column
BH = display attributes for the window or screen lines that are added

Note that it only scrolls the current display page.

AH = 08H   Read character and attribute byte

BH = display page number to use
Returns:
AL = the character on the screen at the current cursor position
AH = the character's attribute byte

AH = 09H   Write character and attribute byte

AL = character to display
CX = number of times to display the
      character
BL = attributes to display character with
BH = display page

The display begins at the current cursor
position.

The cursor position is not moved by the
function.

AH = 0BH   Set color palette

BH = color palette number
BL = color number within that palette

In text modes, if BH is 0, then BL specifies
the color of the border area.

AH = 0FH   Get current video display mode

Returns:
BH = current display page number
AL = video mode number
AH = screen width (40 or 80 columns)

INT 19H   Bootstrap BIOS loader

Reboots the computer. The effect is similar
to turning the power on or pressing CTRL-
ALT-DEL.

Memory check is bypassed.

Memory size and equipment list remain
unreset.

Appendix E - Assembler Rules And Directives

Assembler Coding Rules:

Maximum line length: 132

No continuation lines
One instruction per line
Free-form syntax with blanks or tabs as the delimiters
Null lines accepted (aids readability)
Comment lines begin with a semicolon

Syntax:
name/label   opcode   operands   ; comments

There is no column alignment required; however, for program readability, column-align operation codes, operands, and comments.

Names/labels:
Begin in column 1
Maximum length: 31 characters
Case insensitive (but can be made otherwise)
First character must be alphabetic or one of these: ? @ _ $
Rest of name can also include the digits 0 through 9
No duplicate names and labels
Cannot be one of the reserved words, which include all instruction operation codes, directives, and pseudo-operations

Labels can be NEAR or FAR
If label ends with a colon, it is NEAR
A NEAR label is within +127 to –128 bytes of its use in a conditional branch or loop instruction

Operation codes can be either an instruction or an assembler directive

Operands often take the following forms:

reg8, reg16, mem8, mem16, imm8, imm16

where

8 bit = 1 byte
16 bit = 1 word
reg = register
mem = memory location
imm = immediate data

Storage (memory) can be accessed directly if the address of the area is in one of the three indexing registers: BX, SI, DI.

Syntax:
[BX]

When the length (byte or word) cannot be determined at compile time, use

BYTE PTR [SI]
or
WORD PTR [DI]

BP is used to access storage within the stack segment only (SS:).

Addressing Modes

Addressing mode name	*Coding example*
1. register addressing	MOV AX,CX
2. immediate addressing	MOV AX,1
3. direct addressing	MOV AX,COST
4. register indirect addressing	MOV AX,[BX]
5. indexed addressing (uses SI or DI with optional displacement)	MOV AL,MONTH[SI] or MOV AL,[MONTH + SI] or MOV AL,[SI] + 8
6. based addressing (uses DS:BX or SS:BP with option displacement	MOV AX, ACCTCODE [BX] or MOV AX, [ACCTCODE + BX] or MOV AX,[BX] + 8
7. based-indexed addressing (uses one of SI, DI and one of BX, BP and optional displacement)	ADD AX, COSTTBL [SI] [BX] or ADD AX,[SI + BX + 6] or ADD AX,[SI] [BX] 6

Assembler Directives

ASSUME

Tells the assembler which segment registers are associated with which segments.

Syntax:
ASSUME CS:segname,DS:segname, SS:segname,ES:segname

The segname NOTHING can be used if nothing is to be associated with that register, or the register can just be left out of the statement completely.

Define Storage Directives   DB, DW, DD, DQ, DT

Defines bytes, words, doublewords, quadwords, and tenbytes, respectively.

Syntax:
name DB value

Names are optional.

Value can be

? for uninitialized storage

Decimal number, such as 10

Hexadecimal, such as 0AH

Binary, such as 00001010B

Character, such as "A"

Character strings, such as FRED

single or double apostrophes can be used

A name or label, stores the offset address

Simple expressions, such as

```
BIG_STRING   DB   'THIS IS A
   LONG STRING.'
COST         DW   ?
LEN_BIG_STR DW   COST-
   BIG_STRING
```

effectively store the length of the string.

Stores words, doublewords, quadwords, tenbytes is backwards sequence. The low-order part is in the low-order byte of storage.

DOSSEG

Use simplified DOS segments.

Syntax:
DOSSEG

Version 5.0 of MASM permits a simplified method of defining all segments. This must be done as one of the very first actions, before any segments are defined. When this directive is used, the assembler uses predefined segment definitions and builds the program in standard segment order.

END

This statement defines the very end of the assembly; any lines coming after this cause an error.

Syntax:
END option

If the option is coded, it tells the assembler and linker that this label is the location of the first executable instruction of the program. It can be a segment name, procedure name, or instruction label. If the option is not coded, then the first byte of the program contains the first executable instruction.

EQU

Equate directive.

Syntax:
name EQU value

Read as "This name equates to this value."

Value can be a number, a series of letters, or a dollar sign.

```
ARRAY_SIZE   EQU  5      ; whenever
                        ; ARRAY_SIZE
                        ; appears, it is
                        ; replaced
                        ; by 5
DOS          EQU  21H   ; all appear-
                        ; ances of DOS
                        ; become 21H
```

The dollar sign represents the current offset value.

```
MASTR_REC  EQU  $ ; MASTR_REC
                  ; becomes
                  ; another name for
                  ; the following
                  ; bytes, likely the
                  ; master record
                  ; structure
```

EXTRN

Defines symbols as being external to this module.

Syntax:
EXTRN   symbol:type,symbol,type, . . .

If symbol is a procedure, type is FAR or NEAR.

If symbol is data, type is BYTE, WORD, DWORD, QWORD, TBYTE.

GROUP

Defines large-scale groups of segments.

Syntax:
groupname GROUP segment,segment, . . .

No group can exceed 64K.

LABEL

The coded label is associated with the following common syntax.

Syntax:
name LABEL BYTE

name LABEL WORD

The name becomes another way to refer to the byte or word that follows it.

Often used instead of the EQU to define a data record or structure.

LENGTH operator

Returns the number of elements in an array that has been defined using the DUP operator. If the definition includes nested DUPs, only the outermost value is returned.

PAGE

Ejects the listing to a new page.

PAGE 60,132

Resets the page length from a default of 66 lines to 60 lines and the line length from a default of 80 to 132, then ejects the listing to a new page.

PAGE +

Resets the page number to 1, increments the section number by 1, and ejects to a new page.

PROC-ENDP pair

This pair defines a procedure or subroutine.

Syntax:
name PROC option

The name is used to call the procedure, except the main or driver procedure.

The option can be NEAR (the default) or FAR. A FAR procedure can be in a code segment other than the calling routine; a NEAR procedure must be within the same code segment as the calling procedure.

The syntax for ENDS is

name ENDS

The names on PROC and ENDS must match.

PUBLIC

Named symbols are to be known external to this module.

Syntax:
PUBLIC   symbol,symbol,. . .

SEG and OFFSET operators

mov   AX, SEG cost

moves the segment address of cost into AX.

mov   AX, OFFSET cost

moves the offset address of cost into AX (an alternative to LEA), which is the number of bytes between the item and the beginning of the segment.

SEGMENT-ENDS pair

The pair defines a segment (code, data, or stack)

Syntax:
name SEGMENT alignment combine-type class-name

Delimiters are blanks or tabs, **not** commas.

The alignment defaults to PARA.

The combine-type identifies similar segments to join.

The class-name gives the name to join together.

For code and data segments, the usual coding is

name SEGMENT

For stack segments, usual coding is

name SEGMENT PARA STACK 'STACK'

The ENDS defines the physical end of the segment:

name ENDS

Segments are never physically nested.

The names on the SEGMENT and ENDS must match.

SEGMENT OVERRIDE operator

A segment register can be used as a prefix to another field to override the normal segment address.

To get to the command line stored in the PSP, with ES pointing to PSP, one could address the command line as:

```
MOV  BX,81H        ;OFFSET OF FIRST
                    BYTE OF CMD LINE
```

ES: [BX] will access this byte

```
MOV AL, ES: [BX] ;GET FIRST BYTE
                  OF CMD LINE
```

SIZE operator

Returns the total number of bytes in the definition. That is, it represents the results of LENGTH times TYPE of the field. If the definition includes nested DUPs, only the outer values are used.

standard program entry code

In the housekeeping section, where PGMDA is the name of the data segment:

```
MOV   AX,PGMDA     ; ESTABLISH
                     ADDRESSABILITY

MOV   DS,AX        ; TO THE DATA
                     SEGMENT

MOV   ES,AX        ; AND SET ES FOR
                     STRING FNS
```

standard program exit code

In the return to DOS section:

```
MOV   AX,4C00H     ; SET FOR END
                     PROCESS WITH

                  ; A RETURN CODE
                     OF 00H

INT   21H          ; CALL DOS TO
                     END PROCESS
```

STRUCTURES

1. Define a structure template.

2. Define that structure in memory.

Defining the template is done using the STRUC and ENDS pair. Between the two statements are all the individual fields that the record or structure contains.

Example: Define a Customer Record

```
CREC    STRUC
CID     DB    '00000'
              ; CUSTOMER ID NUMBER
CNAME   DB    'first and last names'
              ; NAMES ARE 25 BYTES
CADDR   DB    '                    '
              ; ADDR IS 20 BYTES
CCITY   DB    '          '
              ; CITY IS 10 BYTES
CSTATE  DB    '  '
              ; STATE IS 2 BYTES
CZIP    DB    '99999-9999'
              ; ZIP IN PROPER FORMAT
CREC    ENDS
```

When the structure is defined in memory, these initial values are applied unless overridden at that time. Also, these beginning values determine the length of the byte fields.

The result of defining the structure in memory is known as a **structure variable**. The syntax of the definition is

name   structure-name   <initialvalue1, initialval2,. . .>

The name is the structure variable name used in the program to reference the actual structure in memory. The structure-name is the name used on the STRUC-ENDS pair that defines the template or pattern.

Any initial values defined in the pattern, or template, are inserted into the defined fields at this point. However, the original template values can be overridden by inserting them within angle brackets. The first entry after the opening angle bracket is the value for the first field in the structure; the second entry, the second;

and so on. A comma separates these values. If a particular initial value of the template should not be overridden, then you must still account for its presence. Hence, commas indicate the end of each field within the structure template. For example, suppose that only the second and fourth field's initial template values are to be overridden. The initial string is coded

<,'new value 2',,'new value 4'>

Even if no values are to be overridden, the angle brackets must be present.

The length of the new value cannot exceed the original field's length in the template. Longer values generate error messages. Shorter strings are padded on the right with blanks.

Fields that have multiple values in the template **cannot** be overridden. This specifically applies to fields created with the DUP operator! Thus, if the field is defined using the DUP operator in the structure template, that field's initial value, if any, cannot be overridden.

Referencing Structures and Fields

The structure in memory can be accessed by name just like any other data definition. Commonly, the address if the structure is needed

LEA   SI,CUST_REC

or

LEA   DI,MONTH

The individual fields within a structure are accessible as well. However, each field reference must be qualified by the structure name that contains it. The qualification syntax is

structure-name.field-name

The period separates the structure name and the field name.

.MODEL

Sets memory model to be used. The syntax is

.MODEL   type

where type is one of the six different types: tiny, small, medium, compact, large, huge.

.DOSSEG DIRECTIVES

The common simplified directives are

.STACK   denotes the start of the stack segment

.CODE   denotes the start of the code segment

.DATA   denotes the start of the initialized data segment

.DATA?   denotes the start of the uninitialized data segment

.FARDATA   start of FAR data initialized segment for large models

.FARDATA?   start of FAR data uninitialized segment, large models

SUBTTL string

Prints the string at the top of every page after the title line (if any), usually found before a PAGE or PAGE +. Maximum string length is 60 characters.

TITLE string

Prints the string at the top of every page. Include only one title per module. The first 6 characters of the string become the module name (unless a NAME directive is used). Maximum string length is 60 characters.

TYPE operator

Returns a number that indicates the number of bytes in the definition type.

Definition is	Return value
DB	1
DW	2
DD	4

VECTOR ADDRESS

Segment address + offset address

segment addresses are stored shifted 1 nibble to the right. When used, the computer shifts the address 1 nibble to left and adds a 0H nibble. Then the offset address from the start of the segment is added to it to create the absolute address.

The vector address is often referred to and shown as DS:offset or CS:IP for the current instruction and SS:SP for the current place in the stack.

MACRO-ENDM pair

These are used to define a macro. The syntax is

name   MACRO   parameter1, parameter2, . . .

.

.   insert the body of the
.   macro here

ENDM

The macro can be called, or invoked, by using its name and providing corresponding arguments for the expected parameters:

macroname   argument1, argument2, . . .

Macro Directives

.LALL   A source listing control directive that lists all of the macro source statements.

.XALL   A source listing control directive that lists only those macro statements that create code or data. It is the default.

.SALL   A source listing control directive that suppresses all macro statements. Only the macro call is listed.

INCLUDE   A directive that tells the assembler to copy another file into the source program at the point where the INCLUDE is coded. the syntax is

INCLUDE file specification

& operator   (substitution operator) Used within a macro definition when a macro parameter follows immediately after other characters or appears within a quoted string. The substitution operator notifies the assembler in these cases that what follows it is to be interpreted as a parameter.

LOCAL   Identifies the list of names as local in scope. The assembler creates substitute names of the form ??0000 from these. In this way, each usage results in a unique name. The LOCAL directive must be the first statement in the macro definition. The syntax is

LOCAL name1, name2, ...

REPT-ENDM pair   The repeat conditional directive. It causes a series of statements to be repeated a predetermined number of times. The syntax is

REPT   number of repeats

.
.   statements to
.   be repeated
.

ENDM

IRP-ENDM pair   The conditional repeat directive. It causes a series of statements to be repeated with specific values. The syntax is

IRP   name, <value1,
        value2,
        value3, ...>
.
.   statements to
.   generate
.

ENDM

The name is replaced with value1 and used in the statements to be generated. Then it is given value2 and used in the statements to be generated, and so on.

IFxx-END   Conditional IF directive. Used to cause conditional assembly of one or more statements. They compose a family of directives.

IFDEF   A name has been defined

IFNDEF   A name has not been defined

IFB   A parameter has been given but with no corres-ponding value

IFNB   A parameter has not been given a value

IFIDN   Two arguments are identical

IFDIF   Two arguments are different

Syntax:

IFxxx   expression
.
.   block of state-
.   ments to be
.   generated if true
.

ELSE
.
.   block of state-
.   ments to be
.   generated if false
.

ENDIF

EXITM   The directive that provides a way to end a macro without branching to the ENDM directive.

Index